The GIANT Handbook of Computer Projects

The GIANT Handbook of Computer Projects

by The Editors of
73 Magazine

TAB BOOKS Inc.
BLUE RIDGE SUMMIT, PA. 17214

FIRST EDITION

SIXTH PRINTING

Printed in the United States of America

Library of Congress Cataloging in Publication Data

Main entry under title:

The Giant handbook of computer projects.

Includes index.
1. Computer-Amateurs' manuals. I. 73 magazine for
radio
amateurs.

TK 9969.G5 621.3819'5 79-5444
ISBN 0-8306-9724-1
ISBN 0-8306-1169-X pbk.

Contents

Introduction

Quite contrary to former beliefs, computers are not totally incomprehensible. They are permeating our society, so you may as well learn to use them. Even if you think you don't have much need for computers now, you will in the very near future. When—not if—they become a necessary part of almost every aspect of life, you will be ready with the help of this book.

First you will be introduced to the technology of computers. The computer's simplicity will convince you that even if you aren't mechanically inclined or a mathematical wizard, you can operate a computer. The mathematical capabilities of the computer are infinite, yet easy to understand. The following chapters will explain how computer arithmetic works, the binary number system, the hexadecimal system and the circuitry of digital equipment.

Microprocessors will be detailed for you including a section on how to troubleshoot them. Several computers and their capabilities will be compared including the Kim-1 and the Z-80.

Then you'll be on the road to building your own pieces of computer hardware equipment. You'll be completing many computer projects—even one on how to put together your own small home computer.

Needless to say, once you've mastered the art of running your computer, you'll want to store vital information. It's easy with memory boards, memory chips and PROM programmers.

You'll enjoy experimenting with projects on clock chips, video boards and even one on an inexpensive paper tape system.

Even if you don't have vital information to store or programs to run, you'll probably enjoy the many computer games you can design from checkers and chess to nuclear attack games.

Various other miscellaneous computer game projects are offered to you as the reader. Among these projects are a bionic clock, a computer-controlled thermometer, a programmable calculator and even a no-cost digital clock.

Each project in this book is supplemented with drawings, schematics and often parts lists.

Chapter 1
Computer Capabilities

Many experimenters are reticent to purchase and build a microcomputer system, even though complete systems can now be purchased for less than $100. This hesitancy on the part of interested experimenters can in most cases be attributed to several factors:

- Temporary depletion of pocket cash.
- Lack of knowledge of computer fundamentals.
- Lack of personal confidence in being able to handle the technology required.

The various components of fundamental computer systems will be discussed, computer terminology will be explained and fundamental, inexpensive breadboard circuits and experiments will be given in order to teach the rudiments of computer technology. The simple circuits and related experiments will give the experimenter the experience and confidence needed to build and debug computer circuitry.

The average experimenter with a basic knowledge of electronics who performs these experiments should be capable of building and using his own microcomputer system.

What Is a Computer?

A computer is a device which accepts information, applies some prescribed process to that information, and supplies the results. This definition can be applied to large classes of devices. For example:

- A series of gears, shafts, axles, cables, etc., such as a speedometer, takes rotation of axle (accepts information), converts the information to usable form (applies prescribed process) and gives reading of speed on dial (supplies results).
- A frequency counter takes input pulses (accepts information), counts them (applies prescribed process-counting) and displays frequency on an indicator (supplies results).
- An amplifier takes a small voltage (accepts information), amplifies it (applies prescribed process-amplification) and gives larger voltage as output (supplies results).

These three devices are all examples of *common computers*.

A computer is not always recognized as a computer, and a computer is not always called a computer. The term computer is a broad term and may be applied to common everyday devices. Computers need not be electronic, but may be mechanical, hydraulic, pneumatic or perhaps biological.

What is a Digital Computer?

Computers are divided into two common classes: *analog computers* and *digital computers*. Both classes of computers are the same in that they accept information, apply a process to that information and deliver results; however, they differ in the types of information which they can handle.

An analog computer processes information within a continuous range or within continuous ranges. Using the amplifier as an example, consider a simple device which will deliver a gain of precisely 100 to voltages in the range of .03V to .08V. In this amplifier an input of .039927V will give 3.9927 volts out. This simple analog computer will operate with any voltage within its specified range. Furthermore, all values of voltage within the range of the device will be processed. The range of the information that the analog computer will handle is continuous—there are no gaps within the range.

A digital computer can process only discrete values (for example, in the range 1-5, the numbers 1, 2, 3, 4 and 5 are discrete values). The digital computer is not capable of handling continuous information. The reason for this is simple. The digital computer uses a series of on-off conditions to store information. The number "one" might be represented by an "on," while the number "zero" might be represented by an "off." But what about numbers such as .5? Can you have half of an "on" or half of an "off?" Certainly not very conveniently. Of course we could change our definition and let .5 be

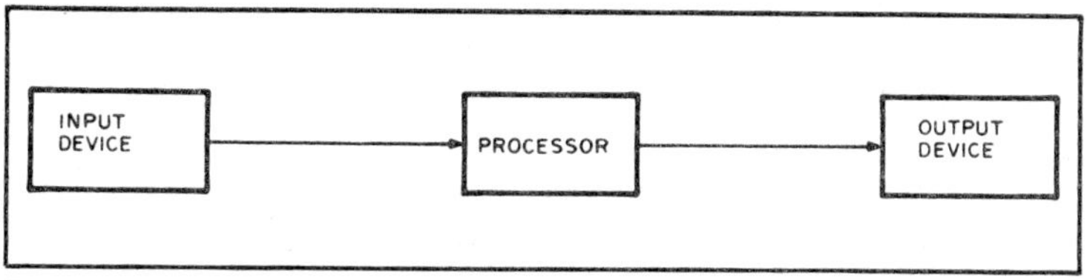

Fig. 1-1. Fundamental computer.

represented by an "on," but then how do you represent .55, .51 and so on? The point is that a digital computer can only handle discrete numbers, regardless of how we define those numbers. It cannot handle *all* numbers in a given range.

The frequency counter is an example of a digital computer. It accepts discrete pulses, counts them and displays the results. In a given one second interval it cannot count ½, or ⅓ or .40497 of a pulse. It can count only discrete pulses.

Components of a Digital Computer

The typical digital computer may have numerous components with a rat's nest of interconnections; however, a fundamental digital computer requires only three pieces: an input device, a processor and an output device (Fig. 1-1).

The input device may be as complex as a graphics input terminal or it may be as simple as a single switch. The output device may be as complex as a video display or it could be very sophisticated, or it could be simple logic used to detect the simultaneous presence of switch closures.

As an example, consider a simple computer which has the sole function of adding two numbers in the range 0 to 9 together and displaying the output on an LED indicator. The block diagram of this simple computer is shown in Fig. 1-2.

This simple computer is a fixed function computer and can do only one function—add. The limitations of this computer should be apparent. It has a small range (0-9), cannot perform other arithmetic functions and cannot compare two numbers for equality.

We could expand the capabilities of our processor by exchanging the simple "addition box" for an ALU (arithmetic, logical unit). This ALU type of processor is a readily available unit and offers additional capabilities such as subtraction, comparison of two numbers for equality, and logical operations such as "and" and "or." The simple configuration has now been expanded to that in Fig. 1-3 by the addition of an extra switch, an *instruction switch*, and by using an ALU for the processor. By varying the position of this switch, the

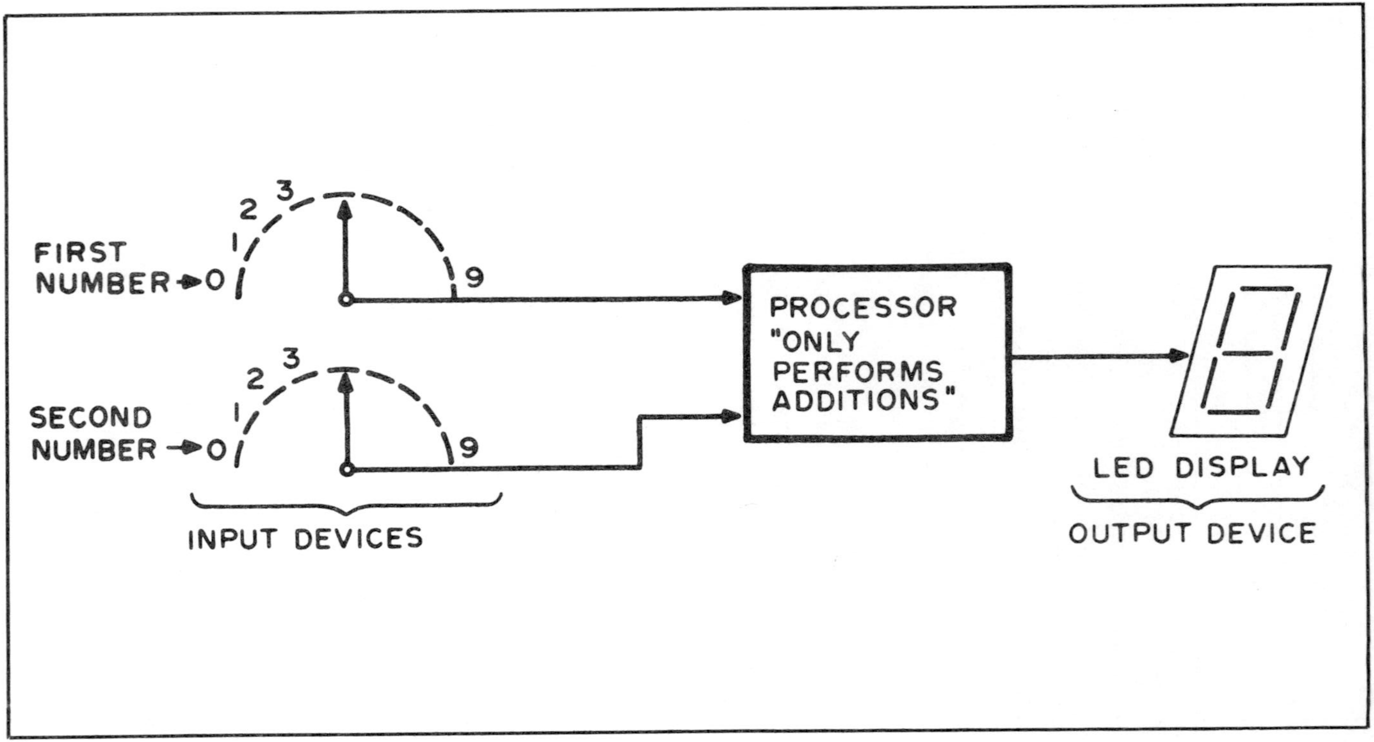

Fig. 1-2. Simple additon-only computer.

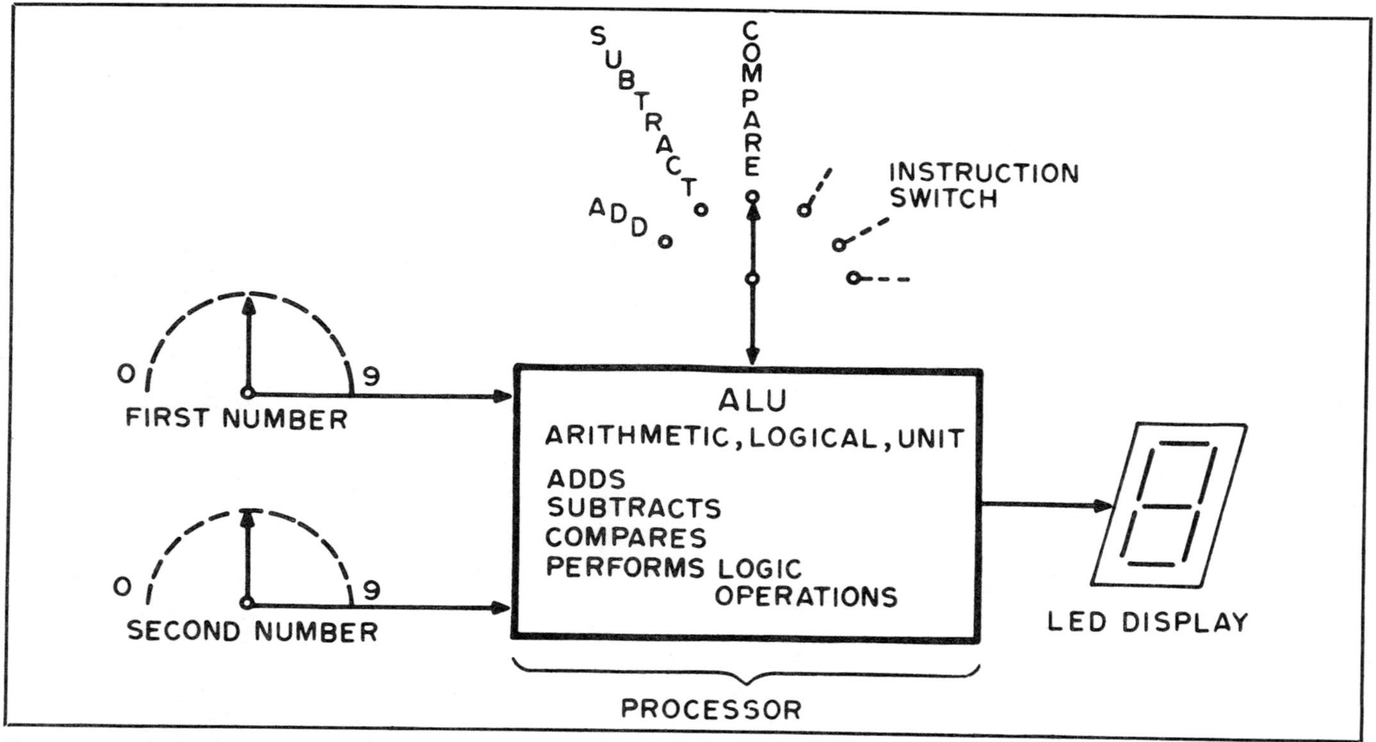

Fig. 1-3. Simple computer using ALU.

various instructions could be selected. We could perform any of the allowable operations on our two input numbers and have the results displayed on the LED indicator. At this point, the fundamental computer has additional capabilities, but still does not have enough capability to be really practical. The ALU by itself can only process two independent numbers at any given time. It is not capable of simple steps such as adding a column of 10 numbers, let alone complex problems involving many steps.

If our problem was to add a column of 10 numbers, we could expand the fundamental computer still further by adding some device to store the column of 10 numbers. The device could be connected to the processor in such a manner that the 10 numbers would automatically be added. This storage device could be in the form of 10 sets of switches, a tape recorder, a rotating magnetic disk, a series of magnetic cores or a series of electronic storage locations. A storage device in one of these classes is commonly called a *memory*. Note that a memory can be of several forms and is not limited to magnetic core or electronic storage. (One of the earliest digital computers used a tank of liquid mercury as a delay-line memory.)

At the risk of appearing to go on and on forever, one last addition will be made to the fundamental computer system—*an instruction memory*. This instruction memory will serve to hold a series of steps for the processor and will give these instructions to the processor in sequence. A clock (in this example, part of the instruction memory) is used to generate pulses to step the instruction memory from one instruction to the next (Fig. 1-4). With this system we could command the processor to perform the following steps in sequence:

- Add the first two numbers.
- Add the last two numbers.
- Compare the two sums.
- Display the smallest sum.

Of course the sequence of commands could be endless. This simple computer system had a lot of versatility and could be very useful. (An example of this type of programmable computer is a programmable calculator.) The process of setting up the instructions for the computer is called programming. The computer as it follows the programmed instructions *executes* or *runs the program*.

A Real-Life Computer

A real-life computer does not differ much in logic or function from that shown in Fig. 1-4; however, the ALU is usually expanded

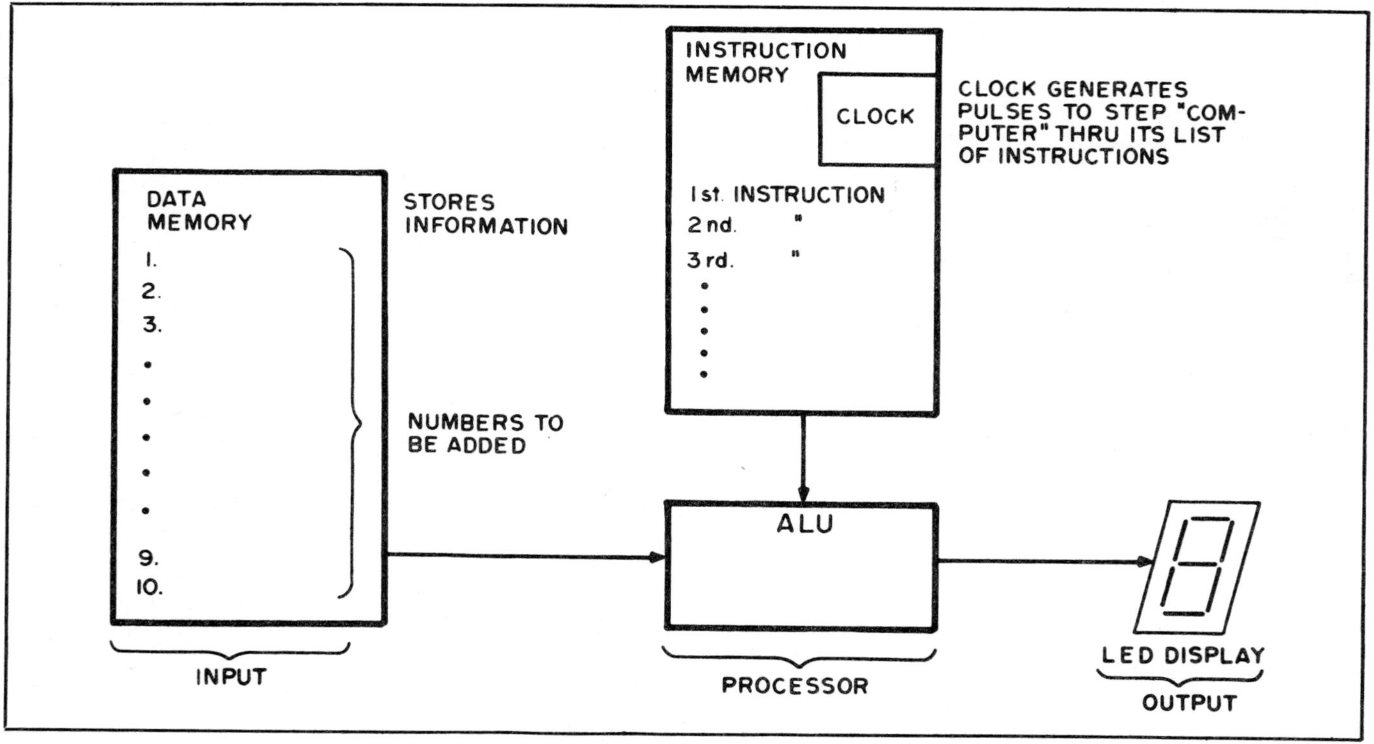

Fig. 1-4. Computer with memory.

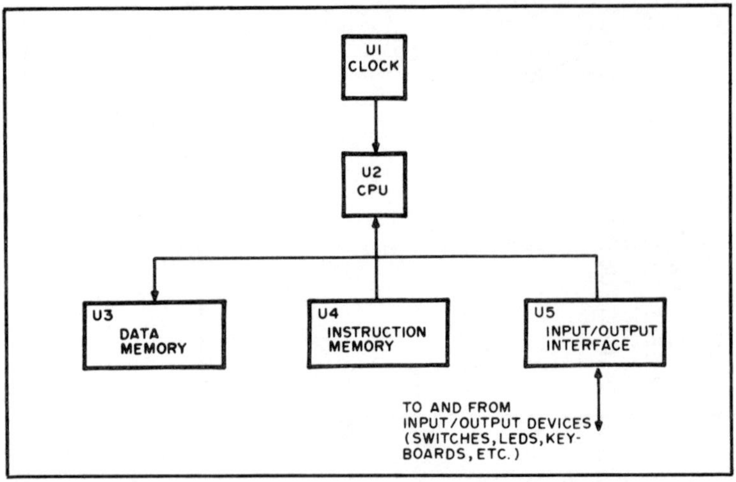

Fig. 1-5. Real-life computer. U1 = 4201 clock chip; U2 = 4040 CPU chip; U3 = 4002 random access memory; U4 = 4308 read only memory; U5 = 4207 (4209, 4211) general purpose I/O.[2]

to provide additional capabilities, and additional circuitry is usually provided to simplify input/output as well as to facilitate the flow of information and instructions within the system. While this last statement may sound like a zinger, it is not, since a device called a *CPU chip* (a single integrated circuit) in most cases contains the additional circuitry as well as the arithmetic and logical functions. A CPU chip (Central Processor Unit) is very unique and versatile device and is commonly called a "microprocessor." Figure 1-5 shows a block diagram for a typical, fundamental microprocessor computer system. The five blocks shown correspond to five integrated circuits. This is a real-life system. An Intel 4040 microprocessor system could be built using just five ICs.

How To Get Started?

It is not difficult to wire five integrated circuits together to form a microprocessor system. It is difficult, however, to make the plunge without first acquiring some important fundamental knowledge. By gathering this basic knowledge first, you can better utilize your microprocessor and you are in a better position to correct a problem should difficulties be encountered.

Fortunately, a large investment is not required in order to get into computers. For a nominal investment in a power supply, a breadboard and a handful of very inexpensive ICs, the experimenter can build up simple computer-oriented circuits to experience firsthand just how things work. While simple circuits will not duplicate all of the functions of a microcomputer system, the experimenter will be able to perform arithmetic and logical operations as well as store and retrieve information with simple memories. If the experimenter is able to understand these basic concepts and is able to duplicate simple experiments, then he should be able to build and use a microcomputer system.

Computers are Simple

There have been numerous examples put forth over the years to illustrate the basic scheme behind the operation of computers. The scheme is deceptively simple and incredibly powerful. The power comes from the speed with which the machines can perform the simple operations. The fundamental concept of the computer is that it is a machine that is capable of doing two fundamental operations at very high speed: First it is able to obtain a piece of information from a storage area and perform a function as directed by the information it obtains; and secondly, based on its current status, it is able to ascertain where to obtain the next piece of information that will give it further directions. This fundamental concept is the key to the operation of all digital computers and while it is a simple concept,

A1	A2	A3	A4	A5	A6	A7	A8
B1	B2	B3	B4	B5	B6	B7	B8
C1	C2	C3	C4	C5	C6	C7	C8
D1	D2	D3	D4	D5	D6	D7	D8
E1	E2	E3	E4	E5	E6	E7	E8
F1	F2	F3	F4	F5	F6	F7	F8
G1	G2	G3	G4	G5	G6	G7	G8
H1	H2	H3	H4	H5	H6	H7	H8

Fig. 1-6. A set of Post Office pigeon holes containing messages.

it can be built upon to arrive at all the complex operations computers of today can perform.

One of the best analogies for describing a computer's basic operations is to consider a bank of boxes, similar to a bank of Post Office mail boxes. A piece of paper containing directions can be placed in each box. A person is directed to go to the bank of boxes, and after starting at a given place, to open each box, withdraw the piece of paper and follow the directions there-on. The boxes are labeled in an orderly fashion, and the person is also told that unless a piece of paper in a box directs otherwise, when the person is finished performing the task directed, they are to replace the paper in the box and proceed to open the next box. Note, however, that a piece of paper may give directions to alter the sequence in which the person is to open boxes.

Figure 1-6 shows a picture of a set of such boxes. Each box is labeled for identification.

To present a view of a computer's operation, assume a person has been told to start at box A1 and to follow the directions contained on the pieces of paper in the boxes until a piece of paper containing the direction *stop* is found in one of the boxes. In this example the person finds the following instructions:

In box A1 is the message: *"Take the mathematical value of 1 and write it down on a scratch pad."*

Since the instruction in box A1 only pertained to some function that the person was to perform, and did not direct the person to go to some specific box, then the person will simply go on to the next box in the row. Box A2 contains the information:

"Add the number 2 to any value already present on your scratch pad."

The person will at this point perform an addition and have a total accumulated value on the pad of scratch paper. The accumulated value would be 3. Since there are no other directions in box A2, the operator would continue on to open box A3 which has the following message:

"Place any accumulated mathematical value you have on your scratch pad into box H8."

Thus the person would tear the current sheet off the scratch pad and place it—containing the value 3—into box H8. Note, though, that while the person was directed to place the accumulated value on the scratch pad into box H8, the person was not directed to alter the sequence in which to obtain new "instructions" so the person would proceed to open box A4 which contains the directive:

"Take the mathematical value of 6 and place it on your scratch pad."

Going on to box A5 the person finds:

"Add 3 to the present value on your scratch pad."

This is obviously just a *data word*. The operator adds the value 6 from the previous box to the number 3, noting the calculation on the scratch pad and proceeds to open box A6:

"Place any accumulated value you have on your scratch pad into box H7."

The person thus would put the value 9 on a piece of paper (from the scratch pad) into the designated box and proceed to open box A7:

"Get the value presently stored in box H8 and save the value on your scratch pad."

This is a simple operation and the person proceeds to open up box A8:

"Fetch the value in box H7. Subtract the value of your scratch pad from the value found in box H7. Leave the result on your scratch pad."

When the operator has performed this operation, the operator will have finished the *A* row and will then continue obtaining instructions by going to the *B* row and opening box B1 where more directions are found:

"If the present value on your scratch pad is not zero go to box B3."

At this time if the person checks the scratch pad it will be found that the value on the scratch pad is indeed non-zero as the last calculation performed on the scratch pad was to subtract the value in box H8 from the value in box H7. In this example that would be:

$$9 - 3 = 6$$

Therefore the directions in box B1 for this particular case will tell the operator to jump over box B2 and go to box B3. For the sake of completeness, however, box B2 does contain an instruction, for had the value on the scratch pad been zero the operator would not have jumped over box B2 and would have found the following message inside box B2:

"The values in box H7 and H8 are of equal value. STOP!"

However, for the values used in this example, the person would have jumped to box B3 where the following directive would be found:

"If the present value on your scratch pad is a "negative number" jump to box B5."

Since this is not currently the case the person will not JUMP to box B5, but will simply continue to open box B4 which contains:

"The value in box H7 is larger than the value in box H8. STOP!

At this point the person has completed the instruction sequence for this example. It should be noted, however, that box B5 did contain the message:

"The value in box H7 is smaller than the value in box H8. STOP!"

This little example of a person opening up boxes and following the directions contained in each one is very similar to the concept used by a computer. Note that each instruction is very short and specific. Also note that the combination of all the instructions in the example will result in the person being directed to solve the problem:

*"Is 1 + X greater than, less than, or equal to : 6 + Y?*For the reader can note, if the data words contained in boxes A2 and A5 for the example were changed, the sequence of instructions would still result in the person being told to STOP at the box that contained the correct answer. The reader can verify this by simply assuming that different numbers than those used in the example are in boxes A2 and A5 and going through the instruction sequence until told to STOP.

The example illustrates how a carefully planned set of directions, arranged such that they are performed in a precise sequence, can be used to solve a problem even though the *variables* (data) in the problem may vary. Such a set of instructions is often termed an *algorithm* by those in the computer field. The example solved a mathematical problem using the algorithm but the reader will find that algorithms can be devised to solve many problems on a computer that are not strictly mathematical!

Any person learning a new skill must of necessity learn the vocabulary of the field in order to proceed to any great extent. You might think that it would be easier if everything was written in plain everyday words, but the truth of the matter is that specialized vocabularies do serve several useful functions. For one thing, they can greatly shorten the time that it takes to communicate ideas or concepts. In today's fast-moving world, that is of significance in itself. In addition, the limitations of the English language often result in a given word having a special meaning when it is used in the context of a particular subject. One must know the new meaning when it is used in such a manner. Fortunately, much of the computer vocabulary is very logically named. This is probably due partly to the fact that computers are of necessity extremely dependent on logic, and hence many persons who helped create the field—and by that fact were rather logically oriented themselves—seem to have had the logical sense to have named many of the parts and systems of computers and computer programs, in a logical manner.

Figures 1-7 and 1-8 are used to demonstrate the analogy between the person taking instructions from a group of mail boxes and the basic operation of a real minicomputer.

POST OFFICE BOXES = MEMORY

A1	A2	A3	A4	A5	A6	A7	A8
B1	B2	B3	B4	B5	B6	B7	B8
C1	C2	C3	C4	C5	C6	C7	C8
D1	D2	D3	D4	D5	D6	D7	D8
E1	E2	E3	E4	E5	E6	E7	E8
F1	F2	F3	F4	F5	F6	F7	F8
G1	G2	G3	G4	G5	G6	G7	G8
H1	H2	H3	H4	H5	H6	H7	H8

PERSON = CENTRAL PROCESSING UNIT

PAD & PENCIL = ACCUMULATOR

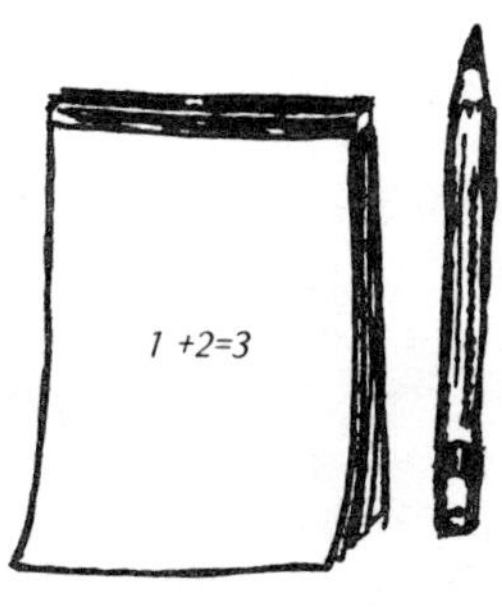

Fig. 1-7. The computer structure compared to the Post Office pigeon holes.

Figure 1-7 shows the Post Office boxes, a figure representation of a person who is able to *fetch* and return the *instructions* or *data* from and to the boxes and a *scratch pad* on which the person can make temporary calculations when directed to do so.

In Fig. 1-8 are three interconnected boxes which form a *block diagram* fo a computer. The uppermost portion of the block diagram is labeled the *memory*. The middle portion is labeled the *central processor unit* or CPU for short. The lower part of the diagram depicts an *accumulator*.

The correlation between the two pictures is extremely simple. The Post Office boxes correspond to the memory portion of a real computer. The memory is a storage place, a location where instructions and data can be stored for long lengths of time. The memory can be accessed. Instructions and/or data can be taken out of memory, operated on and replaced. New data can be put into the memory. A memory that can be *read from* as well as *written into* is called a *read and write memory*. A read and write memory is often referred to as an RAM as an abbreviation. Many times it is feasible to have a memory that is only *read from*. A memory that is never *written into*, but is only used to *read from*, is termed a *read only memory* and is abbreviated as an ROM. For the present discussion the term memory will refer to a read and write memory (RAM).

The figure of a person in Fig. 1-7 corresponds to the central processor unit in Fig. 1-8. The central processor unit in a computer is the section that controls the overall operation of the machine. The CPU can receive instructions or data from the memory. It is able to *interpret* the instructions it fetches from the memory. It is also able to perform various types of mathematical operations. It can also *return* information to the memory—for instance make deposits of data into the memory. The CPU also contains control sections that enable it to sequentially access the next location in memory when it has finished performing an operation, or, if it is directed to do so, to access the memory at a specified location, or to jump to a new area in memory from which to continue fetching instructions.

The pad of paper and pencil in Fig. 1-7 corresponds to the block titled accumulator in Fig. 1-8. The *accumulator* is a temporary *register* or *manipulating area* which is used by the CPU when it is performing operations such as adding two numbers. One number or piece of information can be temporarily held in it while the central processor unit goes on to obtain additional instructions or data from memory. It is an electronic scratch pad for the CPU.

The three fundamental units—the memory, central processor unit and the accumulator—are at the heart of every digital computer

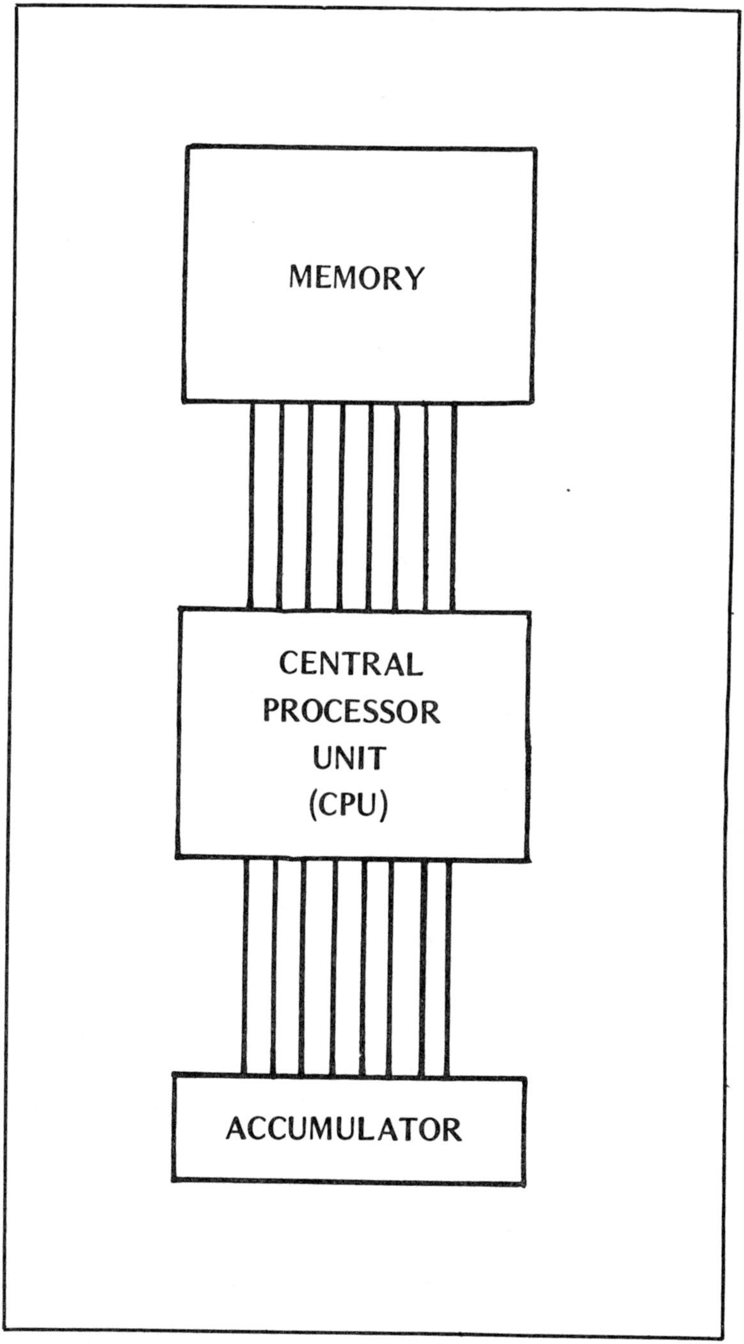

Fig. 1-8. Block diagram of a computer's fundamental components.

system. Of course, there are other parts which will be added in and explained later, but these fundamental portions can be used to explain the basic operation of a digital computer.

The reader should learn the names of the basic parts of the computer as they are presented. Note how easy it is to remember the portions that have been shown. The *remembering element* is a *memory*. The portion that does the work or processing is simply termed the *central processor unit*, and the part that is used to accumulate information temporarily is aptly called the *accumulator*!

The reader should now have a conceptual view of the concept behind a computer's operation and an understanding of the machine's most basic organization. It is simply a machine that can fetch information from a memory, interpret the information as an instruction or data, perform a very small operation and continue on to determine the next operation that is to be performed. Each operation it is capable of doing is very tiny by itself, but when the many operations of a typical program are performed in sequence, the solutions to very complex problems can be obtained. It is important to remember that the computer can perform each little operation in just a few millionths of a second! Thus a program that might seem very large to a person—say one with many thousands of individual instructions—would only take a digital computer a few thousandths of a second to perform. The speed with which the computer can execute individual instructions is what gives the computer its seemingly fantastic capability.

It is now time to start delving into the actual physical manner in which a computer operates. How can a machine be constructed so that it is able to perform the processes of the central processor unit? While it will require a number of pages of text to explain the procedure, it is not nearly as difficult to understand as many people might suspect. The complexity of a computer when first viewed by a person is caused by the fact that it appears to consist of many hundreds of parts. It becomes much simpler when one understands that the hundreds of parts are really made up from a few dozen similar parts and they are carefully organized into just a few major operating portions. The reader is already familiar with the most fundamental portions.

As fantastic as it may sound at first, a digital computer can be thought of as really nothing more than a highly organized collection of *on or off* switches. Yes, computers are constructed from electronic devices that can only assume one of two possible states. The electronic switches can be constructed in a variety of ways. For instance, the switch can be made so that the voltage at a given point is either high or low, or current through a device is either flowing or not flowing, or flowing in one direction and then the other direction. But, regardless of how the electronic switch is constructed, its status can always be represented as being either *on* or *off*. This on or off status can be mathematically symbolized most suitably by a mathematical system based on *binary notation*.

Some people tend to think that computers are very difficult to understand because they have heard of strange types of mathematics that are often referred to in conjunction with computers. In actuality much of the mathematics that are dealt with in computer technology are much easier to understand and deal with than the decimal system that the average person is familiar with. In the decimal numbering system a person must learn 10 different symbols, and in order to manipulate those symbols, they must memorize a lot of information. For instance, look at how students are taught to multiply. The learning process actually involves the student having to memorize a rather large number of facts. Because of the way it is typically taught, most students never realize how much work they have to go through just to learn the multiplication tables! The teacher does not stand up and say, "OK, now you are going to memorize about 100 facts." Instead, over a period of a few weeks or so, the student is made to memorize the 100 or so facts—a few at a time. The student must learn the value of each digit multiplied by all the other digits in the decimal numbering system. The decimal numbering system is far more complicated for the beginner than learning the binary numbering system, and the binary numbering system is the one utilized by computers at their most basic functioning level. The reason the computer uses the binary system is because it is the simplest system around and hence the easiest one with which to construct a computing machine.

Readers know the word *binary* indicates *two*. Computers are built up of electronic switches that can only have two possible states. The switches are binary devices. The status of the switches can be represented mathematically utilizing the binary numbering system. The binary numbering system only has two digits in it. They are zero (0) and one (1). A switch can thus be mathematically symbolized, for instance, by a zero when it is off and a one when it is on. The opposite relationship could also be established, a one could be used to represent a switch being off and a zero used to represent a switch as on. It would make no difference mathematically which convention was used as long as one was consistent. For the purposes of the present discussion, the reader can assume that the first convention (switch off = 0, switch on = 1) will be used.

It should be immediately apparent that working with a numbering system based on only two integers will be a lot easier than working with one having 10 integer symbols. In fact, most problems for people learning the binary system come about because they tend to forget how simple it is, and they tend to keep going towards a decimal solution out of habit when they are working with the binary system. For instance, when one starts to add binary numbers, as soon as the value 1 is exceeded, a *carry* to the next column must be made. The value of the addition of 1 + 1 in the binary system is: 10. It is not 2. There is not such integer as 2 in the binary numbering system. However, when a person who has worked with the decimal system for years first starts working with the binary system, old decimal habits tend to get in the way.

To formally introduce the binary mathematical system one can start by stating that it uses two integers, zero (0) and one (1), and no others. A binary number has a value determined by the value of the integers that make up the number, and the position of the digits.

In the decimal numbering system, the reader is familiar with the location of a digit having a weighted value as follows: A three digit number has a value determined by the unit value of the digit in the right-most column plus the value of the digit to the left of it multiplied by 10, plus the value of the third digit mulitplied by one hundred as illustrated in the following example:

The decimal number 345 is equal to:

5 units = 5
plus (+) 4 times 10 = 40
plus (+) 3 times 100 = 300

In other words, after the right-most column (which has the value of the digit), each column to the left is given a weighting factor which increases as a power of the total number of digits utilized by the numbering system. Note that in this example the 4 representing 40 units is equal to 4 times the number of integer symbols in the decimal system (10) because it is located in the second column from the right. The number 3 representing 300 units is equal to 3 times the number of integer symbols in the decimal system squared because it is located in the third column from the right. This relationship of the weighted value of the digits based on their position can be described in mathematical shorthand as follows:

If the number of different integer symbols in the numbering system is U (for the decimal system U = 10) and the column whose weighted value is to be determined is column number M (starting with the right-most column and counting to the left) and any digit is represented by the symbol X, then the weighted value of a digit in column M is expressed as: X times U raised to the power (M-1) or $XU^{(M-1)}$.

The reader can easily verify that the above formula applies to the decimal numbering system. However, the above formula is a general formula that can be used to determine the weighted positional value of any numbering system. It will be used to determine the weighted positional values of numbers in the binary numbering system.

In the binary numbering system there are just two different integer symbols (0 and 1). Thus U in this formula is equal to 2. For illustrative purposes assume the following binary number is to be analyzed:

101

and it is desired to determine its value in terms of decimal numbers. (Remember its binary value is just 101). Using the above formula for the digit in the right-most column: M is equal to 1, thus (M-1) is equal to 0, and with X = 1:

$$\text{Weighted Value} = X.\ U^{(M-1)}$$
$$= 1.2^{0} = 1$$

(Remember that any number raised to the zeropower is equal to 1.) Going on to the next digit it can be seen that the weighted value is simply 0! Finally, the digit in the third column from the right has the weighted value because of its position:

$$\text{Weighted Value} = X.U^{(M-1)}$$
$$= 1.2^{(3-1)} = 2^{2} = 4$$

Then, by adding up the sum of the weighted values (similar to that done for the decimal example earlier) one can see that the decimal equivalent of 101 binary is 5:

The binary number 101 is equal to:

1 units = 1
\+ 0 times 2 = 0
\+ 1 times 4 = 4

and thus 101 in the binary numbering system is the same as 5 in the decimal numbering system.

There will be more to learn about the binary numbering system. However, the brief information given will be enough to continue on with the discussion that this section is primarily concerned with—the basic operation of a computer. Since the reader is now aware that a computer is composed of numerous electronic switches and knows that one can use a mathematical shorthand to represent the status of the switches (whether they are on or off), and is also aware of the fundamental concept behind a computer's operation, it is now possible to proceed to show how electronic switches can be arranged to build a functional computer. That is, how the electronic switches can be arranged and interconnected in a fashion that will allow a machine to fetch a piece of information from a memory section, decode the information so as to determine an instruction, and also determine where to obtain the next instruction or additional data.

To begin this part of the discussion it will be beneficial for the reader to picture a group of cells (similar to the Post Office boxes shown earlier) arranged in orderly rows as shown in Fig. 1-9. This time, instead of each cell holding a complete instruction, it can be understood that each cell only represents part of an instruction and that it takes a whole row of cells to make up an instruction. Furthermore, each cell may only contain the mathematical symbol for a one (1) or a zero (0)—or, in other words, its contents represent the status of an electronic switch.

At this time a few more computer technology definitions will be illustrated in Fig. 1-9, each box containing a binary 1 or 0 represents what is called a *bit of information*. While each cell may only contain one piece of information at a time, a cell can actually represent one of two possible states of information. This is because the cell can be in two possible states—it either contains a zero or a one. If one starts assigning positional values to the cells in a row, it can be seen that the total number of possible states in one row will increase rapidly. For instance, two cells in a row can represent up to four states of information. This is because two cells side-by-side, containing either a 0 or 1 in each cell can have one of the following four states at a particular moment in time: 1 0, 01, 11 or 0 0. Three cells in a row can represent up to eight states of information as the possible states of three cells side-by-side are: 0 0 0, 0 0 1, 0 1 0, 0 1 1, 1 0 0, 1 0 1, 1 1 0, 1 1 1. In fact, when each cell can represent a binary number, the total number of states of information that a row of N cells can represent is: 2 to the Nth power, 2^n. Thus, a row of eight binary cells can represent 2 to the eighth (256) states of information! That is, the combination of the eight cells can be filled with zeros and ones in 256 different patterns.

WORD #1	1	0	1	0	1	0	1	0
WORD #2	0	1	0	1	0	1	0	1
WORD #3	1	1	0	0	1	1	0	0
WORD #4	0	0	1	1	0	0	1	1
WORD #5	1	1	1	1	0	0	0	0
WORD #6	0	0	0	0	1	1	1	1
WORD #7	1	1	1	1	1	1	1	1
WORD #8	0	0	0	0	0	0	0	0

Fig. 1-9. An array of electronic cells, 8 bits per cell.

A group (row) of cells in a computer's memory is often referred to as a *word*. A word in a computer's memory is a fixed size group of cells that are accessed or manipulated during one operational cycle of the central processing unit (CPU). The CPU will effectively handle all the cells in a word in memory simultaneously whenever it processes information in the memory. Digital computers can have varying *word lengths* depending on how they are engineered. Many microcomputers have a memory word size consisting of eight cells. The number of cells in a word, and the number of words in a computer's memory have a lot to do with the machine's overall capability. In the typical microcomputer system, the memory is available in modules—groups of words which can be plugged into a common set of wires in the system. With current LSI technology, a typical module of moderate price has 1024 bytes in an 8-bit computer system. With the 8008 oriented design serving as the basis for this discussion, one could potentially plug in 16 modules for a total of 16,384 bytes or 131,072 bits. Thus, a large amount of information can be *stored* in the computer's memory at any one time.

The astute reader may have already figured out a very special reason for grouping cells into words in memory. It was pointed out earlier that a row of eight cells could represent up to 256 different patterns. Now, if each possible pattern could be decoded by electronic means so that a particular pattern could specify a precise instruction for the central processor unit, then a large group of instructions would be available for use by the machine. That is exactly the concept used in a digital computer. Patterns of ones and zeros organized into a computer word are stored in memory. The CPU is able to examine a word in memory and decode the pattern contained therein to determine the precise operation that is to perform. Most microcomputers do not decode every one of the possible 256 patterns that can be held in a row of eight cells as an instruction. They have an *instruction set* of over 100 instructions which are represented by different patterns of ones and zeros in an eight cell memory word. Each pattern that represents an instruction can be decoded by the CPU and will cause the CPU to perform a specific function. Details of all the functions a computer can perform are usually found in the manufacturer's documentation.

There is another ingredient necessary for making the machine automatic in operation. That is that the CPU must know where to obtain the next instruction in memory after it completes an operation. That function is greatly aided by having the memory cells grouped as words. The reader should note that in Fig. 1-9 each group of cells represents a word labeled as: "word #1," "word # 2" etc. There is a special portion of the central processor unit that is used to control where the next word containing an instruction in memory is located. This special part is commonly referred to as the program counter. One reason it was given the name program counter is because most of the time all it does is count. It counts memory words. Each word in memory is considered to have an *address*. In Fig. 1-9 each word was given an address by simply designating each word with a number. Word #1 has an address of 1. Word #2 had an address of 2, etc. The program counter portion of the CPU keeps tabs on where the CPU should obtain the next instruction by maintaining an address of the word in memory that is to be processed. About 90 percent of the time all the program counter does is increment the value it has each time the CPU finishes doing an operation. Thus, if the computer were to start executing a simple program that began by its performing the instruction contained in "word #1" in memory—the very process of having the machine start the program at that location in memory would cause the program counter to assume a value of 1. As soon as the CPU had performed the function the program counter would increment its value to 2. The CPU would then look at the program counter and see that its instruction was located in word #2 in memory. When the instruction in word #2 has been processed the program counter would increment its value to 3. This process might continue uniterrupted until the CPU found an instruction that told it to STOP.

A sharp reader might be starting to ask, "Why have a program counter if each instruction follows the next?" The answer is simply that the availability of a program counter gives the freedom of not having to always take the instruction at the next address in memory. This is because the contents of the program counter can be changed when the CPU detects an instruction that directs it to do so. This enables the computer to be able to jump around to different sections in memory, and as will become apparent later, greatly increases the capability of the machine.

The program counter is actually just a group of cells in the CPU that may contain either a binary zero or one. The binary value in the row of cells that constitute the program counter determines the address of a word in memory. Since the number of words in memory can be very large, and since the program counter must be capable of holding the address of any possible location in memory, the number of cells in a row in the program counter is larger than the number of cells in a word in memory. In an 8008 oriented computer design, for example, the number of cells in the program counter is 14. Since 2 to the 14th power is 16,384, the program counter can present up to

16,384 different patterns. Each pattern can be used to represent the address of a word in memory. Figure 1-10 illustrates what the contents of the program counter would look like when it contained the address for a specific word in memory. The address the example displays is *address 0*. which can be considered the first word in memory. The reader should note that an address of zero can actually represent a word in memory.

Earlier it was stated that some instructions can actually change the value of the program counter and thus allow a program to jump to different sections in memory. However, the reader now knows that a word in memory only contains eight cells, and yet the program counter of an 8008 based computer contains eight cells, and yet the program counter contains 14 cells. In order to change the entire contents of the program counter (by bringing in words from memory), it is necessary to use more than one memory word. This can be done if the program counter is considered to actually be two groups of cells connected together. One group contains eight cells and the other six. In order to change the contents of the entire program counter, one whole eight cell word could be read from a memory location and placed in the right-hand group of eight cells of the program counter. Then another eight cell word could be read from memory. Since only six more cells are needed to finish filling the program counter, the information in two of the eight cells from the second word brought in from memory coould be discarded. If the information in the two left most cells of the word in memory were thrown away then the remaining six cells would contain information that could be placed in the six unfilled locations in the program counter. Most of the common eight-bit microcomputers use a similar scheme of breaking an address into two pieces when the program counter is loaded in a jump instruction.

In order to make it easier for a person working with the machine to remember addresses of words in memory, a concept referred to by computer technologists as *paging* is utilized. Paging is the arbitrary assignment of *blocks* of memory words into sections that are referred to figuratively as *pages*. The reader should realize that the actual physical memory unit consists of all the words in memory—with each word assigned a numerical address that the machine utilizes. As far as the machine is concerned, the words in memory are assigned consecutive addresses from word #0 on up to the highest word # contained in the memory. However, people using computers have found it easier to work with addressed by arbitrarily grouping blocks of words into pages. For example in the Intel 8008, pages are considered to be blocks of 256 memory words. The first

13	12	11	10	9	8	7	6	5	4	3	2	1	0
0	0	0	0	0	0	0	0	0	0	0	0	0	0

Fig. 1-10. The program counter of an 8008 based machine.

memory word address in an 8008 system is at address zero (0). Programmers could refer to this word as word #0 on page #. The 256th word in memory as far as the computer is concerned has an address of 255. (Note: Since the address of 0 is actually assigned for the first physical word in memory, all succeeding words have an address that is one less than the physical quantity. A programmer could refer to this word as word #255 on page #0. The 257th word in memory has an absolute address of 256 ("n" th word minus one since location 0 contains a memory word) as far as the machine is concerned, but a programmer could refer to that word location as being on page #1 at location 0. Similarly, the 513th word in memory, when the paging concept is used, becomes word #0 on page #2 for a programmer—but it is just 512 as far as the machine is concerned. Paging at multiples of 256 is a convenient tool when dealing with any eight-bit microcomputer.

The reader might have noted a nice coincidence in regards to the assignment of paging in eight-bit computers. Each page refers to a block of memory words that contains 256 locations (0 to 255). The reader will recall that that is exactly the number of different patterns that can be specified by a group of eight binary cells, and there are eight binary cells in a memory ward. The relationship is more than coincidental. Note that now one has devised a convenient way for a person to be able to think of memory addresses and at the same time be able to specify a new address to the program counter that will still result in it containing an *absolute address* that the machine can use. For instance, if it was desired to change the contents of the 14 cell program counter from an absolute address of word #0, say to word #511, the following procedure could be used: The programmer would first specify an instruction that the CPU would decode as meaning *change the value in the program counter.* (Such an instruction might be a jump instruction in the instruction set.) Following that instruction would be a word that held the desired value of the *low order address* or word # within a page. Since a memory word only has eight cells, since eight cells can only represent 256 different patterns and since one of the patterns is equivalent to a value of zero, then the largest number the eight cells can represent is 255. However, this is the largest word # that is contained on a page. This value can be placed in the right-most eight cells of the program counter. Now it is necessary to complete the address by getting the contents of another word from memory. Thus, immediately following the word that contained the low address would be another word that contained the page # of the address that the program counter was to contain. In this case the page number would be 1. When this value is placed in the left six cells of the program counter, the program counter would contain the pattern in Fig. 1-11.

If desired, the reader can verify by using the formula presented previously for determining the decimal value of a binary number, that the pattern presented in Fig. 1-11 corresponds to 511, and thus, by using the page # and word # on the page, each of which will fit in an eight cell memory word, a method has been demonstrated that will result in the program counter being set to an absolute address for a word in memory. Figure 1-12 provides some examples as a summary.

By now the reader should have a pretty good understanding of the concepts regarding the organization of memory into electrical cells which can be in one of two possible states, the grouping of these cells into words which can hold patterns which the CPU can recognize as specifying particular operations and the operation of a program counter which is able to hold the address of a word in memory from which the CPU is to obtain an instruction.

It is now time to discuss the operation of the "scratch pad" area for a computer—the accumulator and some additional manipulating registers in the typical 8008 based computer.

As was pointed out earlier, there is a section of a computer that is used to perform calculations in and which can hold information while the CPU is in the process of fetching another instruction from the memory. The portion was termed an *accumulator* because it could accumulate information obtained from the CPU performing a series of instructions until such time as the CPU was directed to transfer the information elsewhere (or discard it). The accumulator is also considered to be the primary mathematical center for computer operations for it is the place where additions, subtractions and various other mathematically oriented operations (such as Boolean algebra) are generally performed under program control.

The concept of an accumulator is not difficult to understand and its physical structure can be readily explained. The actual control of an accumulator by the CPU can be quite complex, but these complex electronic manipulations do not have to be understood by the computer user. It is only necessary to know the end results of the various operations that can be performed within an accumulator.

13	12	11	10	9	8	7	6	5	4	3	2	1	0
0	0	0	0	0	1	1	1	1	1	1	1	1	1

Fig. 1-11. The program counter with address 511 represented in binary notation.

The accumulator in an Intel 8008 based machine can be considered as a group of eight memory cells similar to a word in memory except that the information in the cells can be manipulated in many ways that are not directly possible in a word in memory.

Figure 1-13 shows a collection of eight binary cells containing ones and zeros to represent an accumulator. The cells are numbered from left to right starting with B7 down to B0. The designations refer to *bit positions* within the accumulator. Note that the right-most cell is designated B0 and the eighth cell (left-most cell) is designated B7. The reader should become thoroughly familiar with the concept of assigning the reference of zero to the right-most bit position in a row of cells (similar to the concept of assigning a reference of zero to the first address of a word on a page in memory) as the convention is frequently used by computer technologists. The convention can be confusing for the beginner who fails to remember that the physical quantity is one more than the reference designation. The convention of labeling the first physical position as zero makes much more sense once the reader learns to think in terms of the binary numbering system and thoroughly realizes that the zero referred to so frequently in computer work when discussing actual operations actually represents a physical state (the status of an electronic switch) and does not necessarily imply the mathematical notion of nothing. The concept of assigning a bit designation to the positions of the cells within the accumulator will allow the reader to follow explanations of various accumulator operations.

One of the most fundamental and most often used operations of an accumulator is for it to simply hold a number while the CPU obtains a second operator. In an 8008 type of machine the accumulator can be loaded with a value obtained from a location in memory or one of the partial accumulators. It can then hold this value until it is time to perform some other operation with the accumulator. (It will become apparent later that the accumulator of an 8008 can also receive information from external devices.)

Perhaps the second most often used operation of an accumulator is to have it perform mathematical operations such as addition or subtraction with the value it contains at the time the function is performed and the contents of a memory location or one

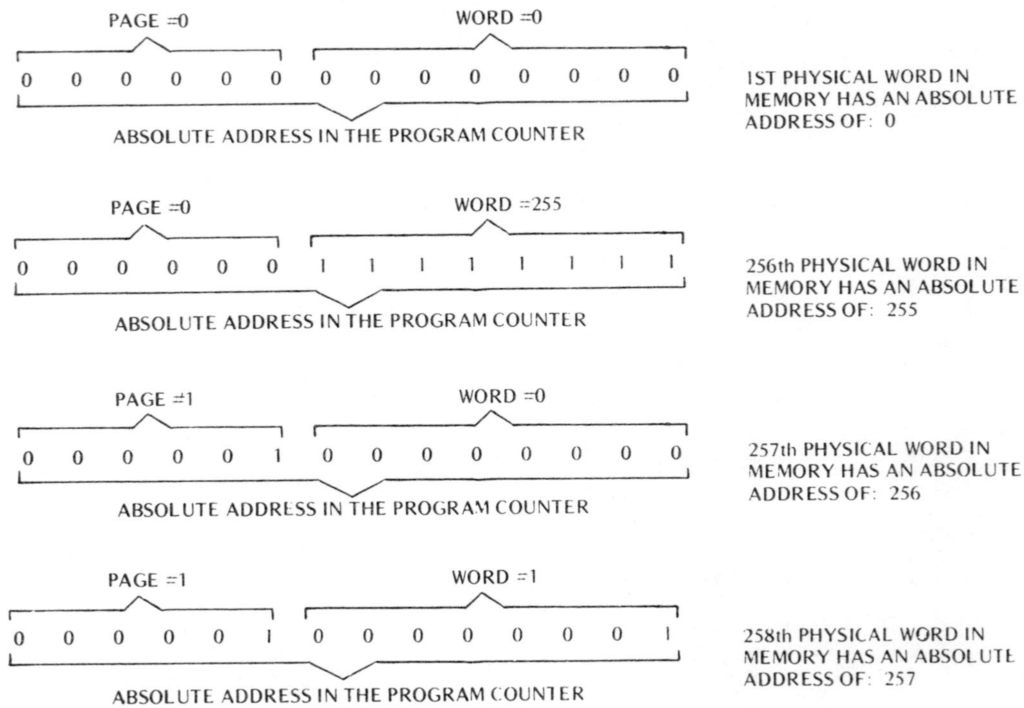
PAGE =0
WORD =0
0 0 0 0 0 0 0 0 0 0 0 0 0 0
ABSOLUTE ADDRESS IN THE PROGRAM COUNTER
1ST PHYSICAL WORD IN MEMORY HAS AN ABSOLUTE ADDRESS OF: 0
PAGE =0
WORD =255
0 0 0 0 0 0 1 1 1 1 1 1 1 1
ABSOLUTE ADDRESS IN THE PROGRAM COUNTER
256th PHYSICAL WORD IN MEMORY HAS AN ABSOLUTE ADDRESS OF: 255
PAGE =1
WORD =0
0 0 0 0 0 1 0 0 0 0 0 0 0 0
ABSOLUTE ADDRESS IN THE PROGRAM COUNTER
257th PHYSICAL WORD IN MEMORY HAS AN ABSOLUTE ADDRESS OF: 256
PAGE =1
WORD =1
0 0 0 0 0 1 0 0 0 0 0 0 0 1
ABSOLUTE ADDRESS IN THE PROGRAM COUNTER
258th PHYSICAL WORD IN MEMORY HAS AN ABSOLUTE ADDRESS OF: 257

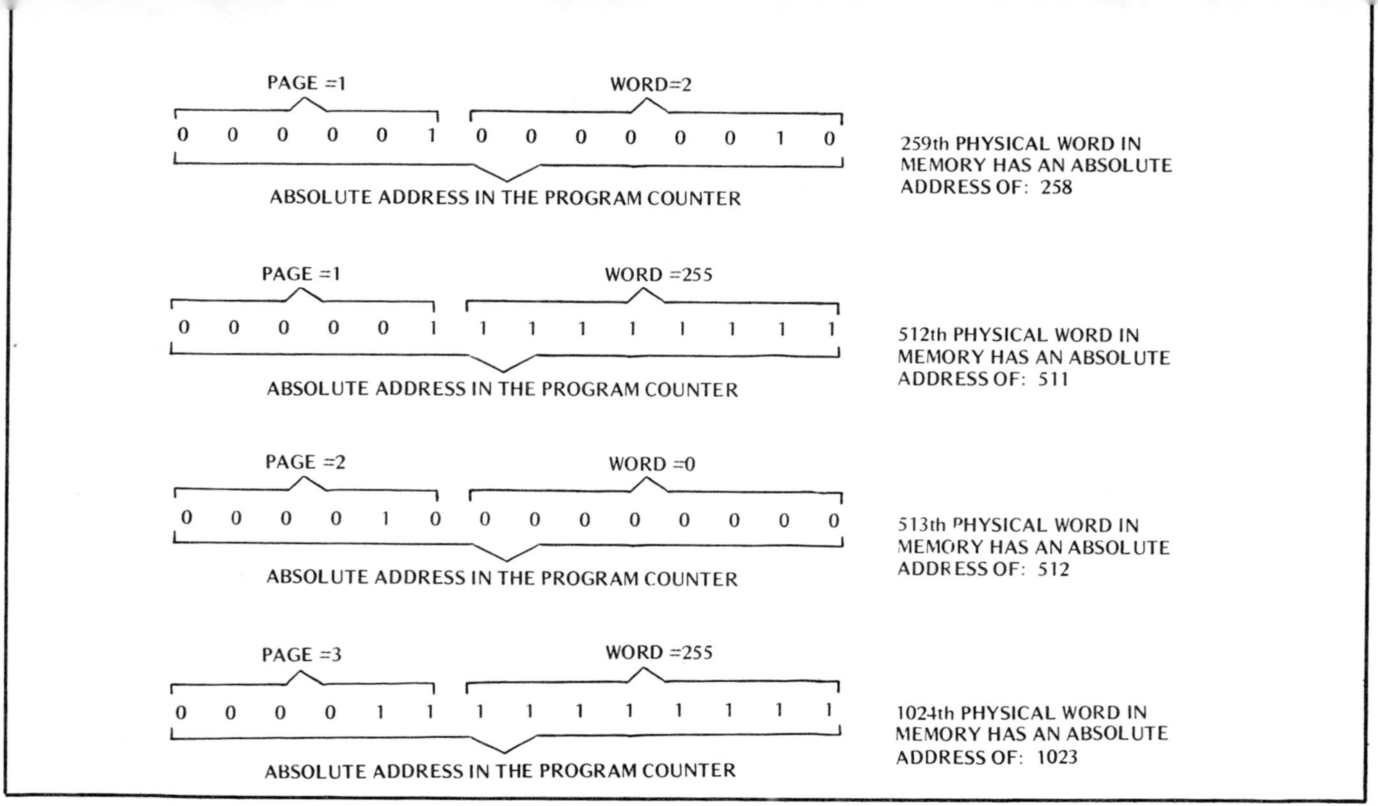

Fig. 1-12. Examples of addresses in an 8008 based system.

B7	B6	B5	B4	B3	B2	B1	B0
1	0	1	0	1	0	1	0

Fig. 1-13. The accumulator, pictured with binary 10101010 (decimal value 160) in its 8 bits.

of the partial accumulators. Thus if the accumulator contained the binary equivalent of the decimal number 5, and an instruction to add the contents of a specific memory location which contained the binary equivalent of the decimal number 3 was encountered, the accumulator would end up with the value of 8 in binary form as shown in Fig. 1-14.

Perhaps the next most frequently used group of operations for the accumulator is for it to perform Boolean mathematical operations between itself and/or other partial accumulators or words in memory. These operations in the typical microcomputer include the logical *and, or* and *exclusive or* operations.

Another important capability of the accumulator is its ability to rotate its contents. In an 8008, as in many micros, the contents of the accumulator can be rotated either to the right or left. This capability has many useful functions, and is one method by which mathematical multiplication or division can be performed. Figure 1-15 illustrates the concept of *rotating* the contents of the accumulator.

The astute reader may notice that the accumulator rotate capability also enables the accumulator to emulate a *shift register* which can be a valuable function in many practical applications of the computer.

The accumulator serves another extremely powerful function. When certain operations are performed with the accumulator the computer is capable of examining the results and will then *set* or *clear* a special group of *flags*. Other instructions can then test the status of the special flags and perform operations based on the particular setting(s) of the flags. In this manner the machine is capable of modifying its behavior when it performs operations depending on the results it obtains at the time the operation is performed!

In an 8008 based computer, there are four special flags which are manipulated by the results of operations with the accumulator (and in several special cases by operations with partial accumulators). These four flags will be described in detail. Other micros have similar condition flags.

B7	B6	B5	B4	B3	B2	B1	B0	
0	0	0	0	0	1	0	1	ORIGINAL CONTENTS OF THE ACCUMULATOR
0	0	0	0	0	0	1	1	CONTENTS OF THE SPECIFIED WORD IN MEMORY
0	0	0	0	1	0	0	0	FINAL RESULTS AFTER THE ADDITION IN THE ACCUMULATOR

Fig. 1-14. Adding the content of a memory word to the accumulator.

B7	B6	B5	B4	B3	B2	B1	B0	
0	0	0	0	0	0	1	0	ORIGINAL CONTENTS OF THE ACCUMULATOR (EQUAL TO DECIMAL 2)
0	0	0	0	0	1	0	0	RESULT WHEN THE ACCUMULATOR IS ROTATED TO THE LEFT ONE TIME (VALUE NOW EQUAL 4)
0	0	0	0	0	0	0	1	RESULT WHEN THE ACCUMULATOR IS NOW ROTATED TO THE RIGHT TWO TIMES (VALUE NOW EQUAL 1)

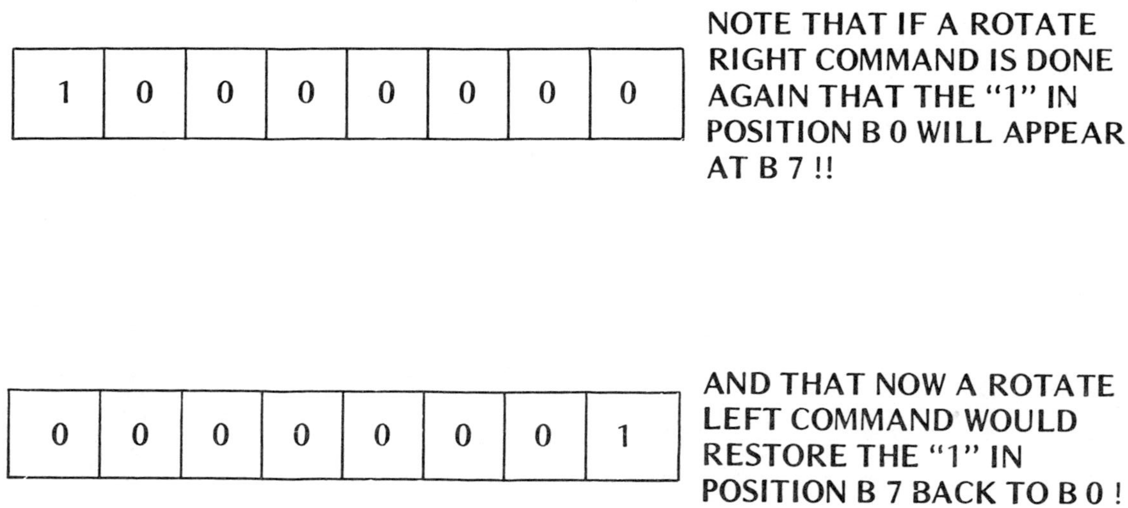

Fig. 1-15. Rotating the content of the accumulator.

The *carry flag* can be considered as a one bit (cell) extension of the accumulator register. This flag is changed if the contents of the accumulator should overflow during an addition operation (or underflow during a subtraction operation). Also, the *carry bit* can be utilized as an extension of the accumulator for certain types of rotate commands.

The *sign flag* is set to a logic state of 1 when the most significant bit (MSB) of the accumulator (or partial accumulator) is a 1 after certain types of instructions have been performed. The name of this flag derives from the concept of using two's complement arithmetic in a register where the MSB is used to designate the sign of the number in the remaining bit positions of the register. Conventionally, a 1 in the MSB designates the number as a negative number. If the MSB of the accumulator (or partial accumulator) is 0 after certain operations, then the sign flag is zero (indicating that the number in the register is a positive number by two's complement convention).

The zero flag is set to a logic state of 1 if all the bits in the accumulator (or partial accumulator) are set to zero after certain types of operations have been executed. It is set to 0 if any one of the bits is a logic one after these same operations. Thus the zero flag can be utilized to determine when the value in a particular register is zero.

The *parity flag* is set to a 1 after certain types of operations with the accumulator (or partial accumulators) when the number of bits in the register that are a logic one is an even value (without regard to the positions of the bits). The parity flag is set to 0 after these same operations if the number of bits in the register that are a logic one is an odd value (1, 3, 5 or 7). The parity flag can be especially valuable when data from external devices is being received by the computer to test for certain types of transmission errors on the information being received.

In addition to the full accumulator previously discussed there are six other 8 bit registers in the Intel 8008 computer referred to as partial accumulators because they are capable of performing two special functions normally associated with an accumulator (in addition to simply serving as temporary storage registers). The full accumulator is often abbreviated as ACC or *register A*. The six partial accumulators will be referred to as *registers B, C, D, E, H and L*.

Registers B, C, D, E, H and L of an 8008 are all capable, upon being directed to do so by a specific instruction, of either incrementing or decrementing their contents by one. This capability allows them to be used as *counters* and *pointers* which are often of tremendous value in computer programs. What makes them especially valuable in 8008 architecture is that when their contents are incremented or decremented the immediate results of that register will affect the status of the *zero, sign* and *parity* flags. Thus it is possible for the particular contents of these registers to affect the operation of the computer during the course of a programs operation and they can be used to guide or modify a sequence of operations based on conditions found at the actual time a program is executed.

It should be noted that registers B, C, D, E, H and L are capable of being incremented and decremented—but the full accumulator—register A—cannot perform those two functions in the same manner. The full accumulator can be incremented or decremented by any value by simply adding or subtracting the desired value. There is not, however, a simple increment or decrement by one instruction for use with the full accumulator of an 8008.

Two of the partial accumulators, registers H and L, serve an additional purpose in the 8008 computer CPU. These two registers can be used to directly *point* to a specific word in memory so that the computer may obtain or deposit information in a different part of memory than that in which a program is actually being executed. The reader should recall that a special part of the central processor unit (CPU) termed the program counter is used to tell the computer where to obtain the next instruction while executing a program. The program counter was effectively a *double word length* register that could hold the value of any possible address in memory. The program counter is always used to tell the machine where to obtain the next instruction. However, it is often desirable to have the machine obtain some information such as a *data word*, from a location in memory that is not connected with where the next instruction to be performed is located. This can be accomplished by simply loading register H with the high address page (portion) of an address in memory, then loading register L with the low address portion of an address in memory, and then utilizing one of a class of commands that will direct the CPU to fetch information into the location in memory that is specified (pointed to) by the H and L register contents. This information flow can be from or to the location specified in memory and any of the CPU registers.

At this time it would be beneficial for the reader to study Fig. 1-16. It is an expanded block diagram of Fig. 1-8 and shows the units of the computer which have been presented in the previous several pages.

Until now no mention has been made of how information is put into or received from a computer. Naturally, this is a very vital part of a computer because the machine would be rather useless if people could not put information into the machine upon which calculations or processing could be done, and receive information back from the machine when the operations had been performed.

Communications between the computer and external devices—whether those devices be simple switches, or transducers, or teletype machines, or cathode-ray-tube display units, or keyboards, or mag-tape and disk systems—or whatever, are commonly referred to as *input/output* operations and are collectively referred to in abbreviated form as I/O transfers.

In the Intel 8008 computer designs all 1/0 transfers are typically made between external *1/10* ports (which connect to external devices via appropriate electronic connections) and the full accumulator in the computer. This 1/0 structure means that a whole group of devices can be simultaneously hooked up to the computer and the computer used to receive information to a variety of devices as directed by a *program*. A special set of commands is used to instruct the computer as to which *1/0 port* is to be operated at any particular instant. With appropriate programming it is then possible to have the computer *communicate* with a large variety of devices in an essentially *automatic* mode—for instance receiving information from a digital multimeter at specified times, then possibly performing some averaging calculations and then outputting results to a teletype machine without human intervention. Or, in other applications, information from a human operator can be typed into the machine using a typewriter-like keyboard. In its simplest form, a group of switches can be used as an input device and a group of lamps used as an output device for the computer!

However, a more sophisticated system used in many applications would be to use a teletype machine or a combination of a keyboard and a cathode-ray-tube (CRT) display attached to input and output ports to serve as the primary means of 1/0. A person can thus type information on the keyboard which will pass it into the computer, and the computer can display the results of its operations on the CRT display (which can, incidentally, be made from an ordinary oscilloscope and a special CRT interface unit).

Perhaps the most wonderful and exciting aspect about a digital computer is its tremendous versatility. It has been said that the computer is the most versatile machine in existence and that its applications are limited only by man's ability to develop programs that direct the operation of the machine. It is undoubtedly one of the best machines for allowing man to exercise and test his creative powers through the development of programs that direct the

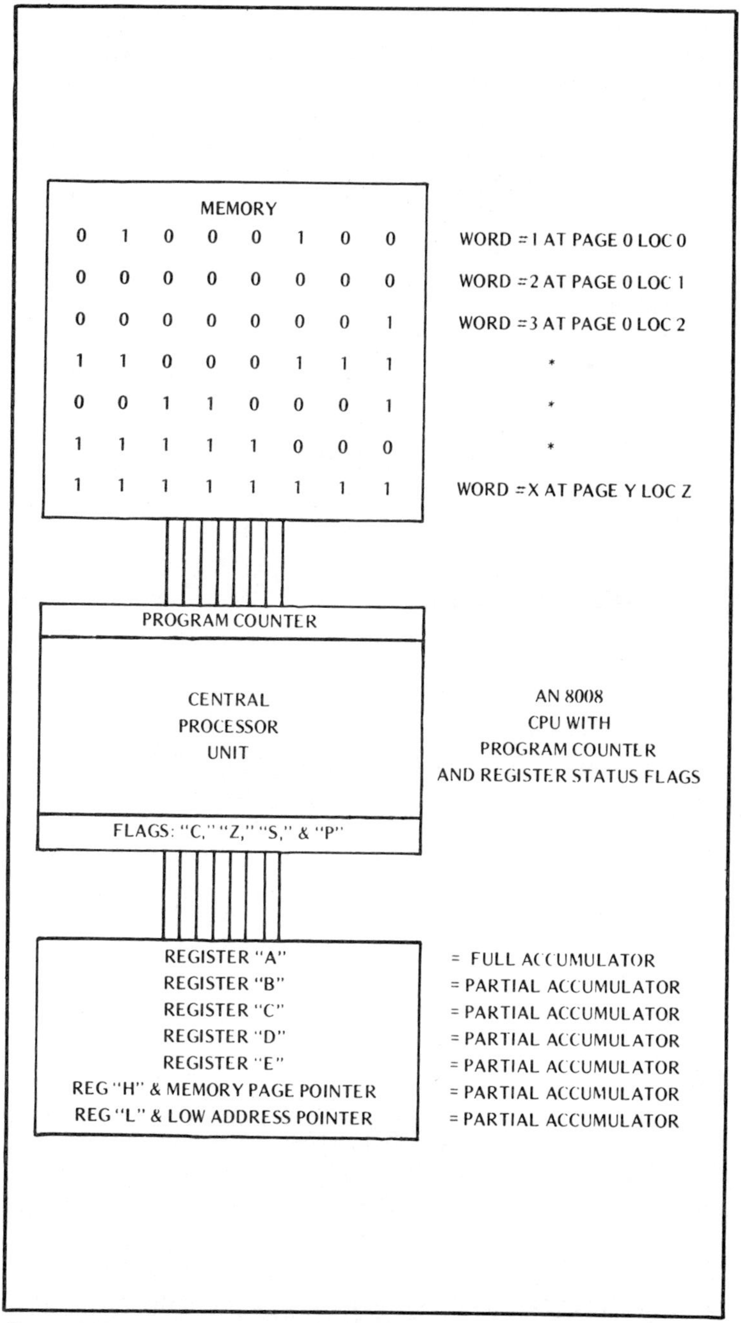

Fig. 1-16. The block diagram of Fig. 1-8 filled in with the designations for an Intel 8008 computer.

machine to perform complex operations that can not only control other machines, or perform calculations many times faster than humanly possible, but because it can be used to *simulate* or *model* other systems that it might be impractical to build for purely experimental purposes. Thus man can create a model in a computer program and actually *play* with the synthetic model without actually building the physical device.

The computer's great versatility comes about because the machine is capable of executing a large group of instructions in an essentially limitless series of combinations. These series on instructions are stored in the memory bank(s) of the computer and a new series of instructions can be placed in the memory bank(s) whenever desired. In fact, the memory bank(s) can often hold several completely unrelated programs in different sections and thus one can have a machine that performs totally unrelated tasks simply by pushing a few buttons and thereby directing the machine to start executing a new program in a different section of memory.

Who Uses Computers

The digital computer is capable of providing services to people from all walks of life. A person need only choose (or develop) programs and connect external instruments that will provide the capabilities desired.

For instance, a scientist might put a mathematical calculator program into the computer's memory and use the computer as a sophisticated electronic calculator by using a calculator-type keyboard as an input device and a CRT display as an output device on which to receive the answers to complex mathematical calculations which the computer performs. After using the computer as a calculator for a period of time, the scientist might decide to utilize the same computer to automatically record data from instruments during an experiment. By simply putting a different program in the computer's memory and plugging some peripheral measuring instruments into the computer's 1/0 ports, the scientist could have the computer periodically make measurements while he went out to lunch and save the results in its memory. After lunch the scientist could have the computer tabulate and present the data obtained from the experiment in compact form. Then, by merely putting a different program in the memory, the scientist could have the computer help him set up and arrange a reference file all sorted into alphabetical order or any manner that would enable him to use the computer to extract information far faster than a manually operated paper file card system.

So the computer can be a valuable tool for a scientist; but, the same machine with a different program in its memory (and possibly different peripheral devices) could be used to control a complex manufacturing operation such as a plastic injection molding machine. In such a case 1/10 units that coupled to transducers on the injection molding machine might be used to relay information to the computer on a variety of parameters such as temperature of the plastic in the feed barrel, amount of feed material in the hopper and injection barrel, available pressure to the mold jaws and feed barrel, vacancy or filled status of the mold and other useful parameters. The computer could be programmed to analyze this information and send back signals to control the operation of heaters, pressure valves, the feed rate of raw materials, when to inject plastic into the mold, when to empty the mold and other operations to enable the plastic injection system to operate in an essentially automatic mode.

Or, a business man could use the same computer connected to an electric typewriter, with a suitable program in memory, to compose, edit and then type out personalized form letters by directing the computer to insert paragraphs from a bank of standard paragraphs so as to form a personalized customer answering system that would handle routine inquiries in a fraction of the time (and cost) that it would take a secretary to prepare such letters. Or, the businessman might utilize the computer to help him control his inventory, or speed up his accounting operations.

However, a computer that costs as little as the typical micro system does not have to be restricted to a business or scientific environment. The computer that can do all the types of tasks mentioned above can also be used to have fun with, or to perform valuable services, to private individuals.

The computer can be used as a sophisticated electronic calculator by almost anyone. It can be used to compose letters (using an editor program) by virtually anyone. Programs that sort data alphabetically or in various other categories can be of valuable service to people in many applications. The computer can be used to monitor and control many household items, serve as a security monitoring system, be connected to devices that will dial telephones and do thousands of other tasks.

The electronic hobbyist can be kept occupied for years with a digital computer. For instance, one can build a little test instrument that plugs into a few 1/0 ports on the computer, then load programs into memory that will direct the computer to automatically test electronic components (such as complex TTL integrated circuits) in a fraction of a second! (Businesses can do this too!)

Or a ham radio operator can put a program into memory that will enable the computer to receive messages typed in from a keyboard, convert the messages to Morse code and then actuate an oscillator via an output port to send perfectly timed Morse code. In addition, the ham radio operator might use the computer with an appropriate program to serve as a *contest logging aid.* The logging aid would serve as an instant reference file whereby the operator could enter the calls of stations as they were worked and have the computer verify if the contact was a duplicate. The computer could do other tasks too, such as record the time of the contact by checking an external digital clock (or by utilizing a program that would enable the computer to be used as a clock within itself)!

And, the computer can be used to play numerous games with, such as tic-tac-toe, checkers, word games, card games and a large variety of other types of games that one can program a computer to perform.

And perhaps most important—for the student, hobbyist, scientist, businessman or anyone interested in the exciting possibilities of its applications—the contemporary microcomputer offers unlimited possibilities for the expression of individual creativity. For the development of computer programs can be extremely creative, exciting and personally rewarding pastime and offers essentially limitless ways to exercise one's creative capabilities in developing algorithms that will enable the machine to perform desired tasks.

Number Systems

Have you ever wondered about the term *binary number*. Since we already have a perfectly good decimal number system, why complicate things with another? If you have a few minutes, here is your chance to learn more about number systems than you ever wanted to know.

One of the most important achievements in the development of science has undoubtedly been the invention of our decimal number system. Counting in units of 10 must certainly be due to the fact that man has 10 fingers. In some cases, some people have counted in units of five or 20, which correspond to the use of one hand or of both hands and both feet.

The main use of numbers in early times was for simple counting and record keeping. The numeration methods were designed chiefly for those purposes. With the development of trade and the sciences, the numeration became more and more inadequate. It took a long time before an adequate number system was devised. The Greeks and the Romans did not succeed in this endeavor even though they achieved a rather high development in science. Just imagine performing simple arithmetic with Roman numerals, like dividing MMDXLVI by CCIX using Roman numerals only. About 600 hundred years ago any simple operations like multiplication and division of large numbers required the services of an expert.

The Hindus and the Arabs are credited with the concept of positional value and the use of the zero, which are explained as follows. Consider the number 74638. We understand this to mean 7 × 10,000 + 4 × 1,000 + 6 × 100 + 3 × 10 + 8 × 1. In the following numbers, the 4 has different values depending on its position: 42,000, 240, 324. In the first number 4 is equal to 40,000, in the second its value is 40 and in the last just 4. Without a 0 to place in some of the positions, how would you write three hundred and six if every position had to have a number? Use of the concept of zero enables us to write 306.

The positional values of the base ten number system are as follows:

$$10^3\ 10^2\ 10^1\ 10^0.\ 10^{-1}\ 10^{-2}\ 10^{-3}$$

You will note that in each case the value of the position is the radix (10) raised to some power. It is necessary to go to the right of the radix point (decimal point) in order to express fractional numbers.

The general expression for a number is then:

$$N = a_1\,(r)^{n-2} + a_2\,(r)^{n-3} + a_3\,(r)^{n-4} + a_4\,(r)^{n-5}$$

In the above expression r is the radix or number base and the a values are the position numbers. In order to have a base ten number system that will translate most practical numbers we would have to make n = 5. Using the arbitrary number 2307.602 as an example, and making n = 5, we derive:

$$2\,(10^3) + 3(10^2) + 0(10^1) + 7(10^0) + 6(10^{-1}) + 0(10^{-2}) + 2\,(10^{-3})$$

Note that any number raised to the zero power is equal to one (i.e., $10^0 = 1$).

Now we can calculate the positional values for the binary (base two) number system. They are as follows:

$2^0 = 1$
$2^1 = 2$
$2^2 = 4$
$2^3 = 8$

$2^4 = 16$
$2^5 = 32$
$2^6 = 64$
$2^7 = 128$
$2^8 = 256$
$2^9 = 512$
$2^{10} = 1024$
$2^{-1} = .5$
$2^{-2} = .25$
$2^{-3} = .125$
$2^{-4} = .0625$
$2^{-5} = .03125$
$2^{-6} = .015625$
$2^{-7} = .0078125$
$2^{-8} = .00390625$
$2^{-10} = .001953125$
$2^{-10} = .0009765625$

We now have the conversion factors necessary to convert a binary number to a decimal number.

Let's consider the base two number 0011100.0 and calculate its decimal equivalent.

$$
\begin{aligned}
0 \times 1 &= 0\\
0 \times 2 &= 0\\
1 \times 4 &= 4\\
1 \times 8 &= 8\\
1 \times 16 &= 16\\
0 \times 32 &= 0\\
0 \times 64 &= 0\\
\hline
&\ 28 \text{ (base 10)} = 0011100.0 \text{ (base 2)}
\end{aligned}
$$

It may not have been apparent from the preceding, but the fact is that binary numbers are made up of 1s and 0s only. If we were to design an electronic computer or calculator to use the decimal number system, we would find that the decimal number system was capable of the high speeds that are necessary—but it would be very difficult to provide ten stable states so that the computer could handle the decimal numbers. Fortunately, any number can be represented in the binary number system, so computers are designed to use it. They might also use the base eight or base sixteen number systems, since these have similar properties.

Electronic circuits have been devised that will add, subtract, multiply and divide in the binary number system.

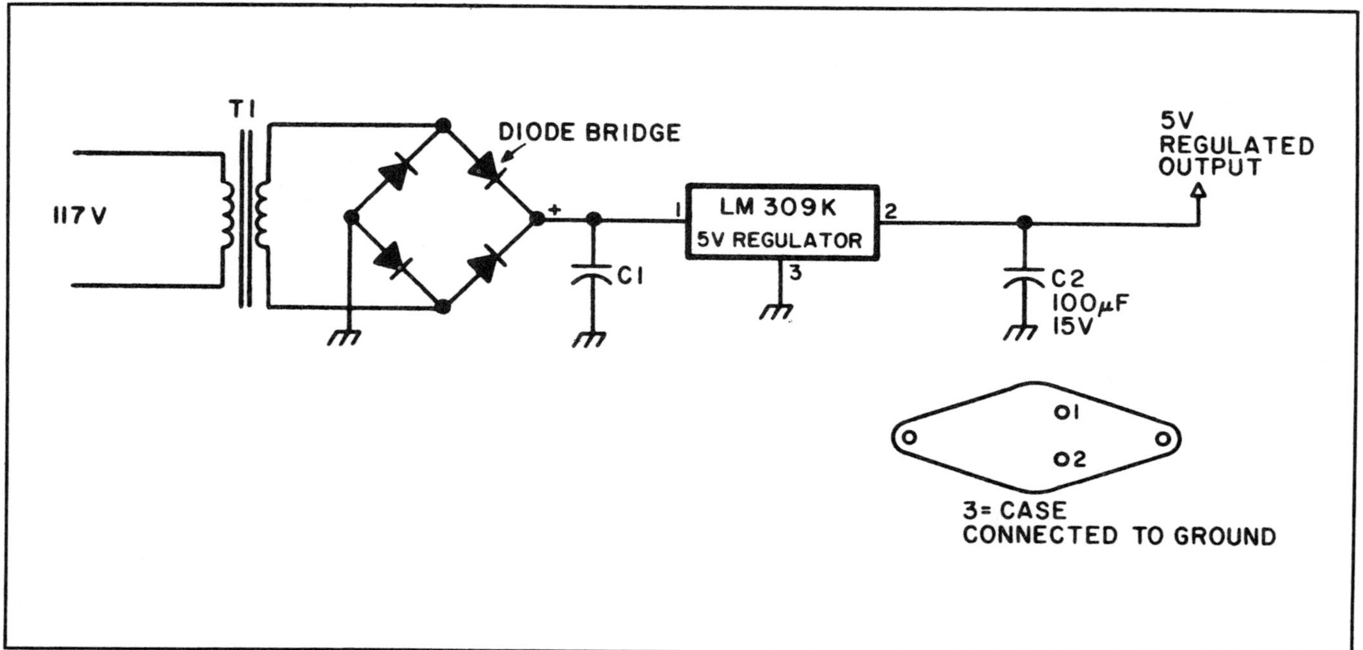

Fig. 1-17. Simple power supply. T1: 12V, 1 A (Poly Paks 92CU2474, $2.95). Diode bridge: 2 A, 50V epoxy (Poly Paks 92CU1346, $.69). C1: 3500 UF (minimum), 25V DC (S. D. Sales, $.79). C2: 100 mF, 15V DC (James Electronics, $.24). LM309K: 5V regulator (Poly Paks, $1.50). Total power supply parts cost: $6.17.

Just to stimulate your interest in the binary number system, let's try working a problem. First we need to know that in the binary system $1 + 1 = 0$ plus a carry. The carry is into the next position (or 2^1) so that properly $1 + 1 = 10$. This happens in the decimal system also; for example, $9 + 9 = 8$ plus a carry into the 10^1 column, so that $9 + 9 = 18$. Now let's try out your new understanding of number systems on this little problem. Calculate the first five positional values to the left of the radix point in the base eight number system (remember, $8^0 + 1$). Then calculate the decimal equivalent of the octal number 40. The answers follow the references. (Answers: 1, 8, 64, 512, 4096; 32.)

How Computer Arithmetic Works

The easiest and most inexpensive way to get started in computers is to begin with inexpensive, easy to use, fundamental building blocks. These fundamental blocks can be used initially for educational purposes to promote understanding and confidence, and later combined to form a fundamental computer.

The arithmetic logical unit (ALU) is a fundamental part of a typical computer system. The ALU is inexpensive, is easy to use and may be operated independently or in conjunction with other devices. The ALU will be a stand-alone device in order to demonstrate computer operations such as addition, subtraction and complement. All necessary details and related information are given so that the experimenter can learn fundamental computer arithmetic.

The dollar outlay required to procure the parts and equipment needed to perform the experiments given in this section should be less than $12, not counting a breadboard or PC board.

The Parts and Equipment

The parts and equipment needed to perform these experiments are as follows:

- 1—5V power supply
- 1—74181 integrated circuit
- 1—breadboard, perforated board, or homemade PC board
- 1—voltmeter or four LEDs

A 5V power supply may be purchased in kit form from James Electronics for $9.95, or a wired and tested supply may be purchased from Micro Digital Corp., for $24.50. A 5V power supply may be built in breadboard fashion, for about $6.00, by using the circuit described in Fig. 1-17.

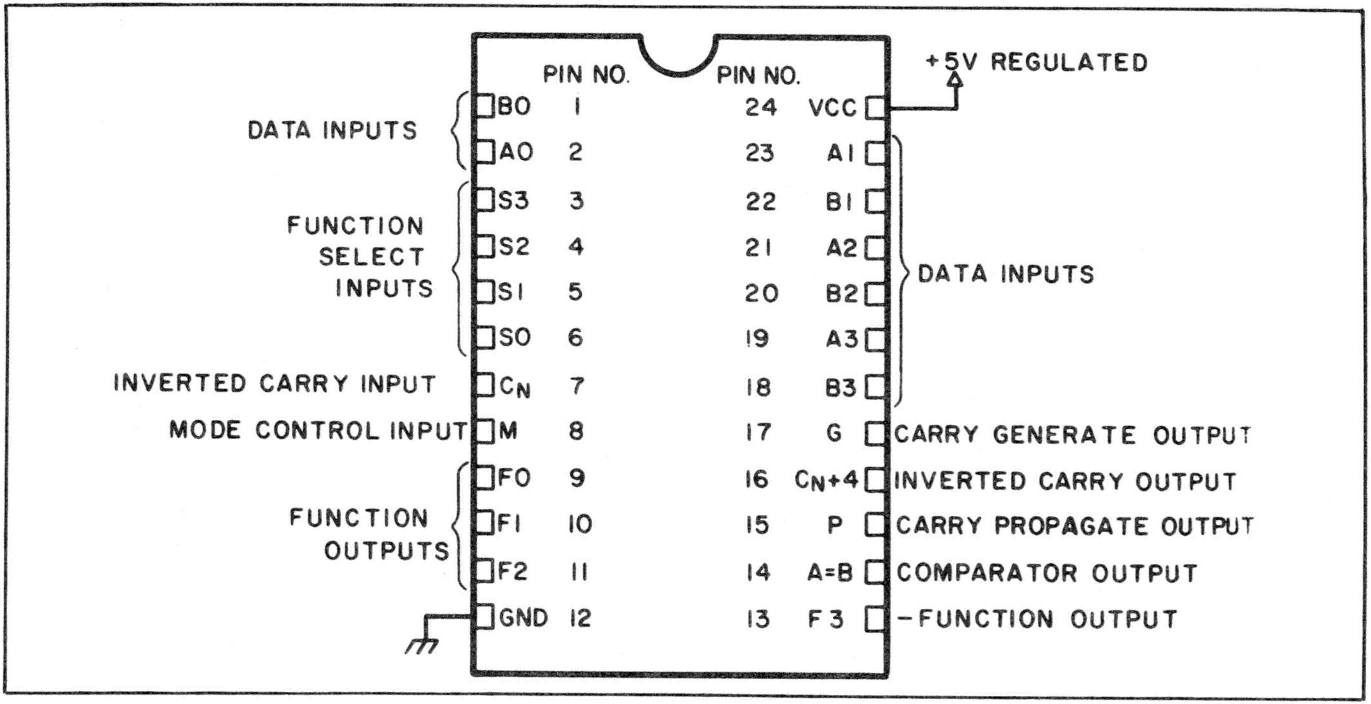

Fig. 1-18. 74181 pin connections.

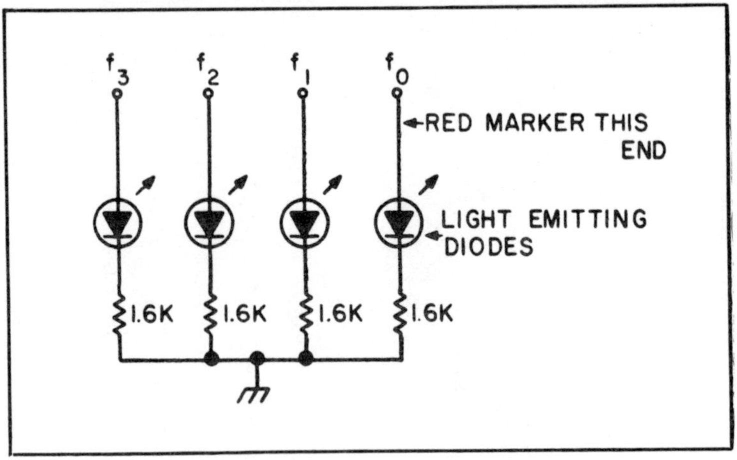

Fig. 1-19. LED readouts. LEDs are Poly Paks 92CU1790 low current LED MV-55.

The 74181 ALU is available from many sources, such as Poly Paks, James Electronics, International Electronics Unlimited and others, for less than $4.00. An illustration of the pin and chip layout is shown in Fig. 1-18.

The user may etch his own PC board or may use perforated board if he wishes; however, a universal breadboard such as a Continental Specialties QT-59S ($12.50) or AP Products 923261 Terminal Strip ($12.50) will make things a lot easier. With the universal breadboard, no soldering is required, as all connections are made with #22 AWG solid hookup wire. The breadboard is recommended to facilitate circuit changes and additions to the experiments.

Some type of indicator is needed to display the outputs of the ALU. A 20,000 ohms/volt voltmeter (which will read 0-5 volts), a DC oscilloscope, or a series of light emitting diodes may be used. The circuit in Fig. 1-19 shows four LEDs connected to the ALU to indicate HIGH (1 bit) and LOW (0 bit). The LEDs used are type MV-55, available from Poly Paks (5 for $1.00, part number 92CU1790).

The Experimental Setup

The basic experimental setup is shown in Fig. 1-20. The instruction lines are brought out to the left, the data inputs are brought out to the right and the outputs are brought out to the bottom, or lower left. The input, output and instruction connections may be made to terminal strips, vacant connections on the breadboard or to

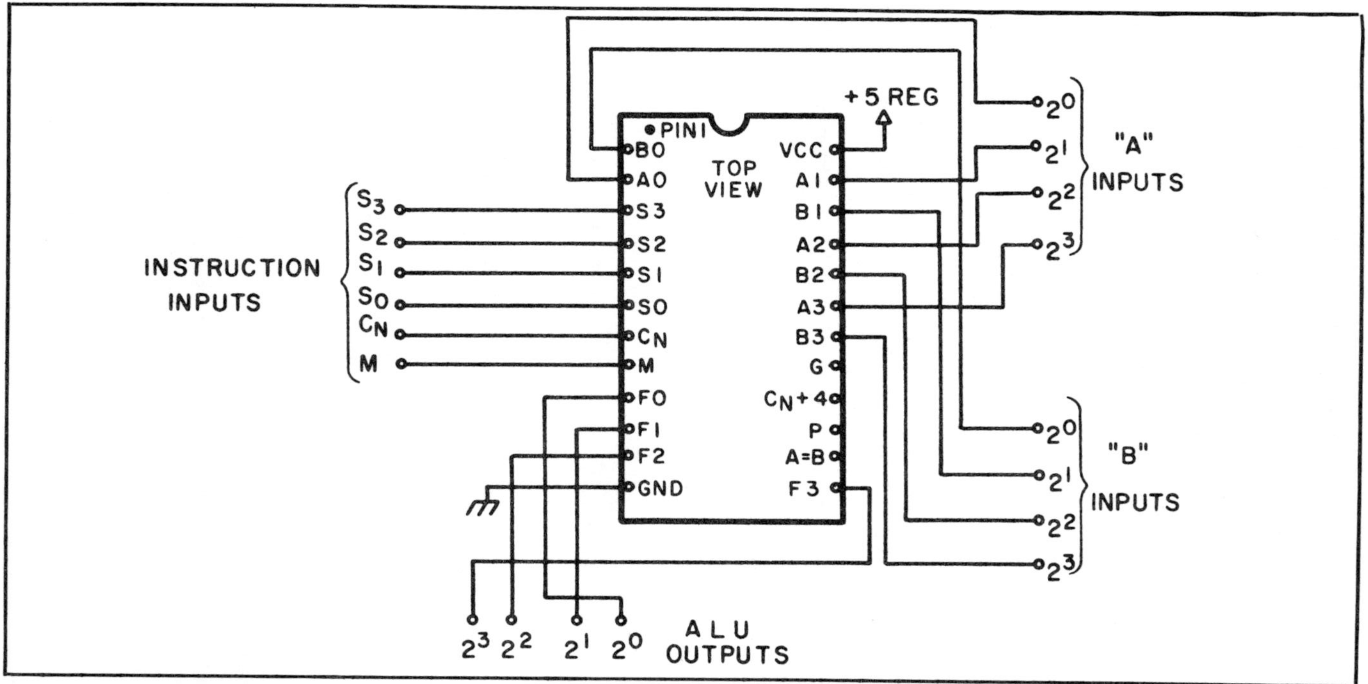

Fig. 1-20. Basic experimental setup. Bring instruction inputs out to left as shown. Bring function outputs either out to bottom or out to left, in order shown. Connect +5V regulated power supply to pins as shown. Bring inputs out to right as shown.

other suitable terminations. Pin 24 is connected to plus 5V from the power supply, and pin 12 is connected to the power supply ground.

The outputs from the 74181 will either be HIGH(H) or LOW (L) voltage levels. A HIGH will be 2.4 volts minimum, but not greater than 5V. A LOW will be .4V or less. A 20,000 Ω/V voltmeter may be used to read the output levels, or LEDs may be connected as shown in Fig. 1-19. If the LEDs are used, a lighted LED will be a HIGH and a non-lighted LED will be a LOW. In these experiments, a *0 bit* is represented by a LOW while a *1 bit* is represented by a HIGH.

Ground Rules

- The 74181 will operate over a range of 4.75V to 5.25V. Operating with voltages outside this range may produce results which are not defined. Operating with a voltage greater than 7V (the absolute maximum rating) may damage the chip.
- Don't short the outputs to ground. If more than one output in a HIGH state is shorted at one time, the chip may be damaged.

EXPERIMENTS

Data Transfers

Connect the ALU as shown in Fig. 1-21. Note that six connections form the instruction word and are used to select the function of the ALU chip. As connected, this instruction will permit data to pass directly from the *A input* to the *output* without changing. The data appearing at the A input is a 0110 and is transferred directly to the output, without change, as a 0110.

The data transfer is a useful instruction within a computer, as it permits data to be transferred from one memory location to another memory location without being changed. Thus, data may be duplicated or placed in a more convenient memory location.

Clear or Set to Zero

Figure 1-22 shows the instruction word (or instruction inputs) required for a clear or set to zero. This instruction sets the output to zero, regardless of the data appearing at either input.

This instruction is useful for setting the initial value of a storage location to zero for counting or other purposes. When counting within a computer, a programmer may add one to the contents of a memory location every time a given event occurs. To insure a

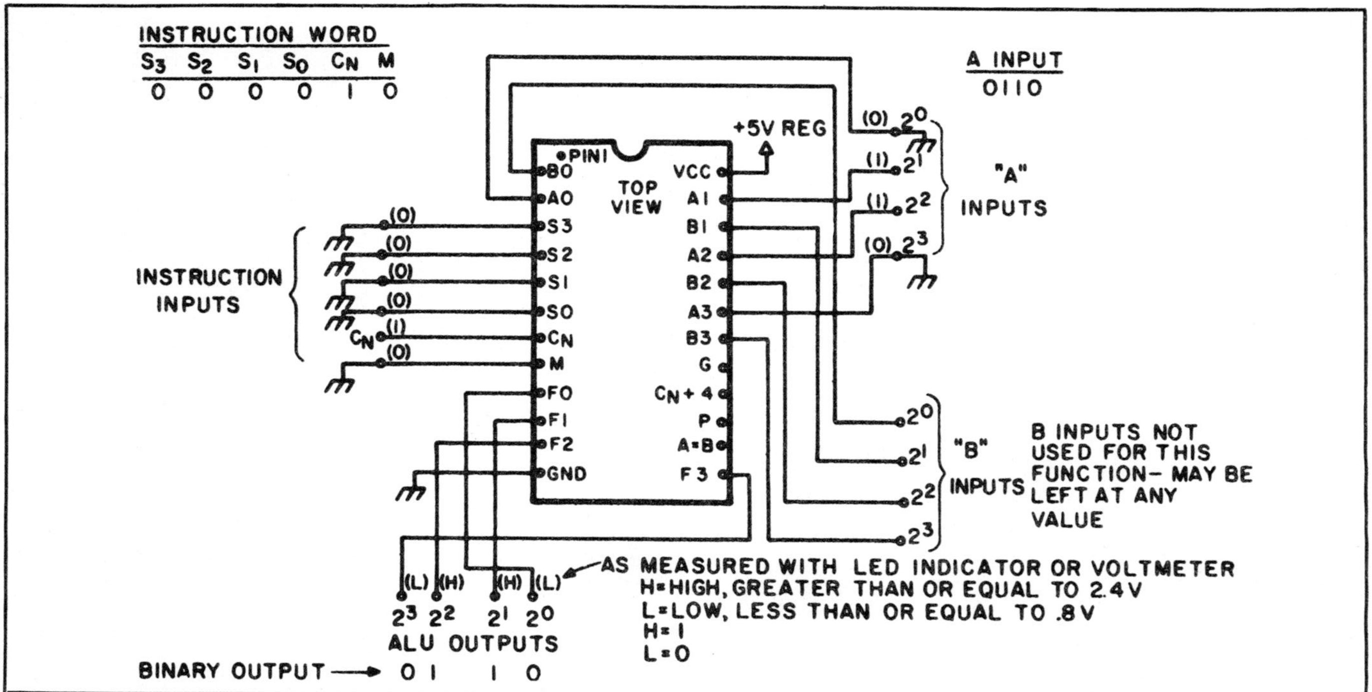

Fig. 1-21. Data transfer. Output = input from A.

correct count, the contents are set to zero or *initialized to zero* before the count starts.

Complement

The complement of a number can be obtained by using the instruction word as shown in Fig. 1-23. The data input is 1011 and the output is 0100, which is the complement of the input.

Addition

Addition is performed by using the experimental setup as shown in Fig. 1-24. The output will be the sum of the data on the A and B inputs. Thus, as shown,

$$\begin{array}{r} 0101\ (5_{10}) \\ +\underline{0011}\ (3_{10}) \\ 1000\ (8_{10}) \end{array}$$

Similarly,

$$\begin{array}{r} 0011\ (3_{10}) \\ +\underline{1010}\ (10_{10}) \\ 1101.\ (13_{10}) \end{array}$$

But now add A and B as follows:

$$\begin{array}{ll} A = & 0111\ (7_{10}) \\ B = & \underline{1011}\ (11_{10}) \\ 1 & 0010\ (18_{10}) \\ \uparrow & \\ \text{carry bit} & \end{array}$$

The ALU has only four data outputs; thus, the results will appear as 0010. This simple arithmetic operation has exceeded the capability of the ACU. We call this an *overflow* condition and say that *overflow* has occurred and that a *carry* has been generated.

Overflow is the phenomenon that separates binary arithmetic. When performing binary arithmetic on paper with a pencil, number size limitations are of little concern (you can always add another sheet of paper). When doing arithmetic with computer elements, number size is a serious concern since there is a hardware limit to the size of the arithmetic word. In these experiments, the arithmetic word size is four bits. If we connected two ALUs together, we would have an 8 bit arithmetic word. With an 8 bit arithmetic word, overflow would not occur and a carry bit would not be generated until a sum exceeding 8 bits was generated.

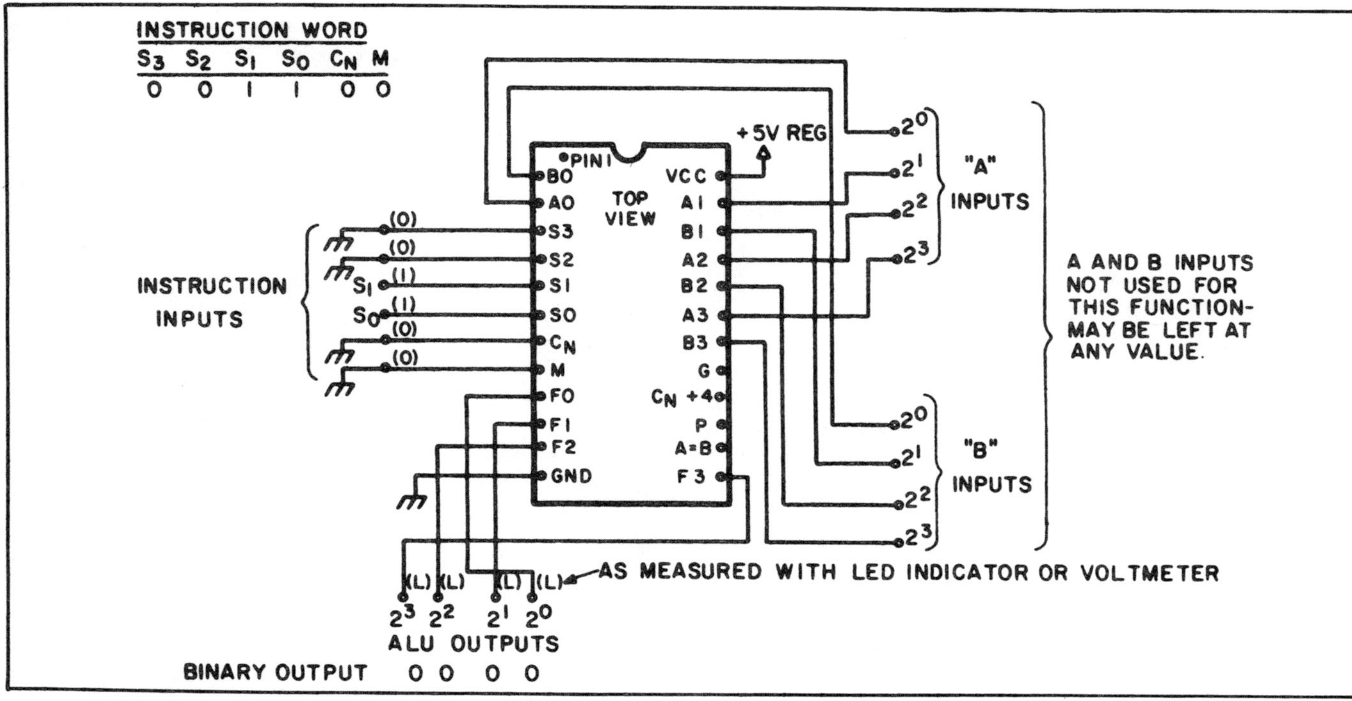

Fig. 1-22. Clear or set output to zero.

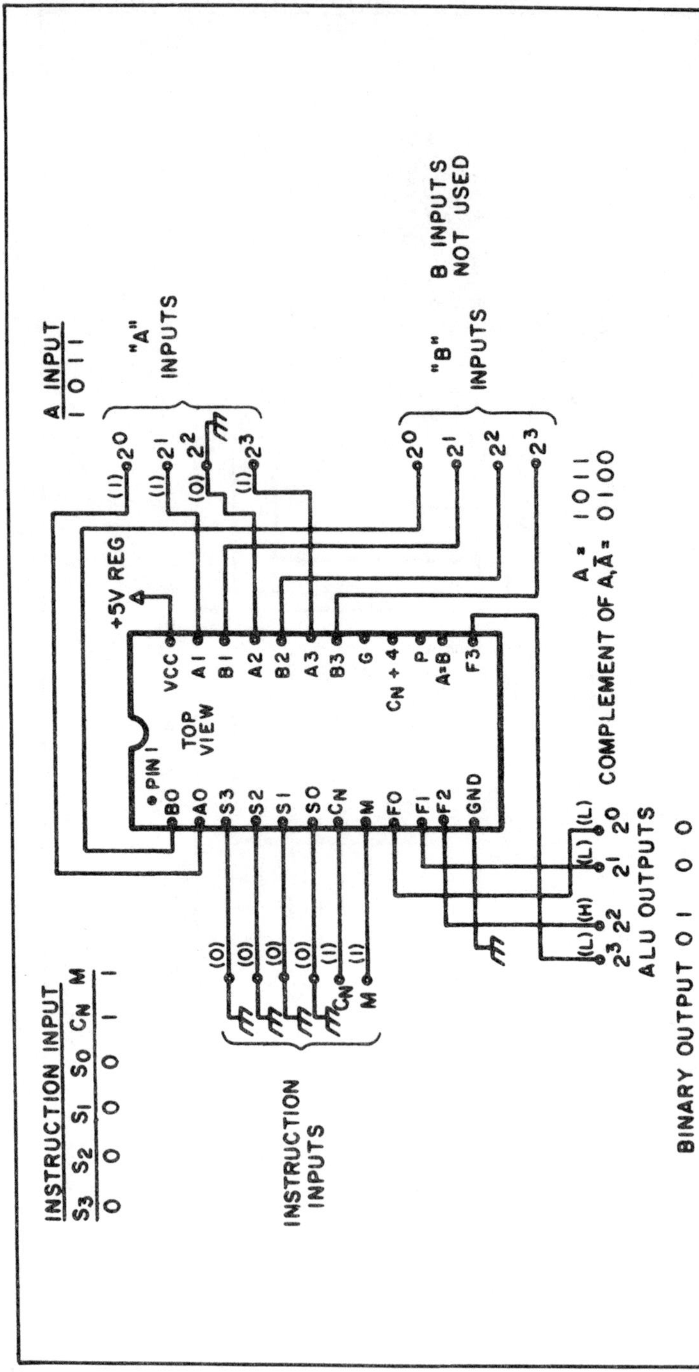

Fig. 1-23. Ones complement of A.

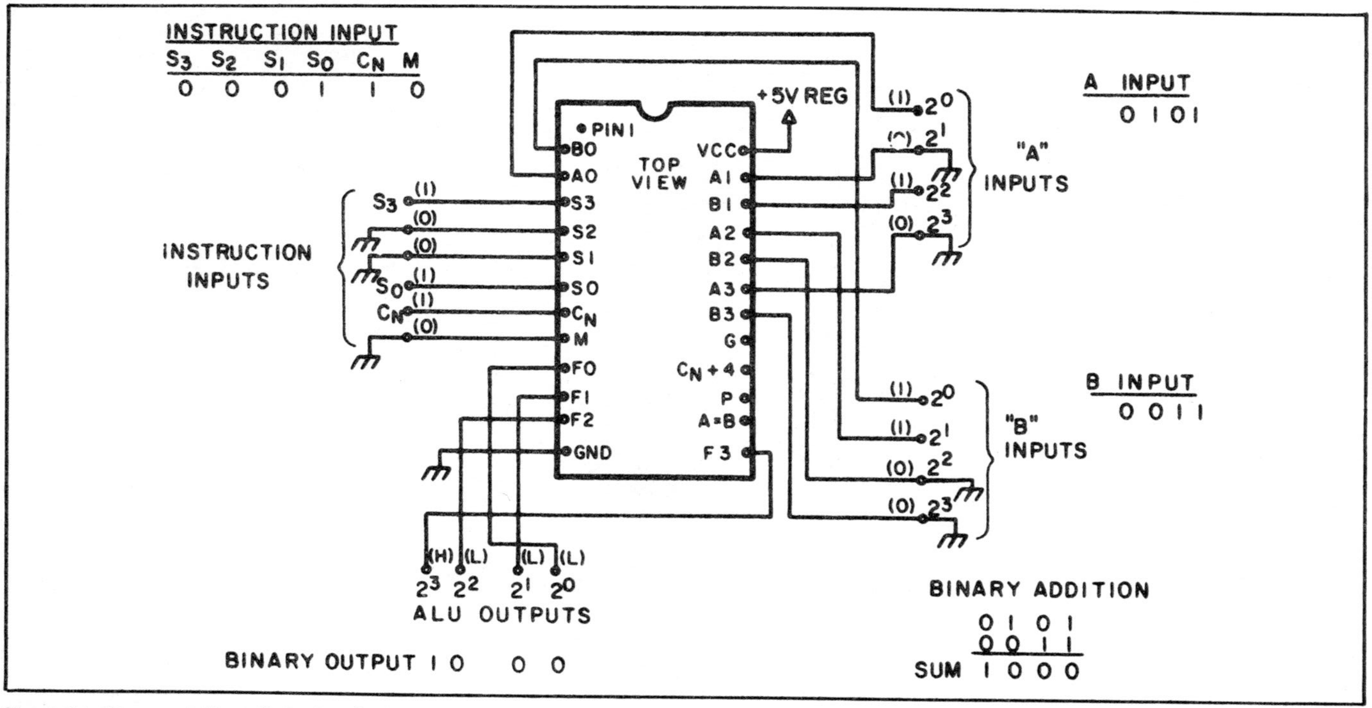

Fig. 1-24. Binary addition. Output = A plus B.

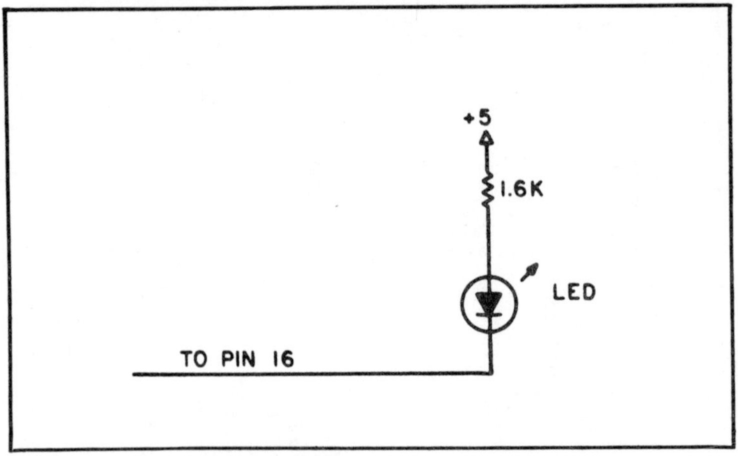

Fig. 1-25. LED connected to carry out.

If overflow were to occur without the user being aware of its occurrence, erroneous results could occur. For this reason, it is important to have the capability to detect the occurrence of overflow. Overflow can be detected on the 74181 chip by monitoring the output of pin 16, the inverted carry output. This output is normally used to feed a carry input on another 74181, but it may also be used to detect the occurrence of a carry bit (overflow). This output is inverted, so it would normally read HIGH with no carry and LOW if a carry occurred. An LED may be connected to the carry output as shown in Fig. 1-25, so that the LED will light if a carry or overflow is present.

By connecting the additional LED as shown in Fig. 1-25, we have gained an additional bit for arithmetic. We have a 4 bit arithmetic word, but we are able to display a 5 bit result.

For example:

```
  1111 (A input)
 +1111 (B input)
 11110
 ↑
 (the fifth bit, the LED for carry, will be lit)
```

Subtraction

Subtraction using twos complement arithmetic is done by using the instruction shown in Fig. 1-26 and 1-27. This experiment shows an example of A-B. The 74181 performs the following functions in order to effect a subtraction:

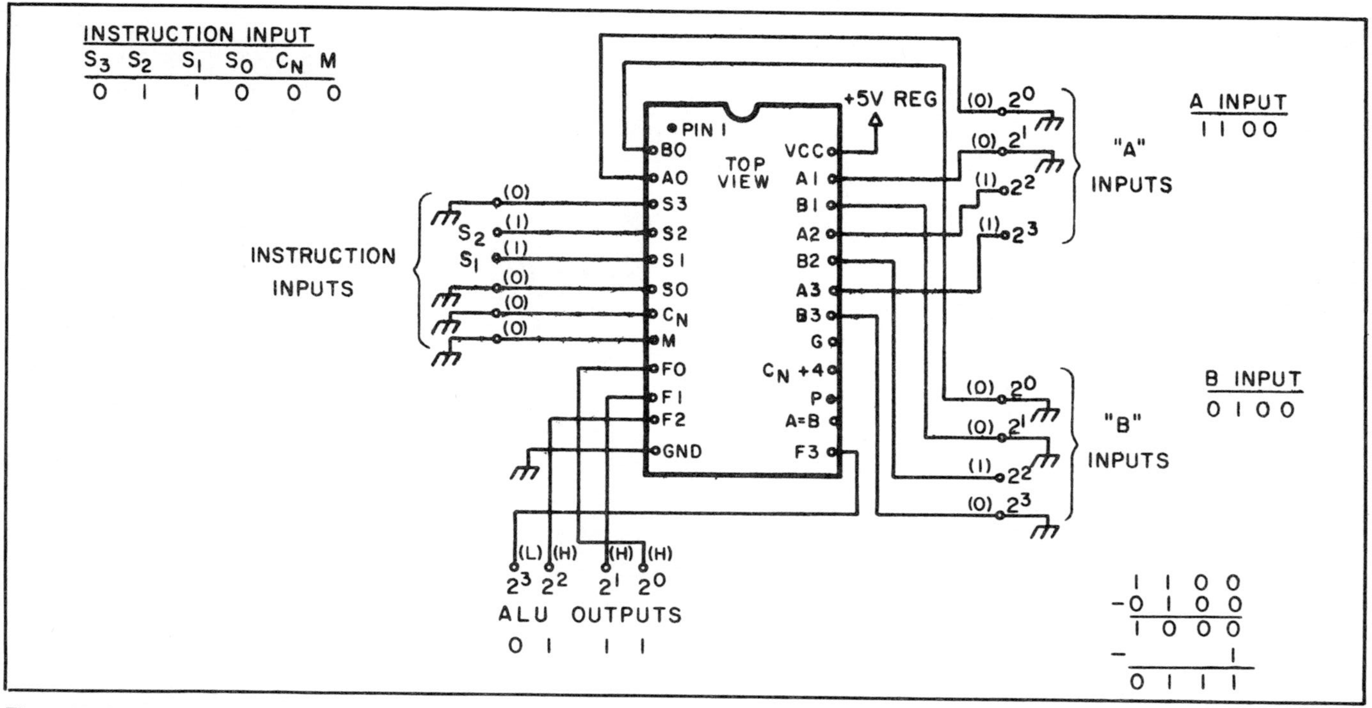

Fig. 1-26. Subtraction. A minus B.

- The twos complement of the B input is obtained by complementing the value and adding 1. The addition of the 1 is a result of making the *inverted* carry in (C_N) a LOW.
- The twos complement of the B input is added to the A input. For example, let us subtract 4_{10} from 12_{10}. The answer, of course, should be 8_{10}.

$$
\begin{array}{lr}
A = 12_{10} = 1100 \longrightarrow & 1100 \\
B = 4_{10} = 0100\text{—2s comp.} & +\underline{1100} \\
 & 1100 = 8_{10}
\end{array}
$$

The result as displayed on the four output bits would be 1000 8_{10}. A=12, B=4 and A-B=8. Carry would occur and the carry LED would be lit, but in this case discarded, because it has no significance.

Do the following problem: 3 – 4 = ? Let A = 3, B = 4. What are the results?

$$
\begin{array}{lr}
 & \text{internal operation} \\
A = 3 = 0011 \longrightarrow & 0011 \\
B = 4 = \underline{0100}\text{—2s comp.}\rightarrow & +\underline{1100} \\
 & 1111 = \text{negative } 1
\end{array}
$$

The result is negative 1 (or minus 1), which is the correct answer for 3 – 4.

It may appear that there is no way of knowing whether a result is negative or positive; however, this is not the case.

Consider the number 1 in binary. On paper, we may write the number one as 1, as 01 or even 0000001 if we wish. To get a negative one, we take the twos complement, which in the case of 0000001 is 1111111. This representation of a negative number is not completely correct, since the 1 really has an infinite number of zeros in front of it. To be correct, 0000001 is really "(infinite number of zeros) 0000001," and the complement is "(infinite number of ones) 1111111."

It can be shown that, in a negative number, the leftmost bit at infinity is a 1 bit. Of course in the real world we can't go on writing down an infinite number of 1 bits to get to the leftmost bit in our arithmetic word as the *sign bit*. Using this definition, the leftmost bit of our four bit arithmetic word is now the sign bit, and in our example the number 1111 becomes a negative number.

Note that, by adopting the leftmost bit in our four bit arithmetic word, our arithmetic is now restricted to 3 bits. The largest positive number that we can generate is $0111 = 7_{10}$. The largest negative number that we can generate is $10000 = 8_{10}$.

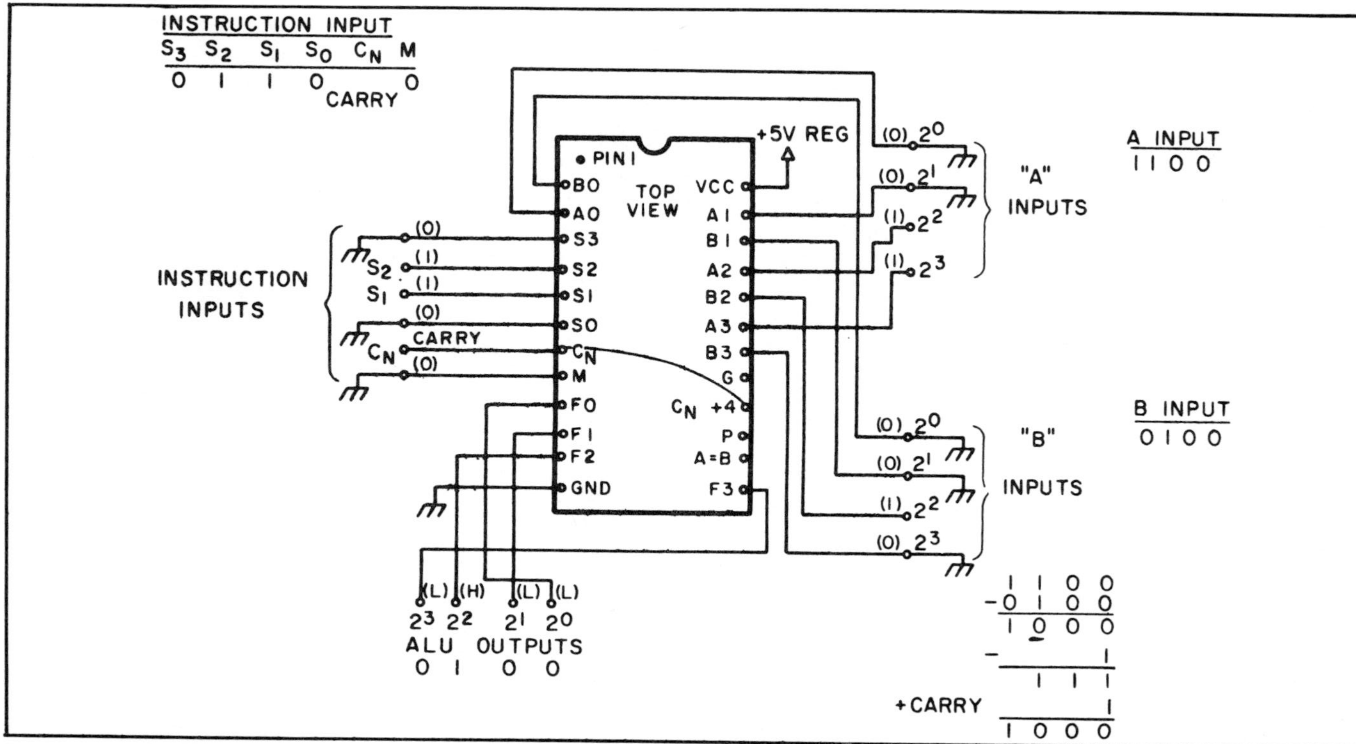

Fig. 1-27. Subtraction: A minus B, plus carry.

Multiply by 2

The instruction shown in Fig. 1-28 is designated an *A plus A* instruction, and has the effect of multiplying *A by 2*. This instruction may also be called a *shift left by 1 bit* instruction, since it shifts the number A to the left by one bit.

This instruction is useful for generating the squares of numbers and may be used as a part of a program to perform multiplication.

ALUs, such as the 74181, are practical building blocks for the computer designer and do exist as important parts of computers available on the market today. These ALUs may stand alone as independent units, or they may be combined with other functions to form a device such as a microprocessor. Thus, the concepts described are applicable to large scale computers, independent ALUs and microprocessors.

Two Finger Arithmetic

The first caveman, when he learned how to count on his fingers, gave us the decimal number system which we use today. Again, while this number system is second nature to us, it is not the only number system with which we come into contact every day. Timekeeping, for example, uses a unique numbering system which is based on the numbers 60 and 24. There are 60 seconds in a minute, 60 minutes in an hour and 24 hours in a day. And of course, the English have blessed us with unique number systems for weights and measures. Who can forget that 4 gills = 1 pint, 2 pints = 1 quart and 4 quarts = 1 gallon? If you stop to think we are involved with many number systems other than the decimal system.

The advent of the computer age has ushered in an additional number system, the *binary system* based on the number two. As previously discussed, this system has come into common use since digital computers can represent information in one of two states—*on and off*. These two states are called binary states and are the basis for the binary system which we use in digital computers.

Man commonly works with the decimal system, computers operate with the binary system and the obvious questions are "How do we get from one system to the other?" And, "How do I represent information in a computer?"

The Decimal System

We are constantly thinking numbers, adding numbers and writing down numbers, but, do we really have an understanding of what we are doing? When we write down a number such as the number 3187, what does it really mean?

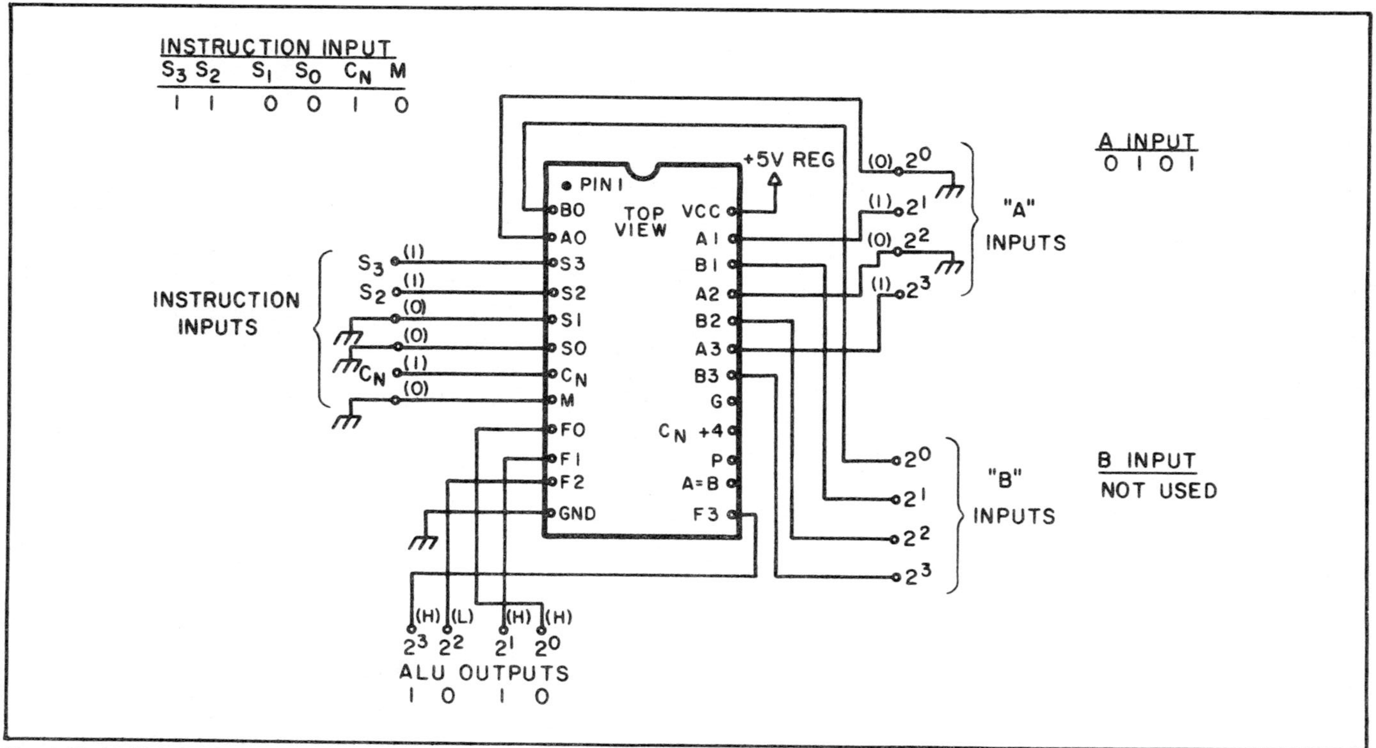

Fig. 1-28. Multiply by 2: A plus A (shift one bit left).

All numbers are made up of a series of digits. A number can have as few as one digit and is not limited to any maximum number of digits. In the decimal system, each place occupied by a digit has a power of ten associated with that place. For example, in the number 3187, we have four places. The powers of 10 associated with the four places are as follows:

digit 3 1 8 7
power of 10 10^3 10^2 10^1 10^0

The number 3187 could be written as the following sum:

$$3187 = 3 \times 10^3 + 1 \times 10^2 + 8 \times 10^1 + 7 \times 10^0$$

and if we remember our basic mathematics we will recall that

$$10^3 = 10 \times 10 \times 10 = 1000$$
$$10^2 = 10 \times 10 = 100$$
$$10^1 = 10$$
$$10^0 = 1$$

When we write the number 3187 we are saying that we have 3 thousands plus 1 hundred plus 8 tens plus seven units (or ones). Similarly, larger numbers such as 5197283 may be represented as

$$5 \times 10^6 + 1 \times 10^5 + 9 \times 10^4 + 7 \times 10^3 + 2 \times 10^2 + 8 \times 10^1 + 3 \times 10^0$$

The Binary System

Computers operate with the binary system because each digit can have only one of two states—on and off. Numbers are represented in a computer by a string of binary digits called *bits*. Consider a number represented by 4 binary digits (bits) when off = 0 and on = 1. Four lights may be used to display the on and off, or one and zero respectively:

number (on) off (on) (on)
numerically $1 \times 2^3 + 0 \times 2^2 + 1 \times 2^1 + 1 \times 2^0$

We know that:

$$2^3 = 8 \qquad 2^1 = 2$$
$$2^2 = 4 \qquad 2^0 = 1$$

Our number represented by the lights above would be:

$$1 \times 8 + 0 \times 4 + 1 \times 2 + 1 = 11_{11}$$

Instead of actually writing down lights to indicate the on and off states, we use the binary numerals 0 and 1. Thus in base 2 our number is written as 1011_2. If it is very clear that you are working with binary numbers, you may omit the subscript 2.

Conversion from Decimal to Any Base

Conversions from a given base to the decimal system can be made by expanding a number to the powers of its base. But, how do we take a decimal number and convert that number to another base? The technique used for this type of conversion is the technique of successive remainders. As an example, convert the decimal value 43 to base two:

$$
\begin{array}{rrl}
 & 21 & \\
2 & \overline{)\,43} & \\
 & \underline{42} & \\
\text{remainder} & 1 & \text{is the multiplier for } 2^0
\end{array}
$$

$$
\begin{array}{rrl}
 & 10 & \\
2 & \overline{)\,21} & \\
 & \underline{20} & \\
\text{remainder} & 1 & \text{is the multiplier for } 2^1.
\end{array}
$$

$$
\begin{array}{rrl}
 & 5 & \\
2 & \overline{)\,10} & \\
 & \underline{10} & \\
\text{remainder} & 0 & \text{is the multiplier for } 2^2
\end{array}
$$

$$
\begin{array}{rrl}
 & 2 & \\
2 & \overline{)\,5} & \\
 & \underline{4} & \\
\text{remainder} & 1 & \text{is the multiplier for } 2^3
\end{array}
$$

$$
\begin{array}{rrl}
 & 1 & \\
2 & \overline{)\,2} & \\
 & \underline{2} & \\
\text{remainder} & 0 & \text{is the multiplier for } 2^4
\end{array}
$$

$$
\begin{array}{rrl}
2 & \overline{)\,1} & \text{(doesn't go)} \\
\text{remainder} & 1 & \text{is the multiplier for } 2^5
\end{array}
$$

Our number expressed as powers of two is $1 \times 2^5 + 0 \times 2^4 + 1 \times 2^3 + 0 \times 2^2 + 1 \times 2^1 + 1 \times 2^0$ or 101011_2. Checking ourselves and converting back to decimal, $1 \times 2^5 + 0 \times 2^4 + 1 \times 2^3 + 0 \times 2^2 + 1 \times 2^1\ 1 \times 2^0 = 32 + 0 + 8 + 0 + 2 + 1 = 43$.

Binary Arithmetic

Arithmetic in the base two is very simple. You don't have to remember a lot of arithmetic facts; all you have to remember is zero + zero = zero, one + zero = one, and one + one = ten. As an example:

$$\begin{array}{r}1\\+0\\\hline 1\end{array}\qquad\begin{array}{r}0\\+1\\\hline 1\end{array}\qquad\begin{array}{r}0\\+0\\\hline 0\end{array}\qquad\begin{array}{r}1\\+1\\\hline 10\end{array}$$

With binary arithmetic, whenever two or more ones appear in a column to be added there will be at least one carry bit added to the next left digit. For example, in adding

$$\begin{array}{r}11\\\underline{+1}\end{array}\quad \text{right digit} \quad \begin{array}{r}1\\\underline{+1}\\10\end{array}$$

we get carry bit ⟶ (the 1 of 10)

carry ⟶ 1

$$\begin{array}{r}11\\+1\\\hline 0\end{array}\quad \text{and then} \quad \begin{array}{r}11\\+1\\\hline 100\end{array}$$

Storing Numbers in a Computer

When we talk about numbers stored in a computer, we don't normally speak of them in terms of bits (binary digits). We usually speak of them in terms of *bytes* or *words*. A *byte* by definition is a collection of sequential bits. A byte can be any number of bits but is most commonly 8 sequential bits. A computer word is a collection of bytes and is defined as the number of bytes pointed to by one addressing operation in a computer. Words and bytes tell us about the organization of the computer. As an example, assume the standard definition of byte, where byte = 8 bits:

- The XDS Sigma 6 computer is a 32 bit computer. It has 32 bits per word. 32/8 = 4, thus there are 4 bytes per word.

- The DEC PDP 11 series of computers have 16 bits per word. It has two bytes per word.
- The INTEL 8080 microprocessor is an 8 bit microprocessor; it has 8 bits per word. Thus it has one byte per word.

The term byte is used very frequently as the definition for a unit of information. Alphanumeric characters (letters, punctuation, printable characters, etc.) are usually stored in coded form in *one byte.*

Numbers written on paper are stored in visual form and for all practical purposes there is no limit to the size of the number on paper. As stated previously, in a computer, there are limts set, due to the word size and due to the aritmetic capabilities of the computer. In large scale computers, it is possible to work with very large numbers such as those which can be represented in 64 bits or more. In microprocessors, however, the limit is very small, usually being 8 bits but in some cases being 4 bits. The arithmetic capability that we are talking about is the type of arithmetic which can be performed in one computer instruction. It is possible to string instructions together and thus handle larger numbersl. This is usually done by software.

Computer Arithmetic

As previously mentioned, computers have limits set on their arithmetic capabilities. They cannot in a single instruction perform simple arithmetic on all size numbers. They are limited to performing arithmetic on some given number of bits. Because of these limitations, computer arithmetic is somewhat different from binary arithmetic. Computer arithmetic is binary arithmetic within limits.

A typical microprocessor, such as the Intel 8080, has 8 bit arithmetic capability. It can perform arithmetic on 8 bit numbers. It cannot in a single instruction operate on a 32 bit number.

The largest number that can be expressed in *8 bit arithmetic* can be determined as follows: Consider an eight bit binary number such as 11111111_2, all one bits in the eight bits. The number can be expanded as $1 \times 2^7 + 1 \times 2^6 + 1 \times 2^5 + 1 \times 2^4 + 1 \times 2^3 + 1 \times 2^2 + 1 \times 2^1 + 1 \times 2^0$, which is the same as $128 + 64 + 32 + 16 + 8 + 4 + 2 + 1 = 255_{10}$. This is the largest number that can be stored in a single 8 bit word (or byte) and also the largest sum that can be accumulated from the addition of two numbers. We can add $250_{10} + 5_{10}$ and get a sum of 255, but we cannot add 250_{10} and 6_{10} to give 256_{10}, since that sum is beyond the arithmetic capabilities of 8 bit arithmetic. Of course this arithmetic restriction only applies to a computer with 8 bit arithmetic. If the computer used 4 bit arithmetic or 32 bit arithmetic, then the actual larges number would be different. In a four bit arithmetic microprocessor, the largest number would be $1111_2 = 1 \times 2^3 + 1 \times 2^1 + 1 \times 2^0 = 15$.

In order to simplify the examples, all discussion in this section will pertain to a microprocessor or computer with 8 bit arithmetic capability.

If our microprocessor can handle eight bit arithmetic and can also store sums up to 255, then what is to prevent us from attempting to add two numbers that will produce a sum greater than 255? The computer doesn't know what the sum will be before the addition, so we can at least make an attempt. The answer is, "Yes, you can instruct the computer to perform the addition, but the results will be wrong." An overflow condition will result. The storage capabilities and the arithmetic capabilities of 8 bit arithmetic will be exceeded. What happens is analogous to trying to pour 3 quarts of water and 4 quarts of water into a five quart container. The container will overflow.

Subtraction and Negative Numbers

Most microprocessors available today have subtraction capabilities; however, the microprocessor user may or may not wish to use those subtraction capabilities, depending on the capabilities available. The user may wish to *complement* the number to be subtracted and then perform an addition, so that the arithmetic techniques may be simplified. Two types of computer arithmetic will be discussed—ones complement arithmetic and twos complement arithmetic.

Both negative numbers and subtraction are used in a computer, but not necessarily in the same manner as with pencil and paper. In order to indicate a negative, instead of writing down a minus sign on paper a *sign bit* is set to *one* somewhere in the computer. This *sign bit* may be stored in a word by itself or it may be stored in the same work in which the number is stored. Most commonly, the sign bit, which indicates a negative number, is stored with the number itself in the leftmost bit position of the word. In an eight bit word, the sign bit would be as shown:

Sign bit ⊗ × × × × × × ×

In a sixteen bit word the sign bit would still be the leftmost bit as:

Sign bit
↓
⊗ × × × × × × ×   × × × × × × × ×

If the sign bit is a 0, then the number stored in the word is positive. If the sign bit is a 1, then the number stored in the word is negative.

The maximum range of numbers which can be represented in an 8 bit computer would be as follows:

Sign bit
↓
0 1 1 1 1 1 1 1 = 127_{10}
(most positive value)
0 1 1 1 1 1 1 0 = 126_{10}
⋮
0 0 0 0 0 0 1 0 = 2
0 0 0 0 0 0 0 1 = 1
0 0 0 0 0 0 0 0 = ZERO
1 1 1 1 1 1 1 1 = −1
1 1 1 1 1 1 1 0 = −2
⋮
1 0 0 0 0 0 0 1 = -127_{10}
1 0 0 0 0 0 0 0 = -128_{10}
(Most negative value)

In an 8 bit word we have defined one bit as the sign bit, leaving 7 bits for the data. This means that the largest number including sign that can be stored in an 8 bit word is 127_{10}. This puts a further restriction on arithmetic operations as can be seen by the example, 64 + 64.

64 in binary	=	01000000
+ 64	=	01000000
		10000000

By definition, we now have negative number! We have changed the sign of our number. As can be seen, the right combination of numbers added together will not produce overflow, but will change the sign. Thus, it is also important to test to see if the sign is changed when performing addition on numbers of like sign. If the sign has changed, the 7 bit capability has been exceeded.

In computer logic, it is easy to complement a word such that all ones become zeros and all zeros become ones. This capability is usually a standard feature within the arithmetic-logical unit of a microprocessor. The complement of the eight bit binary number 01001101 would be 10110010. The number 3 represented in 8 bits is 00000011, and the complement of three would then be 11111100. This type of complement where zeros are exchanged for ones and ones are exchanged for zeros is called *ones complement.*

By complementing a number using the ones complement, we have placed a 1 bit or a sign bit in the leftmost bit of the word, indicating that the number stored in the word is a negative number.

A typical ALU will complement a word internally, and then perform addition in order to effect subtraction. This might happen as follows, for the operation 7-4:

7 in binary = 00000111
4 in binary = 00000100

The ones complement of 4 (negative 4) = 11111011. Adding the two together,

```
      00000111
      11111011
    1 00000010₂ = 2₁₀
    ↑
carry bit
(overflow)
```

But the answer is off by one and overflow has occurred. We got an answer of 2. The answer should have been three. This is the shortcoming of *ones complement arithmetic*, and is the reason all modern computers use twos complement for arithmetic operations and representing negative numbers.

Twos Complement Arithmetic

Twos complement arithmetic operations can be found in all present-day computers, from the lowly 4 bit microprocessor all the way up to the giant large scale systems. The reasons will become evident as we go on and see how effectively negative numbers can be represented in this form.

To find the twos complement of a number, take the ones complement of the number and *add* 1. For example, find the twos complement of 6:

6 in binary	= 00000110
ones complement of 6	= 11111001
add 1	1
twos complement	= 11111010

This value (11111010) represents a *negative* six. Therefore, we can say that when we take the twos complement of a positive number we are changing it to a negative value. To best illustrate that this value is in fact a negative six, let us increment it *six* times (up to zero):

11111010	Negative six
+ 1	
11111011	Negative five

```
         +        1
         11111100        Negative four
         +        1
         11111101        Negative three
         +        1
         11111110        Negative two
         +        1
         11111111        Negative one
         +        1
1        00000000        ZERO
↑
Carry discarded
```

Following are some examples of *subtraction* in twos complement arithmetic:

1.6-5

5 in binary	= 00000101
ones complement of 5	= 11111010
add 1	1
twos complement	= 11111011

Summing,

6 in binary	= 00000110
twos complement of 5	= 11111011
	1 00000001

A carry is produced, but is discarded. The sign (most significant bit) is zero, indicating the result is positive.

2.3-3

3 in binary	= 00000011
ones complement of 3	= 11111100
add 1	1
twos complement	= 11111101

Summing,

3 in binary	= 00000011

twos complement of 3	= 11111101
	1 00000000

And, the correct answer is, of course, zero.

3. 3-4 4 in binary	= 00000100
ones complement of 4	= 11111011
add 1	1
twos complement	= 11111100

Summing,

3 in binary	= 00000011
twos complement of 4	= 11111100
	11111111

The result is negative one in twos complement (no carry produced).

In two complement arithmetic, the addition of two numbers of opposite sign will always produce the correct result. It may or may not produce a carry. The carry or overflow may be ignored.

Notice that, in both ones complement arithmetic and twos complement arithmetic, addition stays the same. The only thing that is changed is the way in which the complement is taken in order to effect subtraction. Some ALUs will compensate automatically for subtraction in ones complement arithmetic, while some won't.

In twos complement arithmetic, the programmer should test for overflow. In any addition of like signed numbers where there is a possibility that the maximum sum could be exceeded, a test must be made for overflow. If the test is not made, there is a danger that erroneous results could occur and that the user might not be aware of that fact. In reality, any addition could produce overflow. While the user may never expect overflow to occur, if his data were erroneous, then an erroneous sum could result. By making the test for overflow under all conditions, those errors *which couldn't possibly happen* would be detected.

All of the examples given here used 8 bit arithmetic to simplify the examples, but the principles and concepts discussed hold true regardless of the arithmetic word length used. On a 32 bit machine, larger numbers can be handled, but the test for overflow (carry) and change of sign must still be made.

Arithmetic Software

Binary arithmetic within a computer is not difficult or mysterious; however, care must be given to making sure that the results obtained from an arithmetic operation are correct. The care required can add additional steps to a program and can conceivably make a simple problem into a lot of work. One way in which some of the work can be eliminated is to choose a microprocessor which provides an automatic *hardware scheme* for testing for overflow or change of sign. Another solution is to choose a microprocessor which provides the same capabilities by software. *Software* in this case is a program furnished by the manufacturer to do the proper testing for you. This software may also offer the capability to work with 16 or 32 bit numbers and may in addition offer other capabilities such as multiplication and division.

What's That in Binary?

My first introduction to the world of computers left me with a terrible reaction. I tend to break out into a rash when real math comes my way, which is not the best reaction when starting to shake hands with computers.

Since others may suffer similar reactions, I have dredged the contents of my memory to recall a simple way of converting a base ten number into the binary numbering system or into the octal system of notation.

Interestingly enough, I was exposed to this method some 35 years ago, in, of all places, a Latin class. The instructor believed in making things come alive by spending some class time showing us how to multiply and divide Roman numerals. Computer stuff, by comparison, is mere child's play—and it is no wonder the barbarians wiped out Rome. It had to be painfully obvious that the Romans were so busy XXVIIing it that they had no time left to fight a mere war.

Here is a little something for my fellow non-math lovers:

$$A_{1b} + A_0 + \sum_{1}^{\infty} a^{-1}\, b^{-1} \ldots$$

It is perfectly obvious that this little bit of razzle-dazzle contains all the wisdom needed to convert a number of any base or radix to a number with any other base. For example, a decimal number to a binary number or an octal number to a decimal number.

Rather than trying to unscrew the unscrutable by translating this little gem into basic English, let me pass on a simple nuts-and-bolts nugget of wisdom.

Specifically, let's examine a way to convert any decimal number, such as 19758 or a number of your choice, to binary or octal. All you need is the native ability to divide by two or by eight.

Decimal to Binary Conversion

- The digits as derived are set down right to left, the rightmost digit being the least significant bit and the leftmost digit being the most significant bit.
- We divide the number first into odd or even by inspection. If the number is even we automatically make the least significant bit a ZERO. If the number is odd, we make the least significant bit a ONE.
- Now we proceed to divide the number by two in a series of successive divisions. We ignore fractional remainders produced by the divisions, i.e., 19 divided by 2 would produce a real world answer of 9½, but we would ignore the remainder or fractional ½.
- Any division that produces an EVEN number gives us a ZERO in our process of converting decimal to binary.
- Any division that produces an ODD number gives us a ONE in our process of converting decimal to binary.
- The process of successive divisions ends when the number is finally reduced to ONE again, ignoring any fractional remainders.

For example, to convert decimal number 38 to binary:

- By inspection, since 38 is an even number the least significant bit is ZERO. 0
- 38 divided by 2 = 19. Nineteen is ODD, hence next bit is a ONE. 10
- 19 divided by 2 = 9 (ignore fraction). Nine is ODD, hence next bit is a ONE. . . . 110
- 9 divided by 2 = 4 (ignore fraction). Since 4 is even, next bit is a ZERO. . . 0110
- 4 divided by 2 = 2. Since 2 is even, next bit is a ZERO. . 00110
- 2 divided by 2 = 1 (divisions end). Since ONE is ODD, the next bit is a ONE. 100110

The final bianry number thus produced is decimal 38 converted to its binary form.

This painless method makes it much easier to generate decimal to binary conversions than remembering the absolute values of each binary bit, particulary for conversions where the decimal number is four or five digits long.

Decimal to octal conversion is a similar process involving successive divisions by eight. However, the signposts in the divisions are different. In the decimal to binary conversion we completely ignored the fractional parts associated with the successive divisions. In the octal conversion we use the numerator of these fractional parts to tell us what the octal bit values are to be.

As you know, in binary or base two, we only have a string of ONEs or ZEROs in the final conversion. In octal or base eight we use the numbers ZERO through SEVEN.

Decimal to Octal Conversion

- As in the bianry conversion, we are using a series of successive divisions. This time the constant divisor is 8. The same rule of bit value applies: rightmost digit is the least significant bit and the leftmost digit is the most significant bit.
- Select a number in decimal to be converted to octal and divide it by 8. This will result in a whole number or a whole number plus a fraction. If the result of the division is a whole number, the octal bit is a ZERO.
- If the division results in a whole number plus a fraction then the octal bit is represented by the numerical value of the numerator of the fractional part.
- The next successive divisions divide the whole number part of the previous division by 8, applying the above rule for determining the bit value of the octal number.
- The successive divisions come to an end when you are left with a simple fraction.

For example, to convert decimal 525 to octal:

- 525 divided by 8 = 65-⅝. Thus our least significant bit is 5. . . . 5
- 65 divided by 8 = 8-⅛ thus our next bit is 1. . . 15
- 8 divided by 8 = 1-0/8. Since ONE is a whole number the next bit is ZERO. The form 1-0/8 is shown to make it clear that the numerator is really still our guidepost even in the case of no fractional remainder. . 015
- We now divide ONE by 8 (which equals ⅛), which produces our most significant bit—and the division process ends as we are down to a simple fraction. 1015

Thus 525 decimal has been converted to 1015, which is its octal equivalent.

These simple conversions will make life a bit more livable when you meet the computer, and you are a giant step ahead of good old Flavius Maximus, who had to MCXVII it all the way to the Circus Maximus checkout. By the time he got his change counted, the show was over!

The Hexadecimal System

By this time words like octal, binary and decimal, plus phrases like base two or base ten have penetrated the consciousness of the reader. The sign of the I/O stands a good chance of becoming the thirteenth sign of the zodiac for many experimenters.

For those so afflicted, here is one more number base family to shake hands with. Hexadecimal or base 16 (hexa meaning six and decimal meaning ten . . . the sum thereof being 16) has a unique quality in that it symbology uses both numbers and letters.

The first 10 states are conventional, using number symbols 0 through 9. The next six symbols in order are A, B, C, D, E, F. These six alpha characters represent number symbols for values 10, 11, 12, 13, 14, 15.

If you encounter this number family in computer literature, you will generally find that hexadecimal is indicated in one of two general ways. H '10' might be one general form. The alternate form drops the H but keeps the single quote before and after the number, '10'.

The place values for hexadecimal, as might be expected, rise rather rapidly due to the fact that we are dealing with base 16.

Confining our discussion to whole numbers, the value of the rightmost figure of any hexadecimal expression ranges from 0 to 15, this compared to 0 and 1 for binary, 0 to 9 for decimal and 0 to 7 for octal notation.

In a two digit hexadecimal expression, we can see the rapid escalation of values. Any digit in the column to the left of the first digit is multiplied by 16 to get its absolute value.

As an example, H '3A' is numerically the sum of A which equals 10, plus 3 times 16 or 48. Thus H '3A' equals decimal 58.

H 'FF' would similarly be computed as the sum of 15 added to 15 times 16. This would equal decimal 255.

If we consider four place values of hexadecimal in the same mathematical fashion as we consider decimal, binary or octal, they would form the usual series:

$$16^3 \; 16^2 \; 16^1 \; 16^0$$

Thus by the time we have something like this, H '3A7B', its decimal value, computed as follows, really climbs.

- The value of 'B' is decimal 11.
- The value of '7' is 7 times 16 or decimal 112.
- The value of 'A' is 10 times 16^2 or decimal 2560.
- The value of '3' is 3 times 16^3 or decimal 12,288.
- The value of the entire expression is 14,971. If you want some exercise you can compute the value of H 'FFFF.'

You may well ask, "Is there a justification for hexadecimal?" The answer most definitely is yes. It is the same reason that octal is of value. You can enter large numbers in a system much faster (fewer key strokes) with octal than you can with binary, and the same is true of hexadecimal by several orders of magnitude. Try expressing the numerical value 14,971 in binary to get the idea of just how time/cost effective the higher valued base systems are.

You can perform basic manipulations with hexadecimal just as you can with any other number family. Take the simple example of adding two numbers such as H '13' and H 'A1':

```
 H '13'
 H 'A1'
 ------
  'B4'
```

How do we arrive at this conclusion? The sum of the rightmost column is fairly obvious, 3 plus one = 4. The sum of the next column becomes equally clear if we remember we are really adding 1 plus 10 which equals 11 which equals B in hex notation.

To prove the answer we get the decimal value of H '13' which is 16 plus 3 or decimal 19. H 'A1' is equal to 10 times 16 plus 1 or 161. The result of the addition is decimal 180. Our answer H 'B4' is the sum of 11 times 16 plus 4, or 176 + 4 which is the same decimal number, 180.

Now let's introduce the element of the "carry" into another simple addition problem, adding H'1A' to H'27'L

```
 H '1A'
 H '27'
 ------
 H '41'
```

How did we arrive at this? The sum of 'A' plus '7' is decimal 17. We deduct the number of sixteens we can get out of this first column addition, and the remainder becomes the right hand figure in the answer. The integral number of sixteens is then added to the next column as a carry. This next column now looks like this . . .

H '1' (the carry)
H '1'
H '2'
H '4'

Checking as before, in the original problem H '1A' equals decimal 26. H '27' equals decimal 39 and the sum of 26 + 39 = 65. Our addition answer H '41' equals 4 × 16 + = 65.

Is Digital all That New?

To meditate on an experiment, a serious experimenter often shelves today's experiment, perhaps never to take it up again. The *light* was in the meditation and not in the experiment. This brings me to the point at hand—meditation as related to digital.

For several years now, a transition from analog to digital has been in the process. To many people, digital is considered as a rather new development, but I ask, "Is it really all that new?" The question may suggest the answer that digital has been around for some time.

Just for the fun of it, let us take a brief and somewhat abstract view of digital devices or communications through the age of man.

From man's beginning, he had a very good calculator at his fingertips as well as a computer with all the software that is necessary for its operation, although he had very little need for either in his primitive culture. It was two to three million years before man saw the need to communicate between computers. Man has, over the last 20,000 years, developed ways to communicate between computers.

If the old axiom is true that a picture is equal to a thousand words, and if we should equate the picture to a computer address and equate the thousand words to the memory of the computer, then the cave man had the basic idea in his cave drawings some 20,000 years ago. Programming his computer to accept more addresses (more pictures), he was able to develop a memory system called *hieroglyphics*, which used approximately 900 pictures. Up to this time man had almost exclusively used *analog*, which is called the spoken language. Hieroglyphic programming was too complex for most computers, so a much simpler system was developed using only about 24 pictures. *Hierotics*, as this sytem is called, was very effective digital-wise, but lacked the ability to communicate with analog systems. About 3,000 years ago a digital-to-analog and analog-to-digital system was developed. This system is often called *phonic writing*. Soon to follow was a digital system that was much more simple and was easily converted to analog. This system was made by the combining of the Phoenician phonic system and the Roman alphabet. Because this system had only 26 digits or letters and could be formed into word groups, it was adaptable to programming. Such programs are placed into a machine called a printing press and are read out into a permanent storage unit known as a book, which is a type of read-only memory. With this type of ROM, the two or three million-year-old old computer design has almost unlimited capacity to perform the most complex problems.

In Aristotle's theory of the universe formulated sometime around 400 BC, it was suggested that a binary system was possible. Such a system would consist of such variables as hot and cold, wet and dry, light and dark, etc.

Much experimenting in digital communications was taking place by the mid-1700s, parallel versus serial as each form was being developed. Static or friction electricity and its pith balls came first as a parallel system (i.e., one set of pith balls for each letter). Soon to follow was a synchronized serial form using only one set of pith balls.

Galvan electricity and the use of magnetic needles went through the same parallel and serial development. However, a new wrinkle was added. The new wrinkle was code—that is, left or right, operated or non-operated. Its form was much like that of Morse code.

From its inception in the mid-1800s, the electromagnetic (telegraph) system used a code in serial form. It was the search for the conversion of the electromagnetic digital system to analog that led to the development of the telephone—which just happens to be an analog device. It was only a few years ago that the conversion of digital to analog and analog to digital was electronically accomplished. Its form is called *pulse code modulation*.

Just as in the addressing of electronic computers, we have been simplifying the addressing to the two or three million-year-old design. Some examples include changing "The United States of America" to USA, and other conversions resulting in terms such as IRS, FCC, IBEW, NAACP, FBI, CIA and others.

What is the answer to the question, "Is digital all that new?" I would say no. I would go so far as to say that at present we are not really in a truly transitional period but rather in a sort of jockeying position, As we turn the corner, I predict that the next big development will be a 3D computer that will make the present computer look like a small contribution to the overall communications system—but I see no way that the old two or three million-year-old design will ever be replaced.

The Ins and Outs of TTL

The design of digital circuits using TTL integrated circuits can be much less frustrating if some simple rules are followed. I am referring to the rules that dictate how and why interconnections between the various circuits and the outside world are made. If you follow the rules, you should be able to put together a digital circuit from TTL ICs and only have to worry about wiring errors, logic goofs and bad ICs. The information is from the manufacturers' literature and my own experiences on the bench.

Ins

The most common and most easily overlooked input of TTL circuits is the power supply. One look at any TTL circuit and you quickly know the value of the supply voltage is +5V. For those who worry about such things, the tolerance is ± percent (military versions are ±10 percent). In other words, the manufacturer only guarantees proper operation of his ICs when the supply voltage is between +4.75V and 5.25V. This is not to say they won't work at other voltages—only that there is no guarantee.

When TTL circuits switch they generate very high frequency current spikes on the power supply lines. These current spikes traveling through the high frequency impedances of the power supply lines cause voltage spikes which can couple into other circuits and trip flip flops, clock counters and do all sorts of nasty (and very difficult to find) things. To protect yourself from this problem these power connection rules should be followed:

- Connect a .01 uF disc capacitor from the +5 connection to the ground connection of each IC. Locate the capacitor as close as is practical and use short leads. A miniature disc with a voltage rating of 10 volts or more is a good choice.
- Use fairly heavy wire (I recommend #18 or larger) for +5 and ground lines and arrange them so there are many connections. Try to simulate a ground plane and a + 5 plane.
- For every 20 ICs or so in your circuit put in one electrolytic capacitor from ±5 to ground. Any value between approximately 4 and 25 μF and 10 volts or more rating is okay. If only one is used, try to locate it where the ±5 first comes into the board. If more are used, distribute them more or less evenly over the board.
- Use a regulated supply for the ±5. There are many circuits for making a regulated supply.

Some of these rules may seem obvious while others are not so well known, especially to the newcomer. Figure 1-29 illustrates one

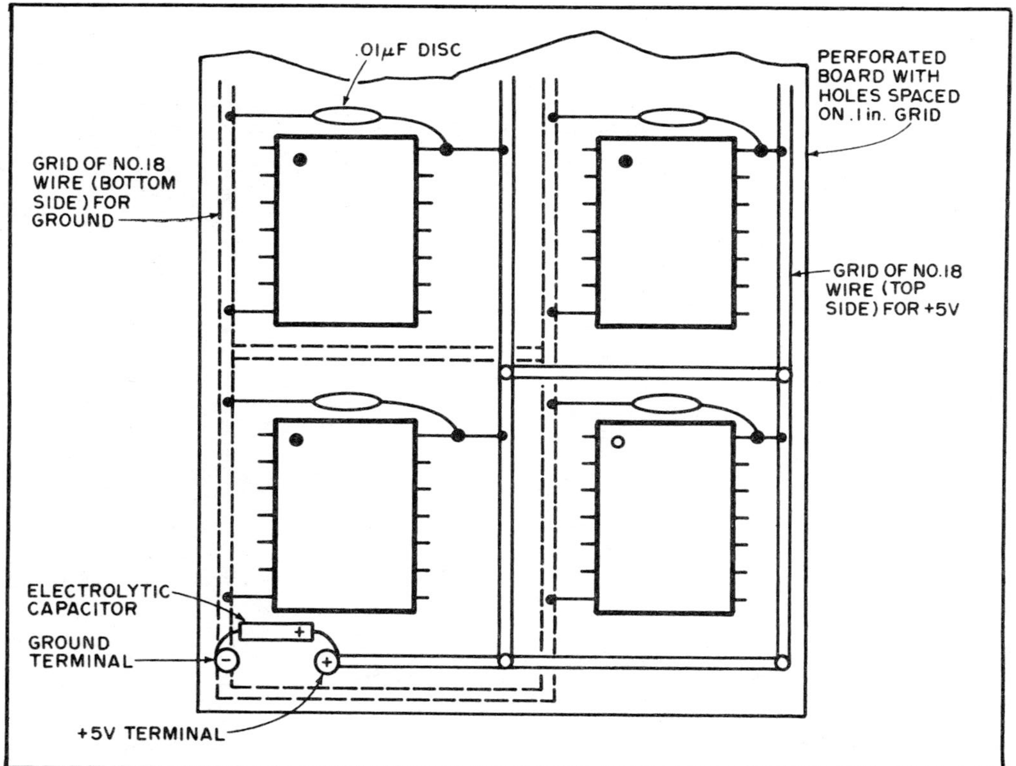

Fig. 1-29. Illustration of rules for power supply connections.

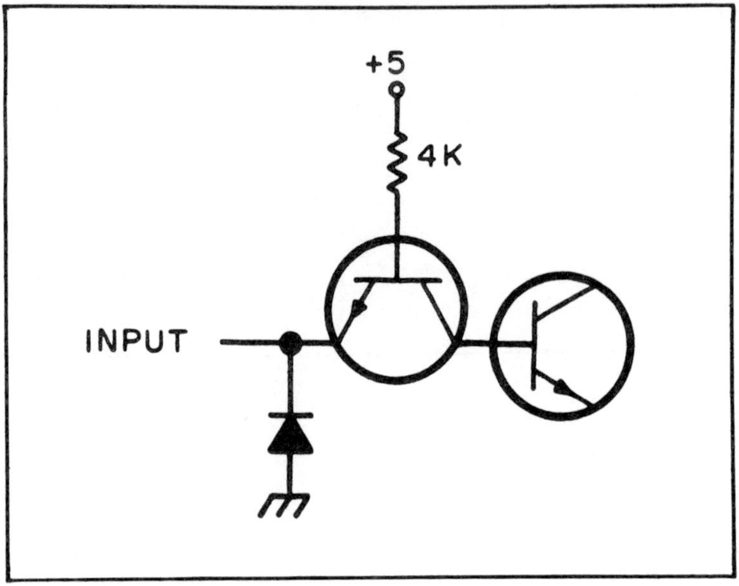

Fig. 1-30. Standard TTL input circuit.

method of construction employing point to point wiring following these rules.

Next on the list of TTL *ins* let's investigate a typical input circuit as shown in Fig. 1-30. In order to guarantee that the transistor is turned on we must do two things. First, we must make the input voltage less than .8V, and second we must draw out of the emitter 1.6mA of current. In order to guarantee that the transistor is turned off we must also do two things. First, we must make the input voltage greater than 2V, and second we may have to supply up to 40 uA of leakage current. The diode is not necessarily present in all circuits. Its purpose is to limit negative pulses on the input that may occur due to transmission line effects on long interconnections. This input characteristic is called one unit load (UL) and a circuit such as in Fig. 1-30 which contains 1 UL is said to have a fan-in of 1.

If a second emitter is added to the circuit of Fig. 1-30, we have a 2-input gate configuration, as shown in Fig. 1-31. Each input has its own protection diode. If either input satisfies the *on* requirements, the transistor will be on. Obviously, both inputs must satisfy the *off* requirements in order to turn the transistor off. By adding more emitters the manufacturers make multiple input gates. The 7430, for instance, has eight emitters.

What about the undefined area of the input characteristic which lies between .8V and 2V? It is just that, undefined. This is a grey area where nothing is guaranteed and, except for some special circuits, it should be passed through as quickly as possible (less than 200 ns). If the input passes through this region too slowly the output can actually break into oscillation. In fact, this is how a TTL oscillator gets started: by being biased deliberately into this grey area until oscillation occurs and then having the frequency of oscillation controlled by external components.

Inputs from the Outside World

TTL circuits connect to themselves very nicely, but the outside world is not necessarily TTL compatible. How do you satisfy these input requirements? It is very easy to get a voltage less than .8V and able to sink 1.6 mA—just short the input to ground with a switch. What about the other limit? How do we get the high voltage and current source? Figure 1-32 shows one way. The 1k resistor guarantees that even with 40 uA being drawn, the voltage will be above the required 2V minimum.

When the input is relatively slow in changing, you can avoid the grey area problem by using TTL ICs which have a special hysteresis built into them. These are called *Schmitt triggers* and have different switching points depending on whether the signal is positive or negative going at the time. The 7413, 7414 and 74132 are examples of this Schmitt trigger type of circuit.

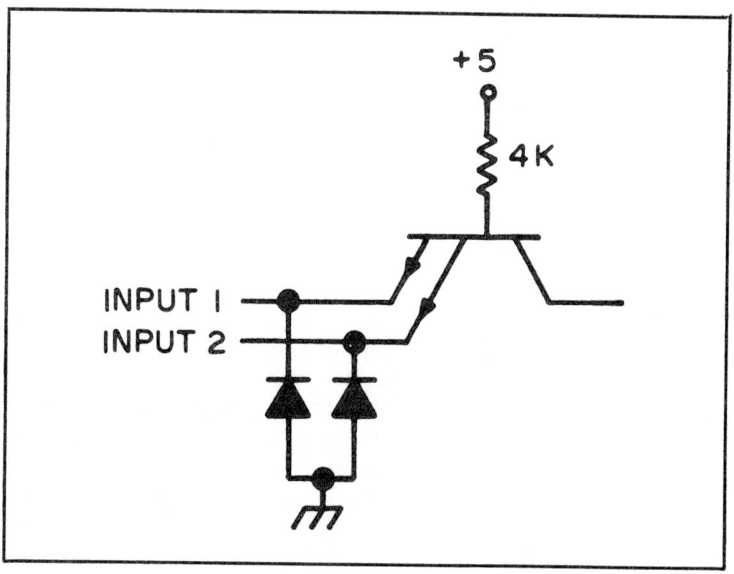

Fig. 1-31. Input circuit of 2-input gate.

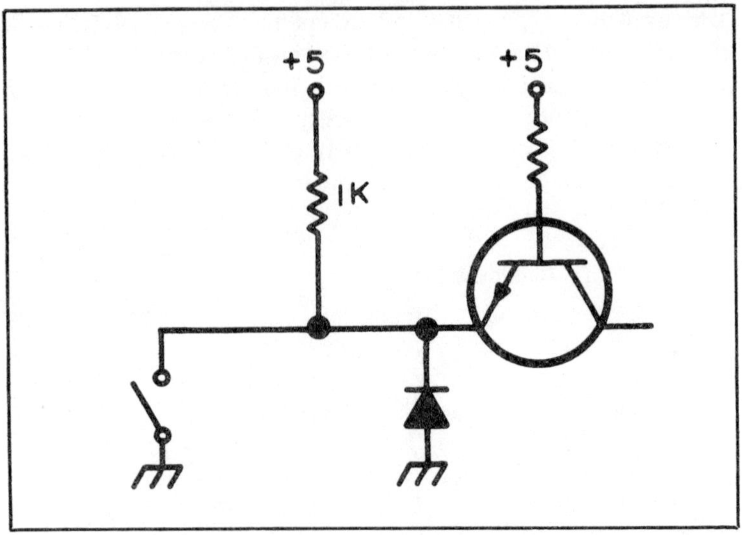

Fig. 1-32. Using a normal switch to drive TTL.

When considering switches as the connection to the outside world another potential problem arises. The contacts of the switch don't close cleanly. They actually hit and bounce apart one or more times before remaining closed. Normally this is no problem, but if you were attempting to count switch closures it would not be possible. Figure 1-33 shows how to use an SPDT switch and two NAND gate elements to form a flip flop which debounces the switch. This is a very common form of circuit configuration called *crosscoupled NAND gates*.

Often when you are finished with a logic design you will find yourself with unused inputs to some circuits. Never, repeat, never leave any unused input to float. It will cause nothing but trouble. Even though an open input is theoretically the same as a high, in practice it is very sensitive to any kind of noise and can cause the output to change for no apparent reason.

What do you do with unused inputs? There are several choices:

- If it will not prevent normal operation of the circuit you can ground the unused input or connect it to a high source.

1. The high can be obtained by connecting directly to +5V. The manufacturers don't recommend this since, if the input goes above +5.5V, it is possible to damage the input if the current is not limited in some way. I do it all the time with no problems (yet). I recommend connecting to the +5V connection on the chip itself.

2. Connect the unused input to +5V through a 1k resistor. One resistor can tie as many as 50 inputs to +5V.
3. Use an unused inverting element and ground the input(s) to force the output high. This high output can then be used to pull as many inputs as its fan-out is rated (see output section).

- Unused inputs of gates can be connected in parallel with used inputs. There is no increase in load for low inputs. The total current required for the two inputs in parallel is still 1.6 mA. Actually you can tie as many in parallel as you wish and the total low fan-in will not exceed 1 UL. The high fan-in does increase, however, as each emitter may require the 40 uA leakage current. As long as the high fan-out capability of the driving circuit is not exceeded you can parallel gate inputs.

One more input characteristic of TTL circuits is worth mentioning. This is the difference between so-called edge-triggered and master-slave flip flops. The outputs of both circuits react according to the status of the control lines at the time the clock pulse occurs. An edge-triggered flip flop output reacts essentially immediately. The small delay is called propagation delay. A master-slave flip flop is more subtle. On the leading edge of the clock pulse the master reacts like an edge-triggered flip flop. The output, however, is from the slave and it does not react until the trailing edge of the clock pulse. Figure 1-34 shows this difference in graphic form. The main point to remember is that a master-slave flip flop requires a complete clock cycle, not just one edge.

Outs

There are three basic forms of output circuit used in TTL. The most common form is shown in Fig. 1-35. This is the so-called *totem*

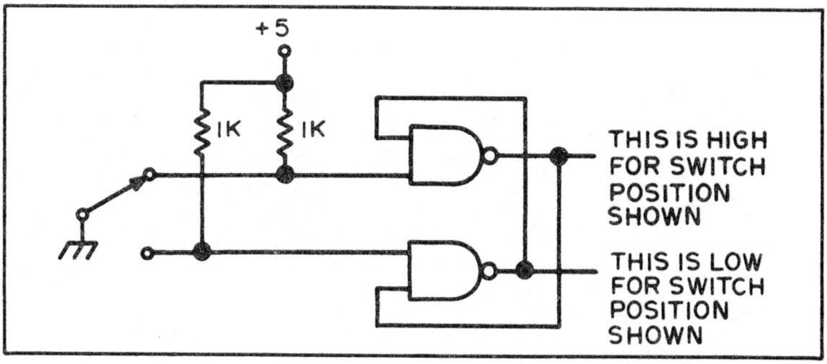

Fig. 1-33. Using cross-coupled NAND gates to debounce a switch.

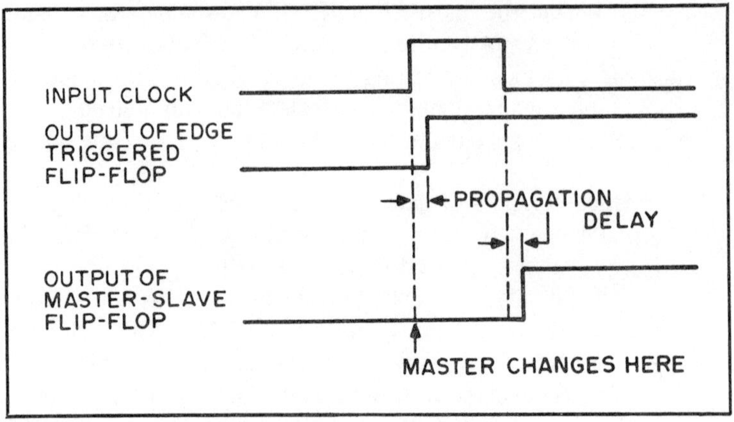

Fig. 1-34. Timing diagram showing difference between edge-triggered and master-slave flip flops.

pole configuration. In the low output state the bottom transistor is on and the top transistor is off. The bottom transistor sinks the current from the connected inputs. In the high state the bottom transistor is off and the top transistor is on. The top transistor now supplies the leakage currents for the connected inputs. This is the normal version. There are minor variations on this circuit but they all operate the same way.

The number of unit loads an output can drive is called its *fan-out*. The standard TTL IC has a low fan-out of 10 UL and a high fan-out of 20 UL. In other words, a standard TTL output can sink 16 mA (10 times 1.6 mA) and the output is guaranteed to be no higher than .4V or it can source 800 uA (20 times 40 uA) and the output is guaranteed to be higher than 2.4V. If you compare these output specs with the input specs you will find there is a .4V safety margin.

There are several ICs which are specifically designed to drive larger loads. The 7437, 7438, 7439 and 7440 will all sink 30 UL. The 7437 and 7440 will also source 30 UL.

The 7438 and 7439 belong to another class of output circuit called *open collector*. In this configuration the top transistor is missing and the bare collector of the bottom transitor is brought out. With this circuit you need an external load resistor of some sort to provide the pull-up to +5V. If the voltage rating of the IC output is high enough (the 7407 is rated for 30V, for example), you can switch much higher voltages, and even drive relays and lamps if the current rating is not exceeded.

The open collector circuit is also used in a logic configuration known as both *wired-and* and *wired-or*. Figure 1-36 shows how this works. All the open collector outputs are tied to a common pull-up resistor. If any output goes low they all go low (wired-or), and the output will only be high when all the output transistors are off (wired-and, hence both terms). There is a practical limit to how many outputs you can connect together. The pull-up resistor must supply the leakage current for all inputs and all outputs when they are all off and still maintain the voltage above 2.4V. However, it must still be large enough to limit the total current of resistor plus inputs to 16 mA (10 UL) when any output is on.

Contrary to what you may have read previously, it is alright to connect TTL outputs in parallel, provided you also connect the inputs in parallel so the outputs are doing the same thing at the same time. In fact, the manufacturers recommend this technique as one way to increase fan-out when the load is too much for one output. However, you should restrict this paralleling to elements in the same package because large transient currents are generated and can cause problems if they are not closely confined.

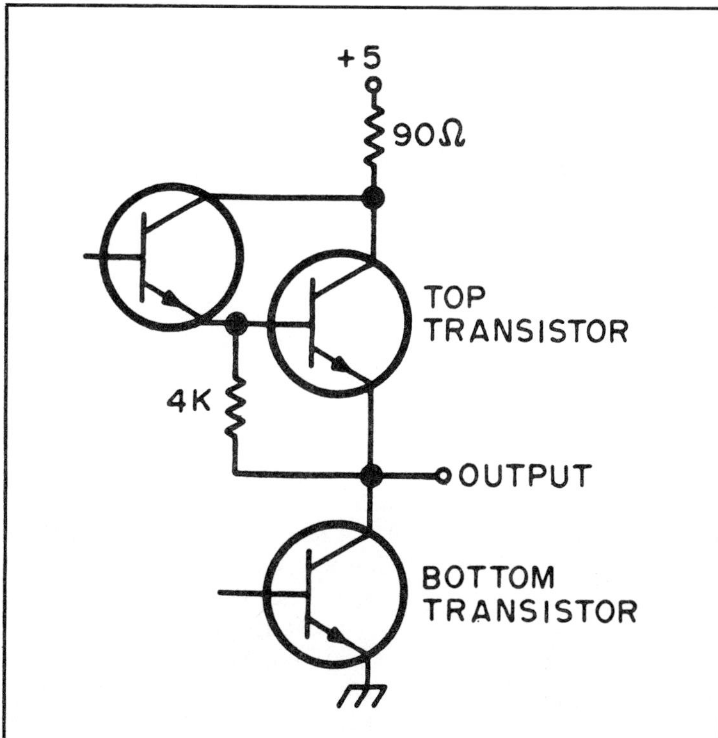

Fig. 1-35. Totem pole TTL output circuit.

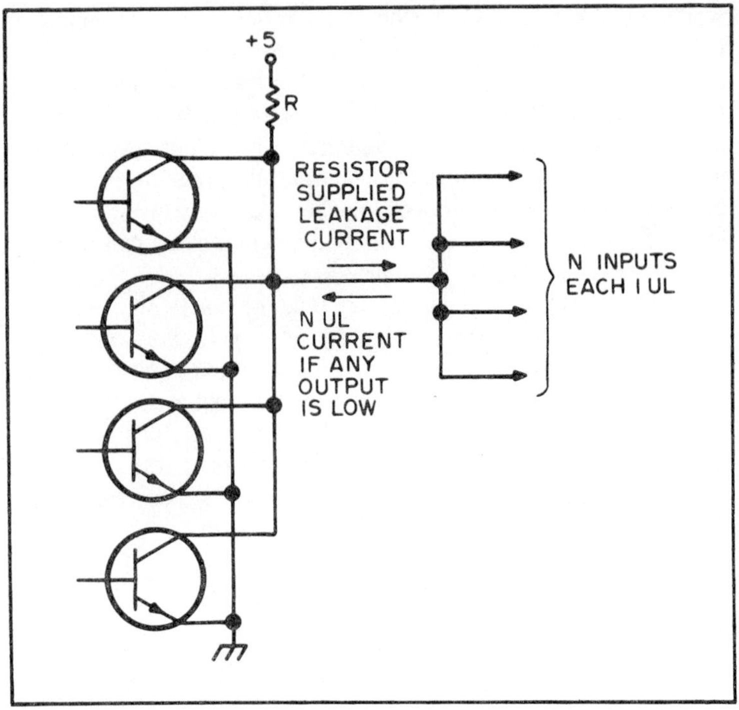

Fig. 1-36. Using open collector outputs for wired-or configuration.

The third and newest type of output configuration is the so-called tri-state or three-state output. This is a normal TTL totem pole output where both transistors can be turned off. An extra *enable input* is added to the the circuit and when enabled the output functions as a normal TTL output. When disabled the output is essentially disconnected. This allows one common wire with many tri-state outputs connected to it to carry all sorts of different information (even in different directions) on a time division multiplex basis. All you have to do is enable the appropriate outputs and inputs at the proper time. This *bus structure* is very common in the world of computers and microprocessors. I have used tri-state circuits to match 336 bits of data at one time and then output them 8 bits at a time. That is 42 different outputs on each data line.

Someplace in your design you have to connect outputs to the outside world. There are special ICs for driving displays of different kinds as this is one of the most common outputs encountered. I have also mentioned using high voltage open collector outputs. If you need more current or voltage, you can use a circuit such as shown in Fig. 1-37. In both versions the resistors limit the base current to a

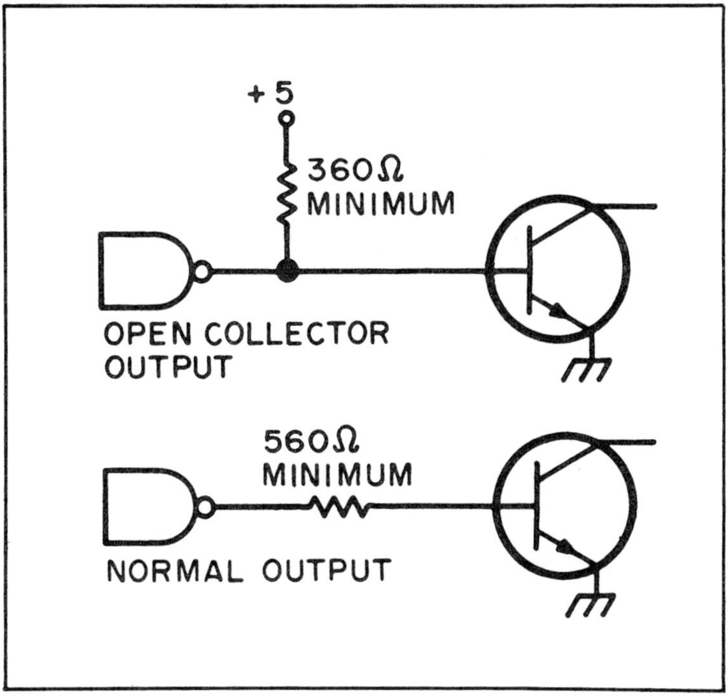

Fig. 1-37. TTL driving transistors.

safe value. When driving an external circuit of any kind it is best to use an ouput dedicated to only that load. That way, if any stray

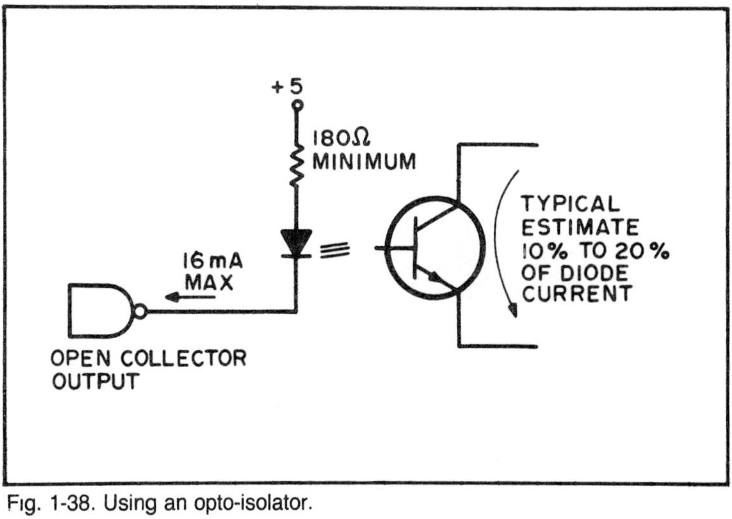

Fig. 1-38. Using an opto-isolator.

too easy for a stray signal to sneak back, get inside the flip flop and do weird things.

When it becomes necessary to switch large output loads, often there are transients generated that ride back in on the ground and cause stray triggers of flip flops and other nasty things. A relatively new circuit element called an *opto-isolator* eliminates this problem completely. Even when driving all eight channels plus sprocket advance of a high speed paper tape punch there is no problem—and that represents 9 A at 24V every 9 ms. The opto-isolator (Fig. 1-38) consists of an infrared LED and phototransistor. The LED is driven from an open collector output and its energy is coupled optically (no physical connection) to the phototransistor, which is then used as a low level switching stage in a totally electrically isolated circuit.

The preceding rules and suggestions will not eliminate all your digital logic problems but they will greatly reduce them, especially those frustrating random ones. Remember the manufacturers only guarantee proper operation if you stay within the specs.

Practical D/A and A/D Conversions

Aside from computers and their peripherals, much of the rest of the world is analog. Computers can perform many valuable tasks in isolation, but application possiblilities are far greater when a computer can communicate directly with the analog world. Communication from a computer to the analog world is normaly done using a *digital-to-analog*, or D/A, converter to change the digital output of the computer to an analog voltage. Similarly, an *analog-to-digital*, or A/D, converter can be used to convert analog voltages to digital words which can be sensed and measured by a computer.

Integrated circuits designed to be the heart of D/A converters are now becoming available from several mail-order parts suppliers. Although these devices were originally developed for use with additional custom control circuits, they can be used in conjunction with a microcomputer to do D/A and A/D conversion. In fact, one of the circuits described can be set by a switch to do either D/A or A/D conversion. Thus, it enables communications to and from the analog world, depending upon application, with a minimum of components.

D/A Conversion

The most basic form of D/A converter is shown in Fig. 1-39. It consists of switches which are used to represent a binary word and binary weighted resistors which contribute current to the output in proportion to the bit posistions of the switches. This particular

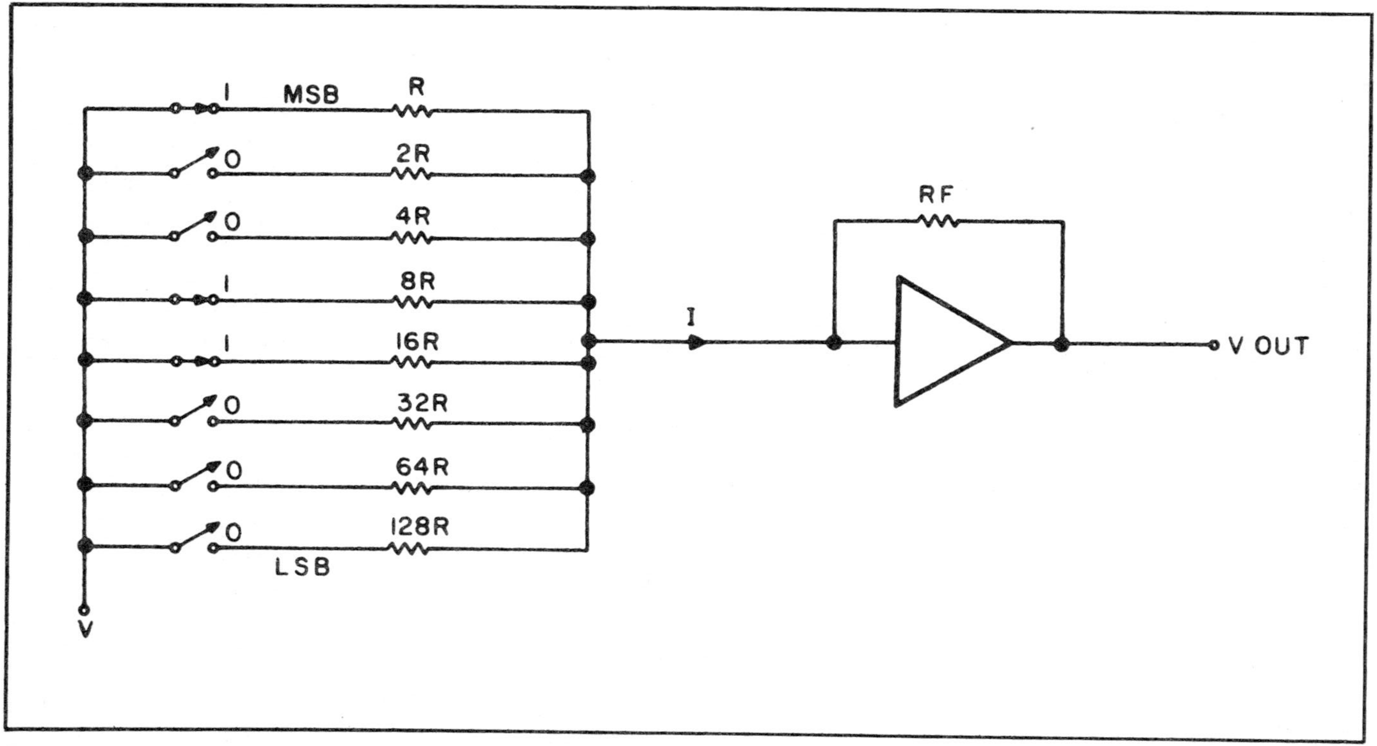

Fig. 1-39. Prototype D/A converter using binary weighted resistors.

signals are picked up and fed back on this line to the outside world they won't be able to couple into another input and disrupt operation. Also you should never use the output of a flip flop (this includes counters, shift registers, etc.) to connect to the outside world. It is converter has eight switches, so it can convert an 8-bit digital word into an output current having $2^8 = 256$ step values. The output current for this type of converter is equal to the voltage source value divided by the largest weighting resistor value (here 128Ω) and multiplied by the decimal equivalent of the digital word. The digital word represented in the figure is 10011000, so the output current would be 152V/128Ω Amperes. The output current could be set to values from 0 Amperes, for a digital word of 00000000, to 255V/128Ω Amperes, for a digital word of 11111111, in steps of V/128Ω Amperes. Notice that we call the output of a D/A converter an *analog signal* but that it actually varies in discrete steps and only approaches an analog signal when the step sizes are small. Usually, it is more useful to have the output be in the form of a voltage rather than a current, and an operational amplifier is included to do the current-to-voltage translation.

A Practical D/A Converter

One disadvantage of using binary weighted resistors to make a D/A converter is that the resistors span a wide range of values. It is difficult to make accurate integrated circuit resistors over a 128-to-1 resistance range, so most integrated circuit D/A converters use a different type of resistor network, known as an R-2R ladder, which can give very high resolution with only two moderately sized resistor values. Figure 1-40 shows an 8-bit D/A converter built around a Motorola MC1408L-8. Internally, this device uses an R-2R ladder, but externally, it behaves the same as the binary weighted resistor prototype converter.

The MC1408 has eight input leads (D7-D0) which control the settings of internal current switches. The inputs are TTL compatible, so they may be driven directly by a microcomputer parallel output port, such as an 8212 or MC6820. As with the prototype converter, an amplifier is included to change the MC1408 output current to a voltage. The amplifier output voltage is given by:

$$V_{out} = 0.0021R_f \left[\frac{D7}{2} + \frac{D6}{4} + \frac{D5}{8} + \frac{D4}{16} + \frac{D3}{32} + \frac{D2}{64} + \frac{D1}{128} + \frac{D0}{256} \right],$$

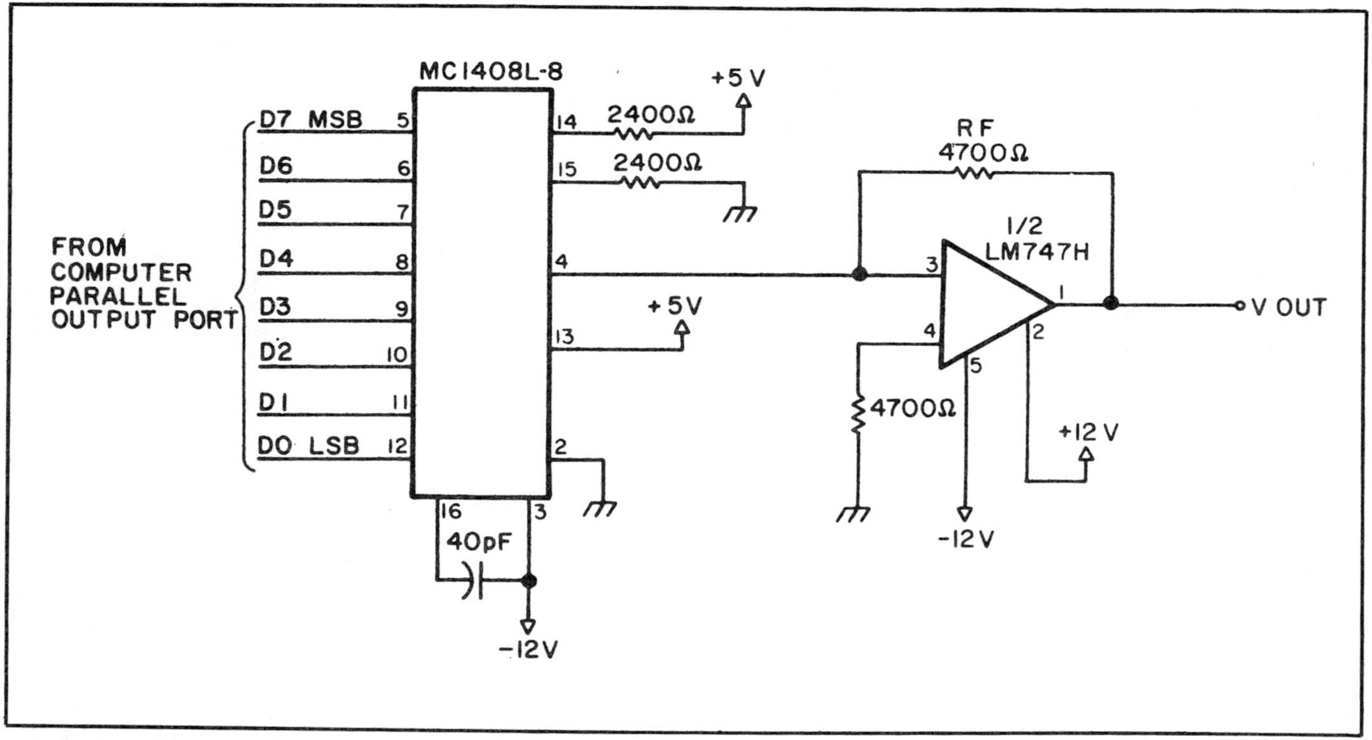

Fig. 1-40. A practical D/A converter having an output range of 0 to 10 volts in 0.039-volt steps.

where D0 through D7 are binary values, either zero or one. Register R_f determines the amplifier gain and, therefore, its output voltage range. With R_f equal to 4.7kΩ, as shown in Fig. 1-40, the maximum amplifier output voltage is approximately 10 volts, and the step size is 0.039 volts. R_f may be decreased if a smaller output range is desired. For example, the maximum output voltage will be 5 volts,and the step size will be 0.0195 volts, if R_f is 2.4kΩ.

Using the D/A converter is straightforward, since it needs essentially no software driver program. All you need to do is output a digital word to the microcomputer parallel output port, and the converter will produce the corresponding analog voltage level at its output.

In many applications, a D/A converter is used to generate a time varying signal, such as a sine wave, by having the computer output a series of digital words. In these cases, it may be important to know how fast the D/A converter can react. The converter shown in Fig. 1-40 can convert a digital word to an analog output voltage in about two microseconds, which is faster than the instruction cycle time of all but bipolar microprocessors. In general then, the microcomputer rather than the D/A converter will limit the maximum frequency which the D/A converter produces.

Adding A/D Conversion Capability

One of the most popular means of performing analog-to-digital conversion is known as the *successive-approximation technique*, and the heart of a successive-approximation A/D converter is a D/A converter such as the one just described. An A/D converter has an analog signal, usually a voltage, as its input, and the circuit tries to find a digital representation for the signal. The successive-approximation converter does this by using a D/A converter to generate an analog voltage which can be compared to the input signal. When the two analog signals are equal, the digital word applied to the D/A converter is also a valid representation for the analog input signal.

A basic block diagram of a successive-approximation A/D converter using an MC1408 is shown in Fig. 1-41. The analog input signal is applied to IC1, which is a high input impedance amplifier that keeps the converter from loading down the analog source. Output currents from IC1 and the MC1408 are compared by high-gain amplifier IC2. Whenever the output current of the MC1408 is greater than that of IC1, the output of IC2 will appear as logic 1 to the computer input port. Conversely, when the output current of the

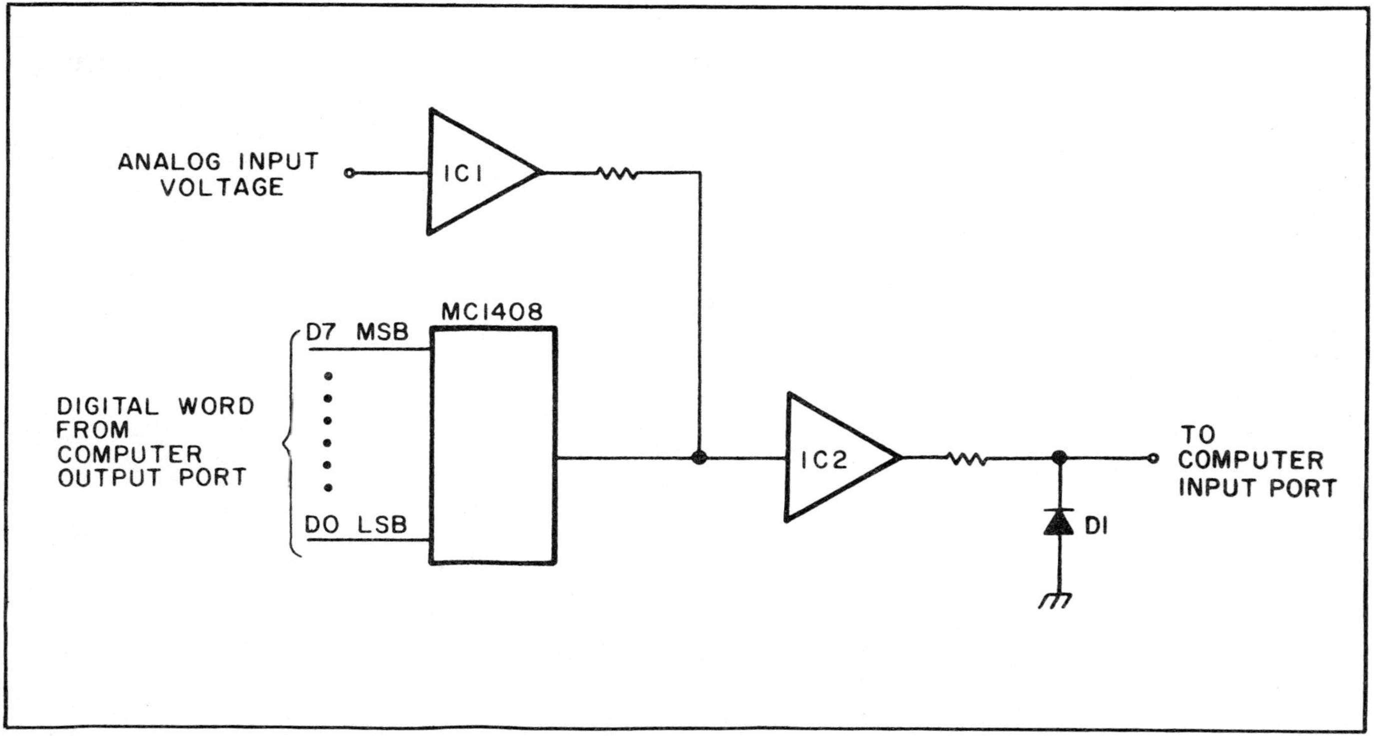

Fig. 1-41. A basic analog-to-digital converter.

MC140 8 is less than that of IC1, the computer input port will see a logic zero (the output of IC2 will be a large negative voltage, but diode D1 will prevent the negative voltage from reaching the computer input).

By comparing Figs. 1-40 and 1-41, you can see that the differences between A/D and D/A converters are small. The circuit of Fig. 1-42 takes advantage of their similarity because it can be used as an A/D converter when desired, and, at the flip of a switch, it can be changed into a D/A converter for use in other applications. In the D/A conversion mode, IC1 is disconnected, and R_f is connected to establish the proper gain for IC2. In the A/D mode, IC1 is connected, and the gain of IC2 is made very high by disconnecting R_f.

Thus far, in discussing the A/D converter, I have ignored the problem of determining the exact digital word which should be presented to the MC1408 input so that its output is identical to the analog signal being applied to the D/A converter. The only way to determine the correct digital word is to sequentially generate digital words in a judicious manner so that each successive word corresponds more closely to the analog voltage. It is this sequential process which gives the successive-approximation converter its name. An algorithm which converges rapidly on the correct digital word is one which individually tests bits, beginning with the most significant bit, to determine whether that bit should be set to a one or zero. Each bit is tested by outputting a word with that bit set to a one. If the output of the MC1408 produced by the test word is less than the analog input signal (IC2 outputs a logic zero), then that bit should remain a one. If the MC1408 output is greater than the analog input (IC2 outputs a logic one), then that bit should be set to a zero. After a bit is tested and its value is known, the next most significant bit is tested in a similar fashion until all bit values are known.

A flowchart listing of the successive-approximation algorithm is given in Fig. 1-43. First, the analog voltage is checked to see if it exceeds the range of the converter. This is done by outputting word FFH (all bits set to one), which corresponds to an analog voltage of 10 volts. If the output of IC2 is a logic zero, then the input voltage must be greater than 10 volts, and an error message is printed. If the output of IC2 is a logic one, you can begin the testing of individual bits. Register B always contains a single one in the bit position being tested. After the bit test is completed, register B is rotated right to move the one into position for the next test. Results of all previous bit tests are combined in register A. An example of how the algorithm proceeds is given in Table 1-1.

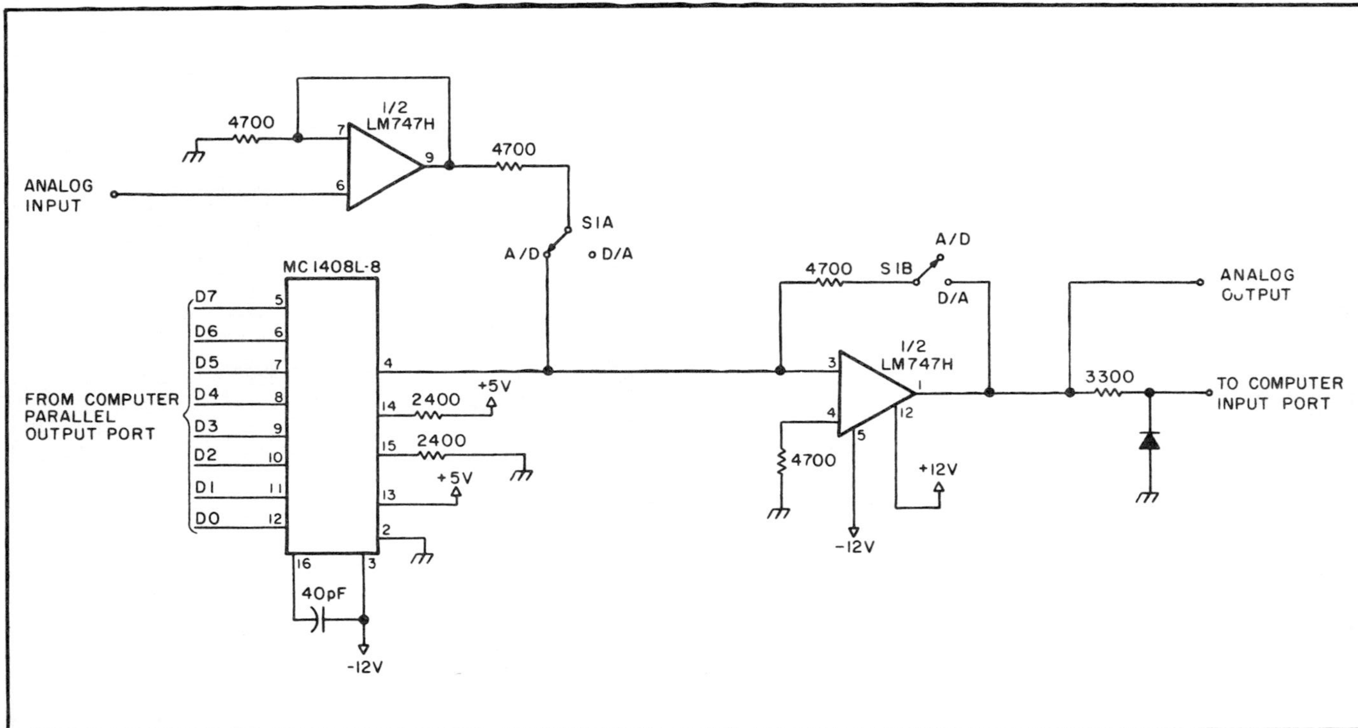

Fig. 1-42. A converter which can perform either D/A or A/D conversion, depending upon the setting of switch S1.

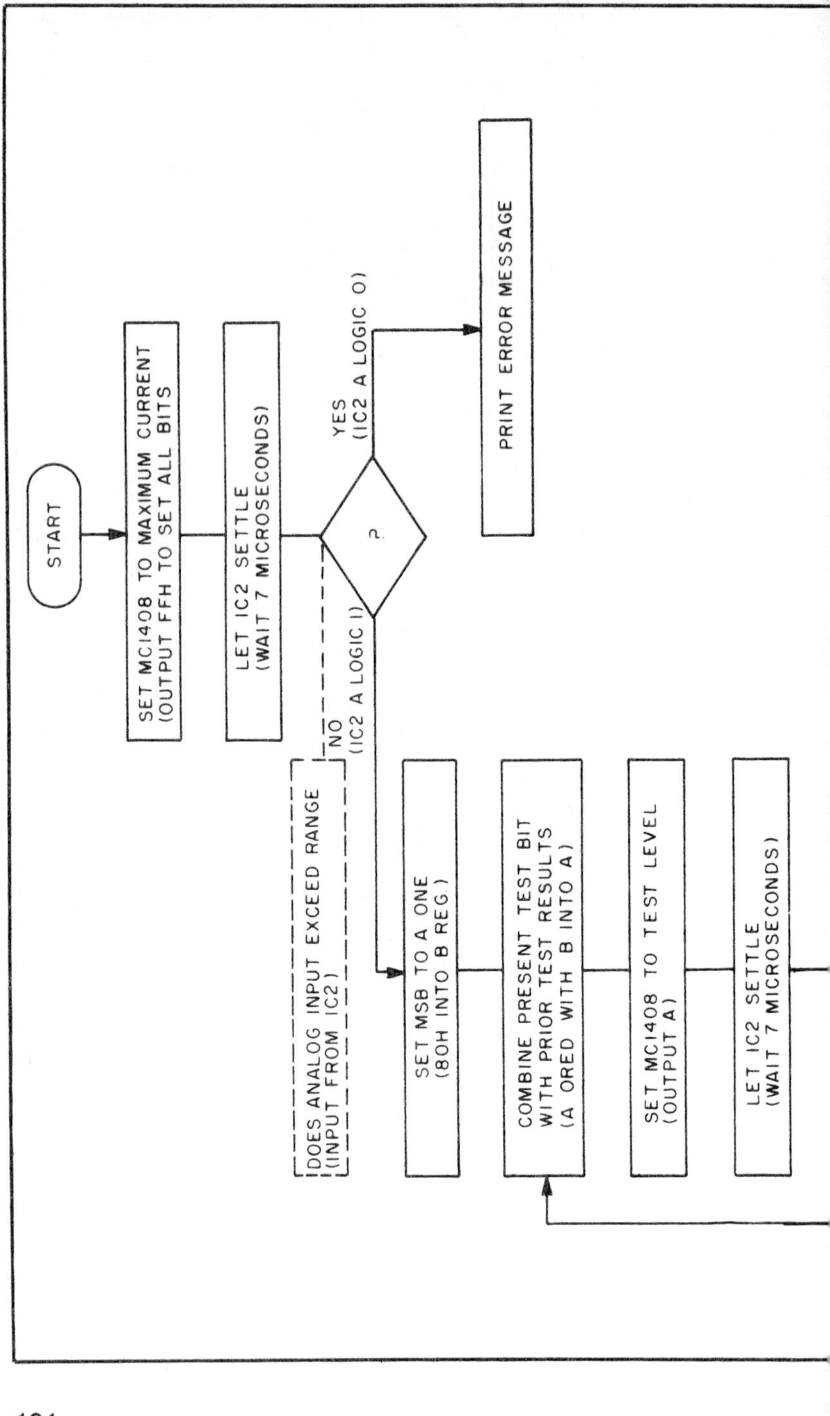
START
SET MC1408 TO MAXIMUM CURRENT (OUTPUT FFH TO SET ALL BITS
LET IC2 SETTLE (WAIT 7 MICROSECONDS)
?
YES (IC2 A LOGIC 0)
PRINT ERROR MESSAGE
NO (IC2 A LOGIC 1)
DOES ANALOG INPUT EXCEED RANGE (INPUT FROM IC2)
SET MSB TO A ONE (80H INTO B REG.)
COMBINE PRESENT TEST BIT WITH PRIOR TEST RESULTS (A ORED WITH B INTO A)
SET MC1408 TO TEST LEVEL (OUTPUT A)
LET IC2 SETTLE (WAIT 7 MICROSECONDS)

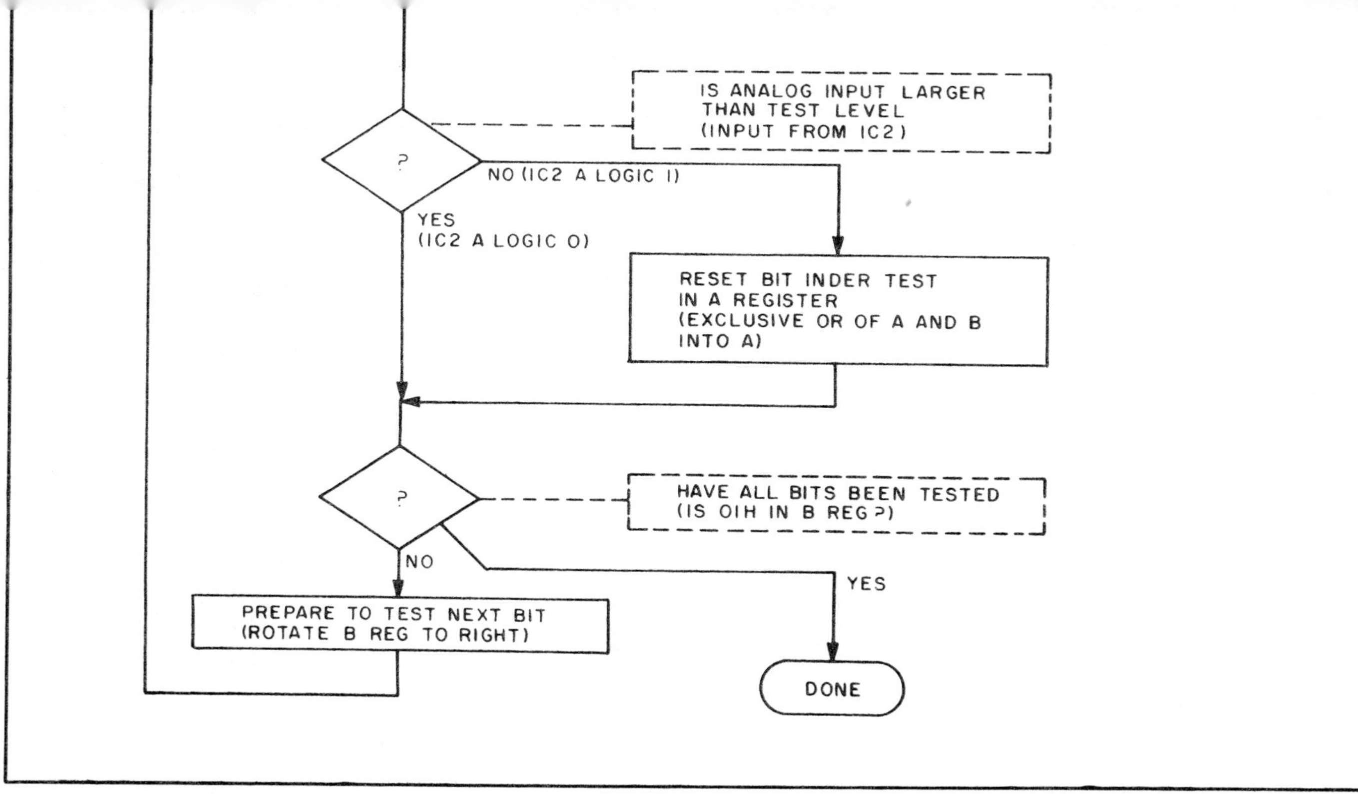

Fig. 1-43. A/D conversion routine. Register A contains results of all prior bit tests. Register B contains a logic one in the bit position under test.

Table 1-1. Algorithm Conversion.

	A-register contents	B-register contents
First test (to see if input is greater than 5 volts)	80H (10000000)	80H (10000000)
	Test passes (IC2 a logic 0)	
Next test (to see if input is greater than 7.5 volts)	COH (11000000)	40H (01000000)
	Test fails (IC2 a logic 1)	
Next test (to see if input is greater than 6.25 volts)	AOH (10100000)	20H (00100000)
	Test fails (IC2 a logic 1)	
Tests continue until all bit positions are tested		

A/D conversion is a slower process than D/A conversion because eight digital words must be generated sequentially (one for each bit test) to complete the conversion of one analog value. After each word is output, a delay of at least seven microseconds should be allowed for IC2 to settle, so the hardware limits the maximum conversion speed to 56 microseconds. To this, you must add the time needed for the microprocessor to cycle through the conversion algorithm instructions. Generally, this will extend the conversion time to several hundred microseconds. Fortunately, changes in the analog world tend to take place comparatively slowly.

Possible Applications

D/A converters synthesize sounds. With them, you can have a function generator of almost unlimited flexibility for amplifier testing, music creation and perhaps even synthetic speech generation. A/D converters have possibilities which may be even more exciting, for they can tell a computer what is going on around it. They can tell it the temperature, how much power the house is consuming, how much sunlight is falling on a solar collector and even whether it should be in pain because a brownout is occurring.

Chapter 2
Microprocessors

Computers are definitely the wave of the future. So says an expert named Hans Napfel. Not only does he work with them at Fairchild, where he oversees 28 people, most of whom are engineers, but he also has been studying them since the early 60s at home, through all stages of their development. And he knows what applications are planned for them in the foreseeable future. No one, he says, can be unaffected by computers. They are a part of everyone's life, and this will be increasingly true.

Hans designed and built a small dedicated computer (one restricted to performing certain functions) in 1973. It was built with the best components available at the time—resistors, transistors, capacitors and some integrated circuits—and had no *microprocessor* (a group of integrated circuits formed into a single component). But most amateur computing did not really begin until more than a year later, when 8008s, the first microprocessing chips, appeared on the market. Now amateur computing is a rapidly-growing hobby, one which Hans nevertheless believes is still in its infancy.

The personal computer is industry's answer to the general demand for involvement with computers. It is diminutive in size, can read from already-prepared tapes to carry out a program, or the operator can write in his or her own programs.

Technical people will find computers extremely useful as a tool, Hans believes. Indeed, it was Hans's technical needs as a radio amateur that created his interest in computers and caused him to begin working with them. "Now," Hans says, "my computer runs my radio station." Not the limited-function computer of 1973, but a second model, built in 1975, which Hans affectionately calls "The Blue Max." It is a general computer, programmable for many things. The Blue Max (which is named for its attractive azure front panel) takes up less than a square foot of space (quite a contrast from the behemoths of the sixties, which were also awkward to use). Max can provide automatic-repeat CW when Hans wants to run a test. It makes contact with a friend on schedule, with or without Hans' presence, and records the Morse code answer received, which it prints, in words, either on the attachable television screen or by radioteletype, or both, as Hans has instructed. It prints the received message at exactly the same speed as the sender gives it.

Hans' computer is helpful to him in other ways with amateur radio. It keeps track of his QSLs for him so that he does not have to wonder whether the contact he's just made should be asked for one. (A bulging QSL file shows why this is helpful!) It keeps track of call-letter changes. And it can be asked to print out all the "Charlies," all the W5s or whatever.

Indeed, with a capability of handling 200,000 full instructions (not bits) per second (yes, that's per second), Hans computer can be asked to remember anything. Hans uses it during contests to keep his log and to eliminate duplications in the log. "It is also useful for field days," he says, "to keep you from repeating stations worked."

Hans also recommends computers as a good way to practice Morse code. For not only does the computer send perfect code every time, at whatever speed you desire, but it also can show you the dots and dashes on screen simultaneously, thus giving you the benefit of involving two senses instead of just one. And it can be programmed to increase the speed gradually, if you wish.

There are other interesting computer applications for the radio amateur. For instance, the moonbouncer will find it "indispensable," Hans says, to keep the antenna positioned at the moon. When an experimenter with a parabolic dish is not at home, a computer can sense the weather and wind and rotate the dish for the least amount of wind resistance.

Hans and three of his friends are working on an even better computer than The Blue Max. It, too, is homemade, but is composed of commercial boards that the four men have modified. (For Max, Hans designed even the routine things.) Hans and his friends are taking care to program their computers the same way and with the same language (they have settled on "super BASIC"), so that they can exchange programs and communicate with each other effectively. The computers can use audio cassettes as well as paper tape. Punch cards, Hans says, are almost obsolete in personal computing.

In addition to paper tape and punch cards, Hans computer can work from a *floppy disk*, with the addition of a floppy bit memory unit. This attachment records information on a flexible record called a floppy disk, and thus gives Hans quick access to what is now peripheral-memory material, freeing space in the computer's central memory. These disks too, are transferable and easily mailed.

When this system is complete, Hans says, it will not only run his radio station, but his whole house as well. Already, Max organizes important dates for him. It tells him when to pay certain bills; it will monitor the water temperature and control the pump and filter of his in-ground backyard pool; it tells him when to send birthday and anniversary cards and when to buy gifts. How does it do this? Not by waiting for Hans to call up its memory. When Hans looks into his conveniently-located equipment room each morning, there is the day's message right on the screen—blinking to get his attention.

"A computer can handle anything to do with numbers," Hans says, "Using it unclutters your memory and makes life easier." If Hans should be late for a class or fail to acknowledge an occasion, it will not be because he was not informed! Max lets him know the flagging date—the day it is necessary to know—if an event is coming up. And Hans can call for a review of the coming month, if he so desires.

The computer is also useful as a telephone directory. It may take a few hours to prepare the program, but to update it later will only take seconds. And you can get the number by first name only, last name only or even by call letters.

Having a computer in the home can be beneficial to non-hams, too. Hans' 12-year-old daughter uses it for games, for educational math workouts and to make musical programs. She will soon have a remote terminal in her room. There is already a remote unit in the kitchen, where Hans' wife bones up on her French.

But the computer can do more. It can adjust the thermostat in the house, for instance. It could even be made to do this *intelligently,* by monitoring the outside and inside temperatures and *deciding* how to adjust the inside accordingly. This could be important when one is away, especially in winter when pipes could freeze, but when an Indian summer could allow a lower-than-usual inside temperature. The computer could also be made to turn lights on and off, water plants, feed the dog, play music and control air conditioning.

The family car will not be unaffected by computers. "In the next two years," Hans says, "cars will have computers to control gas mileage (by noting speed vs. vacuum vs. temperature and keeping the car running at maximum efficiency by optimizing the fuel mixture) and to monitor the condition of the car (letting you know if a light is not working, for instance). In fact, a few cars even have computers now." Signals to the driver will be shown on one light-emitting-diode display, not by means of six or eight meters as we now often see in a car. A computer-controlled warning system will sound a buzzer to alert a speeding or sleeping driver (erratic wheel movements will indicate that the car has left the pavement).

Computers will eventually revolutionize grocery shoping. One could make selections at home, visually (even comparing prices from store to store, right at your own kitchen terminal), and then go to the store to pick up the waiting order. Or it could be delivered to your door. Food, by this system, could be dispensed directly from warehouses. And computers (microprocessors) already control microwave ovens and teaching machines.

But computers will never make it big in the classroom, Hans feels, because "teachers are too threatened by machines. Machines are potentially authority-shattering. What if something goes wrong that the teacher can't fix?" Still, Hans feels that computers could be used by schools successfully as tutors for drill and routine work, if they are housed in a separate room overseen by a competent technician. "But they will never replace teachers," he says.

For handicapped people, they will be especially important, Hans says, becoming the ears of deaf people and eyes of the blind. Already, speaking computers can be purchased. And in the health field, they are already indispensable, but will become even more so.

"And by 1985 or 1990, every house will have its own minicomputer," Hans says. It will be used as an *intelligent* security system (those who live in each house will not set off the alarm), as a telephone answering service and directory (indeed, all forms of paper directories may soon be obsolete), as well as for energy management, bookkeeping, scheduling, providing educational drill and playing games.

"What about using them to communicate with outer space?" we asked Hans.

His eyes twinkled at the unexpected thought.

"They would be essential in a space colony," he answered, "to monitor the station's life-support system and relative positions, and to keep track of supplies. But to communicate with other intelligences in outer space? Let me put it this way: I'm a hardware realist."

For Hans, that's not a limitation. "I keep up with what's being discovered," he says, "and I just take it one step further. That's what makes the difference." In fact, Hans advances the state of computer art through his hobby, then takes his knowledge to the job, where he educates others.

In a pursuit requiring perseverance and thoroughness, Hans' philosophy is clearly the one that works.

Looking for a Micro?

If you are in the market for a complete microcomputer, but your funds are somewhat limited, the KIM-1 is for you.

For $245 the KIM-1 comes complete with CPU, 1024 (1K) bytes of random access (read/write) memory, 2048 (2K) bytes of read-only memory, a 23-pad keyboard for hexadecimal input and limited front panel capabilities, a six-digit seven-segment series of light emitting diodes (LEDs) for output, a cassette interface and a serial teleprinter interface. The only thing the KIM-1 lacks is a power supply. If you are going to run a cassette, you will need a +5V and a +12V power supply; otherwise, +5V at 1.2 Amps will be sufficient. The power supply can be built from a schematic supplied in the back of the KIM-1 *User's Manual,* or you can purchase one at a local radio store for under $50.

The CPU is the MCS6502. It is capable of addressing up to 65,536 (64K) bytes of memory. Although the instruction set of the 6502 is somewhat limited when compared to the 8080A, which is the chip used by the Altair 8800B and others, it is more than sufficient for the person who is just starting to program. (The 6502 has 56 instructions, as compared to the 78 instructions for the 8080A). With some ingenuity, the 6502 instruction set can go quite a long way. The system clock runs at 1 MHz. The instruction execution time runs from two to seven cycles, with four cycles being the average. This means the 6502 can execute up to approximately 250,000 instructions per second. This is only half as fast as the machines that use the 8080A; however, it is still fast enough for most applications.

The 1K of random access memory that is provided onboard is not enough to do much in the way of serious programming. It is, however, sufficient to learn basic machine level programming skills.

Input is through a keyboard located at the lower right-hand corner of the board. If you have an ASR-33 teletype with the 20 mA loop, it can be connected directly to the machine. Lacking this, you are restricted to the keyboard. I would like to take this time to comment on the positioning of the keyboard. I am left-handed; as a result, I find that I must be aware of where I rest my hand, as the two interfaces are directly to the left of the keyboard. This could be improved by having the keyboard remote from the machine itself. This is, however, a relatively minor problem. The keys on the keyboard are as follows:

O-F hex—instruction and data input
AD—enter address mode
DA—enter data mode
+—increment address by 1
PC—restore program counter
ST—generate interrupt (STOP)
GO—begin program at current program counter
RS—reset to monitor control
SST—a slide switch for single-step execution of programs.

Output is through 6 seven-segment LEDs. The left four LEDs are separated from the right two, making it easy to read the display. The display is located directly above the keyboard.

The 2K bytes of read-only memory contain a monitor program which basically controls input/output operations, including cassette operation and serial teleprinter operation.

My main objection to the design of the KIM is the absence of sockets for the 22 integrated circuits. This is not a problem unless one burns out. If one should burn out, it will take a lot of time and patience to replace it. The board has been silk-screened to prevent accidentally shorting out adjacent foils. It should be noted that a potentiometer has been utilized as part of the onboard audio cassette interface. This potentiometer is preset at the factory and should not be adjusted by the user.

The onboard interfaces are for an audio cassette and a serial teleprinter (specifically the ASR-33). The first expansion recommended for the KIM is to add an audio cassette. When you are working on small programs, it is no big deal to key in your program, turn the machine off, and key the program in at a later time; however, when you start to write long programs, keying in a long program every time you turn on your machine becomes a hassle. If you can store that program and load it without having to key it in, you have overcome this problem.

The primary solution to this problem, employed by microcomputers, is storage on audio cassette tape. This is fine—that is, until you drop a bit. Unlike digital recorders in the big machines, an audio recorder does not go back and make sure it has recorded the data properly. You will not discover the error until you try to load the program, and, for some reason, it doesn't work. This is a major problem with audio cassettes and one not easily reckoned with.

The advantage of audio cassette recorders is that they are inexpensive. However, the serious user will soon find that he needs to go to another form of mass storage, such as floppy disk.

The second interface provided is for a serial teleprinter. The ASR-33 is the recommended machine. While this is a fine machine, it is relatively expensive (between $500 and $1000). This is one expansion I don't plan to do for a long while. If I had that kind of money, I would have bought a bigger machine. I would recommend to anyone who is looking toward terminals to consider a CRT (Cathode Ray Tube) terminal, as one can be had for around $250, although you'll have to interface it yourself.

The documentation on the KIM is excellent. It consists of three books, a wall chart and a card listing the instruction set. The books include the *User's Manual,* which should be read first, the *Programming Manual* and the *Hardware Manual.* The wall chart shows how the hardware is connected, and the instruction set card lists the mnemonics and op codes with variations.

Getting the KIM-1 up and running took us almost a week. The main problem was getting the power supply ready to supply power. My power supply is a Control Data Corporation model, supplied by Electravalue Industrial for $50. Initially, upon unpacking the supply, I was terrified by all the cables. However, upon more careful inspection, I was able to determine how to hook it up to the KIM. The problem lies in the number of connectors coming from the supply and the lack of an AC power cord. It took three days of searching over the greater New York area before I finally found one suitable for the job at Westchester Electronics in White Plains.

Once the power considerations were taken care of, I was able to turn on the machine and run the test problem in the *User's Manual*—a simple 8-bit addition routine to check the operation of the KIM. The program worked perfectly, and I have had no problems with my machine yet.

Overall, the KIM-1 is an excellent beginning machine. Among other things, it teaches you how much you can really do with only 1K of memory, something that is forgotten with today's massive machines. More importantly, however, the KIM-1 (at $245) makes computing available to anyone who wants it, and it is versatile enough to satisfy most people's needs.

Kim-1 Can Do It!

Of the several thousand KIM-1 microcomputer systems produced since the system's introduction, many are now being used by experimenters in a number of interesting applications. The KIM-1 may be adapted to function as a versatile RTTY terminal at nominal cost. Methods of interfacing KIM-1 to a typical Baudot TTY loop, as well as some of the software requirements will be discussed. All of the options to be described have been tested and will work successfully. However, there are some considerations to keep in mind before deciding which method might be preferred.

Since all amateur RTTY operation uses the Baudot code, it is necessary to convert the incoming data to the ASCII code for video display presentation, or to operate an ASCII hard-copy printer. Conversely, ASCII characters from the keyboard, or from memory, must be converted to Baudot for transmission. In addition, the system should also perform some of the other functions normally expected of a RTTY terminal.

KIM-1RTTY Functions

The program I am currently using performs nearly all of the required functions, and it can be expanded to accommodate others. These functions may be summarized as follows:

- Baudot to ASCII conversion (receive mode), with unshift on space.
- ASCII to Baudot conversion (send mode).
- Automatic end-of-line (EOL) functions (2 CR 1 LF) in send mode. Keyboard line feed generates the same EOL functions.
- Store messages from keyboard in selected memory blocks. These may be CQ calls and other canned messages, such as the station brag tape. Error correction is provided and case typing errors are made during keyboard entry.
- Read previously stored messages for transmission. CQ calls may be repeated automatically as many times as desired.
- Send "DE (callsign)," followed by the time generated by a real-time clock.
- The real-time clock uses a simple crystal-controlled 1 PPS generator connected to the NMI (non-maskable interrupt) line. The 1 PPS output of some digital clocks can be used for this purpose. The clock is updated from the keyboard with the current time after program execution. The 1 PPS generator is turned on at the exact minute entered.
- CW ID (Morse identification). This routine is a modified version of WB2DFA's KIM-1 Morse keyboard program. However, the CW ID is read from a table, rather than types from the keyboard.

- Keyboard control of all functions. One control key is used to select the receive mode, which is disabled if any other key is depressed.

The RTTY Program

To fully implement all of the above, 892 bytes of onboard memory are presently used with the parallel I/O configuration to be described later. This includes lookup tables for the code conversion. An additional 2K bytes of an S.D. Sales 4K memory expansion board is allocated to message buffer storage. The program is suitable for firmware (ROM or EROM), with the exception of the real-time clock "digit" locations, which must be in RAM. This portion of the program can be modified.

Table 2-1 lists the keyboard control functions. Some ASCII keyboards are not properly coded, so you may have to make some changes to the keyboard control routine, if yours is different.

Table 2-2 is a combination memory map and hex listing of the program. Data in zero page locations 0000-000F is variable and does not have to be saved when making a tape recording of the program. Canned messages may be saved and loaded into memory as part of the program, so they do not have to be reentered.

For my display, Baudot carriage return is converted to a null and does nothing. Line feed is converted to space. The ASCII

Table 2-1. Keyboard Control Functions.

ESC	Sets receive mode.
ETX (CTRL C)	Time update for real-time clock. Type in four digits using 24-hour format.
ENQ (CTRL E)	DE (callsign) and time.
DC1 (CTRL Q)	CW ID.
STX (CTRL B)	Store message (followed by 1, 2, 3, or 4).
(AT Sign)	Read message (Followed by 1, 2, 3, or 4).
*(Asterisk)	End of transmission. Last character typed to end store mode.Also added by store routine, if end of message block, to prevent over-writing into next block.Message is not repeated.
+(Plus sign)	Repeat message. Last character typed, if message is to be repeated. Location 034F contains number of times to be sent. CRLF ends transmission after last line. Error correction. This is effectively a backspace and decrements the message store pointer. Used when stroing a message from keyboard.

Table 2-2. Memory Map and Program Listing.

```
0000-000F  Temporary data and indirect pointers.

     Baudot-ASCII Conversion Table

0010  00 45 20 41 20 53 49 55 00 44 52 4A 4E 46 43 4B
0020  54 5A 4C 57 48 59 50 51 4F 42 47 00 4D 58 56 00
0030  00 33 20 2D 20 00 38 37 00 24 34 27 2C 21 3A 28
0040  35 22 29 32 23 36 30 31 39 3F 26 00 2E 2F 3B 00

     ASCII-Baudot Conversion Table

0050  00 03 19 0E 09 01 0D 1A 14 06 0B 0F 12 1C 0C 18
0060  16 17 0A 05 10 07 1E 13 1D 15 11 00 1F 00 00 00
0070  00 0D 11 14 09 00 1A 0B 0F 12 00 00 0C 03 1C 1D
0080  16 17 13 01 0A 10 15 07 06 18 0E 1E 00 00 00 19

     Initialization.  Set program counter to 0090 to start.

0090  D8 A9 25 8D FA 17 A9 04 8D FB 17 A9 00 85 01 85
00A0  02 A9 3F 8D 03 17 A9 41 8D 01 17 A9 40 8D 00 17
00B0  85 03
     Wait Loop.  Looks for KBD start bit or receive mode enable.
00B2  24 02 30 08 2C 00 17 10 03 20 00 01 2C 40 17 30
00C2  EF 20 00 02 4C B2 00

     Baudot-ASCII Conversion

0100  AD 00 17 4A 29 1F 85 00 C9 04 F0 0F C9 1B D0 07
0110  A9 80 85 01 4C 31 01 C9 1F D0 04 A9 00 85 01 A5
0120  00 24 01 10 02 69 20 AA B5 10 C9 00 F0 03 20 A0
0130  1E A9 00 8D 00 17 A9 40 8D 00 17 60
     Keyboard Control & ASCII-Baudot Conversion
0200  84 05 20 5A 1E A4 05 C9 1B D0 05 A9 00 85 02 60
0210  48 A9 80 85 02 68 C9 02 D0 03 4C 0E 02 C9 40 D0
0220  03 4C 4F 03 C9 05 D0 03 4C 8E 03 C9 11 D0 03 4C
0230  A9 03 C9 03 D0 03 4C 7A 04 C9 0D D0 05 A9 00 4C
0240  86 02 C9 0A D0 03 4C 99 02 C9 20 D0 0D C8 C0 43
```

```
0250  30 03 4C 99 02 A9 04 4C 86 02 85 04 24 04 70 09
0260  24 03 50 10 A9 1B 4C 6F 02 24 03 70 07 A9 1F 20
0270  86 02 A5 04 85 03 29 3F AA B5 50 C8 C0 48 D0 06
0280  20 86 02 4C 99 02 8D 02 17 09 20 8D 02 17 A9 00
0290  8D 02 17 2C 02 17 10 FB 60 A0 00 A9 08 20 86 02
02A0  A9 08 20 86 02 A9 02 20 86 02 60
```

Message Select 1, 2, 3 or 4. Used by Read & Store routines).

```
02AB  20 5A 1E C9 31 D0 13 A9 00 85 07 85 0D A9 05 85
02BB  08 85 0E 85 0A A9 7F 85 09 60 C9 32 D0 13 A9 80
02CB  85 07 85 0D A9 05 85 08 85 0E 85 0A A9 FF 85 09
02DB  60 C9 33 D0 15 A9 00 85 07 A9 0D A9 06 85 08 85
02EB  0E A9 FF 85 09 A9 07 85 0A 60 C9 34 D0 4E A9 00
02FB  85 07 85 0D A9 08 85 08 85 0E A9 FF 85 09 A9 0B

020B  85 0A 60
```

Store Message

```
030E  20 AB 02 A2 00 20 5A 1E 81 07 C9 2A F0 32 C9 2B
031E  F0 2E C9 3C D0 0D C6 07 A9 FF C5 07 D0 E7 C6 08
032E  4C 13 03 E6 07 A9 00 C5 07 D0 02 E6 08 A5 09 C5
033E  07 D0 D2 A5 0A C5 08 D0 CC A9 2A 81 07 20 A0 1E
034E  60
```

Read Message

```
034F  A9 0A 85 0B 20 AB 02 A2 00 A1 07 C9 2A F0 2F C9
035F  2B D0 12 C6 0B D0 03 4C 99 02 A5 0D 85 07 A5 0E
036F  85 08 4C 56 03 84 05 48 20 A0 1E 68 A4 05 20 39
037F  02 E6 07 A9 00 C5 07 D0 CE E6 08 4C 56 03 60
```

continued on page 120

Table 2-2. Memory Map and Program Listing. continued from page 119.

```
      DE CALL
038E  A9 99 85 07 A9 03 85 08 4C 56 03
      Call Table & Time.  Enter ASCII equivalent of call sign in
                          null locations 039C to 03A1.
0399  44 45 20 00 00 00 00 00 00 20 30 30 30 30 5A 2A

      CW ID
03A9  A2 00 BD 18 04 85 0D E8 E0 0B D0 01 60 C9 00 D0
03B9  06 20 EA 03 4C AB 03 29 FC 85 0E A5 0D 29 07 AB
03C9  C0 00 D0 06 20 F1 03 4C AB 03 88 06 0E 90 09 20
03D9  F8 03 20 FF 03 4C C9 03 20 FF 03 20 FF 03 4C 09
03E9  03 98 48 A0 06 4C 06 04 98 48 A0 02 4C 06 04 98
03F9  48 A0 03 4C 03 04 98 48 A0 01 EE 00 17 88 A9 37
0409  8D 07 17 CD 07 17 10 FB C0 00 D0 F1 68 A8 60
0418-0421  CW ID Table.  Enter Morse equivalents for DE (space)
                         (Call Sign).

      Real-Time Clock (NMI routine).
0425  48 E6 0C A5 0C C9 3C D0 4A A9 00 85 0C EE A6 03
0435  AD A6 03 C9 3A D0 08 29 30 8D A6 03 EE A5 03 AD
0445  A5 03 C9 36 D0 08 29 30 8D A5 03 EE A4 03 AD A4
0455  03 C9 3A D0 08 29 30 8D A4 03 EE A3 03 AD A4 03
0465  C9 34 D0 0F AD A3 03 C9 32 D0 08 A9 30 8D A4 03
0475  8D A3 03 68 40

      Time Update
047A  A9 00 85 0C A2 00 20 5A 1E 9D A3 03 E8 E0 04 D0
048A  F5 60

0500-057F  MSG Block 1 (128 bytes)
0580-05FF  MSG Block 2  (128 bytes)
0600-07FF  MSG Block 3 (512 bytes)
0800-0BFF  MSG Block 4 (1024 bytes)
```

carriage return is converted to a blank, since the line feed takes care of EOL functions, as previously noted.

Morse equivalents for the CW ID table are listed in the lookup table in the Morse keyboard program. If any locations in the table are not filled, place word spaces (00) at the beginning or end of the table.

Serial I/O

The type of interfacing required for the external Baudot TTY loop will depend upon the user's choice of serial or parallel input/output. This will, of course, affect the software as well.

The simplest interface, from a hardware standpoint, is the serial I/O shown in Fig. 2-1. The interval timer of the 6530 peripheral interface is normally programmed for 45.5 baud (60 wpm) operation, but it may be changed to any other speed. On the input side, the start bit is sampled at midpoint, 11 ms after detection, and succeeding bits are sampled every 22 ms thereafter. If desired, presence of a stop bit may also be tested, and the character rejected if the stop bit is not received.

The only time a character may be displayed by the video terminal (i.e., TV typewriter) is during the stop pulse, nominally 31 ms at 60 wpm. The video terminal serial interface must be set for something faster than 300 baud, preferably at least 600 baud. The KIM monitor OUTCH routine is used to output characters to the terminal. The keyboard is connected for interrupt operation, as shown in Fig. 2-1, rather than to the terminal input. Therefore, terminal baud rate cannot be determined by sampling the ROBOUT key start bit, as normally done by the KIM monitor program. The data for the KIM monitor CNTL30 and CNTH30 locations (17F2 and 17F3, respectively) was read once with the keyboard connected to the terminal. These locations are then initialized accordingly when the program is executed.

On the output side, keyboard characters are stored in a 256-byte buffer by the FIFO (first in, first out) input routine. Characters are output any time there is something in the buffer. When fetched from the FIFO, and prior to further processing, the character is displayed. This takes a finite time and adds to the Baudot output stop pulse length. Again, the interval timer is used to output serial bits. The length of the stop bit to be added by the serial output routine depends on the character display time. If the TVT clock rate is 600 baud (approximately 17 ms), an additional 22 ms stop bit will give a total of about 39 ms, slightly longer than normal, but acceptable.

Since Baudot figures and letters shift functions are generated by the program and are not displayed, a stop pulse delay to compen-

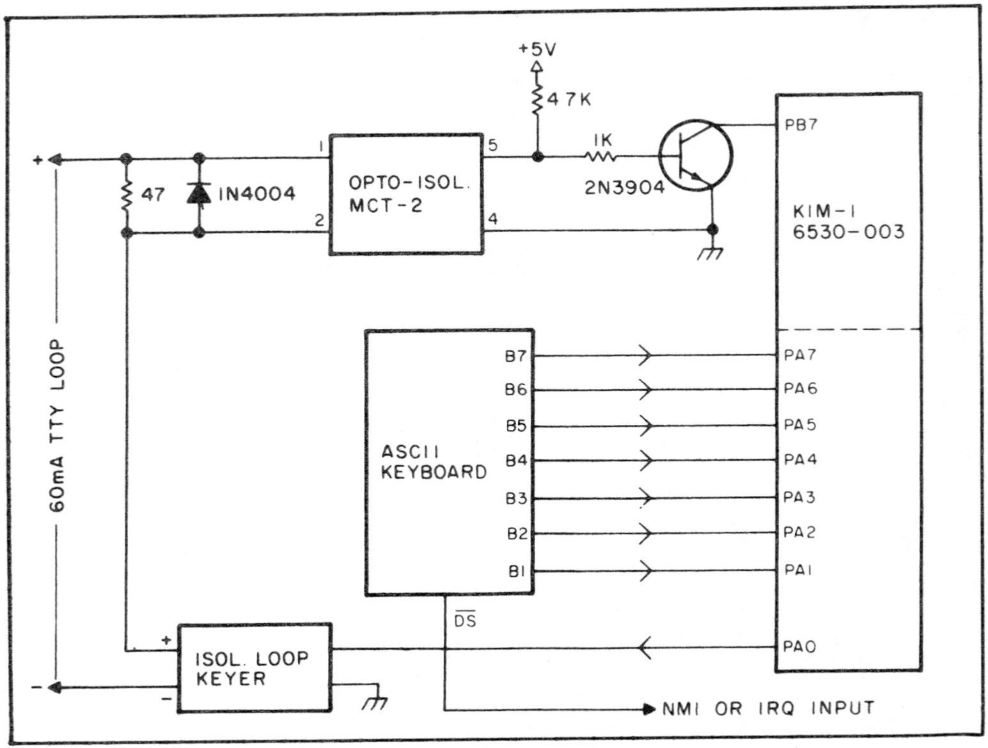

Fig. 2-1. Baudot serial I/O and keyboard input.

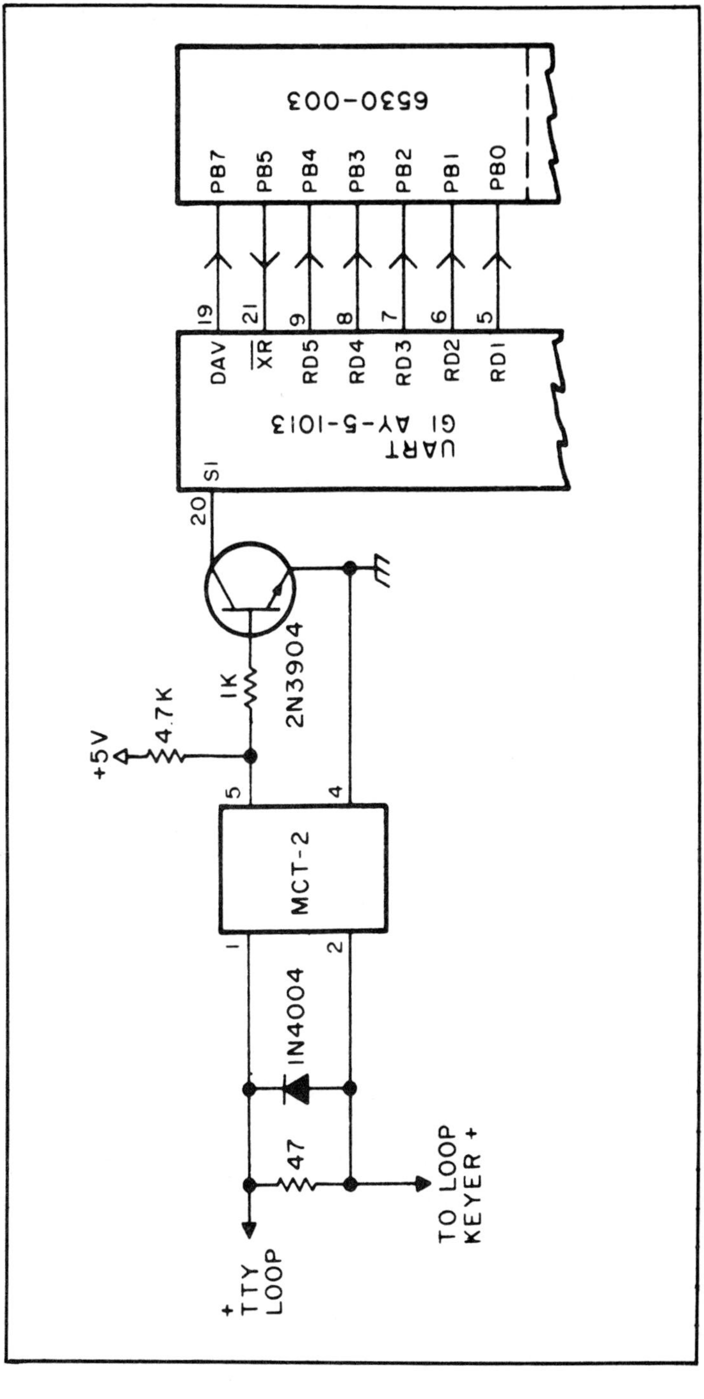

Fig. 2-2. Baudot parallel input.

sate must be added, using a separate interval timer routine. This same routine must be used after the line feed function of the automatic EOL.

Parallel Input

To eliminate possible software timing problems in the receive mode, the circuit of Fig. 2-2 was tried. This uses the receive side of a UART chip to convert the Baudot serial input to parallel outputs, which are connected to the 6530 "B" side inputs. This works somewhat in the same manner as a 6820 or 6520 PIA, but is simpler to program, since there is no control register. PB7 is the input for the "data available" flag, while PB5 is used as an output to reset the flag. This method works perfectly. Serial output and keyboard inputs were left as previously described.

Since the keyboard is not connected to the KIM-1 TTY input when using the foregoing configuration, the hex keyboard and display must be used when loading the program or otherwise using the KIM monitor. The TTY/KB switch should be placed in the KB position and returned to the TTY position after executing the program with the GO key.

Parallel Output

Having gone this far, I decided to change the output to parallel operation also, as shown in Fig. 2-3. To make things easier, the parallel input was changed over to the 6530 "A" side, so PA0 could be programmed for the CW ID output. Now the "B" side is used for the output, as seen in Fig. 2-4.

Obviously, this configuration leaves no parallel input ports for the keyboard. It is connected to the TVT in the normal manner, and the KIM monitor GETCH routine is used to fetch keyboard characters. The software IFO, therefore, cannot be used. The solution to this is to make a trade-off and use a Fairchild 3351 FIFO chip. Note that, in this case, the FIFO is on the Baudot output rather than the keyboard input. Although the 3351 has a capacity of only 40 characters, this is adequate to absorb data at normal typing rates somewhat in excess of six characters per second, as well as providing buffering for the Baudot figures and letters shifts and EOL functions. PB5 is the data strobe for the 3351 shift is (SI) input, and PB7 serves as the input ready (IR) flag.

The UART is configured for five bits per character and one stop bit. The actual time between characters on transmit is set by the 741123 dual MV timing and results in characters being shifted out of

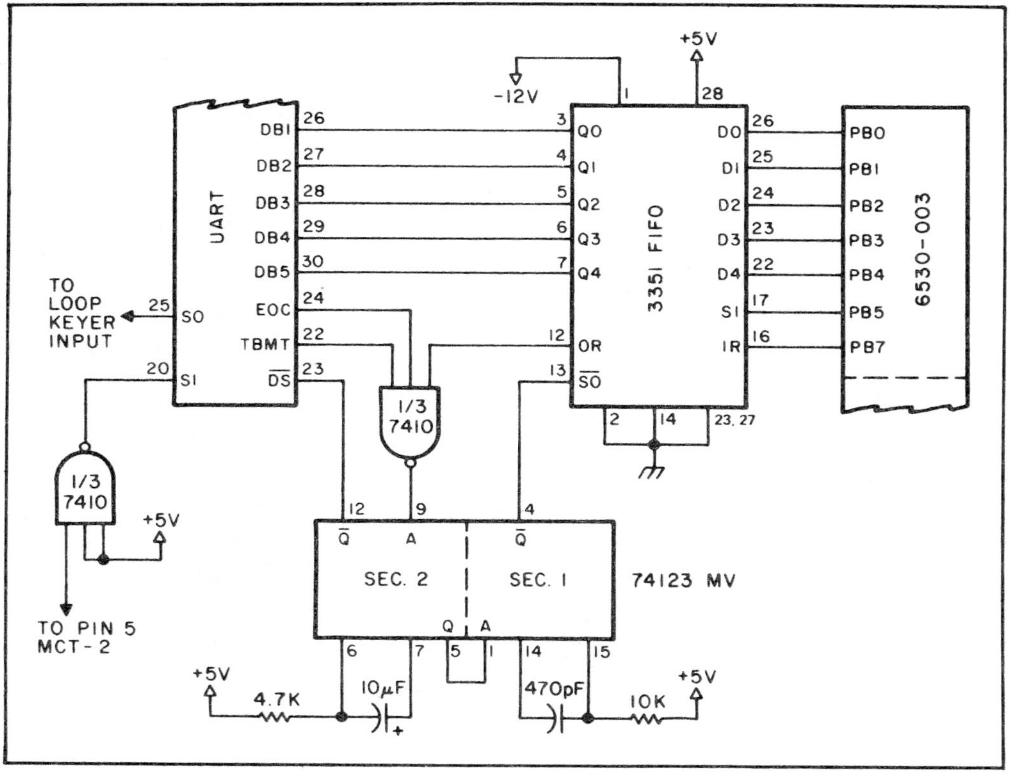

Fig. 2-3. Baudot parallel output with FIFO buffer.

the FIFO at a smooth rate. A crystal-controlled clock is not necessary. At low data rates, a 555 timer clock is perfectly adequate and rarely needs adjustment. The clock is set to 728 Hz for 45.5 baud operation.

Loop Isolation

I use a 60 mA loop, which is common for both send and receive. A printer is always in the line for hard copy. The optoisolator is one of several available types, such as the Motorola MCT2. The loopkeyer output is completely isolated from ground and the input. Figure 2-5 is a schematic diagram of the loop keyer. It's a keyed, balanced multivibrator, running at about 750 kHz, capacitively coupled to a diode bridge rectifier and loop-keying transistor, Q4. The keying transistor can be any high-voltage NPN-type, such as the MJE340, 2N5655 or 2N3440. Q1, Q2 and Q3 can be any small-signal switching transistors. Note that Q3 must be a PNP type.

The loop keyer is sensitive to nearby rf fields when you operate a transmitter at high power, so each side of the loop jack at the KIM-1 end must be bypassed to ground. If CW ID output is used, the output jack should be by passed for the same reason. A shielded cable to the AFSK input should be used. KIM-1 and all associated boards appear to be immune to rf, even unshielded.

Interrupts

For most microprocessor owners, the subject of interrupts is avoided like the plague. This should not be so. Interrupts are among some of the most useful options available to the microprocessor owner.

The very nature of interrupts (i.e., their unpredictability) accounts for the fear and mistrust of using them. A *Dictionary of Electronics* defines an *interruption* as: "In microcomptuers: a halting of the main program followed by the starting of an interrupt subroutine, or returning from the subroutine to the main program."

Either way, it does not make much sense until you realize just how useful an interrupt is.

An interrupt is virtually a "Hey you" followed by an "I want this done now . . ." The loudness of the "Hey you" indicates its priority if more than one arrives at once. When an interrupt occurs, you drop whatever you are doing and go to the interrupter to see what he/she/it wants, and when this is completed, you are free to return to what you left.

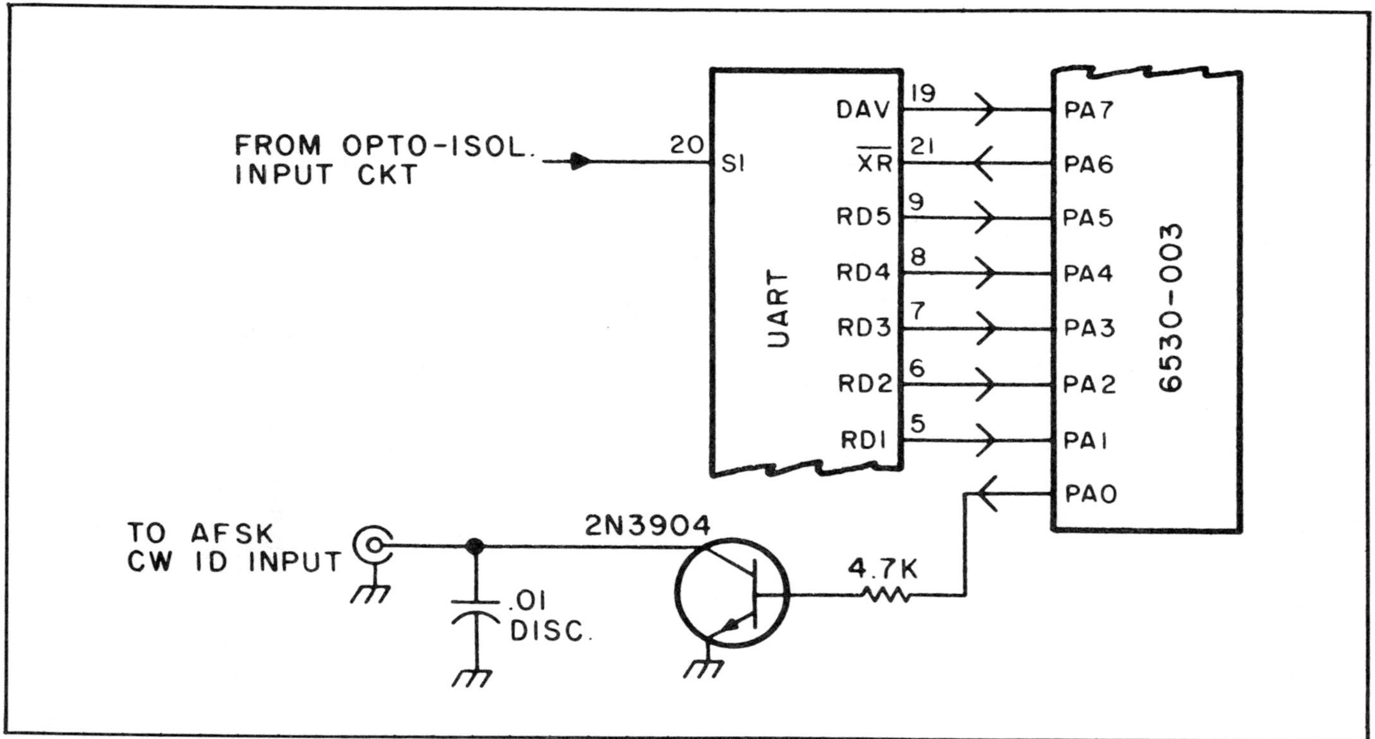

Fig. 2-4. Baudot parallel input and CW ID output.

A more useful analogy when considering interrupts is the telephone. Picture yourself sitting with some friends chatting (main program) when the telephone rings (an interrupt). You excuse yourself and go to answer the telephone (jump to the interrupt location). When you pick up the receiver, the telephone becomes engaged (interrupts are disabled), and you talk to the person calling (execute the interrupt subroutine). When you have finished, you hang up the receiver (enable interrupts) and resume the conversion with your friends (return from interrupt).

Priority and multiple interrupts can also be considered in this fashion, such as the doorbell ringing (high priority), the telephone (low priority, let the XYL answer it), or a call on your experimenting gear (high priority to you, but low to the XYL). The analogy can be carried much further.

In the following description, I have tried to be as general as possible, because with the wide variety of chips, each with its own unique interrupt system, the details are best left up to the programming manual for that particular chip.

However, the basic rules of interrupts are common to all systems. Interrupts were developed to handle a particular type of situation. This situation is when an external device, at some unpredictable moment, requires that the computer do something immediately.

When an interrupt occurs, the CPU (Central Processing Unit) must literally drop everything, but it must remember where it was before the interrupt occurred. To do this in most systems, all of the contents of the register are pushed onto the *stack* (an area of memory or other hardware storage) before the CPU jumps to the interrupt location (the interrupt subroutine). Then the CPU will perform the subroutine at the interrupt location. During this time, the CPU does not want to be interrupted again and, for this reason, most microprocessors have a Disable Interrupts instruction (e.g., DI, hex F3 on the 8080A and SEI, hex OF on the M6800) which allows the CPU to ignore any "Hεy you" no matter how loud, while it performs the current interrupt subroutine.

Systems of interrupts are generally unique to the chip and/or the machine's implementation, but generally there are three main categories:

Single Line Interrupts. Here the processor responds to an interrupt on one line (Fig. 2-6). For more than one, the devices are tied to an OR gate and the individual devices must be scanned by the processor to find out which one generated the interrupt (also referred to as *polling*). Because of this, single line interrupts are slow.

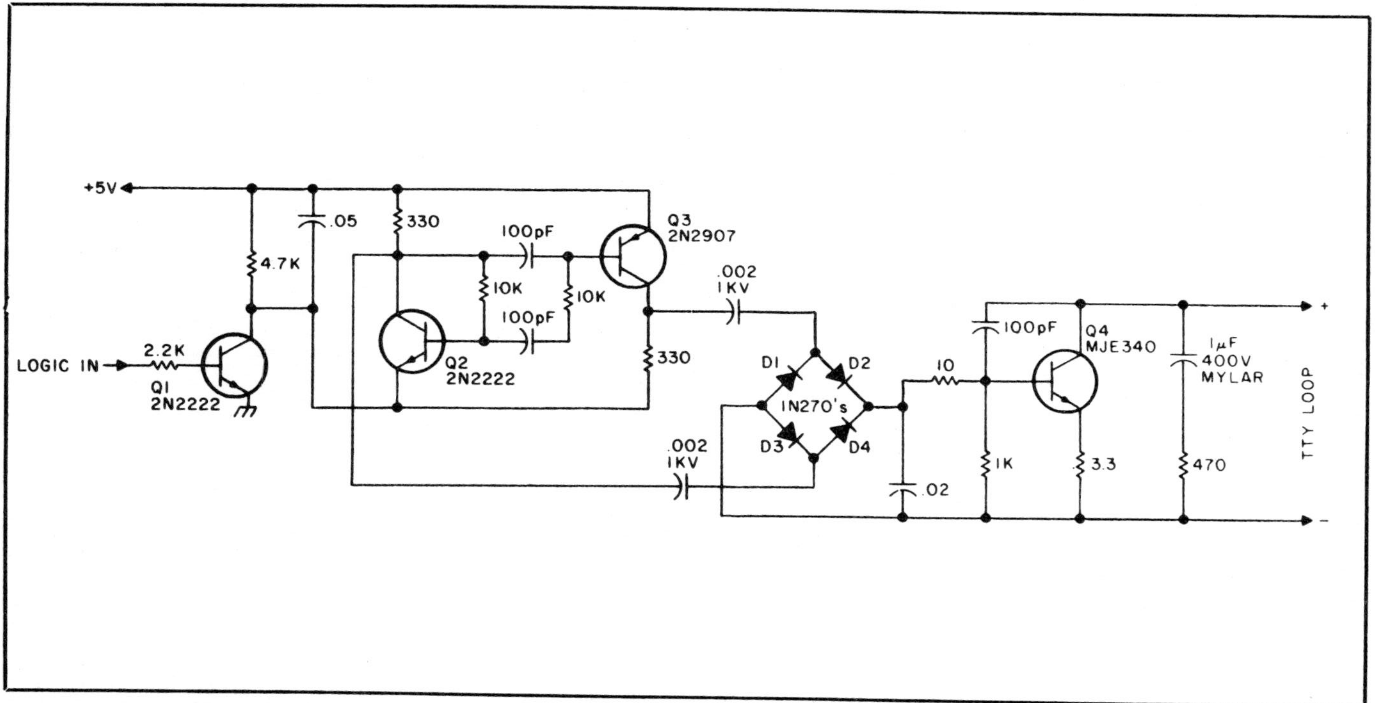

Fig. 2-5. Isolated loop keyer. Mark—high; space—low. Resistors—¼ W; capacitors—disc ceramic, except as noted.

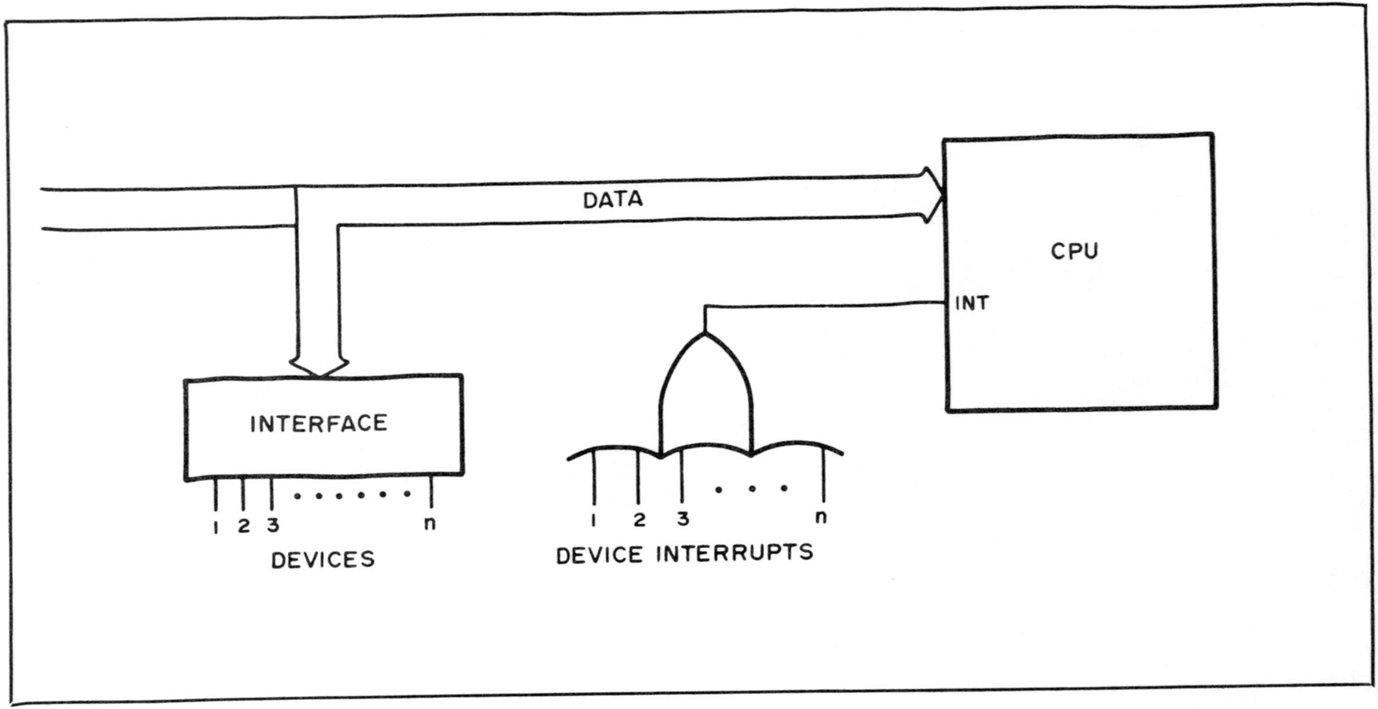

Fig. 2-6. Single line interrupts.

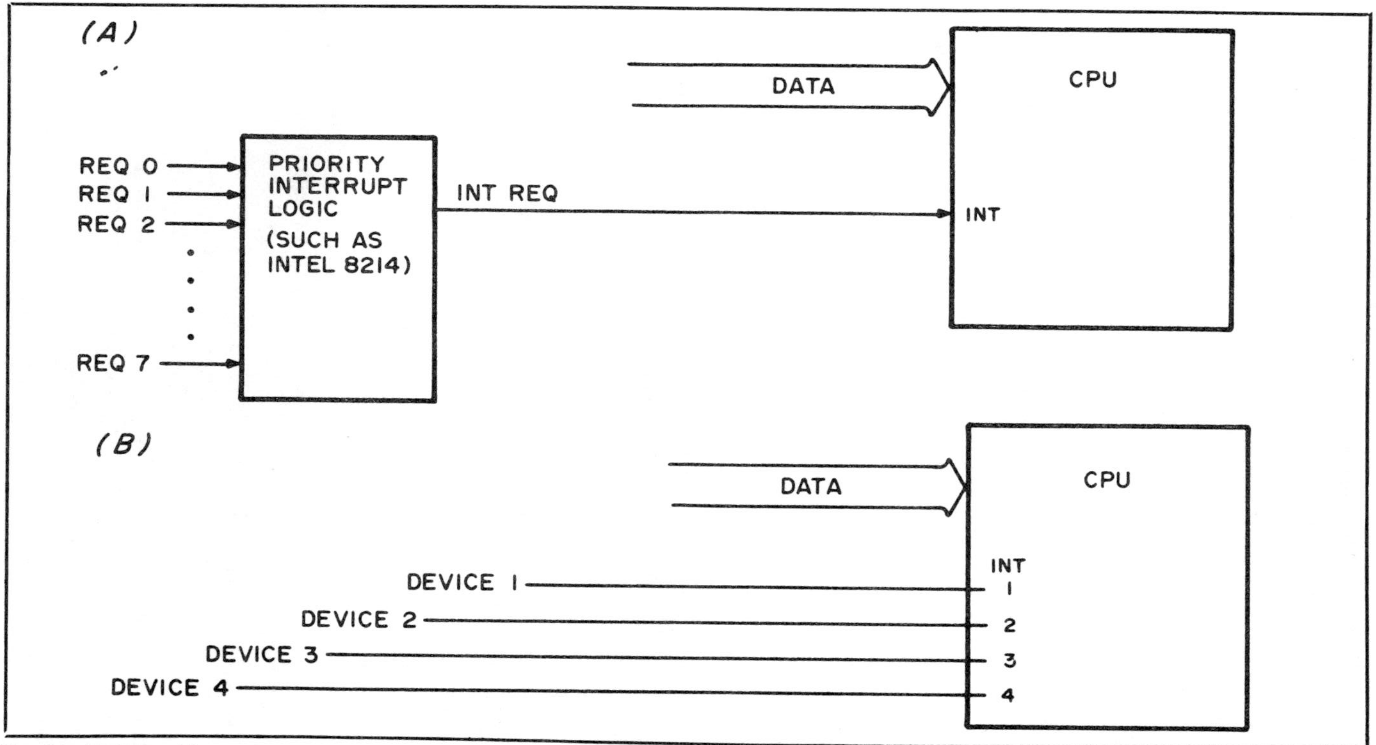

Fig. 2-7. Multi-level interrupts.

Multi-level Interrupts. Here the interrupts could occur on one or several lines going into a priority determination chip or logic (top of Fig. 2-7). If the number of devices generating interrupts is greater than the number of lines, then some lines must be used as in single line interrupts. The M6800 has two multi-level interrupts within the chip, such as in the bottom of Fig. 2-7.

Vectored Interrupts. In this case, only one line is used, but the interrupting device generates an instruction onto the data bus which causes the CPU to jump (vector) to a predetermined subroutine. The device priority must be resolved in hardware external to the CPU (the 8080A has a limited form of vectored interrupts). Figure 2-8 is a block diagram of a vectored interrupt configuration.

On return from an interrupt, the CPU must be returned to the state it was in before the interrupt occurred. This is often done by a specific instruction, Return from Interrupt (RTI, hex 3B on the M6800). This brings the contents of the registers (especially the Program Counter) back from the stack, so that return to the main program can be accomplished.

With a microprocessor, control lines other than the interrupt lines may be used as specific purpose interrupts, and in most systems they are. The control bus lines, HOLD and WAIT (or their equivalents), are normally used for slowing down or synchronizing the CPU to slow memories. They can also be used as Halts for DMA (Direct Memory Addressing) applications.

The RESET line is a major interrupt line with which returns the processor to some initial state to halt the execution of a program. This line could be set by hardware devices any time a major catastrophe occurs (such as tape drive failure).

Such control lines are normally used to provide versatility for the microprocessor in different machine implementations of the chip and to allow it to be used with a wide variety of devices, e.g., in parallel processing, where several processors are using the same memory (Fig. 2-9) and switch each other off or on along the HOLD/WAIT lines. Although these lines were designed for interface with slow memories, they are particularly well suited to allow parallel processing and other DMA applications.

An example of the use of DMA would be for slow to fast scan conversions using a microprocessor. The SSTV analog could be digitized (analog to digital conversion) and stored, and the wideband ATV scanned off the same memories by DMA for display on a normal TV set. Think of the graphics facilities this would allow for both SSTV and ATV!

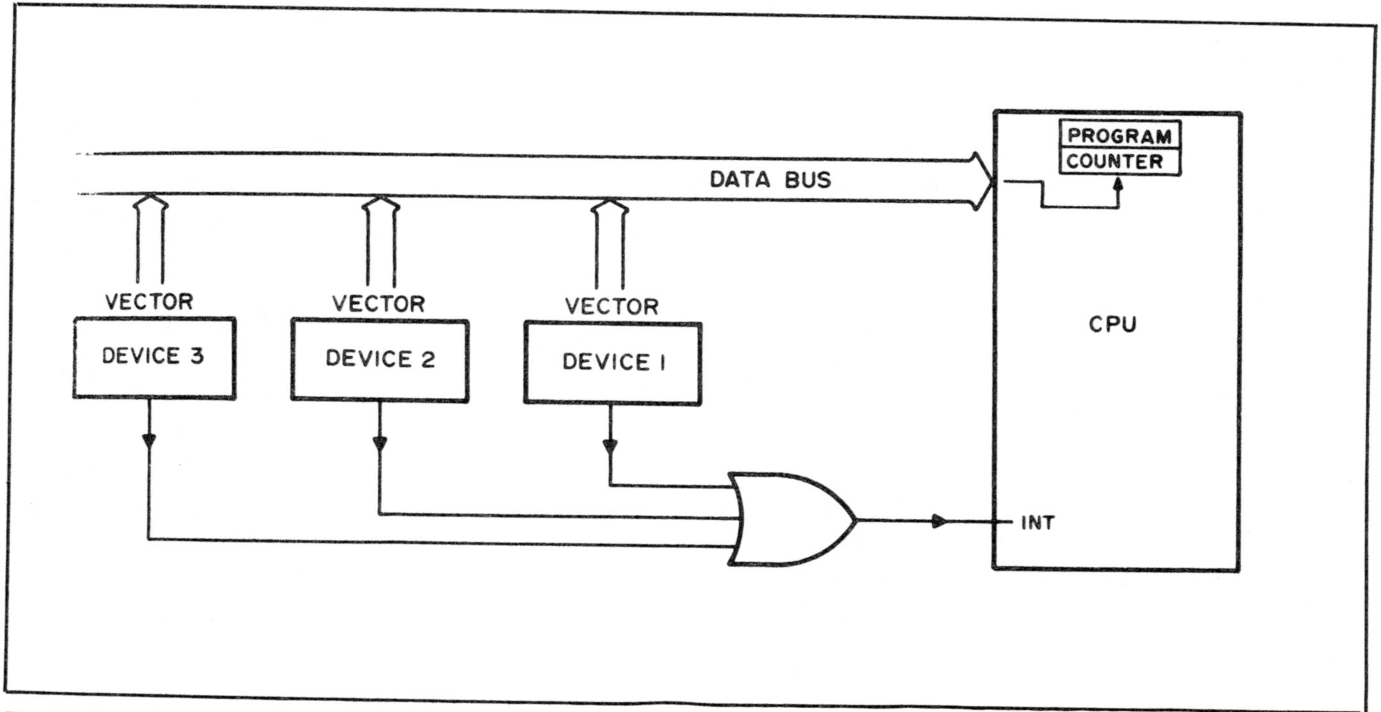

Fig. 2-8. Vectored interrupts.

Similar examples of the use of interrupts can be considered by multi-user computers. An example would be to put the microprocessor up near the local repeater and have it accessible to amateurs with RTTY gear. In this case, the use of interrupts would be essential (for timing users, I/O transmission control, etc.).

Closer to home, interrupts allow the user to have input and output to several devices occurring simultaneously (or almost) and not wasting time while doing this. As in most computers, the actual processing time is very short in comparison to the input/output time. This means the more time taken for input/output during the processing, the less efficient your programming will be. This may not be a major consideration with home systems today, but it will be in the years to come.

Troubleshooting a Micro

While we are often bombarded with propaganda manufacturers proclaiming the wonders of microprocessors and what they can do to automate our station or figure our income tax, we sometimes overlook the problem associated with trying to troubleshoot an ailing system. There is a good reason for this, based on the complexity of the functions that are being performed and the unavailability of test points within the chip. You must be somewhat of a detective to determine what is happening inside from the sparse information that is available to you externally. Fortunately, few of the problems are found within the microprocessor chip itself, but that possibility does exist. While there may be some exceptions to this, it has been my experience that, if the microprocessor will fetch and execute one instruction, it will probably fetch and execute all instructions.

Before starting the troubleshooting procedure, it is important to note whether or not the system is home brew or from a manufacturer. It is also significant whether it has been running and just died, or whether it has never run properly. While the troubleshooting that follows is applicable to all of these cases, there are certain problems that can be ruled out, depending on the previously mentioned conditions. For example, if it is a manufactured system that you are merely assembling, then it is unlikely that it is a wiring error on the cards that you have purchased. If it is your own handwired system, then the likelihood is that you've forgotten some interconnect or connected something up incorrectly.

If the system has been running but now fails, the problem can usually be traced to a faulty bus driver/receiver on the data or address bus. If the system is intermittent, look for temperature effects changing the response of memory, or look at that new

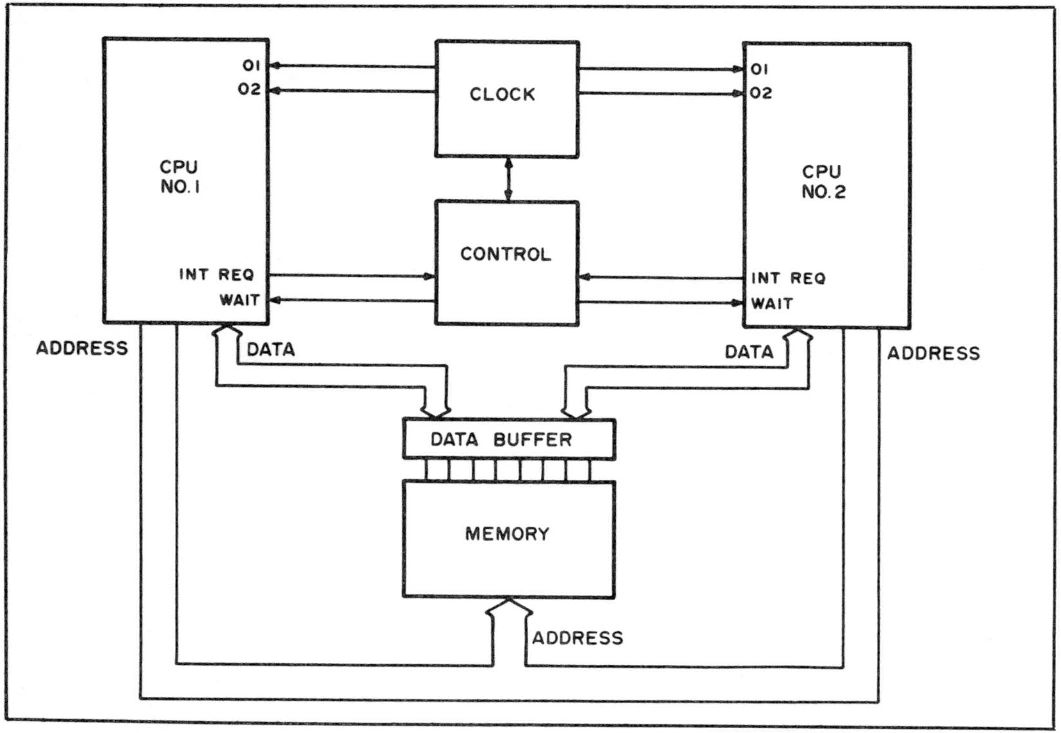

Fig. 2-9. Parallel processing.

interface or memory board that you just hung on the system. Much troubleshooting can be done by merely removing one memory or interface card at a time.

Before continuing, it may also be necessary to note those minimum pieces of test equipment that are required for troubleshooting a system. While some rudimentary checks can be made with a VOM, the system must be looked at dynamically with at least a 10 MHz bandwidth scope. This scope should have at least external triggering and preferably dual trace. Yes, you can look at the buses with slower scopes and see the transitions, but we are looking for problems that may be associated with 50 ns pulses of noise riding around on signal lines, and you will never see them without the prerequisite bandwidth. The microprocessor should also be set up with a hardware restart switch connected directly to the chip itself (or through a peripheral chip designed to do this), so that is can be repeatedly restarted.

There is also one class of problem that is not discussed here, and that is the passing of misinformation by the manufacturer. Occasionally, errors are made in the manuals, or changes are made in the chips that cause them to not function as advertised. This, of course, pertains mostly to the home brew systems. Don't be afraid to call up the local field applications engineer for the company that made the chip and explain your problem. They are, in general, knowledgeable about their product, and may have actually encountered the problem before. If it is a long distance phone call, call them before they are in the office and leave a message with their answering service to have them call you. It may save you quite a phone bill.

As with all electronic problems, beware of the obvious, that is, whether it is a microprocessor that just plain refused to work, or one that intermittently fails to execute its program properly. Start with some of the basic which are often taken for granted.

Power Supply Voltages

The tolerance on power supplies ±5 per cent or 4.75 to 5.25 volts for the 5 volt supply and 11.4 to 12.6 volts for the 12 volt supply. And that is a clean five/twelve volts and a clean ground line. While you wouldn't expect it, most of the digital noise that is found in on the ground line. It should be the first suspect for intermittent faulty operation, assuming that it has never yet worked completely right. Adequate current reserve in the power supply and sufficient bypass capacitors are required for proper operation. As ballpark numbers, 10 microfarads per 20 chips and 0.1 microfarad (for high frequency bypassing that the electrolytic can't handle) near each chip

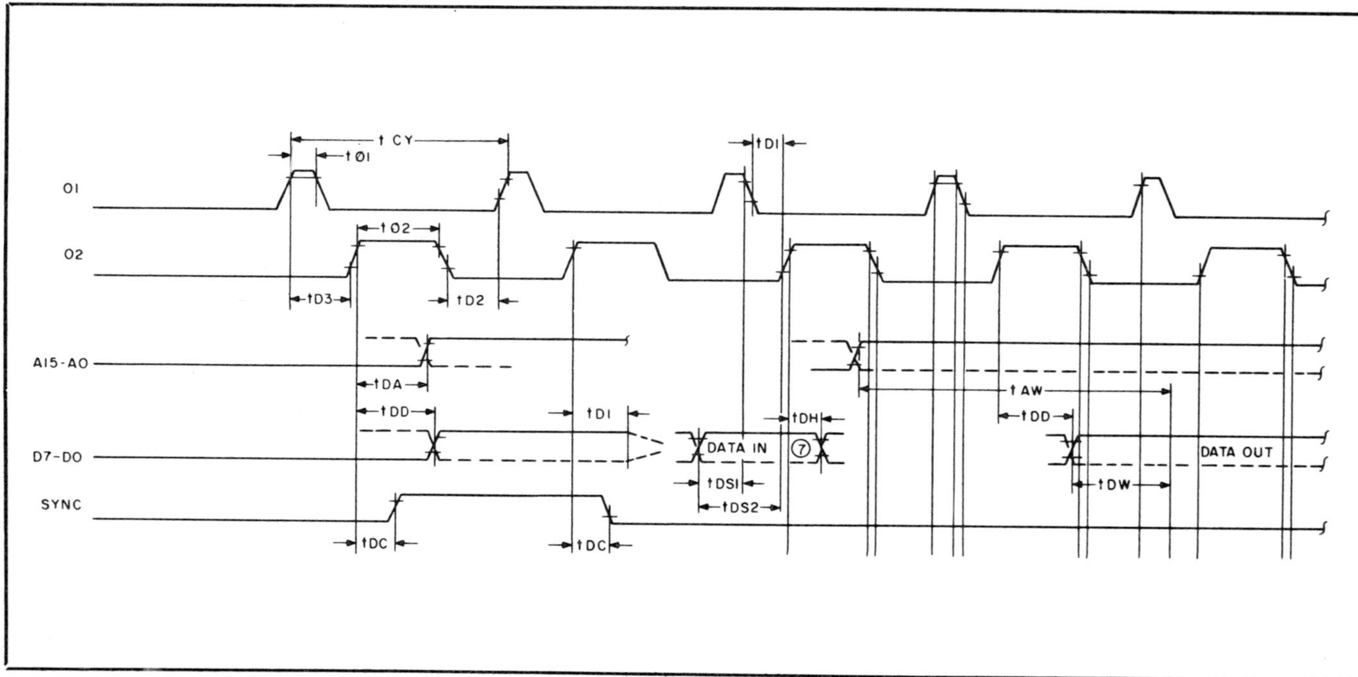

Fig. 2-10. Timing diagram for an 8080A microprocessor. Intel specifies t ϕ 1 as 60 ns minimum, tCY as 480 ns to 2 miscroseconds, tΦ2 as 220 ns minimum, tD3 as 130 ns minimum and tD2 as 70 ns minimum.

that drives signals off of the card or over long distances (bus drivers) should be sufficient.

Another point to remember about checking power supply voltages is to check them at least on the card, if not near the chips themselves, for two reasons. The first is that if a power supply with no voltage sensing is used, the voltage at the power supply may be set to five volts. But, because of losses due to the high currents and small gauge supply wires, the voltage at the chips may, in fact, be below the 4.75 volts minimum. Secondly, if remote sensing is used, the sense line may be open, or the regulating circuitry not operating properly.

Clocks

To operate properly, microprocessors must be supplied with clock signals, since all of the internal functions are performed synchronously. Not only must these signals be present and of the proper duration, but they also must be free from glitches and in the proper timing relationship. Figure 2-10 shows a timing diagram for an 8080 showing a two-phase clock. Note that the duration of phase one must be a minimum of 60 ns, the delay between the rise of phase one and the rise of phase two a minimum of 130 ns and the delay between the fall of phase two and the rise of the next phase one 70 ns minimum. While the clock was being run at 9.5 MHz, rather than the maximum of 18 Mhz, the minimum times were met. A measurement like this can not only be made on a dual trace, 10 MHz scope triggered only by the phase one input, but can also be done on a single trace unit with external trigger. First, phase one is displayed and checked in terms of glitches and minimum pulse width and maximum pulse interval. The triggering is now set up for this signal, and it is moved to the external trigger input (with the scope triggered from this source). Phase two is now connected to the vertical input and displayed, relative to phase one. It may make it easier if phase one is written in on the face of the display with a grease pen.

Instruction Execution

We are now assuming that the microprocessor is hard down and won't do anything. First, disconnect all cards/interfaces/memory, except for Read Only Memory (ROM); then program a ROM with a jump-to-self instruction. In the case of an 8080 the instruction would be as shown in Table 2-3. It is, quite literally, Jump (C3H) to the address (000H) which follows.

While this can be done with other instructions on different machines (such as those with program counter relative addressing),

Table 2-3. Address and Contents.

Address	Contents
0000Hex	0C3Hex
1H	00H
2H	00H

the principle is the same. Try to get the machine to do the minimal amount it can do and still keep fetching and executing a predictable instruction. Now, how do you know if it is running? Look at the synch signal out of the microprocessor. (In the case of the 8080, there is one synch per instruction execution.)

The first check, in this case, is to look at the synch while the reset (a hard reset to the microprocessor through a switch closure) is activated. This reset should set the internal program counter to the starting address where the first instruction will be found (000H in the case of the 8080), and the microprocessor will run for one, two or a number of instructions and then halt. Each of these has a significance. One instruction execution, or synch pulse, means that the microprocessor recognized the rest and has gone out to fetch the first instruction from its starting address. If you don't see at least one synch, it is probably a microprocessor chip problem. If a second synch pulse is found, it means that the microprocessor has output an address, and something has come back. What you don't know for sure is what actually was read from memory. But, you do know that it is going out and fetching. If our dummy instruction is being fetched a number of times (this could be into the hundreds), and then dies, this can probably be attributed to slow memories. To test for this, slow down the system clock. "How?" you say. "It's crystal controlled." First of all, there is nothing that says that is has to be crystal controlled and, second, any experimenter should have miscellaneous crystals around that are less than the value (preferably ½) of the crystal frequency currently being used in the system. Insert the crystal, verify that the clock is running, and see if the microprocessor still dies. If it does, we have to look further.

Address Bus

Whether we are at the one, two, three or more synch pulse stage, it is advisable to check the address bus for proper operation. We are, of course, assuming that the ROM with the jump-to-self instruction is still in the system at the starting address of the microprocessor. One method of checking for proper operation of the address bus would be to synch to the read memory pulse, as this must occur during the time that the address bus is stable. In any event, we should alternately push the restart button and look at each of the address lines to see that the desired starting address is being presented to the ROMs during the time of the read memory pulse. A read memory bar (low is true) is found on the top trace and an address line on the lower trace shows a good zero. No read memory pulse? Probably a bad CPU chip. What you may find is that the leading edge of one of the address lines, either rising or falling, occurs during the read memory pulse. Since this pulse says that the addresses are stable, something is awry. Since there should be nothing on the address bus other than the microprocessor itself and the ROM, the problem is probably not excessive capacitive loading of the bus.

More probably, it's a faulty bus driver/receiver chip if one is used, or a short to Vcc or ground. A lack of noise on an address line is a good indicator of a short to ground. Usually, one address is found to be at fault, and this quickly isolates the offending chip or shorted line. Should all of the address lines be pulling to the required one or zero during the read memory pulse time, then we must look elsewhere for the problem.

Data Bus

The troubleshooting of the data bus can be somewhat more tedious than the previous problems, and so it is left to last. Part of the problem is due to the fact that it is a bidirectional bus and can be transmitting data either to or from the microprocessor. Since the bus is bidirectional, some means must be maintained to keep track of whose data is on the bus at any given time. In a simple system this is easy, because the microprocessor is controlling the bus, and the interfaced hardware has only specific times during which it can put data on the bus.

To digress a moment, although the reader may be familiar with TTL (transistor-transistor logic), to understand the concept of a bidirectional bus, tri-state logic must be brought in (not at the expense of open collector buses, but it is easier to see what is happening on them). Not that understanding them is difficult, for when it is enabled, a tri-state ouput looks like any other TTL signal. When the chip is not enabled, the output assumes a high impedance state. Referring to Fig. 2-11, it can be seen that the normal TTL output is a totem pole arrangement of two transistors, one of which is normally on while the other is off. In fact, what accounts for the large noise spikes in TTL circuitry is that for nanosecond periods of

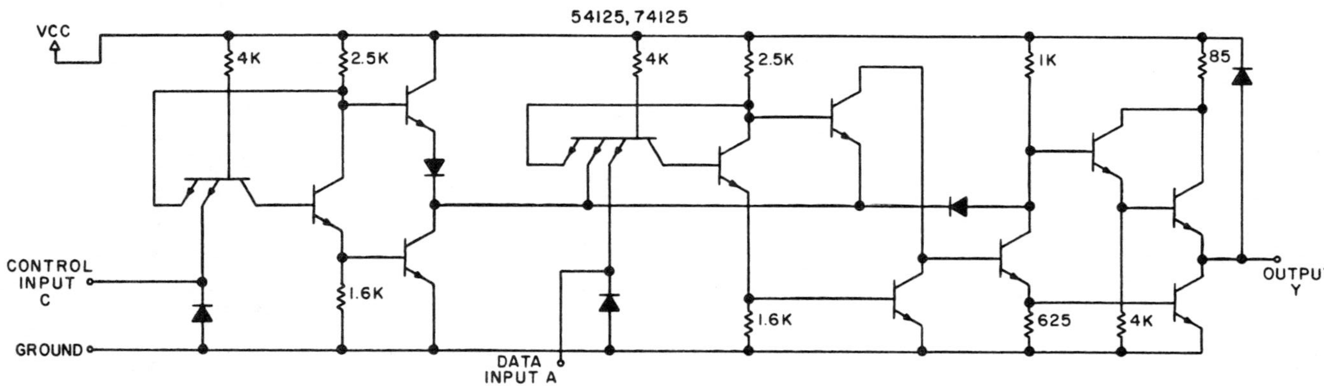

Fig. 2-11. Schematic diagram of a Signetics 74125 quad bus buffer gate with tri-state output. During the tri-state condition, both output transistors are in the high impedance state.

time, both transistors may be on, causing a direct short to ground from Vcc. Looking at it binarily, there is only one other possible state for the two transistors, and that is with both of them off. In this case, looking back into the output of the tri-state device, we see a high impedance to both ground and Vcc and, hence, a very low loading of the data bus.

In the simple case of our jump-to-self instruction, the microprocessor releases control of the data bus during the read memory pulse (and slightly before and after). It is this pulse (read memory) that is logically combined with the decoded address on the address bus to provide a chip enable signal to the ROM so that its tri-state output is enabled and the next instruction put onto the data bus. So the first thing we must do is to look at the pin on the ROM for the chip enable to see if it is, in fact, being enabled. A lack of a chip enable signal says that the problem can now be localized to the chip-select decoding circuitry. If it is present, we continue by looking at the data bus, bit by bit, in synch with the read memory pulse. (At least one should be generated each time the microprocessor is reset.) While it is typically the case that all of the data lines are pulled high (through externally supplied pull-up resistors) so that they go to a known state while they are not being enabled, this is not required, and you may see a data bus without them. Note that the information on the bus is only valid during the read memory pulse time, so both signals must be displayed, or at least synched. Check, as with the address lines, to see that the data is fully a one or a zero during the time that the read memory pulse is there.

During the third read memory bar (low is true) pulse, the data bus is neither high nor low.

If All Else Fails

About the only thing left that can give you fits is an unpredictable interrupt being forced onto the microprocessor through a faulty interrupt controller, an interrupt line that is going low, or one that is not tied high through a resistor (allowing noise to pull it low). Check all interrupt lines for noise. If the chips are mounted in sockets, remove them, use solvent, and reinsert them to allow for a possible faulty interconnect. The same goes for the insertion of the board into its socket. This can be a great source of intermittent aggravation, when it dies every 20 minutes and then starts up with no problems. Another somewhat elusive problem is changing chip parameters with an increase in temperature, especially if the device is being run at close to its rated speed.

So, let's assume that life is not being cruel to you, and the first time that you put the jump-to-self instruction in, the synch pulses and everything else appears to be operating normally. Now is the time to put your rudimentary monitor program ROM back into memory and see if the monitor functions (reads memory, changes registers, etc.). If not, recheck with a scope all of the address lines, data lines and interrupt lines. After a while, you can tell when a line looks correct, even without doing all of the synching, etc. You may want to still check them while you synch with the read memory pulse to check for a slowing of the response of the address and data buses due to capacitive loading increases when additional ROMs are added. If you don't have a small monitor program, put in the minimum amount of software and interface that you need and see if it will work. Slowly add interfaces and memory until the problem occurs. If you are lucky, you should be able to look at each of the address and data lines and see the one that is degraded by the malfunctioning board. If those show nothing, look on the most recently inserted interface/memory board to ascertain if signals are getting through to it. Perhaps it is being enabled all of the time, or conversely, never due to faulty logic on the board. Hopefully, the insertion of boards one at a time will point out the defective board, and a look at all of the lines going to that board will give you a starting place for troubleshooting.

Read the Manual

Since you probably plugged the thing in before you really understood it, and it (miraculously) worked, or it worked after you only read half of the book, read the other half. Experience had shown that the microprocessor is probably not running because you forgot to read footnote number three at the bottom of page sixty-seven, which says that pin five of board six must be grounded for proper operation.

Dial Your Micro

A modem, now that's what I need for my 6800 system! But how about one that has auto answer? Auto answer lets you dial up your phone, and, when it rings, the modem will answer and connect your computer to the phone line. Now you, or someone else, can operate your computer from a remote terminal and modem.

I decided on using Motorola's MC6860 modem IC, and being a fairly-stingy-with-a-buck person, its availability, features and $14.95 price are what sold me.

After spending a week thinking, I decided on the features for my first modem. It was going to do everything the chip was capable of. This overkill approach does have its advantages when you're not positive about what you're going to do with it or connect it to.

Two months later, when the smoke finally cleared, I had built two modems. One was a do-everything, interface-to-almost-everything, and the other was a minimum-parts version, with most of the features.

This section will be about a combination of my two modems which will have the following features: 0-300 baud, self-test, full duplex, originate and answer modes, compatible with various systems via TTL or RS-232 levels and auto answer and disconnect. My total cost for all new parts was under $70, including the case and power supply.

Theory

This modem uses audio frequency shift keying (AFSK). The data to be sent is converted to audio tones. If the modem is in the originating mode, a logic 0 (space) is sent as a 1070 Hz tone (2025 Hz, if in answer mode) and a logic 1 (mark) is sent as a 1270 Hz tone (2225 Hz if in answer mode). See Table 2-4. This might seem a little confusing, but it works just fine. These frequencies are standard for low-speed data communication.

This modem is composed of several logical sections. First is the interface to the telephone company line (Fig. 2-12). This interface must be able to match the characteristic impedance of the phone line, usually 900 ohms, to the modem. It must provide DC isolation from the telephone line and, for automatic answer, must be able to detect when the phone is ringing and be able to answer and terminate the call.

The filter (Fig. 2-13) passes only the frequencies 1070 Hz to 1270 Hz when in answer mode and 2025 Hz to 2225 Hz when in the originate mode. The filter is needed because, in full duplex operation, the modem is transmitting and receiving at the same time, and the signals must be separated. The limiter, IC3, takes the sine wave from the filter and changes it into a symmetrical square wave of a TTL-compatible level. The demodulator in the modem IC compares each half-cycle of this square wave against the crystal-controlled timebase to determine if the incoming frequency is a mark or space. The threshold detector, IC4, is used to tell the modem IC that the input signal entering the limiter is above the minimum detectable level.

The 6860 modem IC is the brains behind the outfit. It takes care of modulation, demodulation and the hand-shaking signals to establish, maintain and terminate the data link. Another section is the

Table 2-4. FSK Transmit Frequency.

Data	Originate	Answer
0 Space	1070 Hz	2025 Hz
1 Mark	1270 Hz	2225 Hz

interface to the computer or terminal. There is a fair amount of flexibility here due to the 6860 signal levels being TTL-compatible. Depending on the exact use you plan for the modem, it can be tailored to fit.

How It Works

IC1 is placed in the answer mode when its pin 19 is grounded. This is done by the ring detector when your phone rings or by pushing the answer switch. This causes IC1, pin 4 to go high, operating RL1, which connects the modem and answers the call. At the same time, IC1, pin 15 goes low. This places RL2 in the proper position to select the answer mode filter. When IC1 detects the mark tone from the other modem, pin 23 goes low. This turns on the clear-to-send (CLS) LED.

The originating mode is initiated when the originating switch is pushed, causing IC1, pin 21 to go low. Next, pin 4 goes high, closing RL1, connecting the modem to the phone line. At the same time, pin 15 goes high, operating RL2 and selecting the originating filter. When IC1 detects the mark tone from the answering modem, it will send out its mark tone from pin 10 to the transmit buffer, T1, and out to the line. Now the CTS LED will light, indicating "ready to exchange data."

If IC1, pin 16 is held low, the modem is placed in the self-test mode. The demodulator is changed to the modulator frequency and loops back to the terminal whatever is typed in.

When a break (150 ms space) is received by the modem, IC1, pin 3 is clamped high and stops data exchange. This positive-going level triggers a one-shot, IC6, which sends a negative pulse to IC1, pin 9, automatically releasing the break condition. This negative pulse is also sent to my SWTP 6800 computer's MRST line. This gives the remote terminal the ability to operate the computer's hardware reset by sending a break.

Construction Tips

I built the modem on four printed circuit boards, consisting of the following circuits: the internal coupler, the filter, limiter and

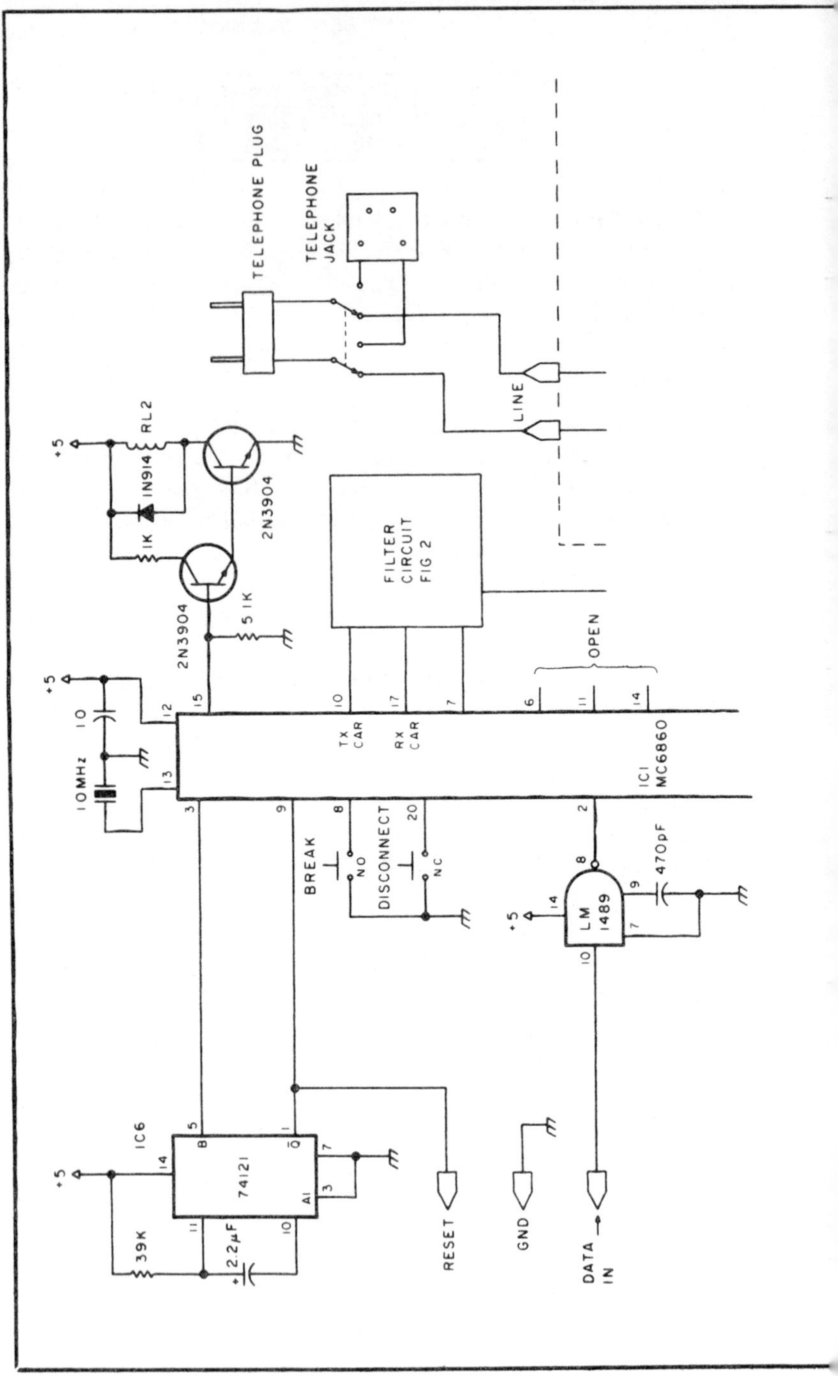
TELEPHONE PLUG
TELEPHONE JACK
+5
RL2
IN914
1K
2N3904
2N3904
51K
FILTER CIRCUIT FIG 2
LINE
OPEN
10MHz
10
TX CAR
RX CAR
IC1 MC6860
BREAK
NO
DISCONNECT
NC
LM 1489
470pF
IC6
74121
39K
2.2µF
RESET
GND
DATA IN

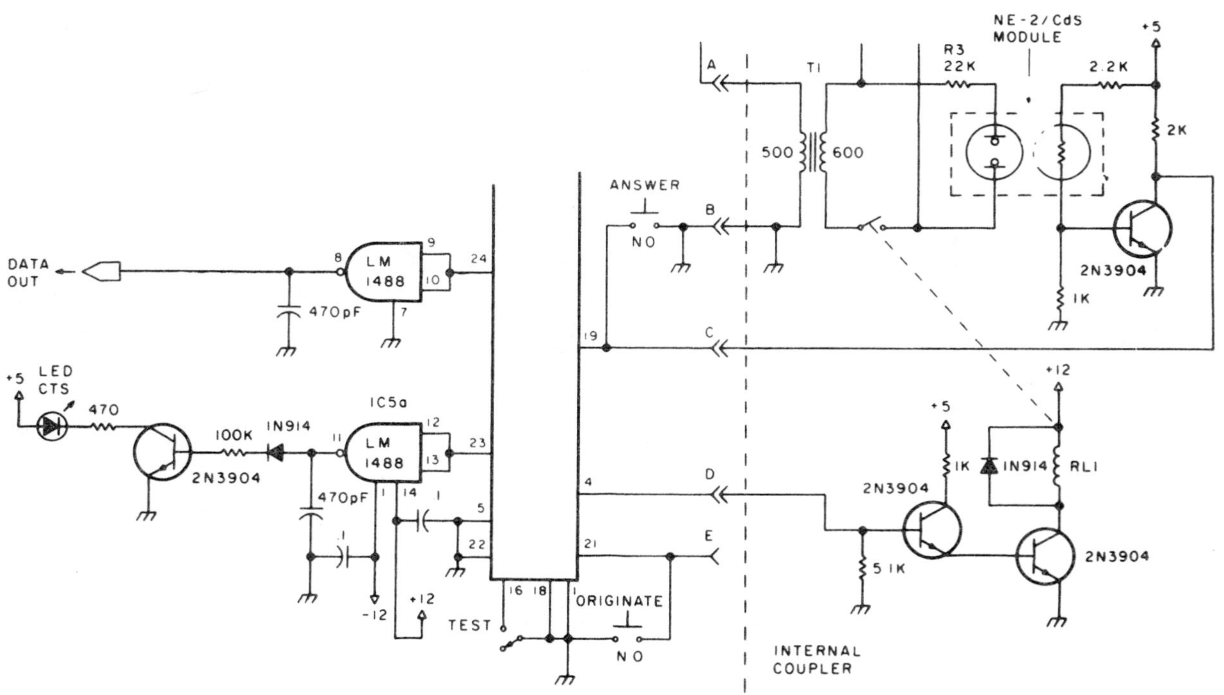

Fig. 2-12. Main schematic with internal coupler.

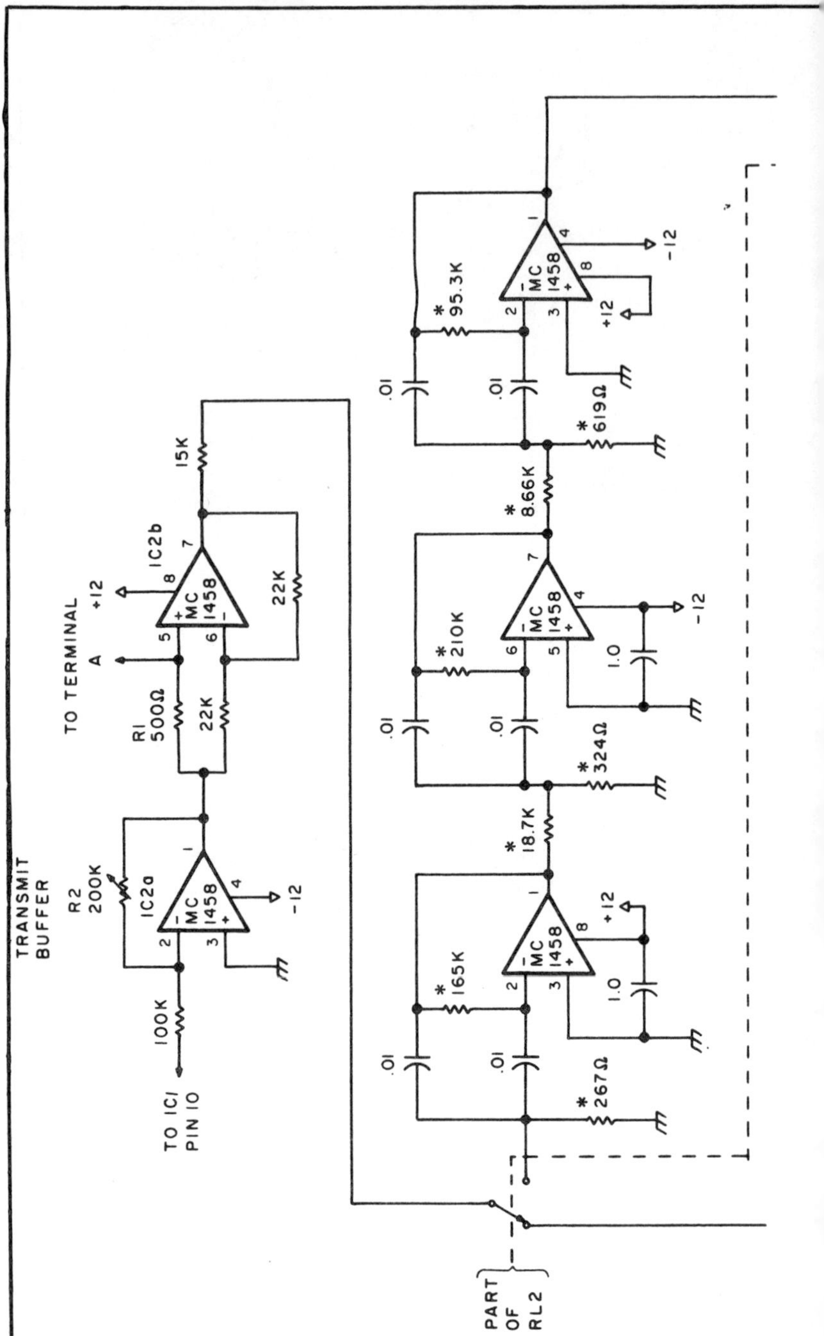
TRANSMIT BUFFER
R2 200K
IC2a
MC 1458
100K
TO IC1 PIN 10
-12
TO TERMINAL A
+12
R1 500Ω
22K
IC2b
15K
22K
PART OF RL2
.01
* 267Ω
* 165K
1.0
+12
* 18.7K
* 324Ω
* 210K
-12
* 8.66K
* 619Ω
* 95.3K

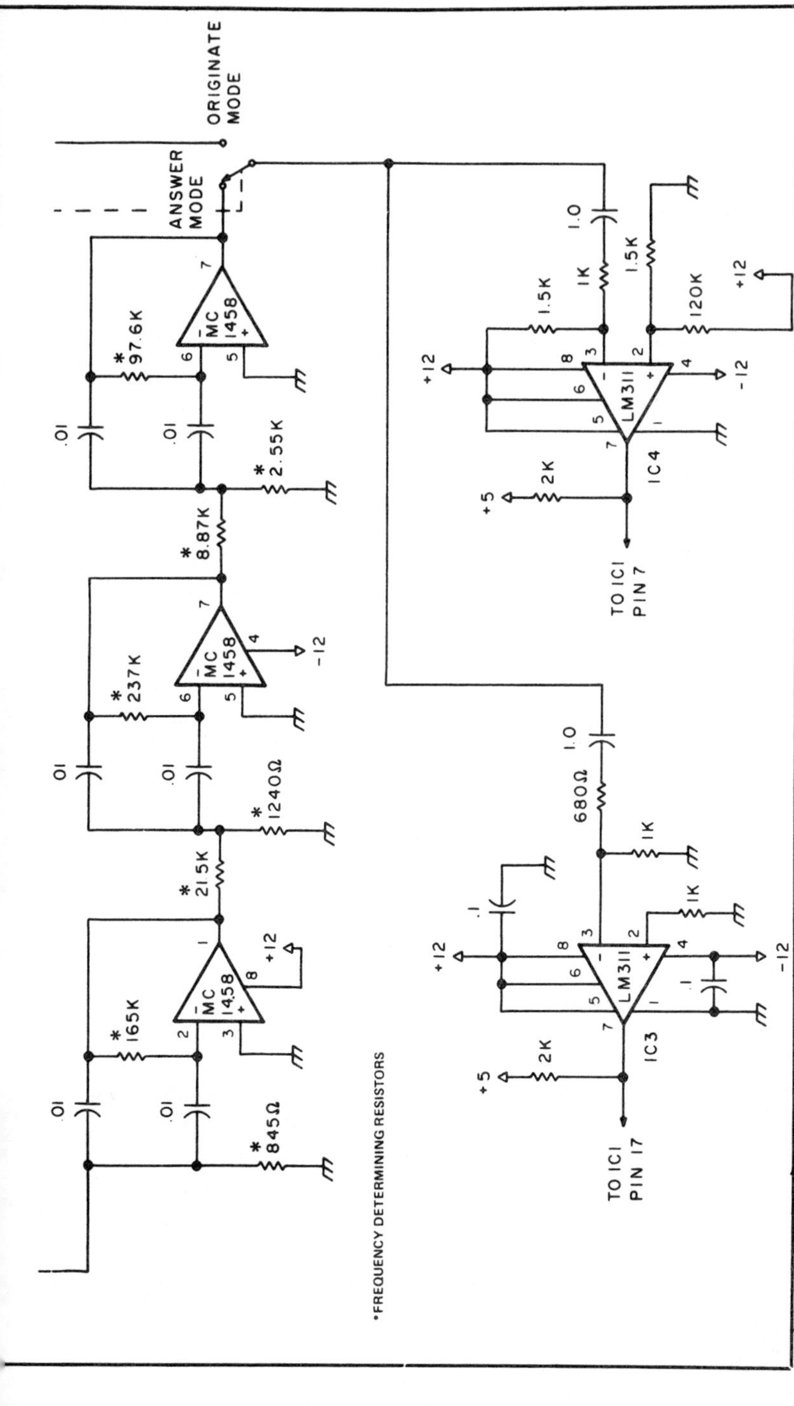

Fig. 2-13. Filter circuit.

threshold detector, the modem IC and RS-232 chips and the power supply. You can use whatever construction technique you prefer. I always socket all integrated circuits. This time I had to replace the 24-pin socket with one of better quality. It caused all sorts of problems, so beware! I guess if I had socketed the sockets, I might not have had that problem.

I made the ring detector by laying an NE-2 lamp on top of a flat cadmium sulfide cell and using hot-melt glue at each end of the lamp to hold them together. Then I wrapped black electrical tape around them to keep out the ambient light. The first one I made didn't work. I found that some NE-2 lamps require about 100V AC before they light. Next I took apart a neon pilot lamp assemble. It had an internal 22k resistor in series with the neon lamp. This combination worked. The series resistor, R3, can be from 22k up to 220k, depending on the wattage rating of the lamp. Pretest your neon-resistor combination to make sure it will light on approximately 70V AC. I bought the cadmium cell at a surplus store. It's about ¾-inch square and ¼-inch thick (any similar configuration you can come up with should work). There are also commercial neon/CdS modules available, such as the Clairex DLM 3120A Photomod.

RL1 is an SPST 12V DC relay with a 1k ohm coil, mounted in a 14-pin IC package. A suitable 5V relay could be used if connected to the 5V supply.

RL2 is a DPDT 5V relay with a 100-ohm coil, mounted in a TO-5 package. You should be able to use any similar relays. In my second modem, I left out RL2 and just used a DPDT switch, mounted between the originate and answer push-buttons. This made construction a lot easier, without losing any real features.

IC5a is just used for inversion to save a transistor.

I used a 500- to 600-ohm transformer for T1. The ideal value for the side that connects to the phone line is 900 ohms. The side of T1 connected to terminals A and B can be anything between 500 and 1k ohms, but, whatever value it is, R1 (connected to pin 1 of IC2a) should be adjusted to match it.

All the frequency-determining resistors in the originating and answer filters should be 1 percent. All the .01 uF capacitors should be 5 percent or better, mylar or polystyrene.

A lot of phone companies require you to rent (from them) a coupling device when connecting external equipment to their lines. There are several types of coupling devices that will give the same auto answer and disconnect features as the internal coupler described here. One is a CBS data coupler which has RS-232-compatible signals. If you use one of these, the optional data coupler

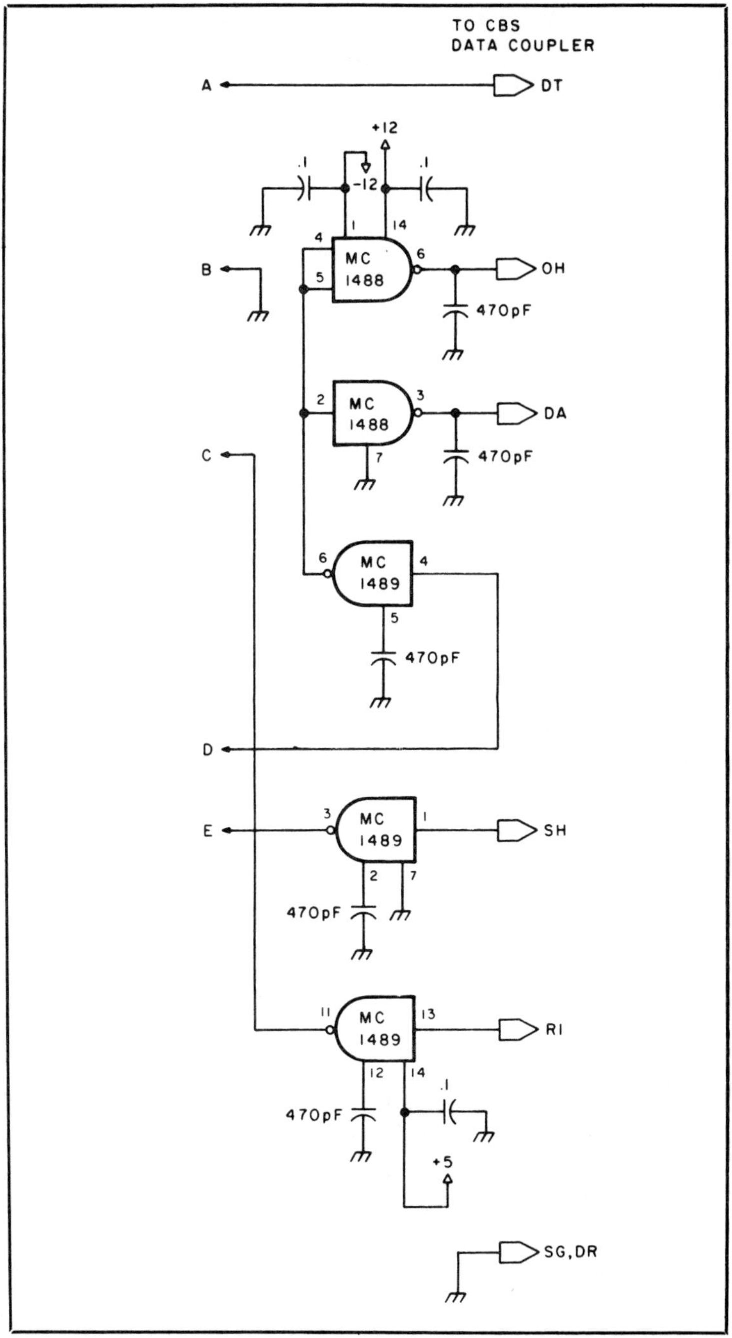

Fig. 2-14. Optional CBS data coupler interface.

interface (Fig. 2-14) is used in place of the internal coupler. This circuit will provide the RS-232 levels needed by the phone company's CBS data coupler. R1 should be changed to a 600-ohm resistor, because the customer sides of their couplers are 600 ohms.

Testing and Adjustment

The modem's handshaking signals should be tested first. Connect a small high-impedance speaker (100 ohm) or frequency counter to the line terminals of the modem. Turn on the power and push the answer push-button. You should hear a 2225 Hz tone. The level can be adjusted by R2.

Next, connect an audio oscillator across the speaker and apply a 2225 Hz signal, push the originate push-button and, if you left out RL2, change the filter switch to originate. You should hear the modem send out a 1270 Hz tone, and the clear-to-send (CLS) LED will light. Next, push the break push-button. The modem should send a 150 ms 1070 Hz tone every time this switch is pushed. Now push the disconnect switch. The modem will send a three-second 1070 Hz tone, the CTL LED will go off and the modem will stop sending.

The transmit level (R2) will be adjusted next. Dial up a friend and have him leave his phone off the hook. With the modem line terminals connected across the phone line, push the answer push-button and hang up your phone, or operate the line switch to the modem. You have 17 seconds to measure the signal level across the phone line with an ungrounded meter. Use the output jack or connect a 0.1 uF capacitor in series with the meter and adjust R2 for a level of −15 dBm, 0.14V rms or 0.39V p-p.

Next have your friend call you back, but, before he does, the modem should be on and connected to the phone line. If you left out RL2, place the filter switch in the answer position. When he calls, the phone should ring once. If it does, wait a few seconds and pick up your phone. The modem should be sending out a 2225 Hz tone. If the phone keeps ringing, the ring detector is not working.

To test the data section, connect the data in and out to something that speaks RS-232 at 300 baud or less. The modem does not care about format. It converts to tones anything that comes into it. I used my SWTP CT 1024 terminal. Turn on the modem and push the answer switch. Turn on the test switch. Now the CTS LED will light, and what you type on the keyboard will be looped back and printed on the screen. If you installed the manual filter switch, change it to the originate position (this is one of the things that RL2 does automatically).

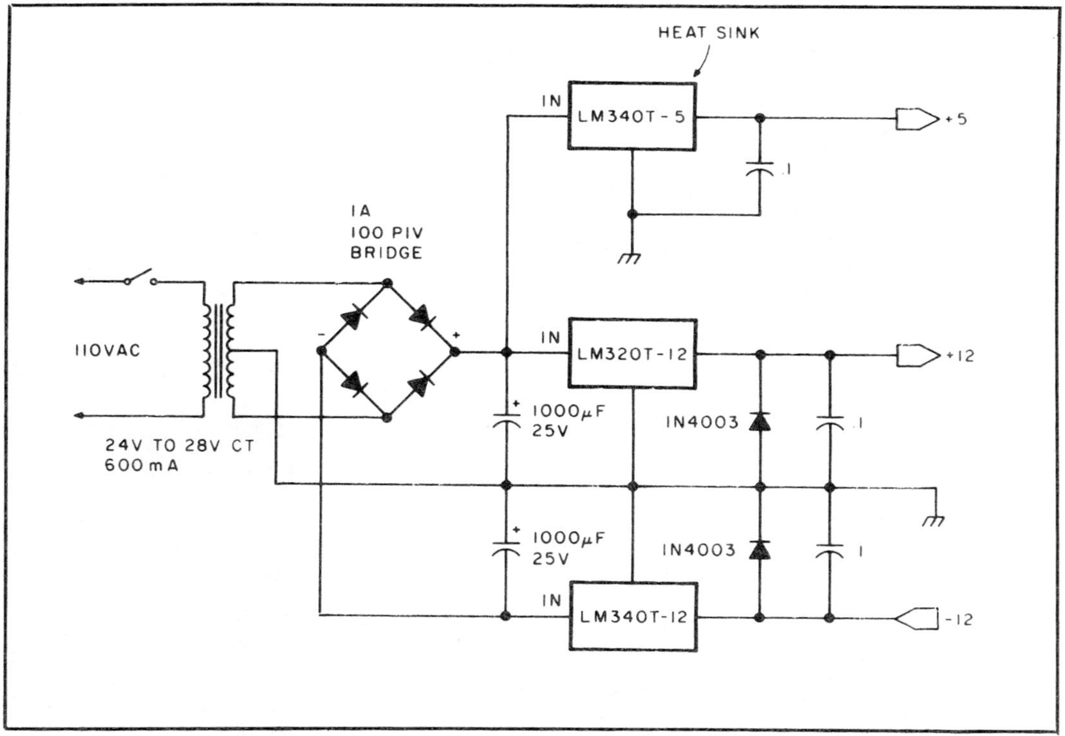

Fig. 2-15. Power supply.

Interface and Operation

I connected the modem to my system by paralleling it across the CT 1024 data in and out lines. This way, it acts like another terminal that can access the computer over the phone line.

To use the modem as a terminal only, like talking to a time-share computer, just connect it to the terminal and disconnect the rest of the system.

When using modems, a point to remember is that one end must be in the originate and the other in the answer mode.

The hand-shaking tones can be lost for up to 17 seconds before the connection will be lost, but data sent when the CTS LED is off will be lost.

During actual use, if you are the originating modem, dial the number you want, and it will be answered by a person or a modem. If you hear a tone, you have 17 seconds to push your originate switch and hang up or change your line switch to the modem. When your modem detects the tone, it will send out its mark tone. The CTS LED will light and the data can now be exchanged.

If you are talking to an SWTP computer whose MRST line is connected to the reset terminal, sending a break will reset the computer to its Mikbug™ operating system. Operating the disconnect push-button will cause the modem at the other end to hang up.

Also remember that, if the modem is on and connected to the phone line, it will answer all calls you get. It could be someone not expecting to get a 2225 Hz tone in his ear, and they could report your phone out of order. The best thing would be if you had a separate phone line just for the modem.

For my acid test, I left one modem at home and the computer loaded with games; the other I took with my terminal over to a friend's home. I dialed up the computer, and we played games for four hours. It worked great!

The power supply schematic for this project can be found in Fig. 2-15.

An 8080 Disassembler

This program was written for a Poly-88 microcomputer (Table 2-5). However, since it is in BASIC, it is easily modified for other 8080-based computers that have a BASIC interpreter or compiler available.

A disassembler's task is very difficult. It must be able to jump into the middle of the computer's memory, help the user to read the mixture of ASCII and numerical data stored there and change the numerical instruction codes into mnemonic assembler code. Instruc-

Table 2-5. Program Listing.

```
90 GOSUB 9000\REM INITIALIZE
100 !"*",
110 C=INP(1)
120 IF C=13 THEN !\GOTO 100
130 IF (C<32) OR (C>122) THEN 110
140 GOSUB 200
145 GOSUB 1000
150 GOTO 100
200 IF C>96 THEN C=C-32\REM MAKE UPPER-CASE
205 C$=CHR$(C)
210 IF C$=" " THEN RETURN
220 IF C$="A" THEN 2000
230 IF C$="J" THEN 400
240 IF C$="B" THEN 500
250 IF C$="C" THEN 450
260 IF C$="R" THEN 600
270 IF C$="P" THEN 700
300 A=A0
310 RETURN
400 IF J0=0 THEN 300
410 !"Jump",
420 A=E
430 RETURN
450 IF J0=0 THEN 300
460 !"Call",
465 S(S0)=A
470 S0=S0+1
475 A=E
480 RETURN
500 !"Back"
510 A=A0-1
520 RETURN
600 IF S0=0 THEN 300
610 !"Return",
620 S0=S0-1
630 A=S(S0)
640 RETURN
700 !"Previous instr."
710 T=A0-12
720 A=T \GOSUB 1200
730 I=B(PEEK(A))
740 T=T+I
750 IF T<A0 THEN 720
760 RETURN
1000 !\REM MAIN LOOP
1005 GOSUB 1200
1010 H2=A\GOSUB 4000\REM PRINT ADDRESS
1020 !":",TAB(T1),
1025 A0=A\REM REMEMBER ADDRESS
1030 X=PEEK(A)
1040 FOR I=0 TO B(X)-1
1050 H=PEEK(A+I)
1055 GOSUB 4200
1060 NEXT I
1065 !TAB(T2),
1070 FOR I=0 TO B(X)-1
1075 H=PEEK(A+I)
1080 IF(H<32)OR(H>126) THEN !"_", ELSE !CHR$(H),
1085 NEXT I
1090 !TAB(T3),
1100 GOSUB 5000\REM DISASSEMBLE INSTRUCTION
1110 !TAB(T4),
1120 RETURN
1195 REM NORMALIZE A
1200 IF A<0 THEN A=A+W\GOTO 1200
1210 IF A<W THEN RETURN
```

Table 2-5. Program Listing.

```
1220 A=A-W*INT(A/W)
1230 RETURN
2000 !"Address: "
2010 GOSUB 2200
2020 A=H2
2030 RETURN
2195 REM GET A HEX NUMBER FROM THE KEYBOARD
2200 H2=0
2210 I=0
2220 C=INP(1)
2225 C$=CHR$(C)
2230 C=C-48\REM ASCII 0
2240 IF C<0 THEN 2220
2250 IF C<10 THEN 2300
2260 C=C-7\REM MAGIC!
2270 IF (C<10)OR(C>15) THEN 2220
2300 !C$,
2310 I=I+1
2320 H2=16*H2+C
2330 GOTO 2220
2350 IF I=0 THEN 2220
2360 I=I-1
2370 H2=INT(H2/16)
2380 !CHR$(127),
2390 GOTO 2220
2400 IF I=0 THEN !"0",
2410 RETURN
3995 REM PRINT H2 AS 4 HEX DIGITS
4000 H=INT(H2/256)
4010 GOSUB 4200
4020 H=H2-256*H
4030 GOTO 4200
4195 REM PRINT H AS 2 HEX DIGITS
4200 N=INT(H/16)
4210 !H$(N+1,N+1),
4220 N=H-16*N
4230 !H$(N+1,N+1),
4240 RETURN
5000 REM GIVEN ADDRESS IN A, DISASSEMBLE 1 INSTRUCTION
5005 J0=0\REM ZERO JUMP FLAG
5010 X=PEEK(A)\REM OPCODE IN X
5015 A=A+1
5020 L=INT(X/64)\REM BITS 6-7
5030 ON L+1 GOTO 5100,7000,6000,8000
5100 REM 00XXXXXX
5120 ON J+1 GOTO 5130,5200,5400,5600,5700,5710,5800,5900
5130 IF X>0 THEN 7200
5140 !"NOP",
5150 RETURN
5200 REM 00XXX001
5210 J=INT(I/2)\REM BITS 4-5
5215 K=I-2*J\REM BIT 3
5220 IF K=0 THEN 5300
5230 !"DAD",
5240 GOTO 6600
5300 !"LXI"
5310 GOSUB 6600
5320 !",",
5330 GOTO 7500
5400 REM 00XXX010
5410 K=INT(I/4)\REM BIT 5
5420 I=I-4*K\REM BITS 3-4
5430 IF K=1 THEN 5500
5440 J=INT(I/2)\REM BIT 4
5450 K=I-2*J\REM BIT 3
```

continued on page 157

Table 2-5. Program Listing.

```
5460 ON K+1 GOTO 5470,5480
5470 !"STAX",\GOTO 6600
5480 !"LDAX",\GOTO 6600
5500 ON I+1 GOTO 5510,5520,5530,5540
5510 !"SHLD",\GOTO 7450
5520 !"LHLD",\GOTO 7450
5530 !"STA",\GOTO 7450
5540 !"LDA",\GOTO 7450
5600 REM 00XXX011
5610 J=INT(I/2)\REM BITS 4-5
5620 K=I-2*J\REM BIT 3
5630 ON K+1 GOTO 5640,5650
5640 !"INX",\GOTO 6600
5650 !"DCX",\GOTO 6600
5700 !"INR",\J=I\GOTO 6400
5710 !"DCR",\J=I\GOTO 6400
5800 REM 00XXX110
5810 !"MVI",
5815 J=I
5820 GOSUB 6400
5830 !",",
5840 GOTO 7700
5900 REM 00XXX111
5910 ON I+1 GOTO 5920,5930,5940,5950,5960,5970,5980,5990
5920 !"RLC",\RETURN
5930 !"RRC",\RETURN
5940 !"RAL",\RETURN
5950 !"RAR",\RETURN
5960 !"DAA",\RETURN
5970 !"CMA" \RETURN
5980 !"STC",\RETURN
5990 !"CMC",\RETURN
6000 REM 10XXXXXX
6030 ON I+1 GOTO 6100,6110,6120,6130,6140,6150,6160,6170
6100 !"ADD",\GOTO 6200
6110 !"ADC",\GOTO 6200
6120 !"SUB",\GOTO 6200
6130 !"SBB",\GOTO 6200
6140 !"ANA",\GOTO 6200
6150 !"XRA",\GOTO 6200
6160 !"ORA",\GOTO 6200
6170 !"CMP",\GOTO 6200
6200 !" ",
6210 GOTO 6500
6400 REM PRINT BLANK, THEN REG. NAME
6410 !" ",
6500 REM GIVEN J, PRINT REGISTER NAME
6510 N=J+1
6520 !R$(N,N),
6530 RETURN
6600 !" ",
6700 REM GIVEN J, PRINT RP NAME
6710 N=J+1
6720 C$=D$(N,N)
6730 !C$,
6740 IF C$="S" THEN !"P",
6750 RETURN
7000 REM 01XXXXXX
7010 IF X=118 THEN !"HLT",\RETURN
7020 !"MOV ",
7040 K=J\REM SAVE J
7050 J=I\GOSUB 6500
7060 !" ",
7070 J=K\GOSUB 6500
```

Table 2-5. Program Listing.

```
7080 RETURN
7200 REM UNDEFINED INSTRUCTION
7210 !"--",
7220 RETURN
7400 REM JUMP OR CALL
7410 REM SET JUMP FLAG
7420 J0=1
7450 !" ",
7500 REM FETCH NEXT 2 BYTES, INTERPRET AS ADDRESS,
7510 REM AND PRINT IN HEX
7520 Y=PEEK(A)\A=A+1
7530 Z=PEEK(A)\A=A+1
7540 E=Y+256*Z\REM E IS EFFECTIVE ADDRESS
7550 H=Z\GOSUB 4200
7560 H=Y\GOSUB 4200
7570 RETURN
7700 REM FETCH AND PRINT NEXT BYTE
7710 Y=PEEK(A)\A=A+1
7720 H=Y
7730 GOTO 4200
7800 REM PRINT RST ADDRESS
7810 ! I,
7820 RETURN
8000 REM 11XXXXXX
8040 ON J+1 GOTO 8050,8100,8200,8300,8400,8500,8600,8700
8050 !"R",\REM RETURN ON CONDITION
8060 GOTO 8800
8100 REM 11XXX001
8105 J=INT(I/2)\REM BITS 4-5
8110 K=I-2*J\REM BIT 3
8115 IF K=1 THEN 8150
8120 !"POP ",
8130 GOTO 8900
8150 ON J+1 GOTO 8160,7200,8170,8180
8160 !"RET",\RETURN
8170 !"PCHL",\RETURN
8180 !"SPHL",\RETURN
8200 REM 11XXX010
8210 !"J".\REM JUMP ON CONDITION
8220 GOSUB 8800
8230 GOTO 7400
8300 REM 11XXX011
8310 ON I+1 GOTO 8320,7200,8330,8340,8350,8360,8370,8380
8320 !"JMP",\GOTO 7400
8330 !"OUT ",\GOTO 7700
8340 !"IN ".\GOTO 7700
8350 !"XTHL",\RETURN
8360 !"XCHG",\RETURN
8370 !"DI",\RETURN
8380 !"EI".\RETURN
8400 REM 11XXX100
8410 !"C",\REM CALL ON CONDITION
8420 GOSUB 8800
8430 GOTO 7400
8500 REM 11XXX101
8510 J=INT(I/2)\REM BITS 4-5
8520 K=I-2*J\REM BIT 3
8530 IF K=1 THEN 8550
8540 !"PUSH ".\GOTO 8900
8550 ON J+1 GOTO 8560,7200,7200,7200
8560 !"CALL",
8570 GOTO 7400
8600 REM 11XXX110
8605 ON I+1 GOTO 8610.8615,8620,8625,8630,8635,8640,8645
8610 !"AD",\GOTO 8650
```

continued on page 159

Table 2-5. Program Listing.

```
8615 !"AC",\GOTO 8650
8620 !"SU",\GOTO 8650
8625 !"SB",\GOTO 8650
8630 !"AN".\GOTO 8650
8635 !"XR",\GOTO 8650
8640 !"OR",\GOTO 8650
8645 !"CP",
8650 !"I ",
8660 GOTO 7700
8700 REM 11XXX111
8710 !"RST",
8720 H=I\GOSUB 7800
8730 RETURN
8800 REM GIVEN I, PRINT RET, CALL, OR JMP CONDITION
8810 ON I+1 GOTO 8820 8830,8840,8850,8860,8870,8880,8890
8820 !"NZ",\RETURN
8830 !"Z",\RETURN
8840 !"NC",\RETURN
8850 !"C",\RETURN
8860 !"PO",\RETURN
8870 !"PE".\RETURN
8880 !"P",\RETURN
8890 !"M",\RETURN
8900 REM GIVEN J, PRINT RP NAME FOR PUSH OR POP
8910 I=J+1
8920 C$=D$(I,I)
8930 IF C$="S" THEN !"PSW",\RETURN
8940 !C$,\RETURN
9000 REM INITIALIZATION
9010 DIM R$(8)
9020 R$="BCDEHLMA"\REM REGISTER NAMES
9030 DIM D$(4)
9040 D$="BDHS"\REM REGISTER PAIR NAMES
9050 DIM H$(16)
9060 H$="0123456789ABCDEF"
9100 DIM B(255)\REM # OF BYTES FOR INSTRUCTION
9105 FOR I=0 TO 63
9110 READ B(I)
9115 NEXT I
9120 FOR I=64 TO 191
9125 B(I)=1
9130 NEXT I
9135 FOR I=192 TO 255
9140 READ B(I)
9145 NEXT I
9150 DATA 1 3,1,1.1,1,2,1,1,1,1,1,1,1,2,1
9160 DATA 1,3,1,1.1,1,2,1,1,1,1,1,1,1,2,1
9170 DATA 1,3,3,1,1,1,2.1,1,1,3,1,1,1,2,1
9180 DATA 1,3,3,1,1,1,2,1,1,1,3,1,1,1,2,1
9200 DATA 1,1,3.3,3,1,2,1,1,1,3,1,3,3,2,1
9210 DATA 1,1,3,2,3,1,2,1,1,1,3,2,3,1,2,1
9220 DATA 1,1,3,1,3,1,2,1,1,1,3,1,3,1,2,1
9230 DATA 1,1,3,1,3,1,2,1,1,1,3,1,3,1,2,1
9300 A=0
9305 A0=0
9310 J0=0
9350 W=65536
9400 REM TAB STOPS
9410 T1=7
9420 T2=15
9430 T3=24
9440 T4=40
9500 DIM S(20)\REM ADDRESS STACK
9510 S0=0
9900 RETURN
```

tions on the 8080 are of varible length, and if the disassembler happens to start in the middle of an instruction rather than at its beginning, what comes out is garbage.

To help cure these problems, this disassembler displays the contents of each location in hexadecimal, in ASCII and in assembler code. It takes into account the variable length of the instructions. The misalignment problem is quite difficult, and if the disassembler is started in the middle of an instruction, it usually takes a few instructions before it is back on the track. However, this program incorporates a heuristic method for obtaining correct alignment. A special code "P," for "Previous intruction," attempts to find the nearest previous instruction that seems reasonable. What it actually does is this: first it jumps back in memory 12 bytes, then it disassembles its way forward to the last instruction that does not overlap the one you started in. The odds are very good that, during this process, the disassembler will find the proper alignment. This feature is, perhaps, the most interesting advance this disassembler exhibits. The other features that make it very convenient to use are explained in the operating instructions.

The disassembler was written by Douglas Wyatt, with a little bit of the code (and probably most of the bugs) supplied by me. A few comments on changing Poly BASIC to your BASIC might help. The exclamation point (!) means "PRINT." Anything shown in lowercase may be changed to uppercase. We think that it is nicer for the computer to talk in standard English if it can, so we use lowercase where appropriate. The function INP(1) grabs a character from the keyboard. Thus, lines 110 and 120 take a character, C, and ask if it is a RETURN (ASCII-13). If it is, the computer does a RETURN and a LINE FEED. The slash (/) allows two instructions to appear on the same line. You can modify this so that they are on separate lines if your BASIC doesn't support this feature.

Knowing the symbol equivalent of various ASCII codes is useful in understanding the program. Your BASIC must have the PEEK function, of course. On some, this is called EXAM. We also use TAB. If you don't have the multiway branch (the ON instruction), you will have to use a list of IFs. It's not all that hard.

Operating Instructions

When the program is running, a press on the space bar disassembles the next instruction. Any key other than a command just repeats the previous instruction. The following six commands form the entire assembler. When they are pressed, no RETURN is required if you use the INP function or its equivalent.

A(ddress). When this command is given, you have to supply a hex address. Disassembly proceeds from that address.

J(ump). If the instruction just disassembled was any kind of jump, this command causes disassembly to proceed at the jump's destination address. Thus, you can use the disassembler to trace through a program.

B(ack). This causes disassembly of the previous instruction.

C(all). If the instruction just disassembled was a CALL then this instruction causes the first line of the called subroutine to be disassembled. Disassembly proceeds through the subroutine until you give the instruction.

R(eturn). Disassembly proceeds with the statement following the CALL. Subroutines may be nested. Use of the R(eturn) instruction is not limited to when you find the subroutine's RTN instruction. It can be used at any time to return to disassembling the calling program.

P(revious instruction). This command has the disassembler go back 12 bytes, then scan forward to the last instruction before the one you started in, trying to align itself to the correct instruction boundaries. If the code you are disassembling isn't making sense, try this instruction. There is a good chance (although it is not certain) the disassembler will now be properly aligned with the program. Of course, if you are in a region of memory that is full of data, then a glance at the ASCII or the hexadecimal columns should show the structure of the data.

Output Format

The address appears at the left edge, followed by the contents of the location (and the next one or two locations if the disassembler thinks that a multi-byte instruction lives there) in hexadecimal. Next is the ASCII representation of those contents, or underlines if they are not printing characters. This is followed by the assembler mnemonic, and then an asterisk.

Hex Notation

Hex smex! It seems that hex notation is the national language of microprocessors. This is understandable, with two hex digits fitting neatly in an eight-bit byte. But oh, my head, after about 10 minutes of converting front-panel binary into hexadecimal. The obvious solution is a hexadecimal front panel. A hex keyboard is no problem, but the hex display is another matter. It's better to have a little skull sweat in the design stage than the long hours of headache during program debugging.

Table 2-6. Human Readable Hex Characters.

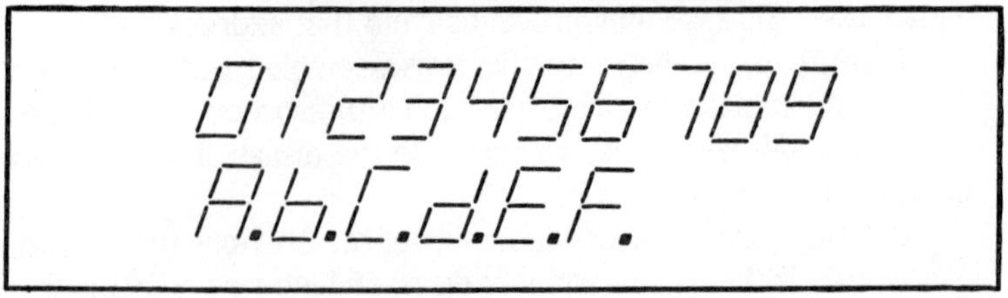

A few minutes of checking prices on hexadecimal readouts proves that their use can be rather expensive. Being the miser that I am, seven-segment displays seem to be the only practical way to go. While most BCD-to-7-segment decoders have unique patterns for the representation of the numbers from 10 through 15, these patterns are almost as difficult to memorize as the binary LED patterns. A little special encoding is required to represent the letters A through F in a human readable form. Table 2-6 shows the proposed character representations for seven-segment displays. These characters are further encoded with the decimal point active for A through F to accent these unusual patterns.

Try as I might, I could not find a standard encoder that so much as comes close to such a pattern. Normally, this situation would call for a 4-to-16 decoder and a handful of diodes to implement such a character generator, but space considerations in my application require a different approach. What is required is a hex-to-seven-segment decoder/driver.

The 8223 is the ideal PROM for such a circuit. Its eight outputs provide control for all segments, including the decimal point. Decod-

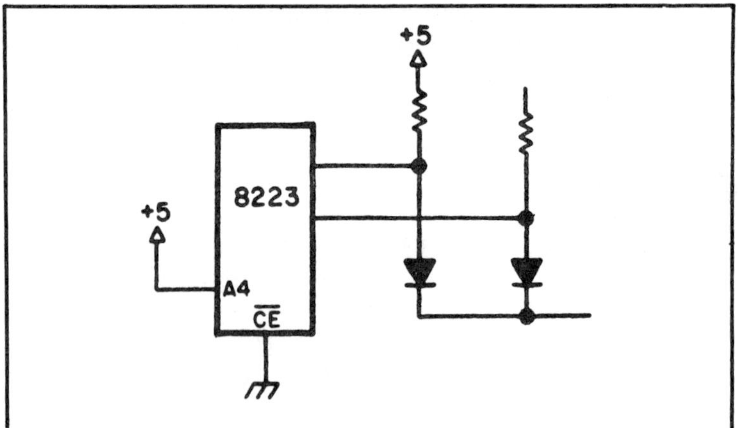

Fig. 2-16. Output connection for common cathode displays.

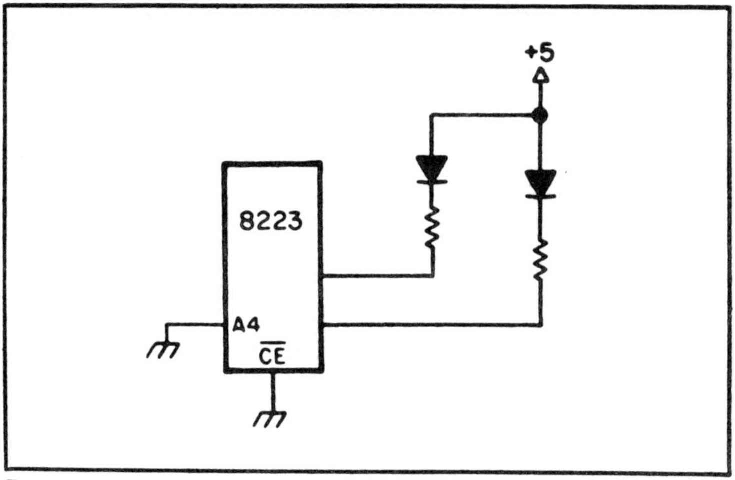

Fig. 2-17. Common anode connection.

ing hexadecimal data uses only 16 of the 32 memory words available in the 8223. By inverting the data for the second 16 words, the encoder is able to drive low or high active seven-segment displays. A0 through A3 define the hex input data, while A4 selects the type of display. With A4 high, the outputs are active high for driving common cathode displays as shown in Fig. 2-16. Figure 2-17 details the common anode connection with A4 active low. The programming code for the 8223 PROM is shown in Table 2-7.

The Bit Explosion

Why settle for eight bits? If you're thinking of building your own microcomputer, take a quick look at what's available before plunging in. For slightly more than what you would expect to pay for an 80-bit CPU chip, you can now get a 12- or 16-bit microprocessor with many more capabilities and features. Those currently available include the 12-bit CMOS chip from Intersil (IM-6100) and Harris Semiconductor (HM-6100) which executes the same instruction set as the Digital Equipment PDP-8/E minicomputer and the 16-bit CPUs from Texas Instruments (TMS-9900), National Semiconductor (PACE) and General Instruments (CP-1600). If you think you're not ready to design your own custom system, several of these companies offer various boards and systems all ready to go.

The 12-Bit 6100

The IM-6100 from Intersil and the HM-6100 from Harris Semiconductor are pin-for-pin compatible 12-bit microprocessors in

Table 2-7. 8223 PROM Encoding Data for Hex-to-Seven-Segment Decoder.

A4	A3	A2	A1	A0	p B7	g B6	f B5	e B4	d B3	c B2	b B1	a B0
0	0	0	0	0	1	1	0	0	0	0	0	0
0	0	0	0	1	1	1	1	1	1	0	0	1
0	0	0	1	0	1	0	1	0	0	1	0	0
0	0	0	1	1	1	0	1	1	0	0	0	0
0	0	1	0	0	1	0	0	1	1	0	0	1
0	0	1	0	1	1	0	0	1	0	0	1	0
0	0	1	1	0	1	0	0	0	0	0	1	0
0	0	1	1	1	1	1	1	1	1	0	0	0
0	1	0	0	0	1	0	0	0	0	0	0	0
0	1	0	0	1	1	0	0	1	0	0	0	0
0	1	0	1	0	0	0	0	0	1	0	0	0
0	1	0	1	1	0	0	0	0	0	0	1	1
0	1	1	0	0	0	0	0	0	0	1	1	0
0	1	1	0	1	0	0	1	0	0	0	0	1
0	1	1	1	0	0	0	0	0	0	1	1	0
0	1	1	1	1	0	0	0	0	1	1	1	0
1	0	0	0	0	0	0	1	1	1	1	1	1
1	0	0	0	1	0	0	0	0	0	1	1	0
1	0	0	1	0	0	1	0	1	1	0	1	1
1	0	0	1	1	0	1	0	0	1	1	1	1
1	0	1	0	0	0	1	1	0	0	1	1	0
1	0	1	0	1	0	1	1	0	1	1	0	1
1	0	1	1	0	0	1	1	1	1	1	0	1
1	0	1	1	1	0	0	0	0	0	1	1	1
1	1	0	0	0	0	1	1	1	1	1	1	1
1	1	0	0	1	0	1	1	0	1	1	1	1
1	1	0	1	0	1	1	1	1	0	1	1	1
1	1	0	1	1	1	1	1	1	1	1	0	0
1	1	1	0	0	1	1	1	1	1	0	0	1
1	1	1	0	1	1	1	0	1	1	1	1	0
1	1	1	1	0	1	1	1	1	1	0	0	1
1	1	1	1	1	1	1	1	1	0	0	0	1

40 pin dual-in-line packages. Both recognize the standard instruction set of the Digital Equipment PDP-8/E minicomputer but cannot accept the Extended Arithmetic Element (EAE) or User Flag (UF) options. Normal memory addressing capacity is only 4K but may be extended to 32K via an Extended Memory Control element. The bus structure of the 6100 can be adapted to provide a subset of the PDP-8/E OMNIBUS signals allowing all PDP-8(E *programmed I/O* interfaces to operate with the 6100 without hardware of software modifications.

The CMOS processor chip requires only a single voltage supply between 4 and 11 volts and is TTL compatible with a 5V supply. There is a built-in crystal controlled oscillator, for system timing, with a maximum frequency of 8 MHz with selected versions of the chip. All control signals are produced by the CPU chip and can interface with up to 64 separate I/O devices with PDP-8/E compatible interfaces. Other features include single clock/single instruction capabilities, Direct Memory Access (which is not PDP-8 compatible), interrupt and dedicated control panel features.

The 6100 does require slightly more support hardware than the simpler 8-bit microprocessors, but its software compatibility with the PDP-8 should make the extra effort well worthwhile. Over a thousand fully developed and documented programs are available from Digital Equipment Corporation, Software Distribution Center, 146 Main Street, Maynard MA 01754. Other user generated programs are available from the DEC User's Society (DECUS) at Parker Street, Mail Stop PK-3/E55, Maynard MA 01754. Besides the usual loaders, assemblers, editors and other utility programs, you can also get various versions of BASIC and FOCAL or even a complete PDP-8 operating system software package. For added troubleshooting convenience, the complete set of processor, memory and terminal diagnostic programs for the DEC PDP-8 can also be used with the 6100. This last feature, the ability to run various diagnostic programs, is lacking in most microprocessors/microcomputers currently available.

The 16-Bit Offerings

The TMS-9900 from Texas Instruments provides a unique approach in micro-system design using a memory to memory architecture with multiple register files resident in memory, similar to some large scale computers. It's available as a single chip, a complete board (similar to the DEC SLI-11) or a complete system. Each has hardware multiply and divide as a standard feature. The rather large 64 pin dual-in-line package requires ±5V and +12V supplies along with a four-phase 3 MHz clock. Figure 2-18 gives a block diagram of the internal architecture of the TMS-9900.

The maximum addressable memory space is 64K 8-bit bytes or 32K 16-bit words. The first 64 words of memory are reserved for interrupt and trap vectors while the last two memory words are used for the LOAD signal trap vector. The remaining memory space may be used for programs, data or workspace registers as desired.

The only three internal hardware registers accessible to the user are the program counter (PC), the status register (ST) and the

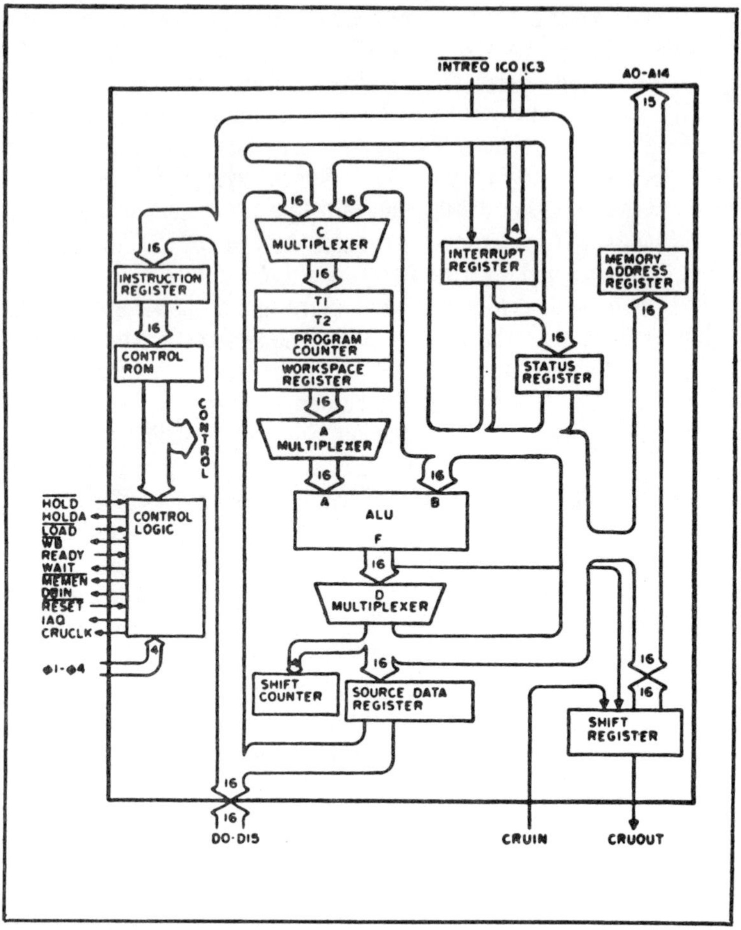

Fig. 2-18. TMS-9900 block diagram.

workspace pointer (WP). The workspace pointer points to the starting address of a 16 register workspace resident anywhere in the external memory space. Each workspace register is addressed by an offset from the current workspace pointer, and the various registers may be used as desired except for a few that have fixed uses as part of subroutine and interrupt linkage conventions.

The CPU provides up to 16 different interrupt level with level ϕ reserved for the RESET function. A built-in Communications Register Unit (CRU) allows up to 4096 I/O bits in fields of 1 to 16 bits in a unique command-driven I/O interface. This interface allows implementing interfaces with exactly the right number of data bits required for a particular application. Other timing and control signals

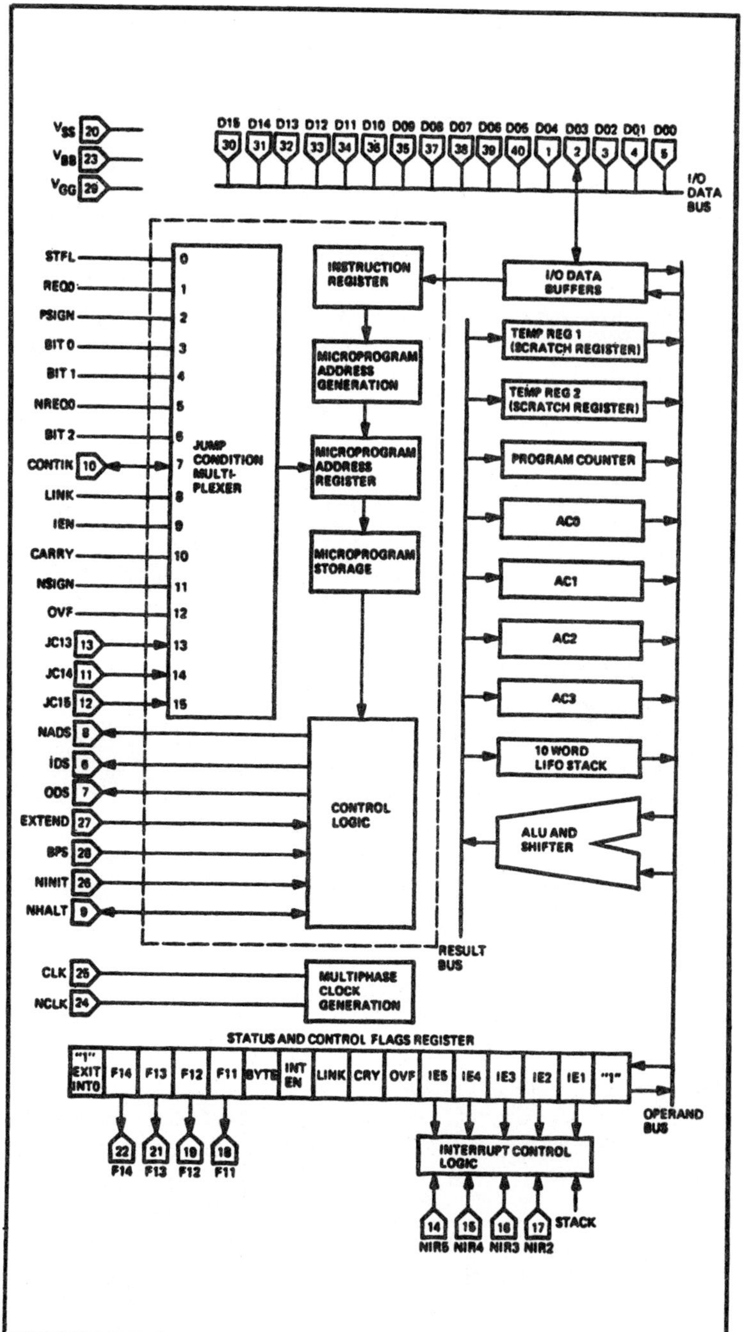

Fig. 2-19. PACE microprocessor functional block diagram.

provide capabilities for ROM loaders, front panel service, CPU hold, slow memory cycles and DMA transfers. Of the 66 general instructions, five provide a means of initiating user implemented external functions for special applications.

Figure 2-19 shows a block diagram of the PACE microprocessor from National Semiconductor, a 16-bit microprocessor in a 40 pin dual-in-line package. The PACE provides for 16-bit general purpose working registers along with a 16-bit status and control flag register that automatically preserves the system status. Return addresses for subroutines and interrupt servicing are automatically saved on a 10 word last-in, first-out stack which may be expanded through software via stack full/stack empty interrupt routines. There is a six level, vectored priority interrupt system with individual interrupt enables in the status register for each level as well as a master interrupt enable for the five lower levels as a group. For direct processor status and control functions, there are four sense inputs and four control flag outputs to the CPU chip itself.

The instruction set consists of 45 instructions in eight classes. Memory reference instructions utilize an addressing scheme that provides three floating memory pages and one fixed memory page of 256 words (16-bit) each. The maximum addressable memory size is 64K words of 16 bits each.

Several support chips are available for PACE which are designed to interface directly with the microprocessor chip and thus simplify system design. The System Timing Element (STE) provides the required MOS clock signals as well as an optional TTL clock. The Bi-directional Transceiver Element (BTE) provides single chip, 8-bit I/O buffering between TTL devices and the PACE MOS I/O lines. The remaining support chips include an Address Latch Element (ALE) and an Interface Latch Element (ILE) that may be needed for more complex systems.

For more complete information, sample system diagram and applications, refer to the PACE Technical Description available from National Semiconductor (publication #4200078A).

The CP-1600 from General Instruments is a single 40 pin chip, 16-bit MOS LSI microprocessor that closely resembles a Digital Equipment PDP-11 in architecture (Fig. 2-20). There are eight general purpose, 16-bit registers with R6 reserved as the stack pointer (SP) and R7 as the program counter (PC) just as in the PDP-11. Unlimited stack depth and self-identifying nested interrupt and subroutine capabilities are provided by the stack pointer in conjunction with external RAM memory.

Instruction execution times range from 1.6 to 4.8 microseconds with a 2-phase, 5 MHz clock. Four addressing modes combined with a 16-bit word length allow direct addressing of 64K bytes or 32K words of memory or peripheral devices. Memory and peripheral interfaces are intermixed in the same address space as desired, and all I/O operations may use any of the 87 available general purpose instructions. For special applications, the Branch on External Condition (BEXT) instruction allows direct testing of up to 16 external digital signals.

The main difference between the CP-1600 and the PDP-11 is that the CP-1600 instruction word format is only 10 bits long in the lower order bit positions of a 16-bit processor word. The higher order 6 bits are ignored; thus only 10-bit wide ROM memory is needed where ultimate ROM bit efficiency is desired for particular applications.

For complete information on the CP-1600 CPU chip showing timing diagrams, programming information and system configurations, the Series 1600 Microprocessor System Documentation is available from General Instruments for $20.

You can readily see that the microprocessor world is not limited to simple 8-bit systems and that some of the larger chips are very attractive from the hobbyist point of view in building a new system from the ground up. The prices currently range from about $30 to over $100 in small quantities, but should continue to drop as more interest develops and second-sourcing becomes more common.

So why build an 8-bit machine and wish you could do more, when 12 or 16-bit CPUs are currently available at reasonable prices with many expanded features? Keep in mind that the larger word size machines make higher-level languages more powerful and easier to implement if you don't intend to write all your programs in machine language—and who in their right mind would?

Z-80 Quality at a Good Price

With the price of hobby computer equipment going from expensive to overpriced and, lately, to outrageous, I have been home brewing most of my computer equipment. This makes it more affordable, as the price of the components plus the cost of a wire-wrap Altair S-100 card is usually a small fraction of the price of the equivalent kit. I have designed and built a complete Altair S-100 bus computer for about $100-150 less CPU card. This computer has all the panel functions of a commercial machine, such as the IMSAI, and performs equally. It was originally designed to use the somewhat obsolete 8080 CPU card that was removed from my other computer

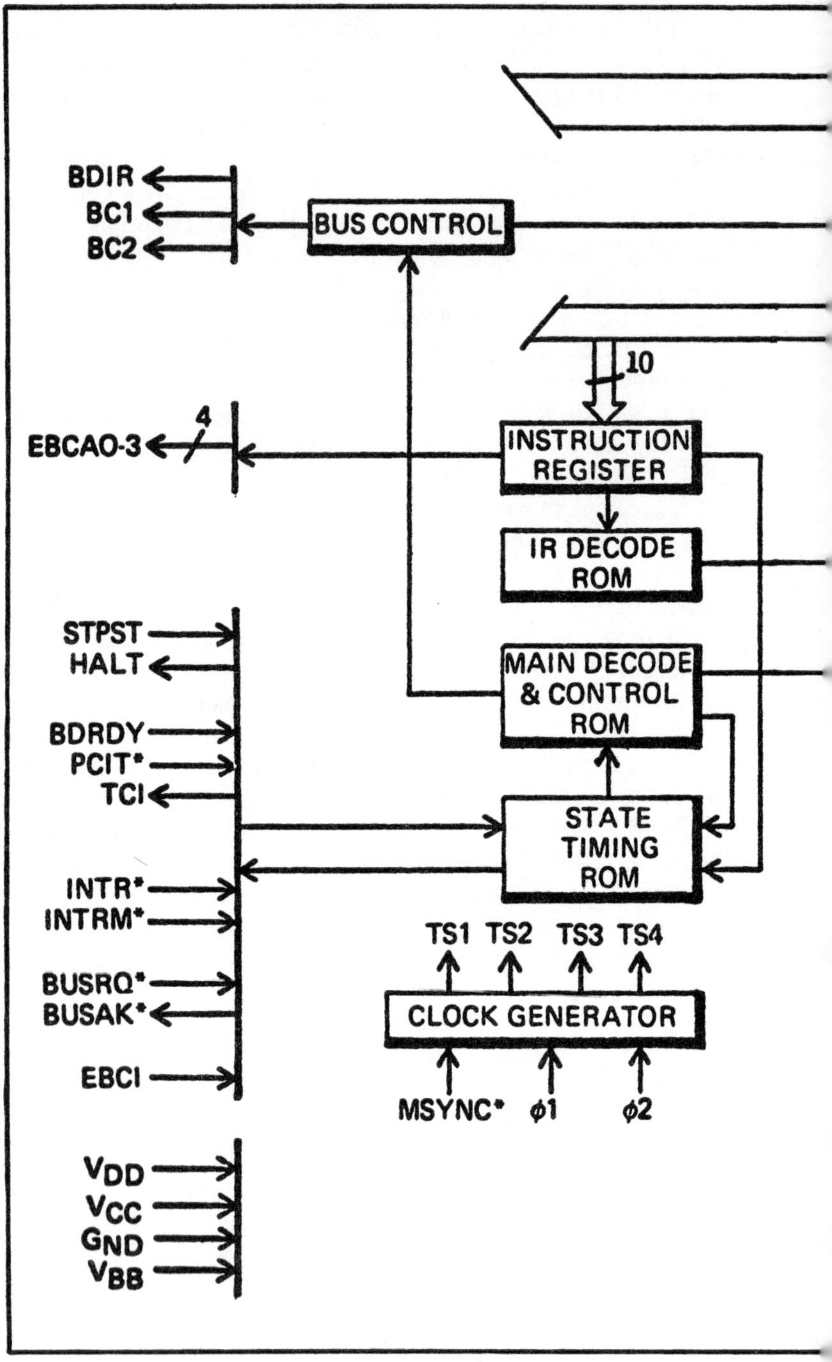
BDIR
BC1
BC2
BUS CONTROL
10
4
EBCAO-3
INSTRUCTION REGISTER
IR DECODE ROM
STPST
HALT
MAIN DECODE & CONTROL ROM
BDRDY
PCIT*
TCI
STATE TIMING ROM
INTR*
INTRM*
TS1
TS2
TS3
TS4
BUSRQ*
BUSAK*
CLOCK GENERATOR
EBCI
MSYNC*
φ1
φ2
VDD
VCC
GND
VBB

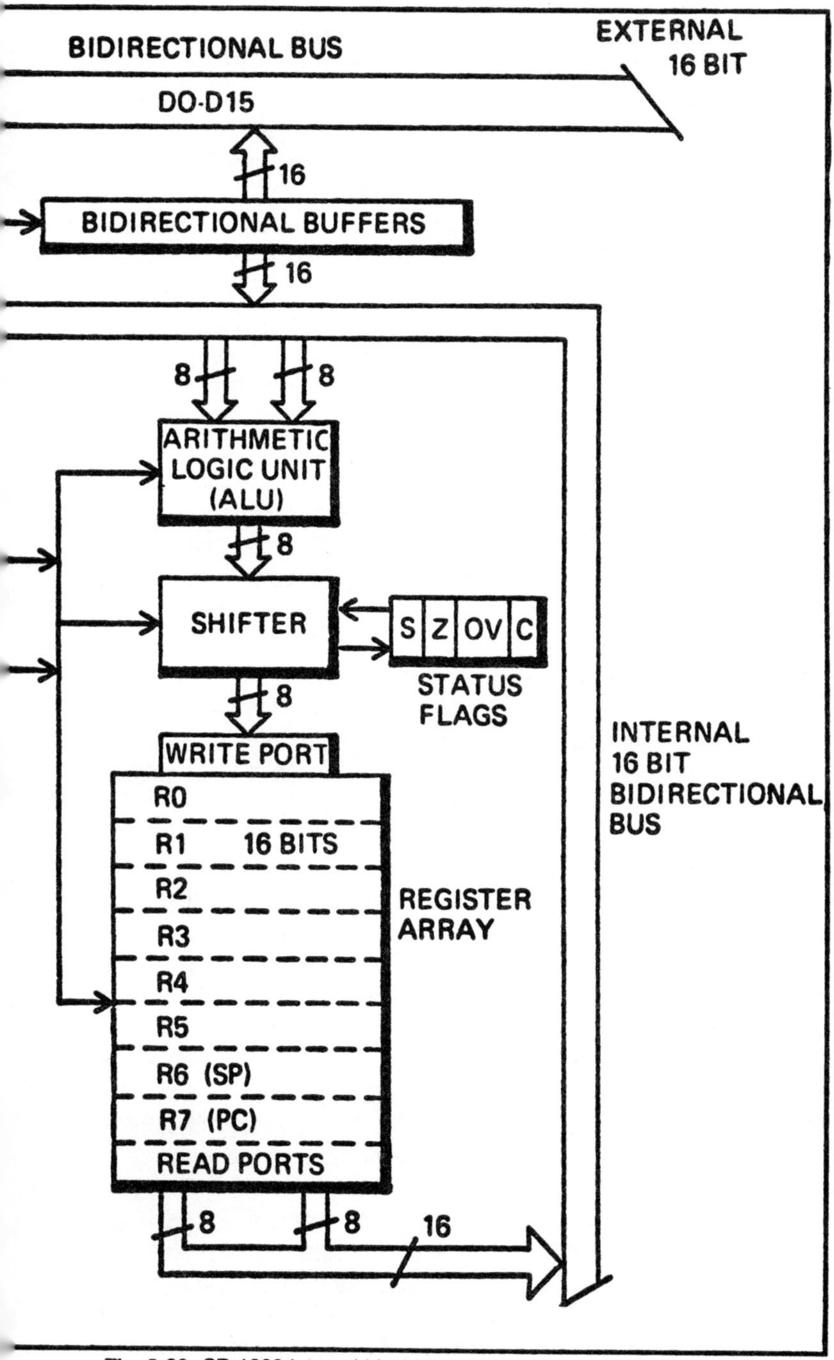

Fig. 2-20. CP-1600 internal block diagram.

when I changed over to a Z-80. However, as anyone who has ever used both chips can tell you, once you have used a Z-80 you will not be able to tolerate the poor instruction set and processing ineffiency of the 8080. About that time I saw an ad for the $149.95 Z-80 CPU card from S.D. Sales. It was fantastic and was at a price that was less than my first Z-80 card cost to build. Of course, the price of the Z-80 had dropped somewhat since I built my first card, but the price was still around the current cost of parts to build a card, so I ordered one.

Having built several microcomputer kits, and lived with poor documentation, poor quality boards, idiotic designs that were very hard to change, etc., I didn't really know what to expect at such a low price. But, past experience with S. D. Sales on parts orders had shown me that they were reputable, quick and generally offered a good value with prime quality parts. This still did not completely prepare me for the surprise that I got when I opened the package.

The PC board was one of the best quality boards I have ever seen. Fully solder masked, high quality plating, plated through holes—everything! The design was really superb—two 5V regulators with heat sinks (most CPUs really need two as the current required for all the buffers really heats one), heavy power buses with a fantastic ground plane, silver mica caps, precut, preformed resistors (most resistors and caps were precut, preformed and ready to insert in the PC board), a very thick book on the design, software and hardware differences between the Z-80 and 8080, complete instructions for assembly and a Z-80 manual. The ICs were all prime quality with very recent date codes. All of the component values (part numbers) were screened exceptionally clearly on the component side of the board, and the IC numbers and component numbers are still visible after installing sockets and components.

The actual assembly of the board was one of the easiest and quickest assemblies of PC boards I've ever done. The instructions were excellent, and the preformed leads and clear screening made everything fall together. One or two resistor locations were somewhat obscure, as they did not wind up in the general numeric order of most of the parts and required a little searching. But there were only a couple of these, and they were solved after a few seconds of searching.

I popped the board into the computer and powered it up. Everything worked beautifully the first time, and with no problems. I did have to make one minor modification to my VDM board (involving the bending of one pin on an IC) before I could initialize the screen. This was mentioned in the Z-80 manual that S. D. Sales provides (the kit manual), but I wanted to try it first to see if it was really necessary. They also mention a few modifications and changes (all very minor) to other boards to get them to work with the Z-80. This is necessary in the case of the VDM because of the timing difference between the Z-80 and 8080 (the Z-80 is in most cases faster). However, it works fine, and it was really thoughtful of S. D. Sales to point all of these differences out. (This is an example of the thorough and complete attention to detail and documentation that is typical of everything involved with the kit.) It is one of the truly fantastic bargains still available on the hobby microcomputer market today.

Speaking of fantastic bargains, S. D. Sales also makes a 4k low power memory board for the Altair S-100 bus that is an equal bargain, in that it has the same quality parts, is equally well documented, easy to build and costs less than the components to wire-wrap one. This is another well-designed, well-implemented piece of hardware. The board uses four regulators and runs very cool. Fast memory chips and good design allow super fast board access time. (The board has no provisions for wait states but works perfectly with a Z-80 CPU running at almost 3 MHz, which is far in excess of specs.) There are sockets for everything. Run to the nearest phone and order a dozen or so right away, before they come to their senses and raise the price to what it should be. At $89.95 you are robbing them blind.

The combination of the CPU and memory gives you the basis for a really super home brew computer with the addition of a panel, back-plane and power supply. This will give you a complete machine, with a Z-80, 16K of reliable, low power STATIC memory and full I/O for about the cost of a bare IMSAI or the same with video output capability for the cost (or slightly less) of an Altair (the case, panel, 8080 CPU and power supply and nothing else).

The Cosmac Connection

A simple 90-byte program can turn your Cosmac microcomputer into an excellent automatic keyer for sending Morse code. It features automatic dash and dot completion, dash and dot memories, adjustable dash:dot ratio, automatic letter spacing, iambic or squeeze keying and adjustable speed from 5 wpm to 80 wpm.

Equipment Required

You will need the Cosmac microcomputer fashioned around the CDP1802CD CPU by RCA. The program requires 90 bytes of memory. In addition, you will need some ICs and perhaps a transistor or relay in order to interface the computer with your transmitter. The program was written for a clock frequency of 1 MHz, but it can be modified for other clock frequencies quite easily.

How the Program Works

After setting subroutine counters and memory pointers, the first thing the program does is convert the code speed entered via the keyboard into hexadecimal form. The program assumes the code speed will be less than 100 wpm. An example will illustrate the method best. Suppose you enter 35 as your desired speed. The program converts this to base 16 by repeatedly subtracting 10_{16} from it until the remainder is less than 10_{16}. In this case,

$$35_{16} - 10_{16} = 25_{16}$$
$$25_{16} - 10_{16} = 15_{16}$$
$$15_{16} - 10_{16} = 05_{16}$$

Each time a subtraction is performed, OA is added to R1, and, finally, the remainder is added to R1. In this case R1 = OA + OA + OA + 05 = 23_{16}. This completes the conversion, 35 wpm = 23_{16}.

Next, I derive a number which is proportional to the length of one dot. Since the length of a dot is inversely proportional to the code speed, I calculate OOF7/code speed in hex form and store the quotient in M(000A). This number sets the length of a timing loop in making a dot. Two times this number is used for letter spacing, and three times this number is used for the dash length. Actually, during execution of the program, a dot or dash is automatically followed by a space of one dot, and, if a letter space of two dots is added to this, you get effectively a letter space equal to the length of three dots.

Spaces were left at M(0048) and M(0049) to enable you to increase the length of the dashes. By inserting the instruction F4 at M(0048), the dashes will be four times the dot length. If you also put F4 at M(0049), the dashes will be five times the dot length. This will change the speed of the code, of course.

The dash length is stored in M(000C), and, since it cannot exceed FF, this restricts the maximum dot length at M(000A) to 1/5 of FF if you use a 1:5 dot-to-dash ratio. This, in turn, places a maximum value on the numerator of the formula quoted earlier, 00F7/code speed in hex form. So, summing up, the number 00F7 was chosen to allow code speeds as low as 5 wpm without exceeding a dash time of FF at M(000C). At M(0036), provision is made for changing this numerator to 01F7 or 02F7, if desired. This is useful when operation will consistently be at high code speeds and when finer resolution is required in the code speed. For example, with the program as is, you get the same speed of code whether you enter 25,

26 or 27 wpm. The speed changes at 28 wpm, but remains at this new speed whether you enter 28, 29 or 30. The problem is accentuated at very high speeds. For example, you get the same speed of code for all entries between 62 and 81 wpm.

The rest of the program is straightforward and is understood best by looking at the flowchart. The key is connected to $\overline{EF1}$ and $\overline{EF2}$. Closing the dot side makes EF1 = 1. Closing the dash side makes EF2 = 1. The program periodically checks the status of these inputs, and the dots and dashes come out on the Q-line, which is interfaced with the transmitter as described later.

The subroutine in the program in simply a timed loop using registers R1 and R2. The initial value of R2 is set before entering the subroutine according to the length of delay required, whether a dot, dash or letter space in being generated. At a code speed of 24 wpm,

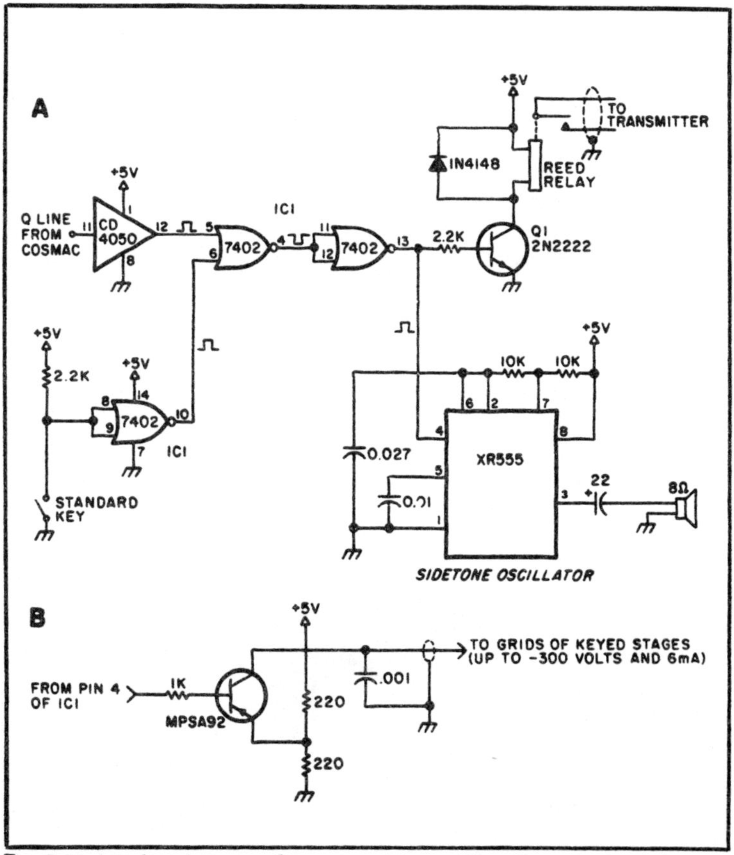

Fig. 2-21. Interface between Cosmac and transmitter; alternate circuit for rigs with grid-blocked keying eliminates relay and Q1.

you should get 10 dots per second. For a 1:3 dot:dash ratio, the length of a dot at 24 wpm should be 50 ms. Accordingly, the values of R1.1 and R1.0 were set at M(009C) and M(009F) so that the dots are the correct length at this speed. They will automatically be the correct length at other speeds because the number in R2 is proportional to the code speed. The values chosen for R1.0 and R1.1 assumed a clock frequency of 1 MHz. It should be a simple matter to adjust these figures for different clock frequencies, although I have not tried anything but a 1 MHz clock.

Interface Circuitry

The connection of the computer to the transmitter is shown in Fig. 2-21. It includes a sidetone oscillator for monitoring your code and also an input for a hand key which I like to use when tuning up the transmitter or when the computer is programmed as an automatic message generator instead of an automatic keyer. Figure 2-22 shows the method used to connect the key to the computer.

If your transmitter is running more than a few watts, you must be careful that your wiring does not pick up rf in your workshop. If it does, it may upset the logic gates, and you'll find that, once the first dot or dash is sent, the transmitter might not shut off. This rules out any long dangling wires running across your desk in front of your transmitter! For best results, use a shielded enclosure and bypass the leads to the transmitter and key with 0.001 uF ceramic capacitors.

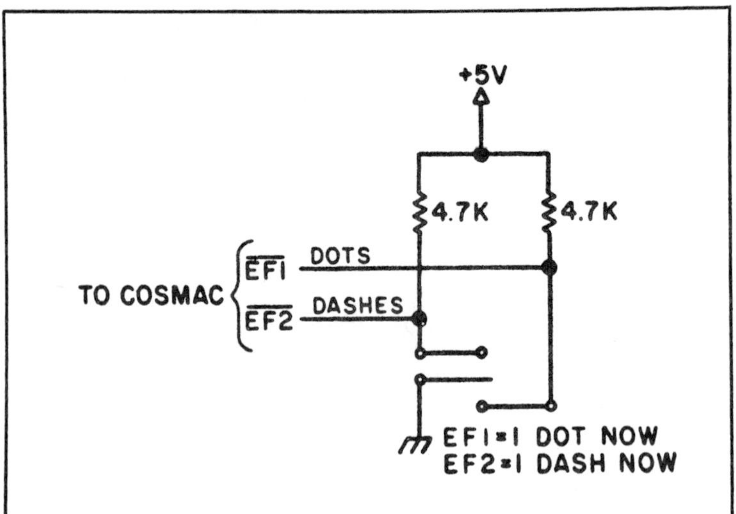

Fig. 2-22. Key connections.

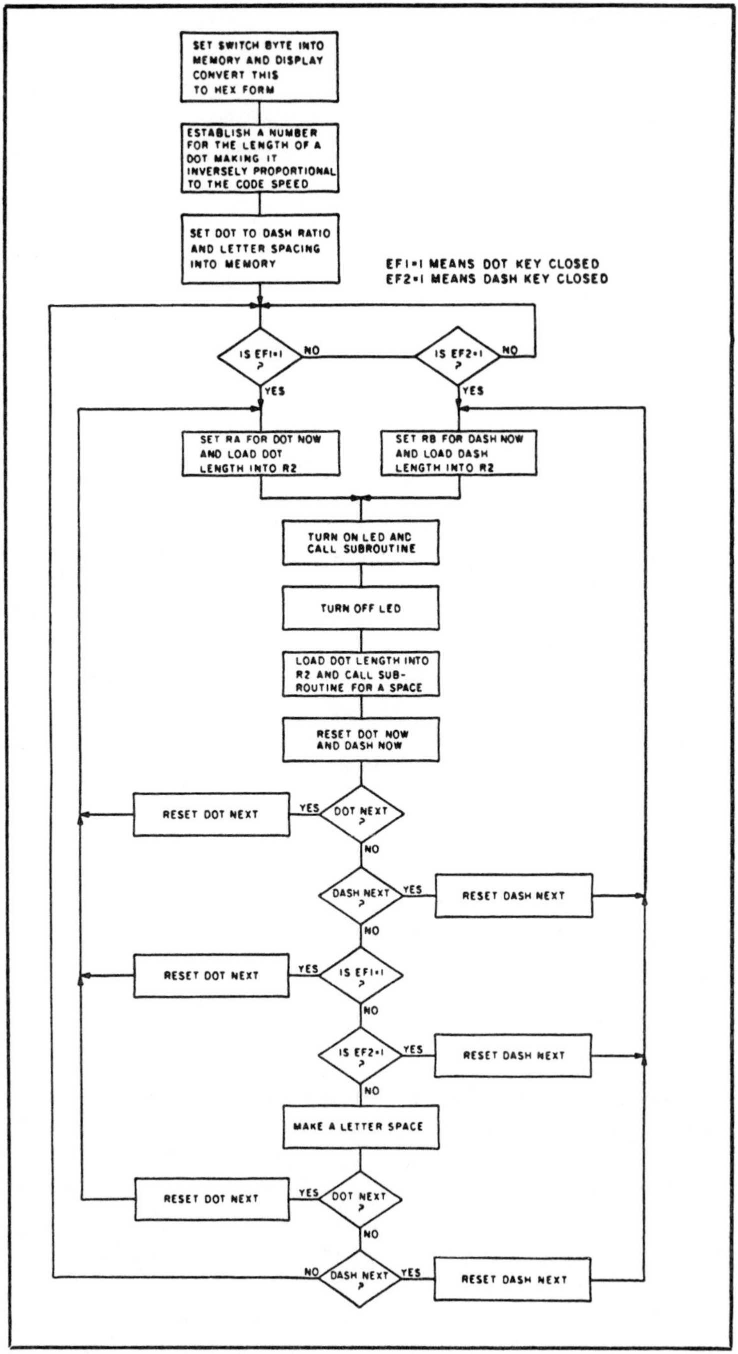

Fig. 2-23. Flowchart for automatic keyer.

Using the Keyer

Enter the program shown (Figs. 2-23, 2-24 and Tables 2-8, 2-9) and, before setting the computer to *run*, enter the desired code speed from the front panel. Set the computer to *run*, and your speed will be displayed on the hex display. To change the speed, just set the switches on the front panel to the new speed and flick the run switch off and then on. Some people find the automatic letter space a bit awkward at first, probably because their fist, like mine, has become a little sloppy over the years. To eliminate automatic letter spacing, enter the instruction C4 at M(007F). C4 means no operation, and the subroutine normally called at that location does not get called.

Program Your Way To CW Happiness

Now you can reduce operator fatigue in that next CW contest by storing commonly used messages in your microcomputer, all ready to be sent automatically at the flick of a switch. Imagine relaxing in your armchair . . . you reach over to your computer, flick a switch, and out comes CQ FD CQ FD DE VE3CWY/3K. No answers? Flick the switch again for a repeat. You've got somebody. You casually call him with your hand key, W1XXX. Then push another button on the computer and presto! Out comes DE VE3CWY/3 QTH HR IS . . . You wait until it's finished. The code is the best you've ever heard. Now how much simpler could things get? Not much, unless you also have an automatic Morse decoder, too! Of course, you don't have to be a contest operator to use this little gem. We use it now for many regular QSOS to put out the initial CQ and to send the first message, which, for most people, is simply a signal report, QTH and operator's name.

This Cosmac microcomputer constructed around the CDP1802CD CPU is used with 256 bytes of RAM of which 105 bytes are used for the main program, the rest being used for storage of the messages. Program timing assumes a clock frequency of 1 MHz, but it is easily adapted for other clock frequencies. The byte stored in M(0004) is selected initially by the operator from Table 2-10. This byte sets the length of a dot and hence sets the speed of the code. The program triples this to get a number that will represent the length of a dash; this is stored in R6.0. Four times the dot byte represents a word space, and this byte is stored in R7.0. Actually, this space gets added to the usual space of three dots that follows every letter so that the actual space between words is equal to seven dots. These bytes are later used to specify the length of a timed loop and thereby set the length of all the dots, dashes and spaces.

The program fetches the first byte of the programmed message from M(0069). It is 45, which stands for the letter C, as you can see from Table 2-11. The first digit, 4, is the total number of dots and dashes in the letter. The second digit, 5, specifies the order in which the dots and dashes appear. Taking C as the example, —.—. can be represented in binary form by 0101, where the 0 represents a dot and the 1 represents a dash. This is the binary code for the number

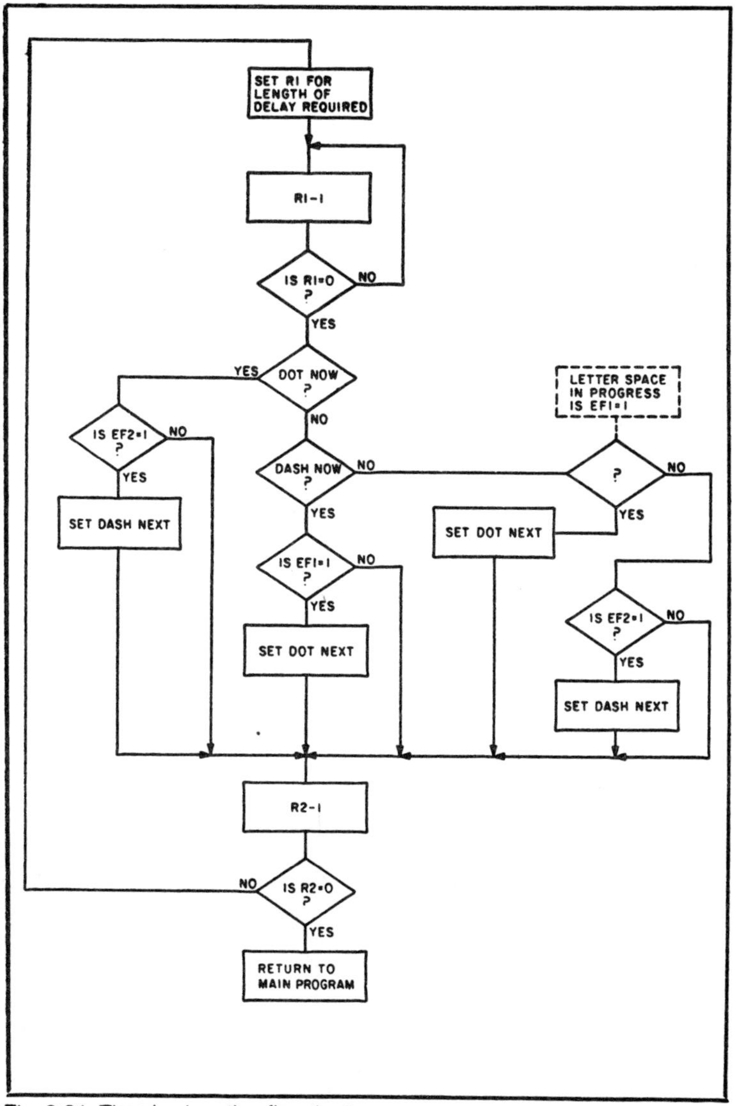

Fig. 2-24. Timed subroutine flowchart.

Table 2-8. Program Listing. Title: Automatic Keyer.

Address	Bytes	Comment
0000	F8	0D→D set main program counter
0001	0D	
0002	A3	D→R3·0
0003	F8	9B→D set subroutine counter
0004	9B	
0005	A4	D→R4·0
0006	C4	no operation; leaves space for setting up
0007	C4	additional subroutine counter
0008	C4	
0009	D3	3→P go to main program
000A		dot time
000B		letter space time
000C		dash time
000D	F8	0A→D
000E	0A	
000F	A5	D→R5·0 R5·0 = 0A
0010	F8	0B→D
0011	0B	
0012	A6	D→R6·0 R6·0 = 0B
0013	F8	0C→D
0014	0C	
0015	A7	D→R7·0 R7·0 = 0C
0016	F8	01→D
0017	01	
0018	AA	D→RA·0
0019	AB	D→RB·0
001A	AC	D→RC·0
001B	AD	D→RD·0
001C	E7	7→X
001D	6C	input switch byte → MX, D
001E	64	MX→display, RX + 1
001F	27	R7-1
0020	F8	00→D start decimal to hex conversion
0021	00	
0022	A1	D→R1·0 sets R1·0 = 00
0023	F0	MX→D
0024	FF	D-10→D, carry→DF
0025	10	
0026	3B	Go to 2F if DF = 0
0027	2F	(if number is less than 10)
0028	57	D→M7 place remainder in M7
0029	81	R1·0→D
002A	FC	0A + D→D
002B	0A	ADD 0A to R1
002C	A1	D→R1·0
002D	30	Go to 23
002E	23	
002F	81	R1·0→D
0030	F4	MX + D→D
0031	55	D→M5 conversion complete

Address	Bytes	Comment
0032	E5	5→X
0033	F8	00→D routine to set dot timing
0034	00	
0035	A2	D→R2·0
0036	F8	01→D
0037	01	
0038	A1	D→R1·0
0039	F8	F5→D limits minimum speed to 5 wpm
003A	F5	
003B	F7	D-MX→D, carry→DF
003C	12	R2 + 1 R2 accumulates quotient
003D	33	go to 3B if DF = 1
003E	3B	
003F	21	R1-1
0040	81	R1·0→D
0041	3A	go to 39 if D ≠ 00
0042	39	
0043	82	R2·0→D
0044	55	D→M5
0045	F4	MX + D→D
0046	56	D→M6
0047	F4	D + MX→D
0048	C4	no operation
0049	C4	no operation
004A	57	D→M7 conversion complete
004B	34	go to 57 if EF1 = 1 (dot now)
004C	57	
004D	3D	go to 4B if EF2 = 0 (no dash either)
004E	4B	
004F	F8	00→D dash now
0050	00	
0051	AB	D→RB·0
0052	47	M7→D R7 + 1
0053	27	R7-1
0054	A2	D→R2·0
0055	30	go to 5D and make dash
0056	5D	
0057	F8	00→D dot now
0058	00	
0059	AA	D→RA·0
005A	45	M5→D R5 + 1
005B	25	R5-1
005C	A2	D→R2·0
005D	7B	1→Q light on
005E	D4	4→P call subroutine for a delay
005F	7A	0→Q light off
0060	45	M5→D R5 + 1
0061	25	R5-1
0062	A2	D→R2·0
0063	D4	4→P call subroutine for delay = 1 dot
0064	F8	01→D

Table 2-9. Register Assignments.

0065	01	
0066	AA	D→RA·0 reset dot now
0067	AB	D→RB·0 reset dash now
0068	8C	RC·0→D
0069	3A	go to 70 if D ≠ 00
006A	70	(no dot next)
006B	F8	01→D
006C	01	
006D	AC	D→RC·0 reset dot next
006E	30	go to 57 and make dot
006F	57	
0070	8D	RD·0→D dash next?
0071	3A	go to 78 if D ≠ 00
0072	78	(no dash next either)
0073	F8	01→D
0074	01	reset dash next
0075	AD	D→RD·0
0076	30	go to 4F and make a dash
0077	4F	
0078	34	go to 90 if EF1 = 1 and make a dot
0079	90	
007A	35	go to 95 if EF2 = 1 and make a dash
007B	95	
007C	46	M6→D, M6 + 1 no dot or dash now
007D	26	R6-1
007E	A2	D→R2·0
007F	D4	call subroutine for letter space
0080	8C	RC·0→D dot next?
0081	3A	go to 88 if D ≠ 00
0082	88	no dot next
0083	F8	01→D
0084	01	
0085	AC	D→RC·0 reset dot next
0086	30	go to 57 and make dot
0087	57	
0088	8D	RD·0→D dash next?
0089	3A	go to 4B if D ≠ 00
008A	4B	no dash either
008B	F8	01→D
008C	01	
008D	AD	D→RD·0 reset dash next
008E	30	go to 4F and make dash
008F	4F	
0900	F8	01→D
0091	01	
0092	AC	D→RC·0
0093	30	go to 57 and make a dot
0094	57	
0095	F8	01→D
0096	01	
0097	AD	D→RD·0

Table 2-9. Register Assignments.

0098	30	go to 4F and make a dash
0099	4F	
009A	D3	3→P return to main program
009B	F8	01→D start subroutine
009C	01	
009D	B1	D→R1·1
009E	F8	58→D fine adjustment of dot length
009F	58	
00A0	A1	D→R1·0
00A1	21	R1-1
00A2	91	R1·1→D
00A3	3A	go to A1 if D ≠ 00
00A4	A1	
00A5	8A	RA·0→D dot now?
00A6	3A	go to AF if D ≠ 00
00A7	AF	
00A8	3D	go to BD if EF2 = 0
00A9	BD	(no dash next)
00AA	F8	00→D
00AB	00	
00AC	AD	D→RD·0 set dash next
00AD	30	
00AE	BD	
00AF	8B	RB·0→D dash now?
00B0	3A	go to B9 if D ≠ 00
00B1	B9	(if no dash now either)
00B2	3C	go to BD if EF1 = 0
00B3	BD	
00B4	F8	00→D
00B5	00	
00B6	AC	D→RC·0 set dot next
00B7	30	go to BD
00B8	BD	
00B9	34	go to B4 if EF1 = 1
00BA	B4	
00BB	35	go to AA if EF2 = 1
00BC	AA	
00BD	22	R2-1
00BE	82	R2·0→D
00BF	3A	go to 9B if D ≠ 00
00C0	9B	
00C1	30	go to 9A
00C2	9A	end of subroutine

R1, R2—part of timing loop and used for decimal to hex conversion
R3—main program counter
R4—subroutine counter
R5—memory pointer for dot length
R6—memory pointer for letter space
R7—memory pointer for dash length
RA = 00 if dot now — RC = 00 if dot next
RB = 00 if dash now — RD = 00 if dash next

5. So byte 45 tells the computer the order of dots and dashes and the number of dots and dashes in the letter. To actually generate the code —.—., the number 0101 is stored in the D-register. D is shifted right giving 0010, and the 1 that peels off the right end of the number tells the computer to send a dash first. D is shifted right again, giving 0001; this time, a 0 peels off the right end, producing a dot. A third shift gives 0000, pushing a 1 off the right end, thus making a dash. A fourth shift gives 0000, pushing a 0 off the right end; this makes the final dot. The computer stops shifting D now because the 4 in byte 45 tells it to make only 4 shifts. A letter space is then generated and the next byte is fetched from M(006A).

Since there are no letters that have more than 4 dots and dashes in total, the order of dots and dashes in any letter can be represented by four binary digits or one hex digit. The numbers, punctuation, and other special characters listed in Table 2-11 contain 5 or more dots and dashes. To handle each of these, two bytes are required. The first specifies the total number of dots and dashes, while the second specifies the order in which they occur.

The rest of the program is easy to follow from the flowchart. Two special bytes were set up. One is EE, which calls for a word space; the other is FF, which halts the program until the input button connected to EF4 is depressed.

Using the Program

Select the code speed desired from Table 2-10 and store this byte at M(0004). Table 2-10 was constructed assuming a clock frequency of 1 MHz. If your crystal is not 1 MHz, simply experiment a little with different hex bytes to get the different speeds. The code speed varies inversely with the size of byte.

After entering the main program, decide on the messages you want and select from Table 2-11 the bytes for each letter, number or punctuation. Note that the numbers and punctuation require two bytes each. Terminate each message with FF so that the program will halt. To initiate one of the messages, enter the memory address of its byte from the front panel of the computer using the toggle switches. Turn on the run switch. When the message terminates,

Table 2-10. Hex Byte for Code Speed.

Speed (wpm)	5	7	10	13	16	20	25	30	35	40
Hex code	3F	2D	1F	17	13	0F	0C	0A	09	08

Table 2-11. Hex Codes for Letters and Punctuation.

One-byte characters

A	22	N	21
B	41	0	37
B	41	0	37
C	45	P	46
D	31	Q	4B
E	10	R	32
F	44	S	30
G	33	T	11
H	40	U	34
I	20	V	48
J	4E	W	36
K	35	X	49
L	42	Y	4D
M	23	Z	43
word space	EE		
stop	FF		

Two-byte characters

1	50	1E	.	60	2A
2	50	IC	,	60	33
3	50	18	?	60	0C
4	50	10	/	50	09
5	50	00	double dash	50	11
6	50	01	end of message	50	0A
7	50	03	end of work	60	28
8	50	07	wait	50	02
9	50	0F			
0	50	1F			

you can make it carry on with the next stored message by pressing the input button which is connected to EF4. This way, you can have pauses inserted in messages to allow you to enter a signal report or callsign manually.

The 7400 Quad NAND Gate

Even a experimenter considers himself somewhat knowledgeable on digital logic can be confused when he glances at a new logic circuit for the first time. Though the logic elements involved in any particular circuit are seemingly simple to understand, their interconnection with other elements and devices often tends to make the circuit as a whole confusing to the point of incomprehensibility, especially to the inexperienced. Circuit analysis is also further complicated when logic devices are utilized to perform functions other than that for which they were primarily intended. Unfortunately, these sources of confusion often appear formidable enough to discourage some of the less experienced experimenters from experimenting with digital logic circuits.

Some of the mystery about the many uses of one of the most basic logic elements, the two-input NAND gate, will now be dispelled. In addition to explaining its primary function, it will be shown how it may be connected to perform the functions of an inverter, a set-reset flip flop, a switch debouncer, a pulse shaper, a square wave oscillator and even a crystal oscillator. In spite of the rather ominous forewarning that this is about a *digital logic* element in an *integrated circuit* package, it will be shown that these applications are extremely simple, making this the ideal device for learning the basics about logic circuits.

Basics

For two important reasons, the NAND gates described will all be of the TTL (transistor-transistor logic) family. First of all, TTL is by far the most commonly used logic in current ham projects. Second, it is the least expensive and the most readily available from surplus dealers. The current price of the 7400 quad two-input NAND gate is a whopping 16 cents.

Figure 2-25A shows the common schematic representation of the two-input NAND gate. Figure 2-25B is the truth table that shows the output of the NAND gate for all possible combinations of inputs. The truth table is the key to understanding the NAND gate, and will be referred to repeatedly in subsequent discussions and applications of this device.

For TTL logic, each 0 in the truth table represents a voltage of 0.8 volts or less. Each 1 represents a voltage of greater than 2.0 volts but less than the NAND gate supply voltage of 5.0 volts.

Figure 2-25C shows the pin diagram for the SN7400 quad two-input NAND gate. As the word quad implies, there are four two-input gates contained in one dual in-line packaged IC. As was previously mentioned, a regulated five volt power supply is necessary to power the IC. Positive is connected to pin 14. Negative is connected to pin 7.

Internal Circuitry

At this point let's digress for just a moment and take a peek into the innards of the IC. If transistor circuitry isn't your bag, simply skip this section. The following discussion of the internal circuitry is not essential in applying the device, but is presented for those who desire further insight into how the gate actually works. For those who are indifferent about this aspect of the IC, the NAND gate can be treated as a black box device.

Figure 2-26 shows the transistor circuitry that actually comprises each section of the SN7400 two-input NAND gate. The inputs are actually the two emitter leads of Q1, a double emitter transistor. The output is connected to the collector of Q4.

First, let's consider the case where both inputs are tied to a 1, or a voltage of between 2.0 and 5.0 volts. This will correspond to the bottom line of the truth table listed in Fig. 2-25B. The base-collector junction of Q1 will be forward biased for this particular set of inputs, allowing I_{BC1} to flow. This current will be sufficient magnitude to saturate transistor Q2. The resulting collector current of Q2 will produce a voltage drop across the 1.6k ohm collector resistor of sufficient magnitude to cause the collector voltage of Q2 to decrease to the point where transistor Q3 is cut off, or effectively open circuited. The rise in potential at the base of transistor Q4 caused by Q2's increased emitter current across the 1k ohm emitter resistor will be sufficient to saturate Q4, causing its collector voltage to drop to near ground potential, or a logic 0. This is exactly as stated by the truth table of Fig. 2-25B.

Now suppose that input A is tied to ground or to a voltage source of 0.8 volts or less. This would correspond to the second line of the truth table of Fig. 2-25B. Now a current I_{BE1} will flow from the emitter of Q1 to the grounded input A. In this case, I_{BC1} will be zero, causing Q2 to be cut off or effectively open circuited. No current will flow in either the emitter or collector circuit of Q2. Therefore, Q4 will not be biased on as in the previous case, and will in effect be cut off, causing its collector-emitter junction to appear to be open circuited. On the other hand, the collector of Q2 will be approximately at the potential of V_{CC}. This will cause transistor Q3 to saturate, presenting a logic 1 voltage at the output terminal that is equal to the

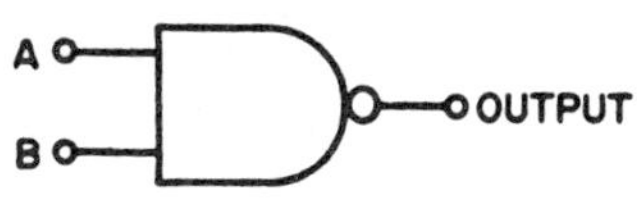

FIG a

INPUTS		OUTPUT
A	B	
0	0	1
0	1	1
1	0	1
1	1	0

FIG b

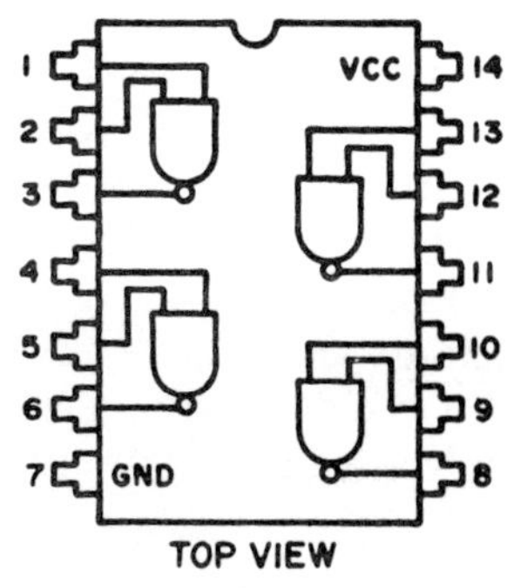

TOP VIEW

FIG c

Fig. 2-25. The two-input NAND gate. (A) is the schematic; (B) shows the truth table. (C) The pin layout of the SN7400.

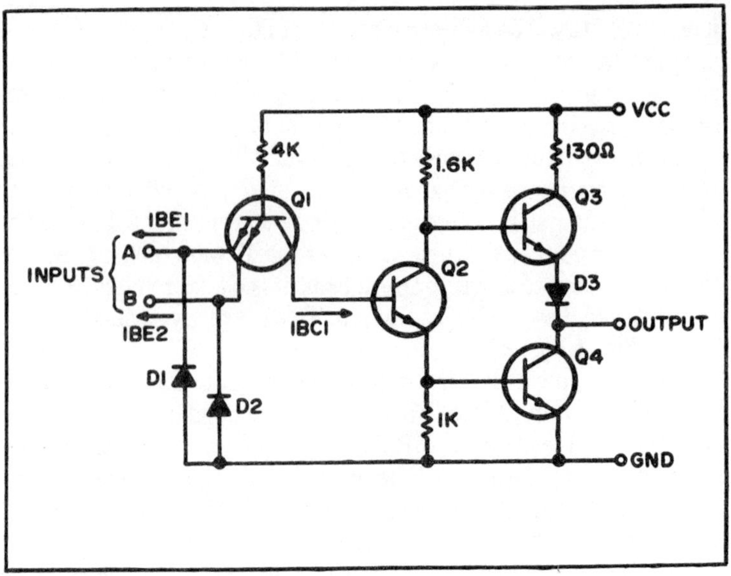

Fig. 2-26. The circuitry for one of the gates in the 7400 quad two-input NAND gate.

supply voltage, V_{CC}, minus the voltage drop across the base-emitter junction of Q3 and the diode, D3. This output voltage is typically about 3.3 volts.

Note that the conditions described in the preceding paragraph apply to the cases where either or both input terminals are connected to a logic 0 as previously defined. This corresponds to the top three lines of the truth table.

Diodes D1 and D2 are included to help protect the gate should the inputs be accidentally connected to a negative voltage.

One important TTL design rule should be evident at this point. An open circuited input of a TTL gate corresponds to a logic 1 input rather than a 0 input. Or in other words, to input a logic 0 you must tie the input to ground or to a voltage of less than 0.8 volts so that transistor Q1's base-emitter junction will conduct. To input a logic 1 you may either tie the input to a voltage of greater than 2.0 volts or simply leave that input open circuited.

Gating

Now that we've taken a look at what's inside the NAND gate, let's discuss some of its many uses. First of all, as its name implies, the NAND gate's primary function is that of *gating*. In a logic circuit, the NAND gate will provide a unique output response of logic 0 if, and only if, both inputs are simultaneously at a logic 1.

Inverter

An inverter is a logic element that provides a 1 output for a 0 input and a 0 output for a 1 input. The two-input NAND gate can be easily converted to perform the functions of an inverter by simply tying the two inputs together. Now, only the top and bottom lines of the truth table apply. The output will always be the inverse of the input.

Like the gating function, the use of the NAND gate as an inverter is very common. The easiest way to gain further insight into the reasons for its use in this fashion is to study current digital logic projects.

Pulse Shaper

A fast switching waveform is necessary to reliably trigger TTL flip flops and counters. Slower switching waveforms such as low frequency sine waves will often result in erratic operation. The circuit of Fig. 2-27 shows how two sections of a 7400 NAND gate can be connected to form a waveform conditioning circuit, providing a TTL compatible square wave output from a slower switching waveform presented at the input.

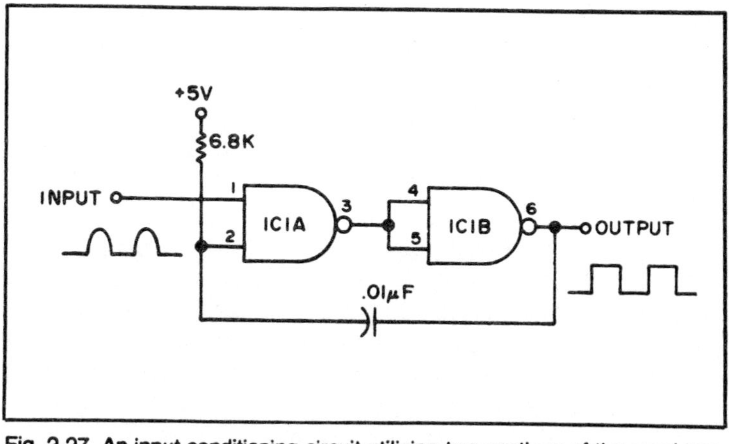

Fig. 2-27. An input conditioning circuit utilizing two sections of the quad two-input NAND gate.

As was discussed in the section on internal circuitry, the NAND gates are saturated logic elements. In other words, the output is either *on* (at a voltage of approximately 3.3 volts) or *off* (at a voltage of approximately 0.4 volts). The circuitry tends to avoid any in-between output states.

This characteristic is utilized in the circuit of Fig. 2-27. As the waveform at the input slowly changes from a 0 to a 1 logic level, and vice versa, the abrupt switching characteristic of the NAND gates transforms this input waveform to a square wave output at terminal 6. The inclusion of the .01 uF capacitor from pin 6 of section IC1B to pin 2 of section IC1A provides a transient feedback that further enhances the switching speed of the trailing edge of each pulse.

The circuit of Fig. 2-27 is often found in digital circuits that contain transistor or unijunction transistor oscillators that do not have TTL compatible outputs. The circuit is also often used to condition 60 Hz half-wave rectified sine waves for use in digital clock circuits.

Set-Reset Flip Flop

A set-reset flip flop is a logic element with two outputs commonly labelled Q and $\overline{Q}$. $\overline{Q}$ is said to be the inverse of Q, since $\overline{Q}$ is always a 1 when Q is a 0, and always a 0 when Q is a 1. A logic 0 applied to the set input of the set-reset flip flop will cause the Q output to go to a logic 1 and the $\overline{Q}$ output to go to a logic 0. The flip flop will then remain in this state when the 0 at the set input is removed. In this respect, the flip flop may be thought of as a memory device. A 0 applied to the reset input will cause $\overline{Q}$ to switch back to a logic 1, and Q to switch back to a logic 0.

Figure 2-28 shows the common logic symbol for a set-reset flip flop, and how NAND gates can be connected to form this device. In this diagram, both SW1 and SW2 are normally open switches or contacts. If SW1 is momentarily closed, grounding pin 1 of IC1A, pin 3 will switch to a logic 1 as dictated by the truth table. This logic 1 is then present at pin 4 of IC1B. Since pin 5 of IC1B is open circuited and therefore also at a logic 1 level, the output of IC1B switches to a logic 0. Now, when SW1 returns to its normally open position, pin 1 of IC1A returns to a logic 1 voltage. However, pin 2, being connected to pin 6 of IC1B, remains at a logic 0. Therefore the output of IC1A remains at a logic 1 state and the output of IC1B remains at a logic 0 state. This is the *set* condition of the flip flop.

Now, if SW2 is momentarily closed, a 0 is applied to pin 5 of IC1B, changing its output to a logic 1. Both inputs of IC1A are then at a logic 1 causing its output to switch to a logic 0. As before, both IC1A and IC1B retain these output states when SW2 returns to its normally open position. This is the *reset* condition of the flip flop.

Even though there are TTL ICs specifically designed as flip flops, it is not at all uncommon to see the 7400 quad NAND gate being used to implement the set-reset flip flop function. In many cases one half of the 7400 IC will be used as a flip flop while the other two NAND gates will be used as gates, inverters, pulse shapers, etc.

Switch Debouncer

We have already taken a look at one of the peculiarities of interfacing TTL logic with the outside world, namely the requirement of waveform conditioning. Another interfacing difficulty is depicted in Fig. 2-29. Mechanical inputs such as switch and relay contacts are relatively noisy. As shown in the illustration, when a mechanical switch or relay contact closes, the contact actually bounces many times before coming to rest in the closed position.

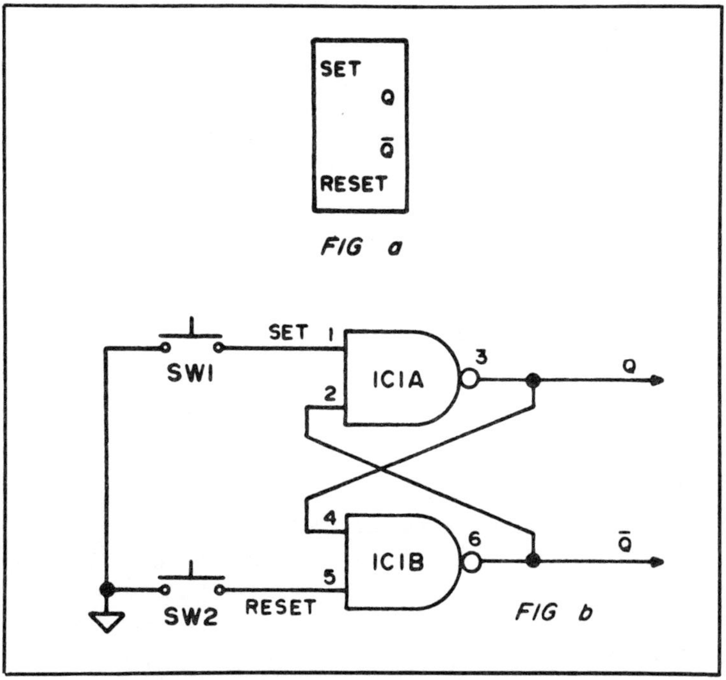

Fig. 2-28. (A) The common schematic for the set-reset flip flop; (B) two sections fo the SN7400 can be connected to form a set-reset flip flop.

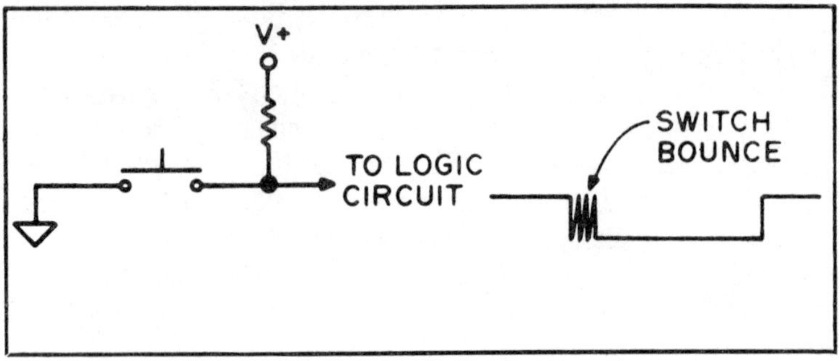

Fig. 2-29. Switch bounce.

These bounces are very fast, being only fractions of a microsecond in duration, and therefore do not affect electromechanical or slower speed electronic circuits. However, to the high speed TTL logic, these contact bounces are a bona fide string of individual input pulses and can cause erratic or unreliable circuit operation. For instance, suppose that a counter circuit comprised of TTL logic elements was constructed to count the number of times the switch contact in Fig. 2-29 was closed. As can be seen from the waveform produced by this noisy switch contact, the counter would actually count the several contact closures that result as the contact *bounces* or *chatters* before coming to rest in the closed position. Obviously some sort of interface is necessary to prevent this type of misoperation.

The circuit of Fig. 2-30 shows how two NAND gates can be connected to form a bounceless switch or interfacing circuit. SW1 can be any SPDT switch or relay contact. As can easily be seen by comparison to Fig. 2-28, the bounceless switch is no more than a set-reset flip flop. Due to the memory action of the flip flop the circuit will always switch on the initial contact closure and will therefore be immune to the subsequent contact bounces. As can be seen from the illustration, the NAND gates will provide one clean pulse for each contact closure cycle even though contact bounce actually occurs at both the normally open and normally closed switching positions.

Square Wave Oscillators

The NAND gate can also be connected as a square wave generator as shown in Fig. 2-31. The particular component values of R_t and C_t shown in this diagram will allow oscillation in the 1 kHz range. To explain the operation of this astable multivibrator circuit, let's first assume that we are starting at the instant that pin 6 of IC1B has switched to a logic 0. Since pin 3 of IC1A is at a logic 1 at this same instant, C_t will begin charging through resistor R_t. When the

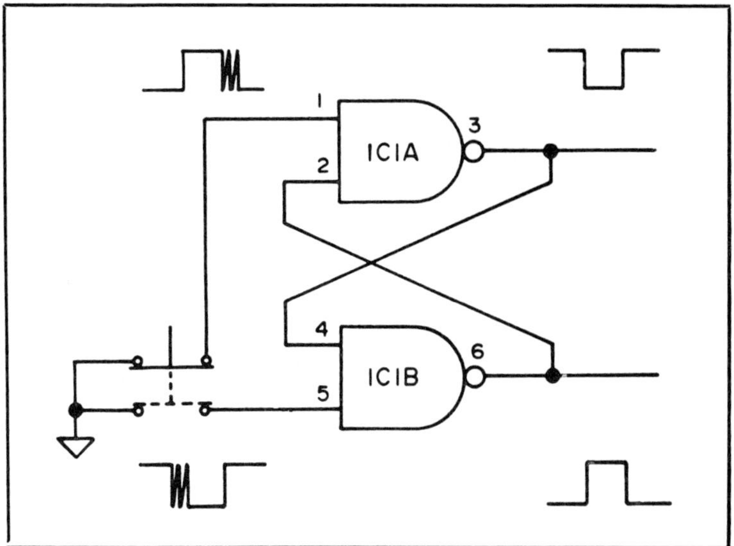

Fig. 2-30. Two sections of the SN7400 connected to form a bounceless switch.

capacitor has charged to a voltage sufficient to provide a logic 1 at pins 1 and 2 of IC1A, the two NAND gates abruptly switch logic output states. Then the logic 1 at pin 6 of IC1B and the 0 at pin 3 of IC1A cause C_t to begin discharging through R_t. When C_t has discharged to a 0 logic level, the gates abruptly change states again. Thus the oscillations continue at a rate dependent on the RC time constant of R_t and C_t.

Provisions for keying the oscillator can be made by disconnecting pin 1 from pin 2 of IC1A. Now, grounding or application of a 0 at

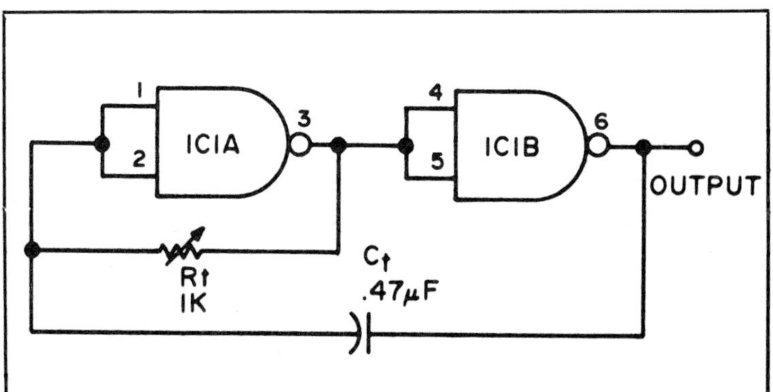

Fig. 2-31. Two sections of the SN7400 connected to form a square wave oscillator.

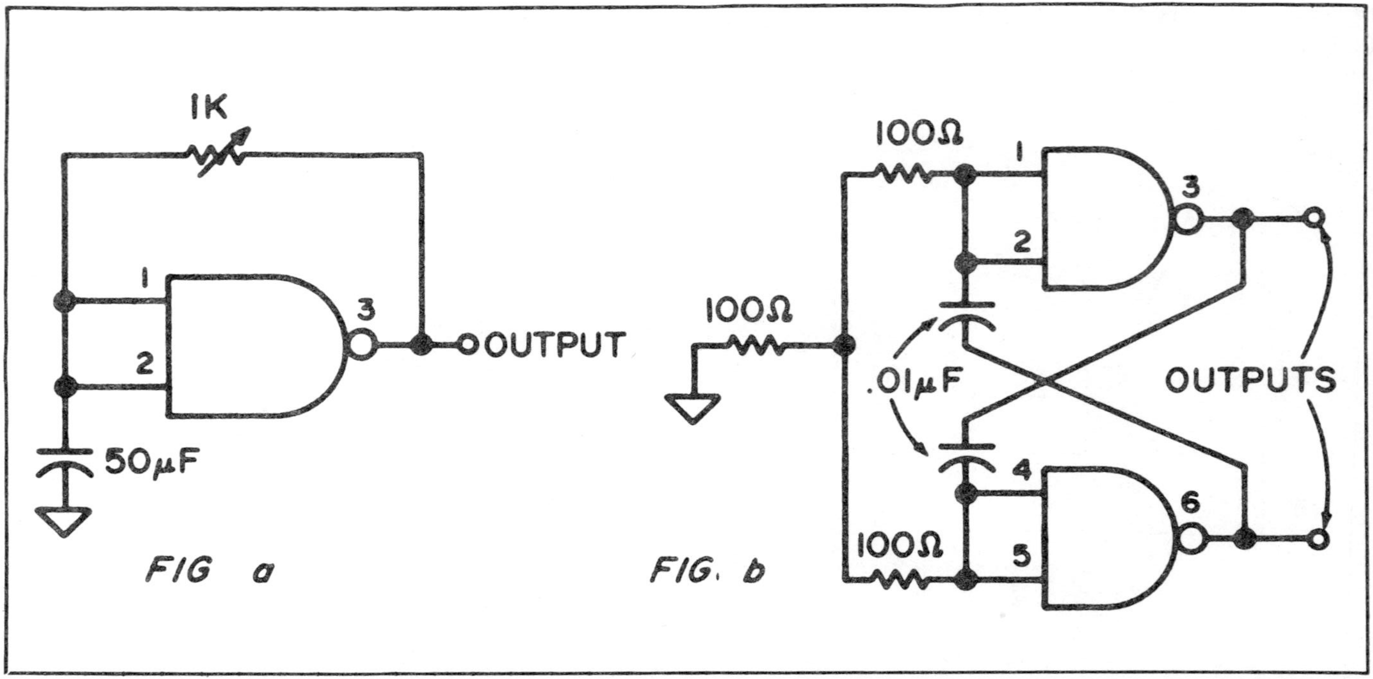

Fig. 2-32. Two more square wave generators. The oscillator of (A) will oscillate at approximately 45 Hz. The oscillator of (B) will have a frequency of about 50 kHz.

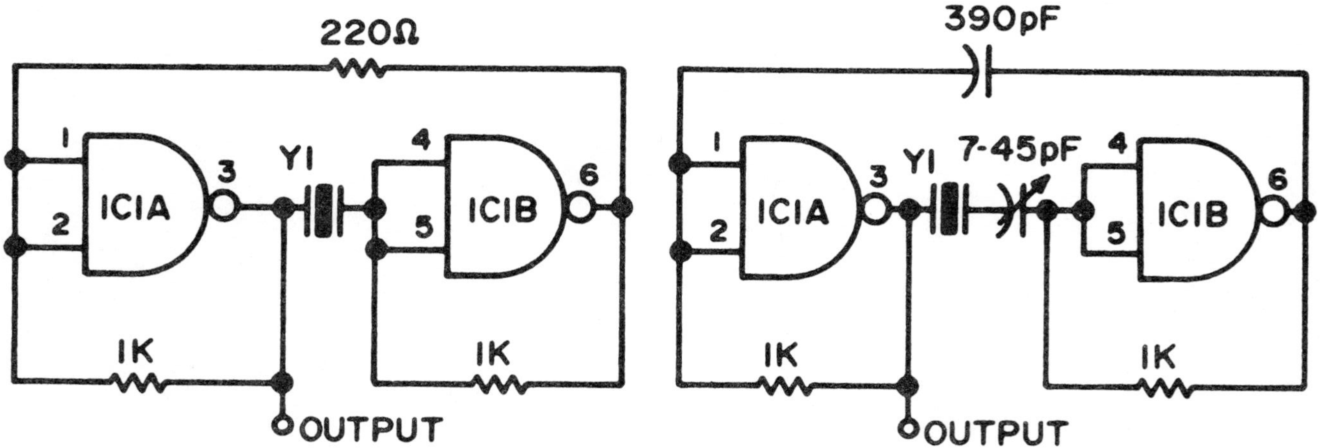

FIG a

FIG b

Fig. 2-33. Two examples of how the SN7400 can be connected to form a crystal oscillator.

pin 1 of IC1A will prevent oscillation, since according to the truth table the output of IC1A must always remain at a 1 as long as one input is at a 0. A logic 1 or an open circuit at pin 1 would allow the oscillator to run.

Two other connections of NAND gates to form square wave oscillators are shown in Fig. 2-32. Like the oscillator just described, these oscillators also rely on the charge-discharge cycle of capacitors to provide oscillation. In all these oscillators the frequency ranges may be varied by the selection of the RC components. The higher the RC product, the lower the frequency range that will result.

Oscillators of the type shown in Figs. 2-31 and 2-32 are often found in circuits that require a TTL compatible clock. Though these oscillator circuits are reliable, some frequency drift can be expected in normal operation.

Crystal Oscillator

Finally, as shown in Fig. 2-33, the NAND gate can be used to make a crystal oscillator for applications that require a more stable clock pulse than that yielded by the previously described square wave oscillators. As can be seen by comparison with Fig. 2-32B, the crystal oscillator is basically the same as the square wave oscillator except for the replacement of one capacitor with a quartz crystal. The upper frequency range of the NAND gate as used in this application is typically 15 MHz though some gates will oscillate at somewhat higher frequencies. The addition of a trimming capacitor in the circuit of Fig. 2-33 will allow for netting the oscillator frequency if this is deemed necessary in certain applications.

This list of presented applications of the 7400 quad NAND gate is by no means complete. Like all other devices, its possible applications are limited only by the ingenuity of the circuit designer. The basic simplicity of the device itself, its low price tag and its versatility make it the ideal device from which the digital logic neophyte can gain valuable insight into digital logic circuitry.

Chapter 3
Memory

While the computer hobbyist faces many trials and tribulations during his quest to get his fabulous (and complex) new toy "up and running," one of the most frustrating problems that he can encounter involves debugging a troublesome memory board. This chapter begins by describing a simple memory diagnostic program, and illustrating its use in tracking down problems in memory. While not a "cure-all" for all memory related problems, especially those that render the complete board inoperable, this will allow the hobbyist to "exorcise" those gremlins responsible for such irritations as memory locations which refuse to store the exact data which you load into them, and addresses which appear to change their contents as though they had a mind of their own.

Checking Memory Boards

The two problems which are presented for illustrative purposes are real-life "bugs" which cropped up following the recent assembly of two 4K memory boards. Note that the program and associated debugging technique which evolved were developed for an Altair 8800 (but should be applicable, with appropriate modifications, to other systems).

At this point, a few words concerning the memory diagnostic program (Table 3-1) are in order. Ignore those parts of the program in parentheses, for the time being. The program, as presented, resides on page 2, address 000-041 (octal). This address was chosen because I already had a simple "MONITOR" residing on pages 0 and 1, and I was certain that page 2 had no "bugs," due to the fact that other small programs which resided there from time to time performed their appointed duties without difficulty. The program can be placed on any other page (change memory references accordingly), assuming that the chosen page has no "bugs" which would interfere with the program's operation. Needless to say, the program can be placed on a correctly operating board, and used to debug all 4K of other appropriately addressed boards. The only restriction concerning placement of the program is that the page(s) to be tested must be different from that page on which the program resides—hence, my choice of page 2.

The program also assumes that you have an octal conversion and print subroutine ("OCTOUT") which it can call. Since this is generally a part of most monitors, it is not included here.

Operation of the program is straightforward. The program loads the value of an address, as data, into that address. For example, address 000 contains data 000, address 001 contains 001, etc. Then the computer compares the contents of the address with the numerical value of the address. If they differ, the program will print out the address and its incorrect contents. Since this method is not infallible, those parts of the program in parentheses are utilized to load and compare specific patterns of data in memory, if necessary. To employ this modification, simply substitute the parts of the program in parentheses for the existing parts. The need for the modified program will be made clear in due course.

The Basics

Before proceeding further, a general discussion of a 4K memory board is in order. These boards usually employ 2102s or a reasonable facsimile thereof, and have the chips arranged in four banks of eight chips each (Fig. 3-1). The particular bank chosen is a function of a two-to-four decoder, which decodes address lines 10 and 11. Figure 3-2 is a schematic and truth table of a typical circuit.

The active output of the decoder circuit pulls down the eight pin 13s of the particular bank of 2102s being addressed, thus enabling that particular bank.

Table 3-2 illustrates the address decoding with regard to each bank and the associated 256 word pages therein. The particular page in a bank is a function of the state address lines A8 and A9. Remember, to activate a given page or address, the appropriate address pins on the chip are pulled down.

Each chip within a bank corresponds to a particular bit, 0-7.

Table 3-1. Memory Diagnostic program.

Label	Address	Code	Alt	Instruction	Comment
DEBUG	002-000	046		MVI H	Load H & L registers with starting address of memory segment to be tested
	002-001	XXX		Page to tested	
	002-002	056	MV	MVI L	
	002-003	000			
	002-004	000	(006)	NOP (MVI B)	Store pattern into entire memory page
	002-005	000	(YYY)	NOP (RAND NUM)	
NEXT	002-006	165	(160)	MOV M,L (MOV M,B)	
	002-007	054		INR L	
	002-010	302		JNZ	
	002-011	006		NEXT	
	002-012	002			
AGAIN	002-013	176		MOV A,M	Compare routine (& jump to "dump" if error found)
	002-014	275	(276)	CMP L (CMP B)	
	002-015	302		JNZ	
	002-016	027		DUMP	
	002-017	002			
CONTIN	002-020	054		INR L	Continue comparisons
	002-021	302		JNZ	
	002-022	013		AGAIN	
	002-023	002			
	002-024	303		JMP	Execute program again
	002-025	000		DEBUG	
	002-026	002			
DUMP	002-027	117		MOV C,A	Print out error address & contents
	002-030	315		CALL	
	002-031	237		OCTOUT	
	002-032	000			
	002-033	115		MOV C,L	
	002-034	315		CALL	
	002-035	237		OCTOUT	
	002-036	000			
	002-037	303		JMP	Continue comparisons
	002-040	020		CONTIN	
	002-041	002			

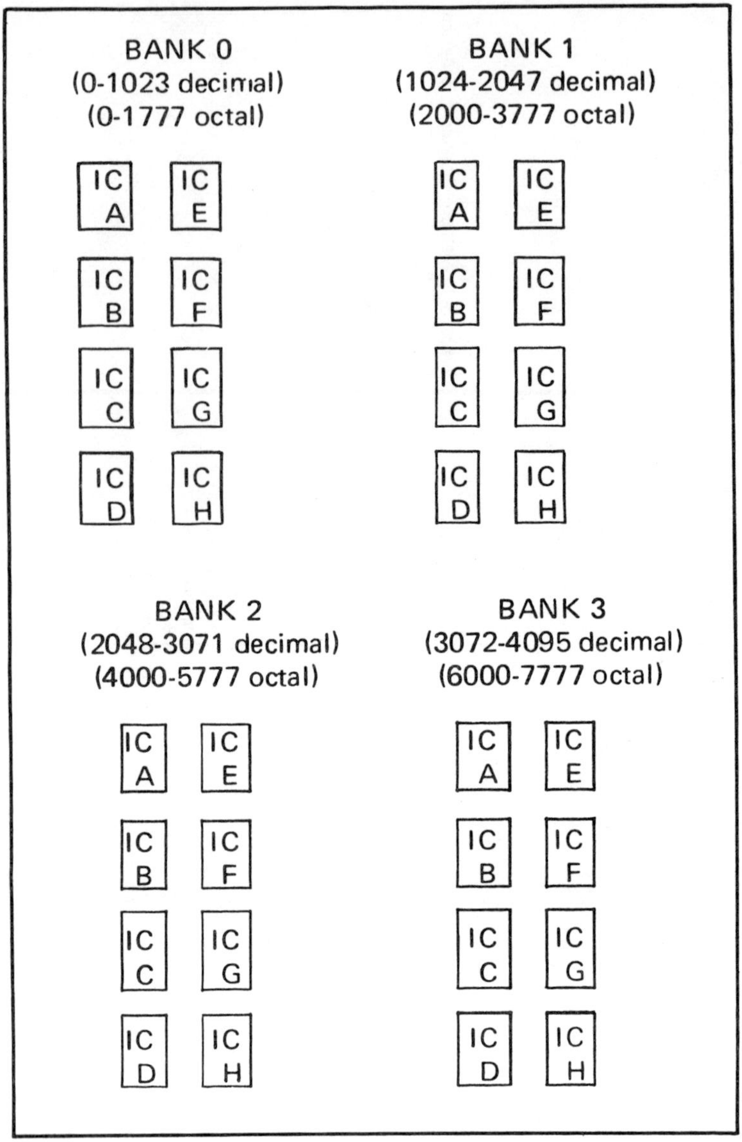

Fig. 3-1. 4K memory segment of 2102s.

Case 1

Symptoms: program data loaded into pages 6 and 7 was full of errors when dumped. Testing of pages 6 and 7 with the unmodified program produced the results illustrated in Table 3-3. Since errors resided in pages 6 and 7, we can localize the difficulty to bank 1 (refer

Table 3-2. Address Decoding with Regard to Bank and Page Selection.

Address Lines—	A11	A10	A9	A8	A7	A6	A5	A4	A3	A2	A1	A0
Decimal Weight—	2048	1024	512	256	128	64	32	16	8	4	2	1
	A11	A10										
Bank 0	0	0			$0—1023_{10}$—pages $0\text{-}3_8$							
Bank 1		1			$1024—2047_{10}$—pages $4\text{-}7_8$							
Bank 2	1	0			$2048—307_{10}$—pages $10\text{-}13_8$							
Bank 3	1	1			$3072—4095_{10}$—pages $14\text{-}17_8$							

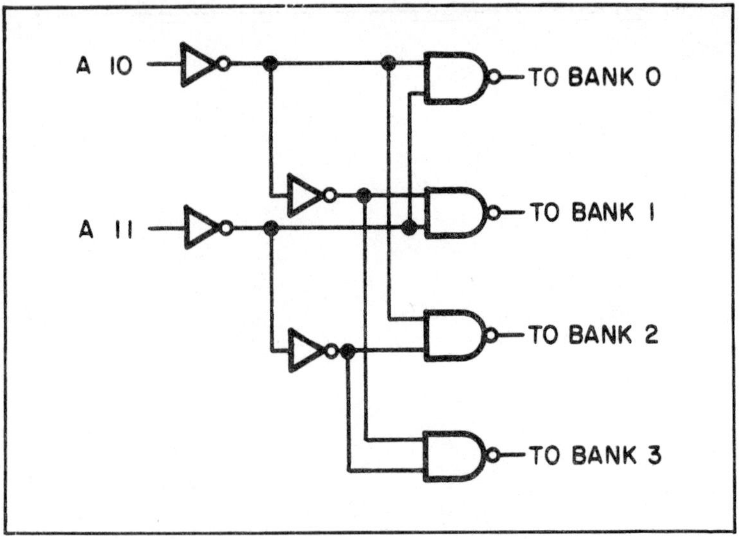

Fig. 3-2. Typical decoder circuit (and truth table) for decoding address lines A10 and A11 to choose the appropriate bank of 2102s.

to Table 3-2). Notice that the contents of the addresses which contain errors are augmented by 004. This points to a problem with bit 2 (chip C) in block 1. The fact that the problem showed up only on pages 6 and 7 seems to indicate that whenever address bit A9 was active, chip C on bank 1 contained a 1, producing the 004. Perhaps it was an internal short in that chip. Substitution of the identified chip corrected the problem.

Case 2

Symptoms: interaction between pages 4 and 5; specifically, data entered into page 4 changed some, only some, data in page 5. Initial use of the memory diagnostic program as in case 1 indicated no errors, although it was known that the pages were interacting. At this point, pages 4, 5, 6 and 7 were loaded with 000 using the modified memory diagnostic. An octal dump of these pages indicated that all were zeroed. The next step consisted of loading the pattern

Table 3-3. Typical Readout from DEBUG.

000	004	010	014
001	005	011	015
002	006	012	016
003	007	013	017

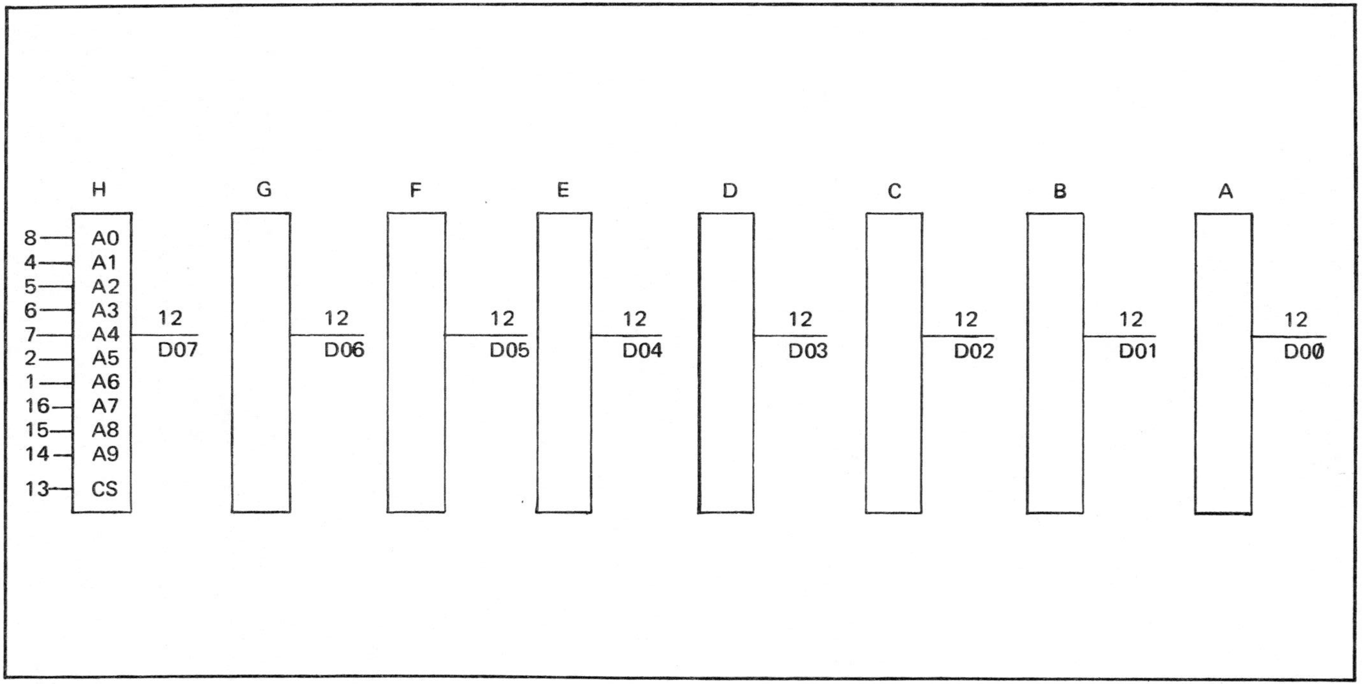

Fig. 3-3. The logic state of each 2102 in the bank of eight contributes to the value of the data word at a given address. Note that each 2102 corresponds to one bit in an 8 bit word.

of 144 into page 4. The memory diagnostic and octal dump confirmed that page 4 contained all 144s. However, an octal dump of page 5 revealed that, although it had not been reloaded, it now contained 040s (i.e., bit 5 was always set). Since it is page 5, our problem resides in bank 1 (refer to Table 3-2), and because it is 040, the problem is associated with chip F in bank 1 (Fig. 3-3). Now, since the error popped up on page 5 although page 4 was the one being addressed, it would suggest that A8 on chip F in bank 1 was going low (remember A8 and A9 determine the particular page in a bank that is being addressed). Manual addressing of page 4 from the display/control board and activation of the examine switch, indeed, showed that A8 on chip F in bank 1 was low. The corresponding pins of other chips in this bank were high. It turned out to be a case of the pin not making contact in the socket. Removal of the chip revealed that pin A8 had been bent underneath upon insertion. Straightening the pin and reinserting the chip (with care) corrected the problem.

This procedure is relatively straightforward and best of all does not require any sophisticated equipment. In fact, you already possess the two most important pieces—the computer itself and ingenuity.

The program also is relatively simple as memory diagnostic programs go. I would recommend that a number of patterns be tried with the modified program to ensure that all possible bits and consequently all possible chips in a bank be tested. Embellishments such as these could be built into the program by the software connoisseurs among us. Space doesn't permit elaborating upon other possible sources of memory problems. However, the technique of isolating the bank, the chip and the appropriate pins has been presented and, hopefully, will be of value when a memory problem occurs.

Short on Memory?

Medical science tells us that only a tiny fraction of the human brain's capacity is used during an individual's lifetime. This excess memory capacity is unfortunately not a feature of the average home microcomputer system, a fact which usually causes the experimenter to seek additional brain power almost as soon as the new micro kit or protype is finished and running. Most of the commercially supplied micro kits provide only minimum memory, usually 1024 bytes (1K) or less. It is in this memory that the user's application programs and language processors (such as BASIC) must reside.

A typical amateur radio application for a microprocessor system is the control of a RTTY station. The micro can be programmed to send CQs, answer calls automatically, detect speed changes, etc. However, it becomes immediately obvious to the operator of the station that more memory than is supplied with most micro kits is required to handle even the simplest functions, such as sending a list of station equipment. For example, the single message:

CQ CQ FROM WB2ZCF—"JOHN"

takes about 33 characters, including shift functions. Taking into account that the machine code to control the system occupies the same memory, it becomes obvious that, when stored in memory, even a short list of equipment, when added to other operator comments, rapidly eats up critical space. Think about some of those other functions that can be controlled by a micro, and you will be ready to consider adding memory capacity to your micro system. There are two ways of making your micro smarter—buying a commercial 2K or 4K board and sliding it into your system or, home brewing a memory system for your setup.

This is a description of the latter approach—a complete do-it-yourself 2K memory system for a Motorola 6800 type microprocessor, including interface and memory board. The design uses popular (and inexpensive) 2102 static memory chips, and the interface design may be modified to support other microprocessors. All parts used in this project are readily available. I have attempted to present in logical order the background required to understand the project, the design criteria, pitfalls, actual construction and logic analysis and finally, the debug techniques used in bringing up the add-on memory. Hopefully, this will encourage those of you who need additional memory for your systems to consider building it yourselves.

The Microprocessor's Nervous System

The Motorola M6800 microprocessor is capable of supporting up to 65,536 bytes of random access memory. The single byte accessed during a machine cycle is selected by 16 address lines. Each address line may be viewed as a digit (1 or 0) in the binary system; therefore, the unique memory address generated by the micro is really a binary number in the range of 0-65,536 (Fig. 3-4). The data to be read or written by the micro is transferred over eight data lines, or the data bus. The memory is directed to read or write by a single line, the R/W line. If the 6800 places a 1 (TTL HI) on the R/W line, the memory sends the single byte of data (whose address

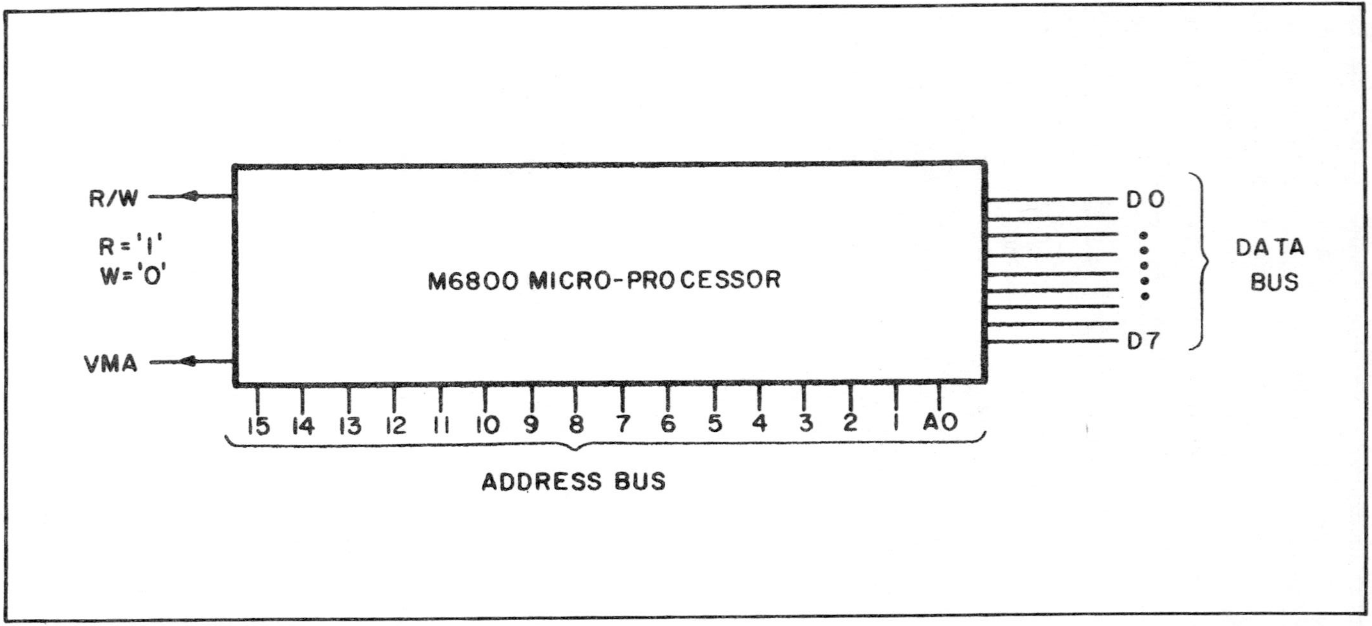

Fig. 3-4. M6800 control lines used by the memory interface. Read/write line (R/W) controls flow of data on 8 bit bidirectional data bus. The valid memory address line (VMA), when HI, allows the interface to respond to the 16 bit address on the address bus. Each address line, when HI, represents a power of two in the binary numbering system. For example, if lines A0, A2, and A10 are HI, the address sent to the interface is equal to ($2^0 = 1 + 2^2 = 4 + 2^{10} = 1024$) or 1029_{10}.

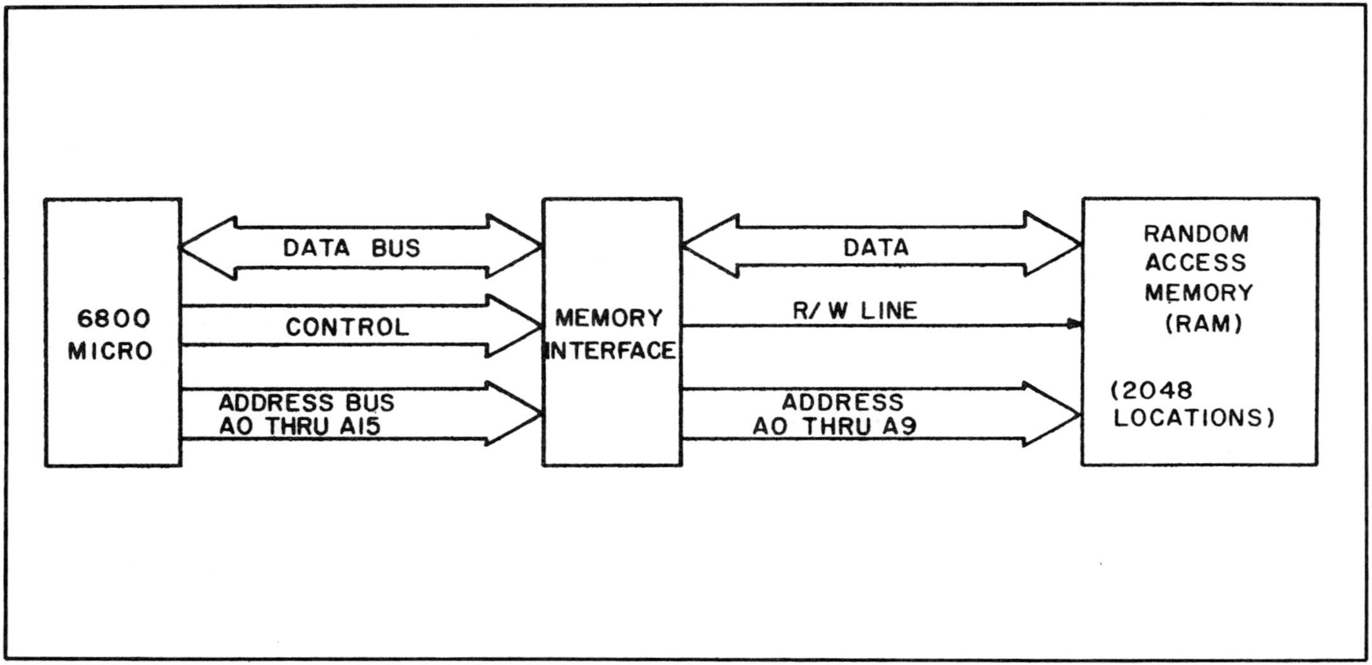

Fig. 3-5. Information flow between micro, interface and memory. Note that only address lines A0-A9 go to memory, as the interface uses remaining lines to decode valid memory addresses.

was presented on the 16 line address bus) to the micro over the data bus. A 0 on the R/W line causes a memory write to occur; the data on the data bus is written into memory. One control line, called VMA (Valid Memory Address), is a 1 if the micro really wants to access memory. These lines, the address, data bus, R/W and VMA, must be used to coordinate data flow between the micro and out planned add-on memory. The logic required to do this is called an *interface*. We will build a simple interface to control our new memory (Fig. 3-5). Since all micros do not have a VMA line or its equivalent, the design of the interface includes a method of removing the VMA function.

Interface Deisgn

The interface has three primary functions. The first and most important function is to determine that the address on the address bus is really intended for our memory. You may wonder how an address could possibly be invalid until you realize that when adding a 2K memory to a system capable of addressing 65K, some means must be employed to channel addresses to the area where memory really exists. This process is called *address decode* and is a concept common to any memory design. There are address decoding techniques that could make our 2K add-on respond to any 2K range of addresses within the allowable 65K, but for simplicity we will place our memory in the range of 0-2047. The actual process of address decode is simple in practice, requiring only a couple of packages in my design.

Recalling that the data bus in the 6800 is bidirectional, we need some method of making the memory correctly receive and transmit data over a common bus when commanded by the R/W line. This, the second feature of the interface, is accomplished by using *three-state* logic. This logic has the familiar 1 and 0 TTL output levels, as well as an *open circuit* state. Thus, upon command, a gate with three-state output capability may appear to be an open circuit to any other device on the same line. This allows us to parallel (OR-TIE) many gates to the same bus, with only one actually driving the bus at a given time. The design presented here uses three-state logic to drive the data bus. On a memory read cycle, the gates driving the bus are turned on (or enabled) by the R/W line, allowing memory data to flow from the 2102s to the microprocessor. On a write cycle, the gates previously enabled are driven into the open circuit mode, allowing data to flow into the memory (Fig. 3-6). The final function of the interface is to buffer the address, data and control lines. Most MOS microprocessors such as the 6800 can drive only one TTL load

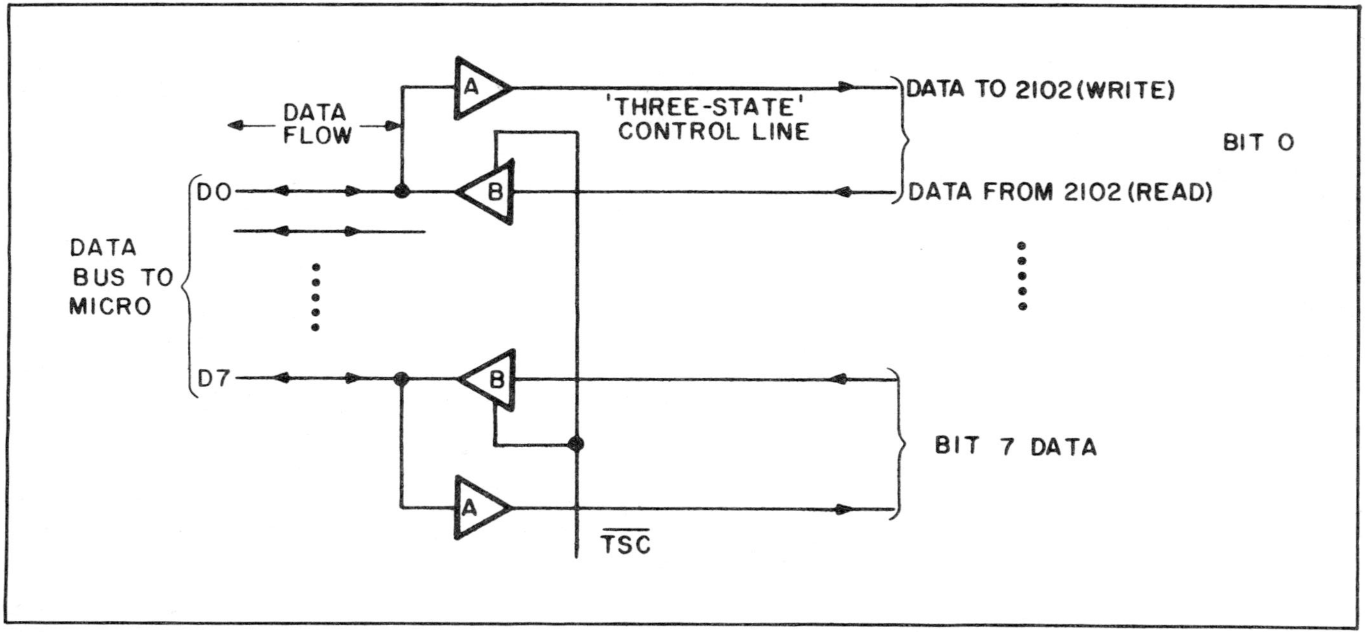

Fig. 3-6. Three-state logic allows devices to be paralleled on the bidirectional data bus. During a memory write cycle, the TSC line is HI, allowing data to pass from the data bus through device A into memory. The B devices are forced into an open circuit condition, thus not affecting data flow. On a read cycle, a LO on the TSC line turns on device B, allowing data passage from memory to the data bus. Device A, although always enabled, is not affected by read data passing through it, as the 2102 memory's write line is off during a read cycle.

per line; thus it is most important not to overload the micro. The interface uses 7400 gates between the NAND gate as a buffer causes the signal to be inverted, a useful characteristic in some parts of the interface.

Pitfalls

One desirable feature of the M6800 microprocessor system can be a possible problem when adding memory. Input and output operations, as well as some system features, use actual memory addresses to initiate and control special functions. For example, micro systems using the MIKBUG® monitor program (such as the SWTP 6800) use locations from $A000_{16}$—$A07F_{16}$ for system storage, and some locations around 8000_{16} are used for I/O control. These locations must not be overlapped by add-on memory. My stem also restricts the use of the upper few memory locations, as they are reserved for system use in a special read-only memory. The point of all this is to be careful where add-on memory is located using address decode techniques. Overlapping system locations can and will cause difficult debugging sessions once the system is running. Good digital construction practices must be used when working with memory systems. No software problem is harder to find than one caused by a hardware glitch. Noise is a problem in systems with add-on memories, as the new memory is seldom on the same board as the original. Liberal doses of power supply bypassing are a must. I used 0.2 uF capacitors in parallel with 0.01 uF ones to bypass power leads. The interface and memory boards are wire-wrapped, but all IC power connections are soldered to the wire-wrap stakes, using #18 bus wire. Interconnection lead length is not critical. Mine are 9 inches between microprocessor and interface and about the same between memory and interface.

Linking Micro and Memory

The interface is represented in Fig. 3-7. All connections between the micro, memory and interface are made using standard 14 and 16 pin wire-wrap sockets. The cables are ribbon cable with IC header connectors used as plugs. The interface functions as follows: Address decode is accomplished in part by keying on the A10 address line to determine if the address is in the range of $0\text{-}1023_{10}$ (Bank 0) or 1024-2047 (Bank 1). Line A10 allows us to select the bank to be accessed. The 2102 type RAM is formatted 1024 bits by one bit wide; thus it takes eight RAMs, each contributing a single bit, to make up one memory bank consisting of 1024 bytes (eight bits to a byte). It takes 10 address lines to resolve an address in the range of

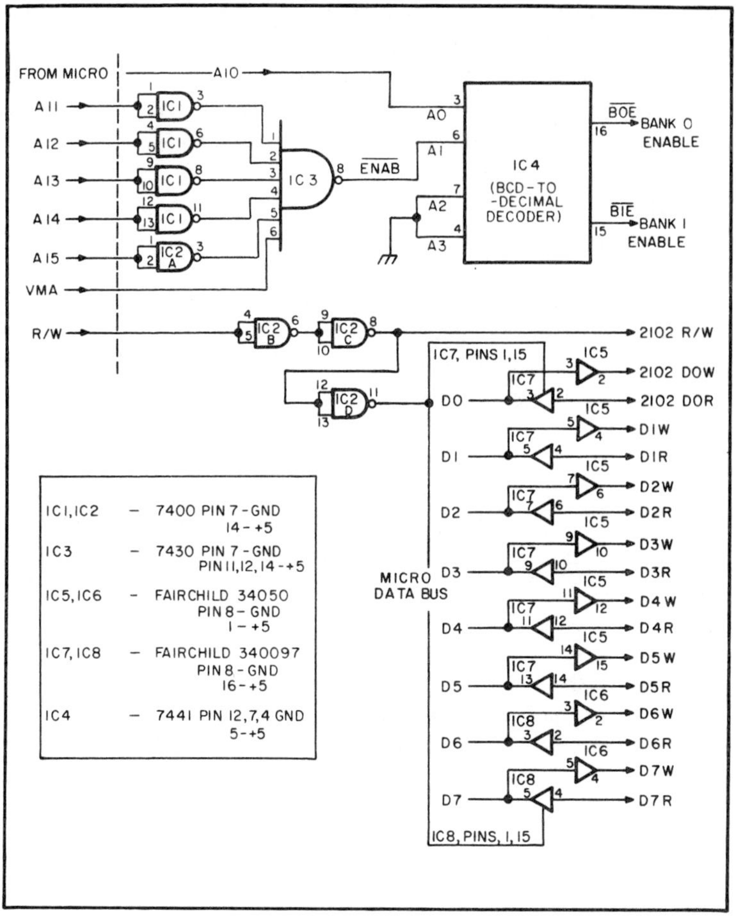

Fig. 3-7. Memory interface schematic.

1024 bytes; therefore, lines A0-A9 are connected to each 2102. A given bank of eight RAMs is enabled or selected by bringing the enable pin (pin 13) low. The eight enable lines of each bank are in parallel to select eight RAMs at once. Since our memory is to respond only to addresses in the range of $0\text{-}2047_{10}$, all other addresses must be *locked out* by our address decode logic, which works as follows: Any address outside the allowable range will have one address line between A11 and A15 activated, IC1 and IC2A invert and buffer the incoming address lines and pass the resulting five signals to IC3, a 7430 eight-input NAND gate. The gate produces a TTL HI output if any of the eight input lines goes LO, a condition caused by one of the inverted address lines containing an invalid (HI) address. If all five of the address lines in question are LO, the output of the 7430 is LO; this signal, called $\overline{\text{ENAB}}$ (ENABLE), will allow the memory bank selected to respond to the memory access. Note that the VMA lines is also connected to IC3. Recall that VMA is HI if the micro really wants a memory access. A LO on VMA disables the memory exactly as an invalid memory address would.

If your micro does not have a VMA line, tie IC3, pin 6, to Vcc along with pins 11 and 12 (the unused inputs). This process satisfies the address decode function described earlier. Now, recall that our 2K memory is actually two banks of 1K, each bank having an enable line formed by interconnecting the 2102 enable lines. We must now select the bank desired, as well as using the $\overline{\text{ENAB}}$ signal formed by the decode process. The key to bank selection is based on the fact that line A10 is LO when addresses 0-1023 are referenced, and HI when addresses 1024-2047 are referenced. This fact allows the easy selection of Bank 0 or Bank 1, if the $\overline{\text{ENAB}}$ signal is active. IC4 is a *data decoder chip*, which provides a unique LO output based upon four input signals. For example, if input lines 10-13 contain data "LO LO LO LO," the first of 10 output lines will be LO. If the input data is "HI LO LO LO," the second output line will be LO; the first returns to a HI state. The remaining input-output correspondence is not used in this design. Since we only desire to monitor one input line (A10), we connect it to IC4 pin 3. Then, when A10 goes LO, IC4 pin 16 goes LO, thus enabling Bank 0. If A10 goes HI, IC4 pin 15 goes LO, selecting Bank 1. Our $\overline{\text{ENAB}}$ signal is fed to the second IC4 input, pin 6. If $\overline{\text{ENAB}}$ goes HI (invalid address), both of the outputs that enable our banks go HI, effectively disabling the entire memory system. It may be seen that the unused inputs and outputs of the data selector IC4 could be used in more elaborate memory systems.

So far we have determined that the address presented to the interface is valid and the correct bank has been selected. All that remains is to control the 2102 read/write function as well as the three-state data bus drivers. The R/W signal is buffered and inverted by IC2B. This output is re-inverted by IC2C and fed to the 2102 read/write lines to direct data flow within the memory chips. This signal is inverted and used to drive the three-state control lines of IC7 and IC8, the data bus drivers. The additional inversion is required as an active LO signal enables the bus drivers, while a HI signal causes the 2102 chips to output data (read cycle). Finally, note that each 2102 receives address lines A0-A9. The interface board was wire-wrapped on a standard perfboard. The memory and interface could have been constructed on a single board, eliminating some interconnections, but I chose to make the interface separate as I had a 2K memory board left over from a former project. The choice is left to the reader.

The Memory

The 2102 RAM device is an economical choice for memory systems under 8K. Eight of the chips are required for each 1K byte of memory. When constructing a memory board, for each 1K bank, tie address lines A0-A9, the $\overline{CE}$ lines, the R/W lines and the DATA IN, DATA OUT lines to form five memory buses. As banks are

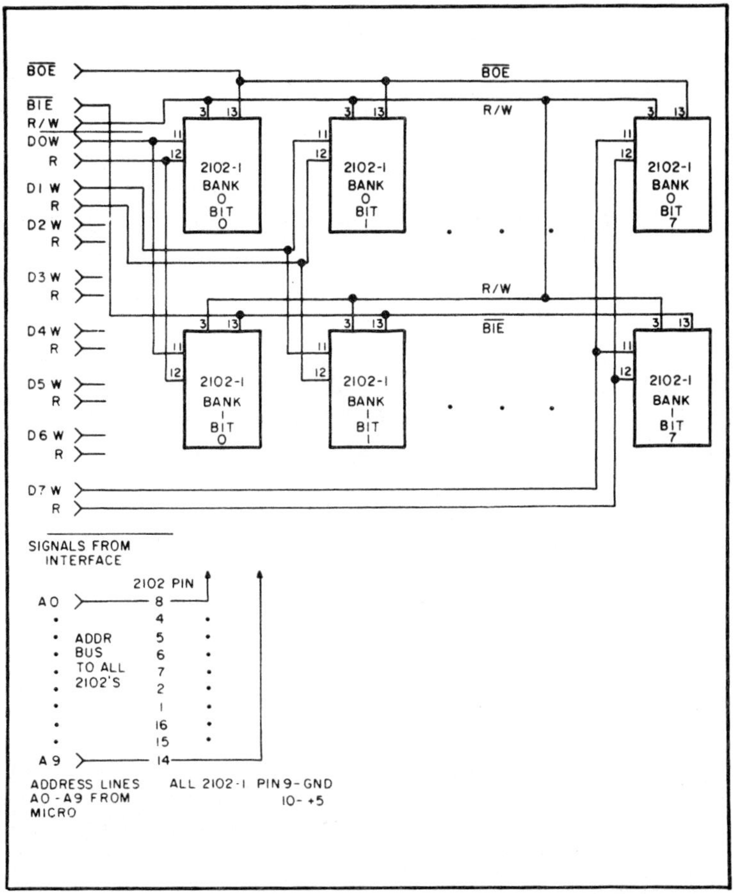

Fig. 3-8. 2K memory consisting of two banks of 1K each. Note that the A0-A9 address bus goes to all 16 2102-1 RAMs, as does the R/W line. The eight enable pins of Bank 0 tied to BOE from the interface (pin 13). All enable lines from Bank 1 go to B1E. Finally, the D0W and D0R lines go to pins 11 and 12 respectively on Bank 0, bit 0, and Bank 1, bit 0. This pattern of interconnections follows for the remaining D-W, R pairs.

formed, all buses are tied *except* the $\overline{CE}$ bus, which is used to select banks. Refer to Fig. 3-8 for details. The memory may be constructed on perfboard and wire-wrapped, but be sure to provide heavy power lines. Commercial memory boards may be used with the home brew interface if the builder so desires. If this approach is taken, be sure that no address decoding is done on the commercial board, or an address conflict will occur.

Testing

Once the interface has been developed and a memory constructed, the system may be connected to the microprocessor board. Connect all buses as indicated in Fig. 3-9. Five volt power (Vcc) for the interface can probably be borrowed from the micro, as the drain is under 60 mA. However, 2K of 2102 RAM requires upwards of 700 mA, dictating a separate supply unless the main supply has the beef. Remember to tie all ground leads if using more than one 5V source. In some cases it is necessary to remove existing memory chips from the micro board if they conflict with the add-on memory. For example, my Motorola MEK prototype board had several 128 byte RAMs in low memory that would have conflicted, so we popped them out and used them in another system.

After making all interconnections and checking for obvious shorts, etc., apply power and check for smoke. If all looks good, insert the ICs, reapply power and then attempt to read a new location. Many 6800 systems use the Motorola MIKBUG® monitor, Which enables the user to execute an *M* command to examine memory. A random pattern should be present. Now attempt to rewrite the location, checking for correct data. Systems with front panel switches, such as the MITS 680, can be checked by manually reading/writing new locations. Next, check the location following the last one supported by the add-on (2048 in this system). It should be zero, indicating correct address decode. Also, try locations that are 2K multiples of the add-on, such as 4096, etc. They, too, should be zero. If all is fine so far, load and execute a program—better yet, write that new application! Don't get lost in all that new memory.

Problems

The most likely problem area is in the address decode logic. If locations read/write erratically, check for address overlap with existing memory or I/O devices. If two devices answer an access request, an error is sure to result. Look for *patterns* in errors. If a single bit of multiple bytes is set or off continuously, check for

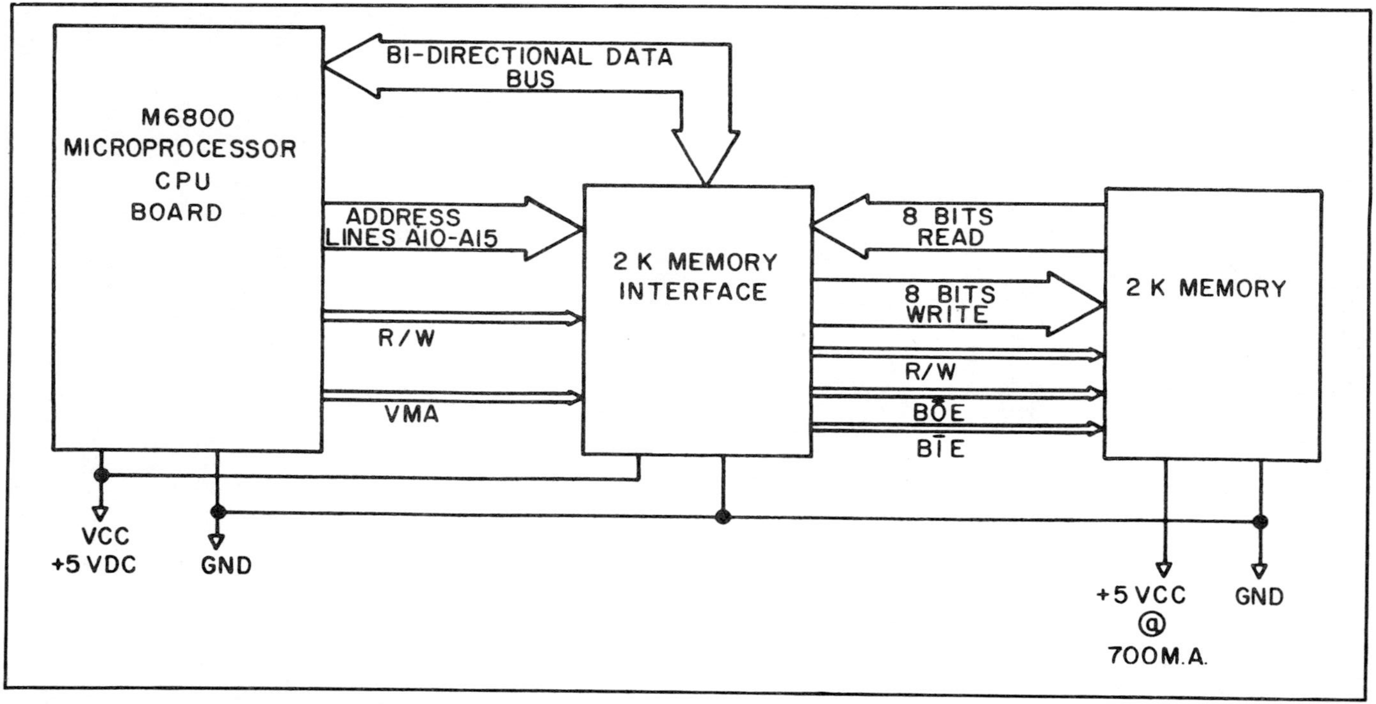

Fig. 3-9. System interconnections.

memory board data line wiring errors. Repetitive errors are easy to isolate due to the fact that so many elements are tied together. Don't discount the possibility of a bad 2102. They are MOS devices, capable of being zapped by static charges during installation. Handle them with care. *Do not* attempt to use old 2102 devices without the "-1" suffix. These are 1000 ns devices and much too slow to be used with 6800 and 8080 systems, especially considering the propagation delays introduced by the interface. Use 2102-1 (500 ns) devices.

After adding a couple of K to your system, applications should suggest themselves at every turn. In order to run BASIC or other language processors, at least 8K will be required. Hopefully, having built the simple 2K system, you will be encouraged to tackle a larger memory system using some of the suggested techniques.

RAM Checkout

This *memory monitor* is a simple assembly language program designed to load zeros or sequential numbers into a block of memory for testing purposes. My original version would only load 256 bytes at a time, which made testing a new 8K board somewhat of a chore, since it had to be run 32 times (256 × 32 = 8K). This final version will load from 1 to 65,536 (64K) bytes of memory. That should be enough to satisfy everyone.

SOL Operations

First, let us describe how my SOL system works so that you can decide how the following explanation pertains to your machine. The SOL has a program in PROM called CONSOL, which handles the keyboard, video and other routines. I can enter data to memory by typing "ENTER—(address)—(data)—CR," and I can dump memory to the video screen by typing "DUMP—(start address)—(finish address)—CR." If the difference between the start address and the finish address is less than 256 bytes, all of the data requested will fill the screen. If more than 256 bytes are requested, the readout will start at the top of the screen and, when it reaches the bottom, will scroll upward until all of the requested data has appeared.

Apparently, the same ENTER and DUMP (examine) operations will work on a computer which uses front panel switches, but they will be done at a much slower rate. Testing a memory board can be accomplished on any machine by first manually loading data into each memory location on the board and then dumping or examining each location to determine that the correct information was indeed written. My memory monitor does it much quicker (Table 3-4). I am

Table 3-4. Memory Monitor Listings.

Address	Op codes	Mnemonics
C900	0E 01	MVI C 01
C902	11 FF 1F	LXI D FF 1F
C905	21 00 00	LXI H 00 00
C908	36 00	MVI M 00
C90A	7E	MOV A M
C90B	81	ADD C
C90C	23	INX M
C90D	77	MOV M A
C90E	1B	DCX D
C90F	3E 00	MVI A 00
C911	BA	CMP D
C912	C2 0A C9	JNZ 0A C9
C915	BB	CMP E
C916	C2 0A C9	JNZ 0A C9
C919	C3 04 C0	CALL TO RESIDENT COMMAND MODE

very much a novice when it comes to programming, so I make no claim that this is the easiest, fastest or best way to get the job done.

Breakdown

If you are not familiar with assembly language, you might be interested in how the memory monitor does what it does. In fact, let's look at it line by line. Since SOL and I talk to each other in a number form called hexadecimal, all numbers in this program are hexadecimal (hex for short).

The first column in Table 3-4. is headed *Address*, and that tells me where this program will be located in memory. When I tell SOL, "EXECUTE C9φφ," it will go to memory location C9φφ, execute the instruction located there and then continue down the list of instructions until told to stop.

The second column is headed *Op code*. These are the instructions, addresses and data that the computer will use to perform its task.

Column three is headed *Mnemonic* (mnemonic means something that helps the memory). Mnemonics are the assembly language abbreviations for the op codes (machine language codes).

I started the program at location C9φφ because the SOL has 1K of onboard RAM beginning at that location. We can put it anywhere

Decimal		Hexadecimal
256		FF
512		1FF
768		2FF
1024	(1K)	3FF
2048	(2K)	7FF
3072	(3K)	BFF
4096	(4K)	FFF
8192	(8K)	1FFF
16384	(16K)	3FFF
32768	(32K)	7FFF
65536	(64K)	FFFF

Table 3-5. A decimal-to-hexadecimal Conversion Table.

you like, but you must rewrite the two JNZ (jump non-zero) instructions. As they stand, a jump will be made to C9ϕA (8080 address and register pair instructions are always written with the address or data backwards). If you wanted to load the memory monitor at location 8ϕϕϕ, for instance, you would change C9 to 8ϕ at each place that it appears in the program. This is called *relocating the program*.

In the first line, ϕ1 in location C9ϕ1 tells the computer how you want it to load the memory locations. ϕϕ here would load all zeros (erase memory), and ϕ1 would load sequential numbers, ϕϕ, ϕ1, ϕ2, etc. ϕ2 would load ϕϕ, ϕ2, ϕ4, etc.

The FF 1F at locations C9ϕ3 and C9ϕ4 tells the computer how many address locations you want to load. FF 1F is actually 1FFF (backwards), which is 8K in the hexadecimal number system (Table 3-5). If you wanted to load a 4K board, then line C9ϕ5 lets the computer know which address to start loading at. The addressing of most memory boards is determined by setting on-board switches or by running jumpers. For this test, we addressed my 8K board to start at address ϕϕϕϕ, but it could be set to start anyplace you want, and instruction C9ϕ5 should reflect this address. If you wanted to locate this board at 6ϕϕϕ because you already had something at ϕϕϕϕ, line C9ϕ5 would read 21 ϕϕ 6ϕ (address reversed as usual).

Enter the program into the memory locations you have selected. Execute the first address, and the computer will load ϕϕ into the starting address on the board to be tested, ϕ1 in the next location, ϕ2 in the next and so on, until it has loaded as many locations as you requested. Then it will stop.

Figure 3-10 is a simplified drawing of the internal makeup of the 8080 microprocessor. Making use of Table 3-4 and Fig. 3-10, let's

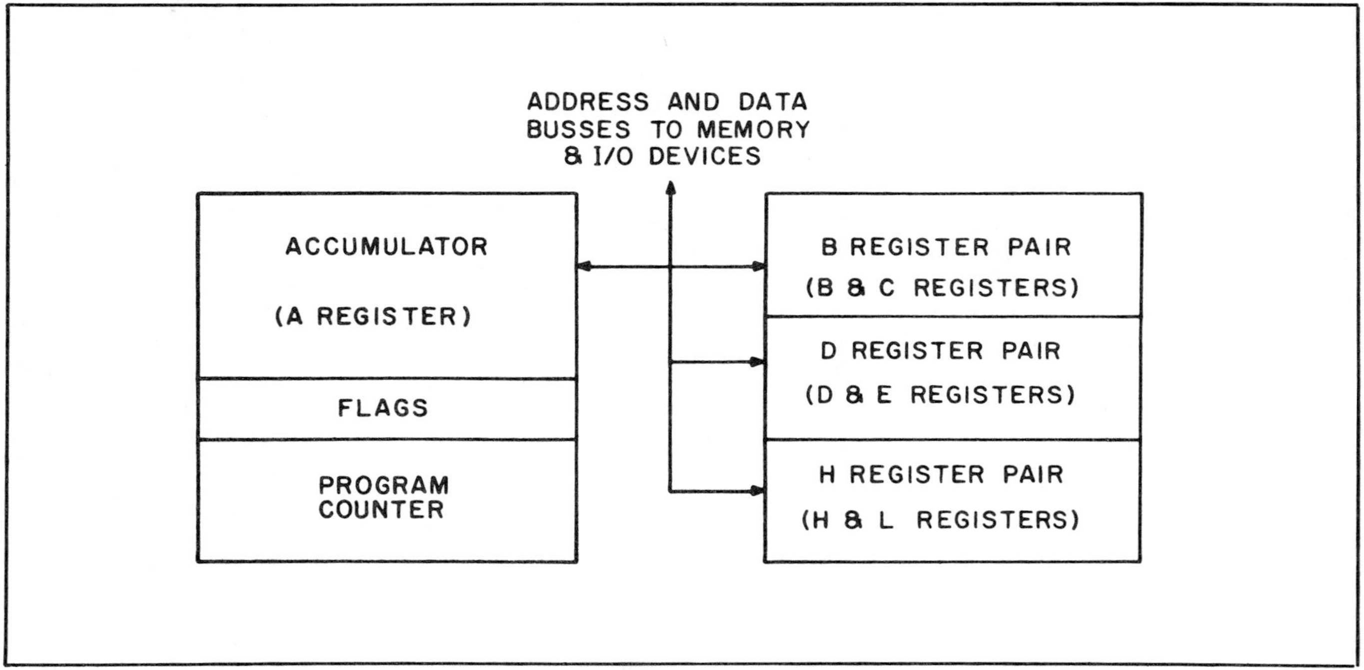

Fig. 3-10. A simplified drawing of the 8080. The registers which make up the B-, D-, and H-register pairs can be used either in pairs or as individual registers, depending on your requirements. The 8080 contains many other features which are not shown here.

step through the memory monitor as the computer would and see what happens. First, my "EXECUTIVE C9ϕϕ" command will load C9ϕϕ into the program counter in the 8080 and start processing instructions from there. The program counter keeps track of which instruction comes next in the program.

The microprocessor can always tell from the first byte of an instruction whether it is a one-, two- or three-byte instruction. As a start, it will fetch ϕE, which is what it found at location C9ϕϕ, and since it knows that ϕE is a two-byte instruction, it will also fetch ϕ1, which is in C9ϕ1. ϕE (MVI C) tells the processor to take the byte that follows ϕE and load it into the C-register. The PC (program counter) then steps to C9ϕ2 and starts a new fetch which is 11 plus FF 1F (LXI D FF 1F). 11 says load the following two bytes into the D-register pair (registers D and E). C9ϕ5—21 ϕϕ ϕϕ (LXI H ϕϕ ϕϕ) loads ϕϕ ϕϕ into the H-register pair (registers H and L), and C9ϕ8—36 ϕϕ (MVI M ϕϕ) tells the processor to load ϕϕ into the location whose address is found in the H-register pair. In other words, you put the address where you want to start your memory board test into the H-register pair (ϕϕϕϕ) and then tell the processor to load ϕϕ at that location.

Next, move the contents (ϕϕ) of the start test location (ϕϕϕϕ) into the A-register (accumulator) C9ϕA—7E (MOV A M), which means that you are about to work on it. The next instruction C9ϕB—81 (ADD C) will add the contents of register C to the accumulator (ϕϕ + ϕ1), and C9ϕC—23 (INX M) increases the address in the H-register pair by one. C9ϕD—77 (MOV M A) takes the contents of the accumulator (ϕ1) and puts them into the location whose address is now in the H-register pair (location ϕϕϕ1). C9ϕE—1B (DCX D) subtracts one from the contents of the D-register pair, and C9ϕF—3E ϕϕ (MVI A ϕϕ) puts ϕϕ into the accumulator.

At the start, the D-register pair contained the total number of locations you wanted to load. After you've gone through the program once and subtracted one from D, check to see if you are finished. The accumulator contains the ϕϕ which you loaded there. C911—BA (CMP D) compares the contents of the D-register with the contents of the accumulator (ϕϕ) and, if they are equal, sets the zero flag. If they are not equal, C912—C2 0A C9 (JNZ 0A C9) will take you back to C90A for another run through the program.

If they are equal (Both ϕϕ), the program counter will move to C915—BB (CMP E) and compare the E-register, which is the lower half of the D-register pair, to see if it is zero also. C916/C2 0A C9 (JNZ 0A) works the same as C912 and reruns the program or passes

```
0000  00  01  02  03  04  05  06  07  08  09  0A  0B  0C  0D  0E  0F
0010  10  11  12  13  14  15  16  17  18  19  1A  1B  1C  1D  1E  1F
0020  20  21  22  23  24  25  26  27  28  29  2A  2B  2C  2D  2E  2F
0030  30  31  32  33  34  35  36  37  38  39  3A  3B  3C  3D  3E  3F
0040  40  41  42  43  44  45  46  47  48  49  4A  4B  4C  4D  4E  4F
0050  50  51  52  53  54  55  56  57  58  59  5A  5B  5C  5D  5E  5F
0060  60  61  62  63  64  65  66  67  68  69  6A  6B  6C  6D  6E  6F
0070  70  71  72  73  74  75  76  77  78  79  7A  7B  7C  7D  7E  7F
0080  80  81  82  83  84  85  86  87  88  89  8A  8B  8C  8D  8E  8F
0090  90  91  92  93  94  95  96  97  98  99  9A  9B  9C  9D  9E  9F
00A0  A0  A1  A2  A3  A4  A5  A6  A7  A8  A9  AA  AB  AC  AD  AE  AF
00B0  B0  B1  B2  B3  B4  B5  B6  B7  B8  B9  BA  BB  BC  BD  BE  BF
00C0  C0  C1  C2  C3  C4  C5  C6  C7  C8  C9  CA  CB  CC  CD  CE  CF
00D0  D0  D1  D2  D3  D4  D5  D6  D7  D8  D9  DA  DB  DC  DD  DE  DF
00E0  E0  E1  E2  E3  E4  E5  E6  E7  E8  E9  EA  EB  EC  ED  EE  EF
00F0  F0  F1  F2  F3  F4  F5  F6  F7  F8  F9  FA  FB  FC  FD  FE  FF
```

Fig. 3-11. A memory dump of the first 255 bytes of memory in the SOL. As can be seen, the computer has counted from ϕ to 256 in hexadecimal.

to the next instruction, depending on the condition of the zero flag. When both registers of the D-register pair are equal to zero, then you have loaded as many memory locations as you originally asked for.

It is now time to exit the program. C919/C3 ϕ4 Cϕ is a call to the command mode in the SOL CONSOL operating system When SOL is turned on or the reset switch is pushed, the computer enters the command mode, puts a prompter (>) on the screen, and waits for me to tell it what to do. This line can be a jump or call to any location you desire and will depend on your machine's operating characteristics.

In order to determine how the test went, I type "DUMP ϕϕϕϕ 1FFF," which covers all of the memory locations of this 8K board, and the screen will scroll through these locations. It's must too fast to really check individual locations, but I'm really only interested in the last location. Since the contents of each location are the contents of the previous location plus one, the contents of 1FFF should be FF, if the test went well. If they aren't, then it is necessary to dump 256 byte pages one at a time until the problem area is found. With this program, I found three 2102 pins that were bent under the IC instead of inserted into the sockets. Figure 3-11 is what the first 256 bytes of memory look like after running the program.

Instruction information for the 8080 is contained in the Intel 8080 Microcomputer Systems User's Manual and the Intel 8080 Assembly Language Programming Manual. The "Intel 8080 Assembly Language Reference Card" is also useful. Anyone who is serious about assembly language programming the 8080 should have all of these.

Any program, whether it is very simple or incredibly complex, is nothing more than a logical progression through a series of instructions. Pick some little chore that you'd like your machine to do, break it down into logical steps, convert those steps into assembly language instructions, and you'll be surprised and happy with the results.

A Simple PROM Programmer

Usually when a PROM is required for a project, a schematic is supplied along with instructions for programming, but not the construction of the programmer. This is a description of the one I built for programming the 8223 PROM. The 8223 PROM is a 32 word by 8 bit memory element. I added a built-in 5 volt regulator and a low current LED to verify the output programming and switches. The only power needed is a regulated 12.5 volt supply or auto battery.

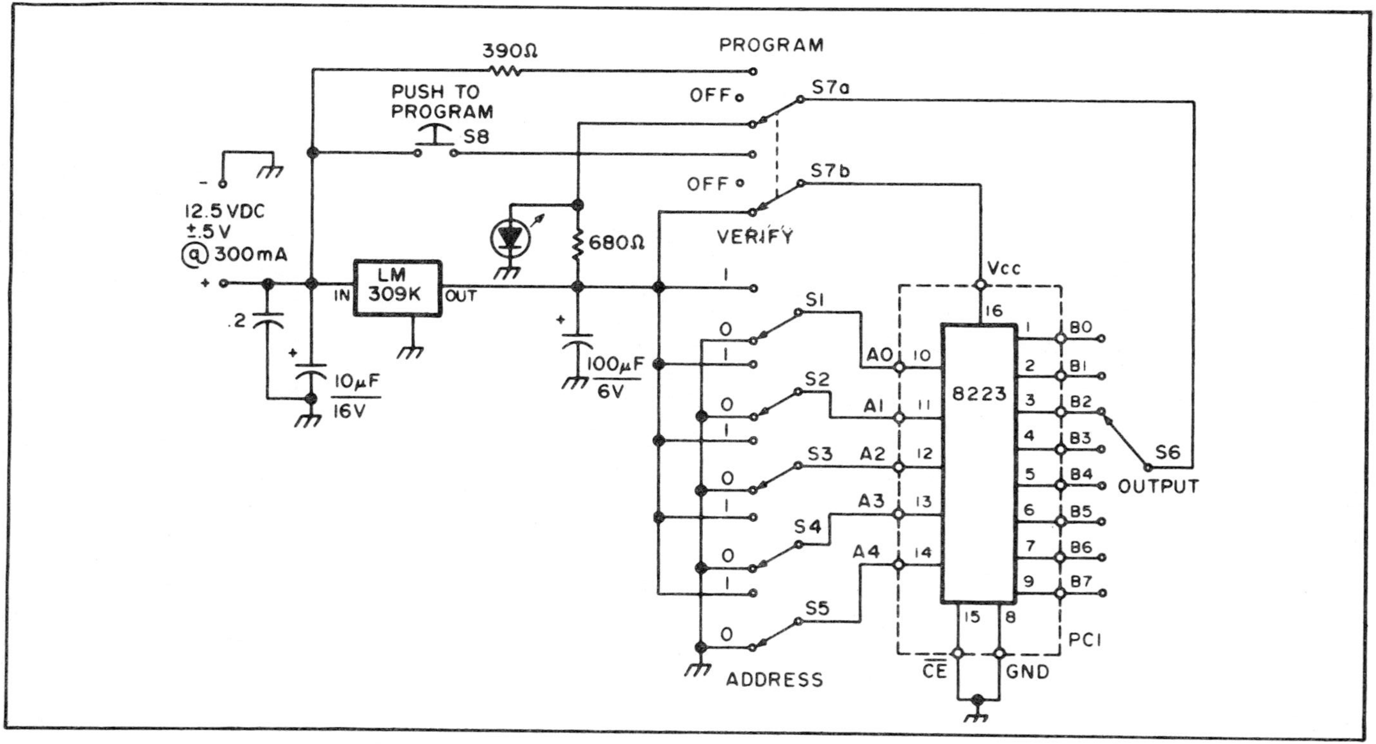

Fig. 3-12. 8223 PROM programmer schematic diagram.

Construction

The programmer (Figs. 3-12 and 3-13) is built in a 4 foot × 6 foot × 2 foot aluminum chassis. A parts layout is given, but may be altered to suit your own taste, depending on the enclosure used. All wiring is point-to-point, with only one PC board used. The PC board has a socket for the 8223 and also provides solder pads for wiring.

First, lay out the top panel. Then drill the holes for the switches and LM309K. Drill two 7/16" holes and file to a rectangular shape for the IC socket to fit snug. Using the PC board as a template, mark and drill the two mounting holes. Drill a hole somewhere on the panel for the LED and two holes on a side panel for the power connections. Deburr all holes and cutouts. Apply lettering if desired.

Mount all the parts on the chassis with appropriate hardware, using insulated washers where necessary. A few ground lugs will also help. Install the resistors, capacitors and LED first, then wire the output selector switch, using color-coded wire to avoid confusion. Then wire the address and program switches, the Vcc and ground lines. For a complete parts list, see Table 3-6.

Operation

Recheck all you wiring and then program according to the following instructions:

- Connect programmer to a regulated 12.5 volt source.
- Set the PROGRAM-VERIFY switch to OFF.
- Insert the 8223 to be programmed in the socket, paying attention to the location of pin 1.
- Set the ADDRESS switches to the proper word to be programmed.
- Set the OUTPUT switch to the output to be programmed for the corresponding word.

Table 3-6. Parts List.

1	LM309K
1	390 Ohm ½W
1	680 Ohm ½W
1	LED
1	.2 uF disc
1	10 uF 16 V
1	100 uF 6 V
1	Chassis RS # 270-245
2	Banana jacks
1	16 pin DIP socket
PC1	Printed Circuit RS # 276-024
S1-S5	SPDT RS #275-326
S6	8-position rotary or thumbwheel
S7	DPDT Neutral Center RS #275-1545
S8	SPST Momentary Contact push-button

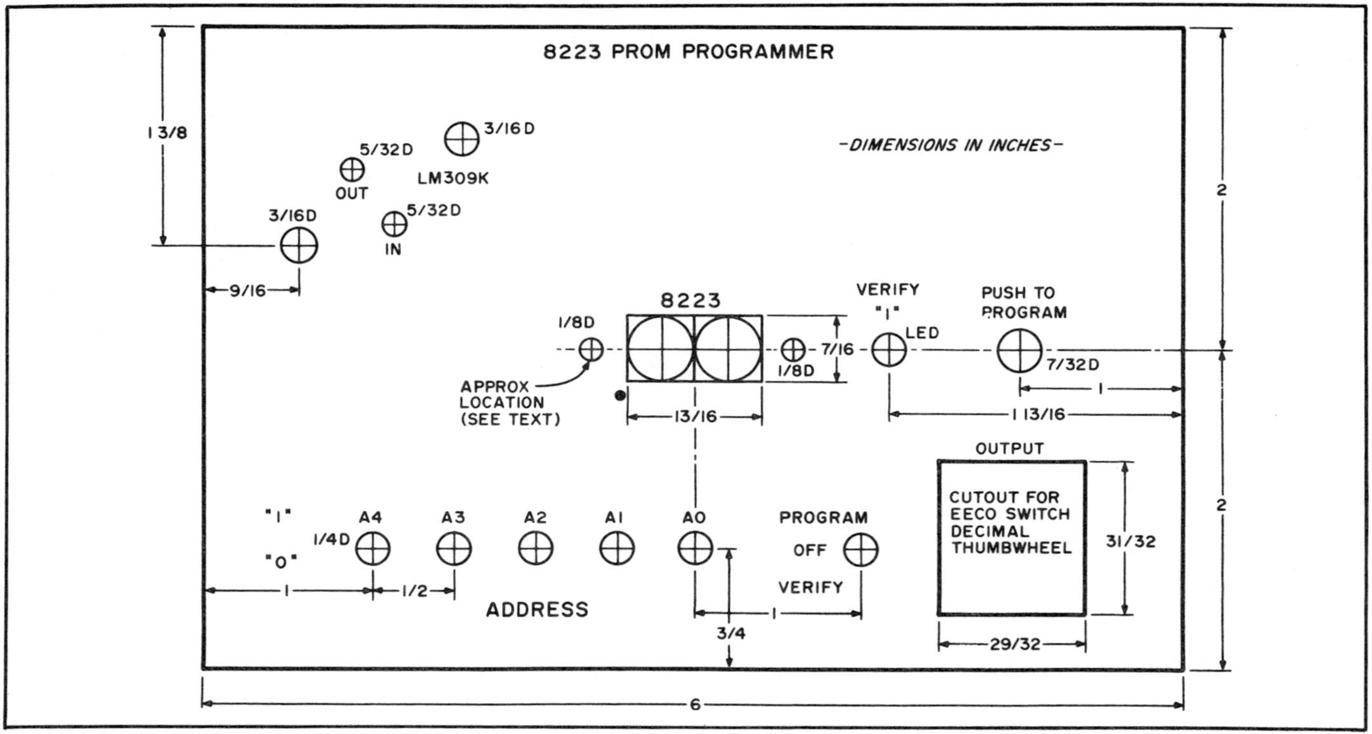

Fig. 3-13. Parts layout of top panel with suggested labeling. Hole for LED should ensure tight press-fit.

- Set the PROGRAM-VERIFY switch to PROGRAM.
- Momentarily depress the PUSH-TO-PROGRAM switch to program a logic 1. (Do not exceed one second.)
- Set the PROGRAM-VERIFY switch to VERIFY. The LED will light indicating a logic 1 has been programmed. Set switch to OFF.
- Repeat steps 4 through 8 to program the rest of the chip.

Only logic 1s need to be programmed as the chip comes with all outputs at a logic 0. Also, by using the V E R I F Y position, pre-programmed chips may be tested and a truth table made up.

Memory Chips

Data processing systems have revolutionized our world, allowing vast amounts of information to be stored, exchanged, updated and utilized in ways undreamed of a few years ago. A chain of department stores can be tied together, for example, by a data network making current inventory, personnel and credit information instantly available at widely separated locations; a railroad can control activity at its switchyard from a control center hundreds of miles distant; switching functions within a telephone company office can be accomplished rapidly and reliably in accordance with stored program instructions. The information involved in each of these examples is different, but the underlying processing principles are the same.

A digital computer or data processor of any type is basically a stored-program machine, in which a memory facility holds a set of operating instructions—the system program. Information is put into a digital format and fed into the machine, which retains it in a data memory. The instructions in the program memory, which are also in digital form, tell the processor what problem is to be solved, or function performed, related to the input data. When the operations demanded by the program memory have been completed, the data is fed out to be utilized in some manner. In practice, program instructions are often stored within the same memory facility as the data; in this way, the program can also be changed if desired.

Despite surface differences, the ways in which memory facilities receive, hold, and feed out information are all based on either sequential or random access principles.

Sequential Memories

The sequential, or serial, memory method requires that the data bits comprising the information be arranged in a particular order. Data stored in this manner—including both programmed

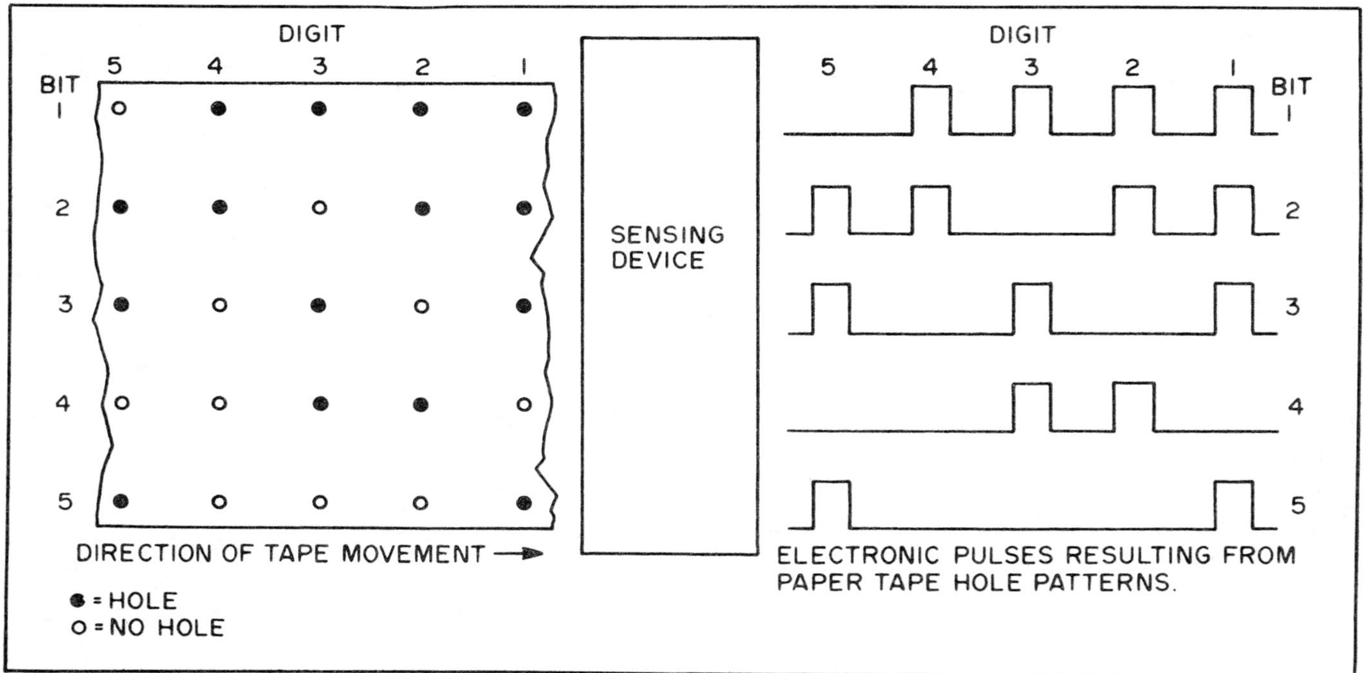

Fig. 3-14. Paper tape is a form of sequential memory storage, in that the bits identifying a given digit can only be retrieved during their allotted sensing time, which may cause delay in finding desired data.

instructions and input information—is retrieved strictly in accordance with its position in a time sequence.

A simple example of sequential memory storage is paper tape, which uses the presence or absence of holes to indicate the condition of a data bit; the combined states of several bits identify a particular digit (Fig. 3-14). The tape is moved through a sensing device to convert the hole patterns into a series of pulses for electronic processing. Each piece of information is retrieved as it passes the sensor. Another form of sequential memory storage is magnetic tape, which stores information as magnetic flux variations corresponding to the 1s and 0s of digital data.

Sequential access memory system, including punched cards and magnetic disks as well as tapes, have been widely used in the area of mass computer memories. They typically contain program instructions and must be physically introduced into the processor system—threaded through a sensing device, for example—so that input data can be operated upon. They may also be used to retain the data for future processing. These devices provide a permanent storage capability since the cards, disks and tapes can be removed and filed for repeated use, and they have non-destructive readouts (i.e., data does not have to be re-entered every time it is used); however, they have some shortcomings which limit their usefulness in high speed memory applications.

For example, sequential access can be a relatively slow process because a large amount of irrelevant data may have to be scanned before the desired bits are found. This delay may be from milliseconds to minutes, which is much too great for many of the uses to which modern data processing equipment is put. Additionally, these sequential mass memory systems require a mechanism to move the data-carrying medium past the sensor. This device is of necessity completely mechanical, and is subject to the adjustment and maintenance considerations which apply to all such devices.

Temporary Memories

Cards, tapes and disks continue to play an important role as high density, longterm mass memory storage elements in such applications as personnel record maintenance, inventory control and retention of performance data for comparison with future achievements.

For low capacity, temporary memory storage, however, structures composed of semiconductor devices have become dominant in recent years. Temporary data storage facilities are used in such areas as office equipment (calculators, etc.) and immediate-use or

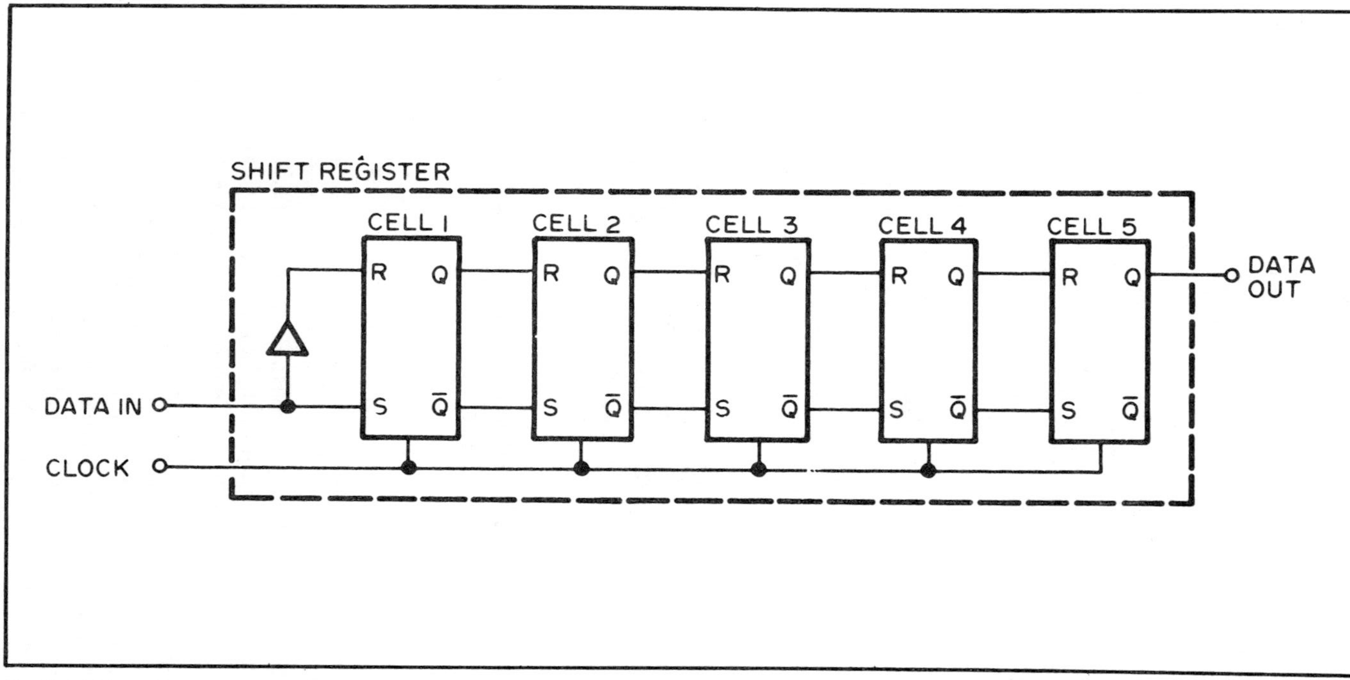

Fig. 3-15. The shift register, which stores data for as long as it takes for the clock to move it through each cell, is typical of semiconductor sequential memory systems.

working memories wherein a data processing device can hold the data with which it is dealing at any given time. It is not uncommon for a data processing system to use tapes and similar elements as permanent, high volume program storage facilities and semiconductor structures for the working memories in which the stored data is operated upon.

Temporary memories are also widely used in data processing terminals, which serve as remote input/output units for a large central computer and may be in any number of forms, from a simple typewriter keyboard to a small computer. Terminals provide a means of encoding data for manipulation by a central computer, and decoding it for use by a human operator.

Interconnection of central computer and remote terminal is commonly made over telephone lines through an interface unit called a *modem*, or data set. The data set may also contain a temporary memory facility which allows it to hold data and either condition it for transmission over the lines or prepare received data for application to the processor.

The semiconductor devices used in temporary memory structures are typically arranged as groups of individual units called memory cells, each of which stores one bit of information as either a logic 1 or logic 0. A cell may consist of as little as one transistor-capacitor combination, or it may be a complex arrangement of several components. But, whatever its composition, it has at least two states that can represent digital data bits.

Shift Registers

A shift register is a device for the temporary storage of digital information. When a shift, or clock, pulse is applied, the register accepts new data and moves every stored bit one step toward the output. Figure 3-15 shows an example of a semiconductor shift register containing five memory cells, each of which is a solid state reset-set (R-S) flip flop circuit. Data applied to the register input in a digital form is stored and shifted from cell to cell in accordance with the clock cycle rate. A logic 1 on the S input of cell 1, for example, will set the flip flop to the 1, or "on," state if a clock pulse is present at input C, thus storing the digit. On the next clock pulse, the stored bit is shifted out of cell 1 to set the second cell to the 1 state, and a new digit is fixed in the first cell. This procedure continues through the register, with the output of the final cell being shifted out for data processing. The clock frequency controls the rate at which the shift register stores and feeds out data bits, with each bit being delayed between input and output by as many clock cycles as there are cells in the register. Since the storage and retrieval are done on a first-in, first-out basis, the shift register is a sequential memory storage device.

Digital data can also be handled by a random access process. This does not mean, of course, that no orderly procedure is involved. It means, rather, that information can be stored in a particular memory cell, or location, and retrieved without regard for any other location.

Random Access Memory Systems

A random access memory (RAM) can be defined as a structure in which any data bit can be stored (written) or retrieved (read out) in any order.

One of the most basic ways to create a memory cell is through the use of the bistable multivibrator, or flip flop. As shown in Fig. 3-16, such a memory cell may consist of only two transistors, two resistors and a power source. In this cell, one or the other of the transistors is always conducting, holding the other one off. When an external signal forces the off transistor into conduction, the initially on transistor turns off and remains in this condition until another external signal resets it. The flip flop, therefore, has two stable states which can be used to store information in the form of logic 1s and 0s.

A RAM is esentially a matrix of such memory cells, with each cell identified by a unique code, or address. The data processing

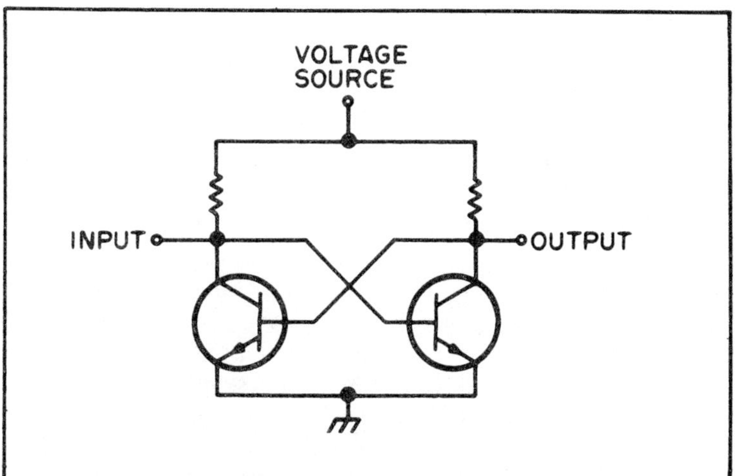

Fig. 3-16. The bistable multivibrator, or flip flop, has two stable states, making it an ideal digital data memory storage cell.

equipment can retrieve a bit of information by addressing the proper location. Because of the matrix structure, the time required to locate any given bit is approximately the same as that required to locate any other bit. For example, in Fig. 3-17 the digit stored in cell 1, at location A1, could be available at the data output in almost exactly the same time as the bit in cell 16, location D4. This rapid access to information makes the RAM ideal for application as a temporary storage facility.

Random access memory structures are of two basic types: read/write and read only. A read/write RAM is programmable; that is, data can be entered into, changed, and removed from the memory at any time. A read only memory (ROM), however, has certain data patterns fixed into it, usually during the manufacturing process. In such a structure, information can be read out—it will always perform the same function—but the stored program does not change. Because the data pattern is fixed, a ROM retains its program regardless of circuit power considerations; that is, it is a *non-volatile* memory device. A read/write memory, however, needs a constant source of power to remain in operation. If power is removed, the semiconductors stop conducting and the stored information is lost, so the read/write RAM is considered to be a *volatile* device.

Although it is not technically accurate to do so, common usage has led read/write memories to be referred to simply as RAMSs, while read only structures—which are, in reality, a type of RAM—are designated Rms.

Bipolar and Unipolar Transistors

The two most widely used devices in memory matrix design today are the bipolar and unipolar, or field effect, transistor. Each can be easily realized as an integrated circuit (IC) component, and they are readily adaptable to virtually any circuit configuration.

Essentially, a bipolar transistor is a semiconductor device whose conductive properties depend upon both majority and minority carriers; that is, current flows in a bipolar transistor because of the simultaneous movement of both positive and negative charges. Negative charges predominate in n-type semiconductor material because there is a surplus of free electrons within the material's atomic structure; p-type material, however, has a shortage of free electrons. The regions in which the electrons would normally exist act as positive, mass-bearing charges called holes; p-type material thus maintains an excess of positive charge carriers. The common

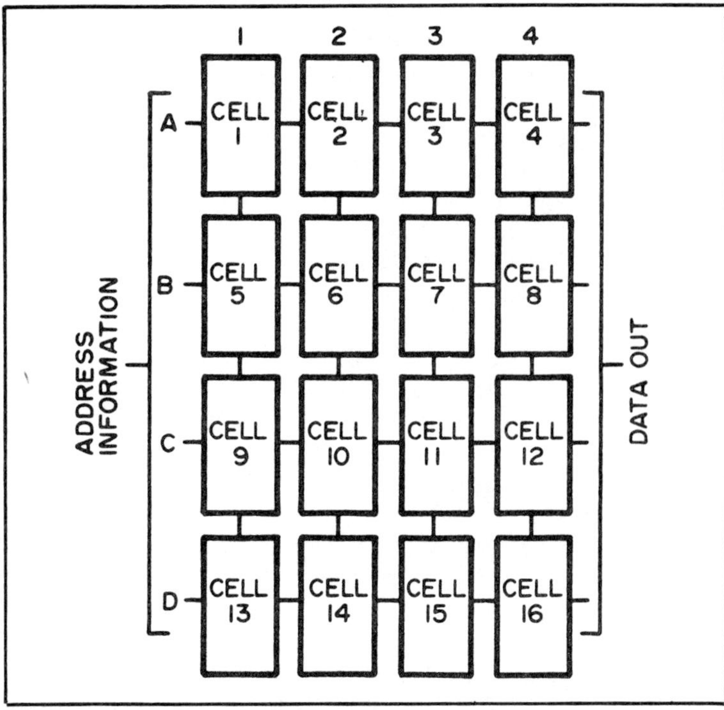

Fig. 3-17. A random access memory (RAM) is a matrix of memory cells, any of which can be accessed without regard for any other cell.

transistor is a general type of bipolar device; since its current flows due to hole and electron movement. Figure 3-18A shows the normal flow pattern within an NPN structure. Figure 3-18B shows a bipolar NPN structure as an integrated circuit. The forward-biased emitter-base junction allows electrons to be injected by the emitter into the base region. Within the base, the greater part of the current flow is caused by holes combining with the excess electrons. The reverse bias of the collector-base junction allows electrons to pass into the collector region. Because there are two n-type regions, electrons are the majority carriers, although the simultaneous action of the minority carrier holes is indispensable.

The field effect transistor (FET) is a unipolar device, in that its current flow is the result of the movement of only one type of carrier. In what is called the p-channel FET, holes are the majority carriers, while the carriers in an n-channel FET are electrons. Figure 3-18C shows a p-channel FET structure operating in the enhancement mode, which is the most common operating mode for FETs. In this mode, there is no conduction within the device when the gate voltage is zero. The other mode of operation is called *depletion*, wherein the semiconductor device is always conducting and requires a proper gate-to-source voltage to turn off.

When the gate in Fig. 3-18C is made negative with respect to the source, it creates an electrostatic field which attracts holes from the n-type semiconductor material toward the area directly below the gate dielectric material. Initially, this n-type area has a surplus of electrons, but as the holes are drawn into it, the electrons are neutralized. At some gate voltage, the holes become dominant and a current-carrying channel is produced between source and drain in which holes are the majority carriers. Because the gate is electrically isolated from the rest of the structure by the dielectric material, there is no current flow into it. The channel, which allows current to flow between source and drain, is created and maintained by the electrostatic field.

The need to provide more electronic function in increasingly small areas has resulted in a great variety of miniaturized circuits. Bipolar transistors, for example, can be realized as discrete items, such as those seen in various entertainment products. In data processing applications, however, the large number of components required to produce a memory matrix makes the use of such bulky devices impractical. A circuit board with several hundred discrete transistors mounted on it, which is what a memory matrix would require, would be too unwieldy to be of any real use.

Bipolar Transistor RAMs

Integrated circuit techniques allow quantities of circuit elements to be realized in a small space. These techniques have been used to produce bipolar transistor memories of various microminiaturized sizes and densities.

The basic storage element in these matrices is the bistable flip flop, which appears in many circuit variations to meet different application requirements.

A bipolar RAM cell which has been widely used is the transistor-transistor-logic (TTL) type, exemplified by the multiple-emitter circuit (Fig. 3-19). In this case, the data processor applies an address code to a decoding circuit. The decoded address raises the voltage on the correct word select line (places it at a logic 1 level), preparing the cell for the read or write function. A logic 1 bit can be written into the cell, for example, by placing the write enable line at a low voltage (logic 0) level while the data bit input is logic 1. This caused the bit line to be low, turning Q1 on and Q2 off, a state which represents a logic 1 within the cell. Once the write function is

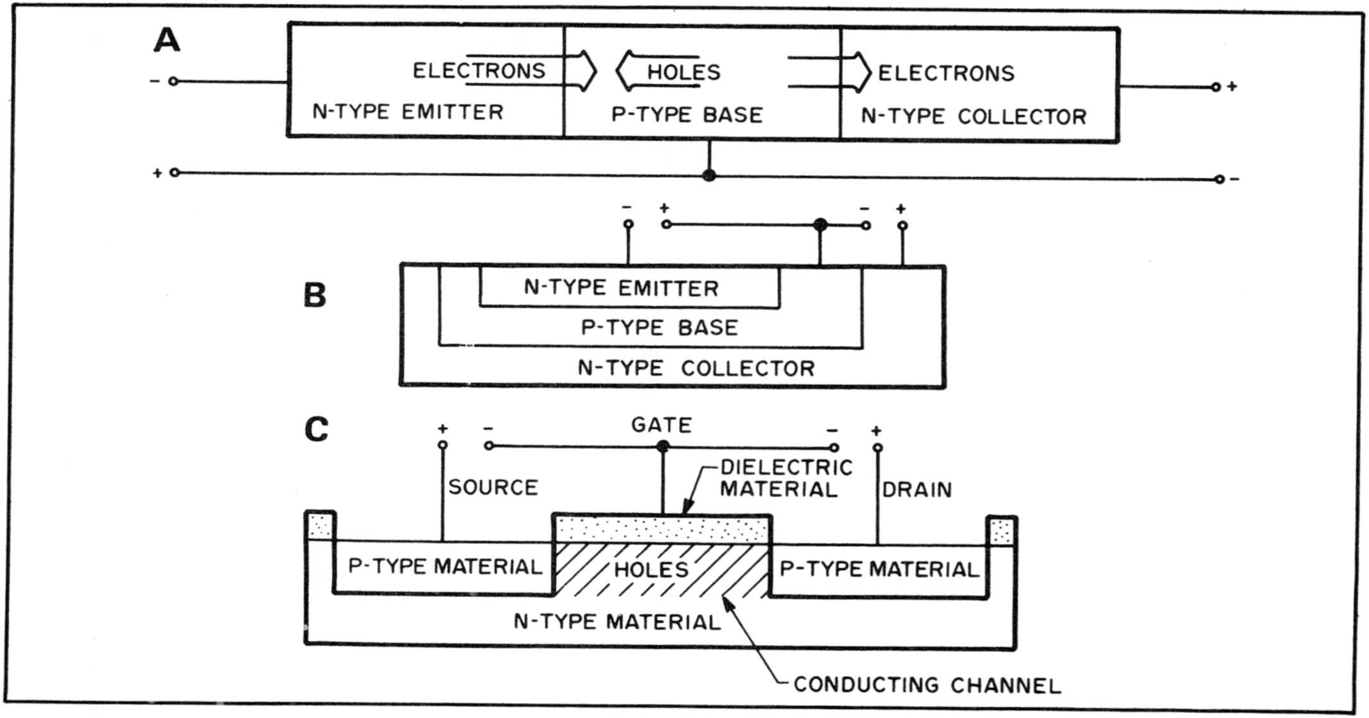

Fig. 3-18. Bipolar and unipolar transistor structures are the most widely used semiconductor memory cell components. (A) Normal flow; (B) bipolar NPN structure; (C) conducting channel.

complete, the address changes, the word select line returns to a logic 0 state and Q1 remains on. To read out the stored digit, the address raises the word select line level and the write enable line and the write enable line is held high (logic 1), allowing read current representing the value of the cell's contents to flow into the appropriate sense amplifier for output to the data processor. Because the read process does not change the state of the flip flop, the stored information is not lost and the cell is considered to have a nondestructive readout capability.

The 2-word, 2-bits-per-word memory shown in Fig. 3-19 is, of course, limited in its application. The same addressing, reading and writing functions, however, are performed in bipolar RAMs containing several times the number of cells. A typical example of expanded capacity is a single integrated circuit capable of storing 16 words of 4 bits each, for a total of 64 bits on one tiny silicon chip. GTE Lenkurt uses nine such chips in both its 262A and 262B data sets. The bipolar RAMs comprise a data memory, in which input data is held to be operated upon. Because of the read/write capabilities of the RAMs, the data being processed can constantly be updated and changed.

Major considerations in memory design include the speed with which a cell can be made to change state (access time) and the amount of power dissipated by the cell's components.

Operating in a saturation mode in which the *on* transistor constantly conducts the maximum possible current, the TTL-type memory cell requires some amount of time to drive the transistor out of saturation before a change of state can occur. This delay is only on the order of nanoseconds, but is enough to concern circuit designers. In addition, the saturation mode consumes relatively large amounts of power. Two of the more successful configurations developed to overcome these disadvantages are the diode coupled and emitter-coupled logic (ECL) cells.

Diode Coupled RAMs

Two gating diodes are used to control conduction in a diode coupled cell (Fig. 3-20). In integrated circuits, these diodes are frequently hot-electron, or Schottky barrier, devices, which become forward-biased at lower voltages than conventional diodes.

If the state of a cell must be changed to store a bit, the address decoder causes the voltage on the word select line to be forced low, while the voltage is raised on the bit line associated with the transistor to be turned off. Referring to Fig. 3-20, in which Q2 is hypothetically to be turned off, raising the bit line B voltage and dropping the word select line (effectively making it more negative) draws addi-

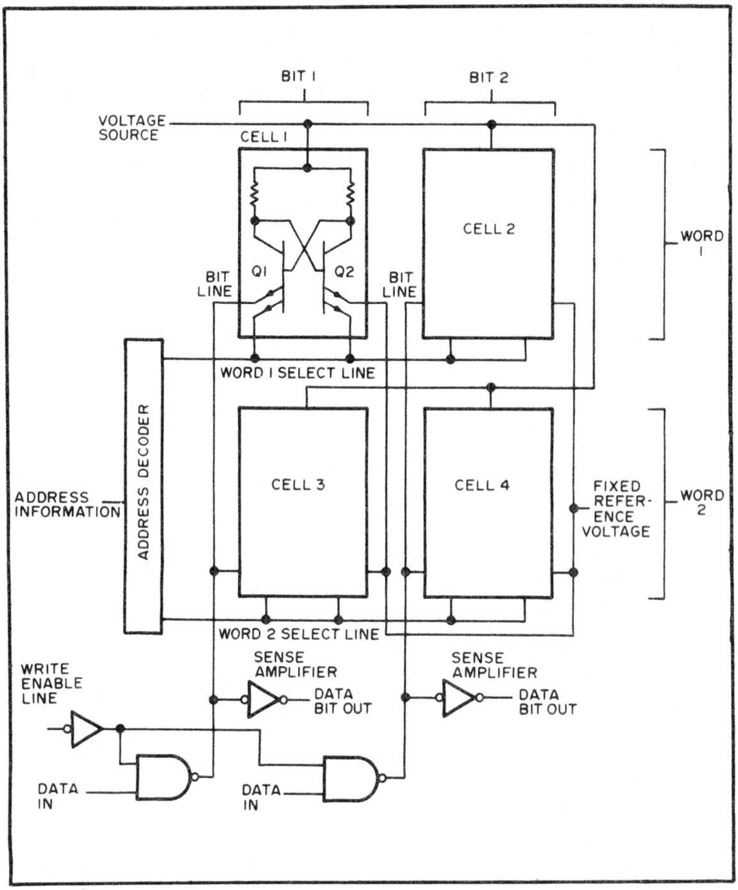

Fig. 3-19. A 2-word, 2-bits-per-word memory array utilizing multi-emitter bipolar transistor structures.

tional current through R4, increasing the base voltage on Q1 to the point at which it begins conducting. The cross-coupling of the transistors then causes Q2 to turn off, thus effecting the cell's change of state.

Reading the stored digit out of a diode coupled cell also requires that the word select line be forced low, but in this case there is no voltage increase on either of the bit lines. The combined effects of the lowered word select line and a bias network cause the diode associated with the *on* transistor to be forward-biased, causing the diode to conduct. Since the diode associated with the *off* transistor is reverse-biased, a differential voltage develops between the bit lines. A sensing circuit determines the cell's logic state from this voltage.

Read current in a diode coupled cell is greater than standby current, which flows when the cell is storing a bit without being addressed, but is substantially lower than write current. Because of this, the voltage developed across the load resistors during the read operation is not great enough to change the cell's state and the readout is a nondestructive process.

Since standby current is lower than read current and is present a greater per cent of the time, overall power consumption in a diode coupled cell is lower than that of a TTL device.

ECL RAMs

The structure of emitter-coupled logic (ECL) memory cells closely resembles that of TTL cells, but biasing techniques are used to keep the transistors out of saturation. This allows the ECL storage element to change state very rapidly. The greatest advantage of ECL over other semiconductor memory configurations is that it has the shortest access time of all. Reading and writing processes are accomplished in essentially the same manner as for TTL, but at a greater speed. Because it constantly draws high current, however, an ECL memory cell has even higher power consumption than TTL, a fact which does impair its usefulness in certain applications.

MOS Technology

One of the major objectives in semiconductor memory design has been to incorporate as much capacity as possible in the smallest area. The greatest size reductions have been achieved with metal oxide-silicon (MOS) techniques, which produce field effect transistor (FET) structures that are considerably more compact than the bipolar integrated circuits (ICs) previously discussed.

An MOS FET is formed by depositing an insulating metal oxide—most often silicon dioxide—on a chip of silicon. Etching processes then remove the oxide from selected areas of the chip, exposing the substrate at source and drain locations while leaving the gate region insulated. Further processing establishes n- and p-type areas within the substrate.

The size reduction possible with MOS techniques allows a much denser memory array to be produced within a given space than is possible with vipolar devices; there are also sbustantially lower power requirements and reduced packaging costs.

Storage cells composed of MOS FETs may be of either a static or dynamic nature. A static cell retains its stored data as long as

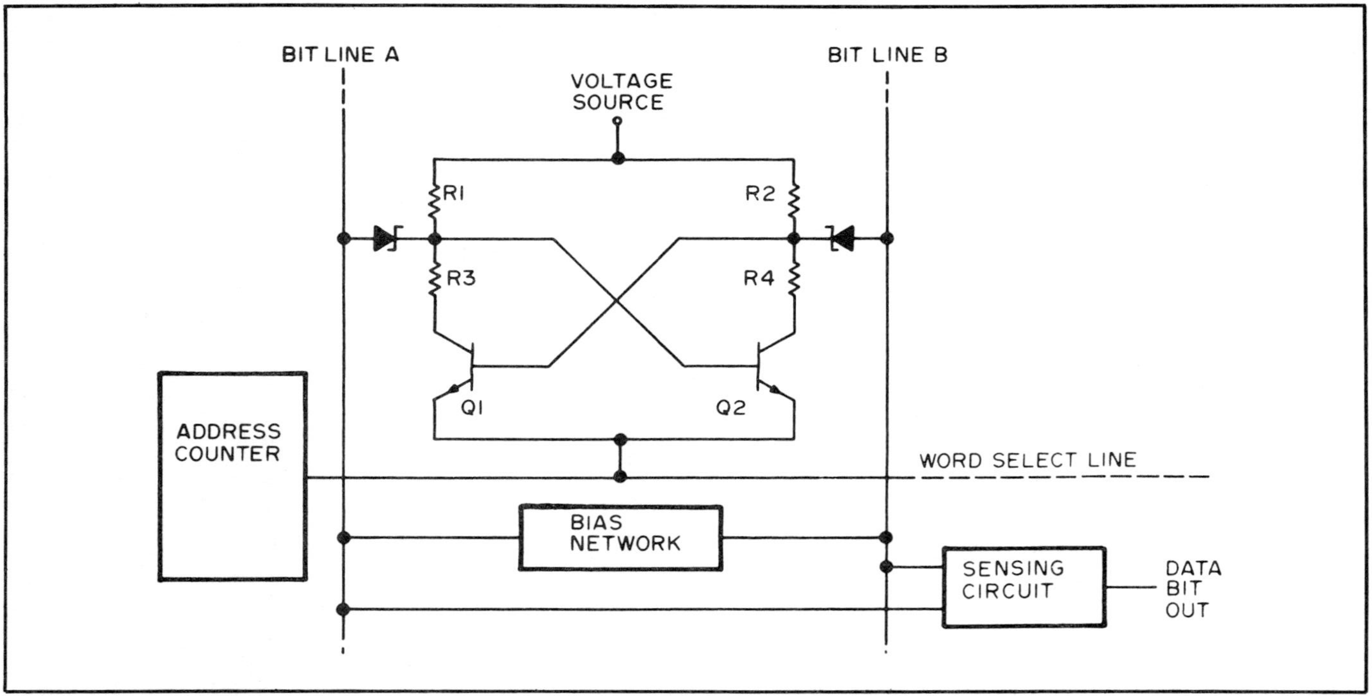

Fig. 3-20. A diode coupled memory cell uses gating diodes to control conduction and reduce power consumption.

power is supplied to the circuit. A dynamic cell depends upon capacitive charge storage to hold its data, and must receive a refresh input to counteract the effects of leakage.

Static MOS RAMs

The basic static MOS RAM cell is a bistable multivibrator (Fig. 3-21) closely resembling the bipolar flip flop used in TTL memories. In an MOS flip flop, however, transistors serve not only as crosscoupled inverters (Q3 and Q4), but also as load resistances (Q1 and Q2). Electrical isolation of the FET gate results in a very high input resistance which can be controlled by the gate voltage. A large-value resistor can thus be produced by an FET in a relatively small space compared to a conventional resistor.

Since only one of the cross-coupled inverters conducts at any given time, the cell has two stable states which can be used to store information in the form of logic 1s and 0s. The state of the cell is determined by external address and data signals. The cell's state remains constant unless changed by an external signal, so no refresh action is required and the circuitry needed to support the operation to support the operation of the cell is simplified.

A static MOS RAM storage unit, however, contains a minimum of four transistors, so it occupies a considerable amount of space on a silicon chip and consumes a relatively large amount of power. Because of these disadvantages, static devices have been largely replaced by dynamic MOS RAMs.

Dynamic MOS RAMs

The basic storage element in a dynamic MOS RAM cell is a capacitor, which holds and releases a stored charge in response to read and write commands. While the capacitor could be an external device, it is much more common for dynamic RAMs to utilize the capacitance existing between gate and source of the MOS FET itself. This capacitance is due to the isolation of the gate from the rest of the structure by a dielectric material. Charging the gate-source capacitance sufficiently to turn the transistor on represents a logic 1 state in most applications, while a lower charge or no charge at all serves as a logic 0.

Inevitably, as with all capacitive devices, the charge stored in the gate-source region drains off due to leakage current. If the charge is allowed to deteriorate too much, the data bit is lost, so some means must be provided to periodically restore, or refresh, the charge; a common requirement is that every cell in a memory matrix be refreshed every 2 milliseconds. Circuits to accomplish this

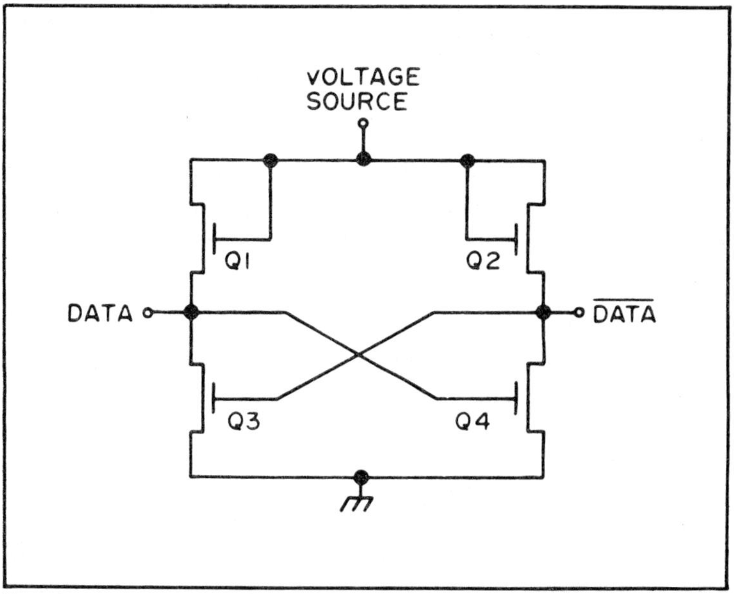

Fig. 3-21. The heart of the static MOS RAM storage cell is the bistable flip flop composed entirely of field effect transistors (FETs). The logic level at one terminal is always the complement of that at the other.

are included in dynamic RAM designs, as are address decoding circuits.

The operation of a typical dynamic MOS RAM cell can be illustrated with the 3 transistor cell shown in Fig. 3-22. In this case, information is stored as a charge in the gate-source capacitance (C_G) of transistor Q2. To write a data bit into this cell, an address decoder produces a write select signal, activiating transistor Q1 and allowing data on the write data line to be transferred to the storage element. Depending upon the state of the data input, C_G either charges or is discharged. When the write select signal is removed at the end of the write cycle, the bit is held in the cell.

At the beginning of a read cycle, both the read and write data lines are preset to some voltage. When the address decoder produces a read select signal, Q3 is ready to begin conducting. If the charge on C_G is sufficient (logic 1), Q2 turns on and current flows through Q2 and Q3, reducing the voltage on the read data line. With no charge on the capacitance, Q2 and Q3 remain off and the read data line stays at its preset level. Because of the gate isolation, C_G is in the same condition (charged or discharged) at the end of the read cycle as at the beginning, making the read process *nondestructive*. An output amplifier senses the state of the read data line and determines what cell condition would produce it (a low-level line generally indicates a stored logic 1) for application to the data processor.

Refresh

Refresh of the stored digit in Fig. 3-22 is accomplished through a clocked amplifier connected between the read and write data lines. Control circuitry provides the timing necessary to keep the refresh cycle separate from the read and write operations.

The refresh process involves reading out the stored digit and writing it back into the cell. To do this, both data lines are preset at the beginning of the refresh cycle. A read select signal is then produced, transferring the bit to the read data line in the same manner as the normal read operation. The refresh amplifier inverts the condition of the read data line and applies it to the write data line. A write select signal then replaces the read signal and the data present on the write data line is entered into the memory. If, for example, a logic 1 (maximum charge) is stored on C_G, the read data line is forced low (logic 0) when the read select signal forces Q2 and Q3 into conduction. The refresh amplifier inverts this and applies logic 1 to the write data line; the presence of the write select signal causes this data to be written into the cell as a refreshed bit. With no charge (logic 0) on C_G, this sequence is repeated, with a logic 0 appearing on the write data line to ensure that the capacitance is not charged by stray circuit currents.

In Fig. 3-22, timing from the control circuitry allows a single amplifier to serve an entire column of cells. One alternative configuration uses a common read/write data line. This lets the cell form a loop within itself and thus eliminates refresh amplifiers.

ROMs

A read only memory (ROM) is a data storage facility into which information is normally written only once. After this entry, a ROM always produces the same output when addressed.

The difference between the read/write RAM and the ROM can perhaps be best illustrated with the example of the pocket calculator. In almost all calculator designs, a RAM matrix serves as a *working*, or data, *memory* and ROMs are used for input/output interface, timing control and program storage (Fig. 3-23).

Each key on the calculator keyboard is identified by a unique binary number. All of these numbers are permanently fixed in the ROM encoder so that, when a key is pressed, the corresponding binary number appears as the encoder output. If a digit key is

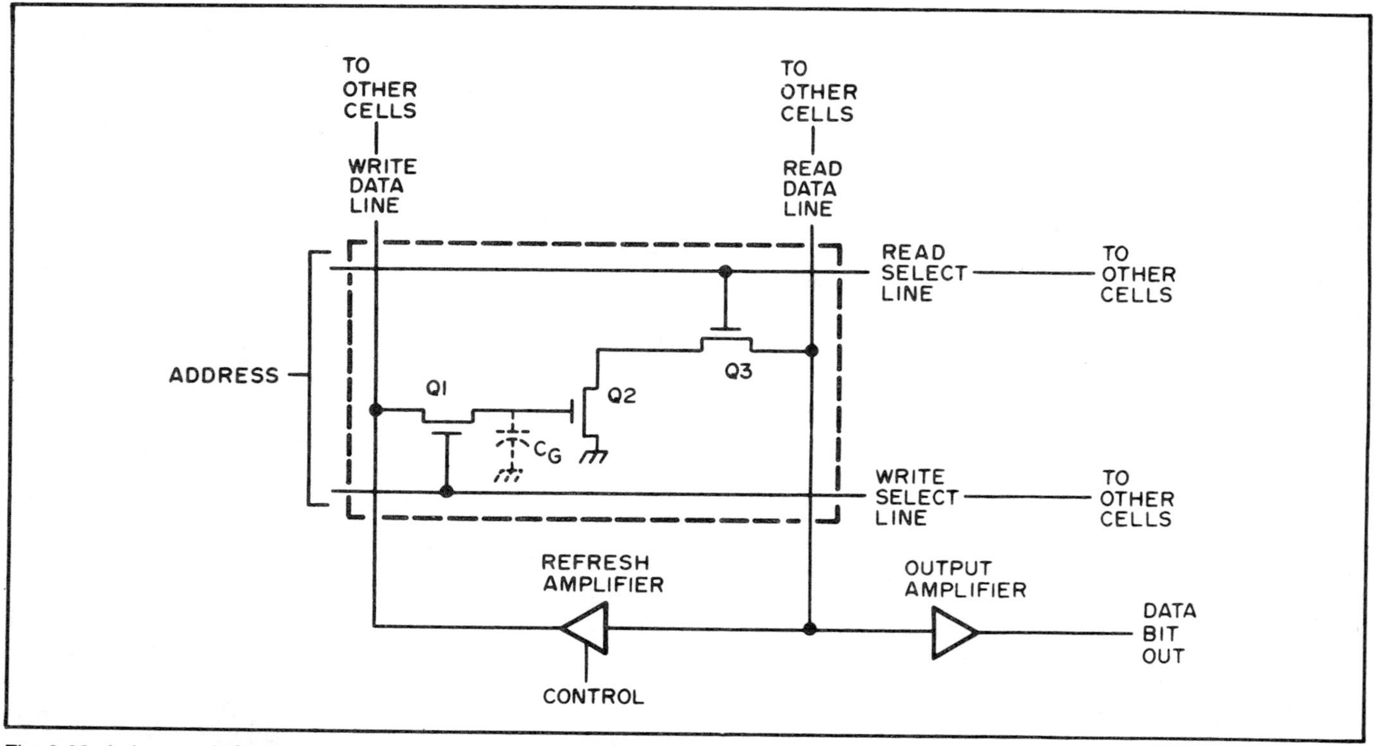

Fig. 3-22. A dynamic MOS RAM cell stores data in the gate-source capacitance of one of its transistors.

pressed, the bits comprising the number are written into the RAM data store. Function key (addition, subtraction, etc.) numbers are applied to the ROM program store as addresses. In the program store are contained instructions for each function. When an address is presented, the proper instructions are read out of the ROM, leading to performance of the desired operation upon the data held in the RAM. When the function has been completed, the result is read out and applied to the decoder, which puts it into a form suitable for display.

The basic ROM structure is a matrix of elements, each of which is accessed by a random address code, allowing approximately equal access time to all bits. The simplest ROM structure is a network of diodes wherein the presence or absence of a diode determines the logic state of a particular location. Such a network is shown in Fig. 3-24. The row address decoder raises the voltage on the appropriate word line to a high positive level, forward-biasing the diodes attached to that line. When the diodes begin conducting, they force their associated bit lines to a high (logic 1) level, while bit lines not connected to diodes remain low (logic 0). Output amplifiers sense the state of each line and present the bits to the data processor's other circuitry.

For example, if the row address decoder raises the word line 1 level, diodes D1, D2, and D3 conduct, raising bit lines 1, 2 and 4. In this case, the matrix output would be the binary number 1101. The next address might raise word line 4, in which case the output would be 0110. In some applications, column (bit line) addressing is added to select fewer than the maximum possible bit outputs.

ROM matrices are also formed with bipolar and MOS devices. In the most common configurations, the presence or absence of conductors establishes logic states.

Figure 3-25 shows a ROM matrix utilizing multiple-emitter bipolar transistors. In this case, the collectors are used as row enabling contacts, replacing the word lines, and emitter contacts are omitted from selected locations to set logic levels. When the row address decoder raises the voltage on the appropriate collector to a sufficiently high level, the transistor segments with emitter contacts begin conducting. For example, if Q2 is selected, the matrix output is 1001 (the level of columns 1 and 4 raised by conduction, 2 and 3 remaining low). In Fig. 3-25, column address and data output decoding selects two of the four bits for application to the processor.

In Fig. 3-26, a ROM matrix composed of static MOS FET devices is shown. Logic states are determined by the presence or absence of gates within the transistor structures. Reading this

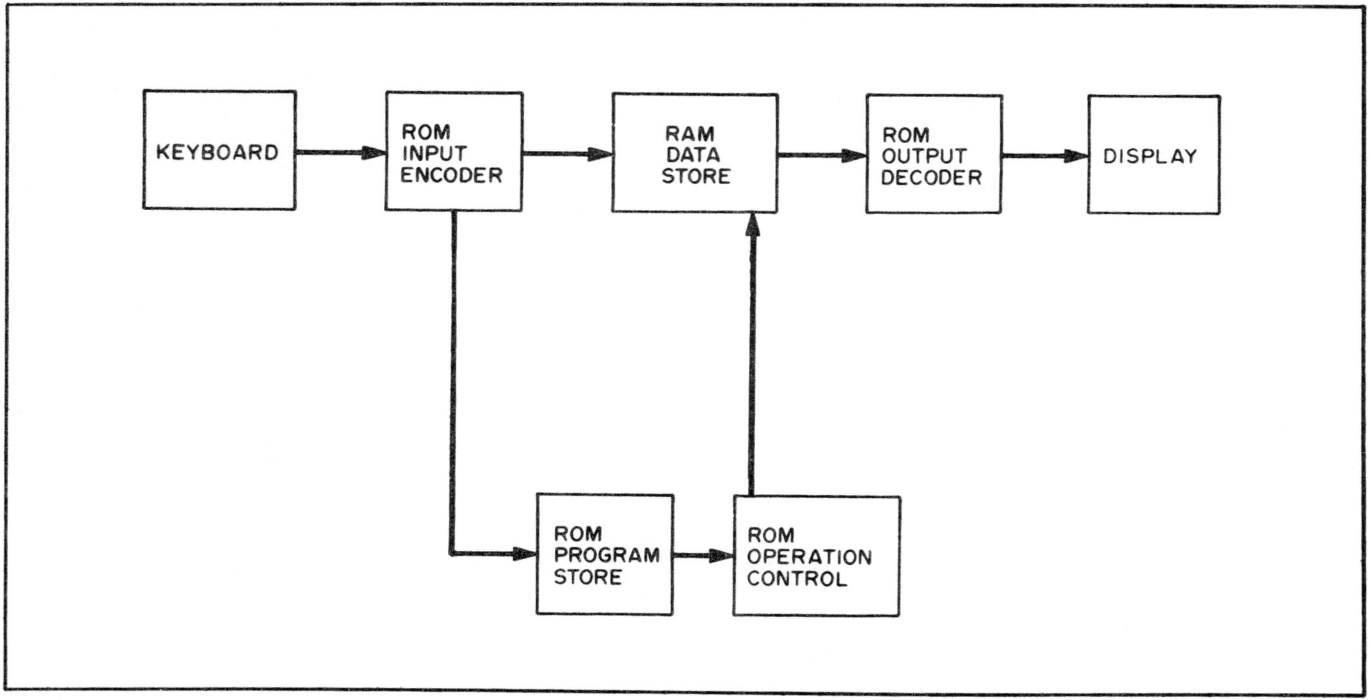

Fig. 3-23. A pocket calculator typically utilizes both RAM and ROM facilities to process input data.

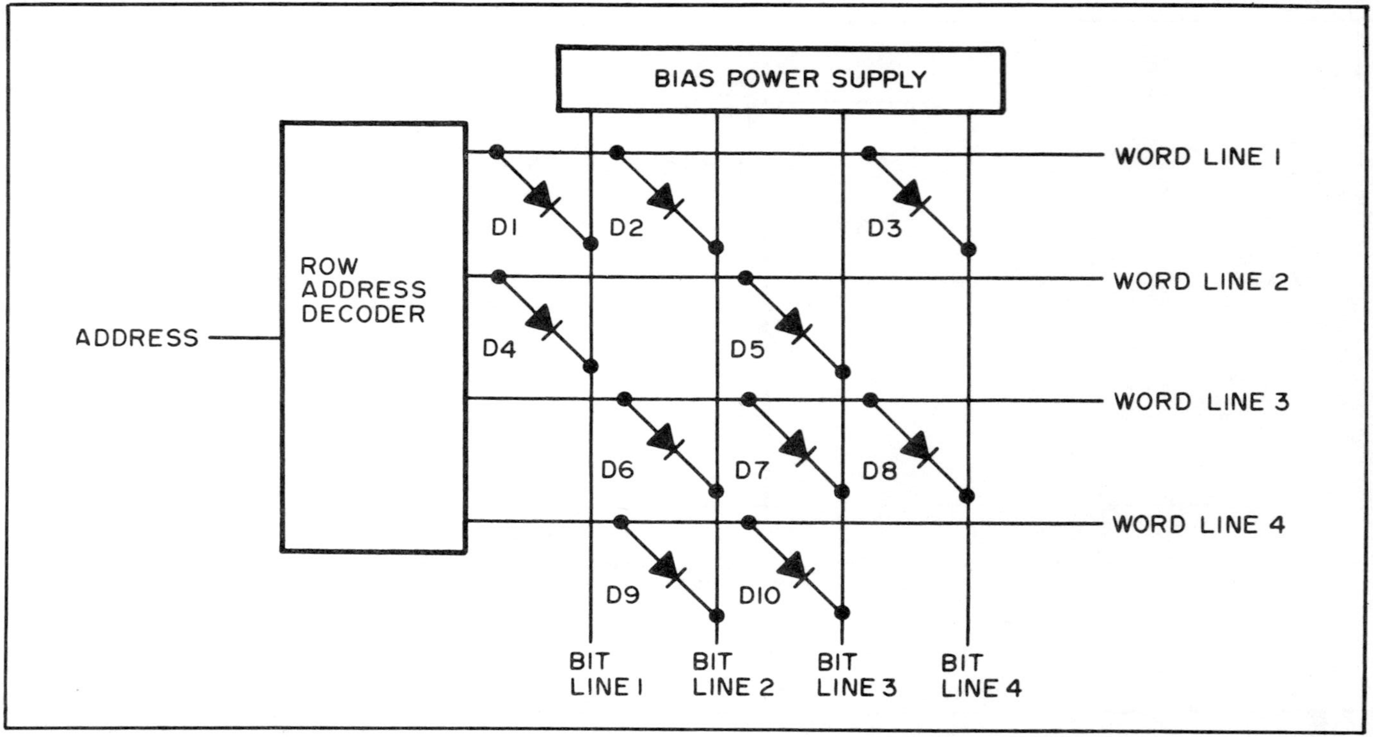

Fig. 3-24. A diode network with random access addressing is the simplest type of semiconductor ROM.

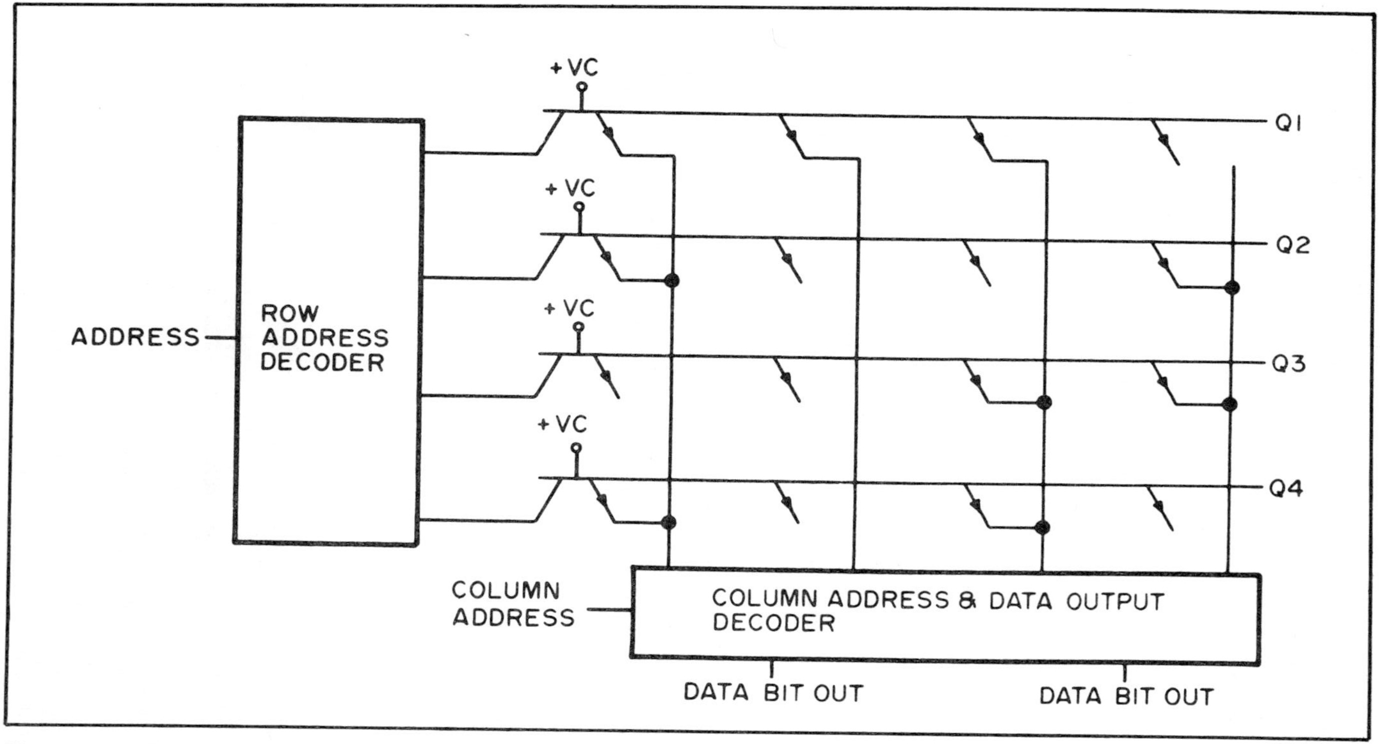

Fig. 3-25. Bipolar read only memory matrix.

memory is accomplished in the same manner as diode and bipolar ROMs, except that the bit lines are driven low (to ground) when the FETs conduct.

Programmable ROMs

Semiconductor memories are almost universally formed on minute silicon chips capable of holding large numbers of integrated circuit devices. The chips often contain complete addressing, decoding and output circuitry in addition to the memory cells.

In the formation of standard ROM matrices—in which the stored data is never to be changed—logic states are established during the manufacturing process by omitting the proper elements to create the desired bit pattern. This is the most prevalent type of read only memory. There are cases, however, in which standard memories are not available to meet application requirements, so programmable ROM (PROM) matrices are also produced.

A PROM is essentially a semiconductor matrix which has its program written into it at some time other than the manufacturing process. The manufacturer provides a chip on which all of the rows and columns (word and bit lines) are linked by conducting devices. Before integrating the chip into a circuit, the purchaser of the PROM uses various techniques—from application of a high-level write current to a laser beam—to eliminate devices from the matrix. In this way, a stored program unique to a given application can be produced.

New Developments

This discussion has covered structures that are representative of devices currently used in data processing memory facilities, and has not attempted to consider all of the variations of the basic structures. Advances are being made at a remarkable rate, and today's technology may be totally obsolete in a few years. Among the new memory devices that may bring this about are charge coupled devices (CCDs), bucket brigade devices (BBDs) and magnetic bubbles. Charge coupled and bucket brigade devices are similar in that both store digits as the presence or absence of electric charge.

A basic CCD is a semiconductor chip, either n-or p-type, over which a dielectric material is laid. A series of gate contacts are placed along the dielectric. Charge is stored as minority carriers under the gate regions. When the substrate is p-type, for example, applying a positive voltage to one gate attracts electrons out of the substrate until they dominate in the area directly beneath the gate, forming a *potential well*. This storage condition is maintained for times up to

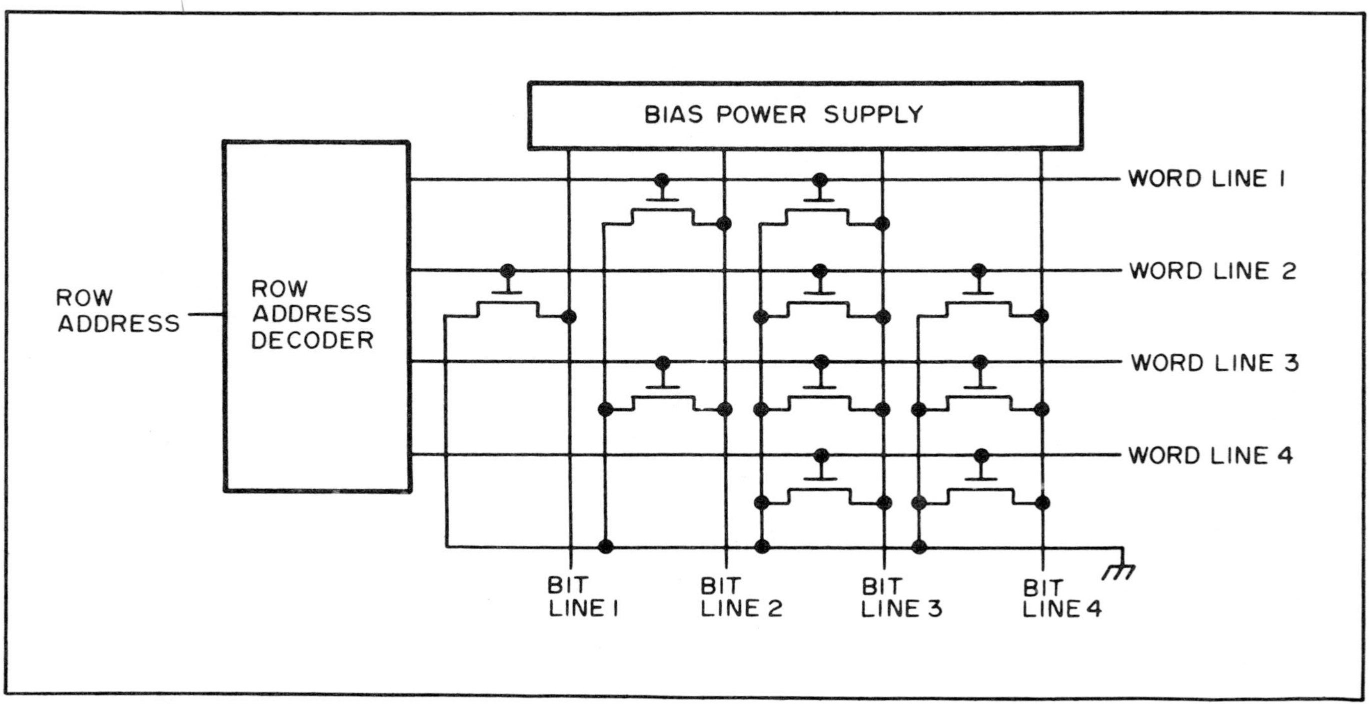

Fig. 3-26. The logic states within a static MOS RAM are determined by the presence or absence of gate contacts.

several seconds after the gate voltage is reduced. Raising potential on the next gate in the series forms a second potential well into which the stored charge is transferred. Gate potentials are sequentially raised by a clocked voltage to move the stored bit through the device. The CCD is thus a sequentially accessed memory facility similar to the shift register.

The movement of charge in a bucket brigade device is the same as in the CCD. Potential wells, however, are replaced by buckets of material unlike the substrate. For example, n-types areas may be embedded beneath the gates in a p-type chip to act as MOS storage capacitors.

Fabrication techniques currently limit the production of CCDs and BBDs, but they hold the promise of extremely small, very fast, low power memories of high density, and many manufacturers are investigating their commercial feasibility.

Magnetic bubble technology is still in the developmental stage, but it also shows great promise. The bubbles, which are tiny, mobile particles whose polarity is opposite to that of the thin film containing them, can be arranged to form coded data patterns, thus providing a storage medium.

Conventional bipolar and MOS devices are being modified to achieve an optimum combination of memory cell size, speed and power consumpion. N-channel and p-channel MOS FETs are being combined on one chip as complementary MOS (CMOS) devices for low power applications, and Schottky diodes are being introduced into various bipolar configurations to decrease power consumption and increase speed. One such modification has resulted in the low power Schottky TTL memory cell, which has access speed approaching that of ECL (the fastest presently available cell type) and power requirements close to those of MOS FETs; GTE Lenkurt uses this family of devices in its 262A and 262B data sets to achieve the most rapid data processing possible with the least power. In another development, metal-nitrade oxide semiconductors are being looked at as possible non-volatile read/write RAMs (memory facilities which would not lose stored data when power is removed).

Whether improvements to existing structures continue at the present rate, or new technologies take over completely, there is no doubt that semiconductors will play an increasingly important role in data processing systems.

Chapter 4
Computer I/O

Contrary to the opinion expressed often in computer hobbyist publications, *Baudot is not dead*! It is alive and well. Frankly, I am glad I learned years ago not to believe everything I find in print. If I had, my Model 15 Teletype® would not be speaking BASIC today. I want to make it clear at the outset that this discussion is not intended to foster a Baudot/ASCII split among computer hobbyists. Nor is it written to argue the relative merits of one system over the other. I wish simply to demonstrate that a Baudot machine can be made an effective and useful hard copy peripheral in a hobby computer system.

Permit me to digress a moment from the main subject—Baudot—to comment in a more general way on these people we call *hobbyists*. Although they come in many varieties depending on interest and ability, there seems to be a common thread running between them: the need to be creative with their hands, heads or both. For instance, there can be no greater pleasure for an electronic hobbyist than to sit back and watch his junk box creation perform like its store-bought counterpart. At that moment he feels a sense of acomplishment unobtainable in many other pursuits of life. This "make do with what you have" philosophy is a reflection of the spirit that has brought man to his stately position among the world's lesser creatures. The hobbyist has the opportunity to foster this spirit each time he digs into his junk box for a new project. Unless you think I am only talking about an electronic junk box, let me remind you that a 16K word memory filled with NOPs is in a sense a junk box as well!

What does all this philosophical wandering have to do with Baudot? Simply this: There are people who say Baudot is obsolete and Teletypes that speak it are junk. Now, can't you see the eyes of some hobbyist light up when the word junk is mentioned? The very word carries with it a challenge he cannot resist. Out to the storeroom he goes to retrieve his old Model 15. The renewing of the hobbyist spirit has begun!

About six months ago, a friend and I were taking just such a challenge. We have made quite a lot of progress since then. In our present state of excitement we want to share some of the knowledge gained and lessons learned. We hope our success will encourage some *junk box digging.*

A Very Cheap I/O

The best place to begin is in the pages of a book on Baudot Teletypes. One good choice is Wayne Green's RTTY *Handbook*, (TAB book No. 597). Learn the theory of teleprinter operation and become familiar with the different machines available.

Next, begin your search for a machine. This will probably require some footwork and a little time. If you live close to a large city start by looking in the yellow pages under junk dealers and electronic surplus houses. Make a few phone calls, ask questions and follow leads. There are mail order companies that have teleprinter equipment. Check the back pages and classified ads of amateur and computer hobbyist magazines. Write a few inquiries, get quotations and ask for the specific machine you want. Get in touch with local radio amateurs and see if they can help. Hams generally have a good attitude toward hobbyists of other persuasions and go out of their way to help. You might find a ham with a spare Teletype that he would be willing to loan out until you can get your own.

Give Western Union and Bell Telephone a call. If you can get through to the right people you may have a chance of getting a free machine. I have heard of this approach yielding success more than once. In these inquiries be sure to emphasize the *hobby* nature of your interest! Above all don't get disappointed and give up too soon. There are thousands of these machines out there—probably one with your name on it!

A Model 15

As the owner of a Baudot Teletype you should take some pride in your new possession. Over the years the Model 15 Teletype has gained an excellent reputation among people who appreciate well-engineered mechanical devices. Most of its moving parts are made of casehardened steel. When a part does wear there is generally an adjustment somewhere to take up the slack. If you can find a maintenance manual, get it and use it. Your efforts will pay off in many years of reliable service. I have often heard Model 15 owners say not to worry with cleaning the working parts—the worse it looks the smoother it operates. A friend has a Model 15 with several more layers of dirt and grease than mine. Not only does his keyboard have a lighter touch but his printer is several decibels quieter! Remember to keep machine oil in the cups and on the clutch felts. With reasonable care your machine should serve you well for years to come.

The Interfacing Problem At the Teletype End

Normally the Teletype will have two connecting cables: one for send (the keyboard) and the other for receive (printer magnet). For testing purposes the two can be series-connected with a power supply and current limiting resistor. Connected in this way the machine will type to itself. Teletype users call this *local loop* operation. For computer use the send and receive cables must be connected separately. Figure 4-1 shows a transistorized switching circuit that provides the necessary TTL level signals for a computer interface.

The following notes refer to Fig. 4-1:

- The use of a high voltage supply (100 to 120 volts) is recommended since it provides the simplest and most reliable operation. Of course, the driver transistor must be a high voltage type similar to the one shown.
- Make certain that the local-line is a *non-shorting* (break-before-make) type. 120 volts is not a TTL level! A telephone type lever switch is ideal.
- The printer magnets (usually there are two mounted side by side) can be connected in series or parallel. The circuit shown assumes a parallel connection. Adjust the slide on the power resistor for 60 mA in the magnet circuit.
- Notice that in the local position the keyboard contacts are switching the full 60 mA at 120 volts. The contact arcing seems to do wonders for cleaning up noise problems in the keyboard. In the line position, the keyboard is switching to ground and the printer will accept TTL logic levels.
- Make absolutely certain that the Teletype and all computer circuits share a good ground system. In fact, connect the Teletype chassis to the computer ground with a separate

ground with a separate heavy wire. We have experienced AC transients on interface lines when the ground connection on the Teletype was inadvertently broken. On one occasion we lost some TTL in our Altair during such an occurrence.

The Interfacing Problem At the Computer End

There are several schemes available to perform the serial input/output function at the computer. A UART (Universal Asynchronous Receiver Transmitter) is readily adaptable to five level Baudot code. The UART represents a hardware solution to the problem. The serial/parallel conversion can also be handled by computer software. This simplifies the hardware requirement but ties up the CPU during input/output operation. The circuit in Fig. 4-2 and the accompanying software listing of Table 4-1 will illustrate this latter technique as applied in an Altair 8800 system.

Although the software I/O system is probably not a good long-term solution to your I/O needs, it does offer a quick and simple approach to getting your Teletype on-line. Figure 4-2 is very similar to the interface circuitry necessary for a cassette interface of the Suding type. If you later change your I/O to a UART type, you can use this circuit to build up a cassette interface.

To check out the software I/O, make the following test:

- At a memory location above the I/O routines, load a main program similar to:

  ```
  LOOP
  LXI SP. LOOP + 10
  CALL INPUT
  CALL OUTPUT
  JMP LOOP
  ```
- EXAMINE the starting location of the main program and begin execution.
- The printer should now echo keyboard entries.

In our Altair 8800 system we have used several home brew I/O interfaces with success. Our original circuit followed in design the "Basic Stunt Box" on page 299 of RTTY Handbook, TAB book No 597. This circuit was modified and improved through several generations. Most recently we have used a MITS SIOC interface board with a few simple modifications. The MITS board is UART-based, with a software controlled interrupt scheme we have found very useful. After a great deal of experimenting, we have little doubt that a UART-based I/O interface is best.

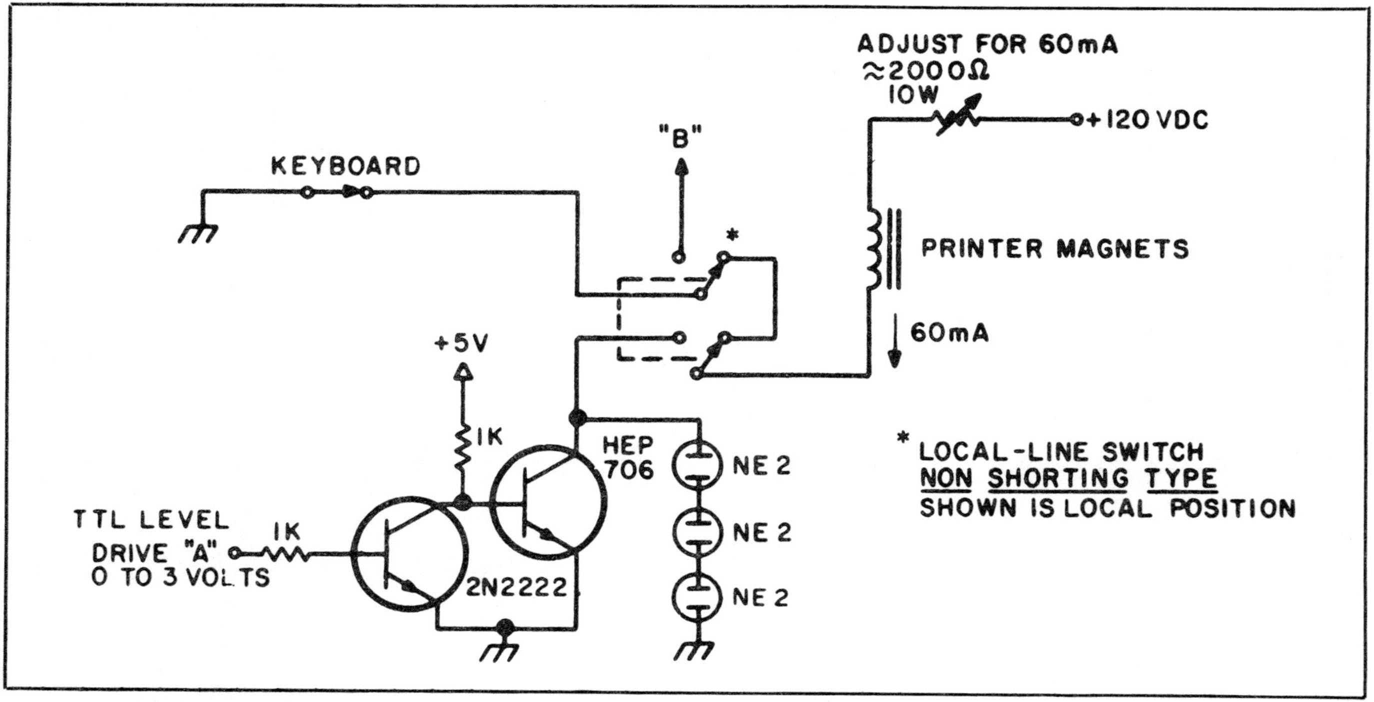

Fig. 4-1. Teletype interface circuit: Model 15 or similar.

Table 4-1. Serial I/O: Software Technique for Fig. 4-2.

LABEL	OCTAL ADDRESS	OCTAL CODE	MNEMONIC	COMMENTS
INPUT	Low- 000	001	LXI B	ZERO C; COUNT IN B
	001	000		
	002	005		
LOOP1	003	333	IN	LOOK FOR START PULSE
	004	376		
	005	037	RAR	
	006	332	JPC	JUMP BACK IF NO START
	007	003	LOOP1(L)	
	010	000	LOOP1(H)	
	011	026	MUI D	SET FOR 1½ TIME UNITS
	012	030		
	013	315	CAL	CALL TIME OUT ROUTINE
	014	110	TMOUT(L)	
	015	000	TMOUT(H)	
LOOP2	016	333	IN	COLLECT 5 DATA PULSES INTO C
	017	376		
	020	037	RAR	
	021	171	MOV A, C	
	022	037	RAR	
	023	117	MOV C, A	SAVE A
	024	026	MUI D	SET FOR 1 TIME UNIT
	025	020		
	026	315	CAL	CALL TIME OUT ROUTINE
	027	110	TMOUT(L)	
	030	000	TMOUT(H)	
	031	005	DCR B	CHECK COUNT
	032	302	JNZ	JUMP BACK IF NOT FINISHED
	033	016	LOOP2(L)	
	034	000	LOOP2(H)	
	035	171	MOV A, C	RETRIEVE A
	036	017	RRC	ADJUST A TO PLACE BAUDOT IN
	037	017	RRC	LOWER 5 BITS
	040	017	RRC	
	041	311	RET	END INPUT ROUTINE
OUTPUT	042	006	MUI B	COUNT IN B
	043	005		
	044	007	RLC	
	045	117	MOV C, A	SAVE A
	046	227	SUB A	CLEAR A
	047	323	OUT	OUTPUT START PULSE
	050	376		
	051	026	MUI D	SET FOR 1 TIME UNIT
	052	020		
	053	315	CAL	CALL TIME OUT ROUTINE
	054	110	TMOUT(L)	
	055	000	TMOUT(H)	
LOOP3	056	171	MOV A, C	
	057	017	RRC	
	060	117	MOV C, A	
	061	346	ANI	MASK OFF ALL BUT Ø BIT
	062	001		
	063	323	OUT	OUTPUT DATA PULSES - 5 IN ALL
	064	376		
	065	026	MUI D	SET FOR 1 TIME UNIT
	066	020		
	067	315	CAL	CALL TIME OUT ROUTINE
	070	110	TMOUT(L)	
	071	000	TMOUT(H)	
	072	005	DCR B	CHECK COUNT
	073	302	JNZ	JUMP BACK IF NOT FINISHED
	074	056	LOOP3(L)	
	075	000	LOOP3(H)	
	076	076	MUI A	
	077	001		
	100	323	OUT	OUTPUT STOP PULSE
	101	376		
	102	026	MUI D	SET FOR 1½ TIME UNITS
	103	030		
	104	315	CAL	CALL TIME OUT ROUTINE
	105	110	TMOUT(L)	
	106	000	TMOUT(H)	
	107	311	RET	

Table 4-1. Serial I/O: Software Technique for Fig. 4-2.

LABEL	OCTAL ADDRESS	OCTAL CODE	MNEMONIC	COMMENTS
TMOUT	110	076	MUI A	ADJUST TIME DELAY
	111	XXX		170_8 for 60 wpm; 135 for 75 wpm
LOOP4	112	075	DRC A	(MITS STATIC MEMORY TESTED VALUES)
	113	302	JNZ	JUMP BACK IF NOT FINISHED
	114	112	LOOP4(L)	
	115	000	LOOP4(H)	
	116	025	DCR D	
	117	302	JNZ	JUMP BACK IF NOT FINISHED
	120	110	TMOUT(L)	
	121	000	TMOUT(H)	
	122	311	RET	

The MITS SIOC board was originally for use with a Model 33 Teletype. To use it with a Model 15 or similar machine, make the modifications shown in Fig. 4-3.

In preparing the MITS board, the number of stop bits must be selected. The five level Baudot code consists of a start, stop and five coded data pulses. The start and data pulses are 22 ms each (60 word per minute machines) while the stop is 31 ms, about one and a half times the others. Theoretically, the stop pulse generated by the serial I/O circuit should be one and a half times the length of the start and data pulses. The MITS SIOC board has provision for one or two stop pulses only. Our experience has shown that both choices work satisfactorily. One stop pulse types a little faster than normal, two stop pulses a little slower. We have used the one stop bit set up for some time without any problems. A UART is available that provides the correct one and a half stop bits but we don't believe you need to be too concerned about getting one.

As you implement a Baudot system, knowledge of the Baud rate will be required. For instance, the MITS serial board instructions do not provide directly the Baud rate hookup for a 60 wpm Baudot machine. After a little head scratching we were able to figure out the circuit connections. For those contemplating a MITS board, Table 4-2 gives the necessary data for strapping the Baud rate counters. If you purchase some other I/O board, be sure to ask the manufacturer for details on setting the Baud rate counters. If you purchase some other I/O board, be sure to ask the manufacturer for details on setting the Baud rate for your Baudot machine. By the way, not all Baudot machines are 60 wpm. Some are 65 and 75 wpm. Gear sets are available from surplus dealers to change speeds. Model 15s work well at 75 wpm. Model 28s are 10 wpm standard.

How Does Baudot Look in the Computer?

The answer to this question depends upon the configuration of the interface system. Consider, for instance, a typical keyboard

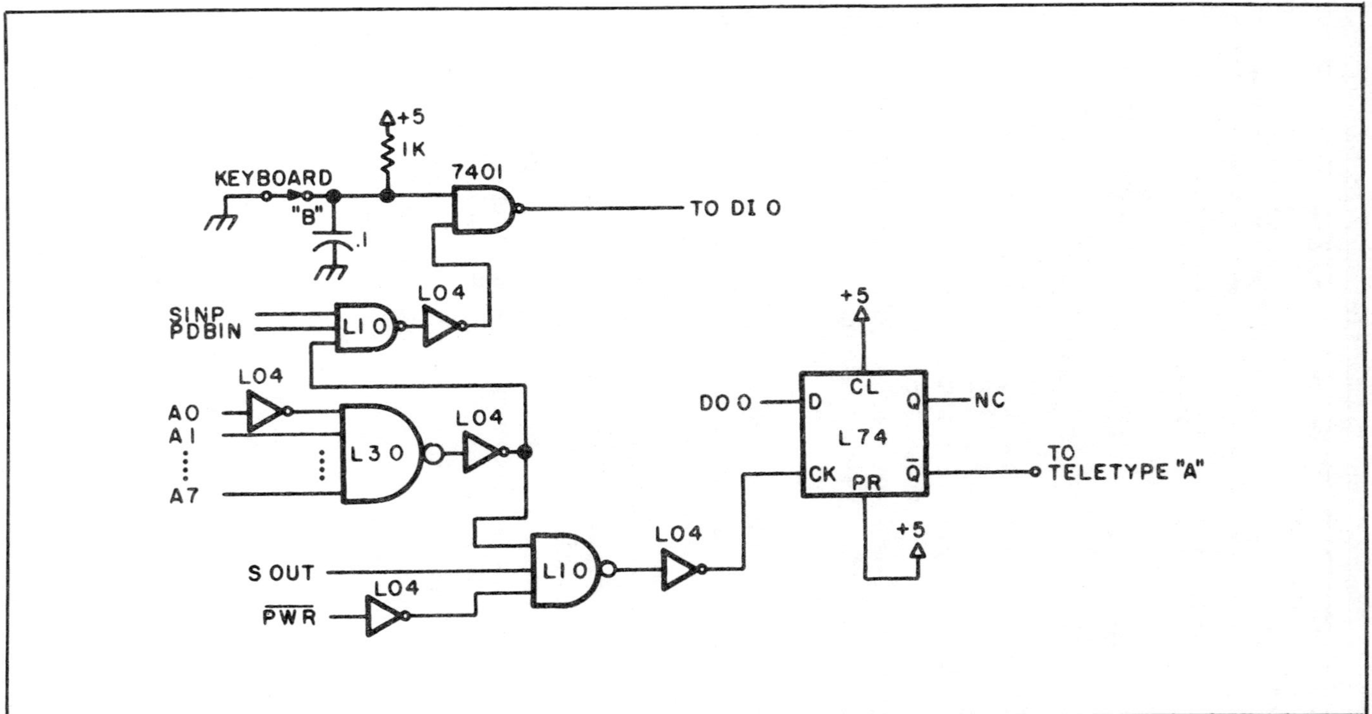

Fig. 4-2. Computer interface for software I/O. Labels reflect Altair 8800 bus. Points A and B refer to Fig. 4-1. All ICs are 7400 series—low power except 7401.

entry to the CPU accumulator. The normally closed keyboard contacts can produce a logic 0 or a logic 1 depending on the number of inversions that take place in the I/O interface. In addition, the interface circuit will determine the location and order of the five level code in the eight bit accumulator. As an example, consider the letter T as it might finally appear in the accumulator:

(T) *020 001 017 036

(*This bracket set will of a five level Baudot character.)

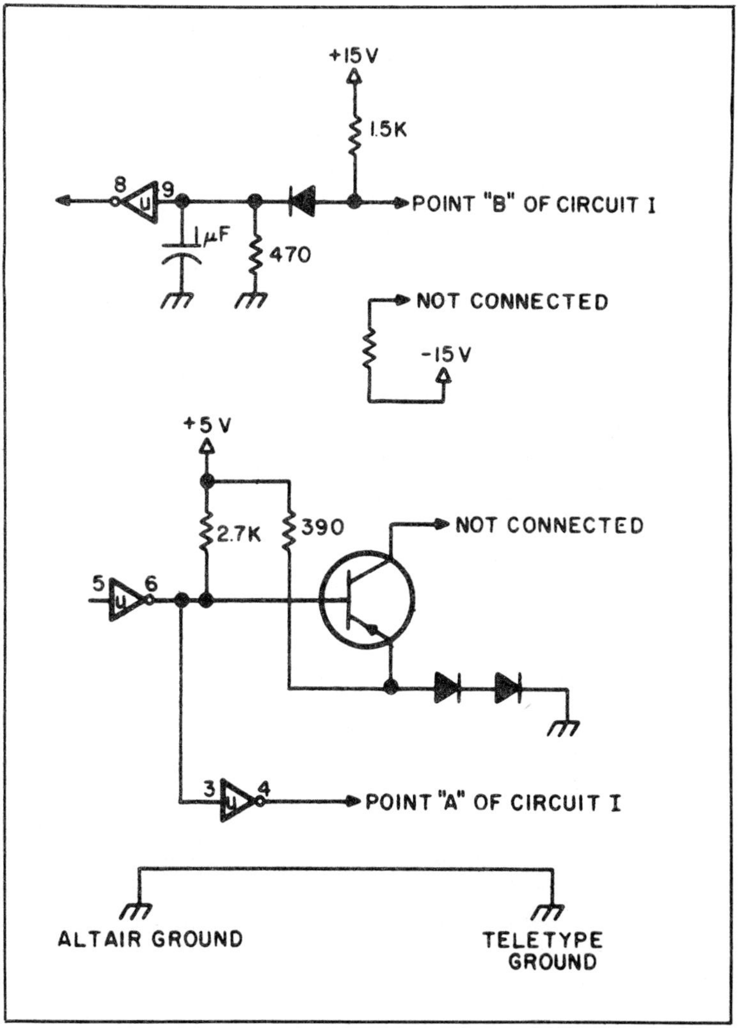

Fig. 4-3. Teletype drive circuits for MITS SIOC interface with modification for connection to a Model 15 Teletype.

Table 4-2. Baud Rate for Baudot Teletypes on Altair 8800 Serial I/O Boards.

	PRESET COUNT											
TELETYPE SPEED	11	10	9	8	7	6	5	4	3	2	1	0
60 wpm	0	1	0	1	0	1	0	0	0	1	1	0
65 wpm	0	1	1	0	0	0	0	1	1	0	1	0
75 wpm	0	1	1	1	0	1	1	0	1	1	0	0
100 wpm	1	0	0	1	1	0	0	1	0	0	1	0

These examples assume the lower five bits of the accumulator are used. A choice must be made from this group if standardization is to be achieved. After consulting a few sources, 020 appeared the best representation. The MITS and Processor Technology boards produce this representation. Table 4-3 presents the full Baudot character set as it would appear in octal notation.

For those not familiar with the Model 15s, upper or lower case is set by FGS or LTR keystroke respectively. A mechanical flip flop holds the case until another FGS or LTR keystroke produces a change. It is convenient in some systems to use a sixth bit to indicate which case is desired or the status of the machine. With the sixth bit, software can be written to control the FGS/LTR function. This relieves some of the difficulties encountered in keeping track of the case.

Blowtorch Your ICs

Have you ever tried to remove 14 or 16 pin DIP ICs from surplus computer boards? Sometimes this can be a very exasperating job, and you may even pass up some good bargains because you don't want to go through all the trouble of removing them.

There are many ways to remove ICs. You can use a special tip that heats all the pins at once, you can clean the solder off the pins one at a time, you can use a special tip with a vacuum line attached or you can even use a special tip with a blower attached. All these methods are slow, cumbersome and expensive, and you will usually end up wishing you had three hands to accomplish very much.

The method that I use may shock you a bit at first, but believe it or not, it really works well.

I remove ICs from surplus computer boards with a blowtorch. That's right, a propane torch that can be obtained in just about any experimenter's workshop.

I turn the flame on the pins from the circuit side of the board and yank the IC out (fast) from the component side of the board using an

LOWER CASE	5 LEVEL	6 LEVEL	UPPER CASE	5 LEVEL	6 LEVEL
A	003	003	-	003	043
B	031	031	?	031	071
C	016	016	:	016	056
D	011	011	$	011	051
E	001	015	3	001	041
F	015	032	!	015	055
G	032	024	&	032	072
H	024	006	#	024	064
I	006	013	8	006	046
J	013	017	Bell	013	053
K	017	022	(	017	057
L	022	034	)	022	062
M	034	014	.	034	074
N	014	030	,	014	054
O	030	026	9	030	070
P	026	027	0	026	066
Q	027	012	1	027	067
R	012	005	4	012	052
S	005	020	'	005	045
T	020	007	5	020	060
U	007	036	7	007	047
V	036	023	;	036	076
W	023	035	2	023	063
X	035	025	/	035	075
Y	025	021	6	025	065
Z	021	010	"	021	061
CR	010	002	CR	010	050
LF	002	004	LF	002	042
SP	004	000	SP	004	044
BLNK	000		BLNK	000	040
FGS	033	033	FGS	033	073
LTR	037	037	LTR	037	077

Table 4-3. Baudot-Octal Conversion.

IC puller or just a plain old pair of pliers. Even when using the torch running full blast, I have yet to damage an IC due to excessive heat. Excessive heat seems to be an old wive's tale on some of these modern ICs. Remember, of course, you can't reuse the boards.

A TTL Tester

Being economically minded by necessity, I have often purchased unmarked, untested semiconductors at really bargain prices. This practice has necessitated the contruction of special test equipment.

One such piece of test equipment was designed to test TTLs. This TTL tester is an expanded version of a very simple diode tester. The simplicity of this diode tester should not be allowed to downgrade its usefulness (Fig. 4-4).

Using this diode tester, the breakdown or zener voltage of a diode or transistor can be quickly determined. Transistors can be classified, after some experience in using this simple tester, into small or large signal, low or high voltage, oscillators, amplifiers, switching, high or low leakage, etc. It also indicates an open or short which makes it useful for a continuity tester.

A built-in calibration source can be added with the addition of one or more zener diodes and switches (Fig. 4-5).

The TTL tester is this same basic diode tester with a few more components and a 5V source (Fig. 4-6). Any 5V DC power supply can be used but should be protected from overload by a fuse or current limited output because of a TTL short or human error. Phone tip jacks are used for test points, with external test connections being made by jumper wires with phone tips (Fig. 4-7).

For an unknown TTL, place the TTL into the test socket and turn power on. The vertical probe is inserted into the CAL TP and the scope adjusted as in Fig. 4-8A. Use an educated guess or flip a coin to choose a TP that would ordinarily be ground, such as TP4 or TP7. Say, for example, that we choose TP7. A jumper would then be placed from a ground TP to TP7. The vertical probe is then moved to each TP, TP1 through TP14. The display on the scope (Fig. 4-9A) may be similar to any figure of Fig. 4-8, but we are looking for one that is decidedly different, or the oddball. Say in our example we have only one that looks like Fig. 4-8H on TP14. It would appear that we have made a wise choice of TP7 for our ground because + and – are usually on 14 and 7 as one combination for TTLs. Reasonably sure that TP7 is our ground, we once again take the vertical probe through TP1 to TP14 with a ground on TP7. A record (mental if you

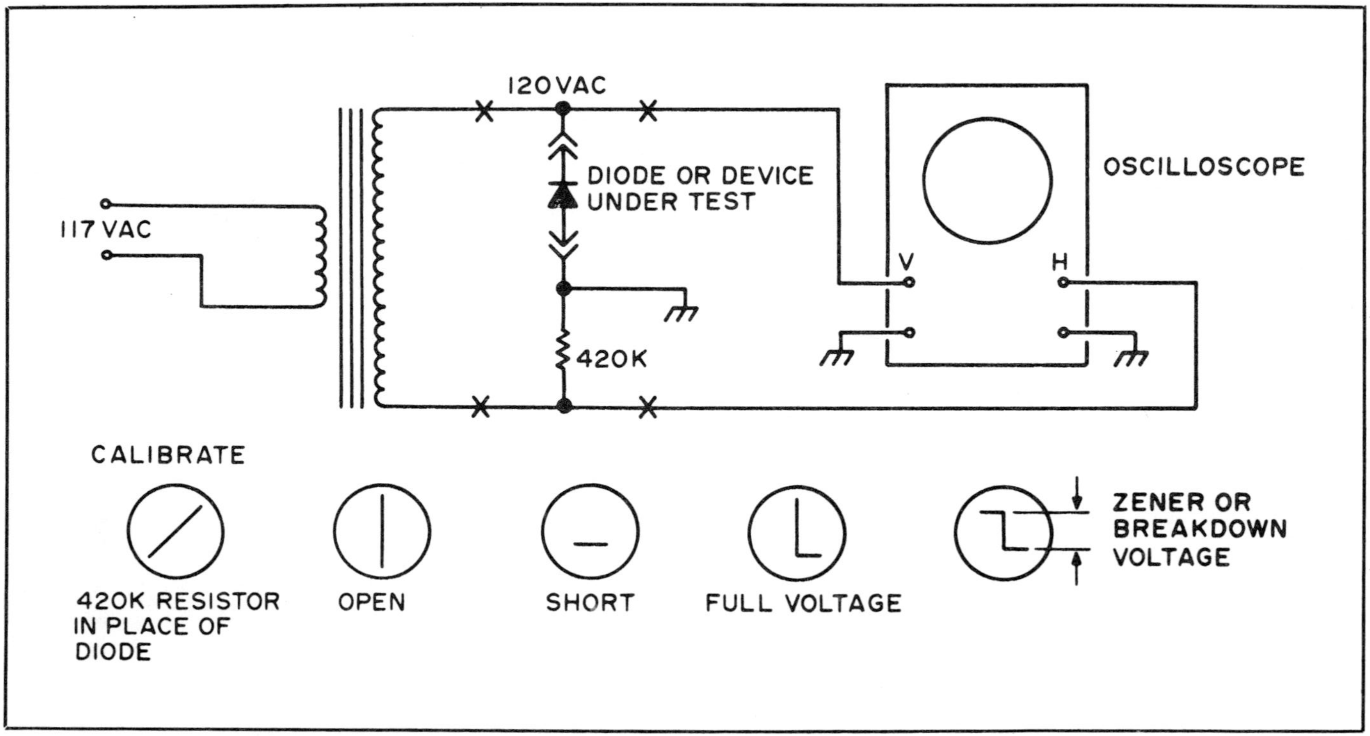

Fig. 4-4. Diode tester.

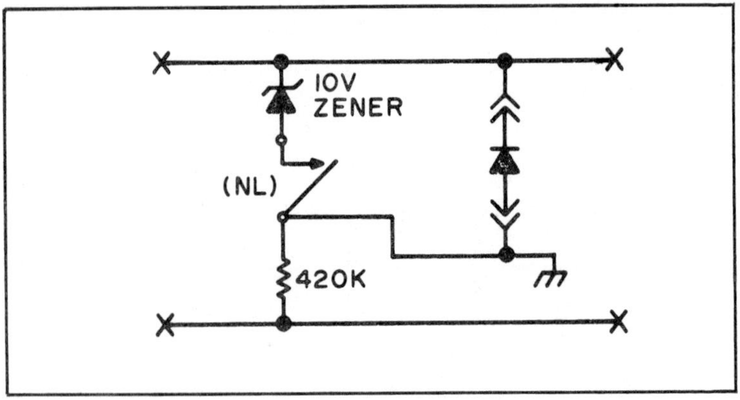

Fig. 4-5. Calibration Source.

like) can be made of each TP test as in Fig. 4-9. Connect +5V to TP14 with a jumper. This will oeprate all gates, etc. Check each test point again with the vertical probe. A change of state will be noted as in Fig. 4-9B. In our example, a change of state occurred at test points 3, 6, 11 and 8 for a total of four changes; thus we may have a quad device. Next we monitor the points of change using the vertical probe. The first in this example is TP3.

A single jumper lead from ground is moved to each test point of no change. In our example, the ground jumper lead of TP1 changes the state of TP3 (Fig. 4-9C). Removing the lead from TP1 restores the state of TP3. Placing the jumper of TP2 changes the state of TP3, etc. (Fig. 4-9C). Moving on to TP4, 5, 13, 12, 10, 9, we note no change on TP3. In our example, we find the same relationship between TP4, 5, 6 and TP13, 12, 11 and TP10, 9, 8. The example was a 7400 TTL (Fig. 4-10) which is a quad 2 input NAND gate TTL. A study of several known TTLs will give you the experience necessary to use this simple tester. The number and type of jumpers will of course depend upon the TTL under test. The 7451 TTL for instance requires two jumpers.

In the end we will know what the circuit is and its maximum breakdown voltage (Figs. 4-8B, C, D, G) as well as whether it is an open collector (Fig. 4-8D) or if the circuit is open or shorted (Figs. 4-8E, H) and most importantly, whether it is working properly.

Cold Solder Joints

The advent of digital electronics in amateur radio has paved the way for a new method of construction practice already widely used in industry. This is called the Wire-Wrap method (The term "Wire-

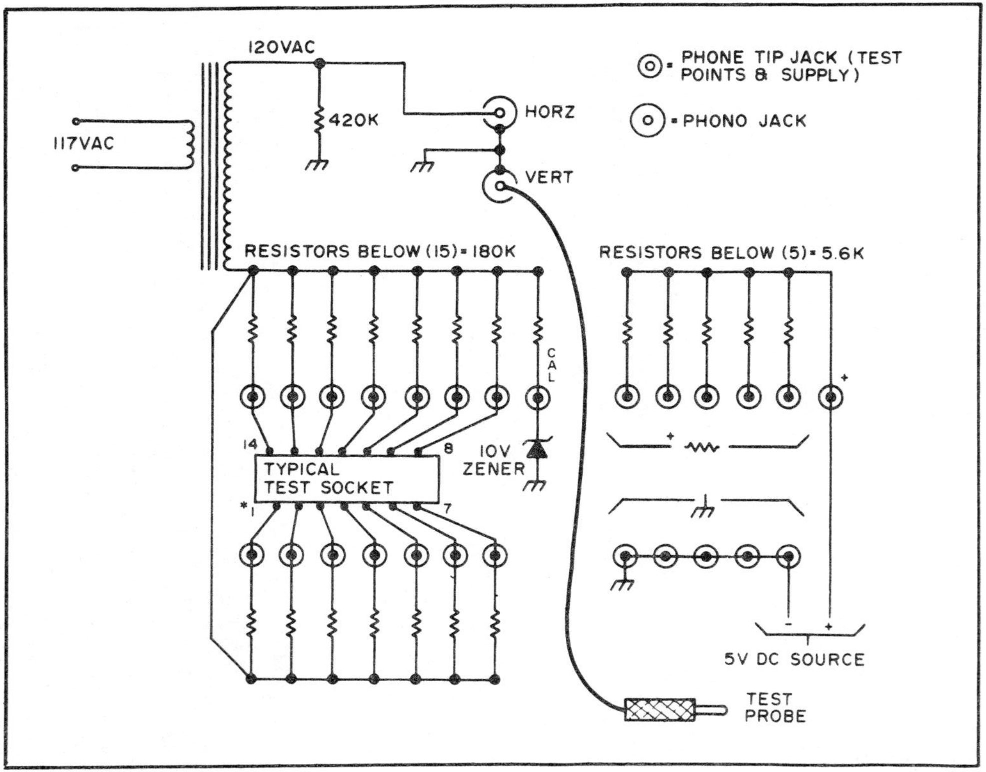

Fig. 4-6. Five-volt source.

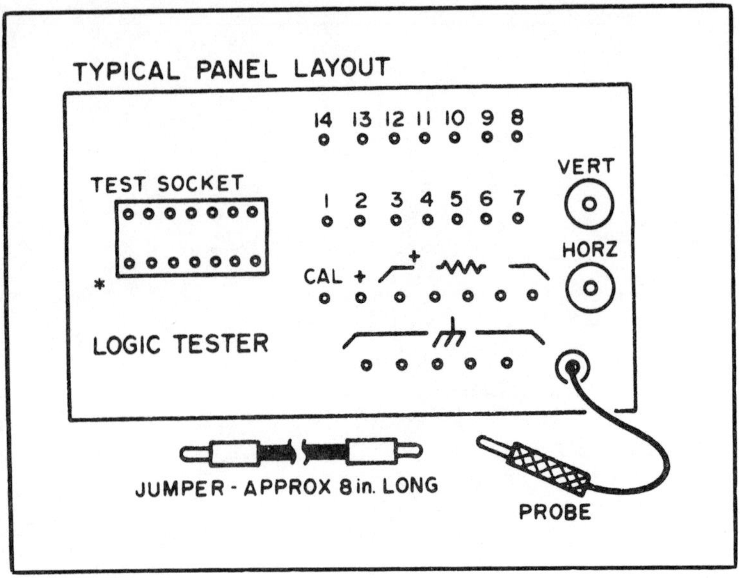

Fig. 4-7. Schematic.

Wrap" is a registerd trademark of Gardner-Denver Co.). One might ask, why Wire-Wrap? Just talking about the number of lines coming from an IC could make one's head reel. For example, let us assume that we have thirty 16 pin ICs, and that we have just one wire per pin as either a voltage, a ground or a signal line. We now have 16 × 30, or 480 lines to interconnect. Can't you just picture the complexity of the printed circuit board required to accommodate such a circuit? Note that I'm talking about a 16 pin IC in this case. Now we are well into LSI and MSI with 24, 36 or 40 pin ICs becoming very popular.

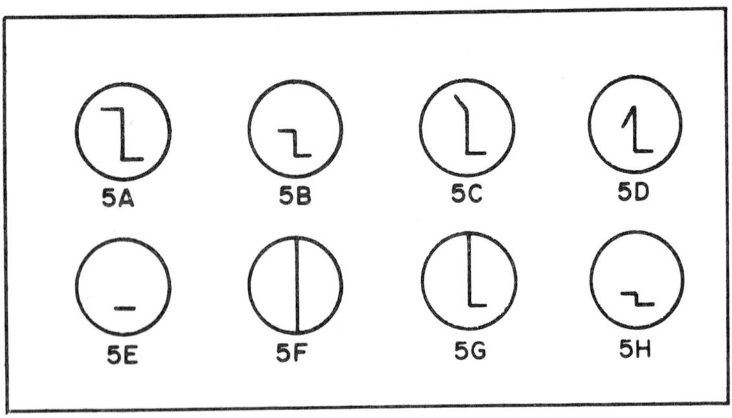

Fig. 4-8. Scope adjustment.

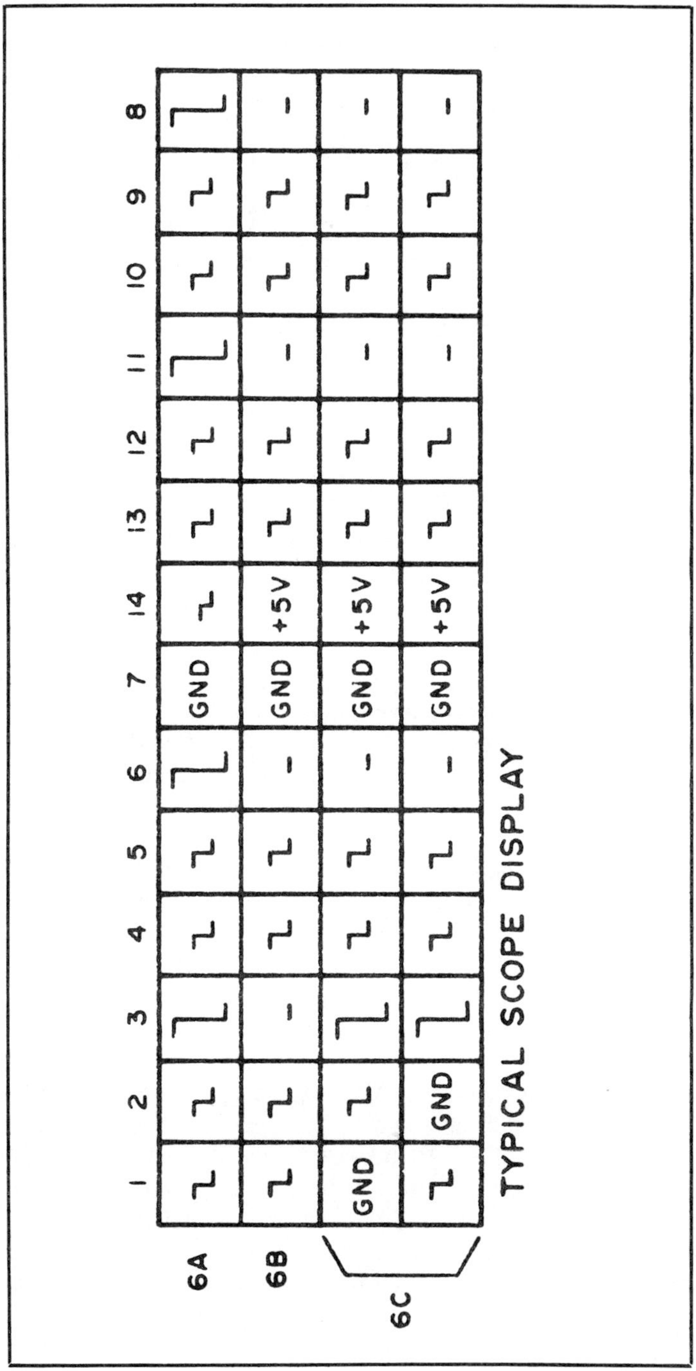

Fig. 4-9. Scope display.

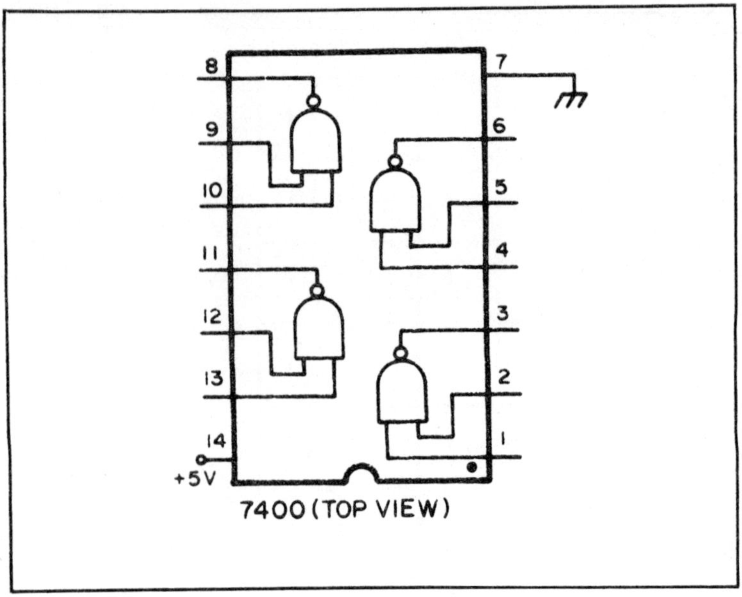

Fig. 4-10. A 7400 TTL.

This is one reason why industry has gone the Wire-Wrap route. The mechanical design effort in laying out such a PC board is a time-consuming, costly operation. Most of the time a double-sided PC board with plated-through holes would have to be used. And in even more complex circuits, multi-layer boards would have to be designed.

A second advantage of Wire-Wrap over PC is the ease with which a design change can be accomplished. All one needs to do is unwrap the wire and put the new one in between the proper two terminals. We all know what it is like to modify a PC board. I have several scarred fingers from a slip of the knife as proof.

Now let's talk about some of the electrical and mechanical attributes of Wire-Wrap. A Wire-Wrap connection consists of approximately seven turns of 30 AWG solid copper wire. The wire is wound about a 0.025 inch square terminal in a helical manner, without the aid of solder. As the wire is wound about the terminal, the corners of the terminal bite into the wire, as the wire notches the sharp corner of the terminal. In this manner, a gastight, oxidation-free joint exists between the terminal and the wire. As the connection ages, a solid state diffusion process takes place, which enhances the mechanical strength of the connection. Through exhaustive tests it has been determined that a Wire-Wrapped connection has a life expectancy in excess of 40 years. This tremendously exceeds the reliable life of a solder connection.

Wire-Wrapping can be accomplished through several methods. There are hand Wire-Wrap tools which are readily available and inexpensive. If many wraps are to be done, I would suggest the electrical hand gun. Where a small run of similar boards are to be Wire-Wrapped, there is the semi-automatic method. A *head* with a Wire-Wrapping bit is indexed over the proper terminal through the use of a numerical controller. The fully automatic method would be chosen on a large run of similarly Wire-Wrapped boards.

Let's go through a step-by-step procedure to show the simplicity of the Wire-Wrap process:

- Insert the stripped end of the wire into the tool.
- Place the tool with the wire over the terminal.
- Twist the tool clockwise, until the stripped portion of the wire is used up in the wrap.

Figure 4-11 shows a completed *modified wrap*. Modified means that there is approximately one turn of insulation around the terminal for strain relief.

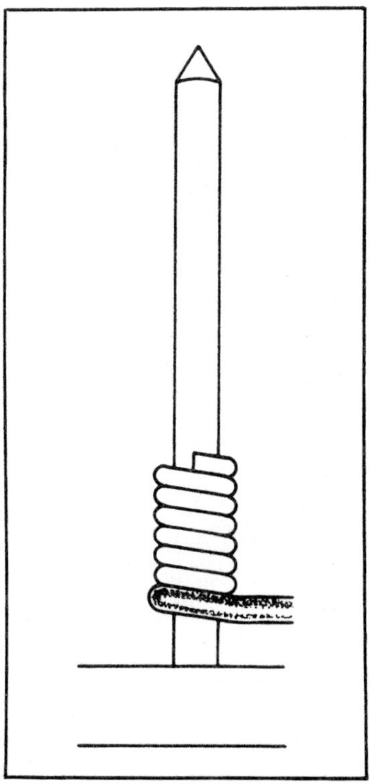

Fig. 4-11. Completed modified wrap.

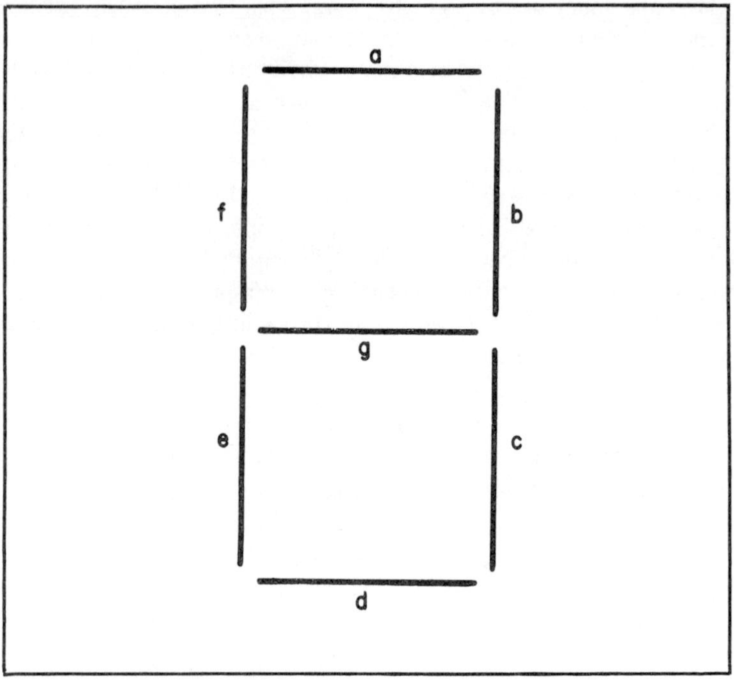

Fig. 4-12. Segment designations.

Interfacing a Clock Chip *

This circuit was developed as the result of a need to interface a clock chip to some other hardware. Unfortunately, the clock chip available had only seven-segment output, and was not equipped with BCD outputs. The first solution required a relatively large number of gates, and because of space restrictions, was inconvenient for the project in hand. To overcome this problem, the gating was replaced with a 32 × 8 PROM, addressing the PROM from the seven-segment output of the clock, with the BCD stored in the appropriate locations of the PROM.

Figure 4-12 illustrates the segment designations of a seven-segment display.

Since the PROM is 32 × 8 bits, it has only five address lines, and it is therefore impossible to use all the clock outputs. But if the seven-segment coding for the numerals 0-9 is considered (Table 4-4), it can be seen that it is still possible to obtain a unique code for each numeral, by using only segments a, b, e, f and g. If segment a is considered as the most significant bit, and segment g as the least

Table 4-4. One-Segment Code.

Numeral	a	b	c	d	e	f	g	PROM location addressed with segments a, b, e, f, g. (Decimal)
0	1	1	1	1	1	1	0	30
1	0	1	1	0	0	0	0	8
2	1	1	0	1	1	0	1	29
3	1	1	1	1	0	0	1	25
4	0	1	1	0	0	1	1	11
5	1	0	1	1	0	1	1	19
6	0	0	1	1	1	1	1	7
7	1	1	1	0	0	0	0	24
8	1	1	1	1	1	1	1	31
9	1	1	1	0	0	1	1	27

significant bit of a 5-bit natural binary code (used to address the PROM), then the ten locations listed in Table 4-4 will be addressed for the numerals 0-9. These locations contain the BCD code.

Although the solution was satisfactory, there is a considerable amount of unused space in the PROM, and since it was desired to link the clock to a microprocessor-based RTTY system at a later date, it was decided to see if any of the remaining locations could be used to contain ASCII or Baudot coding for the numerals 0-9. The first to be dealt with is Baudot. If BCD and Baudot are compared (Table 4-5), it is very clear that element "B" of the BCD is identical to element "E" of the Baudot, except for the numeral 1. If it were not for this one difference, it would be possible to store the BCD (4 bits) and the Baudot (5 bits) in the 8-bit word of the PROM. This problem was overcome by the addition of a 7410 triple 3-input NAND to the output of the PROM, as shown in Fig. 4-13. Then, in any given word of the PROM, the BCD is stored in bits 0-3, and elements A, B, C and D of the Baudot are stored in bits 4-7. Thus all the BCD and elements a-D of the Baudot are directly available at the output of the

Table 4-5. BCD and Baudot.

BCD				Baudot					Numeral
D	C	B	A	E	D	C	B	A	
0	0	0	0	0	1	1	0	1	0
0	0	0	1	1	1	1	0	1	1
0	0	1	0	1	1	0	0	1	2
0	0	1	1	1	0	0	0	0	3
0	1	0	0	0	1	0	1	0	4
0	1	0	1	0	0	0	0	1	5
0	1	1	0	1	0	1	0	1	6
0	1	1	1	1	1	1	0	0	7
1	0	0	0	0	1	1	0	0	8
1	0	0	1	0	0	0	1	1	9

Table 4-6. Seven-Segment Code, with A, B, E and G Inverted.

Numeral	a	b	e	f	g	PROM location addressed with segments a, b, e, f, g. (Decimal)
0	0	0	0	1	1	3
1	1	0	1	0	1	21
2	0	0	0	0	0	0
3	0	0	1	0	0	4
4	1	0	1	1	0	22
5	0	1	1	1	0	14
6	1	1	0	1	0	26
7	0	0	1	0	1	5
8	0	0	0	1	0	2
9	0	0	1	1	0	6

PROM, and element E of the Baudot is obtainable from the extra gating, which works as follows. If the output of U1 is high, then the output of U3 will follow the input of U2 (element B of the BCD). But if at any time the output of U1 should be low (which will happen for numerals 1 and 7), then the output of U3 will be forced high. The output of U3 can then be used as element E of the Baudot. Thus the aim of encoding both BCD and Baudot is achieved, and they are available simultaneously.

Obtaining the conversion to ASCII was accomplished in a totally different way. It was necessary to modify the address inputs in some way, so that the seven-segment would address another set of unique store locations. The only modification of the address inputs which can be done easily is controlled inversion. With the aid of a computer, all the possible combinations of inversion of the address inputs were checked, from which it was discovered there were two. And for reasons which will be given later, the following was chosen. By inverting segments a, b, e and g from the clock, the locations listed in Table 4-6 can be addressed, and it is in these locations that the ASCII (or any other code) is stored. The inversion is carried out with a 7486 quad exclusive OR, as shown in Fig. 4-13. If point X in Fig. 4-13 is brought high, then segments a, b, e and g of the clock are inverted,

Table 4-7. Allowance for Topped 6s.

	a	b	e	f	g	
7-segment	1	0	1	1	1	Location 23
a, b, e, & g inverted	0	1	0	1	0	Location 10

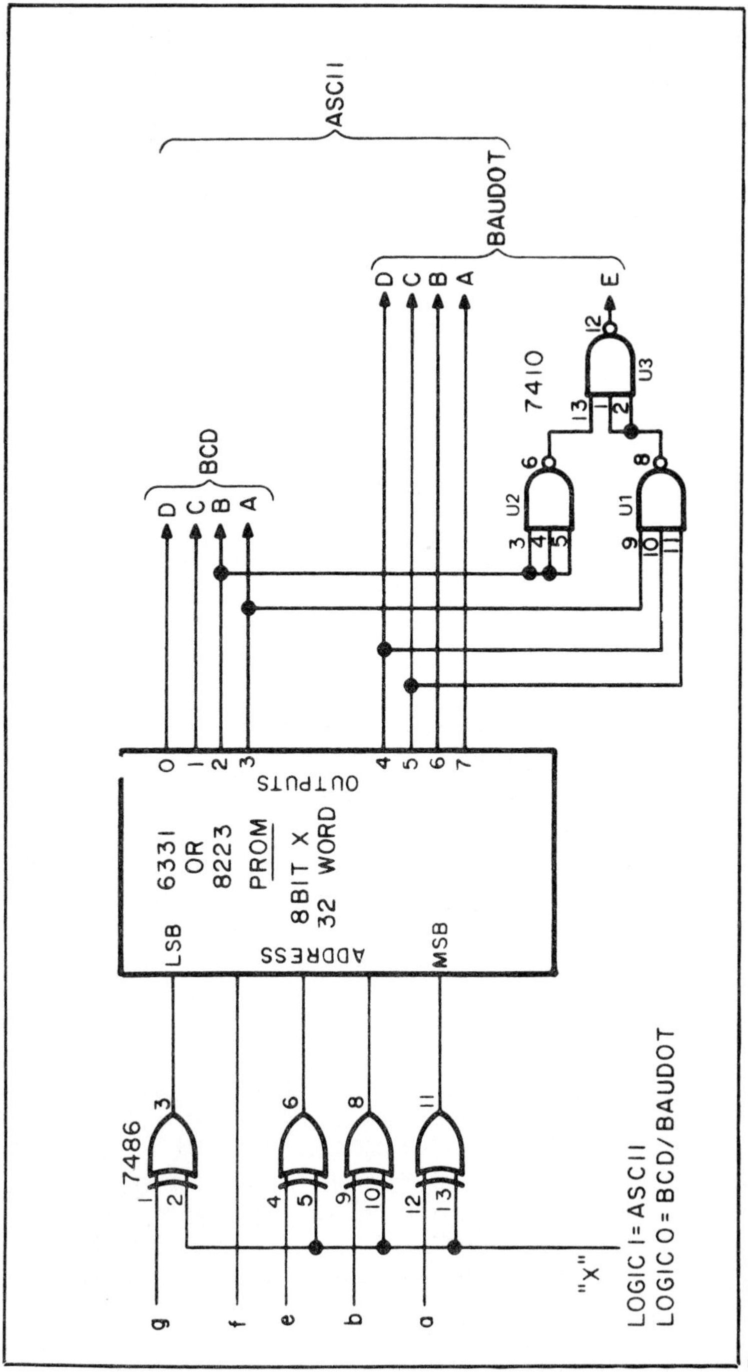

Fig. 4-13. Conversion circuit.

and ASCII can be obtained from the outputs of the PROM. If X is at logic low level, then the outputs obtained from the PROM will be Baudot/BCD.

The circuit given will function perfectly well with any seven-segment coding which produces a 6 without a top, and a 9 without a tail. Since some clock chips produce the 6 with a top, and a 9 with a tail, this was also given consideration. And this is the reason that of the two possible combinations of inversion of the input to the PROM, the one given was chosen. Since the tail of a 9 is given by segment c, it will have no effect anyway. But the top of the 6 will affect the most significant bit of the PROM address line, and it is necessary to allow for it. All that is required is to repeat the BCD/Baudot for the numeral 6 in another location of the PROM, and the same for the ASCII coding of the numeral 6. This information is given in Table 4-7.

Thus it can be seen that with the addition of two extra packages to the PROM, it is possible to cater for the conversion of seven-segment to ASCII/BCD and Baudot, with or without topped 6s and tailed 9s. A complete summary of the layout of the PROM is given in Table 4-8. Although this conversion was designed for use with a clock chip, it could be equally well used to convert the output of other chips, such as digital voltmeters, to another code.

The PROM used was a 6331 from Monolithic Memories, but a Signetics 8223, which is easily obtainable, can be used instead.

Inexpensive Paper Tape System

Serious program development requires the use of nonvolatile mass storage of some type. Cassette tape systems are popular among computer hobbyists, and for good reason. Cassettes are convenient, inexpensive and provide a high density medium for mass storage. Much has appeared in the literature concerning cassette recording techniques. The use of punched paper tape for mass storage has not been adequately treated, although it is readily available to hobbyists interested in Baudot equipment. Paper tape is not nearly as fast or as dense as cassette tape, but it ranks high in convenience and reliability. Programs can be stored on individual strips of tape and labeled for later use.

The Model 19 Teletype comes with a five level paper tape punch and reader. The punch is mechanically linked to the keyboard, so tape must be punched by hand. The keyboard and punch can be physically removed from the printing unit and used separately. The punch magnet requires a 100 volt at 1 Amp supply. The tape reader on the Model 19 is called a Transmitter-Distributor, or TD for short.

Table 4-8. Summary of Layout of Information in PROM.

Address (Binary)	Address (Decimal)	Content
00000	0	ASCII Numeral 2
00001	1	Empty
00010	2	ASCII Numeral 8
00011	3	ASCII Numeral 0
00100	4	ASCII Numeral 3
00101	5	ASCII Numeral 7
00110	6	ASCII Numeral 9
00111	7	BCD/Baudot Numeral 6
01000	8	BCD/Baudot Numeral 1
01001	9	Empty
01010	10	ASCII Numeral 6
01011	11	BCD/Baudot Numeral 4
01100	12	Empty
01101	13	Empty
01110	14	ASCII Numeral 5
01111	15	Empty
10000	16	Empty
10001	17	Empty
10010	18	Empty
10011	19	BCD/Baudot Numeral 5
10100	20	Empty
10101	21	ASCII Numeral 1
10110	22	ASCII Numeral 4
10111	23	BCD/Baudot Numeral 6
11000	24	BCD/Baudot Numeral 7
11001	25	BCD/Baudot Numeral 3
11010	26	ASCII Numeral 6
11011	27	BCD/Baudot Numeral 9
11100	28	Empty
11101	29	BCD/Baudot Numeral 2
11110	30	BCD/Baudot Numeral 0
11111	31	BCD/Baudot Numeral 8

A punched tape is drawn through one portion at a time, and a mechanical parallel to serial conversion produces the correct teletype (TTY) signal. The tape is read at 60, 65 or 75 words per minute, as determined by a gear set inside. The TD is usually connected in series with the keyboard contacts, so that either can be used to generate TTY signals. This is a satisfactory arrangement for computer operation.

With model 19 equipment alone, you will not be able to make paper tapes under computer control. For this capability you will need a Model 14 Typing-Reperforator. The Model 14 accepts standard Baudot TTY signals and punches a corresponding paper tape. In addition to punching, it prints the incoming characters in "ticker tape" fashion. You may wonder how it prints on a tape full of holes. Nothing extraordinary here: The paper tape is chadless (that is, the holes are not punched all the way through). By the way, Model 14s come in a less expensive non-typing version, also. If you already have printer capability, this would be a good choice. Model 14s of both types are readily available on the surplus market.

The Model 14 can easily be connected into the computer I/O system. Since it accepts standard TTY signals, it may be connected in series with the selector magnets of the Model 19 printer.

Paper tapes can be punched with two basic formats: *Baudot* and *binary*. Baudot tapes record the five level Baudot code in five hole positions across the width of the tape. Actually, there is a sixth smaller hole (called the *sprocket hole*), but it is only used for drive purposes. With the Baudot system, a *hole* is regarded as a *mark* and a *no hole* as a *space*. The orientation of the code is shown in Fig. 4-14. Baudot format is that used for communication purposes.

Unlike Baudot, the binary format is not in common use. In such tapes, the five hole positions are used to record five data bits. A *hole* represents a logic 1 and a *no hole*, a logic 0. The hole position corresponding to the least significant bit is indicated in Gig. 4-14.

In a computer environment, Baudot paper tapes are useful for recording programs written in a high level language such as BASIC. Binary tapes, on the other hand, find greatest utility in preserving machine language programs. This is accomplished by simply punching in tape an image of the memory area containing the program. The program can later be re-entered into the same area of memory by reading the paper tape with the proper software. The discussions which follow deal primarily with punching and reading binary tapes under computer control.

The Altair 8800 and similar minicomputers have a basic word length of 8 bits. Since a paper tape can record only 5 bits at a time,

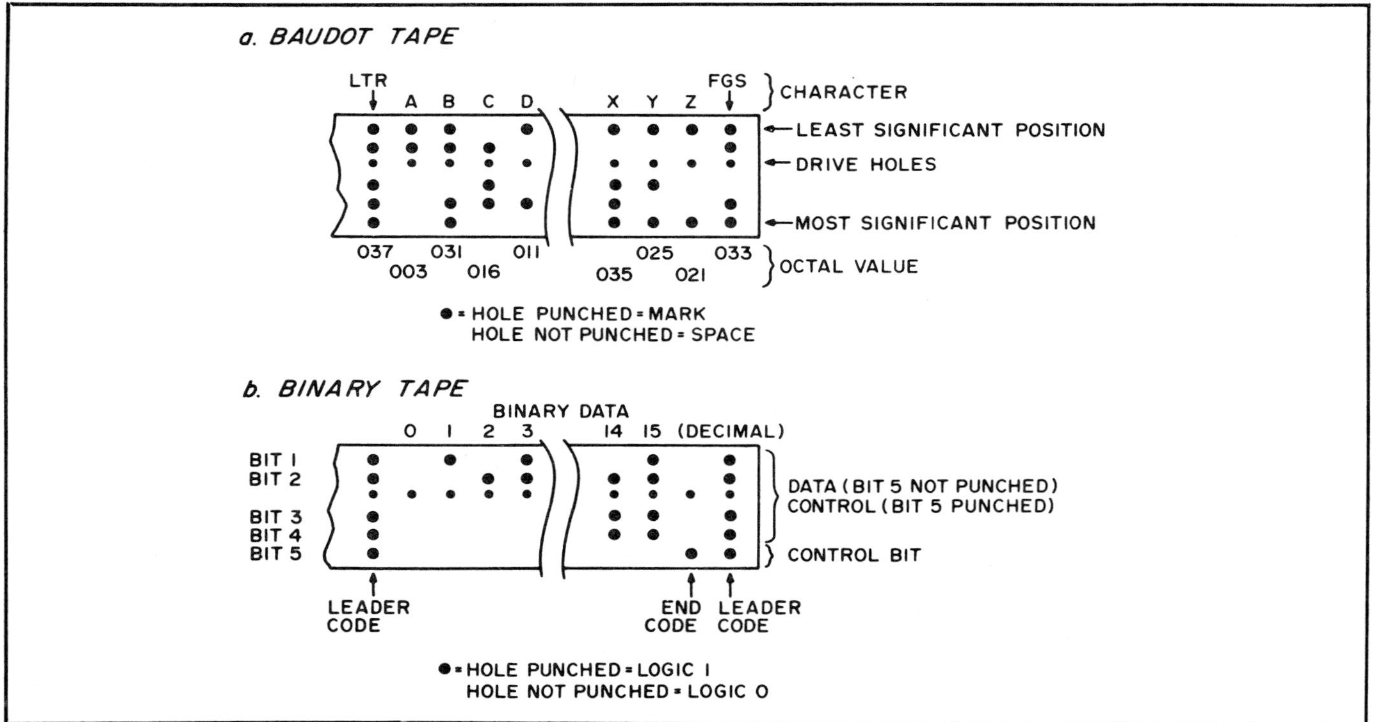

Fig. 4-14. (A) Conventional Baudot paper tape as used in communications service; (B) Binary paper tape for use in computer applications.

two read cycles are required to input the full data word. In this case, one bit of the five can be set aside for control purposes, still leaving the required eight bits with two read cycles. Bit 5 is used for the control function in our system. When bit 5 is not punched, the remaining four hole positions are considered binary data representing half of an eight bit data word. The next character in the tape without a control punch is regarded as the second half of the data word. When bit 5 is punched, the remaining four bits represent a control code. Fifteen possible codes can be used to control various aspects of the reading program. In our systems, one such code is used as the leader at the beginning of the tape and another serves to indicate the end of the tape. Other uses can be made of the control code as well. Suppose you wish to send the computer a 16 bit memory address. You could prefix the four data characters with a special control code that would cause the reading program to branch to an appropriate subroutine. Table 4-9 gives the data and control codes both in octal and their Baudot equivalent.

As further illustration, consider the implementation of paper tape on our Altair 8800 system. A Model 19 TD is series connected with the keyboard and a Model 14 is series connected with the selector magnets of the printer. We choose two control codes: 037 octal for the leader and 020 for the end of the tape. As previously indicated, two character positions are required to store the contents of one memory location. The first contains the least significant four bits while the second contains the most significant four bits. If the leader is encountered within data, it is ignored. This makes it possible to correct a bad punch by simply overpunching with all holes.

The programs we use to punch and read binary paper tapes are given in Table 4-10. The punch program requires the beginning and ending addresses of the memory area that is to be stored on tape. The read program needs only the beginning address, since the end is signalled by an 020 punch.

The punch program is used in the following manner: The beginning and ending addresses to be dumped to tape are placed at 000207 and 000212, respectively. Location 000170 is examined and the RUN switch is toggled. The program genrates a number of 37s for the leader. The contents of consecutive memory locations are then punched. At the end of the tape, an 020 octal is punched, followed by an additional leader. Final termination of the program occurs in a tight loop (i.e., an unconditional jump to itself). At this point, the STOP switch may be toggled.

Table 4-9. Data and Control Codes.

Data CODE		CONTROL CODE	
OCTAL	BAUDOT EQUIVALENT	OCTAL	BAUDOT EQUIVALENT
000	<BLANK>	020	<T>
001	<E>	021	<Z>
002	<LF>	022	<L>
003	<A>	023	<W>
004	<SPACE>	024	<H>
005	<S>	025	<Y>
006	<I>	026	<P>
007	<U>	027	<Q>
010	<CR>	030	<O>
011	<D>	031	<B>
012	<R>	032	<G>
013	<J>	033	<FGS>
014	<N≤	034	<M>
015	<F>	035	<X>
016	fiC>	036	<V>
017	<K>	037	<LTR>

The tape reader program is used in the following way: The address where the tape is to begin storing data is loaded at 000127. Location 000123 is examined and the RUN switch is toggled. After execution has begun, the TD is started with the tape in the beginning leader. When the program is finished, the front panel light pattern will change as a tight loop is entered. STOP may then be toggled. The program or data should be correctly stored in memory.

In the event you have a Model 19 punch and TD but not a reperforator, you can still make programs by hand. Figure 4-15 is a software modification that outputs Baudot characters to the printer as they should be punched by hand. The program supplies automatic carriage returns and line feeds. A "Z" is printed at the end of each line so that SPACEs may be detected. You will note in Table 4-9 that data codes include CR, BLANK and LF (line feed). These would either confuse the printout or not be printed, so the modification software makes the following substitutions:

B is printed for BLANK
L is printed for LF
X is printed for CR

Use the procedure outlined above for punching tape with the modification program loaded at 000271. The characters to be punched will be output to the printer in order. Then use the printout to hand punch the paper tape. A button on top of the punching unit can be used with the LTR key to punch all holes for error correction. When

Table 4-10. Reading and Punch Program: Model 19 and Model 14.

TAG	MNEMONIC	ADDRESS	CODE	EXPLANATION
TREAD*	LXI SP	000123	061	Load the stack pointer
		000124	377	SP (LOW)
		000125	003	SP (HIGH)
	LXI H	000126	041	Load HL with memory load address
		000127	xxx	Low part of address
		000130	xxx	High part of address
LOOP2	LXI B	000131	001	Preset B to 2 and C to 0
		000132	000	
		000133	002	
LOOP1	PSH B	000134	305	Save B and C
	CALL	000135	315	CALL INPUT ROUTINE
		000136	000	INPUT (LOW)
		000137	000	INPUT (HIGH)
	POP B	000140	301	Restore B and C
	CPI	000141	376	Check for end of tape
		000142	020	<T>
SELF	JZ	000143	312	Form tight loop for end
		000144	143	SELF (LOW)
		000145	000	SELF (HIGH)
	JNC	000146	322	Ignore other control codes
		000147	134	LOOP1 (LOW)
		000150	000	LOOP1 (HIGH)
	ADR C	000151	201	First Pass: get least 4 bits
	RLC	000152	007	Second Pass: get highest 4 bits
	RLC	000153	007	
	RLC	000154	007	
	RLC	000155	007	
	MOV C, A	000156	117	
	DCR B	000157	005	Check for second pass
	JNZ	000160	302	Jump back for second pass
		000161	134	LOOP1 (LOW)
		000162	000	LOOP1 (HIGH)

TAG	MNEMONIC	ADDRESS	CODE	EXPLANATION
	MOV M A	000163	167	Store byte in memory
	INX H	000164	043	Increment to next memory location
	JMP	000165	303	Jump back for new byte
		000166	131	LOOP2 (LOW)
		000167	000	LOOP2 (HIGH)
TPUNCH**	LXI SP	000170	061	Load the stack pointer
		000171	377	SP (LOW)
		000172	003	SP (HIGH)
	MVI B	000173	006	Load B with leader count
		000174	036	30 decimal
LOOP1	MVI A	000175	076	Load A with <LTR>
		000176	037	<LTR>
LOOP1	CALL	000177	315	CALL TAPEOUT ROUTINE
		000200	273	TAPEOUT (LOW)
		000201	000	TAPEOUT (HIGH)
	DCR B	000202	005	Decrement Leader count
	JNZ	000203	302	Jump back for more Leader
		000204	175	LOOP1 (LOW)
		000205	000	LOOP1 (HIGH)
	LXI H	000206	041	LOAD Starting Address in HL
		000207	xxx	Low part of Address
		000210	xxx	High part of Address
	LXI D	000211	021	LOAD Ending Address in DE
		000212	yyy	Low part of Address
		000213	yyy	High part of Address
	MOV A, H	000214	174	Check for end of Load
	CMP D	000215	272	Compare High Address
	JNZ	000216	302	If not same, Jump to CONT
		000217	226	CONT (LOW)
		000220	000	CONT (HIGH)
	MOV A, L	000221	175	
	CMP E	000222	273	Compare Low Address
	JZ	000223	312	If same, Jump to END

continued on page 282

TAG	MNEMONIC	ADDRESS	CODE	EXPLANATION
		000224	246	END (LOW)
		000225	000	END (HIGH)
CONT	MOV A, M	000226	176	Get memory byte into A
	CALL	000227	315	CALL TAPEOUT ROUTINE [Special]
		000230	271	TAPEOUT [Special] (LOW)
		000231	000	TAPEOUT [Special] (HIGH)
	MOV A, M	000232	176	Get memory byte again into A
	RLC	000233	007	Reposition upper four bits
	RLC	000234	007	
	RLC	000235	007	
	RLC	000236	007	
	CALL	000237	315	CALL TAPEOUT ROUTINE [Special]
		000240	271	TAPEOUT [Special] (LOW)
		000241	000	TAPEOUT [Special] (HIGH)
	INX H	000242	043	Increment to next memory byte
	JMP	000243	303	Jump back to AGAIN
		000244	211	AGAIN (LOW)
		000245	000	AGAIN (HIGH)
END	MVI A	000246	076	Load A with stop code <T>
		000247	020	
	CALL	000250	315	CALL TAPEOUT ROUTINE
		000251	273	
		000252	000	
	MVI B	000253	006	Load B with Leader count
		000254	120	
LOOP2	MVI A	000255	076	Load A with <LTR> for Leader
		000256	037	<LTR>
	CALL	000257	315	CALL TAPEOUT ROUTINE
		000260	273	TAPEOUT (LOW)
		000261	000	TAPEOUT (HIGH)
	DCR B	000262	005	Decrement Leader count

TAG	MNEMONIC	ADDRESS	CODE	EXPLANATION
	JNZ	000263	302	If not finished, Jump back to LOOP2
		000264	255	LOOP2 (LOW)
		000265	000	LOOP2 (HIGH)
SELF	JMP	000266	303	Jump to SELF to end
		000267	266	SELF (LOW)
		000270	000	SELF (HIGH)
TAPEOUT [Special]	ANI	000271	346	Mask off upper four bits
		000272	017	
TAPEOUT	PSH B	000273	305	Save B
	PSH A	000274	365	Save A
	CALL	000275	315	CALL OUTPUT ROUTINE
		000276	042	OUTPUT (LOW)
		000277	000	OUTPUT (HIGH)
	POP A	000300	361	Restore A
	POP B	000301	301	Restore B
	RET	000302	311	Return to calling program

* TAPE READ PROGRAM
** TAPE PUNCH PROGRAM

making the tape, be sure to use the LTR key to make the leader. This manual way of making a paper tape is quite tedious, but it will allow you to become familiar with the binary tape system. Figure 4-15 shows a paper tape punched by the Model 14 under computer control.

The Polymorphics Video Board

For someone who is primarily a software oriented person, I seem to do a lot of hardware building. In September, 1974, I started building TVT-I. I got it working in December and had it connected to my Altair 8800 in December, 1975. A friend, also with an Altair, built TVT-II and it was so much faster and better designed that I sold my TVT-I and built a TVT-II. I didn't keep detailed notes on the construction of these two projects, but I learn from my mistakes. When another friend showed me his Polymorphics video board, I knew I was doomed. This video board plugs directly into the Altair or IMSAI bus, eliminating a large boxfull of power supply, TVT-II and cables, and frees the parallel I/O port I used with the TVT-II. This time I kept notes on the subject. The kit is of good quality and there should be no more than the normal problems puting it together;

a.

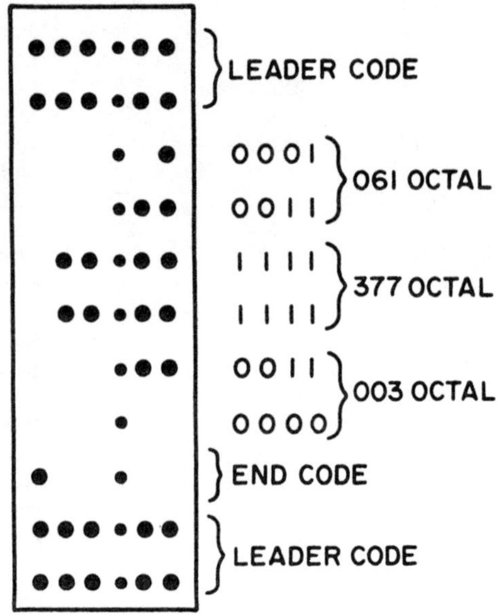

b. EAKKABT

c.

ADDRESS	CODE
000123	061
000124	377
000125	003

Fig. 4-15. (A) Binary paper tape made by punch program; (B) Printout of modified version fo punch program; (C) Memory area used for sample run.

nevertheless, there are some pitfalls. I will explain the ones I encountered and how to solve them.

The video board appears to the program to be a block of random access memory which is constantly displayed on your monitor or modified TV. The display has sixteen lines which may be either 32 character lines ($185) or 64 character lines ($210). The 32 character lines will probably work with a modified TV which has a bandwidth of 2.5 MHz, but the 64 character lines may require a monitor, as they need a bandwidth of 5.5 MHz. The memory uses 91L11 chips and acts as a normal memory. It can be used for program or data storage in addition to its normal uses. Data may be entered into any of its memory locations at any time, giving the capability of scrolling, paging, columns, fixed format eintry or any other display mode you would like to use. This flexibility also requires suitable programming.

An 8-bit parallel input port is built into the video board so that a keyboard may be attached, thus giving both input and output from one board. Unfortunately, there is no corresponding status port for this input port, so the program must check the data to see if it has changed in order to know when new data is available—again, more programming overhead.

The 6572 character generator chip provided with the kit gives 128 ASCII characters, including upper and lower case, numbers and special symbols. Lower case Greek letters print in place of the ASCII control characters. Other chips in the same series may be substituted, giving different special symbols instead of the Greek letters. The graphics display is handled external to the 6572 chip. The character space is broken up into six spaces—three rows of two blocks each, giving 64 possible graphics characters. The blocks cover the entire character space so that the entire screen may be made light with no spaces between characters.

Buying The Kit

When I decided that their kit would satisfy my needs, I called Polymorphics and asked them to send me a kit.

I've learned several things from the boards that I've already built. I use sockets for all ICs (socket come with the Polymorphics video board) and I test all of the parts that I can test. These two things can save hours of time later in the project when it doesn't work.

The first thing I did when I opened the box was to look at the instruction book. This is an impressive manual of about 72 pages and covers assembly, theory, troubleshooting and software. The section on troubleshooting is especially impressive as many kits have no such section. Polymorphics devoted 16 pages to troubleshooting, arranged in a logical manner. Hopefully you won't need it, but it's nice to know that it will help give you a better understanding of the circuits involved.

Building The Kit

The first part of kitbuilding is checking the parts supplied against the parts list. I was missing a 27 pF capacitor and a 150 ohm

Table 4-11. Modification for Model 19 System Only.

TAG	MNEMONIC	ADDRESS	CODE	EXPLANATION
TAPEOUT [Special]	ANI	000271	346	Mask off upper four bits
		000272	017	
TAPEOUT	CPI	000273	376	Check for <BLANK>
		000274	000	<BLANK>
	JZ	000275	312	If so, Jump to PRNTB
		000276	313	PRNTB (LOW)
		000277	000	PRNTB (HIGH)
	CPI	000300	376	Check for <LF>
		000301	002	<LF>
	JZ	000302	312	If so, Jump to PRNTL
		000303	316	PRNTL (LOW)
		000304	000	PRNTL (HIGH)
	CPI	000305	376	Check for <CR>
		000306	010	<CR>
	JZ	000307	312	If so, Jump to PRNTX
		000310	321	PRNTX (LOW)
		000311	000	PRNTX (HIGH)
	LXI D	000312	021	Dummy: Skip instruction
PRNTB	MVI A	000313	076	Place <B> in A
		000314	031	<B>
	LXI D	000315	021	Dummy: Skip instruction
PRNTL	MVI A	000316	076	Place <L> in A
		000317	022	<L>
	LXI D	000320	021	Dummy: Skip instruction
PRNTX	MVI A	000321	076	Place <X> in A
		000322	035	<X>
	PSH B	000323	305	Save BC
	CALL	000324	315	CALL OUTPUT ROUTINE
		000325	042	OUTPUT (LOW)
		000326	000	OUTPUT (HIGH)
	POP B	000327	301	Restore BC
	LDA	000330	072	Place COUNT in A
		000331	364	COUNT (LOW)
		000332	000	COUNT (HIGH)
	INR A	000333	074	Increment COUNT by one
	STA	000334	062	Store in COUNT
		000335	364	COUNT (LOW)
		000336	000	COUNT (HIGH)
	ANI	000337	346	Check for end of line
		000340	077	
	RNZ	000341	300	Return if not
	MVI A	000342	076	Place <Z> in A
		000343	021	<Z>

Table 4-11. Modification for Model 19 System Only. **continued from page 286**

TAG	MNEMONIC	ADDRESS	CODE	EXPLANATION
	PSH B	000344	305	Save BC
	CALL	000345	315	CALL OUTPUT ROUTINE
		000346	042	OUTPUT (LOW)
		000347	000	OUTPUT (HIGH)
	MVI A	000350	076	Place <CR> in A
		000351	010	<CR>
	CALL	000352	315	CALL OUTPUT ROUTINE
		000353	042	OUTPUT (LOW)
		000354	000	OUTPUT (HIGH)
	MVI A	000355	076	Place <LF> in A
		000356	002	<LF>
	CALL	000357	315	CALL OUTPUT ROUTINE
		000360	042	OUTPUT (LOW)
		000361	000	OUTPUT (HIGH)
	POP B	000362	301	Restore BC
		000363	311	Return to Calling program

resistor, but it turned out that neither part was used in the kit. A 1N759 12V zener diode was also missing, but a 78L12 was supplied instead. An extra 10 uF electrolytic capacitor was included and was used in the kit.

Having determined which parts were supplied, the next step was to test all that I could. It is much easier to find a shorted capacitor, for example, when you have not yet mounted it than it is to find it when you discover that your board doesn't work! The resistors supplied with my kit were all within tolerance, but I found that one end of one 10k ohm trimpot was open. I was able to use it for R22, so it caused no problem. I checked the capacitors for shorts and observed the charging of those over .01 uF. All capacitors tested good. All diode and transistor junction resistances (forward and backward) were good. By inspection I found a solder bridge on one of the ICs. This is not uncommon and can cause a lot of grief if it isn't found before the IC is mounted.

The Assembly

The assembly instructions are aimed toward the person who has had some prior kit-building experience. A drawing of the board is given showing the locations of the various parts. Each part is listed with a space to check as each is soldered in place. The drawing in my manual was smeared in places so that I couldn't read the parts labels. I was able to get the needed information from a friend with a

Polymorphics video manual with a clear drawing. There were also two pages missing from my manual which I was able to copy from his. Further confusion can arise from C25, which is labeled .01 uF on the schematic but is given as 4700pF in the assembly instructions (4700 is correct). The polarity is not given for one of the electrolytic capacitors and is shown reversed on the schematic for one of the others. It may be obvious to everyone but me, but I still think that a note should be included telling which way to orient the trimpots so that they can be adjusted while the board is in operation. I also think that instructions on connecting the video output cable should be included.

In all, construction time was probably well under 10 hours, but it is hard to tell when the time available to work on it comes in blocks of 30 minutes or less. In any event, the moment of truth finally came. I plugged it in and turned the power on. A few quick adjustments of the horizontal and vertical controls on my monitor and viola—a screen with funny-looking characters on the left side of the screen and wavy lines running from top to bottom. The characters didn't look too good either. A quick voltage check showed 6.6 volts instead of 5.0. Replacing the 7805 regulator brought the voltage down to an acceptable 5.06 volts. I decided that it is worthwhile to test voltage regulators also. Somewhat afraid that, after the 6.6 volts, I now had a board of write-only memory, I tried again. No ripple this time and the voltage was good, but the characters were still all at the left side of the screen and still looked funny. I could enter characters or change them but they looked like negative images. I had used twinlead to connect the board to my monitor because I didn't have any coax handy. (No cable is supplied with the kit.) My eagle-eyed friend pointed out that I had reversed the connections to the monitor, thus reversing the video. This also caused the monitor to sync on the first white square (black in the negative image) on each line, thus preventing me from centering the display. Changing the cable restored a positive image and fixed the sync. The board now worked just fine with respect to hardware.

Apparently there is a problem with some monitors due to the fact that the video board operates at 17.094 kHz, which is above the normal horizontal sweep frequency. Instructions are given to lower the board's frequency if required. It is also possible to use an onboard crystal to obtain any desired sweep frequency. Normally the signals are divided down from the 2 MHz clock on the CPU board. This modification was not needed with my Sanyo VM-4092 monitor.

Software

Because the board is so versatile, the software to control it is complex and lengthy. For paging, the control software must determine where the character is to be put, control a cursor if desired and watch for end of page. Line feed and carriage return instructions must be intercepted and handled as well as any optional commands you wish to implement, such as backspace or backline, etc. One problem which could have been avoided is the fact that the board looks at the most significant bit to determine whether to display an ASCII character or a graphic character. If the bit is a 1, the ASCII is displayed. Most packaged software, such as MITS BASIC, will mask this bit to a zero so the video control software must also fix this bit.

Polymorphics includes a listing of a program to control their board. It allows for input from their keyboard using interrupts to determine when data is valid. The program offers quite versatile control of the display. Home, erase, right, left, down, delete character, insert character, etc., as well as optional paging or scrolling, are available under software control. The video control routine is 455 bytes long and is given as an assembly listing in hexadecimal. It uses memory locations 0 through 44 and 1D00 through 1E83. The board is assumed to start at memory location 8800 hex. This is a lot more overhead than a simple I/O port which might use 20 bytes. The best idea is to put the driver routine in PROM. Another disadvantage is that this video output will not be compatible with other packaged software such as MITS BASIC, although such programs can be modified to call the video driver.

Another program listing is included in the manual. This one plays the game of LIFE. LIFE loads into memory locations 0 through 0106 hex and also uses blocks of memory starting at 300 and 800 hex.

Since I work in octal, don't have an assembler operating and these routines overlay my control programs, I don't have either of them loaded yet. Both are well-documented with comments, though neither appears to use structured program techniques. It should not be difficult to get them running.

Overall, the kit seems well-designed. Except for a bad part (the voltage regulator) and my own stupidity (the reversed video cable), the board would have worked the first time. Even if it hadn't, the troubleshooting section seems well thought out and requires no test equipment but a voltmeter and your monitor.

Chapter 5
Computers and the Ham Shack

For several years I have experimented with, built and operated different items of SSTV equipment. From that experience I tried my hand at building an all solid state RTTY TVT. In monitoring ham RTTY transmissions on the West Coast, it was noted that the subject of microcomputers and their application to ham radio was being discussed in increasing frequency. My curiosity was aroused about this new development in ham radio.

I was fortunate in being able to visit Dr. Robert Suding WØLMD several times during business trips, and observed the development of the microcomputer that is now marketed by The Digital Group of Denver, Colorado. For my hands-on experiments in microcomputers, I purchased their type 8080-4BD kit. I feel that I was probably like other hams and did not have the slightest notion of how this thing worked, but figured to just jump in and have a go at it. I must say it has been a very interesting project. I am slowly learning to live with the new system and to use it in some practical applications.

A Ham's Computer

The 8080-4BD system as shown in the block diagram of Fig. 5-1 consists of several PC boards and the components that must be mounted on the boards. This includes the standard mother board, a CPU board with 2K of memory, an 8K memory board using 2102 ICs, a video display, cassette interface board and a four-port parallel I/O board. The mother board will accommodate two more 8K memory boards and three more four-port I/O boards. Low profile sockets are used for mounting all ICs. An unmounted surplus keyboard with ASCII encoded output was also purchased from The Digital Group.

A 12 inch transistorized black and white TV set was used for the video display. The display consists of 16 lines of 32 characters per line. For the cassette *read* and *write* modes, I use a Superscope Model C-104 as recommended in the technical literature that accompanies the kit. Power supplies in both kit and assembled form are available from The Digital Group, but I chose to build my own. The cabinet for the mother board, PC boards and power supply was salvaged from an old obsolete tube transmitter. I also fabricated a cabinet for the keyboard assembly. The TV set was modified to accept video input from the computer.

Included in the parts from The Digital Group is a prerecorded tape cassette that is used to initialize the system and to test out the memory card. It also has a game program, a program to make the unit act as a digital counter, a bicentennial demonstration program and a ham CW and RTTY program. The bicentennial program on the tape prints an American flag on the TV screen to the accompaniment of *The Star Spangled Banner*.

Assembly of the System

It is stressed in the data furnished with the kit that the builder should have some experience in building electronic equipment other than assembling detailed kits from Benton Harbor. The data does not give that kind of step-by-step instructions. The quality of the PC boards is first class, with gold-plated connector contacts and double-sided boards with through-plated holes. General instructions on how to assemble each PC board are given with a description of how the circuit works. A schematic diagram is furnished for each board, along with a general parts layout for that particular board. Testing and troubleshooting information is also furnished in the data package.

In assembling my system, I discovered one board that was missing all the bypass capacitors. They were immediately replaced when The Digital Group was advised of the shortage. Another board had one low cost IC missing which I replaced from my junk box. Another board had one extra IC in the kit. After the unit was finally assembled and ready to test, I ran into several bugs. The characters on the video monitor were not complete, and it looked more like a foreign language than English. I found, after consultation with Dr. Suding, that I had a bit missing on the data lines going into the video

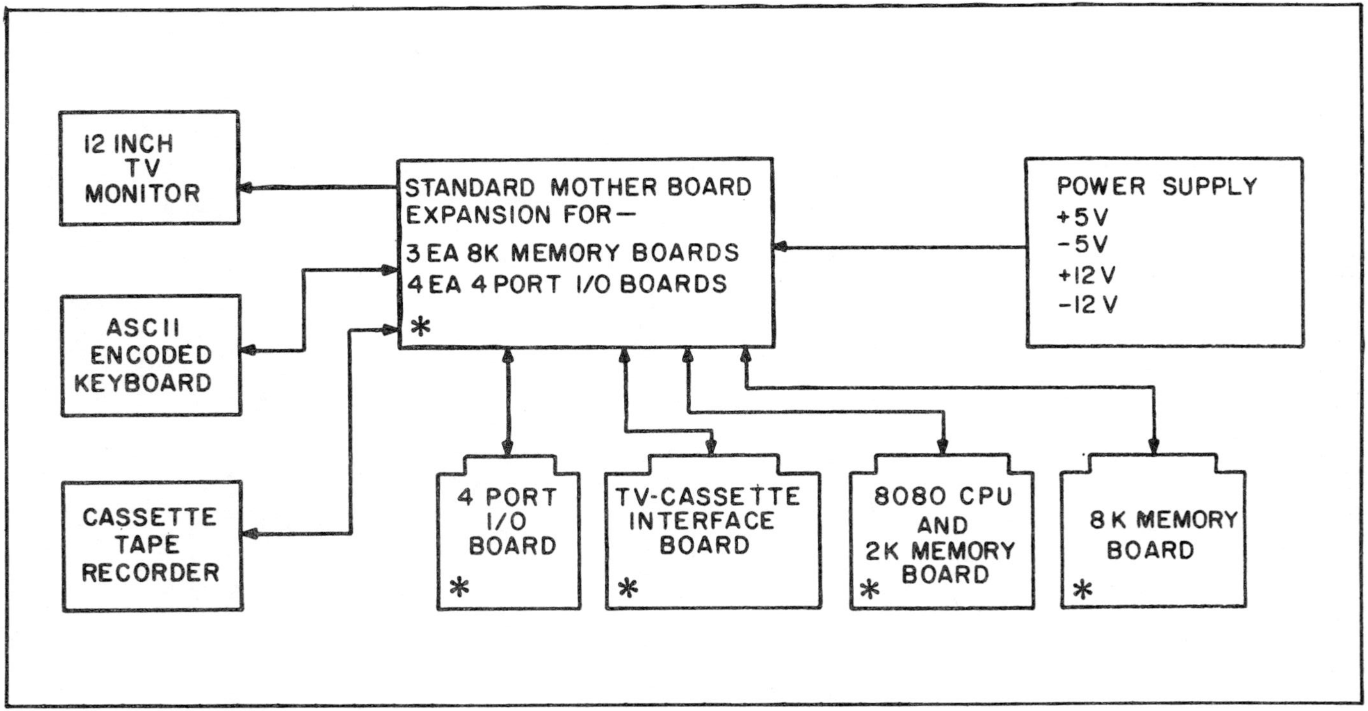

Fig. 5-1. Block diagram of microcomputer system at K7YZZ. *Items basic to the 8080-4BD kit.

board. This was determined to be caused by a lack of through-plating in one of the holes in the mother board. The next bug was that a portion of the dot structure was missing in the characters being displayed. This was found to be caused by a defective Motorola (MCM 6571L) character generator chip which was promptly replaced (once again) by The Digital Group. The last bug was that the encoder chip (T1 TMS-5000) in the keyboard had to be replaced (as one row of keys was dead). With those bugs out of the way the system worked as designed.

The power supply shown in the diagram of Fig. 5-2 was homemade, and provides all the voltages required at the specified current loads. I had to salvage an old 6.3 volt 20 Amp transformer and rewind it with a new secondary for the high current 5 volt load. A second winding was also added for the +12 volt line. The crowbar circuit was added to protect all those expensive ICs on the memory and CPU card. Discussions with Dr. Suding indicated that anything less than 50,000 uF in the 5 volt power supply filter might lead to unwanted noise problems. I located just what was needed in a local surplus store and ended up with a 55,000 uF unit.

The cabinet for the computer is 18½ inches wide by 9 inches high by 12 inches deep. I cut two large square holes in the top and riveted in a perforated grille for better circulation of cooling air. A 4 inch fan is mounted on the compartment divider bulkhead between the power supply compartment and the PC board compartment. The air is directly over those warm memory chips. I have had no problems with overheated ICs. The MPC-1000 5 volt 10 Amp regulator is mounted on a very large heat sink on the back bulkhead, out in the open air. This way it does not dump its heat into the unit.

The 12 inch TV set was modified Fig. 5-3. The level of the video signal from the computer was more than the TV set could handle, and required additional line loading before the set began to display the signal on the screen at an acceptable brightness and contrast level. The builder should not use a TV set that does not have a power transformer providing power line isolation. Be sure that the set does not have a hot chassis with series string heater tubes. That type will really fry the ICs in a computer.

I found that when playing the cassette into the computer I could not monitor the audio signal, so I modified the recorder by adding a 100 ohm resistor across the output jack switch contacts so that the speaker was in the circuit even when an audio line plug was connected to the recorder output. It is convenient to monitor the mark frequency tone as the program playback begins and ends.

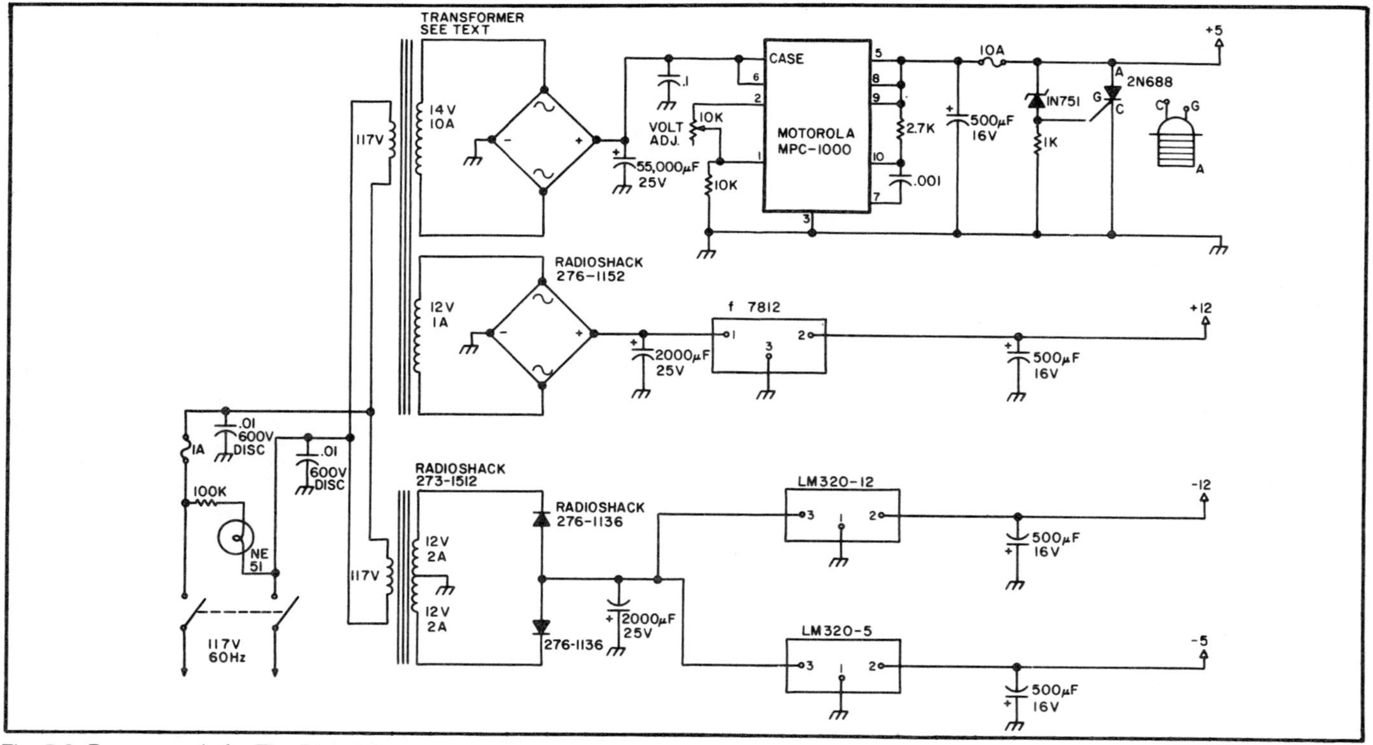

Fig. 5-2. Power supply for The Digital Group 8080-4BD.

Initial Test

When power is applied to the system there should appear on the top of the TV screen "Read 8080 INITIALIZE Cassette." If this message appears, all is well. The first program on the audio cassette furnished with the kit is loaded in the recorder. At the start of the mark frequency tone the *reset* button on the computer is depressed for a moment. The computer then begins to accept the digital data recorded on the tape. As the data is loaded into the computer, the TV screen will display lines of a running series of numbers beginning with 1 through 7, and back to 0 through 7, until the program is loaded. This represents each page of program data being loaded into memory. At the end of the program tape, the mark tone will return and the screen will display "8080 OP SYSTEM" and the options. Selecting item 4 of this listing (hit key 4) will permit the operator to begin generating a program from the keyboard beginning at page 6. Program development using this tape will be in the octal code format. Other prerecorded programs on the tape, such as the *Memory Check* are used to determine if all of the memory ICs are alright. The tape for that program is loaded and key 6 is depressed. The TV screen goes blank until all the memory chips are tested. Then, if all is OK, an alpha sign appears in the upper left hand corner of the screen and another run is automatically begun. Each successful test provides another alpha figure on the screen. For the 2K memory the check time is just a few seconds; for the 10K memory it takes about a minute to run the test. If a defective memory IC is located, it will stop the test and print on the TV screen which IC is defective and on which circuit board the IC is located. This really works, as I tried some known bum chips and it located them very promptly.

At first I was very apprehensive about pushing that RESET button, or switching off the power to clear the memory for a new program entry, but after a while I found that it did not damage the machine. I became more confident of the machine and its operation.

Operation

The Digital Group has established a branch called The Digital Group Software Systems, which supplies cassettes of games and other items, such as a Tiny BASIC Extended. I obtained all the games (that are available to date), including the Tiny BASIC Extended. Most of the games are written in Tiny BASIC and must have the Tiny BASIC program loaded in the computer before they can be played. The machine is turned on, and when the initialization state-

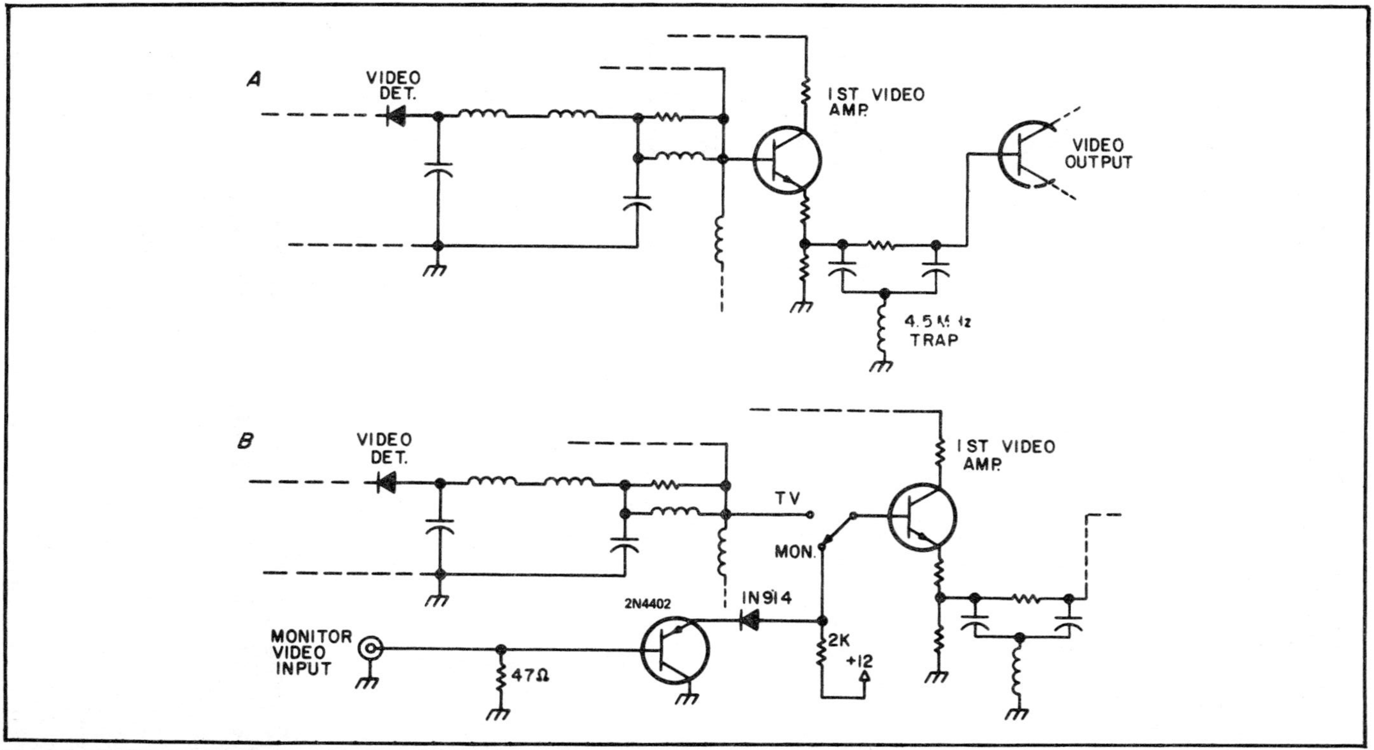

Fig. 5-3. (A) TV circuit before modification; (B) TV circuit after modification.

ment appears on the TV screen the Tiny BASIC tape is loaded. Then the selected game tape is loaded by keying 1 on the keyboard when the mark tone appears at the beginning of the tape.

The blackjack game is fun to play, and some of the locally trained (Las Vegas) experts tell me it is a very well written program. It has all of the game's rules well executed. I condensed all of my games onto two tapes. I recorded the Tiny BASIC program at the beginning of each tape and then recorded around 10 to 12 games on each tape. There is still plenty of tape left for additional games. The magnetic tape cassettes are of the 30 to 46 minute type. Longer tapes are too thin to make good recordings of digital data.

A new ham cassette is in the works at The Digital Group Software Systems and will have expanded capability for both sending and receiving CW and RTTY (with up to eight storage slots of 100 characters each).

I have had some success at trying to program some games using the Tiny BASIC Extended. (Incidentally, the Tiny BASIC Extended does not have floating decimal or square root math capability.) I feel that these programming efforts have been the most informative and effective way to learn just what you can and cannot do with the machine. Also, you can be sure that it will tell the operator when he has goofed, in no uncertain terms.

The construction of the microcomputer turned out to be no more difficult than most SSTV construction projects. The biggest problem is acquiring an understanding of the machine and learning the Tiny BASIC Extended language. Computer terminology is almost like listening to a foreign language. I can assure the reader that after continued exposure to this new technology the terms and functions will begin to make sense. I should also like to warn the reader that this machine is addictive. You will find yourself sitting in front of that keyboard for hours trying out first one thing, then another. It is absolutely fascinating.

The First Computer-Controlled Ham Station

The microprocessor has established itself as one of the most useful and versatile products on the electronic market to date. It is not too surprising that many amateurs are experimenting with and using microprocessors in conjunction with their radio hobby. The applications for microprocessors within amateur radio are as varied as the individual imagination, the best part being that a microprocessor-based implementation of a complex function is relatively simple compared to its discrete component counterpart and is much more flexible. I will attempt to give the reader an overview of what I've done with an Altair 8800 microprocessor-based system and a radioteletype station.

Definitions of Terminology

A few definitions are in order before I get too far. These are my own definitions and are not necessarily rigorous.

- **Microprocessor**—An integrated circuit (sometimes several integrated circuits) which will perform a number of varied operations according to a list of instructions stored in memory; a computer on an integrated circuit. I have been using the words microprocessor, processor and computer almost interchangeably.
- **Instruction set**—A list of logical, mathematical or manipulatory operations that a processor will perform on data stored in memory or within the internal register structure of the processor.
- **Hardware**—The actual collection of electronic components, wire and other assorted items that makes up the computer system.
- **Program**—A sequence of instructions (selected from the instruction set) and data which directs the operation of the processor to accomplish a given task. A program is stored in memory while it is in use.
- **Bit**—The smallest unit of memory. A bit may be either on or off, logical one or logical zero.
- **Byte**—Eight bits. The byte has come to be a standard measure of memory. Hang around a couple computer freaks and you will hear one of them ask how much memory so and so has. If the answer is over 8 thousand bytes you should be suitably impressed. If, on the other hand, the answer is some small number like 256 then you should say something like "What can he do with that?" If the number of bytes is given in so many K, for instance 32K, that is the same as saying 32 thousand except that it is easier. By the way, whenever someone is talking about memory, a thousand (or a K) usually means 1024. It's easier to say 16 thousand, or 16K, than 16,384.
- **Word**—A unit of memory consisting of a somewhat arbitrary number of bits, the number being defined by the particular processor used. It is the number of bits that the

processor operates on at any one time (don't quote me on that since there are always exceptions). The most common word size for a microprocessor is 8 bits, or one byte.

- **Memory**—The medium which stores programs and data such that the processor has access to any word at any time.
- **Mass storage**—A medium which is used for long term or large volume storage of information. Examples are magnetic tape, paper tape and magnetic disc. I distinguish mass storage from normal memory on the basis that information stored on a mass storage device must be transferred to normal memory before it can be used by the processor.
- **Software**—Programs. Programs are called software because they can be modified without too much trouble as compared to modifying a piece of hardware.
- **Firmware**—The exception to the last definition. Sometimes programs are stored in a special type of memory that cannot be modified by the processor (except in very special cases or if the processor begins to burn). These programs are called firmware because it is not as much trouble to modify a firmware program as it is to modify hardware, but it requires more profanity to fix an error in a firmware program than is normally associated with changing software. See the next three definitions.
- **ROM**—Read only memory. A type of memory that is programmed during manufacture. The contents of a ROM cannot be changed except by destruction.
- **PROM**—Programmable read only memory. A read only memory that can be programmed in the field by the user (meaning you). It is more useful to the amateur market than ROM since programming charges for small quantities of ROM (less than several thousand) are prohibitive.
- **EPROM**—Erasable, programmable read only memory. Same as PROM except that it may be erased by high intensity ultraviolet light and re-programmed. There is also a new type of ROM being introduced which is electrically alterable. It is called EAROM for electrically alterable read only memory. The main thing about ROM, PROM, EPROM and EAROM is that it doesn't forget what it knows when the power goes off.
- **RAM**—Random access memory. This type of memory can be read by the processor and modified by the processor. It also tends to forget what it knows if the power goes off unless it is magnetic core memory. Most microcomputers

use solid state RAM since core memory is expensive and comparatively hard to use and uses much more power. Still, you will hear people talk about how much core they have even when they mean solid state RAM.

- **FIFO**—First-in-first-out buffer. A type of memory buffer which stores information (usually characters) in such a way that the characters are expelled from the memory (when requested) in the same order in which they were originally entered. Many radioteletype stations use such devices to stimulate the paper tape punch/paper tape reader combination which can be used to allow an operator to type information ahead of the transmitter.
- **UART**—Universal asynchronous transmitter/receiver. A circuit which converts serial data to parallel data and vice versa.

The Inspiration

When I first got into radioteletype I never imagined that I would ever need or want anything beyond my RTTY converter (ST-6) and my Model 19 teletype machine. After operating my station for a couple years, I had talked to guys who had video displays, selective call-up, time/date prestidigitizers, UARTs, FIFOs and all manner of other equipment better than mine. Hardly anyone knew what a Model 19 was except that it made a lot of noise. Pretty soon my ears confirmed the suspicion that a Model 19 is not as quiet as it could be. Then one day some guy told me what UART stood for and how to use one. I decided to build a super station.

I made a list of all the features I wanted to include in my ultimate teletype station. The major items were to be a video display, a solid state keyboard, use of UARTs and FIFOs, selective call-up, time/date generation and a message board. Minor items were added, deleted and modified almost daily at the outset of the design project.

The first major sign of trouble appeared when I was considering methods to edit a 72-80 character line down to 64 characters so it would fit on my display. The most obvious idea is to break the line on a space if it occurs near the end of the line. For this purpose one has to consider the line feed character to be equivalent to a space. I was talking to some station up in Nova Scotia and telling him about this when I noticed that he, like many amateurs including myself from time to time, had the habit of ending a sentence, sending 10-20 periods (or dashes), and then beginning a new sentence. This could result in split words or lines beginning with umpteen punctuation marks if I simply looked for spaces to break my lines on the display. It began to look like I would have to settle for some funny looking print occasionally. I was willing to accept that, so I plunged ahead. But, by the time I was actually near the point of building anything, the designs had gotten to be so complex and inflexible that I wanted to wander onto I-71 pulling my Model 19 right behind. Then I heard rumblings about the eventual legalization of ASCII for use on the amateur bands and all but gave up on the project.

One day, in the depths of despair, I read an article on recent microprocessor breakthroughs which had brought prices down to affordable levels. It didn't take too long to realize that by simply interfacing the various components of my station to a computer, I would be able to simulate all of the desired features by writing appropriate software. In addition, I would be able to write programs that would do all sorts of other things I had never even considered building because of their complexity (e.g., almost automatic contest operation). Time/date and selective call-up would be trivial. A FIFO could be simulated by software with the addition of elaborate editing capabilities. The legalization of ASCII would cause no problems since I could copy any code (including Morse) by doing the appropriate code conversion. I could even have the system whistle "Dixie."

The Realization

The block diagram of Fig. 5-4 shows the configuration that I finally decided to use. It is not as optimum as it could be, since it would be desirable to have a completely separate interface for the cassette recorder. However, it is reasonable to use the RTTY demodulator and AFSK generator for storing data on an audio cassette since it involves no additional construction other than a switch or two. I needed to get something going to fill the time it would take to get a dedicated cassette interface going. Besides, using normal AFSK for cassette recording will probably turn out to be one of the best ways for amateurs to exchange software.

The keyboard is a solid state keyboard (many types are available from the various surplus houses) which generates a seven bit code (ASCII). The interface for the keyboard is a simple parallel input port.

The Heath SB-301 and SB-401 are monitored and keyed through the ST-6 demodulator and a UART. A control channel allows the processor to select the shift, reverse the shift, select the speed of the UART, turn the transmitter on and off and send make break or narrow shift CW. It is pretty simple, consisting of the UART and some latches to provide the necessary control.

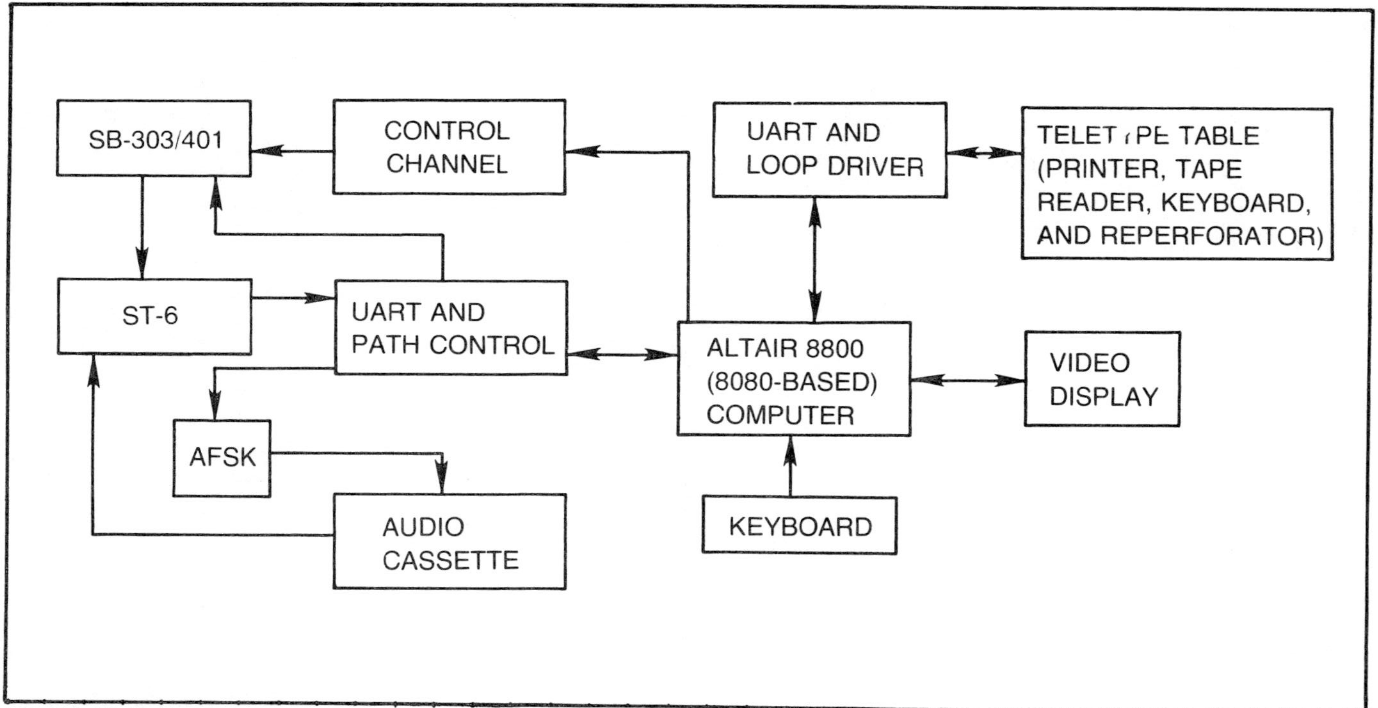

Fig. 5-4. Block diagram.

The video display is a home brew display and is the most useful item in the system next to the processor itself. It will display 29 lines of 64 characters per line in both upper and lower case, plus a few Greek symbols. The memory of the display is large enough to hold 32 lines of information but I have displayed only 29 lines to avoid uncomfortably close line spacing. The processor treats the display as normal memory rather than as an output device, and can read from or write to the display memory at a very fast rate. The actual rate depends on the program controlling the read or write functions. An upper limit for the transfer rate is about 2 million characters per second, the typical rate being closer to 100,000 characters per second. The high read/write speeds mean that there is no need to build extra hardware for scrolling the display—one simply writes a short program that reads each character of the display and re-writes it on the next line up. Scrolling the entire display then takes about 50 milliseconds of processor time. Another advantage of this technique is that the display can be partitioned into several sectors and each sector can be scrolled independently of the other sectors.

Another feature of the display is that each character can be controlled on an individual basis to produce a black character in a box of white. I use the video inversion feature for displaying cursors, which means that I can have as many cursors roaming around as I desire.

The teletype equipment (my old Model 19) is interfaced through a UART and simple loop driver and sensor. I use the teletype for producing hard copy of my programs, my logs and for printing teletype art. It also serves as an excellent backup system for making and reading paper tapes in case the cassette recorder decides to give up the ghost.

The Sting

The first practical use I made of the system was as an operating aid in BARTG RTTY contest. I had just finished putting the system together and had gotten a *resident assembler* running (a resident assembler is an extremely valuable programming tool) when I was invited to bring my system to Albuquerque as a display entry in the Systems Demonstration Contest of the World Altair Computer Convention. It happened that the convention was the same weekend as the BARTG contest. In four long evenings I wrote a contest program that would enable me to operate the contest from the convention while I was devoting most of my attention to telling people about the system.

The processor listened to the receiver through the ST-6 and UART. When I was tuned to a valid RTTY signal, the information was edited and displayed in one area of the video display. If I saw a station that I wished to work, I typed in the call of that station. The computer would instantly tell me if I had already worked the station or not. At the same time it would enter the call of the station, the current time and the contact number on a line of the display that I had reserved for developing log entries. The only other piece of information that I needed to type was the signal report I wished to send to the station. By using special two letter commands, I could have the computer call the station (or answer him if he was calling me), send the entire exchange, tell him that I QSL or ask him to repeat the exchange, or tell him that this was a duplicate contact. Other two letter commands allowed me to request the computer to send CQ and call QRZ. All of the text that the computer generated (which was complete with callsigns and carriage control) was displayed in another area of the screen. Upon completion of a contact the computer would turn on the printer and print a hard copy of all information required in the contest log. If a contact was started and not completed, then no log entry was made. The only information saved in memory after a valid contact was the callsign and a tag byte to indicate which bands the station had worked so the computer could do the duplicate checking. The computer also handled generation of the CW identification, when necessary.

The result was that I walked away with the first place prize in the system display contest, a floppy disc drive. Needless to say, I have altered my plans concerning construction of a separate cassette interface and will be devoting my time to writing software to utilize the disc drive as my mass storage device.

So far I have only scratched the surface of the many possibilities for use of a microprocessor in the RTTY area alone. Other obvious uses for microprocessors within amateur radio include repeater control, CW reception and transmission, antenna control (for OSCAR or moonbounce especially) and who knows what else. A less obvious but equally or more useful application is digital filtering. Slow scan to fast scan conversion would also be another interesting possibility.

A Ham Shack File Handler

This is a simple program in BASIC which will keep track of your QSLs and also give you information on the repeaters that you may wish to use. The program may also be extended to provide other

Table 5-1. A Sample Run of the Ham File.

```
RUN
REPEATER AND QSL FILE
FOR REPEATERS USE LAST THREE LETTERS OR FREQUENCY AS 13/73
OR CITY NAME. FOR AMATEUR STATIONS USE COMPLETE CALL.

STATION? AAA
WR4AAA, 13/73, 190, SALISBURY, NC

END OF SEARCH

STATION? 28/88
WR4ABF, 28/88, 195, SHELBY, NC

END OF SEARCH

STATION? HICKORY
WR4ABF, 25/28 195 HICKORY, NC

END OF SEARCH

STATION? ABQ

NO RECORD IN FILES

STATION? CR6CA
5/26/71, 0015Z, 14MHZ, RTTY, JOE

END OF SEARCH

STATION? K4GV
11/6/75, 0710P, 2M-FM, TED
12/5/75, 0655P, 2M-FM, TED

END OF SEARCH

STATION? W2ABC

NO RECORD IN FILES

STATION? W4BQ
THAT'S YOU, STUPID!

END OF SEARCH

STATION?

OK
```

functions in logkeeping, but it was kept simple to give the hams who are new computer freaks a chance to get acquainted with their new toy. It is written in Altair BASIC version 3.2, but could be easily modified to any other BASIC.

Station Operation

A sample readout (Table 5-1) shows that information about a repeater can be obtained by replying to the initial question of the computer ("STATION?") with the last three letters of the repeater call, such as "AAA" or by typing in the frequency pair as "37/97," or even by typing in the location city as "SHELBY." If your input is a city name, all the repeaters in that city will be printed and the same goes for the repeater frequency pairs, but only one repeater will be printed for each call. If you should be working in an area which crosses district boundaries, and the same last three letters have

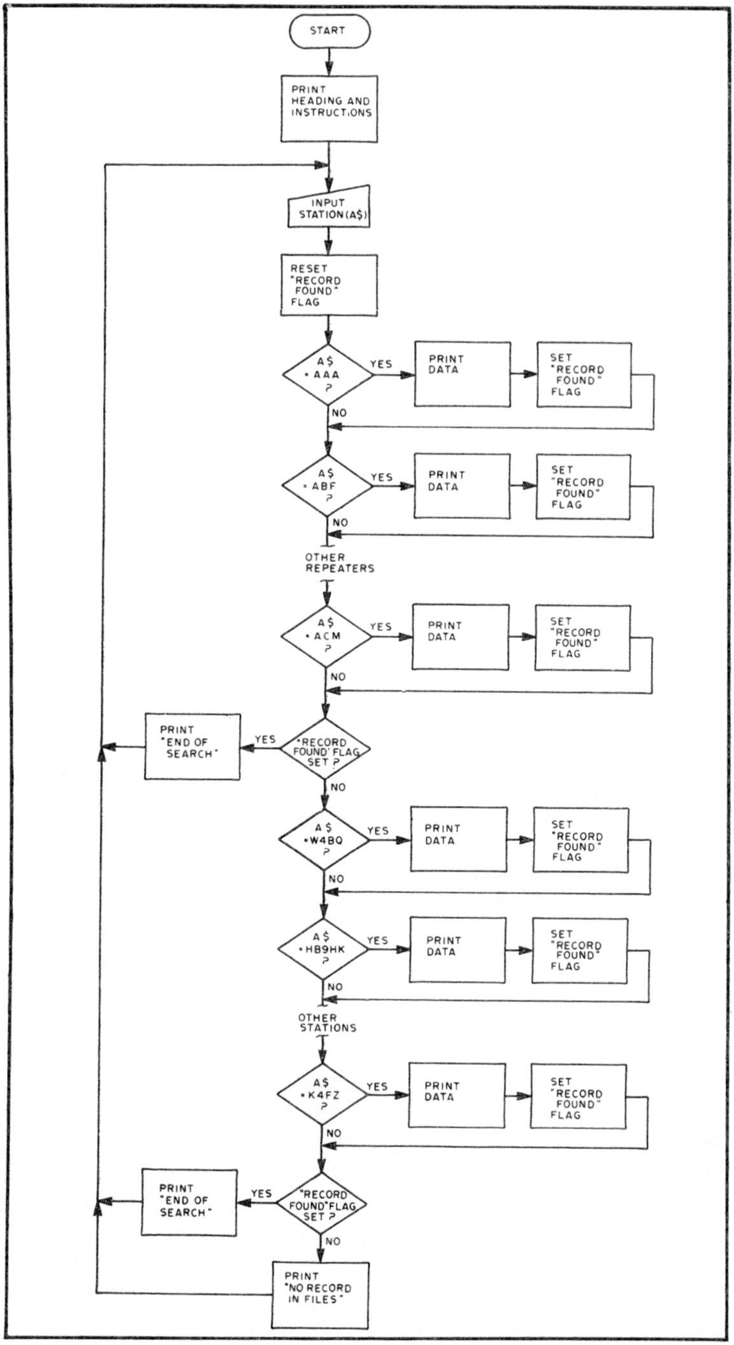

Fig. 5-5. Program flow chart.

been assigned to repeaters that you work, then the identifier should be expanded to include the district number (e.g., "3AAA" and "4AAA").

For information from the log on amateur QSLs, the "STATION?" request is followed by typing in the full call of the amateur station.

After the computer prints the information on repeaters or amateur stations, it will print "END OF SEARCH" and then return to "STATION?" for the next request. If the requested information is not in the file, the computer will print "NO RECORD IN FILES" and go back to "STATION?"

The Program

Additions or deletions to the file are accomplished by using the Altair BASIC command "CLOAD," which brings the program into the computer from cassette. A new entry is made by simply adding a new line for each new station, repeater or even additional QSLs with a previously logged station. After the updating has been performed, the program (Fig. 5-5) is then put back on cassette using the "CSAVE" command.

The memory required for the listing shown in Table 5-2 takes about 1250 bytes and a typical entry takes about 45 bytes. The program could be expanded to provide readouts for summaries of QSLs by districts or foreign countries. This could be done by adding an "OR" phrase as was done in the repeater section of the program, but as mentioned at the start, this program has been kept simple. However, it is a practical operating program and is in use at my station. The listing as shown shows only a small portion of my log files.

Computer Logger

I decided that a computer which prints log sheets was the type of project I'd like to pursue. Unfortunately, I do not have access to a computer using FORTRAN, haven't the foggiest notion of how FORTRAN IV works and was reluctant to impose on people who do. However, I have just finished a half-year course in BASIC programming on the PDP-8/e and decided that this was more my speed. This final fact placed the objective within my grasp.

The program, as shown in Fig. 5-6, is relatively straightforward for anyone familiar with BASIC. Almost all commands in the program have been abbreviated to their three letter abbreviations. The back slashes allow more than one command to be placed on a

Table 5-2. Program List.

```
LIST
5 REM HAM FILE IN ALTAIR BASIC BY GEORGE L. HALLER
10 PRINT:PRINT
20 PRINT "REPEATER AND QSL FILE"
30 PRINT
40 PRINT "FOR REPEATERS USE LAST THREE LETTERS OR FREQUENCY AS 13/73"
50 PRINT "OR CITY NAME, FOR AMATEUR STATIONS USE COMPLETE CALL."
60 PRINT:PRINT
70 INPUT "STATION ";A$
80 F=0:REM RESET "RECORD FOUND" FLAG
100 IF A$="AAA" OR A$="13/73" OR A$="SALISBURY" THEN GOSUB 300
110 IF A$="ABF" OR A$="28/88" OR A$="SHELBY" THEN GOSUB 310
130 IF A$="ACM" OR A$="25/85" OR A$="HICKORY" THEN GOSUB 330
280 IF F>0 THEN 1000:REM IF REPEATER IS FOUND
290 GOTO 400 :REM JUMPS REPEATER SUBROUTINES
300 PRINT "WR4AAA, 13/73, 190, SALISBURY, NC.":F=1:RETURN
310 PRINT "WR4ABF, 28/88, 195, SHELBY, NC":F=1:RETURN
330 PRINT "WR4ACM, 25/85, 195, HICKORY, NC":F=1:RETURN
400 IF A$="W4BQ" THEN PRINT "THAT'S YOU, STUPID!":F=1
410 IF A$="HB9HK" THEN PRINT "7/20/73, 2030Z, 14MHZ, RTTY, WILLY":F=1
420 IF A$="CR6CA" THEN PRINT "5/26/71, 0015Z, 14MHZ, RTTY, JOE":F=1
430 IF A$="OA4BR" THEN PRINT "7/3/74, 0915Z, 14MHZ, RTTY, ZIP":F=1
440 IF A$="JH1TFF" THEN PRINT "5/27/74, 1150Z, 14MHZ, RTTY, DOC":F=1
450 IF A$="KJ6BZ" THEN PRINT "7/6/73, 0200Z, 14MHZ, RTTY, GEORGE":F=1
460 IF A$="K4GV" THEN PRINT "11/6/75, 0710P, 2M-FM, TED":F=1
470 IF A$="W4MYG" THEN PRINT "11/3/75, 0725P, 2M-FM, RAY":F=1
480 IF A$="K4GV" THEN PRINT "12/5/75, 0655P, 2M-FM, TED":F=1
490 IF A$="K4FZ" THEN PRINT "2/17/76, 0430P, 14MHZ, SSTV, BOB":F=1
1000 PRINT
1010 IF F>0 THEN PRINT"END OF SEARCH":GOTO 60
1020 PRINT "NO RECORD IN FILES":GOTO 60
OK
```

- Lines 5–60: Heading & Instructions
- Lines 70–80: Input Station Request & Reset "Record Found" Flag
- Lines 100–130: Repeater Recognition Symbols
- Lines 300–330: Repeater Subroutines (The number after the frequency pair is the antenna direction bearing from my station)
- Lines 400–490: Station QSL Compare Routines

line. Inputs are provided for the number of QSOs per log page and number of pages desired, while string variables are input for the printing at the top of each log page of name, QTH and callsign of the operator. These inputs allows for the user's own information and allow more than one person to use the same program.

I found the elimination of a column for power necessary due to the fact that standard teletype paper is only 8½ inches wide. Not enough room would remain for other information if I included a column for power. Since most people usually use the same power on any given mode, I included the power designation at the top of each page for CW and voice modes. If desired, the power to be used could be entered in the *other* column.

The judicious use of semicolons, commas and quotation marks containing a number of spaces creates the proper spacing in the page heading. This technique also extends the last name of the operator and city name to a maximum of 12 characters (string length is a maximum of six characters with the PDP-8/e).

Obviously, the most efficient way to execute the program would be on a high speed line printer. However, it would be just as easy to set the computer to its task and have it print your log book on a TTY while you sleep (if you can stand the noise).

One final note: This program is by no means hard and fast. It is readily adaptable to the whims of the user. From this basic format, one could print special contest logs to accommodate for special exchanges or print a log expressly for the traffic handler. The possibilities are almost infinite.

Print Your Own Log Book

Several days ago, I stopped in at the local ham store to purchase a log book. And, to my amazement, the ARRL Log Books were priced at $2.00 each. I felt that something had to be done to help combat this inflation, so I decided I could print my own logs (Fig. 5-7) on the computer at work. Agreed, not everyone has access to an IBM 370 Model 165 and 155 back to back. However, there are a lot of computers around, and who knows, the guy down the block just might run the program for you.

The program was written in Fortran IV because of simplicity, and can be compiled by a large number of computers.

The computer program is punched into IBM cards on an IBM 029 Keypunch. The JCL (Job Control Language) was not included because each computer installation has its own unique JCL. And, you will need to know the JCL at the particular computer site you use.

```
READY

LIST

   5 REM PROGRAM BY JIM BERETS
  10 PRI"AMATEUR RADIO STATION LOG BOOK. HOW MANY PAGES";\INPN
  20 PRI"A1 INPUT POWER(WATTS)";\INPC\PRI"A3 INPUT POWER(PEP)";\INPS
  30 PRI"YOUR FIRST NAME";\INPA$
  40 PRI"FIRST 6 LETTERS OF LAST NAME";\INPB$
  50 PRI"NEXT 6 LETTERS OF LAST NAME";\INPC$
  60 PRI"FIRST 6 LETTERS OF CITY NAME";\INPD$
  70 PRI"NEXT 6 LETTERS OF CITY NAME";\INPE$
  80 PRI"STATE";\INPF$
  90 PRI"CALL";\INPG$
 100 PRI "QSOS PER PAGE";\INPA
 105 PRI\PRI\PRI\FORT=1 TO N
 110 PRI\PRI\PRI\PRI"AMATEUR RADIO STATION LOG FOR ";
 120 PRIA$;" ";B$;C$;", ";G$,"LOCATED IN",D$;E$,F$
 130 PRI"EXCEPT AS NOTED ALL A1 QSOS";C;"WATTS, ALL A3 QSOS";
 140 PRIS;"WATTS."\PRI
 160 PRI"                  TIME   EMISS    RPRT
 170 PRI"DATE STATION START END  FREQ  HIS  MINE  OTHER              QSL
 180 FORJ=1TOA
 190 PRI"    I       I     I    I    I     I    I                    S R
 205 PRI"--------------------------------------------------------------------

 210 NEXJ
 215 PRI\PRI\PRI
 220 NEXTT
 230 PRI\PRI\PRI\END

READY

RUN
AMATEUR RADIO STATION LOG BOOK. HOW MANY PAGES? 2
A1 INPUT POWER(WATTS)? 180
A3 INPUT POWER(PEP)? 240
YOUR FIRST NAME? JAMES
FIRST 6 LETTERS OF LAST NAME? BERETS
NEXT 6 LETTERS OF LAST NAME?
FIRST 6 LETTERS OF CITY NAME? STAMFO
NEXT 6 LETTERS OF CITY NAME? RD
STATE? CONN.
CALL? WA1UOU
QSOS PER PAGE? 4



AMATEUR RADIO STATION LOG FOR JAMES BERETS, WA1UOU  LOCATED IN
STAMFORD     CONN.
EXCEPT AS NOTED ALL A1 QSOS 180 WATTS, ALL A3 QSOS 240 WATTS.

                  TIME   EMISS    RPRT
DATE STATION START END  FREQ  HIS  MINE  OTHER              QSL
    I       I     I    I    I     I    I                    S R
--------------------------------------------------------------
    I       I     I    I    I     I    I                    S R
--------------------------------------------------------------
    I       I     I    I    I     I    I                    S R
--------------------------------------------------------------
    I       I     I    I    I     I    I                    S R
--------------------------------------------------------------



AMATEUR RADIO STATION LOG FOR JAMES BERETS, WA1UOU  LOCATED IN
STAMFORD     CONN.
EXCEPT AS NOTED ALL A1 QSOS 180 WATTS, ALL A3 QSOS 240 WATTS.

                  TIME   EMISS    RPRT
DATE STATION START END  FREQ  HIS  MINE  OTHER              QSL
    I       I     I    I    I     I    I                    S R
--------------------------------------------------------------
    I       I     I    I    I     I    I                    S R
--------------------------------------------------------------
    I       I     I    I    I     I    I                    S R
--------------------------------------------------------------
    I       I     I    I    I     I    I                    S R
--------------------------------------------------------------
```

Fig. 5-6. Program.

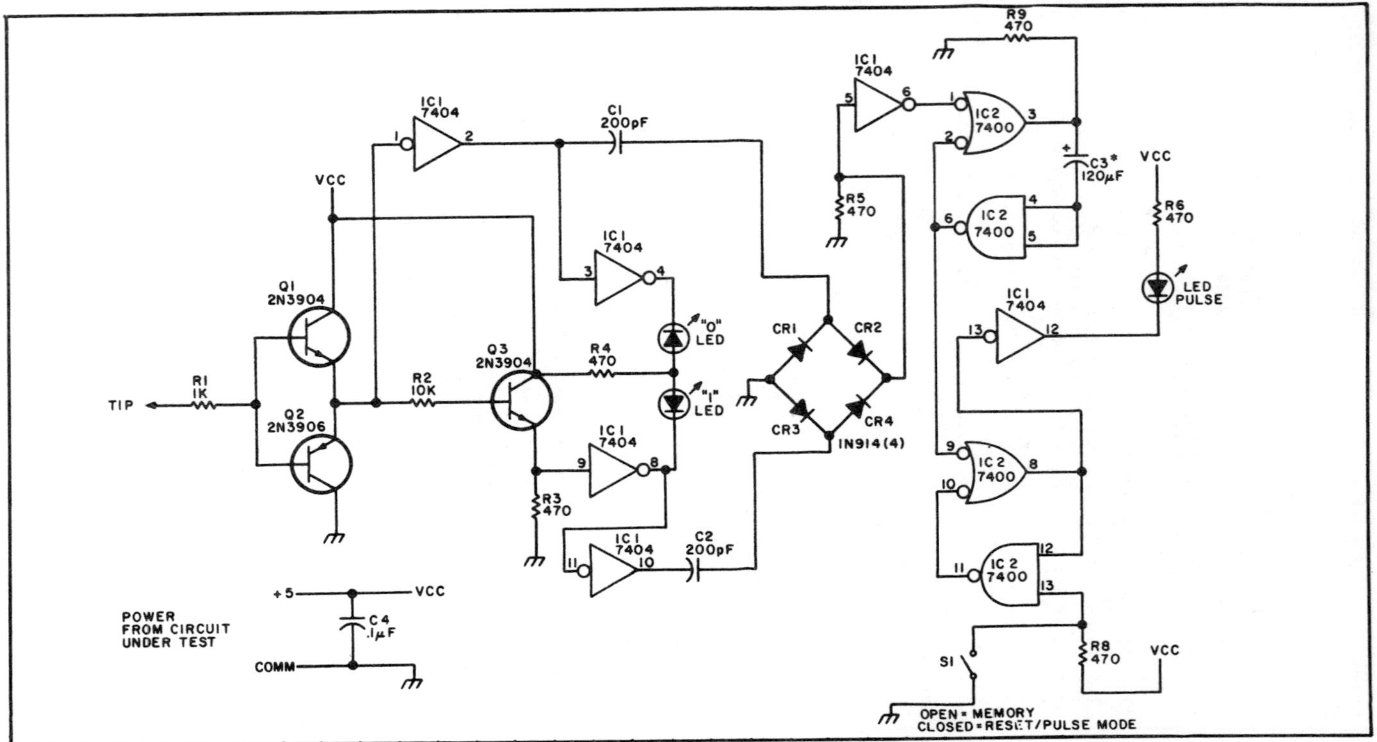

Fig. 5-7. The Superprobe. C3 is two small 60 uF caps wired in parallel.

Table 5-3. Log Book Program.

```
$JOB
      DO 9 M=1,15
      WRITE(6,1)
    1 FORMAT('1')
      WRITE(6,2)
    2 FORMAT(' ',130('-'))
      WRITE(6,3)
    3 FORMAT(' ','|     AMATEUR RADIO STATION LOG OF WAYNE GREEN
     1          CALL   W2NSD/1          TIME IN GMT',33X,'|')
      WRITE(6,2)
      WRITE(6,4)
    4 FORMAT(' ','| DATE &   | STATION   | CALLED    | HIS     | MY      | FR
     1EQ.    | MODE       | POWER | TIME      | COMMENTS',22X,'| QSL |')
      WRITE(6,5)
    5 FORMAT(' ','| TIME      | CALLED    | BY        | RST     | RST     |
     1          |             | WATTS | ENDED     |',31X,'| S|R |')
      WRITE(6,2)
      DO 7 K=1,24
      WRITE(6,6)
    6 FORMAT(' ','|          |           |           |         |         |
     1          |             |       |           |',31X,'|   |  |')
    7 WRITE(6,2)
    9 WRITE(6,8)M
    8 FORMAT(/' ','PAGE',I5)
      WRITE(6,1)
      STOP
      END

$ENTRY
```

So why not punch up the program, find a computer and run off several thousand log sheets on that idle computer?

Superprobe

If the modern technician is going to be successful when working with digital logic, he must have means of looking inside the circuit. The most common way in the industry is with the use of an oscilloscope or logic analyzer. Both of these instruments are great, but the cost puts them out of reach for most experimenters.

The Superprobe was designed to be an inexpensive piece of test gear which will provide the necessary insight into the digital circuit under test. This probe is not a toy, and will provide the user with almost as much information as a $3,000 oscilloscope, when dealing with TTL or DTL logic.

The probe has several desirable features, aside from the expected 1 and 0 indication. The first is a pulse stretcher and pulse memory. Any time a high to low or low to high transition takes place, the pulse LED will flash. The flash will be visible even with very narrow pulses, since the probe will stretch the pulse width to a visible flash. If the probe is in the memory mode, the pulse LED will remain lit until reset by the operator, capturing any stray pulse. Another important feature is high impedance input. It will not load the circuit under test. The input is protected by the zener action of the input transistors, with current limited by R1, in the event the probe is touched to high voltage.

Yet another feature of this probe is that if the tip is touched to an open circuit, or to a chain of floating inputs, no light will light, thus identifying this condition immediately. The entire circuit uses only two inexpensive TTL ICs, three transistors, and can be built into a handy, hand-held probe. The unit shown in Table 5-3 was built by W6ILT. On this very fine unit, Carl used a section of fiber tube for the body, and cast a tip using casting resin (with a glass cigar tube as a mold). A bit of polishing, drilling and handwork gives his probe a professional look. The wire coming out of the top of the unit is for power, which is taken from the unit under test. For a complete parts list, see Table 5-4.

Eight Trace Scope Adapter

Probably the most frustrating problem faced when designing digital circuitry is control of timing. After working out a design on paper, one usually breadboards the circuit to prove it out. In accordance with Murphy's well-known laws, there will be several logic

Table 5-4. Parts List.

IC1—SN7404 IC
IC2—SN7400 IC
Q1, Q3—2N3904 transistor
Q2—2N3906 transistor
CR1, 2, 3, 4—1N914 diode
R1—1k ¼ Watt resistor
R2—10k ¼Watt resistor
R3-9—470 Ohm ¼Watt resistors
C1, C2—200 pF capacitor
C3—120 uF capacitor (2 small 60 uF in parallel)
C4—.1 uF disc capacitor
LED 1-3—Any type/color LED desired

errors which will then be apparent but very elusive. Depending upon the complexity of the design, the errors may be (but usually are not) easily located and corrected.

A number of tools are helpful in tracking down these problems—the logic probe and oscilloscope probably being the most helpful. A logic probe establishes the steady-state status of various points in the circuit, but tells nothing about pulse widths or repetition rates. The oscilloscope is used to visually illustrate these waveshapes, pulse widths and repetition rates. What most scopes do not show is the time relationship between pulses at different locations in the circuit. Sometimes this relationship is crucial in searching out a problem that may be caused by *glitches* (extremely short pulses caused by unexpected and unwanted time overlaps). Well-equipped laboratories use special multi-channel logic scopes for this sort of work, but most of us are not equipped with the kilobuck pocketbook required to manage this. Even a dual channel high speed scope requires a considerable investment.

While such a scope would be most welcome in any experimenter's laboratory, most of us must settle for a relatively inexpensive general purpose scope. Fortunately, it is neither difficult nor expensive to build an adapter to display multi-channel logic signals. The adapter permits viewing up to eight channels of logic signals simultaneously, and thereby examination of the relative timing between them. Although analog waveshapes cannot be displayed (you can use your scope without the adapter for this function), it will show the low or high states, in precise time positions, of any signals present in TTL or DTL circuits.

Almost any general purpose scope should work with this adapter, but it is recommended that it be equipped with a triggered sweep (Figs. 5-8 through 5-10). The viewing of simple repetitive signals without a triggered sweep can be frustrating enough, but attempting to lock onto one of eight channels being displayed may be virtually impossible. If you are using a scope without this feature, I highly recommend that you consider adding a new triggered sweep, even if you do not build this adapter. Scope bandwidth is not critical unless you are working with really high speed, and a 4 MHz bandwidth will let you examine almost all you need to see. You must have a way to externally trigger the scope sweep, and you will have to find the sweep signal or blanking pulse to permit changing the input channels during the retrace interval.

The circuit itself is very simple. A small capacitor couples the scope sweep circuit to a voltage comparator (you may find it necessary to adjust the size of the capacitor for reliable trace switching). The sweep retrace causes a negative excursion at pin 3 of the LM311, forcing its output to go high. Each time this occurs, a 16 stage counter advances one count. Three output bits of the counter are connected to an eight-to-one 9312 multiplexer, which selects each input in turn, and outputs to pin 15. If most of your work is at the lower frequencies, use the low order 3 bits of the counter, instead of the 3 high order bits shown. When using the 3 high order bits, you may use the adapter with a dual channel scope operating in the *alternate mode*.

A ladder network commonly used for digital to analog conversion is used to position each channel on the screen. The resistors should be well matched (i.e., 1 percent), but satisfactory results have been experienced with 5 percent units. If your display is not evenly spaced vertically, try swapping resistors in this network for best spacing. The variable capacitor is used to compensate for the scope input capacitance, and should be adjusted for best waveshapes. The output potentiometer will not be required in most instances, and should not be used unless essential. Note that a 74161 or 9316 synchronous counter is recommended, rather than a 7493 or similar asynchronous type. It is unlikely that propagation delays in an asychronous counter would result in viewable glitches on the scope in this application, but it is good design practice to always use a synchronous counter where the output states are decoded and fed back to the counter.

The adapter may be built on a small printed circuit board (note the IC polarity!) and installed inside your scope. However, it may be very conveniently enclosed in a small box which can be located near and powered from the digital project, and coupled to the scope via cables. You will need the usual vertical input cable and a sweep-out

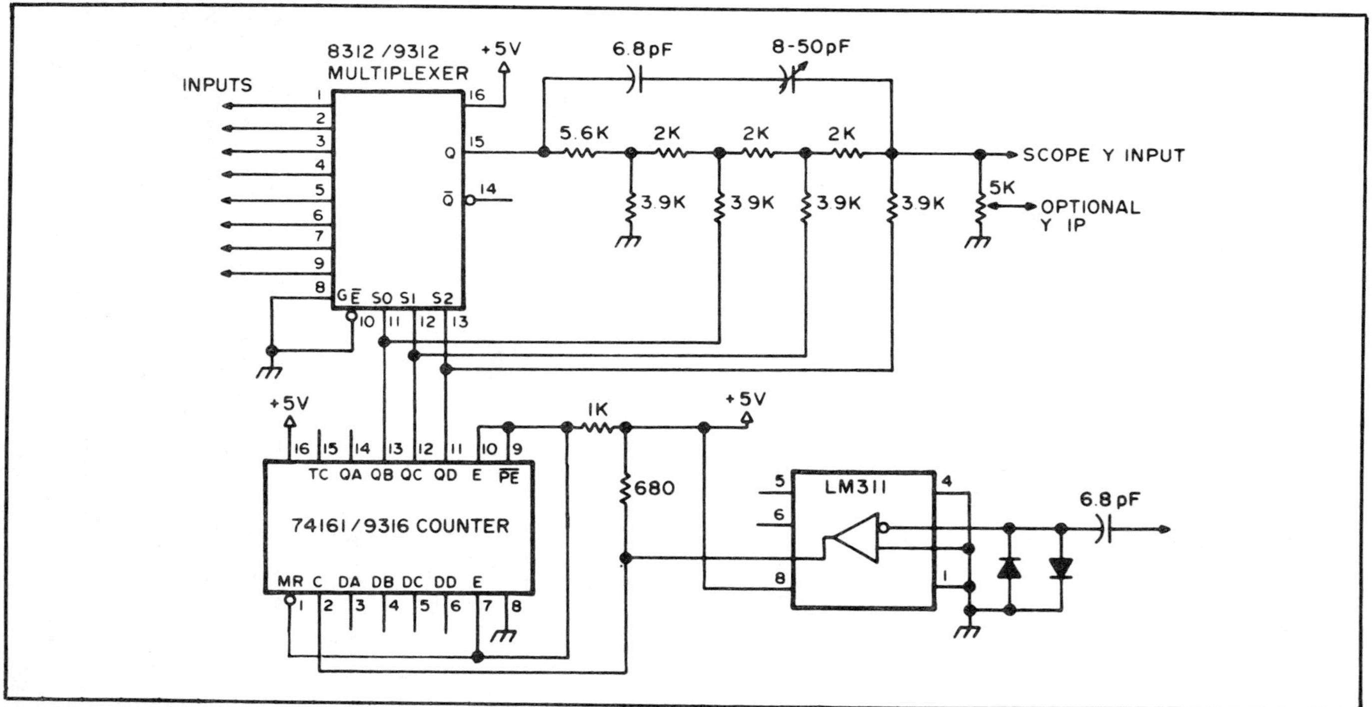

Fig. 5-8. Schematic.

signal. Many scopes have an Ext jack for horizontal input, which is permanently connected to the input of the horizontal amplifier. When the sweep is running, this also happens to be the output of the sweep generator.

Should you experience difficulty in obtaining a stable trace, the sweep circuit may not be advancing the counter properly. Try a different spot in the sweep circuit first. You may find it necessary to invert the signal by using pin 2 of the LM311 (grounding pin 3) if the signal is reversed in polarity. The 74161 counts on a rising edge, and reverse polarity will cause the channel change to occur in mid-sweep, with obvious visible distortion. You may find experimenting with the size of the sweep input capacitor to be helpful, but be careful to avoid distorting the sweep. The scope will not be as bright as usual, as the trace is being timeshared among eight signals. A slight adjustment of the brightness control compensates for this. The variable capacitor is adjusted for best waveform using a 10 kHz or higher digital pulse. A 74151 multiplexer is functionally identical, but not pin compatible, with the 9312 unit. The LM311 comes in either a mini-dip or TO-5 package. As the pin-outs are identical, either may be used with the circuit board shown.

Using your multi-trace scope is a delightful experience: You see all of those signals at the same time, and can really tell what is going on. Remember that you must trigger the sweep from the slowest signal you are viewing; otherwise, you will not be able to sync the slower signals. Also, be aware that the inputs are not protected in any way, and connection to potentials outside of the proper logic levels will destroy the multiplexer IC. Protective diodes may be added on the input lines to give marginal security, but care, plus a socket for the 9312, are probably adequate.

The small investment required to construct this unit will be quickly repaid the first time you use it to track down a problem.

The IC See-er

Having been a dedicated ham and/or electronic freak for many years, I feel that I can speak with some authority on the subject of home construction of electronic projects. Unlike an engineer pal of mine whose motto is, "Never build it if you can buy it," I have one which is, and has always been, "Never buy it if you can build it." I have a shop full of electronic residue to prove it.

Until recently I thought that I had run into every form of frustration possible in the genre—that is, until I started (about six months ago) my love/hate relationship with the ubiquitous integ-

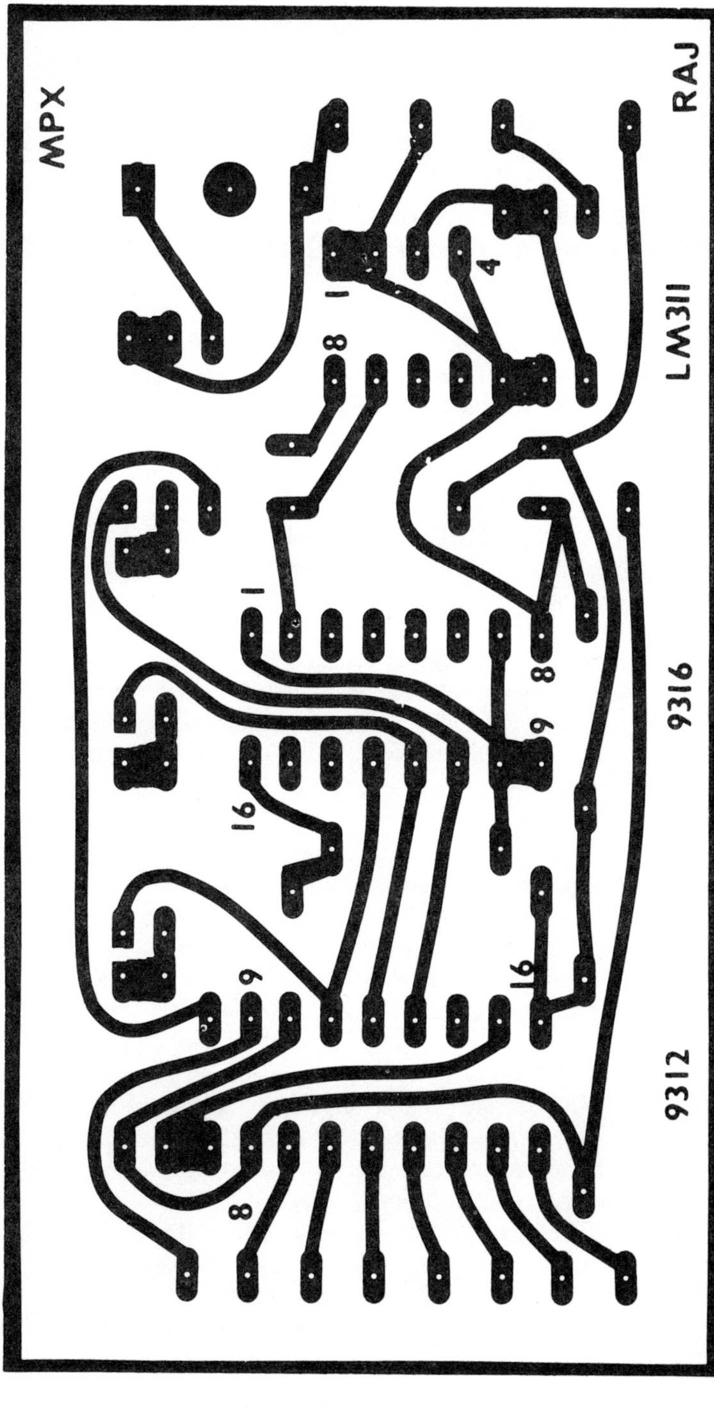

Fig. 5-9. PC board (full size).

rated circuit. It is my considered opinion that no invention in electronics has caused as much fumble-fingered cussing and soldering iron-induced frustration as the IC. Well, since I have always wound up spending more time building the tool to do the job than on doing the job, here is a gadget that will cost you less than $10.00 to build (using all new parts), will cure all of the above mentioned evils and will take the hate out of love/hate.

Yes, I know that there is an outfit that builds a better one, but this is for guys like me who wouldn't buy one even if we could afford the $50.00.

I built this in a 7 inches × 7 inches × 2 inches aluminum chassis. The lens is one of a pair of condenser lenses from a long since defunct 4 inches × 5 inches Omega enlarger. These little tidbits are 6¼ inches in diameter and weigh in at about 2 pounds apiece. I'm waiting for a 7 inch plastic lens to arrive from Edmund Scientific, so I can build a new improved version.

A collar was fashioned (6 inches in diameter by 2 inches deep) from scrap, medium hard aluminum, to hold the condenser lens in place in the chassis (after cutting a 6 inch diameter hole in same).

I do not own a fly cutter large enough to cut a 6 inch circle, so I fell back on the old-fashioned method of drilling a series of small holes and chiseling away the metal between them. Since aluminum chassis are soft, it goes rather quickly and the whole operation took me less than 10 minutes using a drill press. If you have a hand drill it will pay you to center punch at proper intervals so that you will not mess up your nice new chassis. After you have the circle cut, a half round file will dress the rough edges easily. Before I forget, I split a piece of spaghetti tubing lengthwise and used it for an edge liner around the hole. A spot or two of glue and the pressure of the lens keeps it tight, and it makes a very professional looking finish.

I drilled holes in the sides at the point of balance and inserted 3/16 inch bolts and nuts for the side supports. By adding wing nuts and lock washers, I created an easily adjustable mount. Two pieces of ⅛ inch × 1¼ inches × 7 inches aluminum from an old panel were used for side supports, and I bolted them to a scrap plate of 5/32 inch × 8 inches × 8 inches metal that has been kicking around the shop for years. As you might suspect, I never throw anything away, and this base is the living proof that it pays.

I must admit both that I should live in a barn and that my wife is a living, breathing saint (direct from the Old Testament) for putting up with me. Actually, the mounting of this gadget can be done any number of ways and this was just the easiest and quickest, considering the weight of the lens. Besides, I was in a hurry to finish as I had a

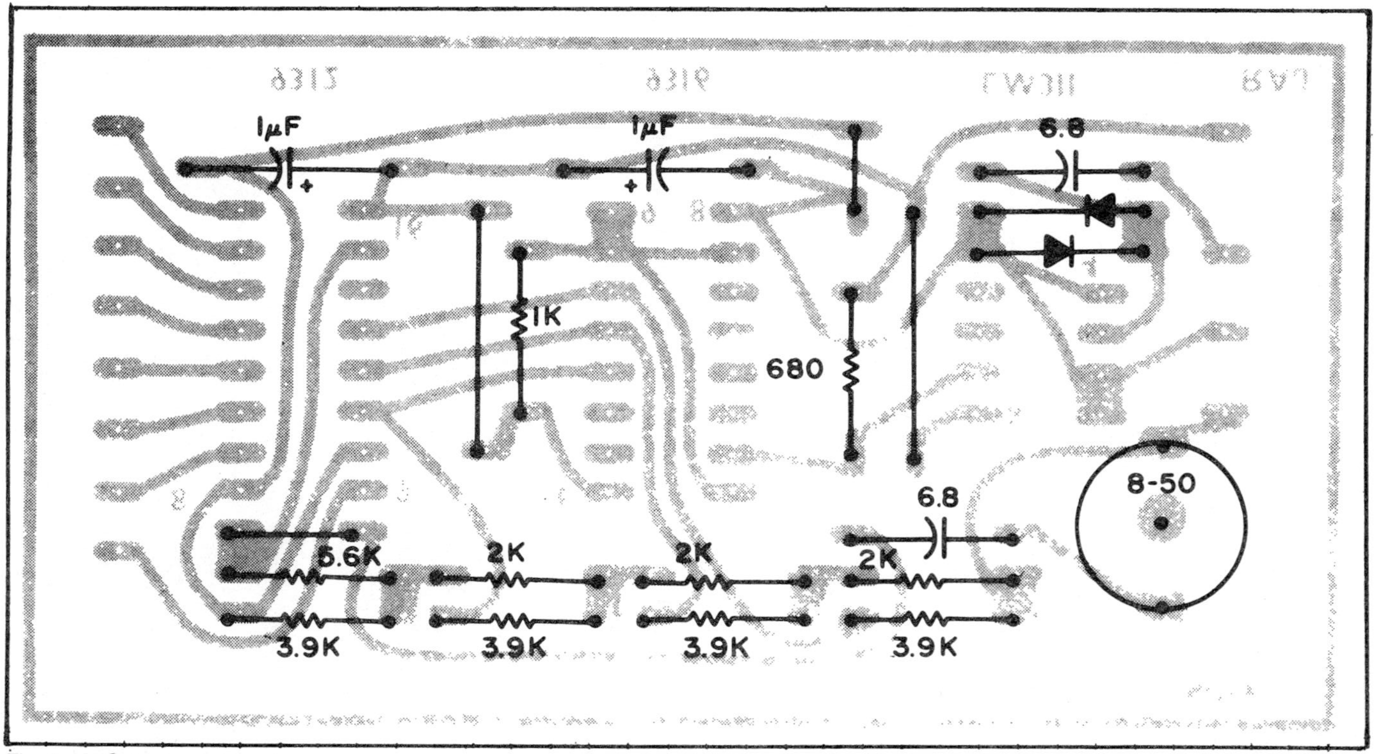

Fig. 5-10. Component layout.

project waiting to be soldered and I wanted to give the IC See-er a workout.

Now for the novel lighting arrangement. There are four pilot light sockets fastened at equally spaced intervals around the outside of the retaining ring collar. If you decide to go my route on this, I want to give you a word of caution right now!

Make sure that the sockets are well insulated from each other and from the metal collar that they are mounted on because I wired them in series and hooked them across the 115V AC line with a switch to turn them off and on. The bulbs are Tung-Sol #T313, 28 volt, bayonet base pilot lights. Twenty-eight times four equals 112 volts, and hooked across 115-120 this gives a not brilliant but very pleasant and quite adequate light for close-up work.

An additional bonus is the high-priced PC board vise (always give them a little extra for their money). It will be obvious that this added luxury feature is the really expensive item of the project, since chromed 2 inch paper clamps are selling in our inflated economy for the munificent price of 27 cents each. I splurged and bought four, so that I would have extras for a vise to hold larger PC boards. The rest of the stand is made from odds and ends of ¼ inch shafting and old shaft collars, plus some assorted scraps of aluminum and radio hardware.

It took me about 2 hours to build this little gadget and, quite honestly, every ham/experimenter who has been in the lab has tried to steal it right off the bench, with me watching yet. Suffice to say I would not part with it for love or money. The one fault it has is that I made the support legs a little short. Still, it is doing a heck of a job for me and in retrospect I don't know how I survived so long without it.

Seals Electronics Memory Board

Upon investigation of the manufacturer of a particular board (Seal Electronics) at the local computer club, I heard a very strange rumor. That is, that it was possible to obtain this 8K static memory board in only 10 days from the date that the order was received. I was quite sure that it was actually 100 days, but the temptation was more than I could resist. On June 16th I placed my order.

As soon as I dropped the order in the box I was gripped with fear, realizing that the interest on my money would probably be collected by the company for some time, at my expense. I resigned myself to receiving the memory board in the next year.

On June 23rd the postman came carrying a box 3 inches deep and 1 foot square. Sure enough, it was from Seals Electronics. I didn't open the box for a long while. I just stared at the box in disbelief and was somehow comforted by its shape. This must be a good sign, I thought.

Finally, I opened the box and peered inside. What a pleasant surprise. I viewed a large plastic envelope that contained four smaller parts packages. All of the components were of top quality. But what about the board? I quickly tore open the package that contained the board and examined it. It was beautiful! Not only was it first class in appearance, but it had no jumper wire holes. It had a solder mask on both sides and was silk screened on the component side. And, there was an assembly manual and two other documents.

I began reading the manual and, to my surprise, I could understand it. It was written in modern English, and even I could understand it. It described the assembly, installation and standby battery hookup. The theory of operation was described so that it could be easily interfaced with a home brew project. Could it be that this manual was written for the hobbyist?

Two more pleasant surprises were yet to come. Upon examining the two remaining documents, I found a multicolor full size printed circuit board layout and a beautifully done foldout schematic of the board circuitry.

My enjoyment increased as I began construction. I followed the instructions and the memory began to take shape. First I installed the diodes, then the resistors, next the regulators and then the address selection switches. Oh yes, and the *sockets*! This kit was supplied with sockets for all ICs! I was becoming convinced that a tremendous amount of thought had gone into the planning of this kit.

Another thing that struck me as I continued to build the kit was that all the holes were the correct size. Not once did I have to file down a lead and stand on my pliers to insert a component lead through the board.

The sockets fell into place and I even tried to make a solder bridge on the board, but was unable to accomplish this due to the almost foolproof solder mask. I was now convinced that anyone could build this kit without error if he simply followed the instructions. The last item of construction was the placement of the capacitors and this also went without a hitch.

Now for the ICs. As I began to insert the ICs in the sockets, another thought struck me. It was impossible to damage them with the old soldering iron.

Finished! I quickly looked the board over with my magnifying glass and, finding no problems, placed it before me with a sigh. After gloating for a few minutes, I picked up the card and headed for the computer. Snapping the address switches into the proper position, I then placed the board in the slot and prepared myself for the big moment. The familiar click of the power switch seemed to be more meaningful and the whir of the fan and lighting of the LEDs joined in to indicate that all was okay.

Now for the test. First I addressed the memory and deposited a few bytes of data. Everything seemed to be working. Next I loaded BASIC into the memory and it worked flawlessly. It worked! And the first time, too.

When my wife called me to empty the garbage I realized that I was not dreaming. I began to consider what performance tests I might use to prove that this memory board was not all that it was cracked up to be. I was really challenged now, and was determined to find a problem with this board. After all, there just had to be some shortcomings somewhere! Besides, my reputation as a skeptic was at stake.

With these purist concepts in mind, I set out to test my newly constructed memory board.

My first plan of attack was to prove that no static memory could come close to my present dynamic memory in low power consumption. To accomplish this, I cut the three power leads between my last extender board and the other boards connected to the computer bus. I stripped ¼ inch of insulation from the free ends of all leads and melted some solder on the exposed wire to aid in soldering them during testing. I then resoldered two of the power leads, restoring normal operation to those two sources of power. I connected my ammeter between the two remaining leads.

The next step was to install two dynamic boards to give a total of 8K of memory. Placing them in the test location, I then applied power and recorded the ammeter reading.

I repeated this process with the two remaining power leads to the boards, and recorded the results.

Now for the new memory board. I installed it in the same manner and measured the 5 volt power line (the only one required for the new memory).

After comparing the results, I was surprised to find that the new low power static board consumed only 20 per cent more power than the two dynamic boards. For all practical purposes, the power consumption is an even swap.

Not being one who gives in easily, I continued my testing. This particular board was advertised as having the memory of an elephant, or something to that effect. So I proceeded to examine this aspect of its operation.

There is a very unique feature built into this board; that is, there is a diode switching network between the normal power line to the memory and the battery standby line to the memory that is brought in on pin 14 of the memory board. (This position is not used on the bus line of the Altair and other similar computers.) This means you can connect a battery across pin 14 and ground, and when power is interrupted, the memory is automatically switched to the standby source to retain memory content.

To test this feature of the memory, I constructed a simple power supply capable of maintaining three volts under load when connected to the memory while the computer was turned off. I then soldered a small piece of wire on the free end of the extender board at location 14. The positive lead from the supply was connected to this wire and the negative lead from the supply was connected to logic ground (pin 50).

Not wanting to start in a small way, I loaded BASIC in the memory and immediately turned off the power. I waited for a few minutes, switched on the power, reloaded the first byte of data (location 0) that was lost by the computer, depressed the run switch and up came BASIC. This was a milestone in the operation of my computer system.

I then decided that a longer period of testing was needed. I followed the same procedure as before, but this time I left the computer off for 24 hours.

When I returned to resume testing I first touched the memory regulator heat sinks to determine whether cooling would be necessary during standby operation. They were cool! When I powered up the machine as before, BASIC came up without a problem.

By this time I was completely sold on my new 8K memory. I was patting myself on the back for what I thought was extremely good judgment on my part in selecting such a nice piece of equipment.

I pondered for some time after the completion of this testing to be sure that nothing else could be done by me to break down the resistance of the memory.

It then occurred to me that perhaps a good test would be to operate the memory with a disc operating system. Since I happened to have a brother-in-law with such a system, it seemed that a trip to his place was in order.

Upon arrival, we installed the memory board in his computer and, as you have probably guessed, it worked perfectly.

In conclusion, I would like to take my hat off to the folks at Seals Electronics, and to what I believe is a long awaited answer to the dreams of the computer hobbyist. It is obvious that they have done their homework in producing a kit which can be built with more than a reasonable expectation that it will work when finished.

If you plan to purchase memory in the future (and who doesn't?), be sure to include this one on your list of considerations.

Chapter 6
Computer Games

The recent arrival of programmable pocket calculators at more affordable prices offers the serious ham a new tool to improve his DX through proper antenna orientation. It also gives him a very good excuse for buying one of those very interesting new calculators that can be taught to perform in seconds what would otherwise be a rather messy calculation. After all, with the investment already made in a two gallon linear, hundred foot tower and stacked yagis, it would be a shame not to get through the pileup because the antenna was pointed wrong. So will buying a programmable calculator fix this? It's not quite that easy, but even if you know nothing of computer programming and aren't too good in math, you can program this very useful computation (Table 6-1).

A Programmable Calculator

Before proceeding further, some mention should be made of current practices among amateurs. All too often an experimenter utilizes great circle maps or azimuth information determined for a location considerably different from that of his QTH. This error, together with the tolerances encountered in orientation toward true north, mechanical drive backlash, and direction indication, can result in an appreciable loss of signal strength in the desired direction. The worst part is that the better the antenna, the less tolerant it is of error in direction.

Table 6-1. User Instructions and Program Form.

HP-55
User Instructions

Title: Great Circle Azimuth Page ____ of ____

Programmer: C. H. Brent WB4GVE

STEP	INSTRUCTIONS	INPUT DATA/UNITS	KEYS				OUTPUT DATA/UNITS
1	Load program						
2	Switch to RUN and		BST				
	load constants						
	λ_1 – Latitude*	NNN.N	N	STO	1		
	of QTH	Decimal Deg.					
	cos λ_1		f	cos	STO	2	
	L_1 – longitude*	NNN.N	N	CHS*	STO	3	
	of QTH	Decimal Deg.					
	180		STO	5			
	270		STO	6			
3	Enter latitude and	Decimal Deg.	B		N	R/S	Azimuth
	longitude* of remote						in degrees
	location*						from north
*	North latitude and						
	east longitude are +.						
	South latitude and						
	west longitude are –						
	(use CHS key).						

The problem of finding true north, orienting the antenna, zeroing out the indicator and backlash error, and using maps and/or formulas for determining direction are all covered in various publications. Assuming proper attention to all the mechanical requirements yields, acceptable accuracy, determination of the proper direction is the next concern. Great circle maps are good if your QTH happens to be near the map center. Otherwise, you are left with the pin,

HP-55
Program Form

Title ______________________________ Page ____ of ____

Press BST in RUN mode, switch to PRGM mode. Then key in the program.

DISPLAY LINE	DISPLAY CODE	KEY ENTRY	X	Y	Z	T	COMMENTS
00.							-180° if 0 < (C_2 - C_1) < 180
01.	34	RCL					
02.	03	3					For Greeneville TN
03.	51	−					λ_1 = 36.167
04.	33	STO					L_1 = -82.687
05.	04	4					
06.	31	f					
07.	13	cos					
08.	34	RCL					
09.	01	1					
10.	31	f					
11.	14	tan					
12.	71	X					
13.	22	X≶y					
14.	31	f					
15.	14	tan					
16.	51	−					
17.	34	RCL					
18.	04	4					
19.	31	f					
20.	12	sin					
21.	81	÷					
22.	34	RCL					
23.	01	1					
24.	31	f					
25.	13	cos					
26.	71	X					
27.	32	g					
28.	14	tan^{-1}					
29.	34	RCL					
30.	06	6					
31.	61	+					
32.	00	0					
33.	34	RCL					
34.	04	4					
35.	31	f					
36.	-46	X <y - 46					
37.	61	+					
38.	34	RCL					
39.	07	5					
40.	31	f					
41.	-46	X<y - 46					
42.	22	X≶y					
43.	23	↓					
44.	51	−					
45.	-00	GTO-00					
46.	23	↓					
47.	23	↓					
48.	-00	GTO-00					
49.							

REGISTERS	
R_0	
R_1	$\lambda 1$
R_2	cos $\lambda 1$
R_3	L_1
R_4	(L_2 - L_1)
R_5	180
R_6	270
R_7	
R_8	
R_9	
$R_{.0}$	
$R_{.1}$	
$R_{.2}$	
$R_{.3}$	
$R_{.4}$	
$R_{.5}$	
$R_{.6}$	
$R_{.7}$	
$R_{.8}$	
$R_{.9}$	

string and globe approach. There are spherical trigonometry formulas one can use, but nobody in his right mind would recommend them. If one is reasonably careful in performing the calculations, a correct angle can be determined. Whether the angle is positive or negative, is referenced to north or south, or is the long or short path, is much in question. After much frustration, I set about to find a means of determining the azimuth from my QTH to any point on the earth without having to perform any calculations, map perusal or thinking. Also, I had to find some good use for that HP-55 I had bought on impulse.

My math was too rusty to rely on, so I engaged a friend and math major to help develop a formula which not only could be programmed with a minimum of key strokes, but also permitted the calculator (not me) to determine the short path with a test and conditional branch. The basic formula is included in case you need to modify the instructions for a different instruction sequence (the algebraic vs. RPN system). For Hewlett-Packard and probably other RPN types, you can go right to the program.

The procedure to follow is simple. The PRGM switch places the calculator in the learn position. The program is loaded into memory by keying in the strokes listed on the Program Form. The switch is placed in the run position, the BST button sets the program at the starting point, and you are nearly ready to start. There is some information that must be loaded into memory (because there wasn't room in the program for it and it can change for different QTH locations). This information is the QTH latitude, cosine of this latitude, QTH longitude and two constants, 180 and 270. The formula was derived with east longitudes and north latitudes being positive numbers. The CHS (change sign) key must be used for south latitudes and west longitudes. Maybe that doesn't sound too simple, but it is only done one time. From then on the calculator displays the short path azimuth to any point if the latitude of the remote location is entered (ENTER), followed by the longitude, and the pressing of R/S.

The calculator can be left on in the shack and used to perform other calculations without affecting the stored program. The HP-55 has a clock for timing QSO IDs or can be used for metric and temperature conversions needed for foreign contacts. One precaution: Run the AC charger cord through grounded braid if there are large rf fields around. A further suggestion: Determine the azimuths to a few places in the manner you currently use, take this program to your friendly calculator dealer and have him check you out before you spend your money.

The basic formula is:

$$\text{Azimuth} = 270 + \tan^{-1}\left[\cos\lambda_1 \frac{\tan\lambda \cos(l_2 - l_1) - \tan\lambda_2}{\sin(l_2 - l_1)}\right]$$

where

λ_1 = latitude of QTH

l_1 = longitude of QTH

λ_2 = latitude of distant station

l_2 = longitude of distant station

If the difference of longitudes ($l_2 - l_1$) lies between zero and 180 degrees, then 180 must be subtracted to get the short path azimuth. Also, to avoid the denominator becoming zero (division by zero not allowed), some small amount can be added to the home QTH longitude (like 0.00001) when that constant is entered.

For example (Table 6-2). What is the azimuth from Chicago to Cairo? (Chicago: 41° 52′ N, 87°38′ W) Converting to decimal degrees, key in 41.87 STO 1, f cos STO 2, 87.63 CHS STO 3, 180 STO 5, 270 STO 6.

To find the azimuth from Chicago to any place, key in the other place's latitude and longitude, available from an atlas, map or world almanac. (Cairo: 30°00′ N, 31°14′ E) Key in 30 ENTER, 31.23 R/S and read the answer displayed as 49.35° or 49°20′, the clockwise azimuth from true north.

A No-Cost Digital Clock

If you already own or are contemplating purchasing a programmable calculator, you may want to try a novel method of using your calculator as a timepiece.

Table 6-2. Practice Examples.

City	Lat.	Long.	Azimuth
Bogota	4.5	-74.3	158.6
Calcutta	23.6	88.4	4.0
Canton	23.1	113.3	339.3
LaPaz	-16.5	-68.4	158.8
Perth	-32.0	115.9	290.3
New York	40.8	-74.0	91.5
Los Angeles	37.8	-122.4	272.9

Table 6-3. Program Listing.

Loc	Code	Key
00	59	*pause
01	59	*pause
02	59	*pause
03	74	–
04	92	.
05	00	0
06	02	2
07	94	=
08	37	X = T
09	01	1
10	04	4
11	22	GTO
12	00	0
13	00	0
14	33	sto
15	00	0
16	15	CLR
17	32	$x \lessgtr t$
18	37	X = T
19	03	3
20	05	5
21	74	—
22	01	1
23	94	=
24	32	$x \lessgtr t$
25	15	clr
26	34	rcl
27	00	0
28	74	—
29	92	.
30	04	4
31	94	=
32	22	GTO
33	00	0
34	00	0
35	01	1
36	54	÷
37	00	0
38	94	=
39	41	R/S

My SR-56 calculator is a versatile piece of hardware, but I have discovered that, much of the time, I use it for simple functions that could be done just as effectively on a less expensive machine. The ability to enter programs that allow the calculator to automatically solve complex equations makes the SR-56 and other calculators like it special. After trying out some of the programs suggested by the manufacturer, I became interested in writing my own software. One item that particularly intrigued me was the pause function. This does just what the name suggests—leaves a short space in the program. Normally one does not worry about the exact length of the pause, but, just on a whim, I checked mine. It turned out to be about .62 seconds long. To convert this fraction into whole units that made more sense, all I had to do was put three pauses in a row, giving a resulting time of just under three seconds.

Now that the basic time unit was established, it became a simple matter to write an addition program where a new time was displayed every two seconds. By using the t-register (conditional branch), where a number is compared with another number in the memory and a predetermined command is given, it was simple to have the calculator replace a .6 with a 1 at the minute mark and start over with 1.02 and so forth.

Between using the t-register and the pause function, it is possible to write a 12-hour clock program or even a 10-minute countdown program that could be used by hams as an ID reminder or possibly a darkroom timer.

The accompanying program (Tables 6-3 through 6-5) is meant to serve as a starting point. It can probably be reworked for almost any programmable calculator. As a novice programmer, I have made little attempt to hone the program down to minimum size. A variety of approaches can be taken. I have shown only the one I found most easy to grasp.

If you need super accuracy, then time programming may not be for you. But, if you enjoy writing your own calculator programs and

Table 6-4. User Instructions.

Step	Procedure	Enter	Press	Display
1	Enter program			
2	Reset and clear		RST CLR	0
3	Set t-register	9	x ≶ t	0
4	Enter initial time	9.6		9.6
5	Start clock		R/S	
6	Ten-minute mark has been reached (flashing)			9.99999999999

Table 6-5. Ten-Minute ID Timer Explanation.

Steps	Explanation
Steps 00-02	This gives a two-second interval.
Steps 03-07	This subtracts .02 (two seconds) from running total.
Steps 08-13	Running total compared to next lowest minute mark.
Steps 14-20	Running total stored, check made to see if it is 0.
Steps 21-25	T-register decremented to next lowest minute mark.
Steps 26-34	Running total lowered to next minute (.4 subtracted).
Steps 35-39	Flashing display for 00 seconds.

would like to show some unique and useful software to your friends, then give it a try.

Computerized Global Calculations

How many of you keep a hand calculator next to your rig? It's great to be able to calculate the distance between two places anywhere in the world.

When you're working that rare DX in Timbuktu, it's always nice to drop a tidbit of information like, "I calculate that our QSO spans a distance of 8346 kilometers, QSL?" Pretty impressive-sounding information, no doubt, and it's a novel topic for conversation.

After a while, though, you can become tired of doing all of that number-crunching every time. No doubt some of you have let the bit bug bite. Either you have picked up some type of microcomputer or are at least interested in them. If so, let the number-crunching bother you no more. Let the computer do it!

This project describes a computer program that calculates the shortest distance between any two points on the globe. All you need to do is type in the latitude and longitude of any two locations on Earth, and it prints out the distance in miles and kilometers.

I call the program GLOBAL, for obvious reasons, and it is written in the programming language BASIC. GLOBAL is listed in Table 6-6. It is very straightforward and takes very little time to run. In Table 6-6, statement numbers 40 through 90 have the computer ask you to input information about your location or the location of the first station. (If you are holding a three-way QSO, you could tell the other fellows how far apart they are.) Statements 100 through 180 calculate the parameters for the first station. Unlike other methods, your station can be located anywhere in the world. So, if you're not in North America, you can still use the program. Statements 200 through 250 ask you questions about the second station's location, and statements 280 through 370 calculate the parameters for his location. The actual calculation of distance is carried out from statement 390 through 410, and then the distance is output in both miles and kilometers.

The language BASIC that I used may be slightly different from the one that you're using, but I've attempted to make it so that the

Table 6-6. Program Listing For GLOBAL.

```
10 PRINT "THIS IS GLOBAL"
20 PRINT " "
30 REM      INPUT DATA FOR MY LOCATION
40 PRINT "MY LOCATION IS"
50 PRINT "LATITUDE(DEG,MIN, 1 FOR NORTH- 0 FOR SOUTH)"
60 INPUT L2,M2,Y
70 PRINT "LONGITUDE(DEG,MIN, 1 FOR EAST- 0 FOR WEST)"
80 INPUT L1,M1,Z
90 PRINT " "
100 REM      CALCULATE CONSTANTS FOR MY LOCATION
110 L1=(L1+(M1/60))*3.14159/180
120 L2=(L2+(M2/60))*3.14159/180
130 K1=SIN(L2)
140 K2=COS(L2)
150 IF Z=0 THEN 170
160 L1=-L1
170 IF Y=1 THEN 190
180 K1=-K1
190 PRINT " "
200 REM INPUT DATA FOR HIS LOCATION
210 PRINT "HIS LOCATION IS"
220 PRINT "LATITUDE(DEG,MIN, 1 FOR NORTH-0 FOR SOUTH)'
230 INPUT L4,M4,B
240 PRINT "LONGITUDE(DEG,MIN, 1 FOR EAST-0 FOR WEST)"
250 INPUT L3,M3,A
260 PRINT " "
270 REM CALCULATE CONSTANTS FOR HIS LOCATION
280 L3=(L3+(M3/60))*3.14159/180
290 L4=(L4+(M4/60))*3.14159/180
300 IF A=1 THEN 330
310 C1=ABS(L1-L3)
320 GOTO 340
330 C1=ABS(L1+13)
340 IF C1<3.14159 THEN 360
350 C1=(2*3.14159)-C1
360 IF B=1 THEN 390
370 K1=-K1
380 REM  CALCULATE DISTANCE
390 A1=(K1*(SIN(L4)))+(K2*(COS(L4))*(COS(C1)))
400 D=(3.14159/2)-(ATN(A1/(SQR(1-A1↑2))))
410 D=69.15*180*D/3.14159
420 PRINT " "
430 REM    OUTPUT
440 PRINT "DISTANCE IN MILES",D
450 D1=1.6093*D
460 PRINT "DISTANCE IN KILOMETRES",D1
470 STOP
480 END
```

Table 6-7. GLOBAL Runs.

```
RUN
THIS IS GLOBAL

MY LOCATION IS
LATITUDE(DEG,MIN, 1 FOR NORTH-O FOR SOUTH)
?40,52,1
LONGITUDE(DEG,MIN, 1 FOR EAST-O FOR WEST)
?73,19,0


HIS LOCATION IS
LATITUDE(DEG,MIN 1 FOR NORTH-O FOR SOUTH)
?22.54,0,0
LONGITUDE(DEG,MIN, 1 FOR EAST-O FOR WEST)
?43.15,0,0

DISTANCE IN MILES                4793.847786
DISTANCE IN KILOMETRES           7714.739241
```

program will work in most machines. Notice that when inputting latitude, you must type 1 for north or 0—zero for south latitudes. If your machine will accept what they call string variables then you could change the program to accept the letters "N" or "S", or the words "North" or "South." The same applies for longitude. You will need to alter the IF statements: 150, 170, 300 and 360. For instance, 150 would become: 150 IF Z$="W" then 170. Also, all of the variables, A, B, Y and Z, would need to be changed to A$, B$, Y$ and Z$, since these usually denote string variables.

One other important point is that GLOBAL converts degrees to radians before calculating. Make sure that your version of BASIC uses radians for angle calculations. If your BASIC needs degrees, then you'll have to eliminate the conversion factors (3.14159/180) from statements 110, 120, 280, 290 and 410, and you'll have to change pi (3.14159) to the value 180 in statements 340, 350 and 400. One last thing you should know is that part of statement number 400 reads like this: SQR (1-A1↑2). The A1↑2 means A1 to the exponent 2, or A1 squared. Some machines may need that written A1**2, or, if all else fails, just multiply A1 by itself (A1*A1). So with these hints in mind, you should be able to get GLOBAL to perform for you, no matter what kind of BASIC your machine eats.

Table 6-7 shows the output for two different runs of the program. The first run calculates the distance between Huntington, Long Island, NY (40°52'N., 73°19'W.) and Paris, France (48.52°N. 2.2°E.) as a total of 3596 miles. The second run calculates the distance between Huntington and Rio de Janeiro, Brazil (22.54° S., 43.15°W.) as 4794 miles.

If you get tired of typing in your own location, you can always calculate L1, L2, K1 and K2 from your location and assign these in the first statements of your program. You could then eliminate statements of your program. You could then eliminate statements 40 through 180. By the way, GLOBAL takes up very little space in memory, less than 1K, and the above measure would reduce it even more.

A Depth Charge Game

The idea for this project came from a game that appeared in our school's time-sharing library some time ago. However, this program has several additional features that can make it very challenging.

Background

Depth Charge is written in BASIC for a Compucolor 8001 which has 8K of user memory. The program itself doesn't take up nearly that much. It uses probably half, so it should run on any machine with 4K of play room.

Use of the Compucolor was generously donated by General Precision Electronics, Inc., in Watertown, Wisconsin, as, at the time, I didn't have access to our school's time-sharing terminal.

The Game

Picture a coordinate system as in Fig. 6-1. Now, make believe that it is a section of the ocean. You may make this section as large or as small as you like, but the coordinate origin (0, 0, 0 as y, x, Depth) will always be in the southeast corner (on the surface) of the ocean.

Somewhere within the boundaries of this section of ocean lies the evil Klingon (Why not? We blame them for just about everything else) torpedo base. The base does not move, but it does pose a threat to world peace (sound familiar?) by torpeoding the passing unfriendly (to them) shipping. However, in typical Klingon style, it takes them awhile to zero in before they can fire. The amount of time it takes to zero in is directly proportional to the size of the section of ocean you have selected. In other words, the larger the area, the more time you have to get them before they get you.

You are the captain of a depth charge carrying destroyer. Your mission is to rid the seas of the evil Klingon torpedo base by destroying it with the ship's depth charges. This is accomplished by entering the detonation coordinates of a depth charge and using ship sonar reports to find the location of the base.

The request *detonation coordinates?* ("SPLASH . . . THUMP") is a request to enter the three numbers where you think the base is. Type a y (north/south) coordinate, an x (east/west) coordinate and a depth (zero is the surface) coordinate, in that order, separated by commas.

You will then get a sonar report telling where your shot was in relation to the target. For example, if sonar reported the depth charge was "SOUTH," "EAST" and "TOO HIGH," the next shot would have more north (larger y coordinate), further west (smaller x coordinate) and deeper (larger depth coordinate). I use y, x, depth instead of x, y, depth because people are used to saying southeast, right?

Anyway, so the game goes until either the evil Klingon base is destroyed by a depth charge ("BLAM"), or the Klingons finally zero in and torpedo you ("WHOOSH . . . KERBOOM!"). Figure 6-2 shows a sample run to illustrate how this can work.

The Program

Figure 6-3 is the program listing. Except for the random number generation at 210 through 230, you should have little difficulty in adapting the program to your system. For the random generation statements, the idea is to generate a random integer between zero and your maximum area value. If you have some trouble getting it going, try this:

```
245 PRINT Y, X, Z
```

That will print your random values to troubleshoot other parts of the program (or cheat at the game, if that's what you want). Most of the program is pretty much self-explanatory.

Nuclear Attack!

Here's another violent and destructive computer game! And it uses nuclear weapons, yet, in this age of detente. I'll bet Texas Instruments never dreamed that their SR-52 would be used to stage World War III battles. Read on, and see how to make yourself a world power! If you don't like the game, at least you may pick up a couple of interesting programming tricks for the SR-52.

The game itself is a new twist on the old *sub search* type of game. Most people get sick of sub searching after a few games, because the game isn't really challenging. It's a simple matter to

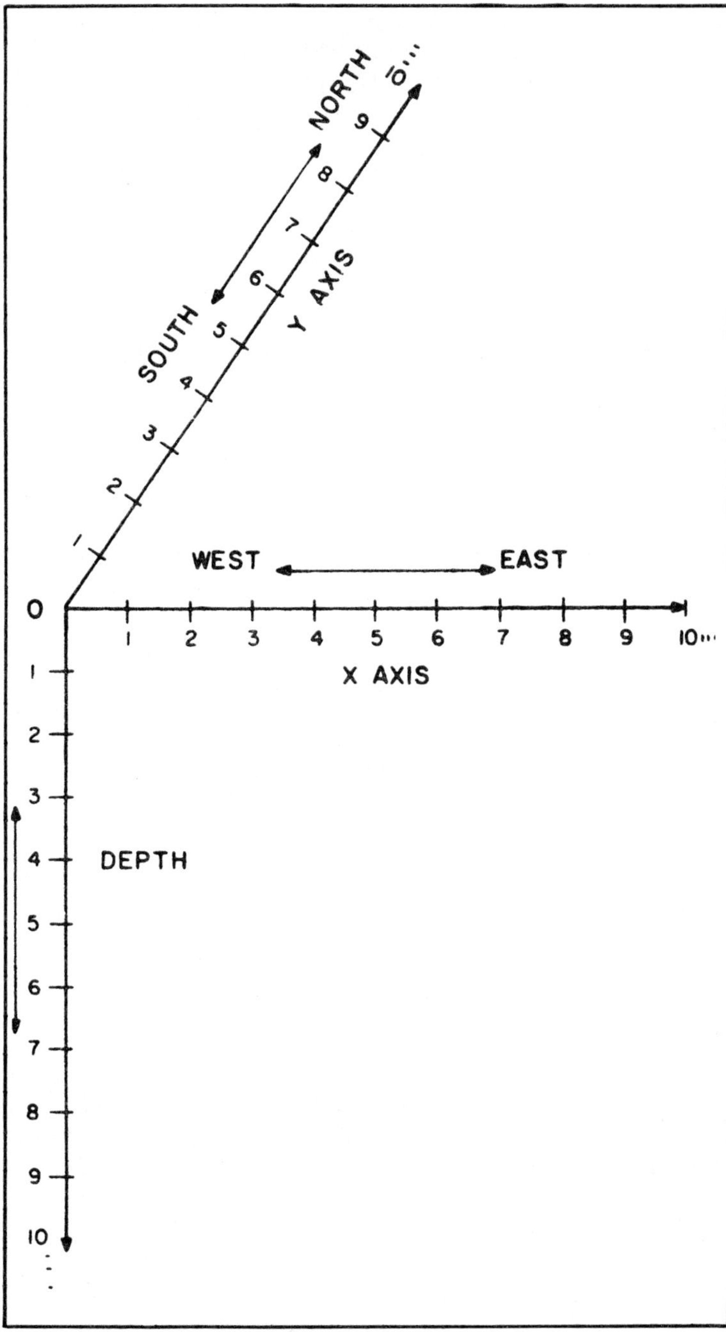

Fig. 6-1. Coordinate system.

```
THIS IS THE DEPTH CHARGE GAME
YOU ARE THE CAPTAIN OF A DESTROYER LOOKING FOR
THE EVIL KLINGON UNDERWATER TORPEDO BASE.

YOUR JOB IS TO DESTROY THE BASE  USING YOUR DEPTH
CHARGES BEFORE THE KLINGONS ZERO IN AND TORPEDO
YOU AND TAKE OVER THE SEAS

YOU MAY SPECIFY THE MAXIMUM SEARCH AREA BY GIVING
THREE NUMBERS--ONE FOR THE Y AXIS (NORTH/SOUTH),
THE X AXIS (EAST/WEST), AND DEPTH.
THE LARGER THE AREA THE MORE SHOTS YOU GET
BEFORE THE KLINGONS ZERO IN AND TORPEDO YOU

TO MAKE A SHOT, ENTER THE THREE NUMBERS (Y, X, DEPTH)
WHERE YOU THINK THE BASE IS.  THE SHIP'S SONAR
WILL REPORT BACK WHERE THE SHOT WAS IN RELATION TO
THE BASE.  GOOD LUCK!!!

MAXIMUM SEARCH AREA (Y, X, DEPTH)? 10,10,10

DETONATION COORDINATES? 5,5,5

SPLASH!
   I
   I
   I
   I
   I
   I
   I
   I
   I
   I
   I
   I
   I
   I
   I

   *----THUMP

NORTH
EAST
TOO HIGH

DETONATION COORDINATES? 3,3,7
```

Fig. 6-2. Sample run.

```
SPLASH!

   I
   I
   I
   I
   I
   I
   I
   I
   I
   I
   I
   I
   I
   I
   I

   *----THUMP


NORTH

WEST

TOO HIGH


DETONATION COORDINATES? 1,4,10


SPLASH!

   I
   I
   I
   I
   I
   I
   I
   I
   I
   I
   I
   I
   I
   I
   I

   *----THUMP


SOUTH

TOO LOW


DETONATION COORDINATES? 2,4,9


BLAM!!------------STATION DESTROYED!!!  THE WORLD

IS SAFE!


TRY AGAIN? (1=YES)? 2

READY
```

```
10 PRINT"THIS IS THE DEPTH CHARGE GAME"
20 REM BY MARK HERRO FOR A COMPUCOLOR 8001
30 PRINT"YOU ARE THE CAPTAIN OF A DESTROYER LOOKING FOR"
40 PRINT"THE EVIL KLINGON UNDERWATER TORPEDO BASE."
50 PRINT
60 PRINT"YOUR JOB IS TO DESTROY THE BASE USING YOUR DEPTH"
70 PRINTCHARGES BEFORE THE KLINGONS ZERO IN AND TORPEDO"
80 PRINT"YOU AND TAKE OVER THE SEAS."
90 PRINT
100 PRINT"YOU MAY SPECIFY THE MAXIMUM SEARCH AREA BY GIVING"
110 PRINT"THREE NUMBERS--ONE FOR THE Y AXIS (NORTH/SOUTH),
115 PRINT"THE X AXIS (EAST/WEST), AND DEPTH.
120 PRINT"THE LARGER THE AREA THE MORE SHOTS YOU GET"
130 PRINT"BEFORE THE KLINGONS ZERO IN AND TORPEDO YOU"
140 PRINT
150 PRINT"TO MAKE A SHOT, ENTER THE THREE NUMBERS (Y, X, DEPTH)"
160 PRINT"WHERE YOU THINK THE BASE IS.  THE SHIP'S SONAR"
170 PRINT"WILL REPORT BACK WHERE THE SHOT WAS IN RELATION TO"
180 PRINT"THE BASE.  GOOD LUCK!!!"
185 PRINT
190 REM SET UP CONDITIONS
200 INPUT"MAXIMUM SEARCH AREA (Y, X, DEPTH)"; A,B,C
210 LET Y=INT(A*RND(1))
220 LET X=INT(B*RND(1))
230 LET Z=INT(C*RND(1))
235 REM SHOT LIMIT
240 LET S=INT((A+B+C)/5)
250 FOR L=1 TO S
260 REM START SHOOTING
270 IF L=S-1 THEN PRINT"BETTER HURRY...THEY'RE ZEROING IN FAST!"
280 PRINT
290 INPUT"DETONATION COORDINATES"; D,E,F
```

Fig. 6-3. Program listing.

```
300 PRINT
310 PRINT"SPLASH!"
320 FOR H=1 TO 15
330 PRINT"    I"
340 NEXT H
350 PRINT"    *----THUMP"
355 REM "DEL" CAN BE SUBSTITUTED FOR THE "*" IN SOME SYSTEMS
360 PRINT
365 REM SONAR REPORT
370 IF D<>Y THEN GOTO 420
380 IF E<>X THEN GOTO 440
390 IF F<>Z THEN GOTO 460
400 PRINT"BLAM!!------------STATION DESTROYED!!!    THE WORLD"
405 PRINT"IS SAFE!"
410 GOTO 530
420 IF D<Y THEN PRINT"SOUTH"
430 IF D>Y THEN PRINT"NORTH"
440 IF E<X THEN PRINT"WEST"
450 IF E>X THEN PRINT"EAST"
460 IF F<Z THEN PRINT"TOO HIGH"
470 IF F>Z THEN PRINT"TOO LOW"
480 NEXT L
490 PRINT
495 PRINT"WHOOSH-------------------------KERBOOM!!!!"
500 PRINT
510 PRINT"YOU'VE BEEN HIT!!!!  ABANDON SHIP!!!!!"
520 PRINT"ITS ALL OVER BUT THE SHOUTING"
525 PRINT
530 INPUT"TRY AGAIN? (1=YES)"; T
540 IF T=1 THEN GOTO 200
550 END
```

narrow down your coordinates with each shot, and the game becomes a sort of three-dimensional high-low. The twist in this game is that you are shooting at more than one target at once (six in this version), and you have to be a lot more clever to figure out where they are.

How To Play

For equipment (besides the calculator), you will need a pencil and a sheet of paper marked off into 100 squares in a 10-by-10 array. This sheet of paper represents your enemy's military base which you are attacking. You don't have to use this paper diagram, but, without it, keeping track of your play is nearly impossible. The columns are numbered 0 through 9, from left to right, and the rows are numbered likewise, from bottom to top (Fig. 6-4). In this way, the board could be looked at as the first quadrant in an x-y plane, so I will refer to the west-east direction as the x-axis and the north-south direction as the y-axis.

Your enemy has six ballistic missile silos hidden at random on this base. You, on the other hand, have a remotely-controlled offensive weapons satellite from which you can drop guided nuclear bombs upon the enemy base. You input the coordinates of the square upon which the bomb is to fall. It is your task to destroy all six silos using as few of your bombs as needed. The only information you are given is the number of silos that lie to the north, to the east, etc., of each bomb you drop. How well you do depends on your skill at organizing and interpreting this information. There is no upper limit on the number of shots you may take.

Each time you load the program, you will have to enter a seed for the random number generator that locates the silos at the beginning of each game. Enter your number and press A. You can use the time of day, your age in minutes, the Dow-Jones average, whatever. I usually just hit the decimal point and then seven or eight digits at random. Any number between 0 and 10^9 will work (except the number one—the random number generator chokes on the number one).

To start the game, press B. The calculator will take about 30 seconds to randomly locate the six silos and will display a zero when ready. You need only randomize once for each series of games you play. Each successive start will give a different pattern of silos.

Now select which square you want to bomb first (example: 5, 6—five is the west-east, or x-, coordinate, and 6 is the north-south, or y-, coordinate). Press 5 and then D to enter the x-coordinate, followed by 6, then E to enter the y-coordinate and run the program.

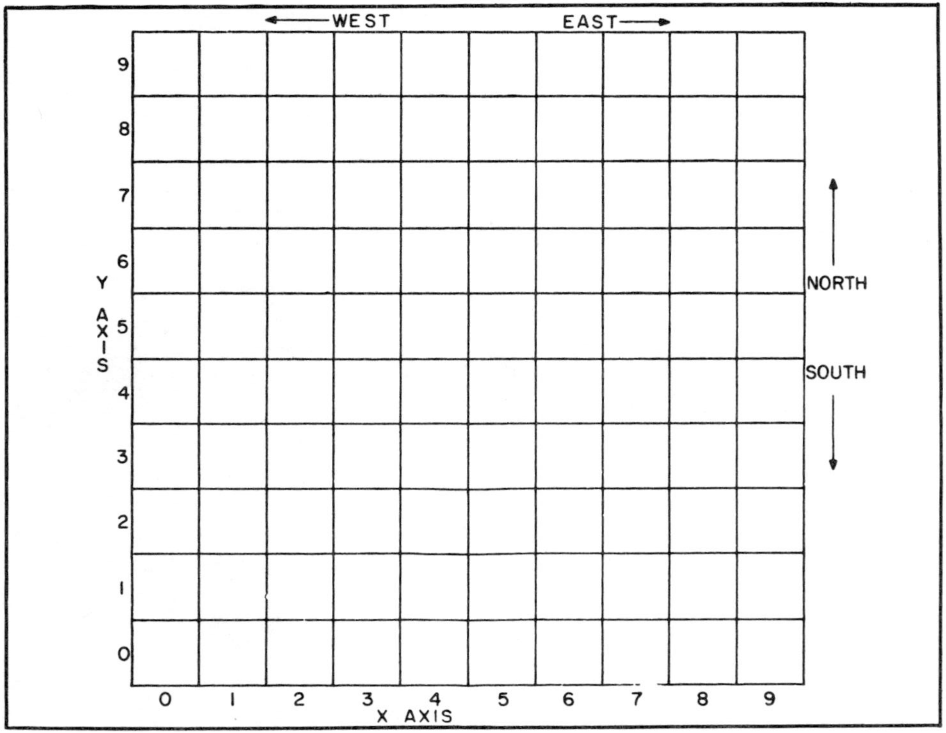

Fig. 6-4. This is how the board is set up. It represents your enemy's missile base.

Congratulations, you have just destroyed everything within square 5, 6. And you didn't even have to file an environmental impact statement! After about 25 seconds, the calculator will come back with a confusing string of digits, like 1562433. Let's break this display down digit by digit and explain what it means.

Taking the digits from left to right, the first digit, 1, means shot number one. The next two digits, 56, are an echo of which square you bombed. The next digit, 2, means that there are two silos to the north of this shot. This doesn't necessarily mean that they are directly north along the same column, but only that their y-coordinates are greater. This is a major point of confustion among new players (Fig. 6-5). The remaining digits are similarly south, east and west, respectively.

Wait a minute! The example says 2433. That adds up to 12 silos. Is there a bug? No, each silo counts twice—once as being either north or south of where the bomb was dropped, and again as being either east or west. Note that, if a silo lies along the same line as your shot, it won't show up in either of the two indicators for that direction. In other words, a silo on the same vertical column as your shot counts as neither east nor west, and one along the same horizontal row counts as neither north nor south.

When you hit a square that contains a silo, the display will flash. Press CE to stop the flashing. When a silo is hit, it is destroyed and will not show up on subsequent shots. Although it doesn't happen very often, two or more of the silos may be placed in the same square. When this happens, they are both destroyed when the square is bombed.

When the last silo is hit, the last four digits will be 0000, and the game is over. To start a new game, press B.

Different people have come up with different strategies for this game, and I will leave you to find your own. Among people I know, the best players average about 13 shots per game. The record low at this writing is eight bombs. However, at the other end of the spectrum, I saw one person give up after 50 shots. That base must have really been smoking!

About the Program

Writing a program for a programmable calculator is very different from writing a program in microprocessor assembly language or a higher level language such as BASIC. The greatest disadvantage of the programmable calculator is its small amount of program memory. The simplicity of pushing each key to enter its function into the program makes coding a program, say from a flowchart, very simple

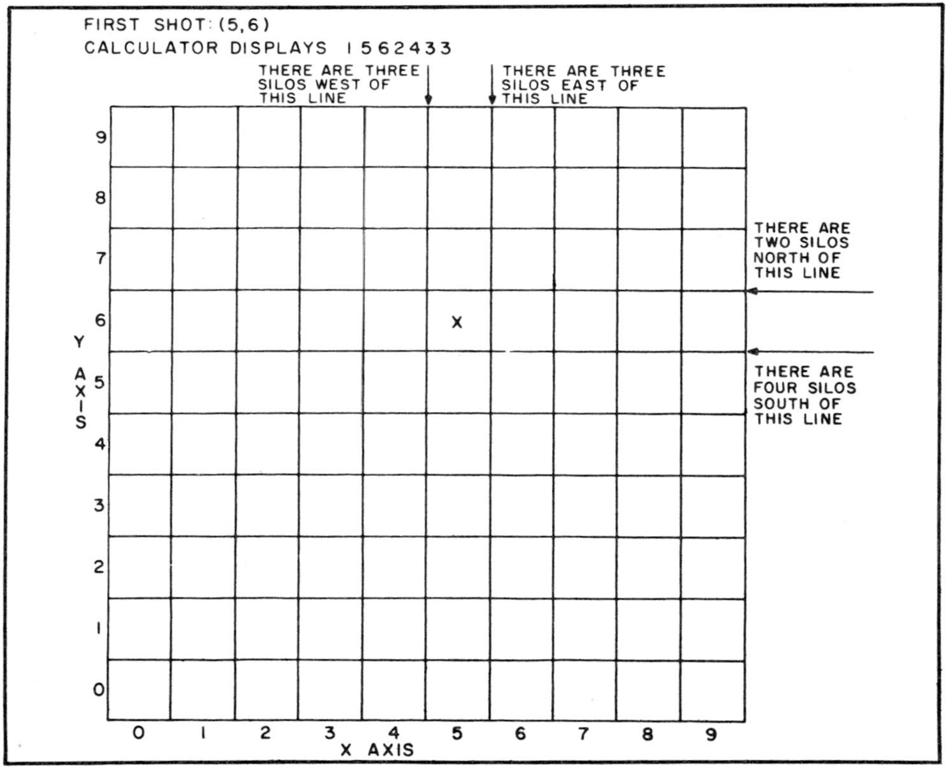

Fig. 6-5. Diagram of example used in text.

Register	Contents
99	random seed
19	number of shots taken
18	x-coordanate of shot
17	y-coordinate of shot
16	number of silos north of shot
15	number of silos south of shot
14	number of silos east of shot
13	number of silos west of shot
12	silo #1 x-coordinate
11	silo #1 y-coordinate
10	silo #2 x-coordinate
09	silo #2 y-coordinate
08	silo #3 x-coordinate
07	silo #3 y-coordinate
06	silo #4 x-coordinate
05	silo #4 y-coordinate
04	silo #5 x-cooridante
03	silo #5 y-coordinate
02	silo #6 x-coordinate
01	silo #6 y-coordinate
00	dsz and pointer

Table 6-8. Register Usage Table.

and straightforward. However, a more complex program will need more keystrokes than there is memory to hold them using the straightforward approach. So the programmer must resort to tricks to condense the program to a usable size. The trade-offs involved with these tricks are:

- They make the program harder to debug and harder for someone other than the programmer to understand.
- They usually slow the program down.

So, as vital as informative remarks and good documentation are for regular programs, they become even more important for the programmable calculator's programs.

In this game, the x- and y-coordinates of each silo are stored in registers 01 through 12 (Table 6-8). When a game is started by pressing B, 12 is stored in register R_{00}, which is used as a pointer. The program generates a random digit, which is stored in the register pointed to by R_{00} using an IND STO instruction (step 197). The IND key is one of the most useful programming functions on the SR-52. It tells the calculator that it is to perform the memory function immediately following the IND (STO, RCL, EXC, SUM, etc.), not on the register specified in the instruction, but on the one whose number is stored in that register. For example, if R_{00} contains the number 9, then the command IND STO 00 would perform the same function as STO 09: The displayed number would be stored in register 09.

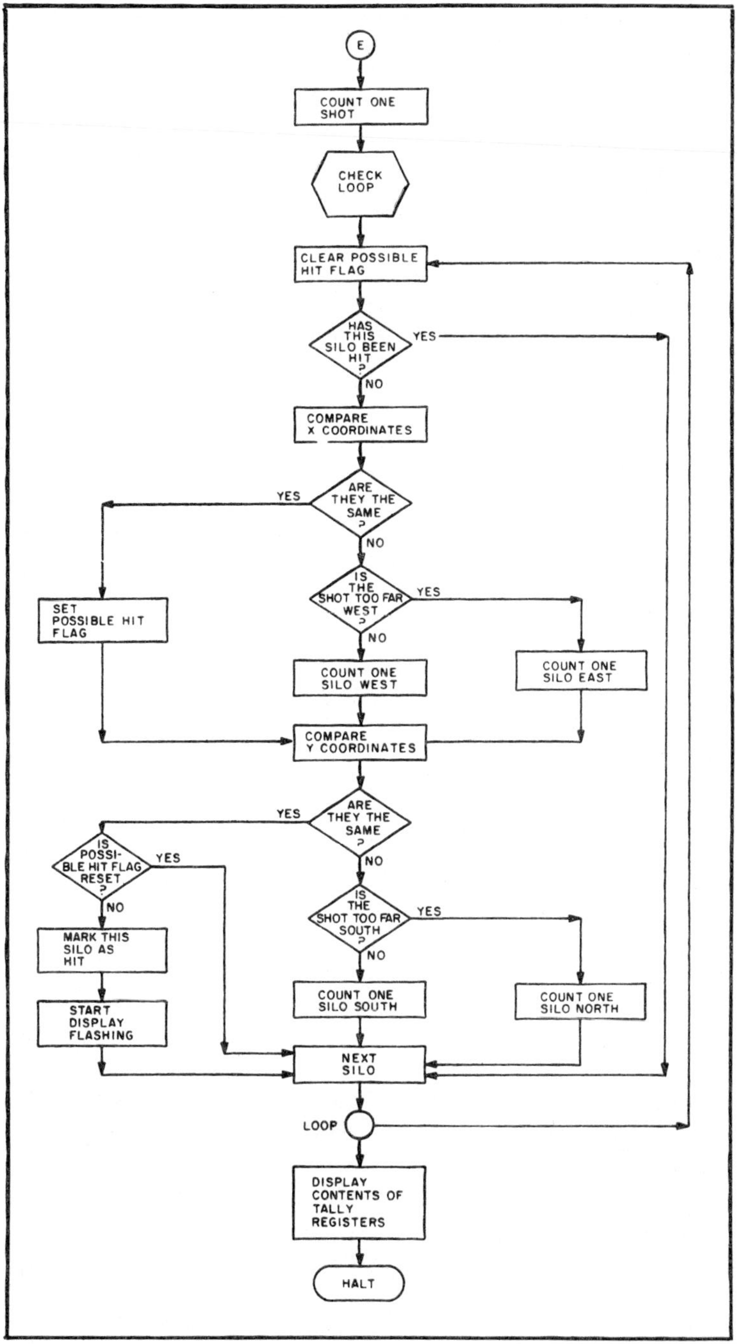

Fig. 6-6. Flowchart.

Using the dsz instruction (decrement and skip or zero) after each random number is stored, the program decrements the value in R_{00} by 1 and checks to see if it has reached zero. If it hasn't, the program loops back to LBL *7′ and repeats the process. So, effectively, the first time through, the loop R_{00} contains 12 and the IND STO 00 stores the random digit in R_{12}. The next time time through, R_{00} contains 11 and the random digit goes in R_{11} and so on. When R_{00} finally reaches zero, the dsz doesn't cause a branch, but just lets the program continue and halt. Now R_{01} through R_{12} each contain a random digit, and these are the coordinates of the silos (Table 6-8). The flowchart can be found in Fig. 6-6.

The Silo Shuffle

The random number generator (steps 179-196) has its random seed stored in register 99. This is because R_{99} and R_{98} are surplus registers which are unaffected by the CMs instruction R_{00} through R_{19}. The seed is recalled, Inxed and then squared and stored back in R_9 as the new seed. This number is multiplied by the degrees/radians constant (57.295779513) and the part to the left of the decimal is chopped off, leaving a decimal fraction. The decimal is multiplied by 10, and the digits to the right of the decimal are removed, leaving an integer from 0 to 9. This approach can be modified to produce random integers from zero to N by replacing the multiplier of 10 in step 193 with a multiplier of N + 1.

Pressing D stores the x-coordinate of your shot in R_{18}. E stores the y-coordinate in R_{17} and continues on to the main body of the program.

Each silo is checked individually. First the xs are compared by subtracting the shot x from the silo x. If the result is zero, then that means that the shot and silo are on the same column. Flag zero is set when this happens so that the calculator will remember later in the program that the xs were the same in case the ys are the same, too, which would mean a hit. If the difference between the x-coordinates is positive, then the silo x was greater than the shot x, and the shot must have fallen to the west of the silo, so R_{14}, which contains the number of silos to the east, is incremented by one. If the difference is negative, then the opposite is true, and R_{13} (west) is incremented instead.

Now, since we are using R_{00} as a pointer to tell which coordinate of which silo we are working on, we must decrement it by one to get the y-coordinate. We do this with a dsz command that branches just ahead of itself. The same procedure as was used on the x-coordinates is applied to the y-coordinates, except that now, if they are the same, we must check to see if flag zero is set. If it is, then both silo coordinates match the shot coordinates, and we have a hit. When a silo is hit, the program changes its x-coordinates to -1 as an indicator that it has been hit and is to be skipped over on later shots. Then a $\sqrt{x}$ establishes an error condition so the display will flash when execution is completed. If the y-coordinates are not the same, then, like before, the north register is incremented, depending on which side of the silo the shot fell.

Now another dsz instruction loops back to the beginning of the check procedure and moves the pointer to the x-coordinate of the next silo, or, if there are no more silos to check, passes control on to the display routine.

The display segment demonstrates a useful way to display the contents of several registers at once. Again R_{00} is used as a pointer, but this time it starts at 19 and is decremented until it reaches 13, and the program halts. The calculator keeps a running total of the contents of each register times a decreasing power of 10. Thus we get $(R_{19}) \times 10^6 + (R_{18}) \times 10^5 + \ldots + (R_{13}) \times 10^0$. Each register contains only a one-digit number, so the resulting sum is a number made by stringing together the contents to registers 19 through 13. Of course, the proper things are stored in each register in order to have the display come out in the order we want.

For the Sake of Speed

Looking over the program listing, you may be wondering about the strange order in which the segments of the program are arranged in memory. The user-defined labels are near the end, and the program branches and subroutines come before the program. The best way I can answer this question is to have you try the following experiment:

Run the four programs in Table 6-9, and time the execution using the second hand of a clock or a stopwatch. Make sure you turn the calculator off to clear the program memory before entering each program.

You can see that the four programs do exactly the same thing. They only differ in their locations in memory and their dsz instructions. Two of them are labeled branches, and two are directly addressed. On my calculator, all programs run in about 10 seconds except number two, which takes more than 40 seconds. It seems reasonable to me to assume that, when the calculator is told to branch to a particular label, it must search through the program memory starting from the beginning. Naturally, the farther down in

Table 6-9. Four Programs.

step	keystrokes		
Program one		**Program three**	
000	*LBL A	000	*LBL A
002	100 STO 00	002	100 STO 00
008	*LBL B	008	*LBL B
010	*dsz B	010	*dsz 008
012	HLT	014	HLT
Program two		**Program four**	
200	*LBL A	200	*LBL A
202	100 STO 00	202	100 STO 00
208	*LBL B	208	*LBL B
210	*dsz B	210	*dsz 208
212	HLT	214	HLT

the program memory (Table 6-10) a label is, the longer the calculator must take to find it and the slower the execution will be. In the program one, the sought-after label B is almost at the beginning, so the calculator finds it quickly, and the loop executes swiftly. In program two, however, the machine must search through almost the entire memory before it locates label B. Consequently, this loop takes much longer to execute. In programs three and four, the branches are made directly to a specified address. The calculator doesn't have to waste time searching, because it has been told exactly where to put the program counter. Thus, both of these loops execute quickly no matter where they are placed in program memory.

As I said, this explanation is an educated guess on my part, and perhaps someone who knows what goes on in the mind of a T1 calculator will clarify this point.

Anyway, this is the reason for placing the branches and subroutines before the main program—the closer they are to the beginning of program memory, the faster the calculator can find them and the faster the program will run. It does make the program more confusing to look at, and I don't recommend that you try to write your programs this way. But, when you finish a long program and have it running, you may find that rearranging things will speed it up considerably.

Go, Team, Go

The game was popular enough in the dorm where I lived during college that we decided to hold a tournament. Each contestant would

Table 6-10. Program Listing.

Step	Keystrokes	Comments
000	*LBL *1'	
002	*dsz *8'	Skip this silo.
004	*LBL *2'	
006	*st flg 0	Set the "possible hit" flag.
008	GTO *5'	
010	*LBL +	
012	1 SUM 14	Count one silo east.
016	GTO *5'	
018	*LBL *9'	
020	1 SUM 16	Count one silo north.
024	GTO *8'	
026	*LBL *3'	
028	INV *if flg 0 *8'	If flag set, then we have a hit.
032	1 SUM 00	Change x-coordinate
036	± *IND STO 00	of silo to -1.
041	*√x *dsz *8'	Start display flashing.
044	*LBL *B'	Integer-part subroutine.
046	(STO - . 5)	Subtract rounding constant.
052	*fix 0 *D.MS	Eliminate fractional digits.
055	*rtn	
056	*LBL E	
058	STO 17 CE	Store y-coordinate of shot.
062	1 SUM 19	Count one shot.
066	0 STO 16 STO 15 STO 14 STO 13	Clear N.,S.,E.,W. registers.
079	12 STO 00	Initialize check loop.
084	*LBL *4'	Beginning of loop.
086	INV *st flg 0	Clear "possible hit" flag.
089	*IND RCL 00	Get x of silo.
093	INV *if pos *1	Branch if it's been hit.
096	- RCL 18 =	Compare to x of shot.
101	*if zro *2'	If same, set flag.
103	*if pos +	If greater, count one silo east,
105	1 SUM 13	else count one silo west.
109	*LBL *5'	
111	*dsz 115	Move to y-coordinate.
115	*IND RCL 00 - RCL 17 =	Compare silo y to shot y.
124	*if zro *3'	If same, check for hit.
126	*if pos *9'	If greater, count one silo north,
128	1 SUM 15	else count one silo south.
132	*LBL *8'	
134	*dsz *4'	Branch back if more silos.
136	20 STO 00 0	Initialize display loop.
142	*LBL *6'	Beginning of loop.
144	+ *dsz 149	Move to next register.
149	*IND RCL 00 X 10 y^x	Get contents of this register and
157	(RCL 00 - 13)	multiply by decreasing powers of ten.
165	INV *if zro *6'	
168	= HLT	
170	*LBL B	Begin new game.
172	CLR CMs	Clear everything.
174	12 STO 00	Initialize setup loop.
179	*LBL *7'	Beginning of loop.
181	RCL 99 lnx *x^2 STO 99	Make a random digit
189	INV *D/R - *B' X 10 = *B'	from 0 to 9.
198	*IND STO 00	Store it as a silo coordinate.
202	*dsz *7'	Branch back for the next one.
204	CLR HLT	Ready to play.
206	*LBL A	
208	STO 99 HLT	Store initial random seed.
212	*LBL D	
214	STO 18 HLT	Store x-coordinate of shot.

play three games and total his scores, lowest score winning. To make things fair, each person would play the same three configuration of silos. This was accomplished by randomizing with the same initial seed before each game. For example, we used sin 1, sin 2 and sin 3. The random number generator then generates the same sequence each time, and the silos come out in the same spots. I find that it's handy to write down the number you initialize with anyway. That way, if the system crashes (batteries go dead), it's simple to set the same game up again after plugging in the charger. It's really frustrating to lose a game half way through, especially when you were just about to blast a silo.

And you certainly don't have to be a computer buff to enjoy the game. The person who won the tournament was a political science major!

A Secret Weapon for Road Rallies

One of the more enjoyable hobbies, I pursue from time to time is that of driving (or navigating) in TSD road rallies. The letters stand for "time, speed and distance." If you run rallies, or know a friend who does, your computer can give you a secret weapon to help you win.

These events are not races, at least not in the conventional sense. You are given a set of instructions. Then you follow them. Sound dull? Well, it isn't! The object of the rally is to exactly follow the instructions, to maintain an exact speed and to get where you are supposed to get after a precise elapsed time. Penalty points are given for being either early or late at the destinations. Usually, there are several destinations—called *checkpoints*—in every TSD rally. To give you some idea of the precision driving required, a penalty point is equal to an arrival time (early or late) of one-hundreth minute (.6 sec) from the scheduled time. A typical winner, in our club, will have a score of 50 to 100, indicating a total error of one-half minute, after three or four hours of driving. Of course, low score wins.

Several things are added for spice. When you start the rally, you don't know how far the first checkpoint is (or any of the others, for that matter). Nor do you even know where the checkpoints are, or the necessary average speed to get there on time, or the time you must expend in getting there. Distances are seldom marked on the instructions. All this information is known only to the rallymaster and his workers.

The instructions are rather like a computer program. Here is a short excerpt from a recent one:

CAST 30
Right at Kenny Road
Left at "Y"
Left after SRIP "Garage"
CAST 42
Right 3d opportunity

This would be interpreted as follows: Change Average Speed To thirty miles per hour; when you get to Kenny Road, make a right turn;, at the next "Y" in the road, after your right turn, take the left fork; you should see a Sign that Reads In Part "Garage"—take the next left (it may be miles down the road); as soon as you turn, Change Average Speed To forty-two miles per hour; at the third chance thereafter that you have to do so, turn right; and so on.

Of course, the sign with "Garage" on it may be faded and half-covered with weeds, the road may be one on which no sane person would go over 20 mph, one of the three "opportunities" will doubtless be impossible to spot (or between the first and second road will be a long private drive that gets counted as an "opportunity" by half the contestants when it isn't) and so on. These are the simple traps you will encounter; rallymasters delight in messing you up. Anyway, you get the point—it is a real job just to stay on course.

Besides helping the driver stay on course and keeping up with the instructions, the navigator has the job of calculating the average speed of the car.

Time, speed and distance problems are all solved by the simple formula: D=RT, where D is distance, R is rate (speed) and T is time. Know any two, and you can find the other. In a rally, you will know distance and time from the last speed change in the instructions. You will be trying to calculate average speed in miles per hour by the formula: $R_{mph} = (D/T)*60$. You will probably want to make a calculation every mile, because tenths of a second are important, and there might never be a chance to make good the loss of even a few seconds.

The navigator is necessarily going to be busy with a stopwatch, pencil, calculator and odometer for the entire rally. He may get so busy that he loses track of where his car is.

You can buy an electromechanical gadget that will keep track of elapsed time and of average speed, but they are very expensive. If you are an experimenter, you might kludge up a small terminal to your mobile rig and have a program running on the computer at home, which will make your calculations for you. But terminals aren't that cheap, either. (And watch sending ASCII over the air!)

The program shown here (Table 6-11) is a cheap and simple answer. It allows you to work in time, not average speed. It is far more helpful to know that you are three seconds ahead of time than to know you are averaging 43.2 mph, when the instructions call for 42 mph.(Why? Because the more miles you drive with a constant error in speed, the further off you become in time. In the heat of a rally, a fraction of mph speed error may not impress you as important, even though you've traveled eight or more miles.

What you get from the program is a printout of speed, distance and time. Your navigator turns to the sheet with the correct speed for that leg, zeros the mileage indicator in your car and zeros the stopwatch. Then, every mile or half-mile, he looks at the stopwatch and compares it with the time next to the mileage which you have traveled. He can then tell you how many seconds you are ahead or behind where you should be at this point. It is then a very simple matter for you, the driver, to make whatever correction is necessary. At the end of the next mile, or half-mile, another check is made and further correction taken. And so on, throughout the rally.

Sure, the formula is not that hard to run on a calculator. But, to get time-error that way, the old navigator is going to run two calculations every mile. Try even the simplest calculation in a rally; I've never known any navigator who didn't mess up at least a third of his calculations on the first try. And he has his eyes off the road for too long.

Yes, I know you can buy time-speed-distance charts at not too great an expense. But, first of all, they can't be tailored for whatever distance interval you wish. This program can. Secondly, they are much harder to read than a computer printout.

The program is written in Dartmouth BASIC. It was run on an IBM 370. It should work on most small BASIC interpreters. It will not work on an integer system.

It is so simple that it almost explains itself. There are two loops, one nested inside the other. The outer loop contains the average speed. It is shown starting at 25 mph, but this could be any figure—it depends on the minimum speed at which rallies in your area are run. This loop terminates at 55 mph because no rally instructions can tell you to drive at an illegal speed.

For each step of the outer loop the inner loop (distance) steps 39 times. Each time it steps, the program calculates time. Then, speed, distance and time are printed out and the inner loop steps again. When distance reaches 20, a blank line is printed, a new heading is printed, and the outer loop steps to the next speed. Then, the whole process is repeated, and repeated and repeated.

Table 6-11. BASIC Program to Calculate Time in Minutes and Tenths of Minutes.

```
05 REM THIS PROGRAM CALCULATES TIME IN  MINUTES  AND TENTHS OF MIN.
10 REM  SET UP THE OUTER LOOP.  R=SPEED IN MPH.
20 FOR R=25 TO 55
30 REM  PRINT THE HEADINGS.
40 PRINT "SPEED","DISTANCE","TIME"
50 REM  SET UP THE INNER LOOP.  D=DISTANCE IN MILES
60 FOR D=1 TO 20  STEP .5
70 REM  CALCULATE TIME
80 LET T=(D/R)*60
90 REM  PRINT IT ALL OUT UNDER THE CORRECT HEADING
100 PRINT R,D,T
110 REM  CYCLE THE INNER LOOP -- WHEN FINISHED, PRINT BLANK LINE AND
115 REM  CYCLE THE OUTER LOOP.
120 NEXT D
130 PRINT
140 NEXT R
160 REM  WHEN R=55, THE PROGRAM ENDS.
170 END
```

About 2 hours after you type *run*, you will have produced 14 feet of copy. This is assuming a step of .5 and a 110 baud printer. By the way, CPU time used on an IBM 370 is just over nine seconds.

If your BASIC does not have the step feature in its "FOR . . . NEXT" statement just leave that out. The program will give you printout for whole miles. This works just as well. Leave out the "REMARKS" to save space. If your system can use multiple statements per line, great.

If you wish to provide for greater mileage in the inner loop, put in whatever you like. You-all in the wide-open southwest might want to go to thirty miles or even more. Frankly, my present version of this printout only goes to 15 miles. I don't need that much, usually, in the rallies I'm in.

If you just like a lot of paper used up, make the inner loop step = .25. This will give you quarter-mile times for each speed. I doubt you'll ever use it, and it triples the length of the printout.

One very useful change to the program is shown in Table 6-12. This gives printout for time in minutes, seconds and tenths of seconds instead of minutes and tenths of minutes. Of course, which you use will depend on how your stopwatch is calibrated. The new code will take the decimal fractions of minutes and convert them to seconds and tenths of seconds. A formatting statement inserts a colon for easier reading.

I use the program's output cut into sheets and staple them at the upper left. The navigator simply flips through the pages for the correct speed, as shown for that leg of the instructions. Then he's set. Those of you handy with tools might want to construct a box-like holder with a dowel at the top and bottom. Then the printout could be scrolled past a window cut into the front of the box. For this display, the printout would be better without the headings before each speed. Change the location of that print statement so that it does not pass by on each execution of the outer loop (i.e., move it to the first line of the program).

Do Biorhythms Really Work?

Do you know what is meant by biorhythm? This project gives you a basic method to compute the values for calculating your biorhythms. A flowchart and a program for the HP-55 programmable calculator are provided (Figs. 6-7, 6-8 and Table 6-13). You should be able to use this information, rewrite it for other calculators or develop a program for your micro.

Table 6-12. The Program Converted to Calculate Time in Minutes, Seconds and Tenths of Seconds.

```
20 REM  SET UP OUTER LOOP.  R=SPEED IN MPH
30 FOR R=25 TO 55
40 REM  PRINT THE HEADINGS
50 PRINT "SPEED","DISTANCE","TIME"
60 REM  SET UP THE INNER LOOP.  D=DISTANCE IN MILES
70 FOR D=1 TO 20  STEP .5
80 REM  CALCULATE TIME IN MINUTES AND TENTHS OF MINUTES, FIRST.
90 LET T=(T/R)*60
100 REM  ROUND THIS TO NEAREST ONE-THOUSANTH OF MINUTE
110 LET T1=INT(T*1000+.5)/1000
120 REM  TAKE MINUTES ONLY AND CALL IT T2.
130 LET T2=INT(T1)
140 REM  NOW, GET JUST THE FRACTION AND CALL IT T3
150 LET T3=T1-T2
160 REM  CONVERT THIS FRACTION TO SECONDS AND TENTHS
170 LET T4=T3*60
180 REM  PRINT EVERYTHING IN RIGHT COLUMN.
190 PRINT R,D,T2:":":T4
200 REM  CYCLE THE INNER LOOP
210 NEXT D
220 REM  WHEN OUT OF DISTANCES, PRINT A BLANK LINE AND CYCLE OUTER LOOP.
230 PRINT
240 NEXT R
250 END
```

The word *biorhythm* literally means movement characterized by regular recurrence of beat, or a pattern of this, in living things. In a more strict sense, it means the study of biological cycles of man. Proper understanding and use of these cycles may help you plan for future events and forecast good days and bad days. It is one of our newer scientific disciplines and concentrates on three natural cycles that influence our physical, emotional and intellectual actions or behavior patterns.

Scientists state that our biological cycles are set in motion at birth. From then until death, we are influenced by these three cycles. (More are acknowledged, but biorhythm study seems to be limited to these three.) The *physical cycle*, requiring 23 days, is said to affect such things as strength, speed, resistance to disease, coordination and other bodily functions. (It is easy to understand why this is one of the more popular cycles!) The *emotional cycle* has a period of 28 days and is given reign over our mental health, mood, creativity, sensitivity and our perception of ourselves and others. Last is the *intellectual cycle*, which requires 33 days to be completed. It affects our ability to recall memorized facts, to learn, to be logical and to analyze.

When the three cycles start at birth, they start at a zero reference, or *baseline*, and proceed on a positive half of the full cycle. Halfway through the cycle, they return to the baseline and enter the negative half of the cycle. At the end of the negative portion of the cycle, the zero reference line is crossed again, and the process will then repeat itself.

There are, therefore, three main parts to consider: the *positive half cycle*, the *negative half* and the *zero reference*. The theory states that, during the positive portion all capacities, energies, talents and skills will be enhanced. The negative portion is described as a rehabilitation period during which all attributes of the rhythms are of reduced magnitude. When any cycle crosses the zero reference line, that day is referred to as a *critical day*. It is during this period that we are most likely to experience accidents, physical harm, arguments, depression, inability to learn, poor judgment, etc. All would depend on the cycle or cycles involved.

It is possible to have single, double and triple critical days. *Double critical days* are to be approached with extra caution. Such days occur when two cycles cross the zero reference line on the same day. They may both be on a negative slope or on a positive slope, or one may be positive while the other is negative. So far as I know, there seems to be no evidence to indicate a need to differentiate between the three types. *Triple critical days* occur at birth and

DISPLAY LINE	DISPLAY CODE	KEY ENTRY	COMMENTS	REGISTERS
00.	//////	//////	(TDA Entered)	R 0 (Used)
01.	33	Sto	TDA stored in memory	Deg. Product
02.	01	1	# 1.	
03.	34	RCL	"360" recalled from	R 1 (Used)
04.	02	2	memory # 2.	TDA
05.	71	x	TDA & 360 multiplied	R 2 360
06.	33	STO	and stored in	
07.	00	0	memory 0. (Deg. Product)	R 3 23
08.	34	RCL	"23" recalled from	
09.	03	3	memory 3 & divided	
10.	81	÷	into Deg. Product.	R 4 28
11.	31	f	Sin of resultant	
12.	12	SIN	angle calculated &	R 5 33
13.	33	STO	stored in memory	
14.	06	6	# 6.	
15.	84	R/S	Physical Value Disp.	R 6 (Used)
16.	34	RCL	Deg. product recalled	Avg.
17.	00	0	from memory 0.	reading.
18.	34	RCL	"28" recalled from	R 7
19.	04	4	memory 4 & divided	
20.	81	÷	into Deg. Product.	R 8
21.	31	f	Sin of resultant	
22.	12	SIN	angle calculated &	R 9
23.	33	STO	added to memory	
24.	61	+	# 6.	
25.	06	6		R.0
26.	84	R/S	Emotional Value Disp.	
27.	34	RCL	Deg. product recalled	R.1
28.	00	0	from memory 0.	
29.	34	RCL	"33" recalled from	
30.	05	5	memory 5 & divided	R.2
31.	81	÷	into Deg. Product.	
32.	31	f	Sin of resultant	
33.	12	SIN	angle calculated &	R.3
34.	33	STO	added to memory	
35.	61	+	# 6.	R.4
36.	06	6		
37.	84	R/S	Intellectual Value Disp.	R.5
38.	34	RCL	Sum of readings	
39.	06	6	recalled from memory	
40.	03	3	6 & divided by 3.	R.6
41.	81	÷		
42.	84	R/S	Avg. Reading Disp.	R.7
43.	01	1	1 added to the	
44.	33	STO	contents of memory 1	
45.	61	+	(TDA)	R.8
46.	01	1		
47.	34	RCL	TDA recalled from	
48.	01	1	memory 1.	R.9
49.	-03	GTO 03	Program goes to line 3.	

Fig. 6-7. HP-55 biorhythm program.

once every 21,252 days, when all three are on a positive slope. So you can expect to be *born again* every 58 years and 67 days. By the way, the number 21,252 is derived from the product of the three cycles.

It should be noted that a great number of well-documented cases have been recorded to support the biorhythm theory. Airplane crashes, train wrecks, automobile accidents and other tragedies have occurred in very abnormal numbers when the responsible people had critical days. Theory tells us to use extra caution, self-control and restraint on critical days. Except things to be subnormal on the negative half cycle. You may not beat world's records, but you will do your best during the positive half of the cycle, especially if two or all three cycles are so positioned. All other days will be *mixed*.

Now let's get to the program itself. The theory states that we complete a physical cycle every 23 days, an emotional cycle in 28 days and our intellectual cycle requires 33 days. It also states that all three start in phase at birth on the positive slope. It is obvious that the three will immediately start to go out of phase with each other. Thereafter, the composite biorhythm situation will vary from day to day. Small numerical values for each of the cycles would seem to be the best method to appraise them.

In order to arrive at some suitable numerical value, we must first divide the total number of days alive (TDA) by the number of days in the rhythm cycle of interest. For example, if the TDA = 10,000, and we are interested in the physical cycle (23 days), the result would be 10,000/23 = 434.78+. In this case, the person would have lived through 434 complete physical cycles and is into the current cycle by .78+. It is this fraction of a cycle that we are interested in. To convert this decimal number to degrees, we multiply it by 360, the number of degrees in one complete cycle. This yields approximately 281 degrees.

With this figure, we can see how far into the cycle we are, but the figure is awkward and, for some, would be hard to position in the mind. If, however, we now take the sine of that angle, we arrive at −.98. This final figure gives us magnitude and polarity in a very succinct way. By using the sine of the resultant angle, the numerical value will start at zero, increase to +1.00 at the top of the positive half cycle, decrease to zero at 180 degrees (a critical day), drop to −1.00 at 270 degrees (the negative peak) and return to zero at 360 degrees for another critical day and the start of another cycle.

The math may be simplified to: sine (TDA × 360/number of days in cycle). This is true because the sine of × degrees or any multiple of 360 + × degrees would give the same result. This

Table 6-13. The Procedure.

1. Enter the program.
2. In the run mode, store "360" in memory register number 2
3. In the run mode, store 23 in memory register number 3.
4. In the run mode store 28 in memory register number 4.
5. In the run mode, store 33 in memory register number 5.
6. Enter total days alive (TDA) in the x operating register.
7. Press BST to place the program pointer to the start of the program.
8. Press R/S to obtain the physical value.
9. Press R/S to obtain the emotional value.
10. Press R/S to obtain the intellectual value.
11. Press R/S to obtain the average reading of the P, E, and I values.
12. For the next day reading and subsequent days, repeat steps 8 through 11. The program automatically increments the TDA value by 1 after each set of readings.

If you forget what day you are reading, you may obtain the current TDA figure by simply recalling memory number 1. This may be done at any time without affecting the integrity of the program.)

method saves steps. Using this formula and the 10,000 TDA figure, the emotional value would be +.78 and the intellectual value +.19. These figures provide us with a mathematical evaluation for each of the three cycles for one particular day. They do not tell us whether the slope is positive or negative.

To find this out, we must take a second set of readings for the following day. In this case the TDA would be 10,001, the physical value −.89, the emotional value +.90 and the intellectual value +.37. If we compare these figures with the previous day, it becomes evident that all three are increasing in value. The P value is becoming less negative, the E value will reach its peak value of 1 in two days and the 1 value is on the way to a positive peak. The program (Fig. 6-7) automatically increments the TDA value by 1 each time a set of readings is calculated with the above formula. With this program, you can obtain a set of readings for a given day and for succeeding days as far in the future as you like. A linear plot of these values will, of course, result in a perfect sine wave.

One additional refinement has been added to this program. It is my personal opinion that it is the totality of all forces acting upon a person that best describes his situation. Which is to say that many factors in addition to biorhythms affect our overall well-being. Those factors are not to be dealt with here, but I felt that an average of the three values might be the best expression of this concept. For this reason, the program will also provide an average reading for each day, after the separate readings have been displayed. With the average reading, we can give a value to a "mixed day" and give it an overall rating. It is very interesting to watch the cyclic gyrations of these average figures. Unlike the other cycles, the frequency and magnitude are constantly varying and might deserve greater study.

As previously mentioned, the critical day happens when the cycle passes through the zero reference line. This will occur when the slope is negative (going from the positive half cycle to the negative half) and when the slope is positive. This should be indi-

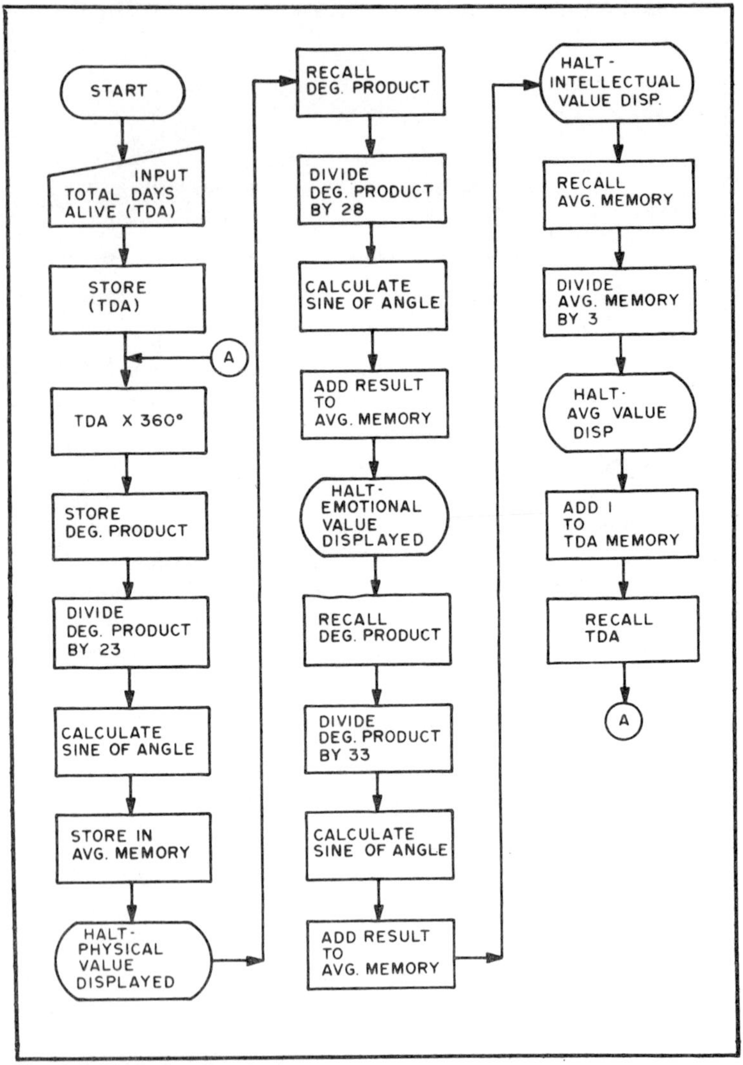

Fig. 6-8. Biorhythm flowchart.

cated by zero, but on the HP-55 with this program, you get things like $-3.18927540 \times 10^{-9}$ and other weird figures close to zero but not absolute. This, I believe, is due to inherent limitations of accuracy. It should also be noted that a critical day occurs not only at the end of a cycle but also at the half-cycle point.

In the case of the emotional cycle, this would be at the 14- and 28-day points and doesn't cause a problem. The P and I values do, because half of 23 is 11.5 and half of 33 is 16.5 For this reason, on these two rhythms, every other critical day point will not be indicated by zero (or a figure very close to it), but rather will be indicated by two contiguous days of low, equal-but-opposite polarity values. .14 and −.14 are good examples. How do we interpret this condition? For the moment, let us assume that birth occurred at noon. Presumably, the critical point of each critical day would then be at noon. This is fine for the emotional cycle, but in the case of the other two, we are forced to assume that the critical time of the half-cycle critical day is positioned ½ day after the birth hour. In this example, that would be at 12 midnight, splitting two days. In any event, you may assume that the critical day, under these conditions, resides between the two low, equal-but-opposite polarity values.

One problem with this subject is the task of determining the TDA figure. You can do this by counting the number of days in your first partial year of life. To this add all the normal 365-day years and the 366-day leap years plus the number of days in the current year. Or you can use one of several "Days Between Two Dates" programs, such as the one in the HP-55 mathematics programs booklet. Texas Instruments also has a similar program for their calculators. However you calculate it, be sure to make a note of the date and TDA figure. For future calculations, you then need only add the intervening days.

A flowchart (Fig. 6-8) is included in the hopes that it will be of assistance to those of you who own microcomputers. I believe that, with proper graphics, you should be able to display each cycle for a month at a time and all three with colors to represent each. The flowchart should also help those with programmable calculators of divergent operations.

So there you have it—a rather uncomplicated procedure to obtain easily-understood numerical values for biorhythm cycles.

Chapter 7
Miscellaneous Computer Projects

Many microcomputer applications require that the current time be available for display or printout, either on demand or when certain events occur. A time system of this type is known as a *real-time* clock, as distinguished from the microprocessor clock used for internal timing. One can think of at least a dozen applications for a real-time clock. For RTTY operation, the current time can be sent at the beginning or end of a transmission, included as part of a contest message when required and used as a 10-minute timer for CW identification. Others may find the clock useful for such things as logging, satellite tracking and timing in conjunction with repeater control, just to name a few.

A Bionic Clock

A practical microcomputer real-time clock is not really a very difficult project. At the time I needed one, however, I could not find much information in the available literature. I had considered interfacing a clock chip such as the MM5312 or 5313 to a 6820 PIA, but neither was on hand at the time. One manufacturer is currently advertising a real-time clock board kit and software for about $100. This is not quite my idea of a cheap clock!

The system I finally decided to use operates on an interrupt basis, using a crystal-controlled timebase and dividers to produce one pulse per second. This is connected to the *microprocessor nonmaskable interrupt* (NMI) line. The IRQ input can also be used, if not otherwise required by the other programs. Component cost is less than $10, and the programs require only a nominal amount of memory. The programs to be described were developed for use with a 6800, using the Mikbug™ monitor and the KIM-1 6502 system. Adapting the programs to other systems should offer no great problems.

In addition to the clock routine, we must have a routine to store the address of the clock routine in the interrupt vector locations, a routine to initialize the clock digit locations from the terminal keyboard and a routine to read out the time. A flowchart to do all this is shown in Fig. 7-1. For the purpose of demonstrating the program, a wait loop is used, so the program is waiting for a keyboard command to either store or read the time.

To start the clock, select the Store Time control character, type in only the four digits for the upcoming time in 24-hour format and turn on the clock pulse generator at the exact minute. To read the current time, select the Print Time control character. The keyboard control characters can, of course, be changed to any others, as you desire.

A flowchart of the NMI routine is given in Fig. 7-2. Tables 7-1 and 7-2 list the programs for the 6800 and 6502, respectively. When the time locations are initialized with the current time, the seconds counter location is cleared. After the clock generator is started, each pulse causes the program to vector to the interrupt routine, and the seconds counter is incremented by one. When 60 seconds are counted, the units/minutes digit is incremented, and the seconds counter is cleared again. The other digits are updated in essentially the same manner, following ordinary clock logic. Since the 24-hour format is used, the hours locations are cleared to zeros when the time increments to 2400 hours.

One note of caution: The clock generator must be off when you are in the system monitor. Until the program is loaded and executed, any interrupt will cause the monitor program to go berserk. After the program is loaded, you can safely return to the monitor if necessary.

If you don't use Universal Coordinated Time (UTC), you can change the time zone to anything else, such as EST, PST, etc. With program modification, the time string can include other data.

A schematic of the clock generator is shown in Fig. 7-3. The timebase reference uses components from a $4.95 60 Hz crystal timebase kit. The 5369 is interfaced to the divider string TTL logic level with nearly any small switching-type NPN transistor. The two 7490s form the divide-by-60 function followed by a 74121 oneshot,

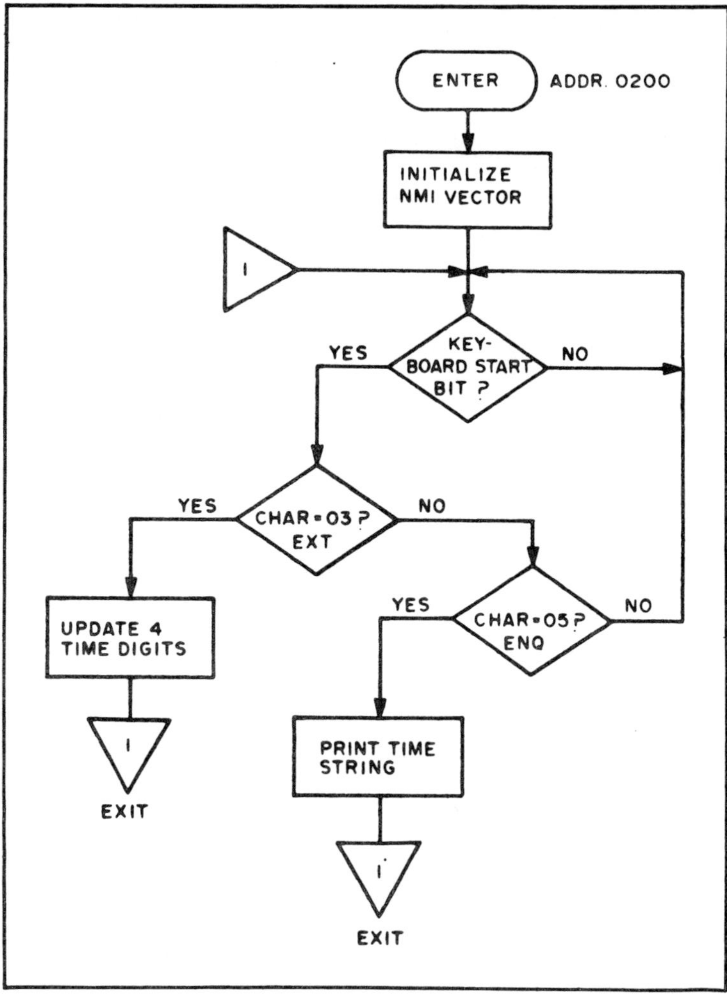

Fig. 7-1. Flowchart—wait loop, time update and print time routines.

to produce a pulse of approximately one ms. The pulse width is not critical, however, since the interrupt operates on the negative edge of the pulse. To reduce current drain, IC2 and IC3 can be replaced by 74LS90s. I could have used 74C90s, but I did not have a CMOS substitute for the 74121.

I discarded that small PC board that came with the timebase kit and made another board for the entire circuit. You can build the circuit on a piece of perfboard, mounting the timebase components on the PC board supplied. Artwork and component layout for the PC board I used are shown in Fig. 7-4.

Table 7-1. 6800 Real-Time Clock Program.

```
0200  D8              START    CLD
0201  A9  50                   LDA    #$50      INITIALIZE NMI VECTOR
0203  8D  FA  17               STA    NMIV (LO)
0206  A9  02                   LDA    #$02
0208  8D  FB  17               STA    NMIV (HI)
020B  2C  40  17      WAIT     BIT    SAD (KIM)  LOOK FOR KBD START BIT.
020E  30  FB                   BMI    WAIT
0210  20  5A  1E               JSR    GETCH (KIM)  GET KBD CHAR.
0213  C9  03                   CMP    #$03      ETX=TIME UPDATE CTRL CHAR.
0215  D0  06                   BNE    RDTIME
0217  20  27  02               JSR    STTIME
021A  4C  0B  02               JMP    WAIT
021D  C9  05          RDTIME   CMP    #$05      ENQ=READ TIME CTRL CHAR.
021F  D0  EA                   BNE    WAIT
0221  20  3A  02               JSR    PRTIME
0224  4C  0B  02               JMP    WAIT
0227  A9  00          STTIME   LDA    #0
0229  8D  A5  02               STA    COUNT     RESET SECONDS COUNTER.
022C  A2  00                   LDX    #0
022E  20  5A  1E      TIMEIN   JSR    GETCH (KIM)
0231  9D  48  02               STA    HOUR10, X  STORE 4 DIGITS.
0234  E8                       INX
0235  E0  04                   CPX    #$04      =SIZE+1
0237  D0  F5                   BNE    TIMEIN
0239  60                       RTS
023A  A2  00          PRTIME   LDX    #0
023C  BD  48  02      PRSTR    LDA    HOUR10, X
023F  20  A0  1E               JSR    OUTCH (KIM)  PRINT CHAR.
0242  E8                       INX
0243  E0  08                   CPX    #$08      =SIZE+1
0245  D0  F5                   BNE    PRSTR
0247  60                       RTS

0248  30              HOUR10          0
0249  30              HOUR1           0
024A  30              MIN10           0
024B  30              MIN1            0
024C  20                              SPACE
024D  55                              U
024E  54                              T
```

```
024F  43                                C

                                        NON-MASKABLE INTERRUPT ROUTINE

0250  48                 NMI      PHA                   SAVE A.
0251  EE A5 02                    INC   COUNT
0254  AD A5 02                    LDA   COUNT
0257  C9 3C                       CMP   #$3C            60 SECS?
0259  D0 48                       BNE   EXIT
025B  A9 00                       LDA   #0
025D  8D A5 02                    STA   COUNT           RESET SECONDS COUNTER.
0260  EE 4B 02                    INC   MIN1
0263  AD 4B 02                    LDA   MIN1
0266  C9 3A                       CMP   #$3A            10 MINS?
0268  D0 08                       BNE   TENMIN
026A  29 30                       AND   #$30            MASK TO ASCII ZERO.
026C  8D 4B 02                    STA   MIN1
026F  EE 4A 02                    INC   MIN10
0272  AD 4A 02           TENMIN   LDA   MIN10
0275  C9 36                       CMP   #$36            60 MINS?
0277  DC 08                       BNE   ONEHR
0279  29 30                       AND   #$30
027B  8D 4A 02                    STA   MIN10
027E  EE 49 02                    INC   HOUR1
0281  AD 49 02           ONEHR    LDA   HOUR1
0284  C9 3A                       CMP   #$3A            10 HRS?
0286  D0 08                       BNE   TENHRS
0288  29 30                       AND   #$30
028A  8D 49 02                    STA   HOUR1
028D  EE 48 02                    INC   HOUR10
0290  C9 34              TENHRS   CMP   #$34            HOUR1 = 4?
0292  D0 0F                       BNE   EXIT
0294  AD 48 02                    LDA   HOUR10
0297  C9 32                       CMP   #$32            HOUR10 = 2?
0299  D0 08                       BNE   EXIT
029B  A9 30                       LDA   #$30            IF HRS=24, CLEAR TO 00.
029D  8D 49 02                    STA   HOUR1
02A0  8D 48 02                    STA   HOUR10
02A3  68                 EXIT     PLA                   RESTORE A.
02A4  40                          RTI
02A5                     COUNT
```

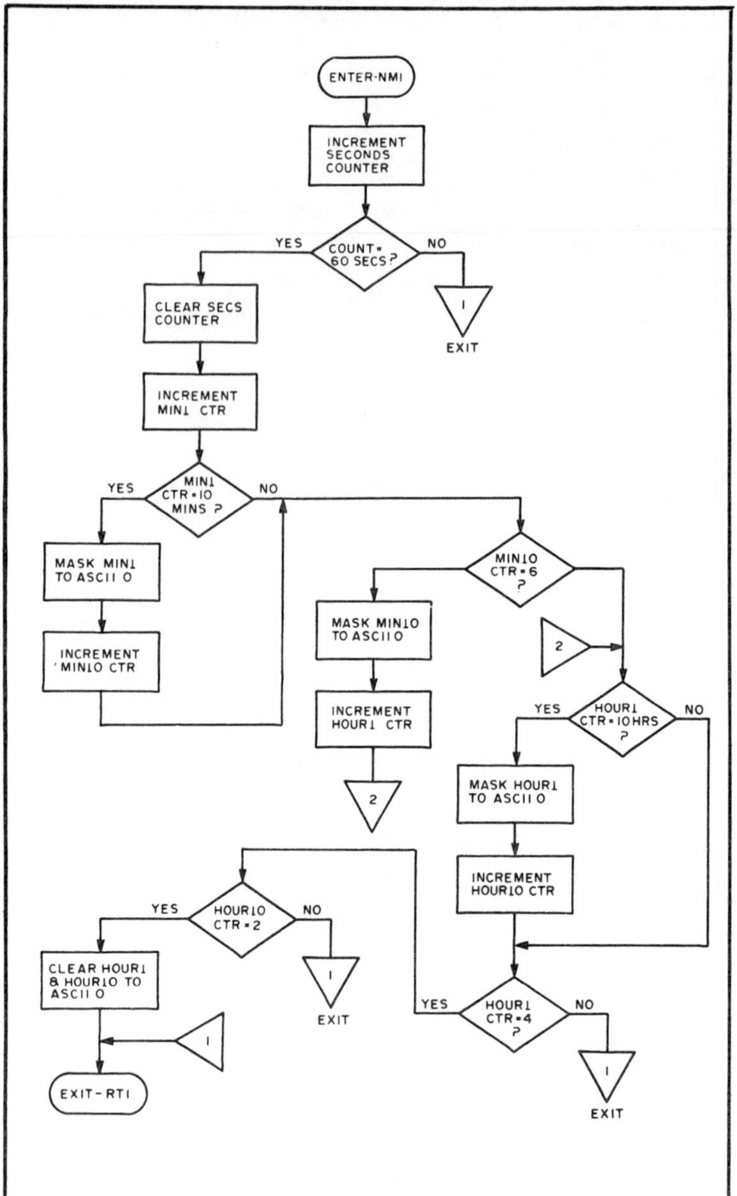

Fig. 7-2. Flowchart—NMI real-time clock routine.

The real-time clock has proved to be a real aid. It's foolproof and reliable, and its accuracy is as good as any digital clock I have used. If your microcomputer needs a clock, try this one.

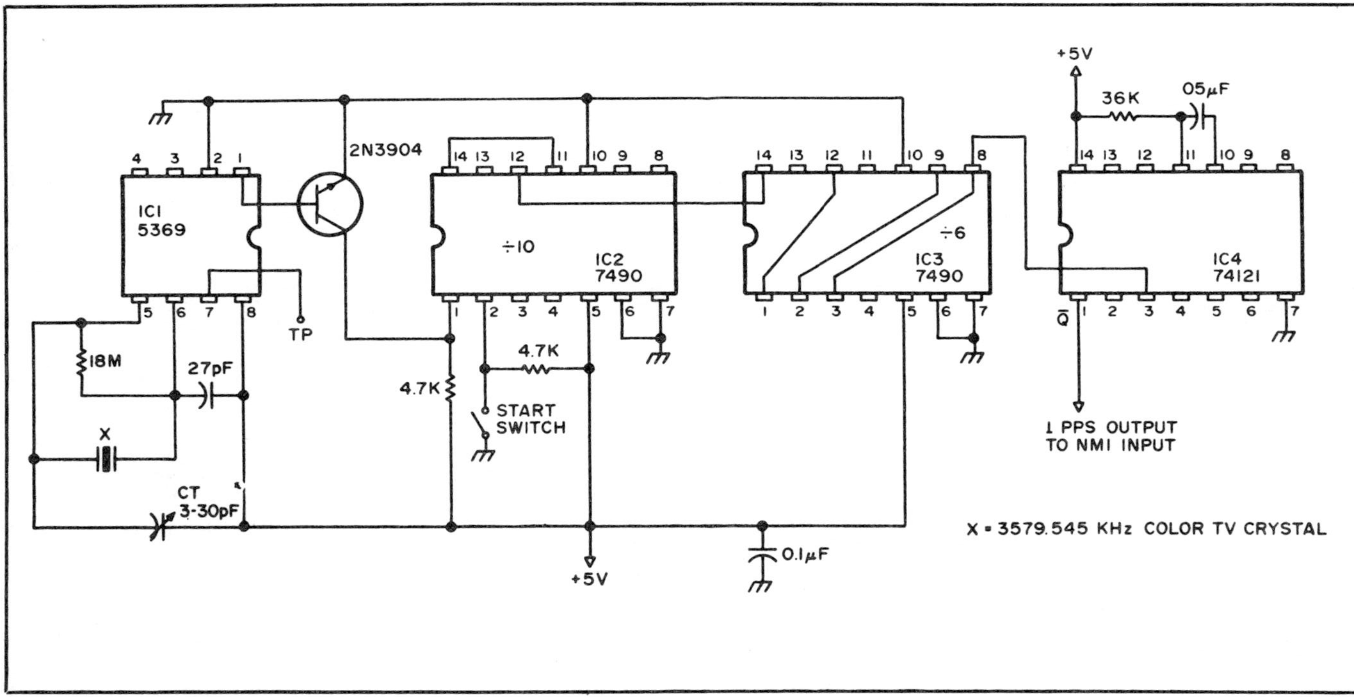

Fig. 7-3. Schematic diagram of the one PPS generator for the microprocessor real-time clock.

Table 7-2. KIM-1 (6502) Real-Time Clock Program.

```
0200  D8              START    CLD
0201  A9  50                   LDA    #$50      INITIALIZE NMI VECTOR
0203  8D  FA  17               STA    NMIV (LO)
0206  A9  02                   LDA    #$02
0208  8D  FB  17               STA    NMIV (HI)
020B  2C  40  17      WAIT     BIT    SAD (KIM)  LOOK FOR KBD START BIT.
020E  30  FB                   BMI    WAIT
0210  20  5A  1E               JSR    GETCH (KIM)  GET KBD CHAR.
0213  C9  03                   CMP    #$03      ETX=TIME UPDATE CTRL CHAR.
0215  D0  06                   BNE    RDTIME
0217  20  27  02               JSR    STTIME
021A  4C  0B  02               JMP    WAIT
021D  C9  05          RDTIME   CMP    #$05      ENQ=READ TIME CTRL CHAR.
021F  D0  EA                   BNE    WAIT
0221  20  3A  02               JSR    PRTIME
0224  4C  0B  02               JMP    WAIT
0227  A9  00          STTIME   LDA    #0
0229  8D  A5  02               STA    COUNT     RESET SECONDS COUNTER.
022C  A2  00                   LDX    #0
022E  20  5A  1E      TIMEIN   JSR    GETCH (KIM)
0231  9D  48  02               STA    HOUR10, X  STORE 4 DIGITS.
0234  E8                       INX
0235  E0  04                   CPX    #$04      =SIZE+1
0237  D0  F5                   BNE    TIMEIN
0239  60                       RTS
023A  A2  00          PRTIME   LDX    #0
023C  BD  48  02      PRSTR    LDA    HOUR10, X
023F  20  A0  1E               JSR    OUTCH (KIM)  PRINT CHAR.
0242  E8                       INX
0243  E0  08                   CPX    #$08      =SIZE+1
0245  D0  F5                   BNE    PRSTR
0247  60                       RTS

0248  30              HOUR10          0
0249  30              HOUR1           0
024A  30              MIN10           0
024B  30              MIN1            0
024C  20                              SPACE
024D  55                              U
024E  54                              T
```

```
024F  43                              C

                                      NON-MASKABLE INTERRUPT ROUTINE

0250  48          NMI       PHA                 SAVE A.
0251  EE A5 02              INC       COUNT
0254  AD A5 02              LDA       COUNT
0257  C9 3C                 CMP       #$3C      60 SECS?
0259  D0 48                 BNE       EXIT
025B  A9 00                 LDA       #0
025D  8D A5 02              STA       COUNT     RESET SECONDS COUNTER.
0260  EE 4B 02              INC       MIN1
0263  AD 4B 02              LDA       MIN1
0266  C9 3A                 CMP       #$3A      10 MINS?
0268  D0 08                 BNE       TENMIN
026A  29 30                 AND       #$30      MASK TO ASCII ZERO.
026C  8D 4B 02              STA       MIN1
026F  EE 4A 02              INC       MIN10
0272  AD 4A 02    TENMIN    LDA       MIN10
0275  C9 36                 CMP       #$36      60 MINS?
0277  D0 08                 BNE       ONEHR
0279  29 30                 AND       #$30
027B  8D 4A 02              STA       MIN10
027E  EE 49 02              INC       HOUR1
0281  AD 49 02    ONEHR     LDA       HOUR1
0284  C9 3A                 CMP       #$3A      10 HRS?
0286  D0 08                 BNE       TENHRS
0288  29 30                 AND       #$30
028A  8D 49 02              STA       HOUR1
028D  EE 48 02              INC       HOUR10
0290  C9 34       TENHRS    CMP       #$34      HOUR1 = 4?
0292  D0 0F                 BNE       EXIT
0294  AD 48 02              LDA       HOUR10
0297  C9 32                 CMP       #$32      HOUR10 = 2?
0299  D0 08                 BNE       EXIT
029B  A9 30                 LDA       #$30      IF HRS=24, CLEAR TO 00.
029D  8D 49 02              STA       HOUR1
02A0  8D 48 02              STA       HOUR10
02A3  68          EXIT      PLA                 RESTORE A.
02A4  40                    RTI
02A5              COUNT
```

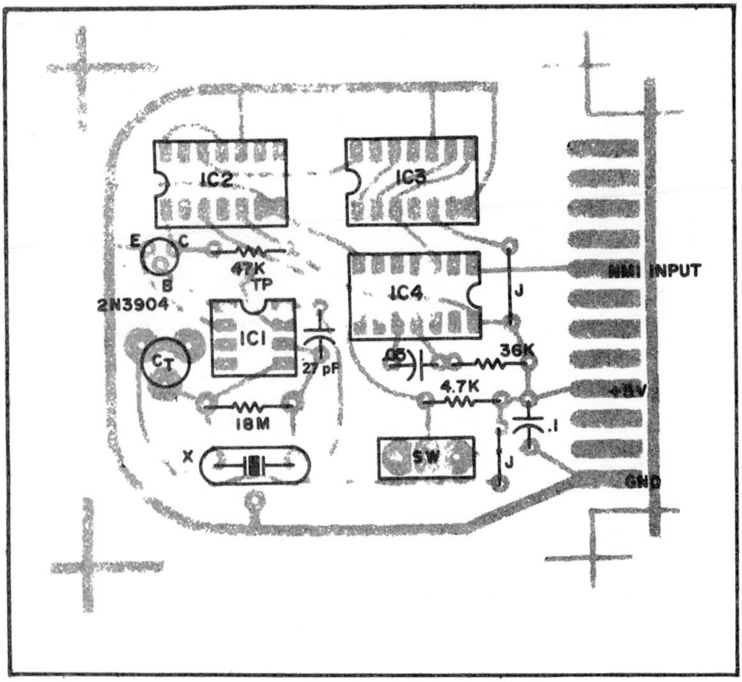

Fig. 7-4. PC board.

Computer-Controlled Thermometer

Browsing through the vast *treasure trove* of literature in our library, a very good article caught my eye. Entitled "How You Can Take Oscar's Temperature," this particular article described OSCAR 7's telemetry information, including formulas to decode the telemetry. After thinking for a bit, a little bug (actually a PROM memory keyer, I think) flew into my ear and said, "You could write a computer program for that!" So I did.

For the few who may not know, both OSCAR 6 and OSCAR 7 are alive, well and broadcasting their onboard Morse code telemetry, transmitting the ship's status to anyone who happens to be listening. So although this project describes the OSCAR 7 telemetry decoding, the same technique can be applied to OSCAR 6 (and future OSCARs) as well. OSCAR 7's telemetry during Mode A (2m/10m) is transmitted on 29.502 MHz. Thus, anyone with a low band receiver is capable of at least listening to the satellite and copying telemetry.

The telemetry itself consists of a cycle (called a *frame*) of 24 numbers divided into a pattern of six *lines*, and divided again into four

LINE #	1	2	3	4	5	6
Channel						
A	1——	2——	3——	4——	5——	6——
B	1——	2——	3——	4——	5——	6——
C	1——	2——	3——	4——	5——	6——
D	1——	2——	3——	4——	5——	6——

Fig. 7-5. Telemetry channels.

channels to each line. Channels are designated A, B, C and D. Thus, any specific number could be referred to as "channel 5C," or whatever (Fig. 7-5). Each number represents a different function or status of the ship. Coming from OSCAR, the telemetry might read like this: HI HI 114 127 143 195 218 223 262 . . . Notice the pattern of 1A, 1B, 1C, 1D, 2A, 2B, 2C, . . . The "HI HI" at the beginning merely separates each full frame of numbers—the telemetry transmits continuously.

The Program

Although the program is written in BASIC for a DEC PDP/11-45, I tried to keep the program straightforward enough to adapt to any of the other forms of BASIC floating around. It shouldn't take that much memory either. See Table 7-3 for the program listing.

A little explanation of the program seems to be in order. First of all, the "Date of Copy" and "Orbit #" inputs (lines 30 and 40) are for the operator's information and convenience only. I included them to keep the reception and orbital data straight for future reference, especially if the output is to a TTY or other hard copy device.

Another possible confusing feature is the request to delete the first number of each channel (line 80). The first digit in each channel—the line number (i.e., *123*. . . *215*. . . *367*. . . etc.)—is for reference only and is not involved in any calculation! So if you use the program as is, you would type "23, 41, 77 . . ." instead of "123, 141, 177 . . ." It's possible, of course, to delete that first number within the program, but for the sake of simplicity (and less hassle for the programmer, not to mention memory!), I chose to do it this way. Table 7-4 shows a sample run to illustrate the program operation (I used a "1" as the input in each case).

Since some of the formulas use the same math equation, instead of just retyping that same thing over and over again while putting in the program, I just stuck in the GOSUB statements for lines 9000 and 9500. Let the computer do the work. This is first demonstrated with the "+X Quadrant Current" statement. There are two separate formulas used repeatedly. The answers to *all* the equations will be in the units specified in the preceding PRINT statement. The usual abbreviations apply: milliamp = mA, milliwatt = mW, temperature in Celcius (later in the program, just "Cel"), etc. If you still don't quite understand the program operation, see the flowchart in Fig. 7-6 for help.

Bells and Whistles

Once you have the program running, it's kind of fun to see for yourself how OSCAR is doing up there. And, of course, you don't

Table 7-3. Program Listing.

```
LIST
OSCAR7     03:06 PM          11-FEB-77
10 PRINT"OSCAR-7 TELEMETRY DECODING PROGRAM"
20 REM BY MARK HERRO, WB9LSS
30 INPUT"TYPE DATE (GMT) OF COPY (DAY, MONTH, YEAR)";D,M,Y
40 INPUT"ORBIT #";O
50 DIM A(24)
60 REM 'A' CAN NOW HAVE 24 INPUTS
70 REM GET READY FOR INPUTS
80 PRINT"TYPE ONE NUMBER PER '?', DELETING THE FIRST NUMBER"
90 PRINT"OF THE THREE NUMBER SET (I. E. USE 23, 43, 77, 80. . ."
100 PRINT"INSTEAD OF 123, 143, 177, 180,. . .)"
110 FOR Y=1 TO 24
120 INPUT A(Y)
130 NEXT Y
140 REM ****DECODING MEAT****
150 PRINT"TOTAL SOLAR ARRAY CURRENT (MA)="
160 PRINT 29.5 * A(1)
170 PRINT"+X QUADRANT CURRENT (MA)="
180 REM LET N=A(2) THEN GOSUB TO RIGHT EQUATION
190 LET N=A(2)
200 GOSUB 9000
210 PRINT"-X QUAD. CURRENT (MA)="
220 LET N=A(3)
230 GOSUB 9000
240 PRINT"+Y QUAD. CURRENT (MA)="
250 LET N=A(4)
260 GOSUB 9000
270 PRINT"-Y QUAD. CURRENT (MA)="
280 LET N=A(5)
290 GOSUB 9000
300 REM SO MUCH FOR THE REPEATS FOR GOSUB 9000
310 PRINT"70/2 OUTPUT POWER (WATTS)="
320 REM IF INPUT IS '00' ODDS ARE 70/2 IS SHUT DOWN
330 PRINT 8*(1-.01*A(6))↑2
340 PRINT "SHIP TIME (HOURS)="
350 REM TIME INCREASES 1 INCREMENT EVERY 14 MINUTES
360 PRINT .253*A(7)
370 PRINT"BATTERY CHARGE/DISCHARGE CURRENT (MA)="
380 PRINT 40*(A(8)-50)
390 PRINT"BATT. VOLTAGE (VOLTS)="
400 PRINT .1*A(9)+6.4
410 REM I DONT KNOW WHY THEY PUT THIS NEXT ONE IN, BUT. . .
```

```
420 PRINT"ONE HALF BATT. VOLTAGE (VOLTS)="
430 PRINT .1*A(10)
440 PRINT"BATT. CHARGE REGULATOR #1 (VOLTS)="
450 PRINT .15*A(11)
460 PRINT"BATT. TEMPERATURE (CELCIUS)="
470 REM START SECOND SET OF REPEATED NUMBERS (9500)
480 LETN=A(12)
490 GOSUB 9500
500 PRINT"BASE PLATE TEMP. (CEL)="
510 LET N=A(13)
520 GOSUB 9500
530 PRINT"P.A. TEMP. 2/10 TRANSPONDER (CEL.)="
540 LET N=A(14)
550 GOSUB 9500
560 PRINT"+X FACET TEMP. (CEL.)="
570 LET N=A(15)
580 GOSUB 9500
590 PRINT"+Z FACET TEMP. (CEL.)="
600 LET N=A(16)
610 GOSUB 9500
620 PRINT"P.A. TEMP. 70/2 TRANSPONDER (CEL.)="
630 LET N=A(17)
640 GOSUB 9500
650 PRINT"P.A. EMITTER CURRENT 2/10 (MA)="
660 PRINT 11.67*A(18)
670 PRINT"TRANSPONDER MODULATOR TEMP. 70/2 (CEL.)="
680 LET N=A(19)
690 GOSUB 9500
700 REM END OF ALL THE REPEATED EQUATIONS
710 PRINT"INSTRUMENT SWITCHING REGULATOR CURRENT (MA)="
720 PRINT 11+.82*A(20)
730 PRINT"2/10 TRANSPONDER POWER OUT (MW)="
740 PRINT A(21)↑2/1.56
750 PRINT"435 MHZ BEACON POWER OUT (MW)="
760 PRINT .1*(A(22)↑2)+35
770 PRINT "2304 MHZ BEACON POWER OUT (MW)="
780 PRINT .041*(A(23)↑2)
790 PRINT"MIDRANGE TELEMETRY CALIBRATION (VOLTS)="
800 PRINT .01*A(24)
810 REM GOSUB EQUATIONS
820 GOTO 9700
9000 PRINT 1970-20*N
9100 RETURN
9500 PRINT 95.8-1.48*N
9600 RETURN
9700 END
```

continued on page 381

```
+X QUADRANT CURRENT (MA)=
 1950
-X QUAD. CURRENT (MA)=
 1950
+Y QUAD. CURRENT (MA)=
 1950
-Y QUAD. CURRENT (MA)=
 1950
70/2 OUTPUT POWER (WATTS)=
 7.8408
SHIP TIME (HOURS)=
 .253
BATTERY CHARGE/DISCHARGE CURRENT (MA)=
-1960
BATT. VOLTAGE (VOLTS)=
 6.5
ONE HALF BATT. VOLTAGE (VOLTS)=
 .1
BATT. CHARGE REGULATOR #1 (VOLTS)=
 .15
BATT. TEMPERATURE (CELCIUS)=
 94.32
BASE PLATE TEMP. (CEL)=
 94.32
P.A. TEMP. 2/10 TRANSPONDER (CEL.)=
 94.32
+X FACET TEMP. (CEL.)=
 94.32
+Z FACET TEMP. (CEL.)=
 94.32
P.A. TEMP. 70/2 TRANSPONDER (CEL.)=
 94.32
P.A. EMITTER CURRENT 2/10 (MA)=
 11.67
TRANSPONDER MODULATOR TEMP. 70/2 (CEL.)=
 94.32
INSTRUMENT SWITCHING REGULATOR CURRENT (MA)=
 11.82
2/10 TRANSPONDER POWER OUT (MW)=
 .641026
435 MHZ BEACON POWER OUT (MW)=
 35.1
2304 MHZ BEACON POWER OUT (MW)=
 .041
MIDRANGE TELEMETRY CALIBRATION (VOLTS)=
 .01

READY
```

Table 7-4. Program Sample Run.

```
READY

RUN
OSCAR7      03:14 PM              11-FEB-77
OSCAR-7 TELEMETRY DECODING PROGRAM
TYPE DATE (GMT) OF COPY (DAY, MONTH, YEAR)? 00,00,00
ORBIT #? 00000
TYPE ONE NUMBER PER '?', DELETING THE FIRST NUMBER
OF THE THREE NUMBER SET (I. E. USE 23, 43, 77, 80. . .
INSTEAD OF 123, 143, 177, 180,. . .)
? 1                          TEST
? 1
? 1
? 1
? 1
? 1
? 1
? 1
? 1
? 1
? 1
? 1
? 1
? 1
? 1
? 1
? 1
? 1
? 1
? 1
? 1
? 1
? 1
? 1
TOTAL SOLAR ARRAY CURRENT (MA)=
 29.5
```

have to stop where the program ends; there are a number of possible modifications. Subtracting out the first number of the channel by the program is one thing, as I said earlier. Or you could try to just calculate one number out of a whole frame. If you really wanted to go all out, you could try getting your system to take the telemetry Morse code off the air (adjusting for the Doppler shift), decode the information and print it out at the same time!!

With a minimum of time and effort, it wouldn't be hard to "take OSCAR's temperature" the easy way. If you have a hard copy printout, all the better. You might even try taking a long-term survey of the satellite's performance by saving the information you collect

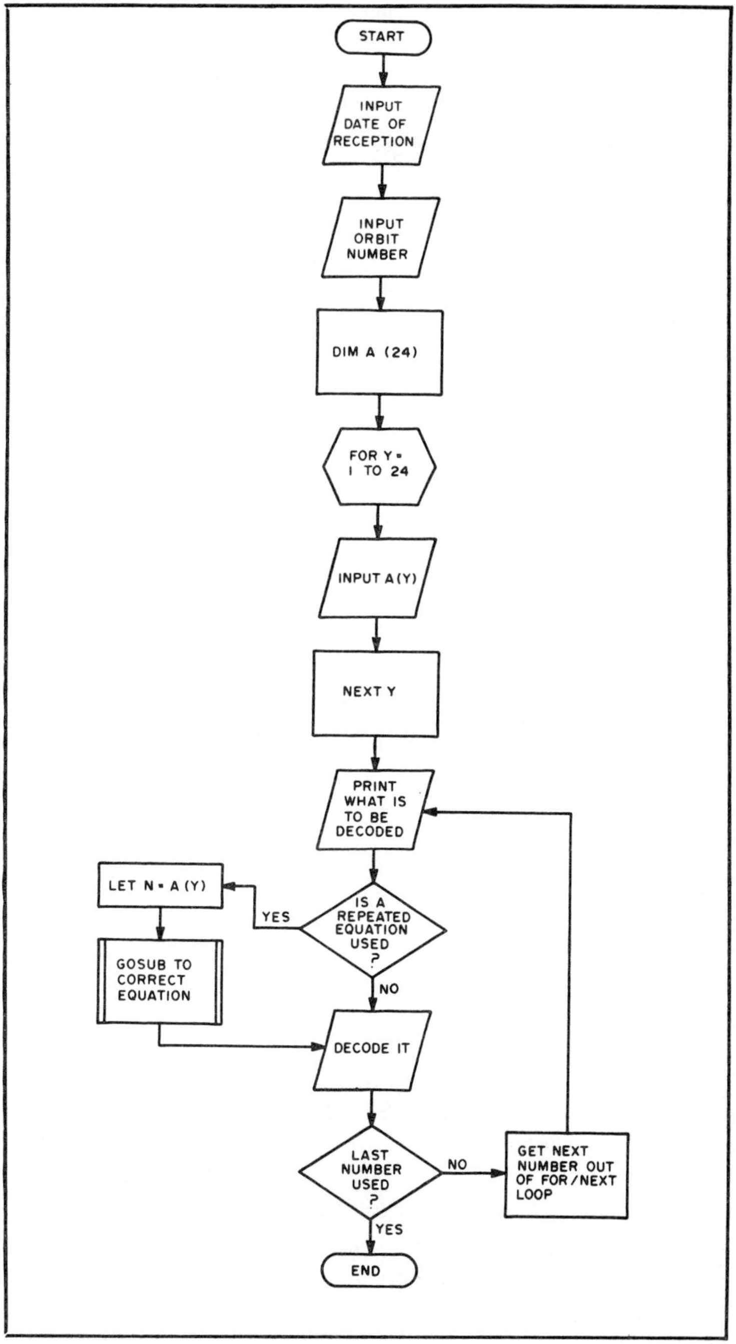

Fig. 7-6. Program flowchart.

for a time, then graphing the data with your new graphics system! Don't forget AMSAT; I'm sure they would be interested, too.

Now, after you have all that set up, try checking into OSCAR 9's telemetry. That'll have 128 channels when it is launched.

Winning the Name Game

Would you like to have a fantastic memory with everyone's name on the tip of your tongue (keyboard)? Whether you are running for office, trying to borrow equipment or just want to appear to be on the ball, this program will fill that need.

The number of newcomers appearing on the repeater scene increases every day. It is extremely difficult to remember everyone's name. Using my program, all you have to do is type in the call of the operator. The computer supplies you with his call and his name. A small piece of information can be included if you so desire.

I wrote this program using SWTPC 8K BASIC to run on my 6800-based machine (Tables 7-5 and 7-6). Southwest BASIC reserves 32 bytes for a string variable. This would allow 6 bytes for the call and 1 byte for a space. This leaves 25 spaces (bytes) available for the operator's name and a key word of information pertaining to that particular operator. If your memory is small, you might consider limiting the length of the string variables by adding DIM statements.

String variables in Southwest BASIC may be named any single alphabetic character or a subscripted letter. The subscripts permitted are 0 through 9 only.

When adapting my program for your own use, be sure to keep some type of line number organization to avoid confusion when adding new calls to memory. Assuming you are using the program for local 2 meter operation data, the call area will probably be the same for the majority of the entries. Therefore, concentrate on the last three letters of the operator's call. In my program, I assigned the line numbers as follows: 100-190 to the calls whose last three (or two as the case may be) letters begin with the letter A, 200-290 to those whose last three letters begin with the letter B and so on through the rest of the alphabet. Those amateur calls contained in statement line 100-190 would be assigned the string variables A$(0) through A$(9). Those in lines 200-290 (beginning with B) would be assigned B$(0) through B$(9) and so on. Line 9000 is inserted as a slight delay loop.

Morrow's Marvelous Monitor

One of the finest, though unheralded, microprocessor boards on the market today is the George Morrow CPU/front panel board,

Table 7-5. Program Listing.

```
10 REM ** 3 X 5 CARD UPDATE **
20 REM ** AMATEUR RADIO NAME DIRECTORY **
30 PRINT "ENTER THE AMATEUR CALL ";
40 INPUT C$
100 LET A$(1) = "WA3AOQ  BILL"
101 IF C$ = LEFT$(A$(1),6)  PRINT A$(1)
200 LET B$(1) = "K3BD  MIKE"
201 IF C$ = LEFT$(B$(1),4)  PRINT B$(1)
300 LET C$(1) = "K3CHD  DON"
301 IF C$ = LEFT$(C$(1),5)  PRINT C$(1)
400 LET D$(1) = "WB3DHB  PHIL"
401 IF C$ = LEFT$(D$(1),6)  PRINT D$(1)
500 LET E$(1) = "WA3ENU  RICH"
501 IF C$ = LEFT$(E$(1),6) PRINT E$(1)
 . . .
 . . .
900 LET I$(1) = "K3IXB  JOHN"
901 IF C$ = LEFT$(I$(1),5)  PRINT I$(1)
 . . .
 . . .
2500 LET Z$(1) = "W3ZCO  KEN"
2501 IF C$ = LEFT$(Z$(1),5)  PRINT Z$(1)
9000 FOR D = 1 TO 50
9010 NEXT D
9020 PRINT
9030 PRINT
9040 PRINT
9050 GOTO 30
```

Table 7-6. Sample Run.

```
READY
#RUN

ENTER THE AMATEUR CALL ? K3IXB

K3IXB  JOHN


ENTER THE AMATEUR CALL ?
```

known as the "Sigma 100." It is being sold directly from Morrow's Micro-Stuff or through dealers around the country. Although it is being advertised innocently enough as a replacement front panel for the Altair or Imsai computers, it does far more than any other CPU system currently being offered. The Morrow board also comprises the brains of the Equinox 100 computer system from Parasitic Engineering.

I first discovered the early version of the board in late 1976, when a friend of mine (computer freak of magnitude 9.9) called my attention to a miniscule ad George Morrow was running which offered a computer board at a ridiculous price. I hustled off a check, figuring at the time that, if computers turned out to be a great hobby, I would soon have a roomful of blinking LEDs (which I now have).

My previous experience in computers was a frustrating FORTRAN course, watching my friend's toggle-switch acrobatics on an Altair, and articles in magazines that I didn't understand. I just plowed ahead and decided to learn as I went. There's a first lesson for beginners here—go ahead, even if you aren't sure that you know what you're doing.

I received my Morrow CPU board in a week. This is a fully-debugged working production model. There's no waiting months until the company gets into production and works out glitches. This is an important point because you see a lot of neat things advertised which aren't being shipped.

The Morrow board itself is a nicely laid out double-sided job. Assembly is straightforward. Stick sockets in, solder and it works.

Then comes the problem: What do you do with a computer when you don't know anything about computers? First of all, you need a power supply, case and mother board with sockets to give the CPU board a home. You can get the works from Parasitic Engineering in their Equinox 100. In addition to what I would best describe as a *moose power supply* (it powers 18 card slots—your money will run out before this power supply will), the Equinox has a specially designed mother board, also from George Morrow.

Next, you need some memory. There's another lesson here for beginners. Pick a CPU that is compatible with your friends', or pick friends who have CPUs and mother boards like yours. That way, you can borrow a board or two of memory when you want to run some large program that uses up memory. You can also swap boards for debugging, at your own risk, of course!

After the memory is in and the power on, you begin tinkering with the keys on the front panel to see what happens. George doesn't swamp you with information, but you do get basic instructions and a little program which makes the seven-segment LEDs count. It helps familiarize you with the operation. The board's operation is so simple that, in about an hour, I had figured out basically what was happening inside the computer. The normal reaction is, "Why aren't all computers designed like this?"

The control of the Morrow panel is set up in a perfectly rational way, so, if you can operate a pocket calculator, you can work a Morrow computer. You don't have to know anything about status lights, memory protect, machine cycles, or nitty-gritty computer design to get going. There's no binary conversion, no flashing lights. The only switch on the board is a reset switch, which sort of sends everything back to home when you mess up the program. There are 12 keys for control functions and 10 LED seven-segment readouts to tell you what's going on.

How Does It Work?

Basically, the Morrow front panel/CPU works like this: There is a combination hardware-software called *firmware* which controls operation of the CPU and does all the work supervising the computer operation. In the normal *run* mode, the CPU will go full speed just like anybody else's 8080 CPU. But now comes the neat part. You can execute the program just one step at a time *single stepping* or let the front panel step through it at any rate you want (*slow stepping*) I will discuss this in detail later. You can also put a *halt* instruction in the program, and the front panel program will stop your program so that you can see what happened so far. Then you can continue from that point, at any speed from single step to full run. Normally, when an 8080 CPU reads a halt instruction, it stops dead in its tracks, and you have to reset the whole works to get going again. Morrow's halt just pauses the program and leaves all the registers, memory, etc., alone, so you can continue from that point on. Now the halt instruction is a truly useful programming aid. Programs can be run in sections to help isolate the bugs more easily.

In addition to the regular speed of operation, the Morrow CPU panel has four modes of operation at stepping speeds. The firmware program lets your program execute just one step, and then it takes over and displays to you what you want to see. You can select the program counter where you look at the memory location and data, any register or pair, any port location or watch one memory location. You select whether it will execute just one step at a time or automatically step through your program.

Pressing the *M* key will run the CPU normally, and the front panel will be in control for halts but will not display any data. The CPU simply runs too fast for any practical monitoring of data in this manner. Pressing *S* will stop the program, and the front panel program will be completely in command. Pressing *S* while the front panel program is in operation will single step your program.

Pressing the *O* and then *M* keys is the normal mode which examines each memory location as the program is stepped. The six LED digits on the left tell you what memory location you are seeing—the first location is 000,000 (octal), then 000,001, etc., on up to 377,377, the last location in memory. The right three digits tell you what is in the memory location displayed. In Fig. 7-7, you see that at location 000,100, there is a 303, which would be executed as a jump instruction. Since this instruction requires two more bytes following for the address, you can press *E* and the next memory location will be displayed (in the example, 000,101 would be displayed) along with the data in that location. Pressing *E* again will display the next location (000,102) and so on. To examine any memory location, enter the location and press *E*. To deposit new data at any memory location, first examine the location (enter the location and press *E*), then enter the data (which might be an instruction or a data byte) and press *D*. If you press *D* again, the same data will be deposited in the next memory location also. It is not necessary to examine each location before depositing data. Each time you deposit data, the memory location will advance to the next location. Thus a long program can be entered in a reasonable amount of time.

The next mode is the register mode. To enter, press the *1* and then *M* keys. Two digits on the left indicate which of the 8080 registers is displayed. The three or six (depending on whether it is a 16-bit pair or an 8-bit register) digits on the right indicate what is in the register. In Fig. 7-7, you are looking at register 15, the program counter. The next location that will be executed is 010,020. You can

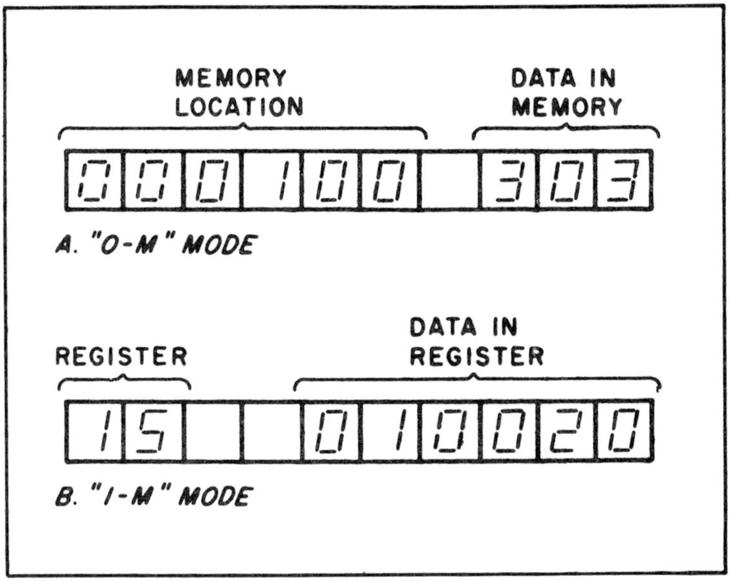

Fig. 7-7. Memory Information.

examine a register and deposit data just like the memory locations. As you single or slow step through a program, you can watch a selected register or pair change. This is an extremely valuable tool in debugging programs. In most computers, it takes an elaborate *trace program* to perform this function.

Since the accumulator (register A) is a standard register, you can watch the accumulator in the register mode. If you are building an interface to the outside world (such as a keyboard), this function can be useful in determining whether a problem lies in the interface circuit or in your computer program. If you aren't getting data into the accumulator, the interface circuit isn't working. If data is getting into the accumulator register, your program is at fault.

In another mode, the *2-M mode*, input ports may be examined and data may be outputted. During any part of your program, while the program is halted and the front panel is in control, data may be sent to any port, just as if you had written a section of computer program which moves data to an output port. For example, if you have just built a device connected to the computer's output port which turns on relays and you want to test the relay interface circuits, you would enter the port mode and then examine the port your relays are connected to. By depositing data into that port, you could see if the relays are turned on or not. Again, you can isolate any problems to the computer program, the device interface circuit or the device itself. As another example, say you've built an analog-to-digital converter board which takes analog values (voltages) and converts them to a digital number. By examining the A/D input port, you can determine if the board is working. By slow stepping a program which inputs the ports, you can watch the values change.

The final mode is the *3-M mode*, which watches a particular memory location. The display looks the same as the *0-M mode*, where the left six digits represent the memory location and the right three represent the data. As the program is stepped through, the memory location will not change in the *3-M mode*, but, if different data is put into the memory location, it will be displayed.

By now, you may have noticed that the Morrow front panel/CPU bears a resemblance to the *trainers* which use similar LED schemes and to the new Heath 8080 computer machine. It should be noted that the Morrow board is the only one with a selectable slowstep rate and with the *controlled halt* which does not require a CPU reset and lose all of the program information. The stepping rate of the slow step is determined by entering a value and then pressing *S*. Entering *1* and then *S* runs the program very fast—it's good for clearing memory areas quickly—and entering *100* and then *S* will execute your program at about one step per second.

An additional plus for the Morrow board is the S-100 bus. There's complete compatibility with the dozens and dozens of other computer boards on the market. The system is totally upward compatible, meaning that, as you begin to squander more and more money on computers, you can use all that you have purchased so far. You might think that 18 slots in the Equinox computer are a lot, but just wait!

It doesn't take long to realize that there's more to a computer than just getting the CPU board and power supply. You need memory and interface boards if you want to communicate with the machine via a keyboard and look at the results on a TV screen. That translates into money. Fortunately, the Morrow board allows you to use all 10 LED readouts and 11 of the keys as input/output ports. When the firmware program is not using them, i.e., when the *M* key is pressed and the CPU is going full blast, you can display any segments of the readouts and input information from the keys. The *S* key is not usable, however, since pressing it anytime stops your programming. You cannot use the readouts or keys during any slow-step mode, since they are dedicated to the firmware program at this time. Still, the keys and readouts do provide at least something. You can devise a frequency counter and use the readouts for frequency display, write a clock program which keeps time (none of this $9.95 stuff), or put input data into the readouts to give you a visual indicator that data is being received.

The LED displays are simply memory locations beginning at 377,000. The eight data lines drive each segment of an LED. By depositing a 117 octal the segments forming a *3* will turn on. With help from Morrow's instructions, you can easily make the readouts count. Remember that, when the front panel program takes over, all the information in the LEDs is lost, so the information needs to be stored at another location.

The keypad is I/O ports 376 and 377. As a key is pressed, a latch is set so that you can input any data combinations from the keys. It's a little bit cumbersome but still better than toggle switches.

Now that you've looked at some of the features of the Morrow CPU board, I will briefly describe several applications for which this computer is ideally suited. The first, and most obvious, is the educational value of seeing what is going on inside a computer as the program is running. Students can easily enter machine language programs (in octal) and then run and debug the programs. As the student becomes more and more proficient, additional boards—memory, analog/digital, interface, etc.—can be plugged in to make the system more sophisticated. I have found that, within the educational realm, the Morrow board is uniquely suited for students to learn computer control applications, beginning with simple programs for simple control applications and progressing into more and more complicated programs. Since data can be read from the LED displays and program parameters changed through the front panel keys, external displays such as CRTs need not be used. This is particularly nice if the computer is going to be used in a laboratory situation, such as machine control, where heat or vibration might cause a TV screen some problems.

George Morrow, in his design of this CPU/front panel board, has pretty well covered all bases. It is a simple-to-operate board for beginners, a sophisticated supervisory-control firmware program for programming and debugging and has complete compatibility with the currently popular S-100 bus structure. Parasitic Engineering, with the rugged power supply and cabinet to house the Morrow board, provides the complementary components for the base for any degree of sophistication.

The North Star Disk

How would you like to be able to turn your system off at night, come back the next morning, flip two or three switches and be running complex BASIC programs in 15 seconds? There are several ways of accomplishing this, ranging from keeping a BASIC interpreter in PROM and files on tape to buying a powerful disk drive and controller.

Commercial computers have used a number of interesting schemes to accomplish an *autoload*—Eniac used a large switch panel organized as memory words. Early Control Data computers used spinning cams to close switches and load data words into memory. Recent modern minicomputers have made good use of direct storage access disk systems to take over the memory system and stuff a bootstrap program from the first sector of a disk to the first few memory locations.

Most of these methods, however, have been too complicated and expensive for home use. But there is at least one happy exception to this trend—the North Star Micro-Disk System. For about $700 (the cost of three disk packs on a large mainframe system), you can have the kind of performance described above.

The North Star Micro-Disk System is similar to other floppy disk systems in many respects, but the price was kept at a minimum by eliminating some of the frills without making major sacrifices in performance. Incidentally, some of these frills have also been eliminated by other manufacturers without comparable price reductions.

One of the differences between the North Star system and more conventional floppy systems is the use of a minifloppy drive instead of a full-sized drive. This decreases the total amount of data that can be saved on a disk. The mini-floppy drive can store 89.6 kilobytes of information as formatted by the North Star controller. Also, this is not a direct storage access device. It uses a memory-mapped I/O system similar to the kind of input/output commonly used in a 6800 microprocessor system. This is, however, still much faster than most tape systems that could be purchased on an experimenter's budget. The North Star minifloppy format is somewhat less capable of storing large amounts of data than other minifloppy systems which utilize double or quad density data packing. Still, 89.6 kilobytes leave sufficient room for a great many programs on a single diskette, and swapping diskettes takes just 5 or 10 seconds. Also, lower data density may result in higher data integrity.

There are four main components in the North Star disk system: the drive, the controller, the disk operating software and the BASIC interpreter. Let's examine them one at a time.

The Disk Drive

North Star uses the Shugart SA400 minifloppy diskette storage drive. This is good news for the experimenter because Shugart is one of the major names in floppy disk technology, and many of the parts (notably the read/write head) have similar or identical counterparts with the very successful SA800 drive. The drive is solidly built and appears very rugged. Most of my disk drive experience has been with huge capacity rigid disks, and I was surprised to notice that there are no provisions for alignment of the minifloppy. I was assured by the technicians at North Star that there have been no problems with diskette interchangeability since one of the recent modifications to their controller board, but I had a great deal of trouble reading the diskette originally shipped to me (containing the disk operating system and BASIC). I took it to my distributor, and he had similar troubles reading it. Autoloading from it took about 20 minutes because so many repeats were necessary due to errors detected with the cyclic redundancy checking software. As it turned out, I can reliably read the diskettes I write, my distributor can read the diskettes he writes, but we can't read each other's diskettes very well and neither of us had much luck reading what came from North Star.

The diskette is hard sectored for 10 sectors per track and 35 tracks per disk, with the first 4 sectors dedicated to the file directory. Two hundred fifty-six bytes of data storage are available on each sector, and a preamble of 16 bytes of zeros and a special sync character precedes the data. The data is followed by one check byte. This format differs somewhat from that used by large-capacity rigid disk drive manufacturers in that it does not allow address verification. This is an interesting area of sacrifice. Many large-disk systems verify the disk address after every seek to make sure the drive has gone to the correct track and sector. Floppy systems do not do this. It has caused no problem in my system and is an example of eliminating the icing while preserving the cake. I think it is worth it for a hobbyist or small business, but, for a big business whose file entries represent thousands or millions of dollars, it may be a serious drawback.

The diskette may be write protected with a piece of masking tape folded over a cutout in the cardboard carrier. When protected, the drive will not write even if (erroneously) told to do so by the disk controller.

The drive comes without a cabinet, but my distributor didn't charge me for one of the pretty (blue) jobs. Incidentally, there is room inside that little box for a small power supply, too, and, even though I didn't pay the $40 they wanted for it, they shipped me the PC board and regulators anyway, so I could tap into the unregulated power from my computer. I was pleasantly surprised at that, but it got me into some trouble later. The +12-volt supply draws a lot of current when the motor starts up, and I had to beef it up before the drive would run reliably.

I was also impressed by the head-seeking mechanism. They have used a stepper motor to spin a disk in small increments. The disk has a spiral groove in it, and what looks like a ball bearing rides this spiral in and out, pushing the head carriage mechanism toward or away from the center of the disk. On long seeks, you can hear the stepped motor make a fluttering sound at each track. Track-to-track access is advertised at 40 milliseconds, which means a 35-track seek will take about 1.4 seconds.

North Star charges about $400 for this disk drive, but, if you order directly from the factory, you can get it for about $355.

The Disk Controller

The disk controller is implemented on a single S-100 compatible PC board which has been silk-screened and solder-masked to increase ease of assembly. Sockets are included for every IC, and, if my experience is typical, it is a good idea. Even though I never had to replace parts, I swapped a lot of them around in order to test them because of timing problems I had.

They used a lot of clever unorthodox hardware tricks on this board. For example, their use of memory-mapped I/O, rather than standard 8080 I/O ports, surprised me. The disk controller looks like a 1K block of variable speed read only memory to the system software, with each disk command decoded not from data sent out from the accumulator, but from the contents of the address bus. Status and disk data are given to the CPU on the memory data in lines as if the data were retrieved from system ROM, and, when data is not available as fast as the CPU wants it, *wait* states are introduced exactly as if the CPU were waiting for slow memory. This scheme does not tie up any of the 256 input or output ports of the 8080, but it does use 1K of address space starting at address E000 in the standard version. North Star may have saved a little money with this method because they don't have to decode the data out lines, but I think there were other reasons for their choice of memory-mapped I/O. It may be possible to use the North Star controller with a minimum of modifications in a 6800 or similar system because of this choice.

Incidentally, I was able to use the North Star controller concurrently with a Godbout 8K PROM board with both addressed at E000, but with the PROMs of the Godbout board removed from E000 to EFFF. Software package 1 owners, take note.

Note a few other interesting hardware tricks. There are three PROMs on the board; two are conventional program storage devices for bootstrap and low-level disk routines, and the third sits on the upper eight address lines to decode board selection, bootstrap PROM selection, status requests or the availability of a byte of data to be written on the disk. There is also an on-board clock instead of an attempt to use the 8080 system clock. This may be due to the current trend of using the Z-80 and other microprocessors with different clock speeds. Also, the engineers at North Star have allowed the option of using XRDY instead of PRDY to sychronize CPU speed with memory speed.

The other functions implemented by hardware are: Sync byte detection is directly decoded from the disk and presented as a status flag to the CPU, and a power-on clear eliminates the necessity of resetting the board at turn-on time. (I wish my memory boards had this feature; most of the 15 seconds it takes to autoload are spent unprotecting RAM.)

A function not implemented by hardware is error checking. Most disk systems use hardware to do a cyclic redundancy check or an error correction code. North Star does a CRC in software. Also, address marks are conventionally written on a disk by the controlling hardware and verified at seek time. This is not done in the North Star system, as previously mentioned.

I found a couple of problems with the disk controller. First, current-model PC boards (#MDC A-2) need a modification which requires cutting a run and adding a jumper. This is documented in an errata sheet included with the kit. Unfortunately for me, this didn't solve all my problems. I found my board was sometimes unable to set a flip-flop used to inform the CPU of *write status*, and the software would just hang in a loop waiting for it. I spent many hours with a scope trying to make this problem go away and finally suceeded by making a minor modification to the PC board. I discussed this with North Star and they were very alarmed, claiming that no one else has ever had a similar problem and that I probably have a bad chip.

The Disk Operating System

I think this is one of the real strengths of the North Star system. It provides the ability to load, save, execute or access files by name or disk location. Names may be up to eight characters long. Up to 256 different file types may be defined, and four are predefined with the system. They are:

Table 7-7. Commands.

1.	L1	List the disk directory of the optionally specified drive. The following information is returned: file names, lengths, starting addresses, and types.
2.	CR	Create a new file. CRT specifies name, length, and optional starting disk address.
3.	DE	Delete a file.
4.	CO	Compact file space, eliminating blank areas.
5.	TY	Change the type of a file.
6.	GO	Load and execute a type 1 file.
7.	GA	Set the "go address" of a type 1 file.
8.	JP	Jump to the address specified in HEX from the CRT
9.	LF	Load a file to RAM.
10.	SF	Save a file from RAM.
11.	CF	Copy a file (same or different disk, different names).
12.	CD	Copy an entire diskette (multiple drive systems).
13.	RD	Read a # of blocks from disk to RAM.
14.	WR	Write a # of blocks from RAM to disk.
15.	IN	Initialize a new diskette.
16.	DT	Drive test: writes a changing pattern all over the diskette, then reads and checks it. This is useful for checking a diskette for bad spots.

- Type 0: Default type. All files are type 0 until explicitly changed.
- Type 1: Machine language (executable) program.
- Type 2: BASIC program. Can be loaded or saved from BASIC.
- Type 3: BASIC data file. Can be read or written by BASIC.

Interfacing with system hardware is provided by a good documentation package and memory space for the user to write his or her own I/O and initialization routines. The guidelines provided are thorough, and I have seen the DOS successfully interfaced to a POLY-88, a 3P+S, and a line printer with relative ease.

There are 16 commands available from the CRT. Most of them specify the file name, and some also specify drive number (1 to 3), disk addresses, RAM addresses and number of sectors to be operated upon. These commands are shown in Table 7-7.

I am so pleased with the DOS that it is hard to specify a weakness of any kind. But it would be very nice to have the ability to flag and skip over bad tracks on a diskette. I really don't know if this should be called a weakness of the DOS or of the controller hardware, but it would certainly be helpful.

North Star BASIC

I am also quite pleased with North Star's implementation of BASIC. It is much better than the 5K version I had been using, even though it uses 10K of RAM to do it.

I have noticed that it is much slower at number crunching than I had expected, but it calculates eight significant digits instead of the more common six, and the slower speed is probably a good marketing strategy for North Star, whose second major product is a hardware floating point board designed to speed up number crunching.

As shipped from the factory, North Star BASIC expects to find 16K of RAM starting at address 2000 hex. It does not overwrite the disk operating system, although some commands of the DOS bomb BASIC. (It's a small loss when it only takes 5 seconds to reload.) BASIC uses the upper 4K (approximately) for program storage, and documentation is provided for expanding or moving the program storage space.

Major strengths of the BASIC package are shown in Table 7-8. Additionally, all of the standard features you'd expect to find in a good BASIC package are available with North Star BASIC.

As for its weaknesses, once again, it is hard to criticize a package as sophisticated as this one, especially at this price. Less capable BASIC interpreters have been sold for thousands of dollars with no hardware and very little documentation provided.

For a price which I considered very reasonable, I recently received from the factory a software update on a diskette. This time I was able to read the diskette perfectly. Included are ARCTANGENT and CHAIN, the latter allowing one BASIC program to call and execute another BASIC program from the disk. I consider this an indication that they intend to give good support to this product.

Table 7-8. BASIC Package Strengths.

1. A line editor which has several commands for copying or changing portions of old lines.
2. Formatted output similar to FORTRAN.
3. Multiple-line user-defined functions.
4. String and substring manipulation.
5. Boolean operators: and, or, not.
6. Memory examine and fill (decimal memory values).
7. 8080 in and out capabilities.
8. Machine language subroutine calling with interface to DE and HL register pairs.
9. # of bytes of program storage remaining can be calculated.
10. Natural logs and antilogs.
11. Random and sequential disk file accessing.
12. Trigonometry (sine and cosine only).
13. Multiple dimensioned arrays.
14. Renumber.

Overall, I am very pleased with the North Star disk system. I am convinced that, dollar for dollar, it is the best investment to be had in the area of mass storage for computers today. Extra bonuses are the great disk operating system and the good implementation of BASIC.

Nevertheless, it is a big project. I have built each part of my system from the ground up, and this has been, by a big margin, the most difficult of all, including home brewing my own CPU from Altair PC boards and home brew components,cabinet, power supply, back plane, etc.

I recommend to those of you interested in buying this product that, if you don't have a solid background in hardware and access to a good dual-channel oscilloscope, buy it assembled and tested. It may have been just bad luck on my part, but, even though I never had to replace a bad component or redo a connection, it still took me almost two weeks to get it running flawlessly.

Timing Diagrams

A timing diagram is one of several road maps for digital circuits. Aside from providing us with a picture of what a waveform should look like at the output of a circuit, it can also tell us the exact conditions which exist within a circuit for any particular instant in time. The latter can be very helpful information when troubleshooting a circuit. Being able to generate a timing diagram to the point of determining what the output waveform looks like is a useful tool in analyzing and learning digital circuits.

We're going to be discussing timing diagrams from two different angles. First, we're going to take a look at some of the fundamentals and techniques involved in *generating* a timing diagram. Secondly, we're going to examine a couple of manufacturers' diagrams and discuss the *intepretation* of same.

A Basic Timing Diagram

Figure 7-8 illustrates the fundamentals of a simple timing diagram. Perhaps one of the first things worth pointing out is the desirability of using *graph paper*. This will help you establish a time reference (by assigning a time period for each division) and certainly help in keeping events lined up vertically, which is one of the objectives.

The arrow at the bottom of the diagram indicates *time* is going from left to right. It's the only way to go. There aren't many things as

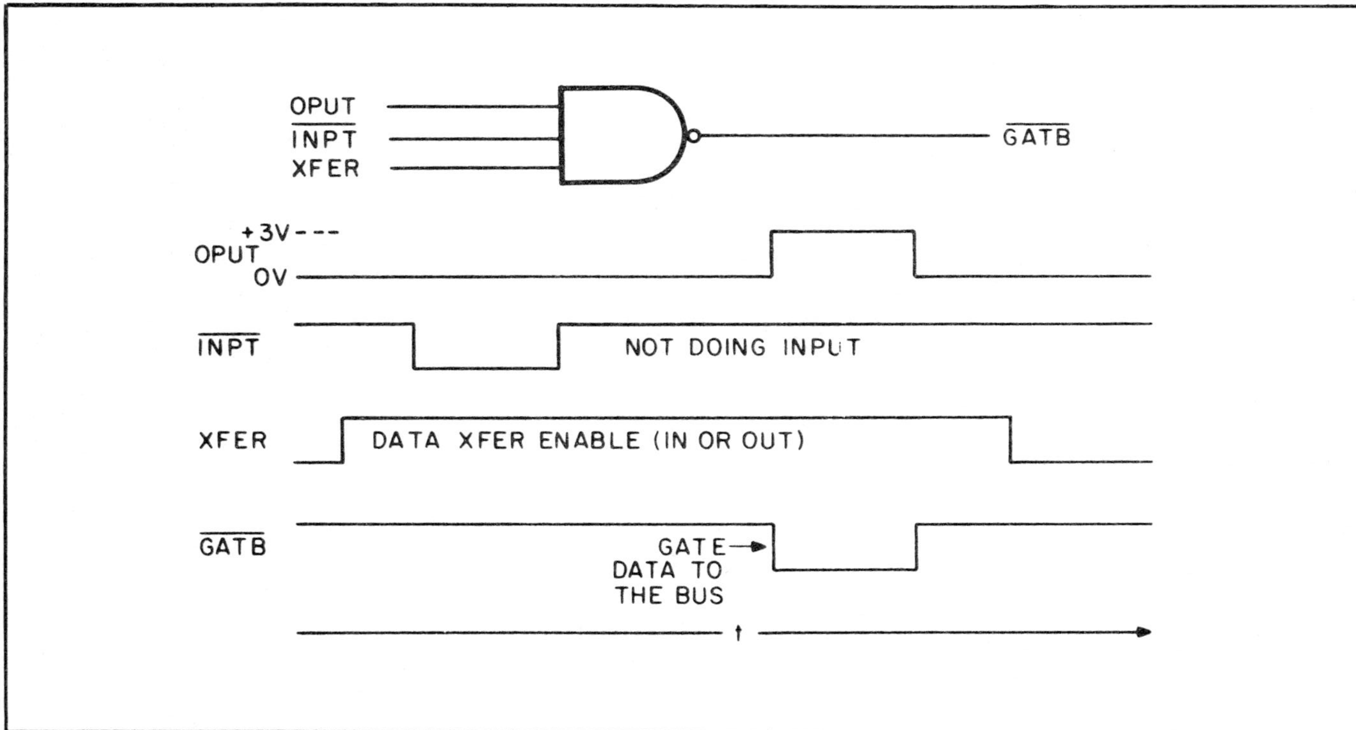

Fig. 7-8. A simple timing diagram illustrating the output of a 3-input NAND gate.

confusing as trying to use a timing diagram drawn the other way. (Keep in mind that an oscilloscope display is also from left to right with respect to time.)

The diagram illustrates the inputs and outputs of a 3-input NAND gate. Assuming we had the three input signals down on paper our next step would be to generate the output. Remembering the rules for a NAND gate (that is, the output will go low only when all of the inputs are high), we begin examining the input signals from the left. As long as any of the inputs are low, the output will remain high. And, as you can see, the output drops low when all three are high. Signal OPUT ("OUTPUT") is high, indicating an output function is to be performed. $\overline{\text{INPT}}$ ("INPUT " NOT) is high, indicating, an input function is not currently being done. And, XFER ("Transfer") goes high to enable the data transfer. The output signal, $\overline{\text{GATB}}$, ("Gate to Bus" NOT) is low when we're gating data to the bus.

One more point before leaving this basic diagram. Notice the comments. Now, it doesn't matter if you put comments with the signal mnemonic or with the waveform, as shown. But, it's a good idea to do it. This timing diagram is to the hardware man what a program and/or flowchart is to a software man. All of them will be easier to read and understand by others (and yourself, a year from now) if there are comments included.

By the way, the reference to "hardware" and "software" shouldn't imply that this discussion is aimed toward computers. We're dealing with *digital electronics*, and that covers a wide range of equipment and applications.

Timing Diagram Generation

It was evident from Fig. 7-8 that we needed to know what the input signals were before we could start. This will, of course, hold true for any timing diagram we wish to generate (i.e., the inputs will be our known values, and the other signals—including the output—will be our variables, or unknowns).

We have three signals coming into the circuit shown in Fig. 7-9. These are Θ1 (Phase 1), Θ2 (Phase 2), and $\overline{\text{RST}}$ (RESET NOT). As you can see, this circuit has a flip flop, and it is very important that you establish in the beginning the state of that flip flop (either set or reset). Note that $\overline{\text{RST}}$ goes true (low) in the beginning to put the flip flop in a reset condition. And, as part of the comments in this diagram, the arrow illustrates this.

As a suggestion why don't you take a piece of paper and cover the waveforms below the three inputs, and we'll see if you can

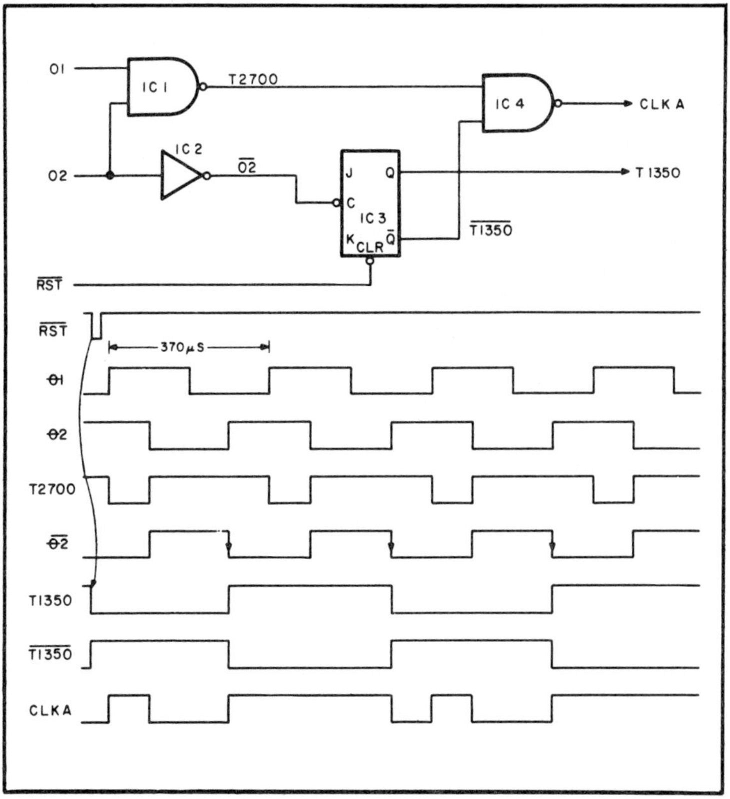

Fig. 7-9. Generation of a nonsymmetrical clock.

anticipate the outputs as we go along. Or better yet, draw them on the paper.

Θ1 has a period of 370 microseconds. If you grab your handy-dandy little calculator and take the reciprocal of that, you should come up with a frequency of 2700 Hz. The ANDing of 01 and 02 (through NAND gate IC1) produces the signal T2700. So much for IC1. Doing it first was strictly arbitrary. Now, let's take the inversion of 02 (through IC2) and generate the clock for the JK flip flop. On the trailing edge (or *down clock* or *one-to-zero transition*) of $\overline{02}$ the flip flop will change state. It started off in the *reset* condition (because of $\overline{RST}$) and is clocked set (i.e., O output high, and $\overline{Q}$ low) on the first trailing edge of $\overline{02}$. And, as you can see, it is toggled (change of state) two more times during the duration of the diagram. The outputs of the flip flop are labeled T1350 and $\overline{T1350}$. The signal names in this case are derived from the frequency of the output, which is 1350 Hz. (The flip flop divided the input frequency of 2700 Hz by two.)

In order to complete the timing diagram for this circuit, we need to AND together (through NAND gate IC4) the signals T2700 and $\overline{\text{T1350}}$. Once again, remembering the rule that the output goes low only when the inputs are both high, we generate the signal CLKA (which is, of course, a non-symmetrical clock, or signal).

Figure 7-10 is an interesting circuit, a divide-by-three. Note that in this case we didn't show the reset signal ($\overline{\text{RST}}$) in the timing diagram. Regardless, it's very important that you establish the starting conditions for the flip flops (either set or reset). The labeling of various timing points (t_0, t_1 . . . t_5) can be very useful for reference when discussing the diagram. Also notice the comments, the period of the input waveform (7.716 usec), the period of the output waveform (7.716 usec), the period of the output waveform (23.15 usec) and the arrows indicating which transition caused which change of state. The divide-by-three function of the circuit is evident when you see that it took three cycles at the input to develop one full cycle at the output. If you haven't seen this circuit before, and you find it interesting, it's suggested that you examine it more closely, because it is definitely tricky.

Figure 7-11 is an *exercise circuit* for those of you who would like to try your hand at generating a diagram from scratch. The answer (*timing diagram*) is shown in Fig. 7-12. Assume that all three flip flops are in a reset condition initially, and the input frequency of 10.8 kHz is a symmetrical square wave. Be sure to have at least 10 full cycles of the input signal across the page.

Interpretation

There are several techniques regarding timing diagrams which haven't been mentioned (but are very common) and will help you in interpreting others. For example, we've been using the bar (or vinculum) over the signal mnemonic to indicate the not term (e.g., $\overline{\text{INPT}}$ = "INPUT NOT"). There are several methods in use today for representing the true and false terms in signal notation. Most of them are listed in Table 7-9.

Figure 7-13 illustrates several techniques used to indicate various conditions or states. The first line (DAL 0-7) represents the data and address lines of an 8 bit computer. The crossing over of the lines simply indicates that the data and address will be either ones or zeros. This is especially true for multiple lines (as per the example) but can also be used for a single line. The signal called SYNC in the second example is depicted with a broken line, which means that the signal may or may not occur at that particular point. The third line (ADDR) illustrates the *settling time* for a signal. Settling time is the

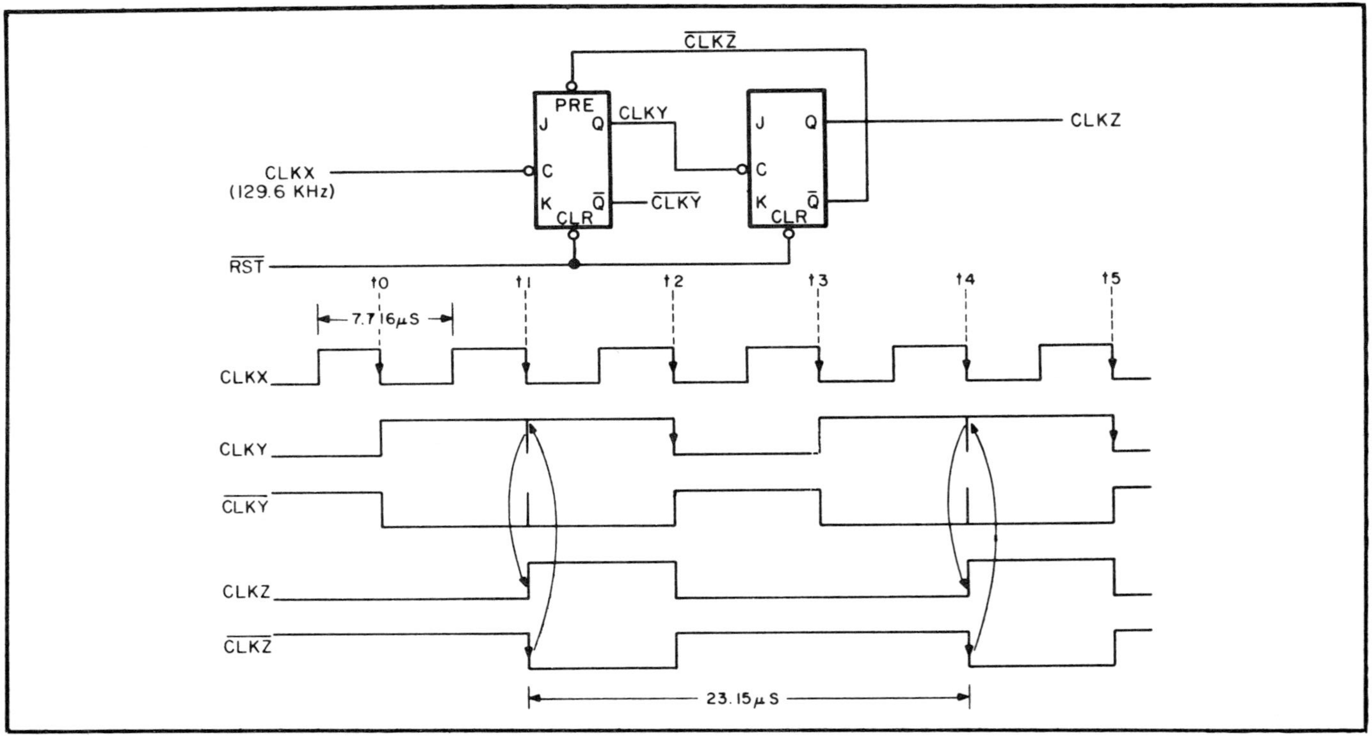

Fig. 7-10. A divide-by-three circuit.

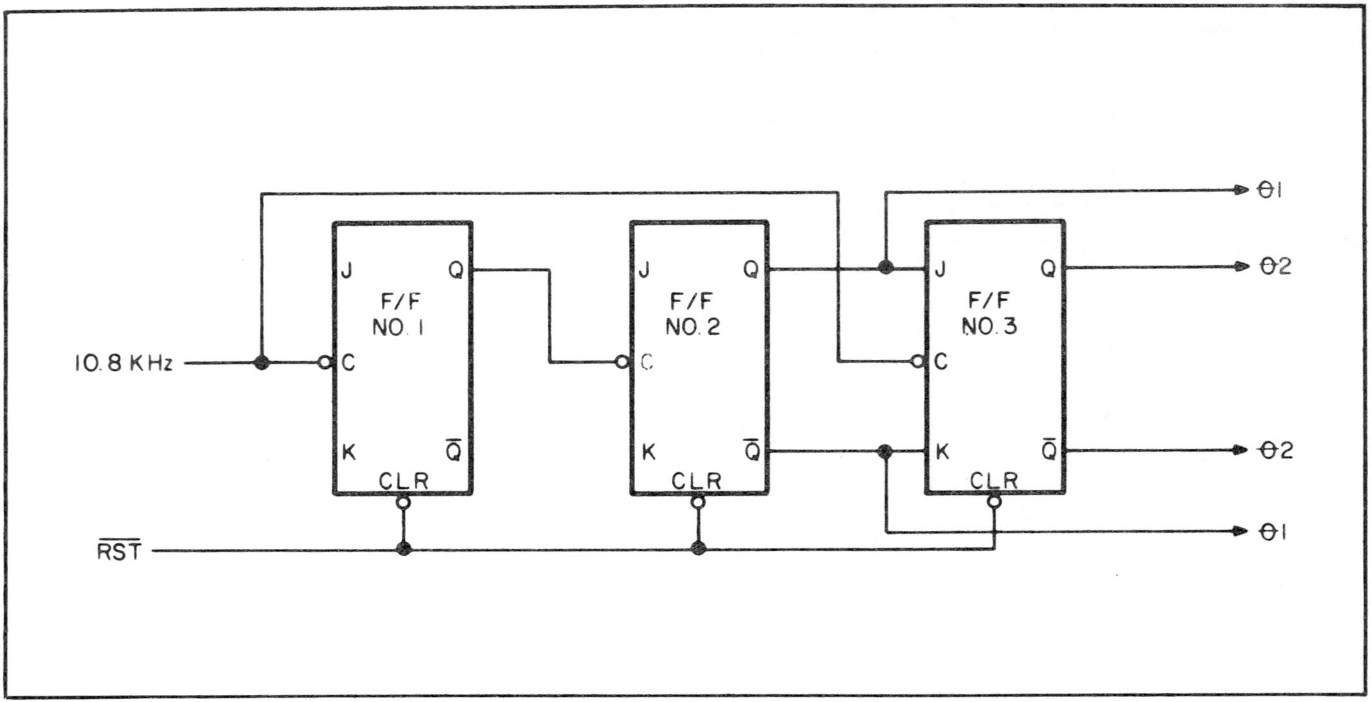

Fig. 7-11. Exercise circuit.

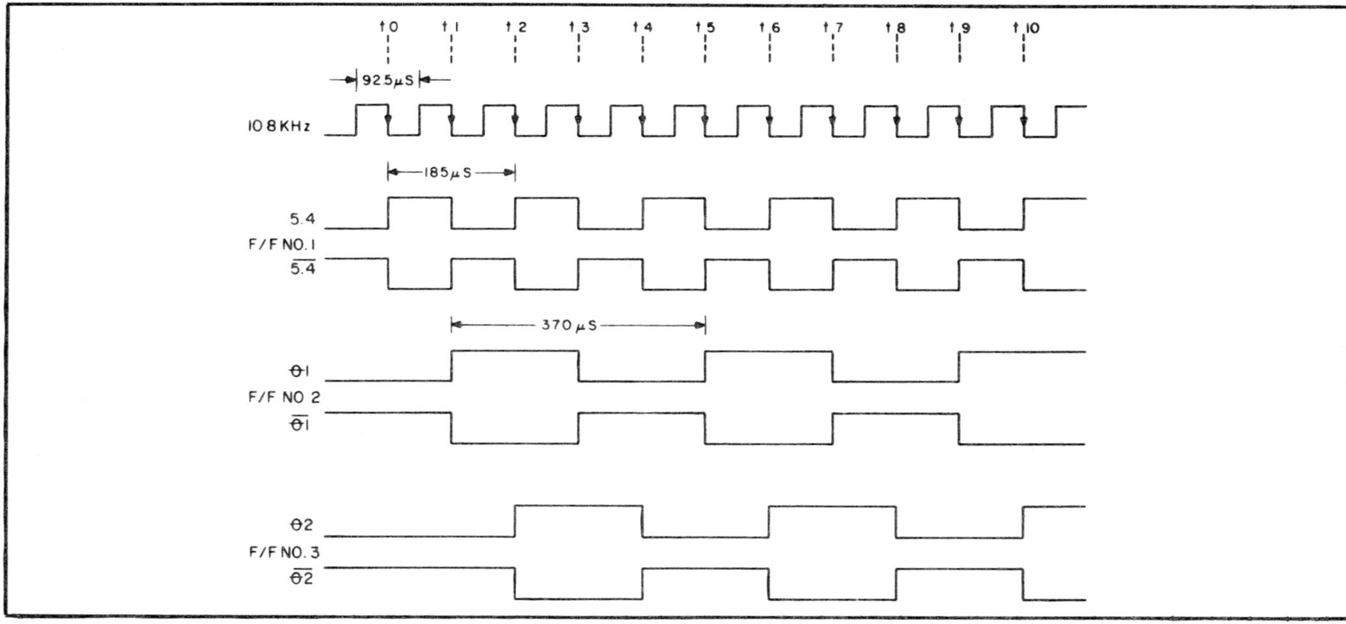

Fig. 7-12. Timing diagram for exercise circuit. Flip flop #1 divided the input frequency by two, and we came up with 5.4 kHz. Flip flop #2 divided the 5.4 kHz by two and we now have a frequency of 2700 Hz. In order to make this circuit work you must take the input conditions to flip flop #3 prior to the trailing edge of the t_1 clock pulse (i.e., a low should have been clocked to the "Q" output, as shown here). The high output (Θ 1) from flip flop #2 won't be clocked into flip flop #3 until clock t_2. This circuit has generated a frequency of 2700 Hz at four different phases. Consider signal "Θ1" as 0° Phase, and "Θ1" will be the 180^2 Phase. "Θ2" is 90° removed from 0° Phase (and is therefore the 90° Phase). Signal "Θ2" is 180° removed from 90°, and must therefore be the 270° Phase.

Table 7-9. Examples of Signal Notation.

High True Condition	Low True Condition
STRB+	STRB–
STEP	$\overline{\text{STEP}}$
EADR	NEADR
CRST	CRST'
INTF	INTF L
INIT	*INIT

time it takes for a signal to become stable after being applied to a line or bus. This is of primary concern when the signal is initially applied to a line, and therefore the fourth line illustrates another method of showing this, but only at the beginning of the signal.

Timing diagrams are just one of several useful tools for evaluating, designing and analyzing logic circuits. It's like anything else—the more you use it, the better tool it becomes.

Interrupts Made Easy

When my Intel 8080-based S-100 bus system was finally up and running, I began looking around for ways to increase its flexibility. The first thing I needed was a means of getting out of a program that was running and back into the monitor without using front panel switches. Interrupt capability was clearly needed. Unfortunately, parts of my software resided in the section of memory that the 8080 uses for its restart instructions, so I couldn't use an interrupt controller such as Intel's 8214.

After a few minutes of thumbing through data sheet catalogs, I discovered my problem—Intel's 8259 programmable interrupt controller. The 8259 uses a call instruction instead of a restart instruction, which allows the interrupt-handling routines to be located anywhere in memory. As an extra bonus, the 8259 also allows interrupt priorities to be changed or individual interrupt lines to be disabled at any one time during processor operation.

I will now describe how interrupts work in an 8080-based system, the 8259 chip and how to interconnect the 8259 to the S-100 bus.

Interrupts and the 8080

Basically, an interrupt is a request by a peripheral device for immediate service by the central processor. In an 8080-based system, the sequence of events following an interrupt is as shown in Fig. 7-14. You must first assume that the processor is busy executing some program, which I have called *Main*, for lack of a better

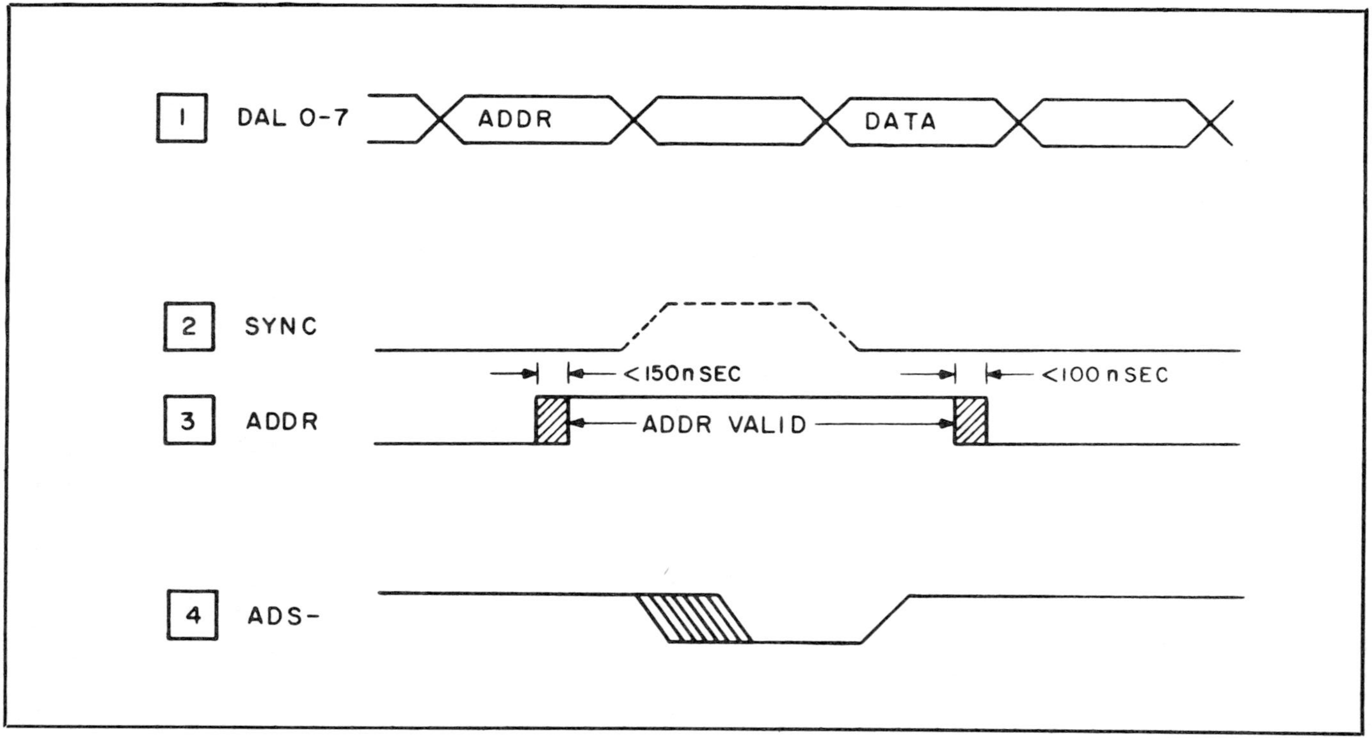

Fig. 7-13. Some miscellaneous techniques.

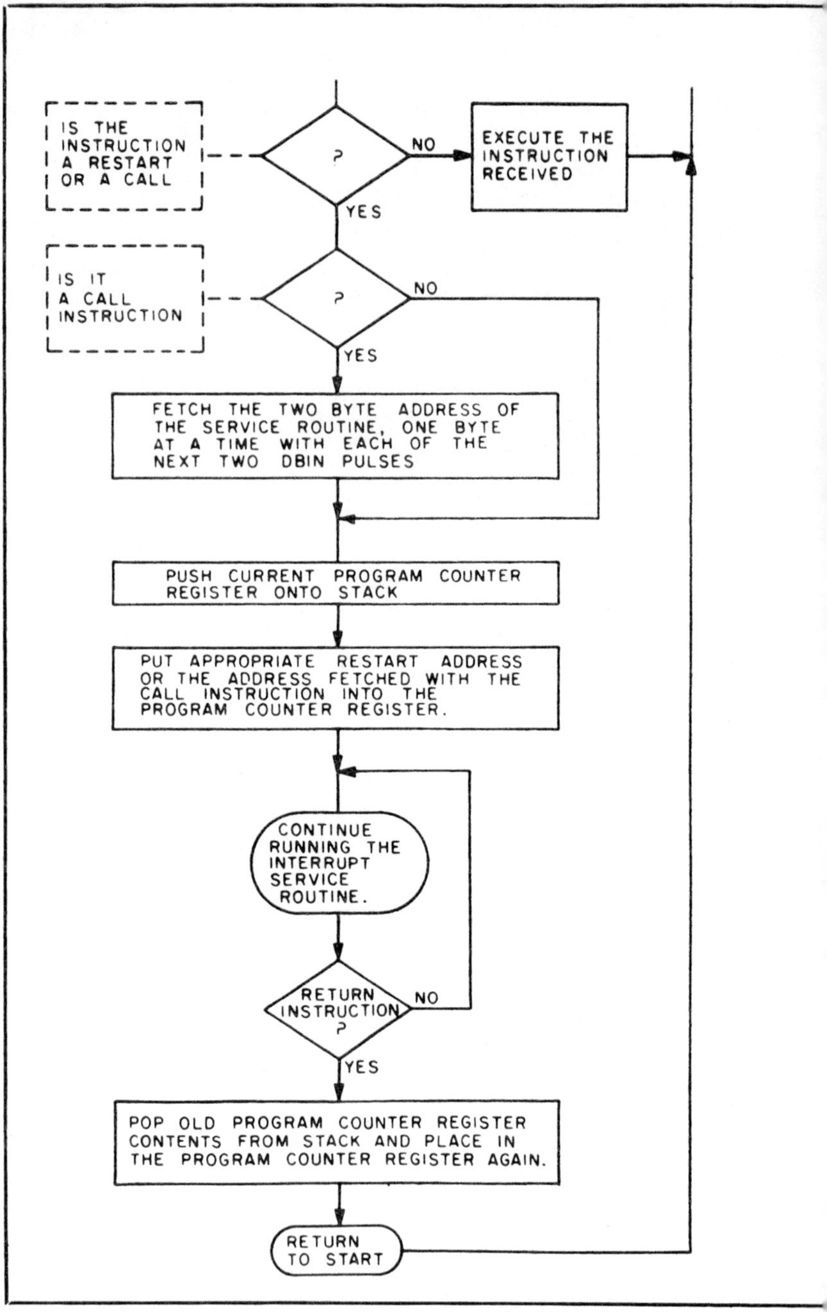

Fig. 7-14. Flowchart of the event sequence for interrupts in an 8080-based system.

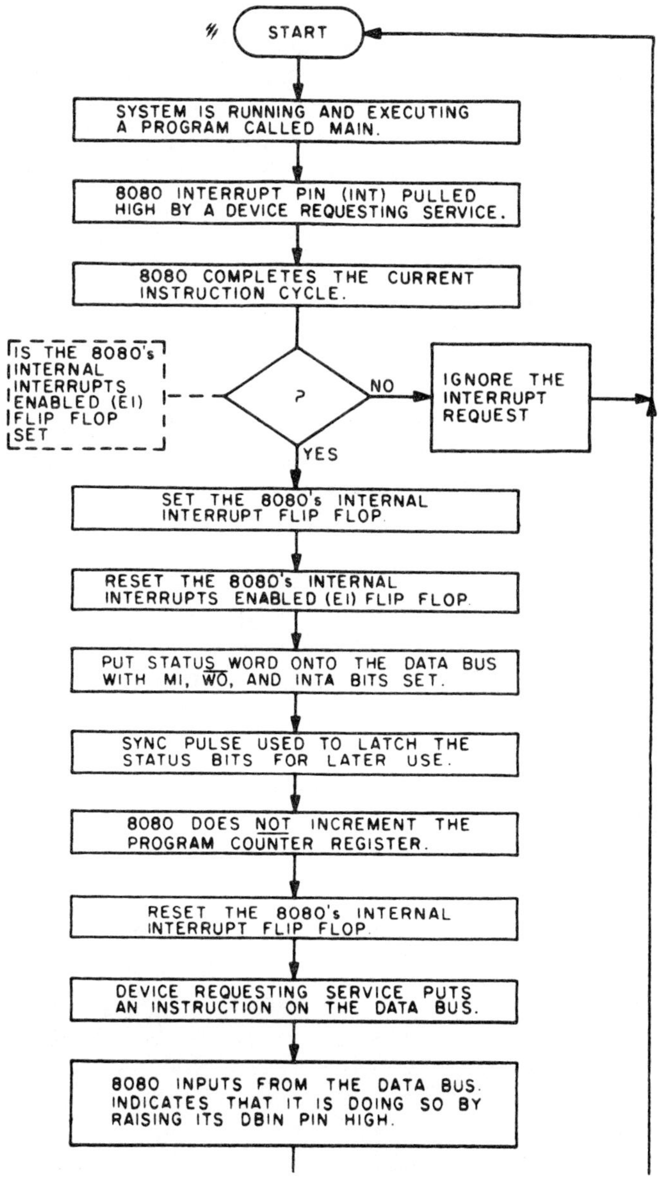
START
SYSTEM IS RUNNING AND EXECUTING A PROGRAM CALLED MAIN.
8080 INTERRUPT PIN (INT) PULLED HIGH BY A DEVICE REQUESTING SERVICE.
8080 COMPLETES THE CURRENT INSTRUCTION CYCLE.
IS THE 8080's INTERNAL INTERRUPTS ENABLED (EI) FLIP FLOP SET
?
NO
IGNORE THE INTERRUPT REQUEST
YES
SET THE 8080's INTERNAL INTERRUPT FLIP FLOP.
RESET THE 8080's INTERNAL INTERRUPTS ENABLED (EI) FLIP FLOP.
PUT STATUS WORD ONTO THE DATA BUS WITH MI, WO, AND INTA BITS SET.
SYNC PULSE USED TO LATCH THE STATUS BITS FOR LATER USE.
8080 DOES NOT INCREMENT THE PROGRAM COUNTER REGISTER.
RESET THE 8080's INTERNAL INTERRUPT FLIP FLOP.
DEVICE REQUESTING SERVICE PUTS AN INSTRUCTION ON THE DATA BUS.
8080 INPUTS FROM THE DATA BUS. INDICATES THAT IT IS DOING SO BY RAISING ITS DBIN PIN HIGH.

name. When our external device decides that it needs to be serviced, it pulls the INT (interrupt) line (pin 14) on the 8080 chip high, providing an interrupt request to the 8080. The 8080 ignores this line until it has completed the current instruction cycle.

For those unfamiliar with the 8080, and instruction cycle consists of everything the 8080 must do to get and to process a single instruction. Each instruction cycle is subdivided into smaller parts called machine cycles. The first machine cycle in any instruction cycle is the instruction fetch, or M1, cycle. Whether or not any more machine cycles are required depends on the type of instruction the 8080 obtained while in the M1 machine cycle. Many 8080 instructions do not require more than one machine cycle, while some require up to five.

After the current instruction cycle is completed, the INT line is examined. If it is high, the 8080 also looks at its internal interrupts enabled (EI) flip-flop. This flip-flop is software controllable, using the EI (enable interrupts) and DI (disable interrupts) instructions, and must be set before interrupts will be accepted by the 8080. If the EI flip-flop is not set, the 8080 ignores the interrupt request on its INT line and continues running the program Main. If the EI flip-flop is set, the 8080 sets its internal interrupt flip-flop, resets the EI flip-flop (disabling any further interrupts) and begins an interrupt-instruction cycle.

The 8080 tells the outside world what type of machine cycle it is entering by placing eight status bits onto the data bus at the beginning of each machine cycle. The first machine cycle in the interrupt-instruction cycle is indicated by having status bits M1 (instruction fetch), $\overline{\text{WO}}$ (processor write, active low) and INTA (interrupt acknowledge) high and all others low. These bits are latched into an 8-bit register by the SYNC pulse sent out by the 8080 on pin 19 when the status bits are stable on the 8080 data bus. The status bits can then be used to control circuitry external to the 8080.

During a normal instruction fetch, the 8080 would increment its program counter register at this time. Following the interrupt, however, the program counter register is not incremented. This allows you to keep track of the address of the next instruction to be executed in program Main so that you can continue execution after the interrupt is processed.

Next, the 8080 resets its internal interrupt flip-flop and inputs an instruction from the data bus. It is assumed that the interrupting device has placed an instruction on the data bus for the 8080 to get. The external circuitry associated with the device-requesting service has the repsonsibility to see that the right instruction is placed on the data bus at the right time.

The type of instruction that the 8080 receives from the data bus determines what happens next. If the instruction is not one of the 8080's restart instructions or a call instruction, it is simply executed, and the program Main then continues where it left off. This feature is useful if it is desired to increment or decrement one of the 8080's internal registers in response to some outside trigger while a program is running, for example, a counter. There are probably lots of clever ways to use this feature of the 8080 that have not yet been tried.

If the 8080 gets a call instruction, then it fetches two more bytes which are the address of the routine being called. This is normally the address of the service routine for the interrupt. It may not be immediately apparent, but a lot has to take place in the circuitry external to the 8080 for this to occur. That's what the 8259 is for.

If, instead the 8080 gets a restart instruction, the address of the service routine is automatically set by a three-bit pattern imbedded in the single-byte restart instruction itself. Obviously, only eight such 3-bit patterns exist, so you only have eight places in memory to locate your service routines. These start at address 0000 hex and are spaced every eight bytes in memory. These addresses correspond, in order, to the restart instructions RSTO through RST7.

Regardless of whether the instruction was a call or a restart, the 8080 now pushes (stores) the current program counter register contents onto its stack (the area of memory devoted to keeping addresses for future use) so that it will be available after completion of the interrupt service routine. This is necessary because the program counter register contains the address of the next instruction to be executed in program Main. The appropriate address from the call instruction or restart instruction is then placed in the program counter register, and the 8080 continues executing instructions, only now it is in the interrupt service routine instead of the program Main.

When (if ever) a return instruction is encountered by the 8080, the old program counter register contents (address of the next instruction in the program Main) that was pushed onto the stack earlier is popped (removed) from the stack and placed in the program counter again. The program Main now continues executing at the instruction that would have been executed next if the interrupt had not come along, just as if nothing at all had happened.

This is more or less how the 8080 was designed to handle interrupts. Normally, you will use more than one interrupt request line in a system to allow several devices to be serviced as they require. The request lines are usually arranged in some order of priority, with the most important devices taking precedence over less important devices.

All of this is intended as a review if you are already familiar with how the 8080 handles interrupts, or as a brief introduction if you are encountering this for the first time.

The 8259

The 8259 gets around most of the limitations that the 8080 has in handling interrupts. Figure 7-15 is a block diagram of the 8259. The chip has its own internal bidirectional data bus and is interfaced to the 8080 data bus through the eight-bit bidirectional data-bus buffer.

The interrupt-request register (IRR) is basically an 8-bit positive edge-triggered latch that holds a record of those devices that have requested service. The *positive edge-triggered* business means that, when the interrupt-request (IR) pulse is making the transition from low to high, the flip-flop is set.

The priority resolver determines which (if any) of the interrupts will be serviced next and then sets the appropriate bit in the in-service register (ISR). The in-service register then determines which address is to be placed on the data bus in response to the $\overline{\text{INTA}}$ pulses from the 8080.

Individual interrupt request lines may be masked off, which simply means that they can be inactivated, by setting the appropriate bit in the interrupt-mask register (IMR).

The control logic block takes care of synchronizing the various internal parts of the chip. Its primary duty is to issue an interrupt to the 8080 in response to a valid interrupt request at one of the 8259's eight interrupt-request lines and then gate the three bytes of the call instruction onto the 8080's data bus in response to the three $\overline{\text{INTA}}$ pulses from the 8080 support circuitry.

Programming and reading the status of various registers in the chip are handled by the 8080's I/O (input/output) instructions and the read/write logic block of the 8259. The chip requires two I/O port addressed for proper operation.

More than one 8259 can be tied together through the use of the cascade buffer/comparator. One 8259 is designated as the master, and all other 8259s in the system are designated as slaves to the

PIN CONFIGURATION

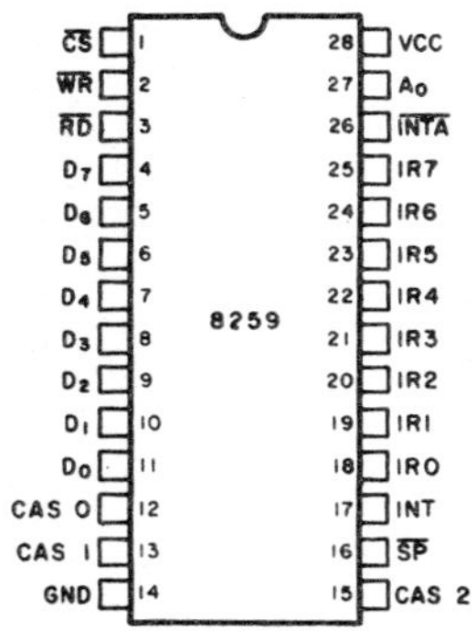

BLOCK DIAGRAM

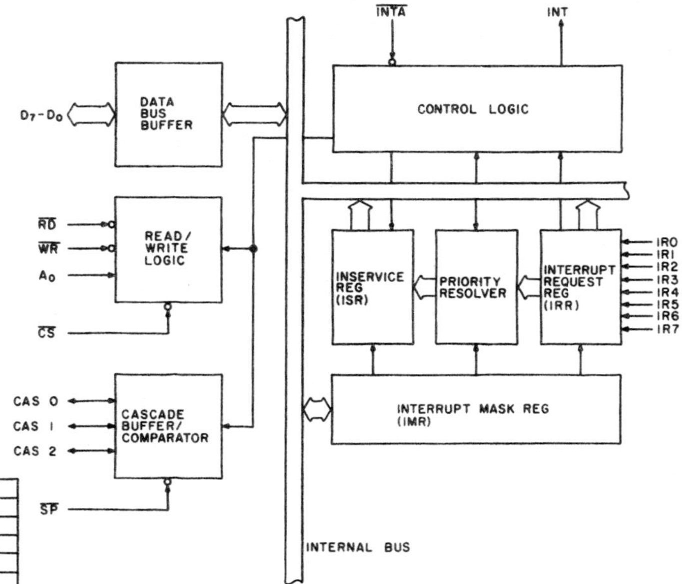

PIN NAMES

D_7-D_0	DATA BUS (BI-DIRECTIONAL)
$\overline{RD}$	READ INPUT
$\overline{WR}$	WRITE INPUT
A_0	COMMAND SELECT ADDRESS
$\overline{CS}$	CHIP SELECT
CASI-CASO	CASCADE LINES
$\overline{SP}$	SLAVE PROGRAM INPUT
INT	INTERRUPT OUTPUT
$\overline{INTA}$	INTERRUPT ACKNOWLEDGE INPUT
IRO-IR7	INTERRUPT REQUEST INPUTS

Fig. 7-15. Pinout and block diagram of Intel's 8259 programmable interrupt controller. (Coutresy of Intel.)

master. The slave's INT line is connected to one of the master's interrupt-request lines so that, when the slave chip gets an interrupt request on one of its interrupt-request lines, it sets the master 8259's interrupt-request register flip-flop. The master 8259 then issues an interrupt request to the 8080 on its INT line. An 8259 chip is designated as a master by tying its slave program ($\overline{SP}$) pin high or as a slave by tying the $\overline{SP}$ pin to ground. Up to eight slave 8259s may be used with a single master.

When a slave 8259 receives an interrupt request, the slave outputs a high on its INT pin which is connected to one of the master 8259's interrupt-request (IR) pins. If that IR pin is not masked off by the master 8259's interrupt-mask register (explained later), the master 8259 issues an INT to the 8080. When the 8080 acknowledges with the first of the three required $\overline{INTA}$s, the master 8259 puts the call instruction onto the data bus. The master also puts the address (one of eight) of the slave 8259, the one which received the interrupt request from the device needing service, onto the cascade buffer/comparator output lines, CASO through CAS2. This address (connected to the slave's cascade buffer/comparator lines) enables the slave 8259 to put the required service routine address onto the 8080 data bus with the next two $\overline{INTA}$s from the 8080.

Clearly, since a call instruction is used instead of a restart instruction, the service routine may be located nearly anywhere in the 64K of memory available to the processor. The master/slave feature allows as many as 64 interrupt-request lines to be serviced by 64 different routines, if desired.

The interrupt-mask register (IMR) allows for maskable interrupts. Again, this means that the user can disable any or all of the interrupt-request lines to any 8259 chip. To accomplish this, you set the desired bit(s) in the interrupt-mask register. You thus have the option of turning off any particular interrupt(s) without turning them all off.

The priority resolver allows the user to change the priority of any interrupt-request line at any time during system operation. Suppose, for instance, that, after servicing a particular device, you wish to assign it to the lowest priority, giving the remaining devices in the system a higher priority. This is easily accomplished with a single command to the 8259, which reprograms the priority resolver to do what you want.

By this time, you must already realize just how versatile the 8259 is. The chip has exactly the kind of flexibility that I needed to solve my interrupt problems. The next step was to get the chip operating in the S-100 bus environment.

Interfacing to the S-100 Bus

This section deals specifically with the S-100 bus standardized by the Altair 8800.

All of the interfacing is fairly straightforward, except for one small part. Intel designed the 8259 to work in a system that employs the 8228 system controller and bus driver chip. For those not familiar with this chip, it is basically a status bit latch and bidirectional data-bus driver all in one chip. It also has another unique function. When a call instruction is issued in response to an INTA status bit, the 8228 issues three INTA pulses, one during each of the next three machine cycles, so that the 8080 will get all three bytes of the call instruction. Since S-100-based systems do not use the 8228, I needed another method of producing these pulses.

A very simple solution to this problem is shown in Fig. 7-16. When the $\overline{\text{INTA}}$ status bit is valid, PDBIN is allowed to give the first of the three INTAs to the 8259 and also to clock the 7474 dual flip-flop. Clocking the 7474 keeps the 7400 NAND gate between the PDBIN bus pin and the 7474 enabled (i.e., pin 1 of the 7400 is high) so that the next two PDBINs can give the 8259 the next two $\overline{\text{INTA}}$s that it requires to gate the address onto the data bus.

After getting all three bytes of the call instruction, the very next thing that the 8080 will do is push the contents of the program counter register onto stack. Since the $\overline{\text{INTA}}$s must be stopped after the 8259 has received three of them, the stack-status bit (Stack) is used to reset the 7474 flip-flop, turning off the 7400 NAND gate between PDBIN and the 7474 (i.e., making pin 1 of the 7400 low), stopping the $\overline{\text{INTA}}$ pulses to the 8259.

The entire logic diagram is shown in Fig. 7-17. The INTA pulse generator of Fig. 7-16 is shown in the upper left-hand corner of Fig. 7-17. As shown in the diagram, the 8259 is selected ($\overline{\text{CS}}$ low), and the appropriate set of data-bus buffers is enabled as soon as it is apparent that the 8259 will be accessed. This is known when the status bits have been latched and the address has been decoded. The bus drivers to the S-100 data IN bus are also enabled when a status INTA bit is received in response to an interrupt request, allowing the 8259 to give the three-byte call instruction to the 8080.

Address decoding is done using two 7485 four-bit magnitude comparators and an 8-bit DIP switch, which allows the interrupt controller to be addressed at any pair of the 8080's 256 input/output ports. Notice that, since two I/O ports are required for operation of the 8259, address bit A0 has been connected directly to the A0 pin of the 8259.

$\overline{\text{Read}}$ ($\overline{\text{RD}}$) or $\overline{\text{write}}$ ($\overline{\text{WR}}$) strobes (active low) are obtained by NANDing PDBIN with SINP (the status input bit) or PWR (processor write signal) with SOUT (the status output bit), respectively. This gives the necessary delay time between chip select ($\overline{\text{CS}}$) and the $\overline{\text{RD}}$/$\overline{\text{WR}}$ strobes to the 8259 (50 ns minimum).

Since my system presently uses only one 8259, I have programmed it as a master by tying $\overline{\text{SP}}$ high. The three cascade buffer/comparator lines, CASO through CAS2, are left unterminated, since they serve no purpose when only one 8259 is used.

The eight interrupt-request lines to the 8259 from the S-100 bus are inverted to provide positive pulses to the 8259 from the negative pulses used in my system for interrupts. This is necessary since my system's interrupt-request lines (V10 through V17) go low and stay low until reset by software commands. The 8259, on the other hand, only acknowledges an interrupt if the interrupt-request register flip-flop is set by the rising edge of a pulse. Clearly, if I did not invert the interrupt-request lines before applying them to the 8259, the 8259 would never acknowledge an interrupt.

That completes the interfacing of the 8259 to the S-100 bus.

Build a CW Memory

While building a random access memory (RAM) for my keyer, it occurred to me that my CW operating habits did not require the versatility of the RAM and that my memory requirements could be satisfied with one or more programmable read only memories (PROMs).

Although the control logic for the read modes are similar for RAMs and PROMs, PROMs offer a non-destructible memory (within their recommended operating parameters) after their initial programming, without the need to frequently refresh the memory as is necessary with RAMs.

The memory described is self-contained and need not be used with a keyer. The output circuitry is designed to drive gridblock keyed transmitters with key-up voltages not exceeding -100 volts. TTL inputs are available for keying the transmitter from an external source (i.e., the digital output from additional memories, a keyer, or CW identifier).

Circuit Description

Figure 7-18 shows a simplified block diagram of the PROM memory. The memory uses four Intersil IM5600C PROMs. These PROMs are fully decoded TTL Bipolar 256-bit custom programmed

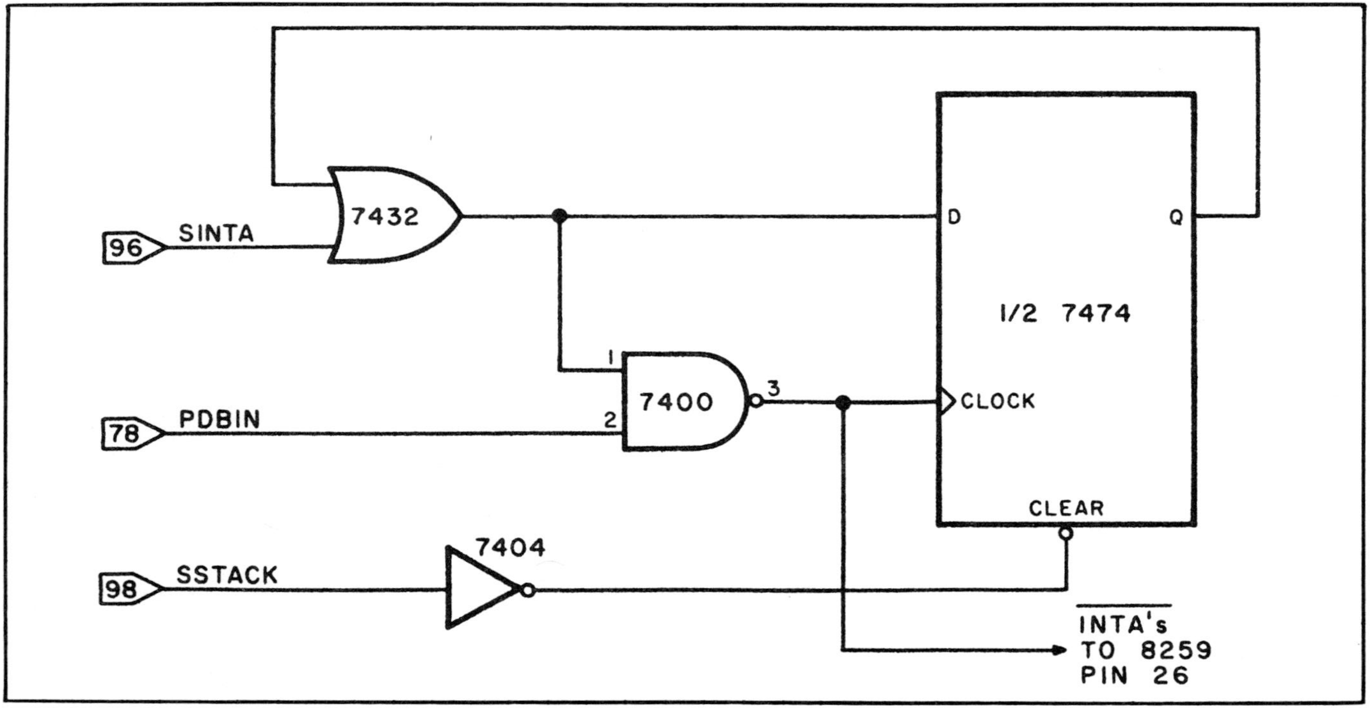

Fig. 7-16. INTA pulse generator circuit. (Bus pin numbers are those of the S-100 bus.)

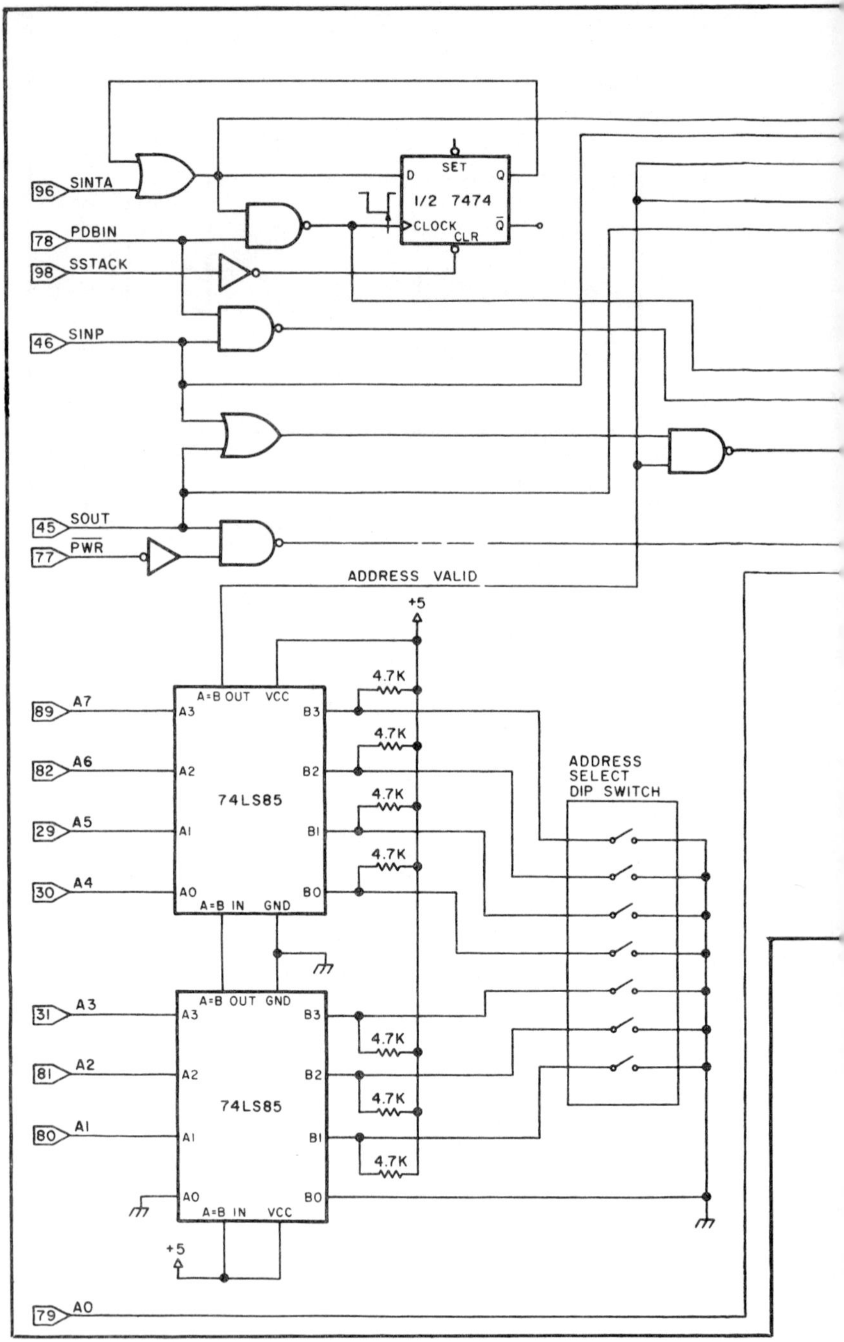

Fig. 7-17. Logic diagram of the 8259 implementation in S-100 bus systems.

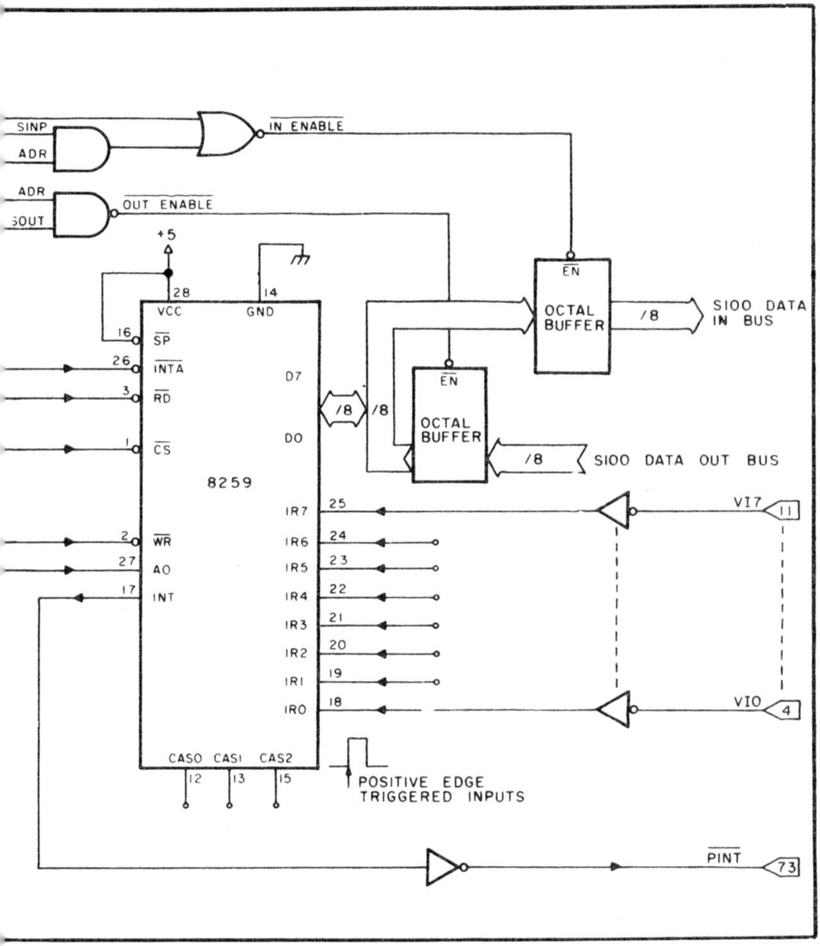

read only memories organized as 32 words by 8 bits (U7-U10). Open collector outputs and chip enables insure simple memory expansion. An effective memory capacity of 1024 bits is obtained by ORing the four 256-bit chips together. I chose a 256-bit PROM because it offers a convenient memory length of approximately 22 characters. Memory retrieval is initiated with the appropriate program select push-button switch (S2-55). The program can be stopped at any point with the stop push-button switch (S1).

U3 and U4 are 7476 Dual J-K flip flops with preset and clear, used as start/stop flip flops. The stop push-button switch, S1, is connected to the preset inputs (ins 2 and 7) of U3 and U4. Grounding this bus forces the Q outputs to logic 1, disabling the clock and U6, stopping the program (a logic 1 on pin 7 of U6 forces pin 5 low). The clock inputs (pins 1 and 6) are connected together. A negative edge at the clock inputs, corresponding to the end of the 256th bit, will clock Q to logic 1, disabling the clock and U6, ending the program. Individual program select switches are connected to the clear inputs (pins 3 and 8) and U3 and U4. Grounding *one* of these pins will start the program corresponding to the PROM selected. The Q outputs of U3 and U4 (pins 11 and 15) are connected to the chip enable inputs (pin 15) of the four PROMs. The appropriate PROM is enabled by forcing one of the outputs of U3 or U4 to logic 0, enabling the clock and U6, starting the program. Starting the program resets the eight bit binary address counter U1 and U2.

U1 and U2 are 7493 TTL MSI 4-bit binary counters used to address PROMs U7-U10 and U6, a 74151 TTL MSI 8-line-to-1-line data selector. The first three bits from the counter address U6, while the remaining bits address PROMs U7-U10. In this fashion U6 multiplexes the PROM outputs of eight lines to one line before the address counter selects the next word.

U5 is a 7420 TTL Dual 4-input positive NAND gate. It is the enable/disable gate for the clock and U6 and the reset gate for the eight-bit binary address counter. U11 is a 7403 TTL Quadruple 2-input positive NAND gate with open collector outputs used as the input for the transmitter keying circuitry.

Clock pulses for the memory are generated by a relaxation oscillator consisting of Q1 and Q2 and associated parts. The oscillator is the same one used in my keyer and was selected so that the speed controls could be ganged and would track in the event that the keyer would be packaged with the memory (it wasn't).

Programming

PROMs are fabricated with all logic levels at zero. The programming procedure open-circuits metal links which results in a logic 1 at selected locations in the memory. Intersil, instead of using a metal link, forces a resistive shaft through the junction of one diode in the memory cell resulting in a logic 1 at selected locations in the memory. Once the memory cell has been programmed to a logic 1, that bit cannot be altered (reprogrammed).

Distributors of PROMs offer custom programming services or the reader may program his own. Design data sheets and application notes describe the programming procedures in detail. Read these instructions carefully and fully understand the address methods as programming errors can be costly.

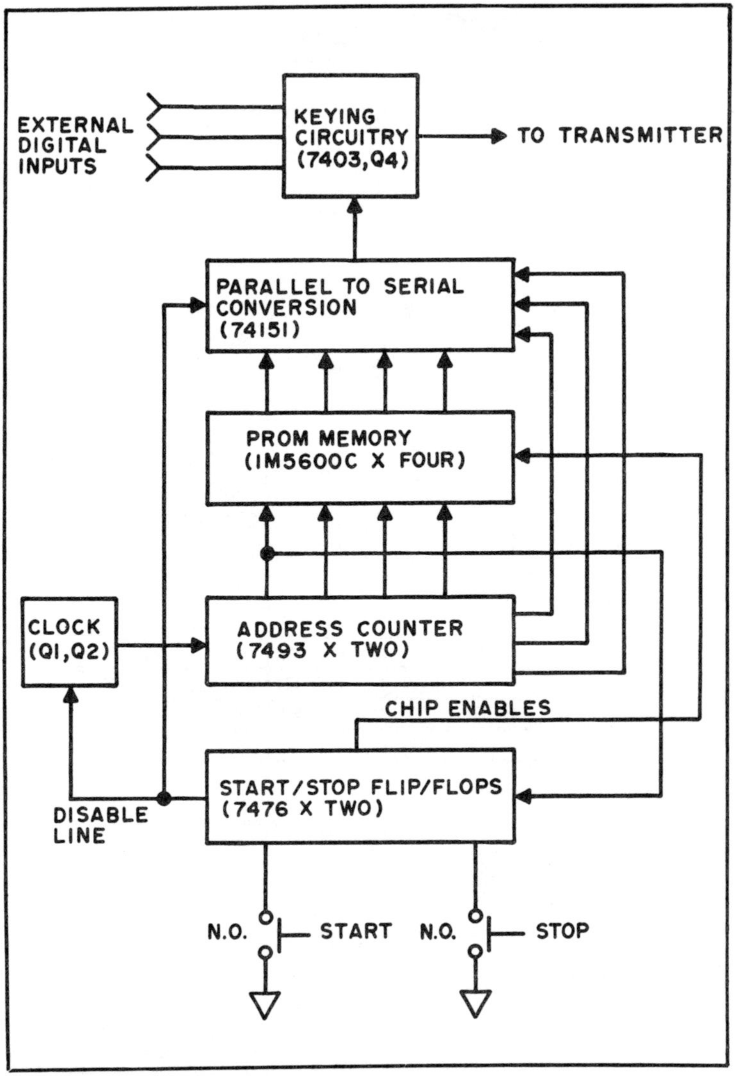

Fig. 7-18. Block diagram of the PROM CW generator.

Figure 7-19 illustrates a typical programming card for the following program: DE WA6VVL WA6VVL WA6VVL K. Standard spacing should be used in writing the program. For example, use 7 bits for a word space, 3 bits for a letter space, 3 bits for a dash and 1 bit for a dot.

The quoted price from R.V. Weatherford included programming costs. One advantage of a distributor programming your PROM is that they verify its program before they send it to you.

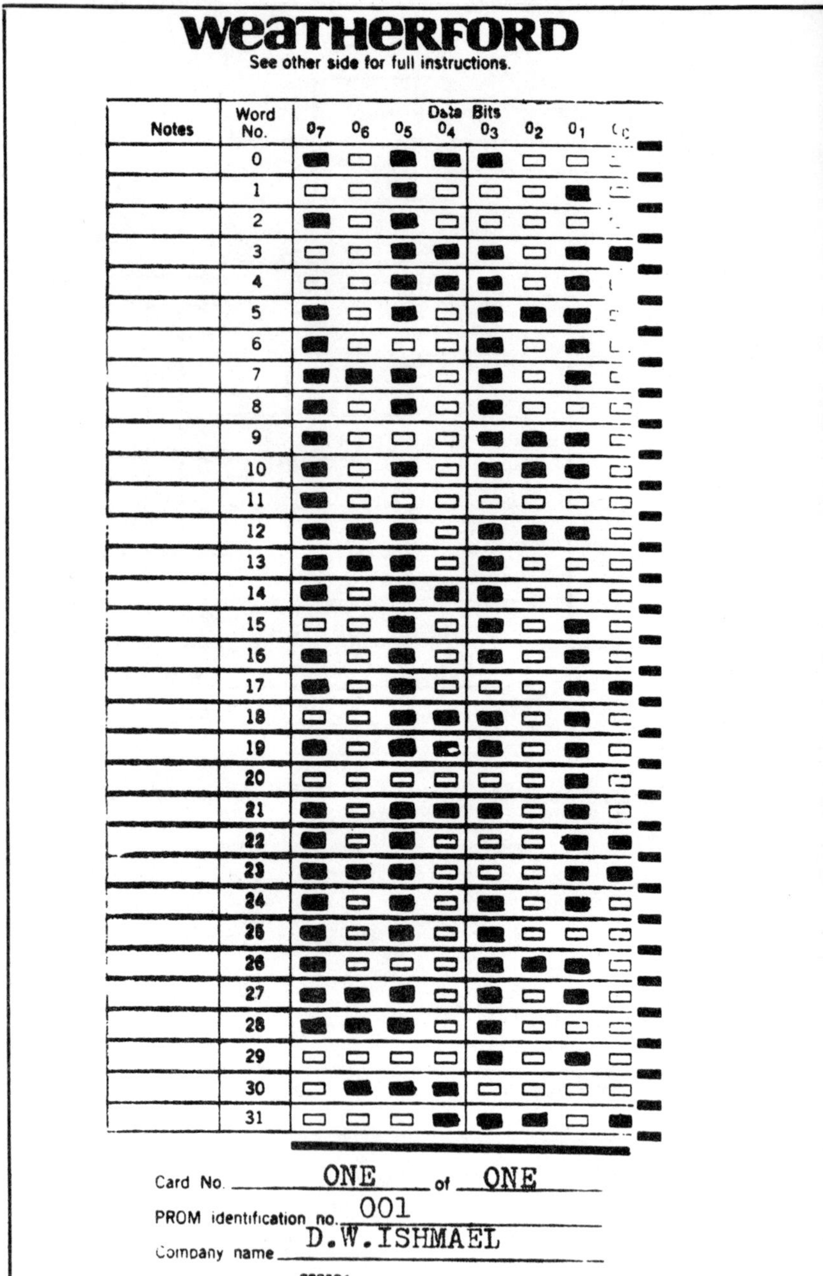

Fig. 7-19. The above program, DE WA6VVL WA6VVL WA6VVLK, is read from right to left, top to bottom. The program is written in the same fashion.

Weatherford P/ROM Programing Card

Ordering Information

1. Company name D.W. Ishmael
2. Company address 1118 Paularino Ave., Costa Mesa, Calif
3. Requisitioner's name Above
4. Telephone number (714)979-5858
5. P/ROM manufacturer's part number IM5600C
6. Quantity of P/ROMs required 1
7. Quoted price per P/ROM $6.00
8. Requisitioner's purchase order number ______
9. Special P/ROM marking instructions 001
10. Shipping instructions UPS

How to use this card

1. Use a soft pencil (No. 2)
2. On the "program" side of every card mark blank spaces for the logic "1" (high output state) data-bit locations in your program.
3. Write anywhere on the shaded portion of the card. DO NOT mark in the unshaded portion unless you are indicating a "1" data-bit location.
4. DO NOT ERASE in the unshaded data-bit portion. If an error is made, destroy the card.
5. On card No. 1 of each program, complete the "Ordering Information" section above.
6. Pack cards with stiff backing to avoid damage.

Take completed cards to your nearest Weatherford sales office or send to:

Weatherford Programing Center
6921 San Fernando Rd.
Glendale, CA 91201

IBM K12882

Power Supply

The 5 volts supply illustrated in Fig. 7-20 can be built to satisfy the requirements of the memory circuitry. U12 should be mounted on a heat sink similar to the Wakefield 680-.75A or 621-A.

U12 dissipates only 1½ watts at nominal line using a 6.3V transformer. However, at low line, ripple feeds through the regulator. No problems with the memory have been experienced under low line conditions to date. A slight improvement in low line operation can be gained by using a 12.6 VCT transformer and a full wave center-tap rectifier.

If you anticipate using your keyer with this memory, do not attempt to power the memory circuitry from your keyer power supply unless it is capable of supplying an additional 450-650 mA.

Construction

The memory is housed in a Cal Chassis 7 inch × 11 inch × 2 inch aluminum chassis base. The majority of the memory components (Figs. 7-21 through 7-23) are mounted on a single-sided 8 inch × 5 inch glass-epoxy circuit board. The board is fabricated to fit a standard 22-pin card edge connector.

Since the memory utilizes four PROMs in parallel on a single-sided board, there are a number of jumpers (92) and holes (434) on the circuit board. The jumpers are installed first with the rest of the components following. Sockets are advisible due to the cost of the integrated circuits and PROMs. They not only speed troubleshooting when the need arises, but also prevent overheating during the soldering operation. The power transformer, filter capacitors, regulator, panel switches and controls are mounted on the aluminum chassis.

Total assembly time for the board, including drilling the holes, was under 4 hours. Mechanical and chassis wiring consumed another 10 hours.

After assembly, connect pins 1 and 20 together on the connector. This connects the digital output of the memory to the first input of the transmitting keying circuitry. If there are no additional inputs, ground pins 2, 3 and 4.

After checking the power supply voltage, connect the power supply, start/stop push-buttons and speed control, and the memory is ready for use.

Two open-circuit phone jacks have been provided on the rear apron of the chassis. They are connected in parallel providing an input for my keyer and an output for the transmitter.

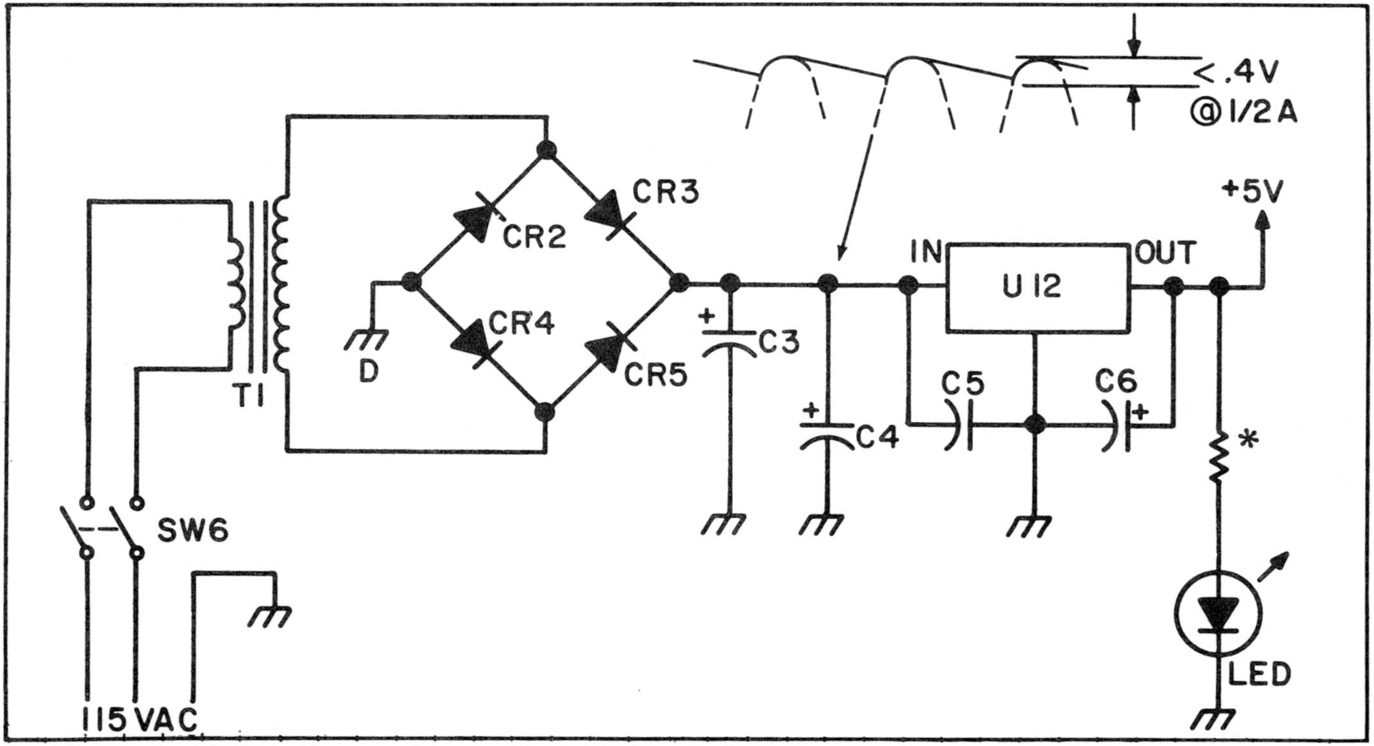

Fig. 7-20. Power supply. *Select for appropriate current through LED selected. 150 ohms was adequate with a Hewlett-Packard 5082-4440 LED.

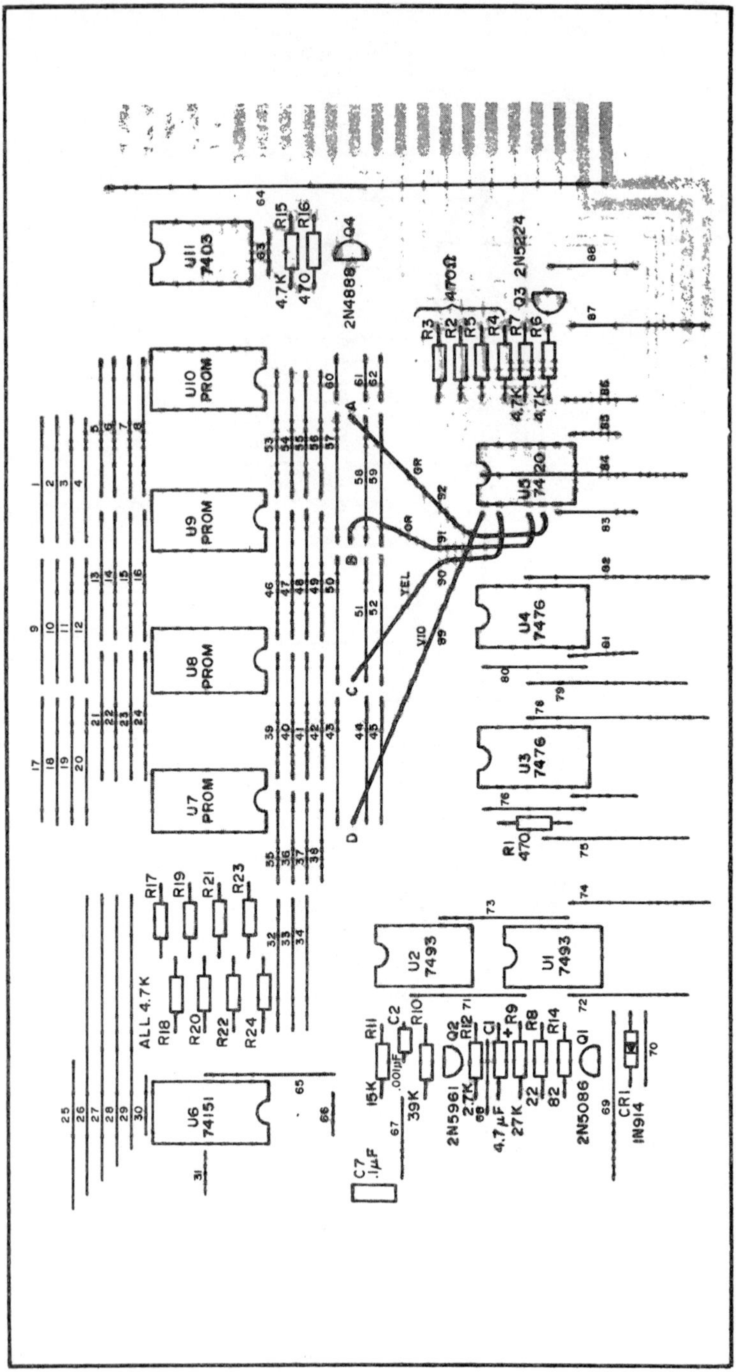

Fig. 7-21. Component layout.

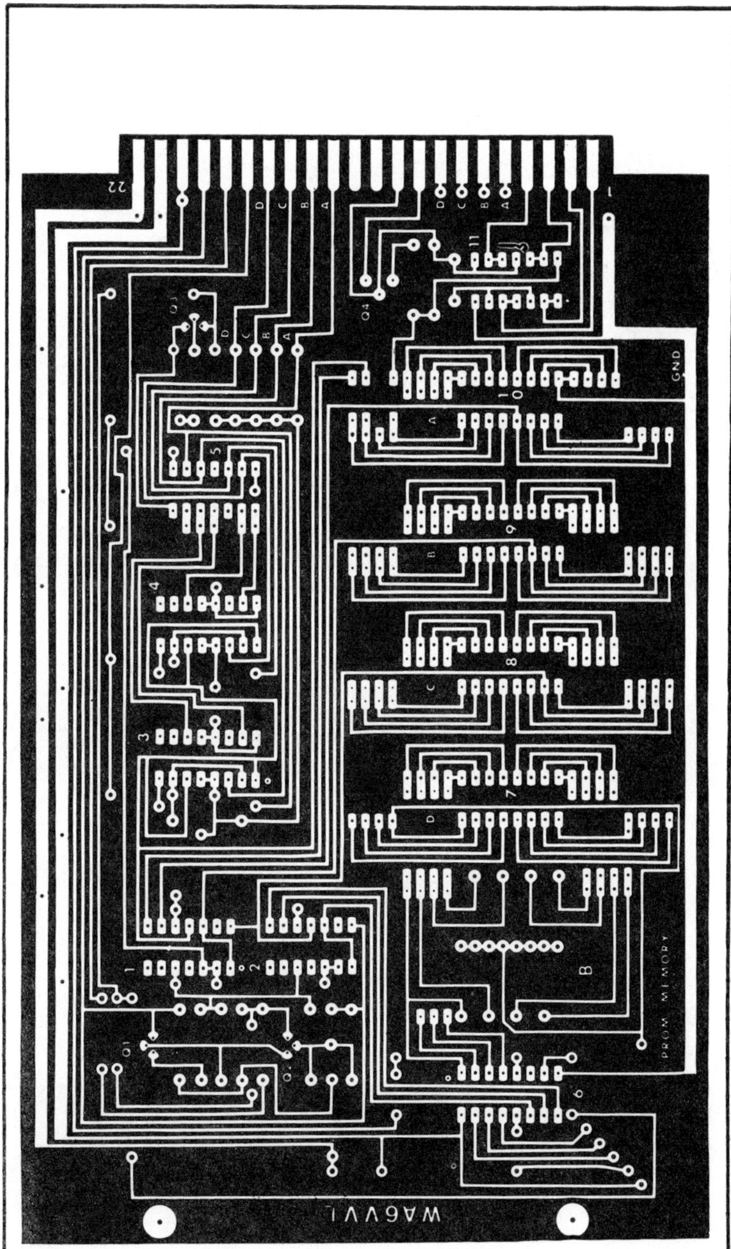

Fig. 7-22. PC board.

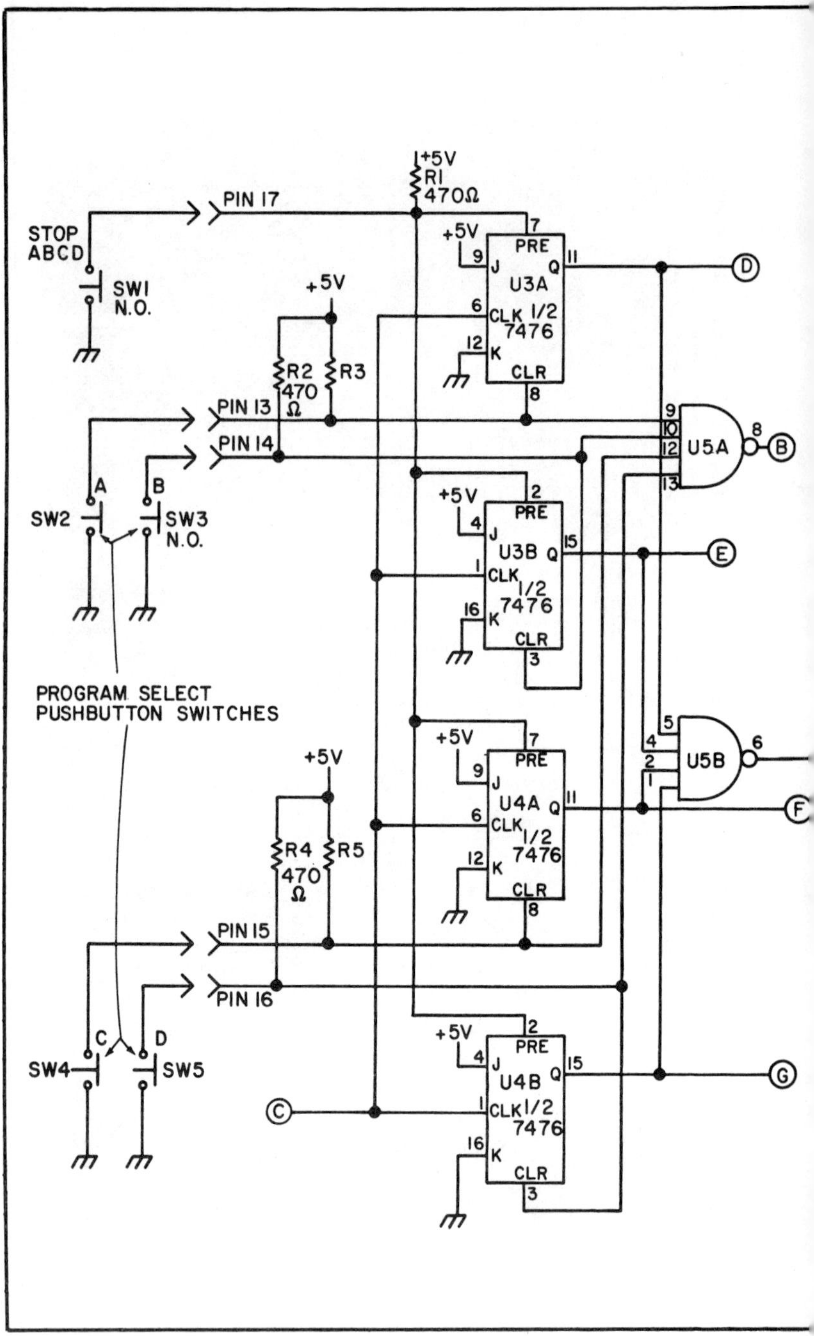

Fig. 7-23. Schematic of the PROM CW generator-keyer.

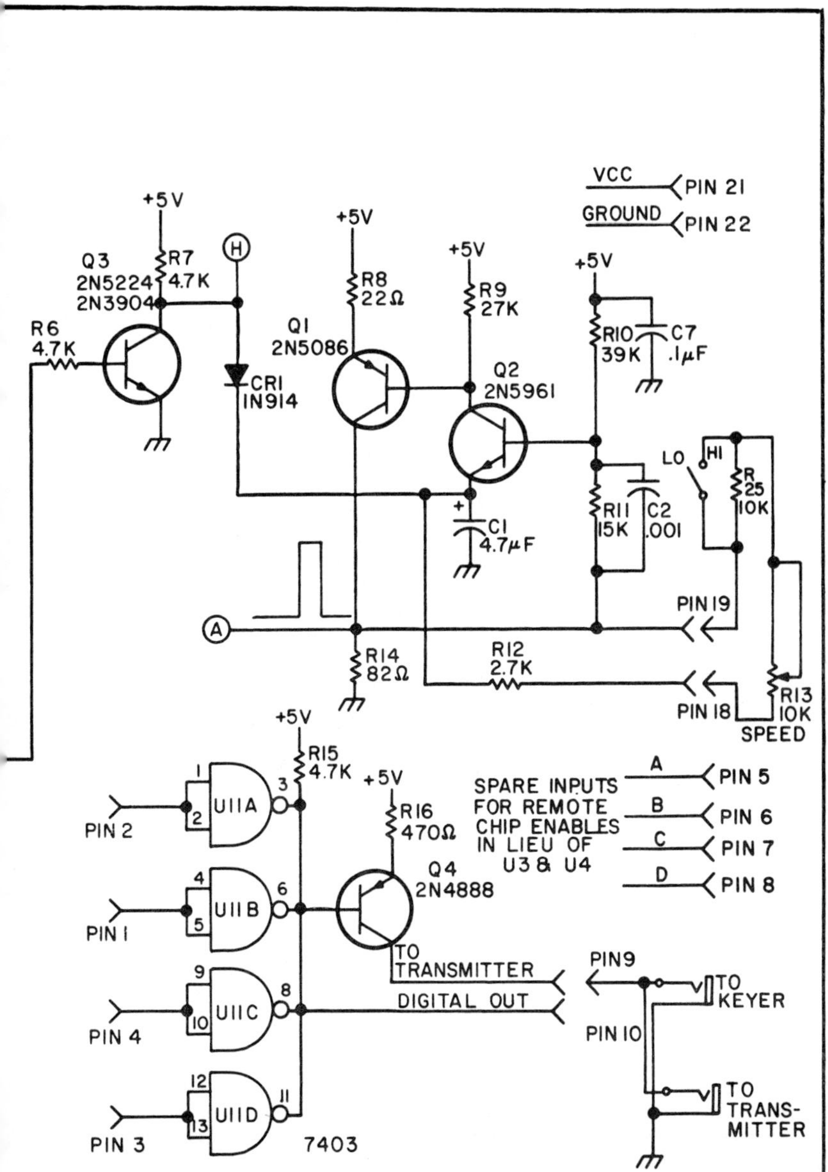

Ground unused inputs.
Connect pin 1 to pin 20 (PROM digital output).

Table 7-10. Parts List.

C1	4.7 mF 10 W V dc tantalum capacitor
C2	.001 mF ceramic capacitor
C3-4	4700 mF 16W V dc electrolytic capacitor
C5	.33 mF ceramic capacitor
C6	2.2 mF 10 W V dc tantalum capacitor
C7	.1 mF 10 W V dc disc ceramic capacitor
CR1	1N914 silicon signal diode
CR2-5	1N4001 or equivalent 50 V piv rectifier diode
Q1	2N5086 or equivalent PNP transistor
Q2	2N5961 or equivalent NPN transistor
Q3	2N5224 or equivalent NPN transistor
Q4	2N48888 or equivalent HV PNP transistor
R1-R5, R16	470 Ohm ½ Watt carbon resistor
R6, 7, 15, 17-24	4700 Ohm ½ Watt carbon resistor
R8	22 Ohm ½ Watt resistor
R9	27,000 Ohm ½ Watt carbon resistor
R10	39,000 Ohm ½ Watt carbon resistor
R11	15,000 Ohm ½ Watt carbon resistor
R12	2700 Ohm ½ Watt carbon resistor
R13	10,000 Ohm 2 Watt linear taper potentiometer
R14	82 Ohm ½ Watt carbon resistor
R25	10,000 Ohm ½ Watt carbon resistor
SW1-5	Normally open push-button switch. Similar to Alcoswitch MSPS-103C SPST.
SW6	DPST miniature rocker switch. Similar to Alcoswitch MSL-203N-7
T1	6.3 V ac Filament Transformer, 1 A. Similar to Allied 6K9HF or Triad F-14X.
U1-2	7493 TTL MSI 4-bit binary counter
U3-4	7476 TTL Dual J-K flip flops with preset and clear
U5	7420 TTL Dual 4-input positive NAND gate
U6	74151 TTL MSI 8-line-to-1-line data selector
U7-10	Intersil IM5600C 256-bit PROM
U11	7403 TTL Quadruple 2-input positive NAND gate
U12	7805 or LM309 Three terminal regulator

Alternatives

If the reader was not satisfied with using these PROMs, there are a number of PROMs available from which the reader could choose. Texas Instruments, for example, offers the 74186 (512-bit, 64 words by 8 bits), 74187 (1024-bit, 256 words by 4 bits) and the

Turn the PROM memory on *off the air* as it will take a few seconds for the memory to clear itself, the actual time dependent upon the setting of the speed control.

74188A (256-bit, 32 words by 8 bits). There are pin-compatible equivalents available from other manufacturers. The Intersil IM5600C is pin-compatible with other 256-bit PROMs including the Texas Instruments 74188A and Signetics 8223.

If the reader was reasonably sure that his program would not change, the 1024-bit PROM might be a better choice with simpler supporting logic. Additional benefits include less than 2¢/bit (compared to about 2½¢/bit for 256-bit PROMs) and one third the board area. One possible disadvantage is the eight programming cards which need to be filled out.

The memory described here has been designed specifically for my CW operating habits. Many variations in construction, chip enable and address circuitry, memory size (bits) and PROMs are possible.

Using my board, total construction costs should not exceed $60.00 assuming the reader had to purchase all the parts. Approximately 40 percent of the cost is for the PROMs. For a complete parts lists and for pin assignments, see Tables 7-10 and 7-11.

Table 7-11. Pin Assignments.

Pin	Assignment
1	TTL input. Logical 1 (+2.5-5.25 V) will key transmitter. Ground if not used.
2.	TTL input. Logical 1 (+2.5-5.25 V) will key transmitter. Ground if not used.
3.	TTL input. Logical 1 (+2.5-5.25 V) will key transmitter. Ground if not used.
4.	TTL input. Logical 1 (+2.5-5.25 V) will key transmitter. Ground if not used.
5.	A spare — May be used to externally enable
6.	B spare — the PROMS instead of U3 & U4,
7.	C spare — or connected to the chip enables.
8.	D spare — to drive external LED displays.
9.	Keyer output. Disigned to drive transmitters utilizing negative grid-block keying. The PNP driver transistor specified will withstand-100 volts under key-up conditions. Do not use with cathode keyed transmitters.
10.	Digital output. Do not use for keying transmitter. Output is low as transmitter is keyed. Logical 1, +2.5-5.25 V. Logical 0, 0 to + .4 V.
11.	N.C.
12.	N.C.
13.	Start program A. Momentary contact closure to ground to start.
14.	Start program B. Momentary contact closure to ground to start. The PNP driver transistor specified will withstand-100 volts under key-up
15.	Start program C. Momentary contact closure to ground to start.
16.	Start program D. Momentary contact closure to ground to start.
17.	Stop program ABCD. Momentary contact closure to ground to stop.
18.	To speed control.
19.	To speed control.
20.	Memory digital output. Do not use for keying transmitters. Output is high as transmitter is keyed. Logical 1, +2.5-5.25 V. Logical 0, 0 to +.4 V.
21.	DC volts input. +4.75 V to +5.25 V.
22.	Digital Ground.

A TV Game Chip

There are very few things which are universally entertaining to children, or adults for that matter—except maybe the boob tube. Today's generation of children has grown up spending more time in front of a television than in school. The TV has become a cheap babysitter and the primary source of entertainment for most American families.

One husband, trying to keep peace in the family, scans the TV listings and sees that he has a choice of Peyton Place reruns, a subtitled movie in Swahili and Jimmy Durante doing impressions of Walter Cronkite. His only wish at this point is that the TV set would show something that he wanted rather than what Smell-o Deodorant or Slippery Lip Ice Cream was willing to sponsor. In a search through books and magazine articles, he spies something describing the construction of a TV ping pong game and decides this may be the answer to his problem. Such a system would use his existing TV—no re-education necessary—and all parts are available from a supplier.

He spends his $140 and obtains a kit by mail a month later. He carefully lays out all the parts for the basic game plus the optional scoring board and power supply: 90 TTL ICs, assorted resistors, capacitors and hardware. His wife surveys this and pipes in with, "Do they sell that junk by the pound?"

Completely undaunted, he spends the next week, three telephone calls to the kit manufacturer and one very expensive and frustrating visit to a TV repairman for him to set and align all the timing circuits. The kids have been thoroughly entertained in the meantime watching Daddy yelling at each individual component as he assembled the massive board.

Then came the moment of truth. Power on. It would be unfair to say that it didn't work. It did work and the kids were completely occupied for about three weeks. They then got tired of just bouncing the ball back and forth in the same ping pong game all the time.

This painfully familiar story serves as our introduction to the world of TV games. There are TV games sold in every discount store and almost every major electronics publication has had a construction article on them. The commercial units cost between $75 and $100 and the construction kits are about the same cost, but there are considerable differences among them. Some may be using older designs which may have as many as 100 chips to perform only one game, or at the other extreme one chip to perform six games. Obviously, this husband would have been better off buying a unit which performed more than one game and allowed variations within each. Fewer parts would necessarily mean a lower price and increased reliability.

The ultimate in perfection (so far) is the subject of this project: the AY-3-8500-1 made by General Instruments. This is a 24 pin MOS integrated circuit TV game chip capable of playing six different TV games. The features are as follows:

- Six selectable games—tennis, hockey, squash, single player practice and two rifle shooting games.
- Automatic scoring.
- Score display on TV screen: 0-15.
- Selectable bat size.
- Selectable ball speed.
- Selectable deflection angles.
- Automatic or manual ball service.
- Realistic sounds.
- Shooting forwards in hockey game.
- Visually defined playing area for the four ball games.

Game Descriptions

Tennis. The tennis game picture on the TV screen have one bat or player per side, a playing field boundary and a center net. Scoring position is at the top center of the screen. After reset is applied, the score is 0 to 0 and the ball will serve arbitrarily from one side toward the other. It is the opposing player's objective to intersect the path of this ball and deflect it back toward his opponent. If no intersection occurs, a point will be automatically scored against the erring player and the ball will again be automatically served toward him again. Serve will not change until he scores a point and gains the advantage. A game concludes when one player's score totals 15 points.

The exact details of the game are a function of the optional speed, size and angle selections. While the game is in progress, three audio tones are output to indicate boundary reflections, bat hits and scores.

Hockey. The rules of the hockey game are exactly the same as the tennis game except that each human player controls two bats or players on the screen. These players are referred to as the goalie and the forward respectively. The goalie defends the goal, while the forward is located in the opponent's playing area. When the game starts, the ball will be arbitrarily served from one goal toward the other side. If the opponent's forward can intercept the ball, he can shoot it back toward the goal and score a point. If the ball is missed it will travel to the other half of the playing area and the opponent's forward will have the opportunity to deflect the ball toward the goal. If the ball is saved by the goalie or it reflects from a boundary, the same forward will have an opportunity to again try to deflect the ball back toward the goal. This method of jamming the ball between the forward and the goalie is a very effective scoring method and makes for an exceptionally exciting game.

Scoring and audio are the same as the tennis game.

Squash. In this game there are two players who alternately hit the ball against a back court boundary.

Scoring and audio are the same as the tennis game.

Practice. This game is similar to squash except that there is only one player.

Rifle. Rifle 1 game results in a large target which randomly shoots across the screen while Rifle 2 requires that the target bounce around within the area defined by the TV screen. External circuitry listed in Fig. 7-24 conditions optical input to a photocell located in the barrel of a toy pistol or rifle which is aimed at this random target. When the trigger (PB3) is pulled, the shot counter is incremented. If the rifle is on target, the hit counter is incremented.

After 15 shots the score is displayed.

Circuit Description

The simplest circuit utilizing this game chip is illustrated in Fig. 7-25. A DIP switch (S1-S8) is used for rarely changed functions such as game selection, rebound angle and bat size. A $2.00 eight section switch such as this serves to lower overall costs by replacing about $8.00 worth of toggle and rotary switches while maintaining miniaturization. S1 through S6 are the game selection switches. Only one of the switches is enabled or placed in the ON position. The others must be left open or the game chip will try to play more than one game simultaneously. The correct procedure for selecting a game is to turn the currently programmed game off (all six switches open) and then close the particular switch for the desired game. Switches 1 through 6 will select the following games respectively: Rifle 1, Rifle 2, tennis, hockey, squash and practice.

Bat size and ball deflection angle are controlled by DIP switch sections S7 and S9 respectively. With S7 open the larger bat size is selected. On the 21 inch television screen this will appear to be about 2 inches. When this switch is in the closed position, small bats of approximately half the previous size will be displayed.

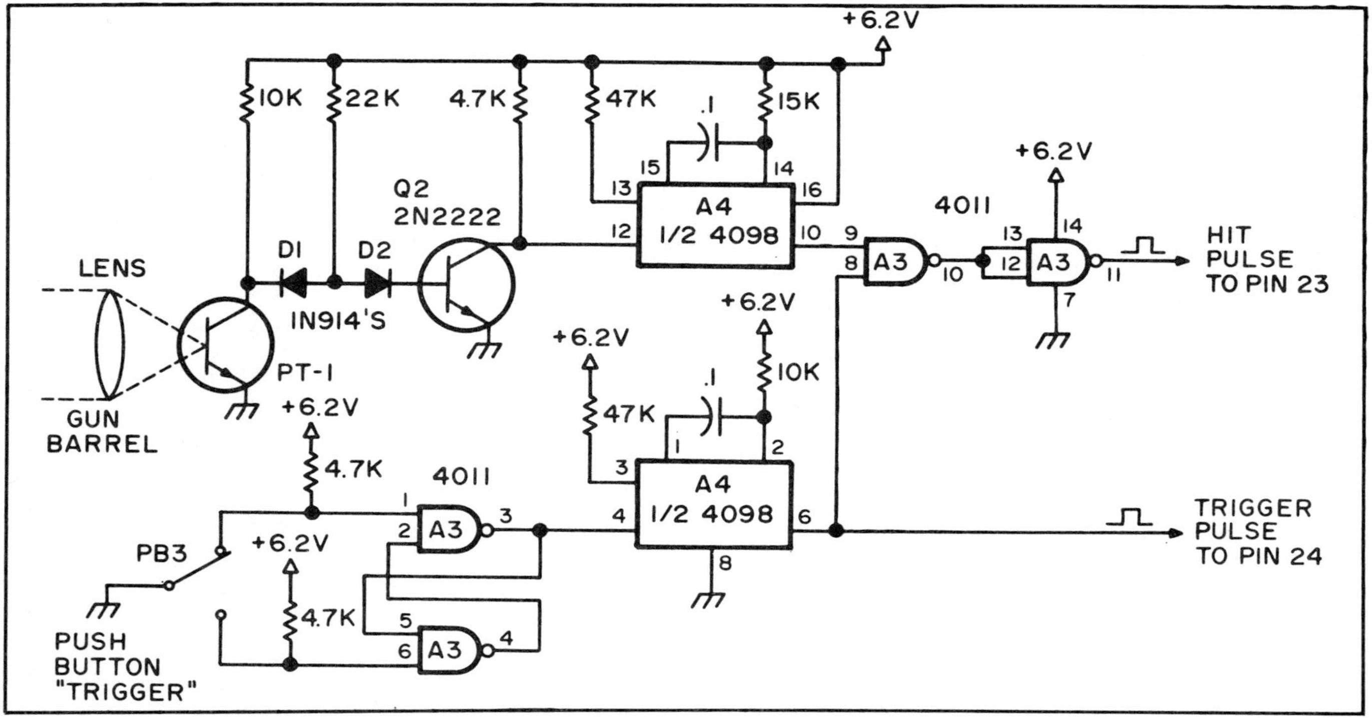

Fig. 7-24. Rifle circuit. PT-1—phototransistor TIL64 or equivalents 4098—dual monostable; 4011—quad 2 input NAND; all resistors ¼ W 5%; all caps minimum 25V DC ceramic.

When first playing a TV game, a player may want to find his bearings and fine tune his eye-hand coordination. For just this reason General Instruments provided for selectable bounce, or deflection angles. When S8 is open, three rebound angles are enabled—plus and minus 20 degrees and straight back at 0 degrees. With S8 closed, five rebound angles are possible—plus and minus 20, plus and minus 40 and 0 degrees. This latter selection requires considerable player skill and dexterity and adds new dimensions to otherwise repetitious games. If that were not enough, selectable ball speed is also available. The ball speed switch SW1 is used more often than the game select switches and therefore should be a more easily used slide switch. When this switch is open, low speed is selected. In this mode the ball takes 1.3 seconds to traverse the screen. When the switch is closed, high speed is chosen and the ball will dart across the screen in .65 seconds. There is a complete understanding of the concept of human fallibility after playing a game which combines small bat size, full rebound angles and a fast ball speed. With this combination, the cure for boredom becomes electronically induced insanity.

If these features were not sufficient, there are more—realistic sound and automatic scorekeeping. All games consist of 15 points with both players starting with a score of zero after pushing the game reset button (PB1). With pin 7 grounded through the manual serve push-button (PB2), play will resume automatically upon the release of the reset button. Automatic start is signified by the game ball being arbitrarily served into the playing area, and each time a point is scored, the ball will come into play into the court defended by the player having scored the point. If automatic start is not desired, the reset and serve buttons should be pressed simultaneously when resetting a game. The reset button is then released while still depressing the serve button. This will allow complete player readiness and will only put the ball in play when the serve button is finally released. Score is incremented (up to a high of 15) each time a player fails to deflect a ball away from goal.

All of this rebounding and scoring results in some very interesting game sounds. A ball hit upon a paddle results in 32 milliseconds of 976 Hz tone. A boundary reflection is 32 milliseconds (msec) of 488 Hz tone and score is 160 msec of 1.95 kHz tone. This square wave oscillation is amplified by a 2N2222 transistor and applied to a 100 Ohm .2 Watt speaker. (An 8 Ohm speaker may be used with proper current limiting in the collector circuit.) SW2 is provided to switch off the sound without having to shut off the game. Player positioning is remotely controlled through cables attached to pins 10 and 11 of the game chip. Each player control consists of a 1 meg pot and .1 microfarad capacitor which combines to form a variable time constant utilized by internal timing circuitry. Longer or shorter time constants will result in relatively different vertical player positions. To reduce noise, this extension cable should be shielded; otherwise, a display malady referred to as "herringbone effect" will result.

For a TV game to be properly displayed on a raster scan television, the proper video signal, similar to that of any commercial TV station, must be applied to the antenna. Such a video signal results from synchronized dividers inside A1, which divide the 2 MHz master clock (Fig. 7-25) and output the required 60 Hz vertical and 15750 Hz horizontal sync signals. These signals from pin 13 are combined with those of the ball output, right player output, left player output and score and field output (pins 5, 8, 9, and 21 respectively) in a two bit digital to analog converter formed with a 4072 CMOS dual 4 input OR gate. This type of video output is referred to as composite video output and is suitable only for use on video monitors and not standard televisions. This video output may in turn be used to amplitude modulate an rf carrier suitable for a standard television receiver. Figure 7-26 illustrates a sample circuit of this basic type of modulator. Figure 7-27 is the necessary schematic. With the components chosen, the frequency is approximately that of VHF channel five.

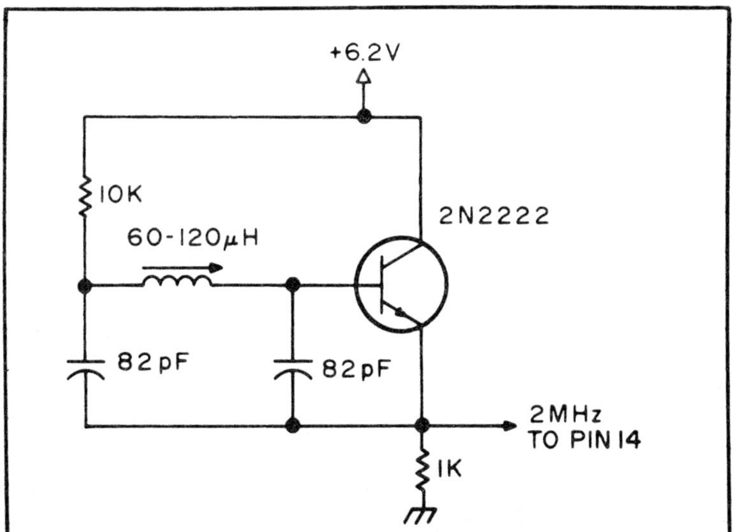

Fig. 7-25. 2 MHz oscillator. Miller 9055 miniature slugtuned coil; all resistors ¼ W 5%; all caps minimum 25V ceramic.

This circuit is intended for illustration only and acceptability by the FCC as a proper class 1 rf modulator is not inferred. The modulator output is connected directly to the TV antenna terminals, with the antenna disconnected, and adjusted for the best reception.

This game is a marvel of engineering ingenuity through which General Instruments has succeeded in enlightening the average American to the latest advantages in electronic technology. It is easy to overlook 16K bit RAMs and microprocessors, but it is hard to ignore such a marvelously exciting TV game when presented on your own home television. For a parts list, see Table 7-12.

Table 7-12. Parts List.

A1	AY-3-8500-1 MOS game chip General Instruments
A2	4072 Dual 4 input OR gate CMOS RCA
A3	4011 Quad 2 input NAND CMOS RCA
A4	4098 Dual monostable CMOS RCA
Q1, Q2	2N2222 or equiv.
S1-S8	8 position DIP switch Gray Hill or equiv
PB1, PB3	SPST momentary push-button
	C & K Subminiature
PB2	DPST momentary push-button
	C & K Subminiature
SW1, 2	SPST slide switch
	Alco Subminiature
SW3	SPST toggle switch
	C & K Subminiature 3 A 115 V ac
PT-1	TIL 64 phototransistor or equiv
	Texas Instruments
D1, D2	1N914 diode Texas Ins
C1	100 uF electrolytic 15 V dc
Z1	1N753A or equiv.
R1, R2	1 meg composition potentiometer 2 Watt
	Allen-Bradley or equiv.
SPK	100Ω .2 Watt speaker
LED	NSL5053 LED or equiv.
All resistors are ¼ Watt 10% unless otherwise indicated	
All capacitors are ceramic type with min. voltage ratings of 25 V dc unless otherwise indicated	
MISC	extension cable, batteries, box, hook up wire, etc

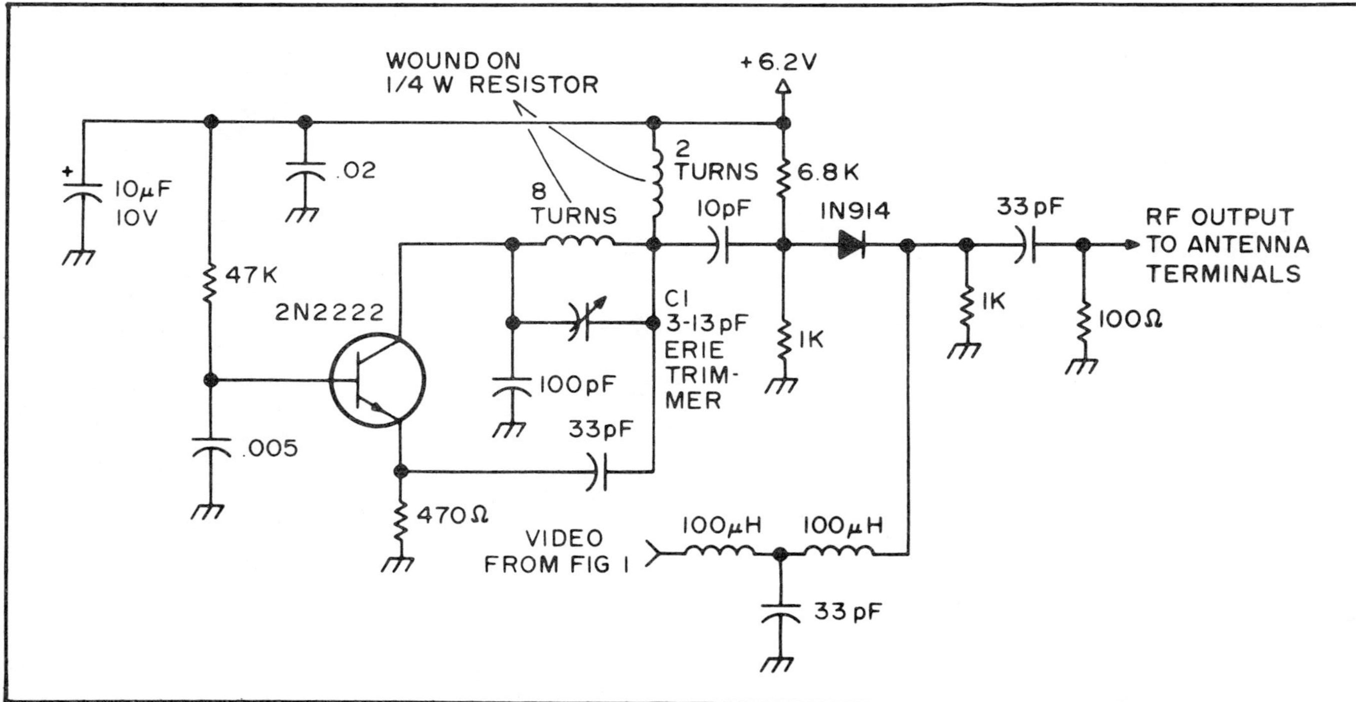

Fig. 7-26. VHF modulator sample circuit. All resistors ¼ W 5%; all caps minimum 25V ceramic unless otherwise noted.

The shipping carton measures 18 × 18 × 13 inches and checks in at about 40 pounds. It will fit in the car nicely for the trip home. I would suggest that the gals let the salesperson place the carton in the car for them. You can wrestle the thing into the house after you get it home.

If you have been waiting for the Heathkit to get their act together before you take the plunge, you can stop waiting. This one puts the whole show together and packages it in a neat console, just a little larger than the typewriter that put the words on this manuscript.

Shipping Carton Packaging

One of the things that I look for in kits is how well the manufacturer packages his kit. All kinds of things can be inferred from this information. The computer nut on the receiving end wants the kit components well protected. After all, he has already paid for them. How well the contents are protected also reflects how much the manufacturer thinks of his product. He should want to get it to the buyer without any damage whatsoever to the contents.

This kit is exceptionally well packaged. Inside, there is ample packing material, and each individual item is protected from its neighbors, so there is no chance of components rubbing and bumping together. Short of dropping the shipping carton from a height of 4 feet onto a concrete floor, you can't hurt things at all. Normal shipping handling should not affect this carton's contents.

Unpacking

When you slit the top tape holding the upper flaps closed, the first thing you see is the thick binder. This is exactly the way it should be. Leave the rest of the kit packed, and take the binder out of the carton, relax in the easy chair and read it.

The first thing you are going to see is a page that says *"STOP! Do not pass Go without reading this page.* We have a number of revisions to incorporate into the manual first. This is par for the course. Even Heath has to do this with their products for a while, until all the kit builders feed back the necessary information to get all the errors out of the assembly manual before the second printing of the manual. (Sometimes, it's the second or third printing before you get an error-free manual to work from.) Don't panic. The revisions are quite minor and already reflect some of the feedback from the kit-building fraternity.

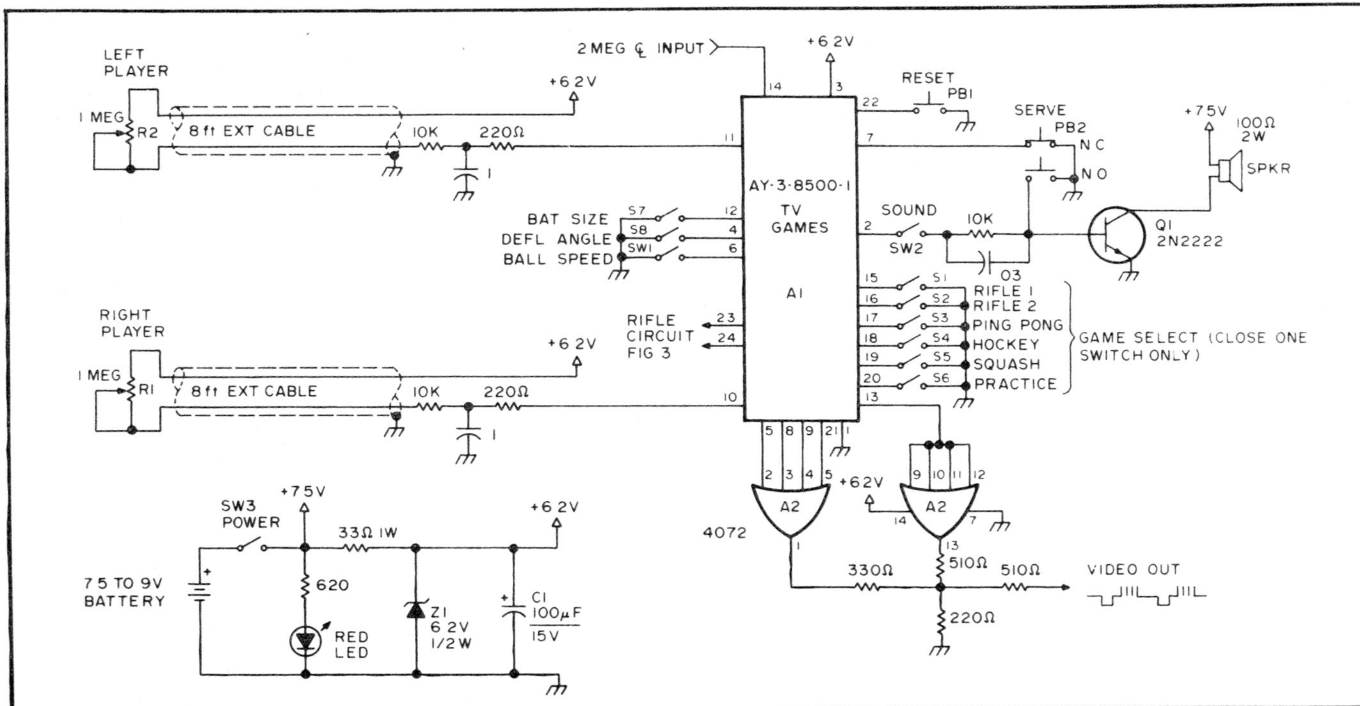

Fig. 7-27. TV game schematic.

Manual Revisions

I want to revise the assembly manual even further, but this revision has to do with the nature of the kit builder rather than any errors that I uncovered. In Step 3 of the revision page, add an (aa) before the manual's Step 1. For the (aa) step put in: Go to section VI, page VI-9. What I want to do is to get you to the part of the manual concerning the finishing of the walnut side panels at the very start. These solid walnut side panels have to be finished with some type of protective coating, and this will take some time. It could take several days to put on the finish of your choice. If you don't have them all done, finish dry and ready when you get to that particular assembly step, they will probably end up getting put on without any finish whatsoever, and you'll make the excuse that you'll take them off later and finish them. If this step is not taken at the onset of the construction process, then we kit builders know what will happen.

Assembly Tools and Test Equipment

A list of tools and necessary test equipment is given at the beginning of each section. Almost all of these tools will already be on hand for any serious kit builder. A good #2 Phillips screwdriver is an absolute must. A good volt ohmmeter is a must. An oscilloscope is desirable, but Processor Technology Corporation (hereinafter called PTC) shows you how to build an rf probe from some of the kit parts to bypass the scope, if you don't have one.

One of the things you are going to have to get for your computer system is a video monitor. In fact, you are going to have to have one for the assembly of this kit. This can be a commercial monitor or a modified TV set. If you modify a TV set, then modify one that has a transformer in it. Don't even try to use a so-called *transformerless* set. These are often called *hot-chassis sets* and rightly so. A transistorized black and white TV is around $100. Since you are going to have more than a kilobuck invested in your system, it is not economically sound to try and use a hot-chassis TV set with the possibility of destroying your $1000 investment. The details on how to convert a TV to make yourself a good monitor are in the back of your binder.

The assembly of the power supply and what PTC calls the Personality Module will not require the video monitor. As soon as you start the assembly of the main board, you will need it. PTC is going to have you assemble and test the built-in character generator chip and all its associated circuits at the beginning, to make sure they work before you proceed with the microprocessor section. This is sound procedure, and, after you see the entire character set displayed on the screen, you will be feeling quite good about your decision to build the SOL.

So, as soon as you place your order for your kit, get shopping for your monitor. Until the kit arrives, you can enjoy the little black and white transistorized TV in its more conventional application.

Problems

This usually turns out to be the longest portion of my kit building experiences. This time I am going to have to get picky on the finest details, because I had no problems. I suppose a good deal of this lack of problems could be contributed to luck. However, Murphy usually doesn't treat me any differently than he treats you.

The first unit assembled is the power supply module. It went together smoothly and without problems. A test of the assembled power supply module showed all the right voltages in the right places, except one. I'll get to that incorrect voltage in a moment. PTC even includes a spare fuse in case you aren't as lucky as I was. This unit now has a spare fuse.

There is one feature in the power supply that I feel is needed and is state of the art. This is the inclusion in this power supply of overvoltage protection. Consider what will happen to all your precious chips, throughout the entire computer, if the series pass regulator transistor fails. The most common failure is a collector-to-emitter short. Such a failure places unregulated DC on all chips connected to the +5 volt line. TTL chips don't like to see anything over about 5.5 volts. They are most unhappy with 8 volts applied to them. There are a lot of TTL chips in this computer.

This power supply has overvoltage protection built in, and this feature is often called *crowbar overvoltage* protection. I feel that this feature is so important that I deliberately left this circuit *energized*, or operational, to make certain the overvoltage circuitry was functional. By leaving out R2 on the power supply, you can leave the overvoltage circuit functioning, and you will not have +5 volts out of the power supply. Since R2 is involved in one of the modifications that PTC is going to have you make, it is relatively simple to leave out R2 and the modification, to insure that the circuit will offer the desired protection. This is why I had one incorrect voltage, as stated above. It was not because I had a problem; it was because I deliberately introduced a problem, so I could test something. It involves a little extra work on your part, but I feel that it is worth the extra work.

Assembly

I implied earlier that this was a kit that was comparable to a Heathkit. I still wish to imply that you do not need to wait for

Heathkit to come out with their product. This one comes close to their line in simplicity of assembly. You should have assembled several Heathkits, including some of their more complicated ones. This is not an easy kit and certainly not one that you should try to cut your teeth on. Assembly time for me ran to 40 hours, and I had no problems. With any problems, you should plan on at least twice that much time. The factory charges $500 more for the assembled kits. So that is how much you are going to save (earn?) by assembling your own kit. That's what I would charge to put one together for you, and I would be earning every penny of it, too.

You need to be able to solder and solder very well. You need to be able to make a good solder connection quickly, with no more heat than is necessary to do the job correctly. You need a good, temperature-controlled soldering iron with a small point. If you don't have one, then I suggest that you allow an extra $50.00 for your system and purchase one. That's only 5% of your investment, and I can't see how you can get around it.

This kit will challenge all the skills you have built up assembling all the other kits. It is extremely well designed mechanically. They have squeezed an awful lot into that package, and I am still amazed at how all the parts fit. Somebody there at PTC has a lot of skill in the mechanical engineering department.

Problems? I couldn't find one transistor. I couldn't find the tape that goes in the finger wells. (The tape is packaged in with the plexiglas in the lid.) I won't say that the transistor was not in the kit. I suspect that I lost it somewhere here on the workbench. With several thousand parts in the kit, a track record of just one missing item tends to make me think I was at fault and not PTC. I replaced the missing transistor from my own stock and did not even ask PTC for it. Thus, with no missing parts, my assembly was not held up at all. (The walnut end panels still don't have any finish on them.)

The Keyboard

I really like this keyboard. It has everything on it, and I especially like the way it is constructed. The keys have what appears to be aluminum foil bonded to a spring-type sponge pad. As you press down on a key, this foil shorts two contacts on the keyboard PC board under the key. This is my kind of circuit—simple, effective, and almost foolproof. If you don't buy the SOL, buy the keyboard (if PTC will sell you one separately). It's a winner. The feel is almost perfect. The keys are arranged beautifully and functionally.

The Video Display

If you assemble any computer, or even if you buy one already assembled, the first thing you will find when you finish assembly is that you can't do anything. You have to have some way to get data into the machine and some way for the machine to get data back out to you. The keyboard takes care of the data input. I have already indicated that you'll have to have a video monitor in order to assemble the SOL. You would have made it the first purchase after assembling SOL anyway, so you already have the output device on hand. The video monitor circuitry is built into SOL, and you have verified its operation during assembly. All you need to do now, to be up and running, is to connect the video monitor to the machine. The assembly sequence and testing procedures also assure you that, after you get the kit all put together, it will do something immediately.

The video display is based on the 6574 character generator chip, and this gives you the full ASCII character set, both upper and lower case letters and all the other symbols. Provisions are made for your choice of letters as well. You can have black letters on a white background or white letters on a black background. And you can have combinations of the two options. You will not have the Greek alphabet with the character generator, but I doubt that this lack will dismay very many of us. The lower case letters are offset. That is, the descenders, such as on the letter *p*, extend below the line the way they are supposed to. The display is 64 characters wide, and, although this crowds the letters a little on my 5-inch monitor, each character is clean and quite readable. On a larger screen, the characters are better separated and more legible. I like this video monitor display.

Input/Output and Expansion Capabilities

A serial data input/output port is built in. A parallel data input/output port is built in. All the circuitry to control these ports is built in. A cassette input/output port and its associated circuitry are built in.

There are only five slots in the card cage. Is this going to be a limiting factor? Every function that you want your machine to perform requires the filling up of a mother board slot. Most computers have as many as 20 or even 22 slots for you to plug cards into to get these functions. Only having five available slots may seem to be quite a limitation, at first. But, if you stop and think for a moment, PTC has built in almost all the circuitry that you need for almost all the functions you are going to want immediately. One of those slots is going to get either an 8K or 16K memory board. As soon as it is filled, you can load PTC BASIC via the built-in cassette recorder circuitry and begin programming in BASIC. Another slot can be filled with a floppy disk controller. A third slot can contain the interface circuitry for a hard-copy printer, if you can't interface either through the serial I/O or parallel I/O circuitry that you already have. You may just have to *hunt* (or wait until something else is invented) for something to fill those other empty slots in the card cage.

What Will It Do?

A better question might be: What won't it do? Attach the monitor and apply power. Inside, a small plug-in board that PTC calls their Personality Module, which contains four EROMs, provides the firmware to get operational. The board is a small one, but it's big on performance and takes the place of still another one of those boards that would normally go in a mother board slot. When you order your kit, get their best Personality Module, which PTC calls SOLOS™. It does everything.

Software Support

PTC has indicated that a full line of software support will be available as soon as all the bugs are out. That's nice—most of us would much rather wait a little longer for them to debug in exchange for the time it would take us to debug. In the meantime, since this is an 8080-based machine, all the 8080 software that has been written can be loaded from cassette and we can do anything with this computer system that we can get into programming. The speed of this machine is optimum. Running a machine at 4 MHz costs dollars. We have to use memory that is very fast and, therefore, costs more money. By running the system at a slower speed, we save money on almost every device that we want to add to the system. Most of the time that a computer system is operating is spent waiting for a cassette to load, the printer to print out or the operator to program. For the home computerist, there is seldom a time that running at 4 MHz is cost effective. The trade-off of speed versus dollars is still very much on the side of dollars. My system uses a 750 kHz clock. It waits 90 percent of the time for me. I am the factor that limits the speed of my system.

Operation

As soon as you complete assembly, connect the monitor and apply power. You can do something. Power on produces auto reset, the prompt character appears, and the system awaits your instructions. Typing *DU*mp followed by the entire address range from 0000 to FFFF will cause the entire contents of memory to flash by on the screen. The addresses change so fast that the last two hexadecimal digits are nothing but blurs, and the entire screen is nothing but data in hexadecimal form. In couple of minutes, the entire 65K of addressable memory is dumped. If a high speed printer were hung on the parallel data port, the paper in the printer would literally fly out of the printer and across the room.

Many other commands are already programmed into the EROM firmware. You'll have to get yourself a SOL with SOLOS and see for yourself.

Project Summary

Been waiting for Heathkit to come out with their kit? They are too late. Processor Technology has stolen the ball game. If you have already built several kits, and at least one of the more complicated kits, and you can solder quickly and well, then wait no longer. Write: Processor Technology Corporation, 6200 Hollis Street, Emoryville CA 94608; or call them at (415) 652-8080, and get the scoop. Get yourself a video monitor or a small black and white transistorized TV set that has a transformer in it, get a schematic for the thing, modify it, assemble the SOL and you will have an operational computer system. Add 8K of BASIC via the cassette input already provided, and you can start programming in BASIC immediately. Add a floppy and a floppy controller, and you can have the whole ball game on the road for about $2k with enough memory to play all the games and even do the books for the corporate business.

Outstanding Computer Bargain

Have you seen the BYT-8 on display in the Byte Shops? This little machine, with its rather plain black and beige aluminum cabinet with wrap-around top is not much larger than a portable typewriter case, measuring approximately 15 inches wide, 7 inches high and 11 inches deep. Inside it contains a 10-slot, S-100 bus mother board and has a 10 Amp power supply (+8V DC, ±18V DC) and an MWRITE logic circuit. It uses an optionally provided fan. The front panel is uncluttered, having a start/restart switch and an LED to indicate that the power is on. The power master switch is located on the back panel to lessen the temptation of curious switch flippers who may visit the computer room.

At first glance the kit appears simple, so putting it together should be a snap, even for the novice. However, the manner in which the assembly instructions are written makes it more of a challenge. If you can spare the time, I'll tell you all about it.

My BYT-8 is the first of several building projects which I hope helps provide me with a fully-operational home computing system.

I must point out that I have not yet accumulated all the components necessary to get it operational, so that, at this point, it hasn't been fully tested. Therefore, all the comments made here relate strictly to my experience in selecting and building the mainframe assembly.

I was attracted to the BYT-8 initially because of its compactness and apparent simplicity. It affords one the opportunity to get started in this new hobby in a modular way without a large initial capital outlay. It also gave me some time to study various optional paths I might take while getting my feet wet in kit-building activity. Once I had taken the initial plunge, I was reasonably certain I would pursue the activity until I had a complete system. That first commitment, for me, was a difficult hurdle to overcome.

The First Steps

Before making my initial selection, I suppose I did the normal amount of agonizing over the offerings of the many computer companies. I even attended two large home computer shows on the West Coast and hung out at the local computer shops. I joined a computer club at work. I read everything I could get on the subject; little did it matter that I understood only a small part of what I read. In the end I was confused and indecisive, but I did know lots of buzzwords and could smile and nod knowingly when people spoke of such things as dynamic memories, EPROMs, machine cycles and the like. By doing some home studying, I even got to know something about BASIC programming. I became aware of BASIC's general capabilities, though I still cannot claim any proficiency in the language. The point of this is that I began to look at the various systems offered in terms of both their hardware and software capabilities.

After considerable soulsearching, I finally narrowed my selection down to equipment offered by The Digital Group, Processor Technology and Technical Design Laboratories. All of these systems appeared to best meet my basic objectives for a system, both from the standpoint of the hardware and from software availability. In the end, TDL's Z-80 CPU (ZPU) with its S-100 bus compatibility, won out over the others. However, this immediately posed another problem, since, at that time, TDL did not offer a complete package to house their card. I had to seek a solution to that problem.

At this point, I recalled having seen the BYT-8 at a nearby store, and I really became interested in it as a possible part of my system. I wondered if a 10-slot mother board would be large enough to meet my ultimate needs. The arguments of the Byte Shop people convinced me that it would do. Currently my initial system is comprised of the Z-80 CPU board supported by the TDL Z-80 monitor board (this contains 2K ROM, 2K RAM, 2 serial and 1 parallel input/output ports, plus a cassette interface). To this I plan to add a 16K memory board and a video interface. This should afford me plenty of expansion room, especially in light of the high-density memory boards which are currently available. Since most boards use one Amp or less per board, the 10-Amp power supply should be sufficient.

Before making the decision to buy the BYT-8, however, I looked at the possibility of purchasing an Imsai mainframe assembly without the front panel. I am convinced that the front panel is not needed for my application and is simply a source of additional trouble. It appeared to be cost effective to eliminate the front panel if I could. The Imsai sans the front panel would have cost about $70 more than the BYT-8 (priced at $299). Since I had comvinced myself that I only needed 10 slots, the larger cabinet and 28-Amp power supply didn't hold much appeal for me. The only other alternative was to pick up a mother board here and a power supply there and find a cabinet somewhere to mount it all in. Since I am new in the hobby, I wanted someone to hold my hand a bit, so I opted for the BYT-8 kit. I slapped down my Mastercharge card and walked out of the Byte Shop with the kit under my arm.

Once I had the box home, I opened it and began to read the instructions. I was prepared for the worst, since I had heard from others that computer kits are a far cry from Heathkits. At this point I can say they were not exaggerating with respect to the BYT-8. (Since constructing the BYT-8, I have put the TDLZPU together and found it to be almost Heatkit-like in its approach.) At this point, I want to make it clear that the criticism presented here is aimed principally at helping the novice builder—either directly, by giving him the benefit of my experience, or indirectly, by prompting the manufacturer to improve his assembly instructions to make them easier to follow. Those experienced in this field may feel I am nitpicking, but I feel this is not so. I have thrown out a number of lesser criticisms which I felt were too inconsequential to mention here, but which, in the interest of product improvement, should be considered. The kit manufacturer states early in his instruction manual, "For the most part, our discussion will be aimed at the

Intermediate, but we will constantly give references and repeat things for the Neophyte and Novice." At times, the instructions fail to keep this promise. The manual defines five categories of builders, from the neophyte and novice through intermediate, advanced and expert. By Byte Shop definitions, I should be classified as a novice.

My criticisms fall into two classes—those dealing with hardware design and those relating to documentation. I feel that those in the first class are not of a serious nature, if one is aware of them, and that those in the latter are mainly a nuisance which tends to take some pleasure out of the kit-building experience and could cause those unfamiliar with electronics to blow a few components if they are not careful and observant. The hardware aspects will be covered first, followed by the documentation deficiencies.

Hardware Shortcomings

The most serious hardware problem results from the manufacturer's recent change to a PC board which is twice as thick as that used in his original design. This change is noted in the errata sheet, where it is stated that the change was made to provide proper board rigidity without the use of supporting struts since the struts were found to be a source of short circuits to the mother board. While the substitution appears reasonable, the manufacturer has not properly considered the consequences of this decision on the IC sockets provided. The pins on the sockets are too short to penetrate the board far enough for reliable soldering. It is extremely difficult to apply heat to these short pins to assure a good solder joint. Since the traces are on only one side of the board, the holes are not plated through, and solder does not tend to wick up the hole along the socket pins. This condition occurs only in the MWRITE logic portion of the board. If this optional circuit is going to be used, the builder should exercise care here or purchase wire-wrap sockets whose longer pins will easily penetrate the board. The pins on the 100-pin edge connector present no problem, since they are long enough to properly penetrate the board.

However, I should caution that the mother board requires the 100-pin connectors to have a lateral (across-the-connector dimension) pin spacing of 5/32 of an inch. This proved to be rather costly for me, since I found a ready supply of the ¼-inch dimension connectors for only $3.50 each, but the only 5/32-inch connectors I could acquire cost $7.35 each! (Maybe I should have bought the Imsai! Half of my saving by not buying the Imsai went for the more expensive connectors.)

Apparently, when the new board was manufactured, two errors crept into the design regarding the connections to the power-on LED. The first of these is minor. The pads for the plus voltage supply, obrained through a dropping resistor, were changed to a new location, and the pictorials were not properly updated. The other problem results from neglecting to drill the hole for the LED ground return. This simple operation must be done by the builder.

One other design deficiency relates to the power-on LED. The BYT-8 design solders the two leads of the LED to wires running to the mother board without any terminal strip to provide proper support of the leads. The unsupported leads are subject to damage or shorting whenever one works in the chassis or inserts or removes boards. To eliminate this problem of hanging leads, I installed a two-lug terminal strip on a nearby chassis attach screw. This strip is close enough to the LED so that the leads would reach, and no additional holes were required in the chassis. Only one note of caution: One should take care that the solder lugs of the terminal used are not grounded through the terminal's mounting lug, in order to preserve the BYT-8's ground independent of the cabinet.

When it came time to install the top and bottom covers of the cabinet, I discovered that the top was about 1/32 inch too short! The top is a wrap-around affair, and the curvature was slightly off, so two of the mounting holes for the attaching screw didn't quite line up with the threaded holes on the chassis side rails. I attempted to fix this condition by reaming the holes out slightly, but this failed to give enough relief to line the screws up with the holes. To have continued on this tack would have required holes too large for the screw heads and would have necessitated the use of large washers. Instead, I elongated the holes on one side, difting them down and back with a small file. This made the top fit acceptably well, but still, there is a narrow gap along one side.

My final hardware comment is directed to the manufacturer. I recommend strongly that the mother board be solder masked to make it less likely that we novices will bridge the traces when we solder in the bus sockets. Those traces are really very close together!

Additional Shortcomings

None of the documentation deficiencies cited below are considered highly critical, but, by being aware of them, the inexperienced builder may avoid time-consuming, if not costly, pitfalls.

The construction notes are contained in an attractive vinyl loose-leaf notebook. Unfortunately, the instructions are somewhat disorganized. The manufacturer should hire a programmer to write the assembly instructions, since programmers should be orderly in their thinking processes and would appreciate the need for logical progression in assembling the kit. The writer of the instructions provided apparently did not put organization very high in his order of priorities. The document contains much irrelevant text and a number of meaningless photographs and sketches. These and a number of redundancies can be overlooked. However, some of the photographs needed for an understanding of the assembly are of poor quality, and proper highlighting of necessary details has been omitted. For example, the master diagram is a top view photograph of the mother board installed in the cabinet. Most of the components show up well enough in this view, but the jumpers blend into the background and are difficult to see. Small (less than 1/16 inch) labels are penned in, but even these are difficult to see—in some cases, they are black written on dark grey. This is one area that the manufacturer should seriously consider for improvement.

At this point, follow me as I flip through the pages of the instruction manual and point out some of the areas where problems may be avoided. Parenthetical numbers refer to the page numbers in my instruction manual. (Possibly, later editions will have different page numbers and will, hopefully, have clarified these points.)

The assembly instruction section has an overview which lists the steps from unpacking the kit through the final testing (ASI-4). This overview is important, since it is the only place where I found an unambiguous description of the construction steps required to assemble the kit. It was here, for example, that I found that I should have mounted the power transformer to the back panel before I assembled the cabinet. Unfortunately, I hadn't remembered that bit of wisdom at the critical point and proceeded to put the cabinet together first, as later instructions implied. This out-of-step assembly caused only a little difficulty in bolting in the transformer and making the solder connections that otherwise would have been easy. Therefore, I suggest to those building this kit that they take this list of steps out of the book and consult it for each major operation along the way.

Several pages in the overview of the assembly are devoted to explaining the electrical characteristics of a number of the components, such as capacitors, diodes, etc. (ASI-8). These pages may be of value to the neophyte kit builder, but they are not complete enough with respect to diodes, as I will explain later.

The expenditures for the two pictures showing how to unpack the kit could have been better used elsewhere to clarify construction steps (ASI-17 and 18.)

The detailed installation pictorial (ASI-26) contains an error on the bridge rectifier polarity (BR2). This picture shows the BR2 plus pin as a minus. However, this should cause only minor confusion, as the PC board has the correct polarity printed on it, as does the as does the pictorial on page ASI-25. Also on page ASI-26, the builder should be aware that the center tap of the 30V AC winding of the power transformer (white/red) is inserted in the top-most hole on the PC board, while the 9V AC and 30V AC leads are installed below it in that order. This detail is not shown clearly anywhere in the instructions and only is apparent if one refers to the wiring schematic and compares it with the PC board. In the earlier discussion of diodes, the instructions failed to tell the neophyte how to identify the anode and cathode of the diode. When he comes to the point where he must insert it into the PC board, he has a 50-50 chance of being right. It would be helpful if he were told (back on page ASI-8) that the diode has a band on one end of its package which corresponds with the straight bar (cathode) on the symbolic representation of the diode. One last comment about page ASI-26—the document persists in saying that the transformer 30V AC leads are orange, except for one place, the schematic of the transformer, where they are correctly identified as red.

On the next page (ASI-27), the voltage regulator circuit components are photographed and super-imposed on the photograph as a schematic of the circuit. As so frequently happens in kits, components change in physical shape from time to time. In my kit, the 10-uF capacitors were not the same type as shown in the pictorial. Instructions such as *caution polarity* are not very enlightening if one is unaware of what the polarity is supposed to be. It would be helpful if the polarity were indicated explicitly on the photograph. The schematic, while helpful to some, may be confusing to the uninitiated, since the relationships between the components in the photograph and those in the schematic are upside down.

Page ASI-28 is a photograph of the bottom of the mother board which is captioned *inspect and clean away residue*. The text relating to this step (ASI-24a) is only slightly more informative than the picture. The builder should be told to thoroughly clean the resin residue and solder splashes from the board with alcohol and a small stiff bristle brush (acid brush obtainable at the local hardware store). The board should be thoroughly wet with the alcohol in a small area and brushed until all resin is dissolved. Before the alcohol dries, the board should be blotted with a clean absorbent cloth. Several cleanings may be necessary to remove all residue. After cleaning, each solder joint should be inspected with a magnifying glass for solder bridges and cold solder joints. Cold solder joints may be identified as areas where the solder has a frosted appearance.

The transformer installation is indicated on page ASI-32. Here one gets the impression that the transformer is installed after the front and back panels are in place. This is wrong! This impression stems from a picture showing the back panel already in place.

After reading page ASI-33, the neophyte may have some trouble installing the power cord grommet/strain relief, if he has never installed one before. He should have a pictorial to go by and a bit of encouragement that the task is at least possible. Attempting to push the two parts of this grommet together with the heavy line cord between them and to insert the entire assembly in the hole in the chassis is almost like trying to put a one-inch-square peg in a ½-inch-round hole!

The schematic of the power transformer (ASI-34) should have a note to instruct the builder to scrape the paint away from the lug mounting screw hole so a good connection can be made for the ground wire of the line cord. This isn't made clear, and I imagine that some builders may wonder why there is no ground on the chassis when they come to that part of the checkout in later steps.

Page ASI-40 has a much better view of the jumpers that were installed earlier in the assembly process (ASI-25). The photo has increased contrast, and the details stand out more visibly. Here one realizes that the board has some changes in the location of the LED power connections from those pictured. Also on this page, one is instructed to connect the start/restart switch. The switch in my kit was a double-throw spring-loaded center switch. The picture doesn't make it clear whether the second connection to the switch is made to the top or bottom terminal. Since the function implemented here is the restart, and the front panel shows this in the *up* position, I reasoned that the connection should be made to the lower terminal on the switch. This means that the *start* position has no effect. Possibly this puzzle is the result of substituting a double-throw switch for what was originally a single-throw switch.

There is one last item. In providing instructions for the cabinet assembly, very little text is available; the manual relies almost totally on the pictorials. This is fine. However, it would be helpful if the size of the screws was specified in the drawings. I found that I used a wrong screw size when I later discovered that the remaining screws wouldn't work. Thus, I had to disassemble a few things and reassemble them with different size screws.

One might gather from all the gripes above that I would hesitate to recommend the BYT-8 to my freinds. This is not the case. In spite of the problems, I feel that it is worth what I paid for it, and, for those forewarned of the deficiencies, it should pose no real problems. At this point, I have tested every part of the board that I can without the rest of the computer components, and it appears to work as advertised. But who knows what I'll find when I plug in all the other components?

A Cassette-Computer System

The most practical and economical way to store programs and large quantities of data for small computer systems is with the common tape cassette recorder. Cheap and plentiful, audio-type cassette equipment is capable of storing several times the amount of data that an equivalent volume of paper tape can hold, with the added benefits of erasability and easier operation. Floppy disks may be faster, but are beyond the price range of most hobbyists.

While computer manufacturers have long been supplying their programs on audio cassettes, there has been a major problem with compatibility. Every manufacturer has had his own pet system of recording, and a tape recorded for use with one brand of computer is utter gibberish to another brand of computer. For this reason, several manufacturers decided to adopt a standard system of tape interfacing.

The proposed standard, as implemented by Pronetics Corp., calls for a frequency-shift keying standard. The two tones to be recorded are ideally to be square waves, with Mark (logic 1) to be 2400 Hz and Space (logic 0) to be 1200 Hz. With a standard tape exchange speed of 300 baud (bits per second), Mark would consist of eight cycles, Space of four. This could be divided to 600 or 1200 baud, in which case one cycle would be a space (1/1200 seconds). Higher density would be impractical. For comparison, 300 baud corresponds roughly to 30 characters per second.

Within each character, the first recorded tone should consist of a Space (start) bit, followed by eight data bits (least significant bit first, parity last) and two Mark (stop) bits. All undefined bits, as well as the interval between characters, would be Mark (2400 Hz).

This system aas several beneficial features. It is self-clocking. The first bit of any character is Space and must follow the Mark tone that ends previous characters and exists between characters. It is possible to tolerate as much as a 30 percent speed variation with this system, which can be an important factor with inexpensive tape equipment.

Do You Need a Good Recorder?

Almost any cassette recorder can be used for data storage

using this FSK standard system. But for convenience and accuracy, there are a few criteria for selection that differ from hi-fi quality.

You want a clean, reliable machine. Dirty heads and mechanisms can soil data very easily. If you don't have a cassette recorder already, a used model is adequate, but it shouldn't show signs of mistreatment. It should also have capstan drive—a few miniature units don't.

A digital tape counter is also a great convenience. Without one, identifying programs on a tape can be difficult, and could lead to accidental erasures. These are found on many hi-fi type machines, and occasionally on portable units.

An important electrical feature is AC bias/erase. Some recorders, and most of the under-$100 category, use DC for erasing and record biasing. This results in higher noise and less frequency response. While frequency response is not as critical with this system as with music recording, it still helps to have a good clean treble response, which can help preserve the square wave shape. Low noise means fewer errors, so a high signal-to-noise ratio aids reliability.

Stereophonic capability is unnecessary. If you have a stereo recorder, be sure to record both tracks simultaneously, and bulk erase the tape before using it.

Your tape recorder must have an auxiliary or microphone input jack, as well as an earphone or line output. Acoustic coupling is unsatisfactory. The choice of levels can be performed in the computer interface circuitry, so either mike, line or speaker levels can be used.

What About Tape?

While the choice of tape recorder is uncritical, the tape itself is the weak link in the chain. Do not skimp on tape. Use the best tape you can get your paws on. Since dropout on the tape means loss of data, the tape must have a high manufacturing standard. Some cassettes jam easily, and the thin tape found in C90 and C120 cassettes is too thin and fragile to be reliable. A premium grade C60 tape is ideal. Perfectionists might want to spend the extra money for chromium dioxide tape. The extra response can't hurt.

Store the tapes in a dust-free location, in their own container. Do not smoke near the tapes or the recorder, and clean the heads frequently. Tape cleanliness and quality are far more important in digital applications than in music.

The Recording Interface

Digital information from your computer is generally available as 8 bits parallel from either an I/O port or data bus. The tape is

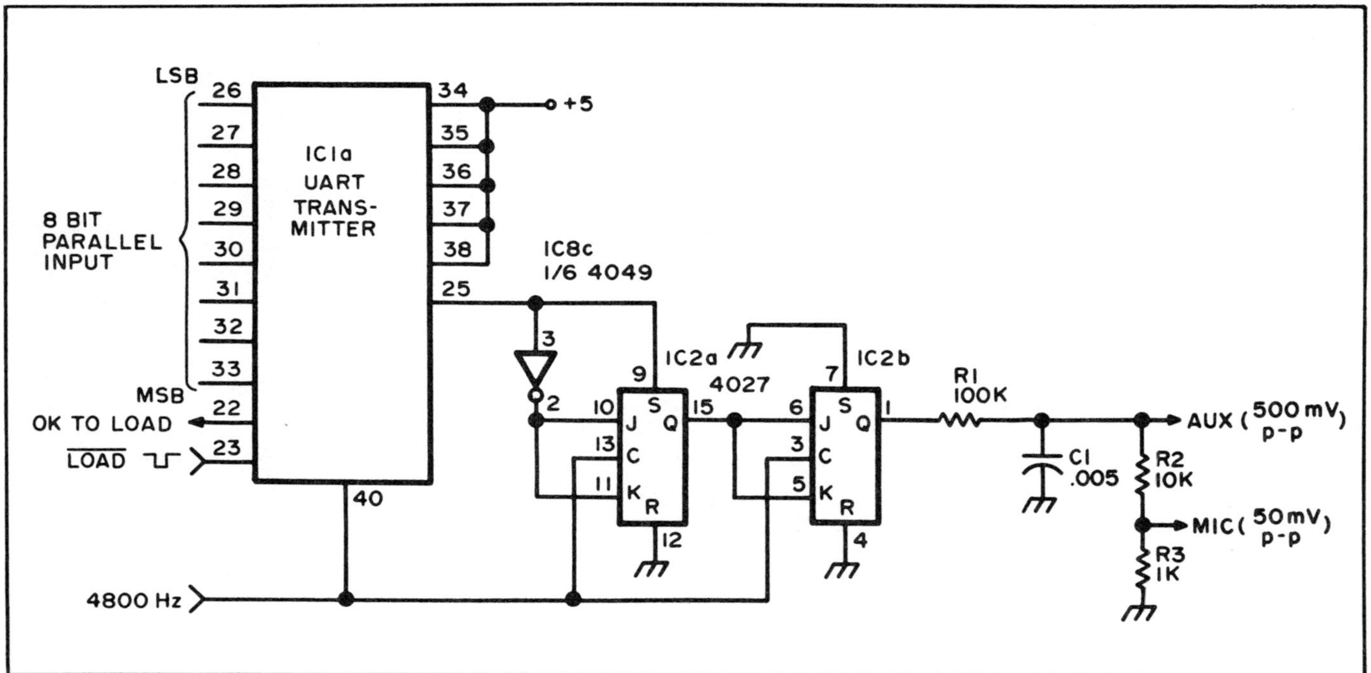

Fig. 7-28. Cassette digital modulator. This circuit converts 8-bit parallel input data to a series of 2400 and 1200 Hz tones for recording on cassette tape.

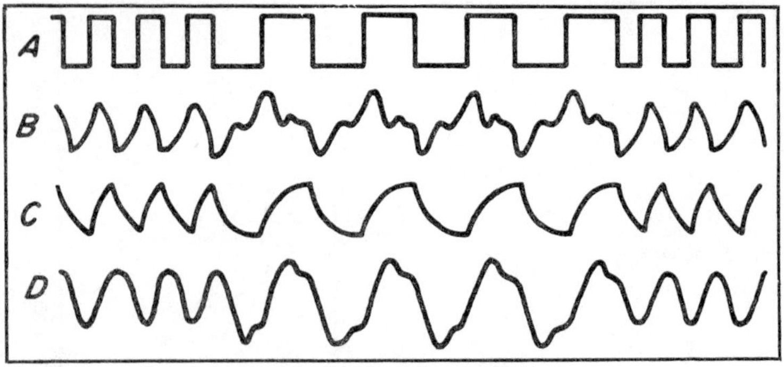

Fig. 7-29. If a square wave signal such as a waveform A is recorded on a low cost cassette recorder, the playback response may look like waveform B, which is very difficult to demodulate. If the square wave is filtered with a low pass filter before recording (waveform C), the playback response will appear like waveform D, a usable signal.

recorded serially; the conversion is best accomplished with a Universal Asynchronous Receiver/Transmitter (UART) IC.

The modulator is shown in Fig. 7-28. The serial output of the UART has logic 1 as a high level and logic 0 as a low level. IC2a and IC2b form a clock divider circuit, dividing the 4800 Hz clock signal by 2 or 4, depending on the UART output level. The output is a series of square waves which feed the tape recorder's input.

The poor frequency response of some tape recorders, especially those with DC Bias, causes the manufacturers to exaggerate the treble being recorded, which distorts the square wave. Sine waves record better, but are harder to generate digitally. In some cases using a low pass filter makes the waveform usable; R1 and C1 perform this function. A smaller value for C1 may increase effectiveness with better recorders. Figure 7-29 shows the effect of the recording process on digital waveforms.

The AUX output of the interface is 500 mV peak-to-peak and is for use with high impedance high level inputs. The MIC output is 50 mV, suitable for most units with microphone inputs.

The 4800 Hz signal must be capable of driving two TTL loads. While a crystal oscillator and divider chain work best, and a phase locked loop referencing the 60 Hz power line is also very good, the oscillator in Fig. 7-30 is simple and quite satisfactory (but requires calibration with a frequency counter).

If the available digital information from the computer is already in serial form with the necessary start and two stop bits, and is properly timed at 300 baud, the UART is not necessary. However, the 4800 Hz clocking signal should be synchronous with the serial data, with 16 clock pulses per bit. If the serial data is not at 300 baud, a UART receiver must first be used to convert the data to parallel form. It then is clocked through the UART transmitter as shown.

The OK TO LOAD line on the UART goes high when it is ready to accept a byte of parallel data. The data is then loaded into the UART transmitter by pulsing the LOAD line low for at least one usec or until the OK TO LOAD line goes low. The transmitter will then start transmitting the byte when the LOAD line is returned to the high state. When not transmitting, the output is high, causing the modulator to generate the 2400 Hz Mark signal.

The Playback Interface

There are several possible ways to recover the FSK signal from the tape. An FM discriminator or a phase locked loop demodulator can be used, just as with an amateur RTTY signal. Users of previous nonstandardized cassette interfaces can readjust them to decode the 1200/2400 Hz tones, but the most accurate system uses digital recovery to extract timing information from the recorded signal and uses that information to retime the recovered data.

Figure 7-31 is a complete schematic of the playback demodulator. Figure 7-32 shows the resulting waveforms. The signal from

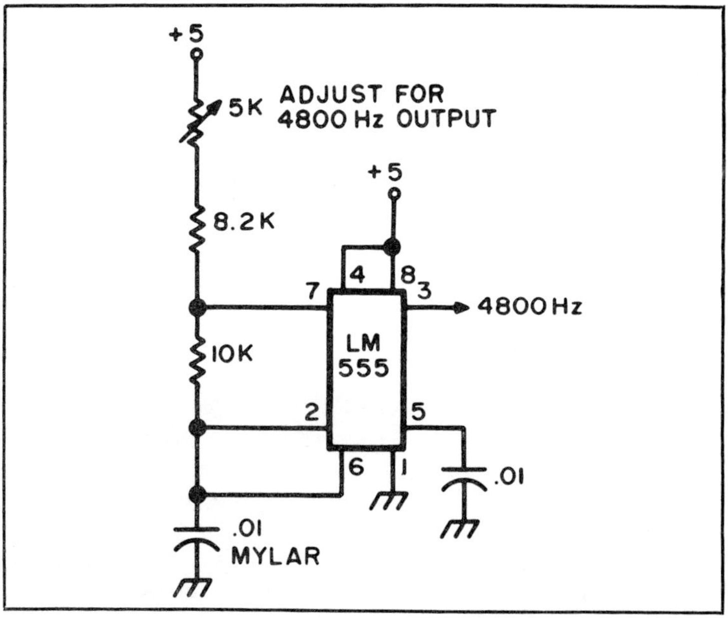

Fig. 7-30. Circuit of 4800 Hz oscillator. Use this circuit if a more precise and stable source of 4800 Hz is not available.

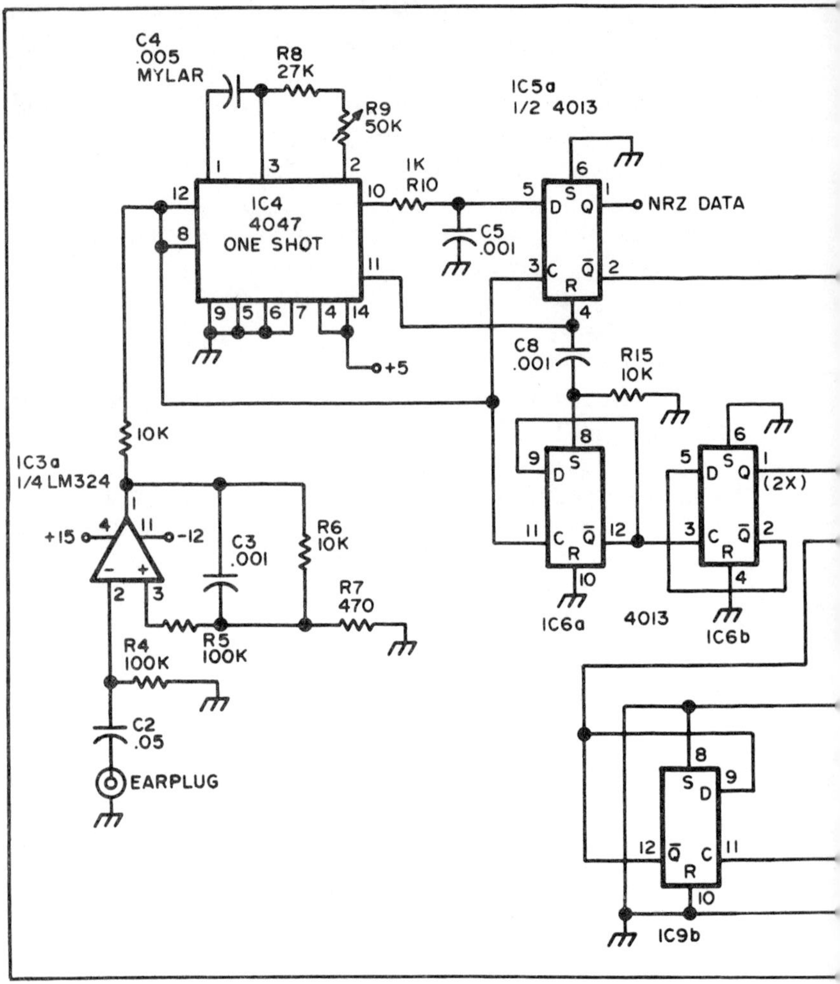

Fig. 7-31. Cassette data recovery circuit.

the cassette player is conditioned by IC3, an op amp used as a Schmitt trigger. The output of a Schmitt trigger is, by definition, either fully high or low, so it regenerates pure square waves from the distorted tape input. IC4 is a retriggerable one shot with a period set to 555 microseconds. As long as the input signal is 2400 Hz, the one shot is retriggered before it times out. Flip flop IC5a remains high, which is interpreted as logic 1. The 1200 Hz signal, on the other hand, has a period between pulses of greater than 555 usec, so the one shot times out, resetting IC5a. It stays at logic 0 as long as 1200 Hz is being received because the one shot is timed out

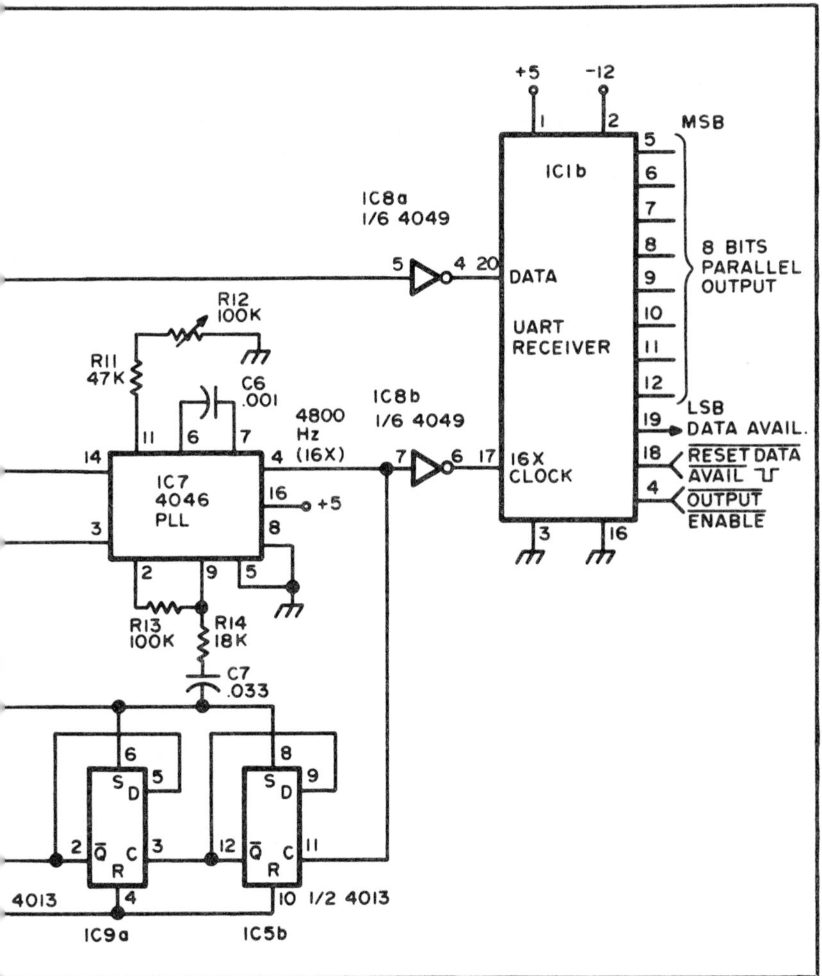

whenever the next triggering edge occurs. When the 2400 Hz signal returns, the one shot stays high, permitting IC5a to switch back to high state. The output of this flip flop is the serial data.

While that simple circuit will work well if the tape speed is accurate to better than ±6%, such is frequently not the case. Since tape speed variations will be reflected in pitch variations in the recovered tones, it is possible to use the 1200 and 2400 Hz signals from the tape to retime the recovered data. Flip flops IC6a and IC6b extract this timing information. When the 1200 Hz signal is received, IC6a is preset with a pulse generated by C8 and R15 every time the one shot times out. The effect is to cause IC6 to divide by two. When 2400 Hz is being received, the one shot does not time out and IC6 divides by four. The result is a clock at the output of IC6b, at 600 Hz.

Instead of clocking the data into a shift register, the receiver portion of UART IC1 is used. It has built-in circuitry to identify the start and stop of each byte automatically. It also has three-state output (logic low, logic high, and functionally disconnected), which permits direct connection to most data buses and I/O ports. The UART needs a 16x clock, which is formed by phase locking a 4800 Hz oscillator to the 600 Hz output of IC6b. The PLL is adjusted to oscillate at 4800 Hz in the absence of any input signal. IC5b and IC9 divide the PLL output by 8 to drive one of the phase detector inputs, while the other input is driven by IC6b.

The UART receiver raises its DATA AVAILABLE output to logic 1 when it recognizes that it has received a complete character. Since the UART outputs are three-state, it is necessary to drive the RECEIVED DATA ENABLE input to logic 0 to read the parallel output data. After the parallel data has been read it is necessary to pulse the RESET DATA AVAILABLE line to prepare the UART to output the next byte. The pulse must remain at logic 0 for at least one usec, or until the DATA AVAILABLE line drops to logic 0.

Circuit Adjustments

The only adjustment necessary for the recording modulator is to put the 4800 Hz signal exactly on frequency. Since a Mark byte consists of eight (not seven or nine) cycles at 2400 Hz, this is fairly critical.

The data recovery one shot and PLL oscillator must be accurately adjusted for best results. The one shot is critical. To adjust it, set a well calibrated audio source to 1800 Hz with 1.5 to 3.5V rms output. Adjust R9 until the data output of IC5a pin 1 just changes, measured on a high impedance voltmeter. Adjust R9 to as close to the point of change as possible.

The PLL oscillator is adjusted by R12 with no input to the playback input. If no counter is available, the oscillator output at IC7 pin 4 should be compared to the 4800 Hz signal used for the UART transmitter.

Circuit Operation

The circuit as shown will recover data most accurately if the earplug output signal of the tape recorder is between 4 and 10 volts peak-to-peak. Most portable recorders have that capability. If the

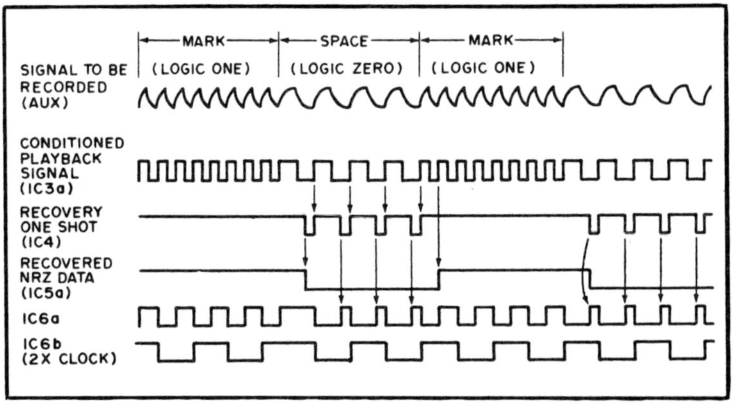

Fig. 7-32. Cassette modulator/demodulator waveforms.

cassette deck does not have a speaker amplifier, a low gain amplifier may be necessary. If the recorder uses DC bias, there may be too much tremble, which necessitates turning down the tone control.

To comply with the standard for tape exchange, the recorded data should be preceded by at least 5 seconds of 2400 Hz tone before the data begins. This is accomplished by operating the recorder in the record mode for five seconds or longer before sending data to the UART transmitter. With the UART idle, the modulator generates 2400 Hz.

During playback, wait a couple of seconds before allowing the computer to accept the UART receiver output, to avoid reading the garbage generated by turning the recorder on and off. It is possible to have the computer control, via a relay, the remote control switch of the tape recorder under program control. It is still necessary to wait a few seconds before accepting data, due to the time spent starting and stopping the tape. The 2400 Hz leader provides that interval on the tape.

Using this type of hardware for tape cassette modulation and demodulation simplifies programming for a cassette-oriented computer system. In some circumstances it may be possible to connect the interface hardware directly to the computer, while some computers may require peripheral interface adapters to get the data in and out of the computer.

The Cheaper Beeper

While the idea of a tone generator for a microprocessor is great and the circuit is simple, $7.95 for the DIP-alarm seems a bit steep. While it is probably best for the computer freaks, it can be done less

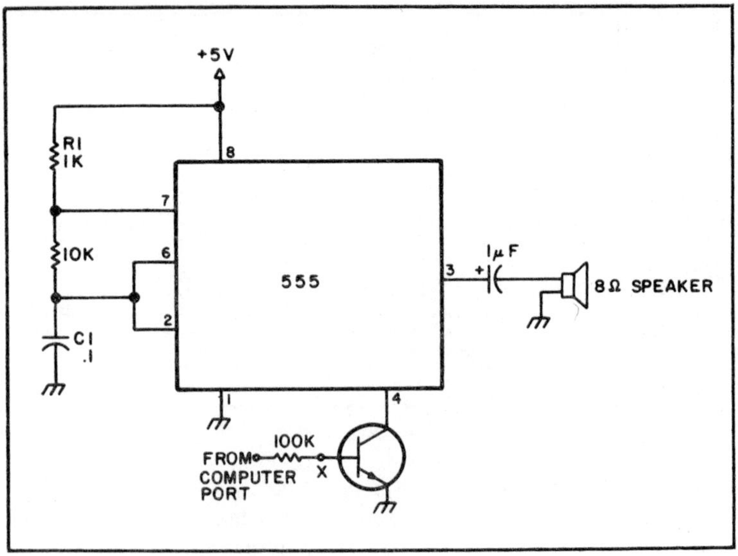

Fig. 7-33. Schematic.

expensively by using junk box parts (Fig. 7-33). While it isn't all that original, it is different from a lot of keyed 555 tone generators. I have often noticed with distress that people enable a 555 by grounding pin 1. Pin 4 is actually labeled *enable*, and this circuit makes use of it. The transistor acts as an inverter.

Perhaps the easiest method of construction would be to find a junked transistor radio and use the speaker and case from it. This would save you having to go to the trouble of mounting the speaker in some other box along with the extra trouble of drilling holes for sound. None of the component values are critical. By changing either R1 or C1, the frequency can be changed. With the values shown, the frequency is about 600 Hz. For the transistor, I used an unmarked type off a computer circuit board, and just about anything will work.

If you want a tone when a high is applied to the tone generator, just disconnect the transistor and apply the signal from the uP directly to pin 4. For those of you interested in using the generator as a code practice oscillator, connect the side of the 100k resistor marked from computer port to the 5-volt supply, and connect your key from point *X* to ground.

Also, note that this circuit does not have to be run off 5 volts. It will work on anything from about 5 volts to 15 volts. As a CPO, it would probably be easier to use a 9-volt battery. If you're using CMOS in your uP and don't have a 5-volt supply, this circuit is particularly nice.

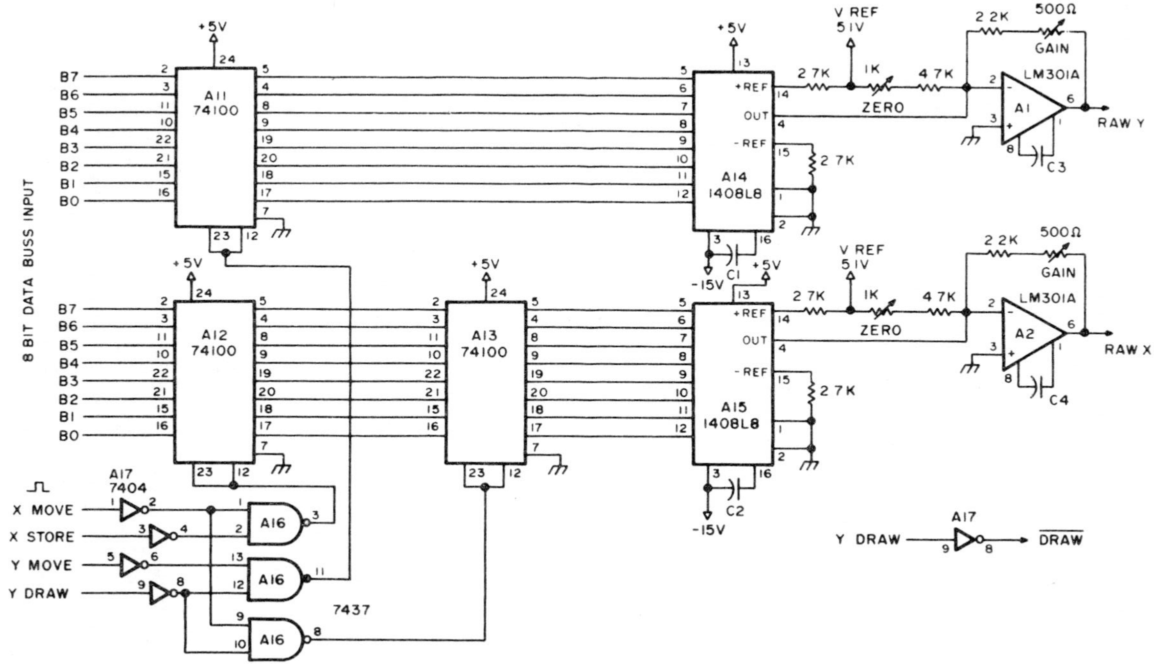

Fig. 7-34. Input register and DAC.

Simple Graphics Terminal

Several designs have been presented in the past that would, in one way or another, allow the display of graphical data on a CRT. Although these several approaches will accomplish the stated objective, each has the shortcomings of requiring the builder to fend for himself when it comes to the actual output device to be used. This graphics display described takes advantage of a group of ready-made subassemblies, which when interconnected and properly interfaced with the graphics driver portion of this project, will result in a first class graphics display with capabilities far in excess of those attainable with a simple oscilloscope adaptation or a raster-scan television readout device (Figs. 7-34 through 7-39).

To illustrate that point, consider the following. The raster-scan home television type display, such as that used in several popular alphanumeric displays, can be used. But, the display is overly complicated and will appear as a connection of blocks rather than as pure line segments. Consequently, since graphics display implies a random display, a single memory cell is required for every defined location on the screen, with the block size determining the maximum number of locations and hence, the resolution. The finer the detail required, the smaller the blocks and the more memory cells required. If the complete screen is to have 256 elements or blocks, these individual units could be defined by four bit X and Y addresses and 32 bytes of 8 bit memory. The resolution in a display with these few points would be terrible.

An 8 bit microprocessor works best with multiples of 8 bits. If we, therefore, made a display incorporating an 8 bit X address and an 8 bit Y address, it would fit nicely and be easy to work with. This display would be of fairly high resolution since it now has 65,000 discrete locations. The only complication is that it will require 8K bytes of memory to store, regardless of the picture being displayed. This will always be the case in any digital storage system. The computer must account for every dot on the screen (65K) and, depending on whether there is a one or a zero stored in the memory location defining that spot, it will make it either black or white. Additional information is required if gray tones are involved.

A much better system is one which incorporates this same high resolution but does not have to provide storage for anything other than the actual displayed points. The one described here is just such a system.

What Is Graphics Display?

Everybody knows what a graphics display is, right? We all know that a graphics display will allow us to observe phenomena in that

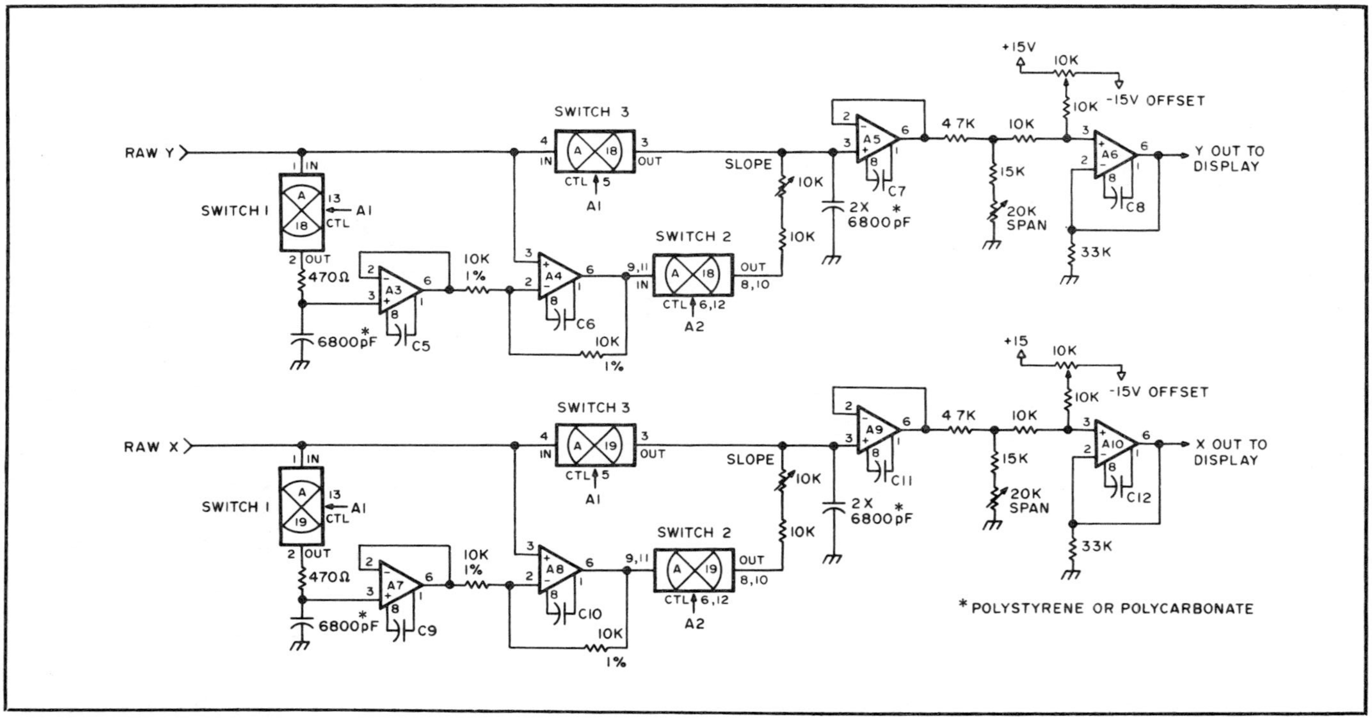

Fig. 7-35. Vector generator. Note: A1-A10-pin 7 to +5 V, pin 4 to – 15V, A16-A17, A21, A22—pin 14 to +5V, pin 7 to ground; A20—pin 16 to +5 V, pin 8 to ground.

familiar Etch-A-Sketch format drilled into us since kindergarten days. Using appropriate input signal conditioning, a graphics display can be just about anything we want it to be . . . from a simple tic-tac-toe pattern to a very complex schematic or logic diagram. We can even play games such as Space War and tennis, display a graph of the current stock market trends, plot temperature and humidity and on and on.

That's terrific. Everyone should have one, you say? Agreed. The following paragraphs will describe, in sufficient detail, a method whereby the average experimenter can acquire all of the parts and subassemblies needed to construct just such a device. Basically, this graphics display consists of a group of ready-made subassemblies which, when modified per the instructions contained herein, will result in a very high performance X-Y display. The readout device is a 12 inch diagonal TV-like CRT with a very bright green-blue trace. This CRT has a medium persistence, which is desirable in the interests of flicker reduction. Additional electronics are described to transform the output instructions from any microprocessor into the analog voltages and positioning signals used to actually produce the various line segments that will make up the desired display of information.

It should be noted that the graphics display described is the result of the many bits and pieces of pertinent information and ideas which abound in the field today. We've drawn on ideas, and in some cases used portions of previously described circuits to arrive at the final configuration presented here. We have integrated these various data into a workable, practicable and *available* piece of equipment intended to do a specific task well, but also have a degree of expandability for new techniques of the future.

So much for the commercial. Now it's time to get on with the description of the project. We'll start with the basic CRT display, since that is the easiest portion. What could be easier than simply sending off an order for a couple of boxes full of already constructed gear and waiting patiently for the order to arrive? Well, there's a wee bit more to it than that, but not much. Suntronix Company (Londonderry, H.H. and Lawrence, Mass.) is once again selling a package of electronic subassemblies that include all of the basic electronic items needed to construct the X-Y display portion of this project. These subassemblies include all of the power supplies, both high and low voltage, the vertical and horizontal deflection amplifiers, a special yoke for the magnetically deflected 12-inch CRT, four PC cards, a chassis and base to hold these subassemblies and a neat enclosure to hide all of the above. Also included in the

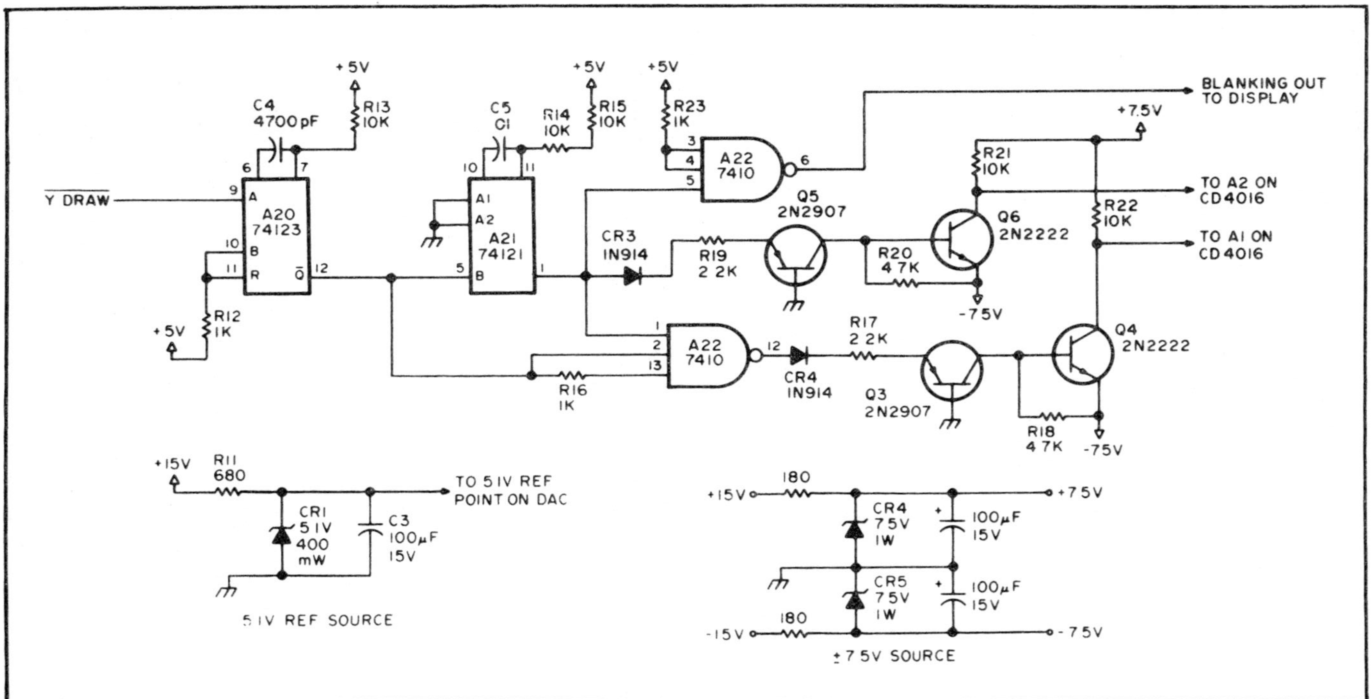

Fig. 7-36. Schematic.

package price is a keyboard, ASCII encoded, with an enclosure that fits nicely with the rest of the equipment. Complete data in the form of schematic diagrams for each subassembly is included. As received from Suntronix, these subassemblies will interconnect without major modification to provide the basic X-Y display. So, first thing to do is fire off an order to Suntronix for the complete package of subassemblies.

Now the hard part. You must decide whether you want to build the CRT driver from scratch or order one from Suntronix. Whichever route you choose, you should read the following technical description anyhow, so put off the hard part (the decision-making) and continue to read.

CRT Graphics Driver

The graphics driver is the interface between the actual display and the microprocessor. It translates the binary coded coordinates presented to it through software routines to analog voltages which position the CRT beam appropriately. This driver is a fairly simple system designed to draw line segments with a very high degree of resolution, yet requires only beginning and ending cartesian coordinates to define that line segment. For example, a line running diagonally across the CRT screen from upper left to lower right (−X, +Y to +X, −Y) requires only four eight bit bytes to define the line. Beam position is proportional to the analog voltages applied to the inputs of the deflection amplifiers. The digital to analog converters (DACs) in the graphics driver convert the eight bit coordinates to the analog voltages they represent. Continuous scanning of a series of these values connects many individual line segments to produce the desired figures or pictures or whatever. Additional circuitry is included to assure a relatively uniform beam intensity regardless of where the beam is commanded to go. Also, blanking of unwanted beam movements is included.

Input Registers and DACs

The graphics driver has been designed to be driven by any eight bit microprocessor such as the 8008, 8008-1. It is compatible with any faster eight bit machine so long as the software scanning routines do not exceed the processing and analog conversion time of the driver. Though somewhat modified, this circuit is based upon a similar design by Hal Chamberlin. Basically, the design is a software graphics driver. Computer instructions are used to output the binary position coordinates to the driver eight bits at a time; first an X position, then a Y position. Together, these sixteen bits represent the X, Y beginning position of a line segment. Next, the computer outputs the X, Y values of the ending position of that line segment and the driver unblanks the CRT beam to allow display of this motion between the start and end positions. Since this display is software driven, the total number of displayed lines is a function of the computer's speed. Refresh of the display is accomplished by having the computer scan the coordinates continuously. If there are too many points, the display will appear to blink or jitter. The CRT's P31 phosphor helps to correct this condition by allowing more time between refresh cycles. This will be helpful to people with slow computers!

Four instructions are used: Xmove, Ymove, Xstore and Ydraw. They are actually four output strobes from the computer which are enabled by the transfer of position data to the graphics driver storage registers. When Xmove (the I/O instruction outputting data to whatever output port is chosen) is executed, the contents of the microprocessor's accumulator are transferred via the eight bit data bus to an eight bit register, A13. Next a Ymove is executed and the accumulator contents are transferred to All. Connected to these registers are two eight bit DACs, A14 and A15. The converters free run and will follow any change in value of the input registers. Within a few microseconds of data input, the respective raw X and raw Y voltages will have settled out and now represent, in analog form, the digital X and Y coordinates from the computer. As the instructions implied (Xmove and Ymove), the beam position changes to follow this new input but is not displayed since the beam is blanked during this period.

The actual analog voltage is a function of the 1408L8 DAC. This device behaves like a programmable current source set by the reference current at pin 14. In this particular design, the reference current is approximately 2.0 mA. Binary inputs to the DAC provide the equivalent fraction of the reference current at the output. For example, if the input to the DAC were 00100000, the output current would be 32/256 of the reference current. This signal is more useful and manageable in voltage form. That's the job of op amps A1 and A2. These op amps are configured as current to voltage converters with adjustable gain and offset. With an input of 00000000 binary, the output should be adjusted to a value of −2.5 volts. Adjusting the gain and offset trimmers alternately will produce the desired results. Conversely, an input of 10000000 should produce an output of +2.5 volts. This voltage range is not compatible with the display deflection amplifiers as received, and will be scaled by additional circuitry in the display driver electronics.

Vector Generator

The raw X and raw Y voltages from the DACs go to the vector generator which uses CD4016 quad analog switches. These switches are controlled by Q1, Q2, Q3, and Q4, a level shifter that changes the voltages from TTL levels to MOS levels, required by the CD4016s. Each switch section consists of a signal input and output terminal and a switch control terminal. When this control terminal is at +7.5 volts, the switch is on, and when the control terminal is at −7.5 volts, it is off. A DM8800 level shifter could be used in place of the four transistors and associated components if you can find it. The Suntronix graphics driver uses the transistor version in the interest of simply being able to obtain the parts readily.

In the quiescent state, switches 1 and 3 are on, 2 is off, and the output of the vector generator is equal to the raw input voltage. When a Ydraw is executed, A20 fires for approximately 20 microseconds and turns off switches 1 and 3. During this one shot period, raw X and raw Y voltages are settling toward the new input values loaded into the registers. These values correspond to the end point of the line segment. The display is still in a blanked state, and with switches 1 and 3 off, the vector generator is acting as a sample and hold circuit in a hold condition with the output constant.

When the first one shot times out, it fires A21 which has a period of approximately 100 microseconds. While A21 is on, the beam is unblanked, switch 2 turns on, and switches 1 and 3 remain off. In this state, the integrating capacitor at A9 starts charging through switch 2 along an exponential curve. Even though this voltage is actually 2 times the new raw value minus the original raw value, the one shot's period is adjusted to time out at the correct end point voltage and provide the appearance of a straight line. The fact that the output voltage changes along an exponential curve is irrelevant as long as both axes are identical. At the conclusion of this one shot period, switch 2 turns off, switches 1 and 3 turn on, and the display blanks again. The output voltage readjusts itself to exactly the new voltage through switch 3.

The driver electronics, to this point, have been set to produce minus and plus 2.5 volt signals for octal inputs of 000 and 377 respectively. This five volt magnitude is incompatible with the deflection amplifiers as purchased. The purpose of A6 and A10 is to scale and offset the vector generator outputs so they are within 0 to −3 volts as required. Each op amp is configured as a non-inverting summing amplifier. The span adjustment alternates the 5 volt absolute magnitude from the vector generator to 3 volts (plus 1.5 volts to −1.5 volts). The offset pot is then set to produce an offset of −1.5

volts with no signal in. The resulting signal level will be minus 3 volts for an octal 000 input and 0 volts for an octal 377 input. These two settings, as well as the gain and offset adjustments of the D to A converters, are best done by loading single values in the registers and not trying to program an actual display.

The vector generators will need slope and end match calibration. It is easiest to adjust the vector generator if a square with diagonals from corner to corner is displayed. The worst case for the driver, and hence the optimum case for calibration, is the display of a square with full scale coordinates. A square with two diagonals can be drawn with 6 line segments and is illustrated with full scale octal coordinate numbers in Fig. 7-37. The brute force display method is to write a program which treats each line segment as a separate entity and outputs the display coordinates to the driver sequentially. For this particular square, the program would do successive outputs from the accumulator of Xmove, Ymove, Xstore and Ydraw, respectively, for the following series of octal coordinates: 000,000,000,377 (line segment 1); 000,377,377,377 (line segment 2); 377,377,377,000 (line segment 3); 377,000,000,000 (line segment 4); 000,000,377,377 (diagonal line segment 5); and 000,377,377,000 (diagonal line segment 6). Repeat continually for a constant display.

This again is the worst case display and requires optimum performance from the driver. End point timing problems will appear either as under-or over-shoot of line segment length and can be

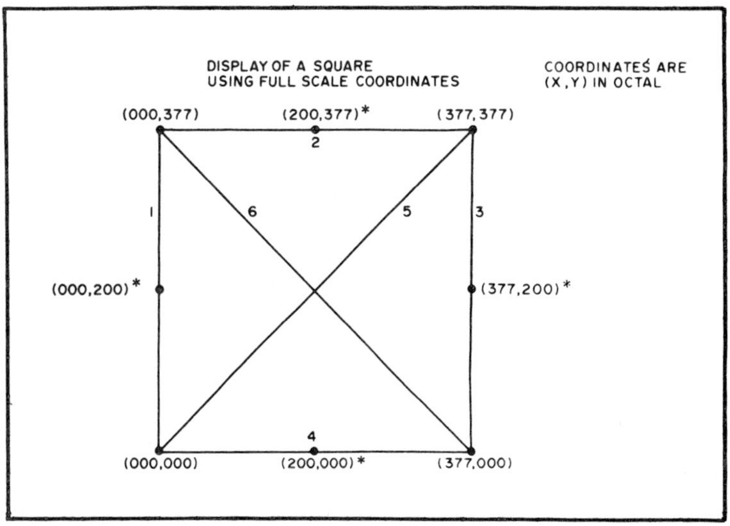

Fig. 7-37. Example of a square for calibration.

compensated by adjusting the end match pot on A21. Slope problems will result in the diagonals of the square pot meeting in the corners. Slope adjustments are made with the appropriate pots at A5 and A9. It is important not to substitute any operational amplifiers which may have a slower frequency response than the LM301A's because this will compromise the driver's ability to track large changes in input coordinates and will attenuate full scale response. An additional area of concern is power supply bypassing and grounding. The largest ground plane and thickest wire appropriate for connecting grounds will result in the least noise and the cleanest display. Bypass capacitors (.1 microfarad/25 volt) should be placed between supply voltage points and the ground plane at a number of locations on the display driver board. Too many is always better than too few when it comes to bypass capacitors. Make the layout orderly and neat to reduce crosstalk and avoid ground loops. If separate power supplies for the +5 volts, +15 volts and −15 volts are built and connected by a cable, it is a good idea to put extra filter capacitors (100 microfarad or higher/25 volts) on these power lines where they enter the display board. Tantalum capacitors are the best choice but aluminum foil capacitors are adequate.

Now that you know how it works, it has once again come to the hard part; a decision must be made whether to *build or buy.* Obviously, the quickest and easiest way to get this fascinating and useful instrument up and running is to purchase the graphics driver and the set of subassemblies being offered by Suntronix Company. Certainly that is not the only way. You may choose to build the graphics driver from scratch. With the printed circuit card available from Suntronix it should be a relatively simple and even enjoyable task. Merely follow the instructions in the following paragraphs and those that come with the PC card.

If you want to build the driver and elect not to purchase the driver PC card, some additional comments are in order.

Much of the electronics on the four PC cards that come with the subassemblies is superfluous when used as an X, Y display. The two 6 bit digital to analog converters previously used for character placement can be eliminated, as well as the actual starburst pattern generator. The only other alteration is to isolate the blanking signal. When these few tasks are completed and external voltages applied where the DAC inputs had been previously, one will have an operational 12 inches X, Y input CRT all ready for graphics.

Testing the Unmodified CRT Subassemblies

Before any modifications can be made, the operational integrity of the terminal must be established. Even though the refrigerator sized controller necessary for alphanumerics is missing, the unit is capable of self-scanning through a combination of positions and blanking control with the D to A cards as they are. To test the unit, install the four cards. The card closest to the screen is the horizontal DAC and the next card behind it is the vertical DAC. Both cards are identical. The third card in from the tube end is the integrator, clock conditioner and starburst generator card. Behind it is the digital position and unblanking card. On the back connector, labeled J103, it will be necessary to put in a 1 MHz clock signal and an unblanking signal. The 1 MHz clock, which is required both for the high voltage generation and character position, is applied to pins 8 and 9 (8 ground and 9 high). A suitable TTL circuit to feed the 50 Ohm load presented by the CRT is illustrated in Fig. 7-38. It is not necessary that it be crystal controlled, but a clock input is required at all times to operate this unit. The unblanking signal is applied to pins 10 and 11 (10 ground and 11 signal in). With the clock signal applied, and −5 volts from pin 11 to ground, turn on the display. A fairly noticeable high pitched tone should be heard. This is the high voltage oscillator. Slowly rotate the intensity control (same shaft with the on/off control), and a pattern should appear. This pattern will appear as though one were looking at ten layers of chicken wire, but it is actually all starburst locations unblanked and displayed. Removing the −5 volts from the blanking input will leave one starburst pattern displayed on the screen in a random location. Repeated applications of the blanking input will make this single pattern appear to jump around the screen.

At this point, initial checkout is complete and modifications can begin. Although not absolutely necessary, it was determined that all of the modifications to this terminal could be carried out on the four PC cards. The easiest approach is always the preferred method when dealing with surplus electronics because of the numerous

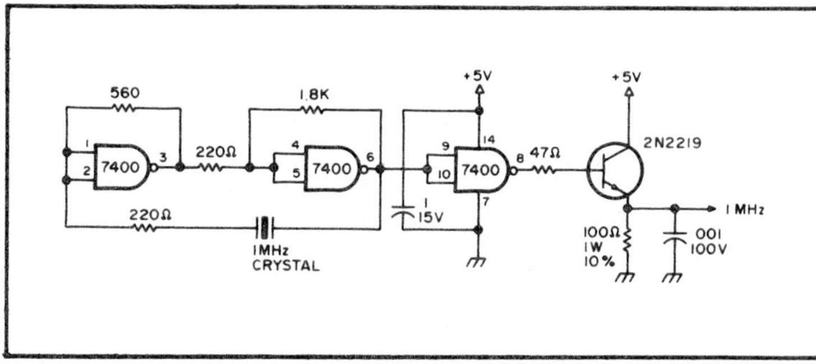

Fig. 7-38. MHz oscillator. All resistors ¼ W 5% unless otherwise noted.

design revisions such equipment has had over the years. The latest schematics are always hard to find.

TTL Level Blanking Input

One of the first modifications necessary is to change the blanking level input from the previous level of –5 volts into 50Ω which is inconvenient to use. This negative voltage is an external requirement only. From there it feeds a level translator on the integrator card which converts it to a +4.5 volt blanking level compatible for use in the digital logic of the position and unblanking board. After transferring through all the logic, this signal leaves the board as an unblank to video amp signal on pin 3 of connector J107 on the base of the card. Between terminal E31 (connected to pin 3) and E30 is a jumper. By removing this jumper and attaching a separate TTL level input to terminal E31, this unblanking option can be externally controlled. The card itself cannot be discarded and has to be inserted for the unit to be operational. There is additional logic on this card necessary to generate the high voltage for the CRT. This concludes the modifications necessary to allow external blanking.

Eliminating the Starburst Generator

The starburst generator is located on the integrator and clock conditioner card. The output of this generator feeds directly to the video amplifier and must be disabled or a moving starburst will be displayed rather than a line segment when the beam is moved. This simple modification can be accomplished by removing a transistor, Q9, and cutting a tape between pin 15 and the junction of R21 and the emitter of Q8. By cutting these two signals to the video amp, we are eliminating a 2 bit D to A converter which continually causes the beam to trace a starburst pattern. What is left is a single dot on the screen whose position is completely controlled by the vertical and horizontal deflection voltages generated on the vertical and horizontal D to A cards. As in the previous case, there is other circuitry on this card, such as the clock conditioner, which requires that the card be inserted for the display to be used. This concludes the integrator card modifications.

Vertical and Horizontal Deflection Inputs

The modification to the deflection amplifiers to allow external deflection voltage input is indeed simple. It essentially means throwing away the two D to A converter cards and applying the external input voltages directly to the connector pins. Unfortunately, getting at these pins is difficult and requires removing the high voltage section. An easier method is to disconnect the DAC outputs on each card and attach the external input on the card in its place. The two cards are identical and require the same modification. Each of these boards is a 6 bit digital to analog converter card. The output of the converter is jumpered from terminal E1 to terminal E2. Terminal E2 is also the output pin M on the base of the card. By removing this jumper, the card electronics is disconnected. A coxial cable can then be attached to terminal. E2 on each board to provide the external input. There is plenty of foil grounding area on the cards to which to solder the coax shield directly, and this serves to reduce input noise considerably.

Warning! With all these modifications, the automatic blanking and sweep circuits of the unit have been defeated. This is of no real consequence, but extreme care must be taken not to damage the CRT. The blue-green phosphor is exceedingly bright, and has to be protected from over-intensity which would otherwise burn a permanent mark on the screen. The graphics driver is designed to prevent this occurrence, but at this stage of the checkout process, none of those protective circuits is involved.

It is important to check the display terminal as it stands now. For all practical purposes, it is a 12 inch oscilloscope at this point and can be checked out as such. The deflection voltage which must be externally applied to both horizontal and vertical inputs is in the range of 0 to –3 volts. It is of the *gravest* importance that the polarity not be reversed or the magnitude exceeded on these inputs.

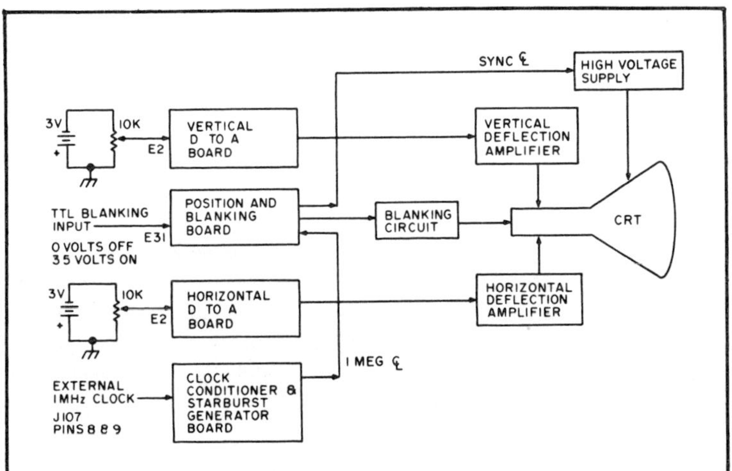

Fig. 7-39. Deflection amp subassembly checkout.

Schematically, it would appear quite acceptable to do this, but in actuality it is disastrous. The deflection yoke resistance is less than .1 Ohm and demands considerable current to drive it. This deflection current is directly proportional to the input voltage. When a 0 to −3 volt signal is applied, the deflection current sweeps from −2 Amps to +2 Amps approximately. The low voltage power supply is a real brute capable of better than 10 Amps. When voltages of other than the optimum are applied, the deflection will try to follow. The unfortunate problem is that the manufacturer didn't build the deflection amplifiers to handle this much current and they go poof! They, of course, never were concerned with this problem because the D to A converter cards could not have produced these voltages. It is a wise idea, if this display is not going to be permanently attached to a driver of some sort, to put some clamping and voltage limiting circuitry on these inputs. It wasn't without hard reality that these facts were determined.

To continue the deflection checkout, it is necessary to have two 3 volt supplies. Two pair of "C" cells in series are quite adequate and safest. Figure 7-39 is a sketch of these checkout requirements. Each 3 volt supply should be placed across a 10k Ohm pot with the positive side of the battery connected to the display chassis ground. The output voltage at the wiper of the pot will go from 0 to −3 volts with respect to chassis ground. When this fact is agreed upon, one can feel fairly safe in attaching this variable voltage to the horizontal and vertical inputs as described previously.

Now comes the acid test. Using a meter, set each input to −1.5 volts. This will correspond to a null or no deflection condition and should place the beam position directly in the center of the screen. The blanking input should be ungrounded and open and the 1 MHz oscillator turned on. Very carefully turn on the display, but don't immediately rotate the intensity adjustment. After allowing about 30 seconds warmup, and taking note the high voltage is on, slowly increase the intensity. Eventually there will appear a single dot near the center of the screen. Do not make it too bright because it will burn the screen. When this phase is accomplished, increase the voltage applied from the battery sources and notice that the beam moves proportionally with the voltage change. The horizontal input obviously is driving the beam in an X direction from left to right and back, while the vertical is driving it in the Y direction which is up and down. If both pots are turned simultaneously, the beam will move at an angle.

That's all there is to it. Be sure to use coax between the driver and the horizontal and vertical inputs and watch the ground loops.

Table 7-13. Parts List.

A1-A10	LM301 A Op amp
A11-A13	741oo 8 bit Reg.
A14-A15	1408 8 bit D to A converter—Motorola
A16	7437 Quad NAND
A17	7404 Hex inverter
A18-A19	4016 CMOS quad analog switch
A20	74123 One shot
A21	74121 One shot
A22	74103 input NAND

All resistors 1/4 W 5% unless otherwise noted.
All variable resistors are trimpots or equivalent.

Properly adjusted and imaginatively programmed, this graphic display will very quickly become your favorite form of entertainment as well as an extremely useful tool. For the parts list for this graphics drivers, see Table 7-13.

High Quality Display with Cursor and Video Control

This video display is a high quality display with large capacity (2048 characters), extremely high speed (normal memory cycles are used to enter or read data from display memory) and unlimited formatting capability. I have assumed the reader has at least a basic working knowledge of digital logic and is familiar with typical uses of a video display.

The display itself consists of 32 lines each containing 64 characters for a total of 2048 characters. The character set includes both upper and lower case characters and the Greek alphabet, in addition to some special characters. Normal display of a character is white on black, but the video may be inverted on a character by character basis to produce a black character in a field of white.

The display memory is accessed directly by the microprocessor as though it were normal memory. This allows information to be written to or read from any location of the display memory at any time. Scrolling the display then becomes a software process, and as such allows the display to be arbitrarily partitioned into several segments, each being scrolled independently of the others. In fact, programs may be loaded directly into display memory and executed.

The display does not, however, steal cycles from the processor (as many who have seen my display immediately ask). Display memory is normally isolated from the processor bus and is used by the display control circuitry in parallel to normal processing. When the processor performs a read or write cycle utilizing a location within the display memory, control of that memory is automatically switched to the processor. This means that the processor steals cycles from the display when needed.

A Basic Video Display

Before I go into a detailed description of my display, I'd like to go through a simplified description of the fundamental process of creating a raster scan display.

A raster scan CRT (Cathode Ray Tube), an example of which is a normal TV set, produces an image by moving a electron beam horizontally across the screen 262½ times (from left to right) while moving it once from top to bottom. On every other vertical trace of the beam, the start of the horizontal tracing is delayed slightly to produce a field of horizontal lines between the lines drawn by the previous trace. Each of the two fields of lines is called a *frame*. The process of causing the lines of the second frame of the first frame is called *interlacing*.

Movement of the electron beam is synchronized by special pulses which are part of a video signal, the horizontal and vertical sync pulses. For instance, suppose that the beam has just completed a trace across the face of the CRT. The horizontal sync pulse will cause the beam to go back to the left side of the tube (retrace) and begin a new sweep. Likewise, a vertical sync pulse causes the beam to move back to the top of the screen. Another part of the video signal is the blanking. Blanking pulses follow each of the horizontal and vertical sync pulses and servo to blank out the retrace of the beam so that it does not show up as unwanted light on the screen. The final part of a video signal is just the video information itself. This information controls the intensity of the electron beam as it is being swept across the CRT. The sync, blanking and video information are all combined to produce a single signal which controls the CRT monitor.

Producing a display of characters on a raster scan CRT involves only the synchronization of an appropriate train of pulses with the horizontal and vertical information. I have shown a simplified block diagram to accomplish this in Fig. 7-40.

The clock and timing information block is responsible for generation of the horizontal and vertical sync and blanking pulses. This information is fed directly to a video combiner and is also used to control the operation of several counters. The row counter and the column counter provide an address to the memory (which contains the characters to be displayed). The data from the memory serves

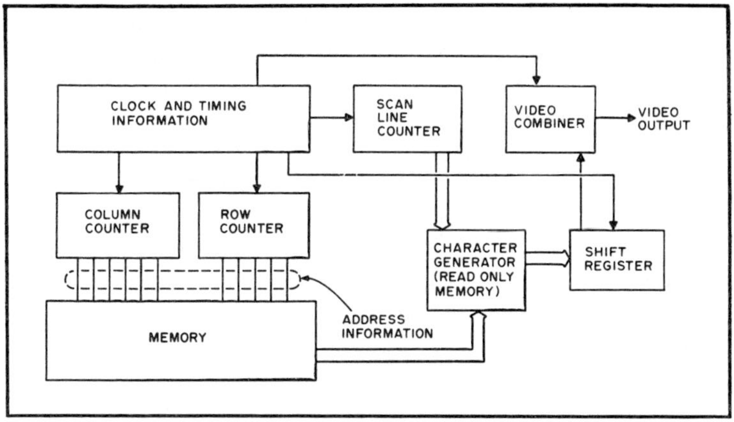

Fig. 7-40. Video display simplified block diagram.

as one input to a read only memory called a character generator. The character generator contains a matrix of dots for each character (Fig. 7-41). Since only one row of dots for a character may be produced on a given scan of the electron beam, a scn line counter is needed to tell the character generator which particular row of dots is currently being called for. The outut of the character generator is loaded into a shift register and shifted out to be combined with the horizontal and vertical information to produce white dots on the screen.

My display writes 32 lines of 64 characters per line. I allow 15 scan lines per row of characters. This means that it takes 15 traces of the electron beam to produce one row of characters. A simplified flow of events would be:

- The system is reset by the vertical sync pulse.
- Several horizontal sweeps are allowed to happen before anything else to space the characters down from the top of the raster, which is usually distorted.
- Data from memory is presented to the character generator. At the same time, the scan line counter tells the character generator which row of dots within a character is needed.
- The output of the character generator is loaded into a shift register and shifted out into the video combiner one bit at a time.
- The column counter is incremented and the same process takes place over and over until the end of a line.
- At the end of a horizontal trace, the scan line counter is incremented by the horizontal sync and the same line of characters is presented to the character generator to pro-

duce the second row of dots on the screen. This process repeats until the first row of characters has been completed.

- A few horizontal sweeps are allowed for spacing. Then the row counter is incremented and the above process repeats for the next row of characters (and so on, until all the characters have been completely displayed).

The operation of my display follows this basic outline, except where I have taken advantage of peculiarities within the circuit. I also have had to play tricks because of the interlacing of the two video frames, so that I would have enough scan lines available to produce 32 lines of high quality characters.

Conventions

For simplicity I have adopted a few conventions in drawing the schematics. First, all crossing lines are *not* connected. Connections are drawn to produce *T* junctions.

A logic gate with an 00 in it is a 7400, one with an 04 in it is a 7404, and so on.

ICs drawn as boxes have their part numbers inside the box.

I have not numbered pin connections on common logic gates; I leave this to the builder, since it is unlikely that his layout will make it convenient to use the same pin numbers.

My display is wire-wrapped. I highly recommend going that way, as a printed circuit layout on this scale would be a great undertaking for the hobbyist. I have not numbered or shown power connections for any but special ICs. Figure 7-42 contains all pin number and power information for the ICs used. Where I have numbered pins on counters, flip-flop and special ICs, there is little choice (except for the flip-flops which have two gates per package). Numbers in small square boxes refer to Altair bus numbers and are the only off board connections to be made except for the video connection itself. If you are not using an Altair-compatible bus, then you will need to make appropriate corrections to the memory control part of the schematic (note that the only connections to the external world are those appearing on the memory schematic—except for power and the video connection).

The Memory

I'll start my discussion of the actual display circuit by describing the memory schematic shown in Fig. 7-40, since it is relatively straightforward.

I have used 2102s for memory, since they are cheap and readily available. There is nothing sacred about this choice, and any other

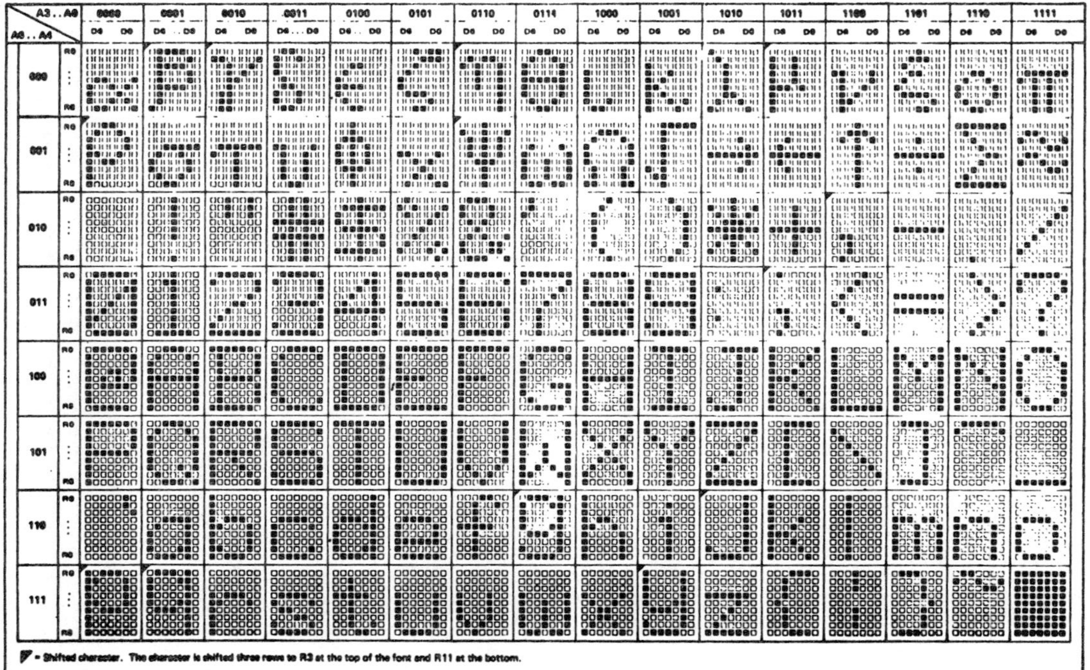

Fig. 7-41. Character set for the MCM6571A character generator. This read only memory is also available with other character sets.

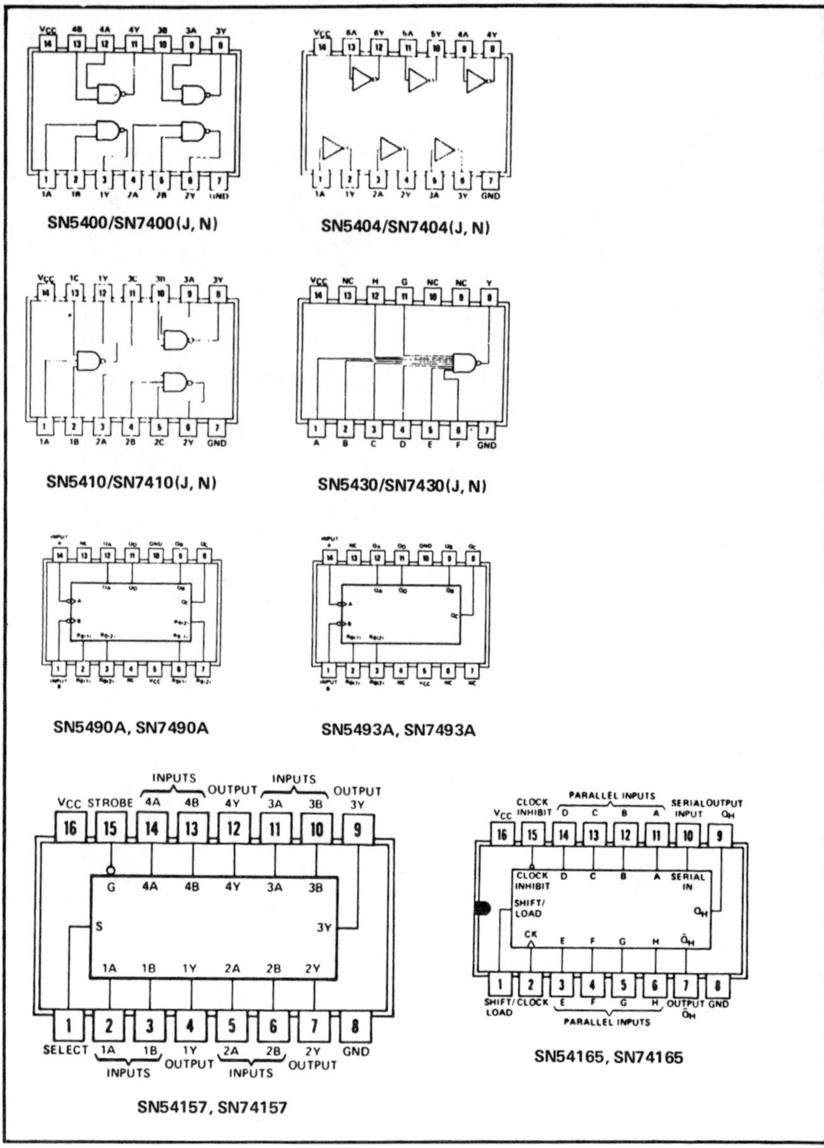

Fig. 7-42. Pin configurations for the various ICs used in the display.

memory could be substituted if it were fast enough. I recommend buying memory which is guaranteed to at least 500 nanosecond access time (to insure reliable operation).

The address lines of the memory chips are tied in parallel and connected to the outputs of the 74157 multiplexers, whose function

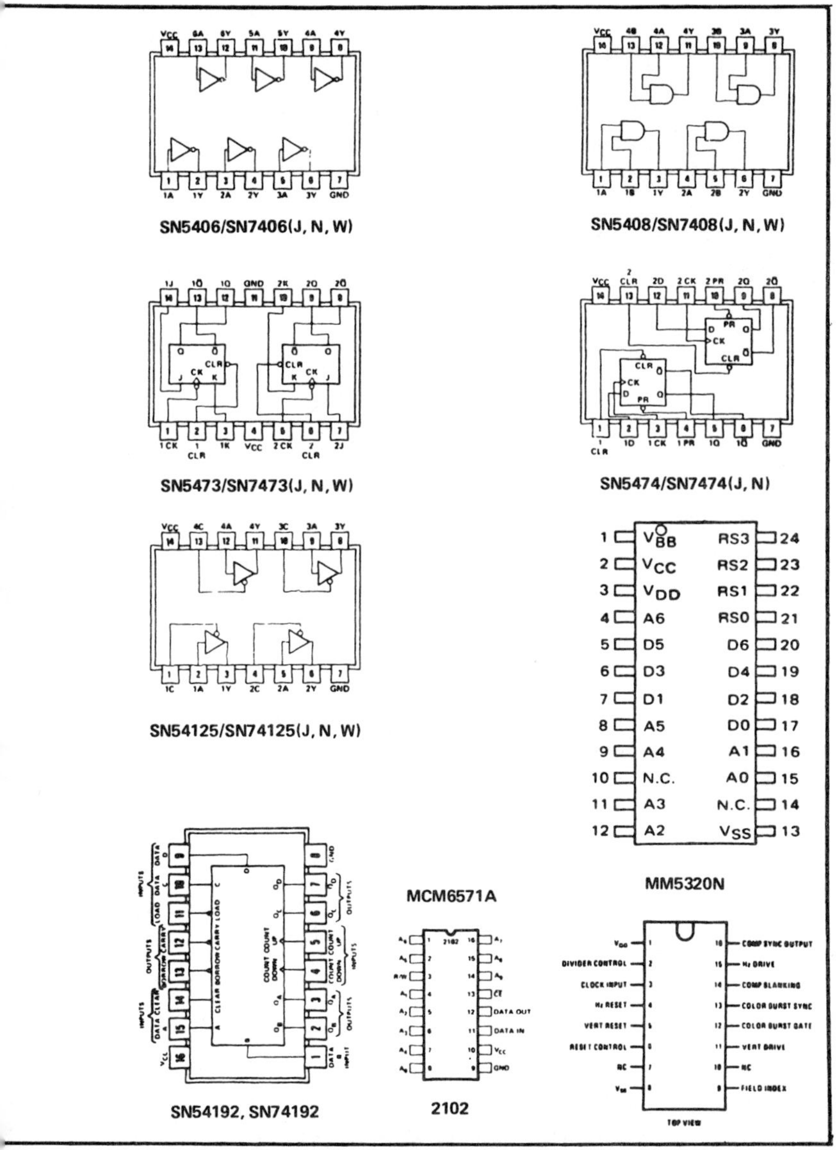

I'll describe soon. Data inputs of the memory are simply connected to the data out bus of the processor. The data outputs of the memory are connected to the charactr generator (Fig. 7-43) and to some tri-state bus drivers (74125). The purpose of the tri-state bus drivers is to allow data to be read from the display memory by the processor. If you wish to use another tri-state gate (such as an 8T97), it will make no difference.

The memory control circuit serves to distinguish between valid memory requests and random states of the Altair bus which occasionally look like memory requests if enough care is not taken. The gates in the upper left of the left memory schematic decode valid processor requests for the memory by monitoring three status lines and five address lines. If SOUT and $\overline{WO}$ are both low, then the processor is about to write memory. If MEMR is high, the processor is about to read from memory. If, at the same time, address lines A11 through A15 are high, then the byte of memory being addressed is within the two kilobytes of display memory. One half of a 7474 flip-flop is used to latch the request status during sync time of the processor, with the $\emptyset_1$ clock being used to clock the flip-flop at a time when all address and status signals are stable. While my display memory is located in the high order two kilobytes of the Altair's memory addressing range, it is by no means a sacred choice. You can put your display memory anywhere you wish by appropriate decoding of A11-A15.

When a valid processor request has been decoded and latched, the three 74157 multiplexer chips shift control of the memory address lines from the display's own counters to the computer's address bus. The MWRITE Altair bus signal is gated by the output of the request latch to allow the processor to write data into memory. Similarly, the MEMR signal is gated with the output of the request latch to enable the tri-state bus drivers for a read cycle.

Address bit 2^{10} (from the multiplexers) is used to enable either the high order kilobyte or low order kilobyte of display memory.

When the processor is finished with its request for use of the memory, the multiplexers shift control of the memory back to the display control.

The Character Generator

Before I get into the actual description of the control schematic, I would like to take time to go over the character generator I chose and attempt to explain why I did some of the things I did with the control circuitry.

The character generator stores a 7 × 9 matrix of dots for each of its 128 characters. Some of the characters (like j, y, g) should extend beneath the line for best results, so the character generator contains circuitry which shifts the matrix automatically on such characters. What this means is that for a normal character, the dots of the character will appear when lines 0 through 8 of the character

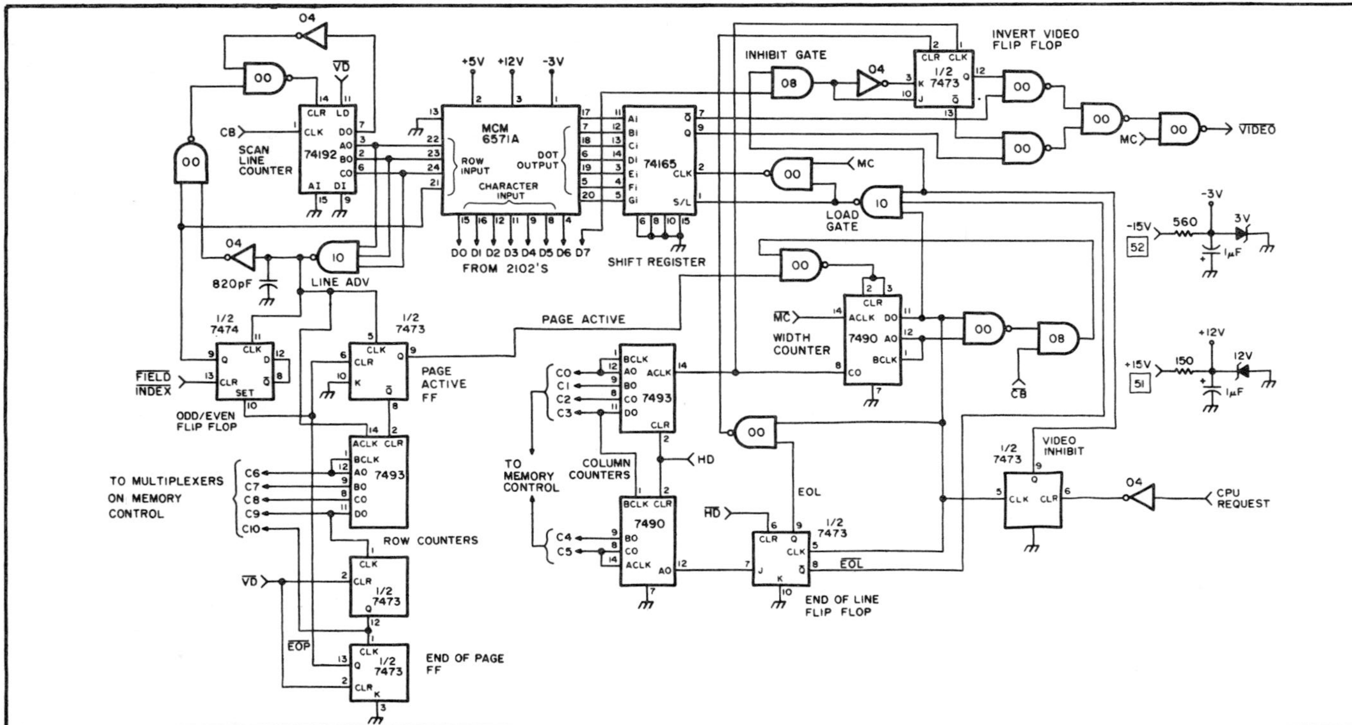

Fig. 7-43. Schematic diagram of display control circuits.

generator are addressed. For a shifted character, lines 0 through 2 will come out blank and the 9 lines of the matrix will appear when lines 3 through 11 are addressed. In addition, if lines 11 through 15 are addressed, blanks will result at the output.

What this really means is that from the designer's viewpoint I don't have to know that the information is stored in a 7 × 9 matrix. I can make believe that it is in a 7 × 16 matrix where the last four lines are always blank. Motorola, I love you for the MCM571A!

I use 15 scan lines per row of characters in my display (originally I used 16 but could not achieve 32 lines of characters). Multiply 32 lines of characters by 15 scan lines per character line and you get 480 scan lines (see how nicely the units cancel—high school physics, eat your heart out!).

Now remember from my earlier discussion that there are only 262½ scan lines per frame. Since I need 480 lines, I must use the fact that alternate frames are interlaced by causing my control circuitry to do every other scan line and alternate between frames. Since I am using 15 scan lines per character line, I must in one frame write the eight even number lines of the first row of characters, then the seven odd numbered lines of the second row of characters, the even of the next, etc., etc.

In the next frame, I must start with the seven odd numbered lines of the first row, the eight even numbered lines of the second, and so on. I also have to be sure that I am using the correct frames of the raster to avoid producing some weird characters. It turns out that only about 482 lines of the raster are useful. The rest are contained within the field of the blanking pulses, and attempting to use them results in a rolling display or worse. Otherwise I would have stayed with 16 scan lines per character. I might also mention that the choice of 14 scan lines per character was appealing to me until I tried it and found that the lines began to be uncomfortably close together.

Display Control

Several signals within the control circuitry are important, and discussion of their functions will help to explain the operation of the display control (Fig. 7-43). These are PAGE ACTIVE, FIELD INDEX (FI), LINE ADVANCE, END OF PAGE (EOP), END OF LINE (EOL), MASTER CLOCK (MC), VERTICAL DRIVE (VD), HORIZONTAL DRIVE (HD)and COMPOSITE BLANKING (CB). VERTICAL and HORIZONTAL DRIVE are really just vertical and horizontal sync, but the sync generator manufacturer labels them as drive. Any signal shown on the shematic with a bar above it (as $\overline{\text{CB}}$ or

$\overline{VD}$) is the complement of the signal indicated. The signals VD, HD, CB, and FI originate from the sync generator (Fig. 7-44). The other signals are generated within the display control.

Sync Signals

I have used a National Semiconductor MM5320N TV camera sync generator to generate timing signals needed to produce a raster. It produces the VERTICAL DRIVE signal, which (along with its complement) is used mainly to reset various counters and flip-flops of the display control. The HORIZONTAL DRIVE output of the sync generator serves the same purpose. The FIELD INDEX output of the sync generator identifies field number 1 of the raster. It

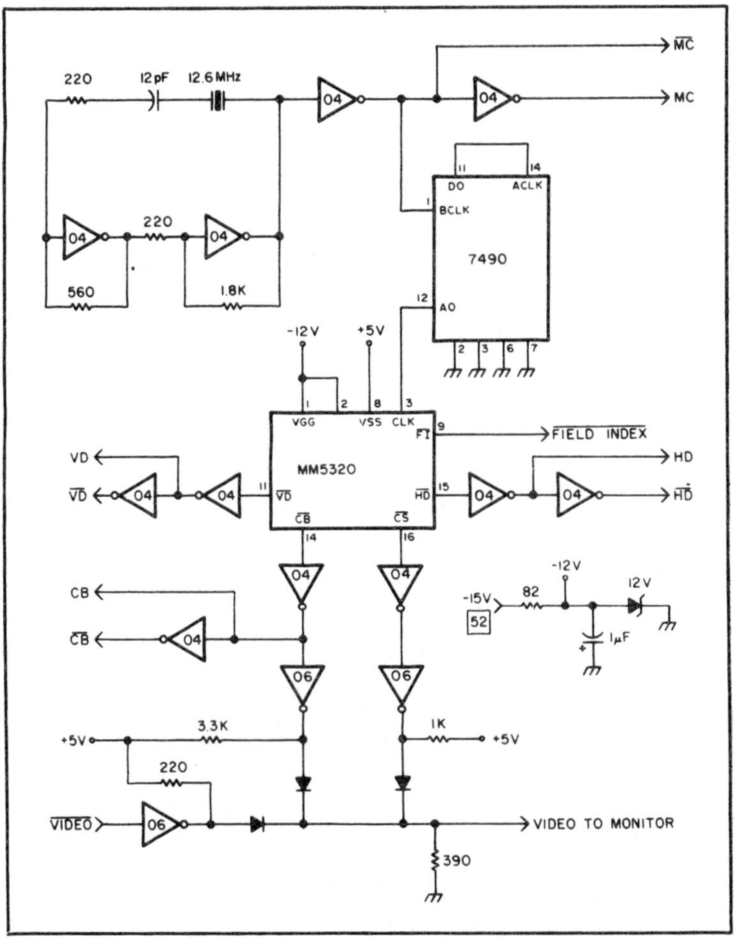

Fig. 7-44. Sync generator, video combiner and clock circuits schematic diagram.

is a pulse which occurs for two clock cycles at the leading edge of the vertical blanking for field one. I will discuss the sync generator in more detail when I get to the description of that schematic (Fig. 7-44), and mention it here only as a prelude to describing the control circuitry.

Page Active

PAGE ACTIVE is a signal which goes high during the writing of a frame of information on the CRT. Thus, it will be low until the electron beam is in position to trace out the top scan line of the first row of characters and it will remain high until the last scan line of the last row of characters has been produced. When it is low, all video output is suppressed and the control circuit is mainly idle.

Here is the sequence of events which results in the clocking of the PAGE ACTIVE flip-flop (which in turn enables the rest of the display):

- $\overline{\text{VD}}$ occurs (resetting other things which I will mention later) and causes the scan line counter to be loaded with a five. I will try to explain why I had to do this in a few lines.
- The CB signal will begin clocking the scan line counter. When this counter reaches seven, the 7410 connected to the A, B, and C outputs of the scan line counter will go low, causing the PAGE ACTIVE flip-flop to be clocked, setting it high.

The reason that I load the scan line counter with a binary five is to cause a fixed number of scan lines to be ignored before clocking the PAGE ACTIVE flip-flop. Remember that I said earlier that only 482 scan lines were useful? This is because 21 of the 262½ lines per frame occur during the vertical blanking pulse. This leaves only 241½ useful lines per frame. By using the COMPOSITE BLANKING signal to clock the scan line counter, I already ignore the first 21 lines since no clocking of the counter will occur during the vertical blanking pulse. By presetting the scan line counter to five, it will take only a couple of lines to get it to seven where it causes the PAGE ACTIVE flip-flop to come on, thereby wasting as few as possible lines. It turns out that the counter will count the vertical blanking pulse so that I am in fact only wasting about one half of a line at the top of the display. In any case, there are not many lines to waste and this method utilizes the maximum amount of useful raster.

Once the PAGE ACTIVE flip-flop has been set, the row counters and the width counter are enabled (follow the logic on the schematic to convince yourself of this). The PAGE ACTIVE flip-flop is ultimately cleared by the END OF PAGE signal.

Odd/Even Flip-Flop

The FIELD INDEX is used to keep track of which frame is being written at any given time. Remember that I mentioned earlier the necessity to alternate even and odd scan lines of the characters being displayed. The alternation must occur between rows of characters and also between frames. The FIELD INDEX is used to control the starting point of the odd/even flip-flop within a given frame. This is accomplished by setting the odd/even flip-flop with the END OF PAGE signal. The EOP flip-flop, however, is cleared by $\overline{VD}$, causing the EOP signal to go away at the beginning of the VD pulse. The FI pulse hangs around for a couple of clock cycles after the beginning of the VD pulse, so that if it (FI) is present it will clear the odd/even flip-flop. Thus the odd/even flip-flop will be set or reset at the beginning of a frame.

The output of the odd/even flip-flop serves as bit zero of the line input to the character generator, causing it to generate the appropriate dot information. The output of the odd/even flip-flop also serves to control the number of scan lines allowed for a row of characters by causing the scan line counter to divide by either seven or eight. This is relatively straightforward and I leave it to the reader to verify that this is so by examining the schematic. Upon completion of two complete scans, there will have been 15 scan lines allotted for each row of characters.

Line Advance

The LINE ADVANCE signal is the same as used to enable the PAGE ACTIVE flip-flop, except that once the PAGE ACTIVE flip-flop is set, the LINE ADVANCE will clock the row counters. I had trouble with a glitch on the LINE ADVANCE, so I had to put in an 820 (or so) pF capacitor to get rid of it.

Row Counter

The row counter consists of a 7490 decade counter and one half of a 7473 flip-flop. The row counter provides the high order five bits of the memory address to the multiplexers.

End Of Page

The EOP flip-flop is clocked by the row counter after 32 rows of characters have been displayed in a given frame. It is used to clear the PAGE ACTIVE flip-flop (which inhibits the world) and also to set the odd/even flip-flop as described above. EOP is reset by VERTICAL DRIVE.

The Character Generator Again

The character generator accepts a row input from the scan line counter to tell it which row of a matrix to present to its output. The character code is the rest of the input to the character generator and comes directly from the memory. Te seven bit output of the character generator represents part of the dot pattern of a character and is presented to the 74165 shift register. Clocking of the shift register to dump the dots out in serial fashion is by the MASTER CLOCK. Loading of the shift register is controlled by circuitry associated with the width counter.

Width Counter

The width counter is a 7490 decade counter which is really dividing by nine because of external gating (shown in the schematic). The width counter is held at zero whenever the PAGE ACTIVE line is low. It is also cleared by the COMPOSITE BLANKING to insure that it begins every line from zero.

The width counter is clocked by the MASTER CLOCK and is responsible for determining the number of clock pulses allowed for each character in a row. I have allowed nine clock pulses per character. Seven pulses are needed to display the seven dot width of a character, plus one leading and one trailing pulse to allow for spacing between. I have arranged the loading and clocking of the shift register to achieve both leading and trailing blank dots, as opposed to simply allowing two blank dots between character. This distinction is not too important when displaying normal video, but when the video is inverted on a given character, it assures that the character will be centered in the field of white.

The D output of the width counter is used to provide a load signal to the shift register. The C output is used to clock the column counters, which count the number of characters per row. Note that the column counters are advanced before the shift register is loaded. This is to allow sufficient time for the two memories (the main character memory and the character generator) to stablize. The data loaded into the shift register will be data from the last character, because of the memory access time.

Column Counters

The column counter, a 7493 and part of a 7490, counts the number of characters within a row and provides the low order six bits of address information to the memory control board. The column counter is reset by the HORIZONTAL DRIVE pulse to insure that it begins counting at zero for each row. The C output of the width counter is used to clock the column counter as discussed above.

One half of the 7490 used in the column counter is a divide-by-four counter, while the other half is used as a flip-flop. To see this, note that the D output of the 7493 is connected to the B clock of the 7490 (the B clock is the input to the divide-by-give stage of a 7490). The C output of the 7490 is used to clock the A input, which will cause the output to go high after the fourth time the B input is clocked. The A output is connected in turn to the J input of the END OF LINE flip-flop. The END OF LINE flip-flop will be clocked on the falling edge of the D output from the width counter. The output of the EOL flip-flop then inhibits any further loading of the shift register, hence ending the current line.

The reason for all this playing around with the column counter is to allow the last character to be loaded into the shift register. If you remember the discussion about the column counter being clocked to the next character before the data from the current character is loaded into the shift register, you will see that the column counter will be at 64 (representing the 65th character since the counters start at zero) when the load pulse for character 63 (the 64th character) occurs. Since I have to allow the 64th load pulse to occur, I came up with the above scheme to delay the clocking of the EOL flip-flop.

I might mention at this point that there is really no good reason to bother using the C output of the 7490 to clock the A input. The internal D flip-flop of the 7490 is already clocked by the C output, so the D output could serve as the J input to the flip-flop. In fact, by gating together the D output of the 7490 section of the column counter with the D output of the width counter (using a 7408 AND gate with the output of the AND gate clocking the A input of the 7490), the EOL flip-flop could be eliminated, the A output of the 7490 replacing the EOL signal. But you would have to use a NOT gate to derive $\overline{\text{EOL}}$ and then you would have one half of a flip-flop left over elsewhere. I mention this possibility partly for the benefit of anyone who might be making changes where it would be nice to have an extra flip-flop, and partly to illustrate that there is nothing sacred about the way I have done things. As long as you understand the purpose of each part of the circuit, you can modify it to suit your particular requirements or supply of parts.

Video Inversion

The Invert Video flip-flop controls inversion of the video signal to produce a black character within a field of white. Note that by inverting the video, I am referring only to inverting the character part of the video, not the sync and blanking signals.

The video may be inverted character by character, allowing the use of multiple cursors (I use an inverted blank for a cursor) or techiniques such as inverting important messages (or flashing them between normal and inverted video). The display also makes a dandy checkerboard. The eighth bit of the display memory is used to control the state of each character.

Since the memory has already been advanced to the next character during the time in which dots for a given character are being drawn by the electron beam of the CRT, it is necessary to latch the eighth bit of memory in the Invert Video flip-flop. This bit is clocked into the flip-flop at the same time the load pulse for the shift register goes high. The outputs of the flip-flop control a multiplexer made from 7400 gates, thereby selecting either the Q or $\overline{Q}$ output from the shift register. The Invert Video flip-flop is forcibly cleared after the EOL signal comes on (EOL and the D output of the width counter are gated to produce a clear pulse), to assure that the brief part of a line traced by the electron beam after the last character is blank.

Note that the output of the video inversion multiplexer (the 7400 gates) is clocked by the MASTER CLOCK. The main reason for this is to eliminate the possibility of generating a wide video pulse (the top of a *T* or an inverted blank would be examples) which would cause the trace produced by the electron beam to bloom or, at the very least, appear brighter than other parts of the display. Clocking the video makes all video pulses the same width (the top of a *T* would come out as seven consecutive short pulses rather than as one long pulse) and results in a very uniform brightness over the entire display.

Video Inhibit

The Video Inhibit flip-flop prevents generation of random video pulese which would otherwise result from decoding of wrong information by the character generator during times when the processor is using the display memory. Whenever the processor makes a request for the memory (as indicated by the CPU REQUEST signal from the memory control schematic), the Video Inhibit flip-flop is cleared. The Video Inhibit flip-flop inhibits further loading of the shift register and forces the Video Invert flip-flop to the off state the next time it is clocked. Once the processor request has been cleared, the Video Inhibit flip-flop will be clocked by the end of the next load pulse, setting it back to normal. Note that the load pulse which clocks the Video Inhibit flip-flop will be ignored by the shift register, since it does not clock the flip-flop until the trailing edge. The next load pulse will cause the shfit register to be loaded. The result is that video is inhibited during processor requests for memory and for at least one complete character cycle after control is restored to the display (to assure that the memory is back in step with the display control).

The loss of a row of dots from random characters around the screen during processor requests is not a problem, since it is hard to notice the absence of a single row of dots within a single character for 1/30th of a second. The only time that the display is noticeably degraded is when the processor is making requests at a very rapid rate. But the rate is so great that it would not be possible for most people to read the display anyway.

One instance where the degradation of the display caused by cycle stealing becomes noticeable is during a line feed. The line feed, or *scroll* is a software function and involves reading and rewriting almost all 2048 characters of the display. The process is very fast (50 to 100 milliseconds, depending on your software and memory cycle time) and results in a noticeable display degradation because of the large number of requests within a short time. But the degradation during a line feed is not a problem since the display would be non-readable during a line feed even if it was not degraded. Also, it happens so fast that one does not really perceive the display to have lost anything unless he is really looking for it.

One other thing to remember (to prevent heart seizure the first time it happens) is that if you stop the processor and examine the contents of a location within the display memory, then you are in effect requesting 100 percent of the memory's time, resulting in a completely blank display.

Sync Generator and Video Combiner

The sync generator schematic includes the MASTER CLOCK and the video combiner. The MASTER CLOCK is a simple oscillator made from 7404 gates, a few Rs and Cs and a 12.6 MHz crystal.

The National Semiconductor MM5320 sync generator requires a 1.26 MHz clock, so I divided the 12.6 frequency by ten. Note that the 7490 is used as a symmetrical divide-by-ten counter by going through the divide-by-five stage and then into the divide-by-two stage.

I have buffered all outputs of the 5320 except the FIELD INDEX output, which is only connected to one gate anyway. As I discussed earlier, the sync generator does all the timing necessary to generate the appropriate sync and blanking signals to produce a raster.

Putting the COMPOSITE SYNC, COMPOSITE BLANKING and VIDEO (from the display control schematic) to form a single video signal is the function of the video combiner. The video combiner is built from 7406 open collector inverters and some diodes. The resistors shown at the junction of each of the 7406 outputs and its respective diode determine the weight of the given signal. The resistors I have shown are not too critical and may be changed for best results. The resistor for the blanking component is chosen to produce about a .2 to .3 volt change in the output level when the blanking turns on and off. Similarly, the sync component should be around .7 volts and the video component should be a couple of volts (or whatever produces good contrast). These values seem to work well with the monitor I use, as it has a 75 Ohm input impedance.

The video monitor is a Motorola M2000-1SC. It is a good quality 9 inch monitor having a bandwidth of about 12 MHz. If you plan to use an old black and white TV, you may experience problems with overscan (which is built into most TV sets to make the picture look bigger) or bandwidth. The Motorola monitor costs around $115, but is well worth it for this application.

Power Supplies

The logic components will require a good five volt supply. I used two 7805 regulators (the same as used by MITS and other Altair board manufacturers) to regulate power from the Altair bus. I use one for powering the memory and one for the logic. Be sure to install plenty of .1 uF capacitors at various points on the board, to prevent noise problems from messing up the display. If you are building the display for use outside an Altair type computer, I will assume that you can also manage the power supply.

Various other voltages required by the sync generator and character generator are provided by the zener diode regulators shown on the schematics. The amounts of current needed at these voltages are very small. The schematic of memory circuits is found in Fig. 7-45.

Use of the Display

There are several ways for utilizing the display. I will try to present a few simple ideas to get you started.

The first thing is to think of the display as a window to memory rather than as an output device. Any manipulation of data on the

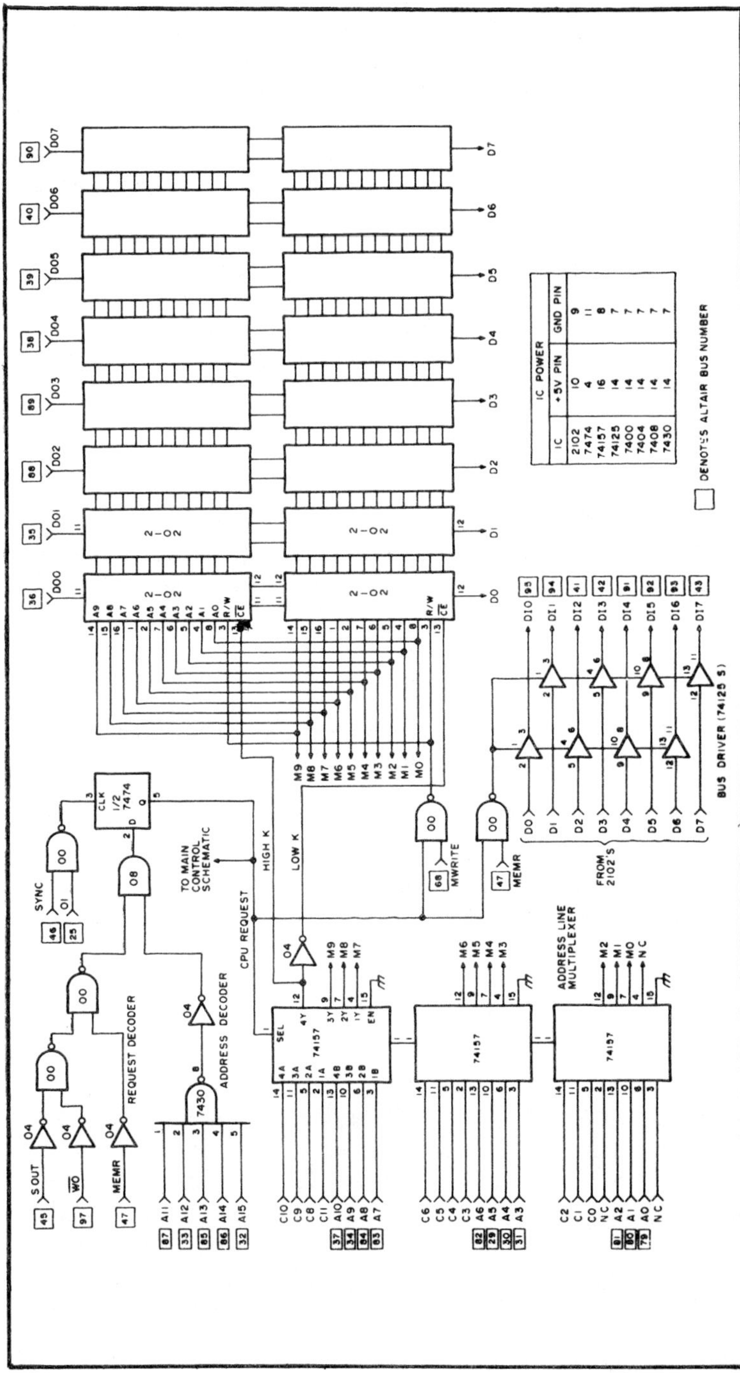

Fig. 7-45. Schematic diagram of memory circuits.

display (writing, erasing, updating, scrolling) involves a software process to put the desired information into the right location within the memory. There is no line feed function, nor are there any cursor positioning functions. Characters are simply stored at the correct locations. Cursors, if used, are simulated by appropriate software for the benefit of the person looking at the display. This allows the display to be configured any way you see fit. Some of the photographs depict displays where my Altair was being used as a terminal to a DEC PDP-10. A simple program was written which made the display behave as though it were a Hazeltine 2000 video terminal.

Some specific methods to accomplish normal functions are:

- Erasing—Simply store blanks throughout the display memory. Note that selective erasing is just as easy.
- Scrolling—Read a character from the second line and write it back in the same location on the first line (i.e., move it back 64 places). Continue reading and writing characters until you have rewritten the last line into the second to last line. Then erase the last line. Note that it is a simple matter to scroll only a part of the display instead of all of it.

Construction Ideas

Before you begin building the display, you should make copies of the schematic and make any changes you think necessary to adapt the display to your system. Then assign numbers (or letters) to all of the ICs and number the pins. If the IC numbering scheme is devised to represent a socket coordinate, you will have less trouble when you begin to wire-wrap the board. Then make all power and ground connections. Then finish the board by making all wraps associated with a node on the schematic at the same time, indicating (by small colored slashes or otherwise) that you have completed a node.

TESTING

There is very little I can mention here, as there are so many things that can be wrong from a misplaced wire-wrap. I suggest checking the sync generator to be sure it is working and then proceeding to the various counters and flip-flops to see which are working. The memory may be tested for proper operation by writing a memory diagnostic program. Obviously, for any real troubleshooting or debugging you will need an oscilloscope—and you will need to be able to think through the operation of the display.

Index